You have the potential to make a difference!

WileyPLUS is a powerful online system packed with features to help you make the most of your learning potential, and get the best grade you can!

With Wiley**PLUS** you get:

A complete online version of your text and other study resources

Study more effectively and get instant feedback when you practice on your own. Resources like self-assessment quizzes, tutorials, and animations bring the subject matter to life, and help you master the material.

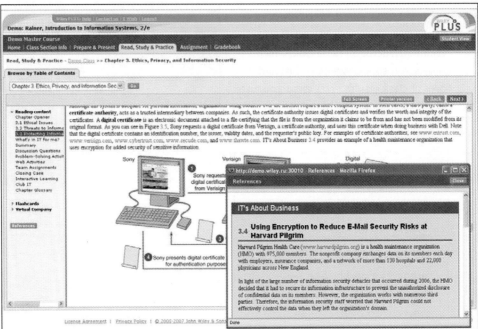

Problem-solving help, instant grading, and feedback on your homework and quizzes

You can keep all of your assigned work in one location, making it easy for you to stay on task. Plus, many homework problems contain direct links to the relevant portion of your text to help you deal with problem-solving obstacles at the moment they come up.

The ability to track your progress and grades throughout the term.

A personal gradebook allows you to monitor your results from past assignments at any time. You'll always know exactly where you stand.

If your instructor uses *WileyPLUS*, you will receive a URL for your class. If not, your instructor can get more information about *WileyPLUS* by visiting www.wileyplus.com

---

"It has been a great help, and I believe it has helped me to achieve a better grade."

Michael Morris, *Columbia Basin College*

74% of students surveyed said it helped them get a better grade.*

Achieve Positive Learning Outcomes with WileyPLUS...

Every one of your students has the potential to make a difference. And realizing that potential starts right here, in your course.

When students succeed in your course—when they stay on-task and make the breakthrough that turns confusion into confidence—they are empowered to build the skill and confidence they need to succeed. We know your goal is to create a positively charged learning environment where students reach their full potential to become active engaged learners. *WileyPLUS* can help you reach that goal.

WileyPLUS is an online suite of resources—including the complete text—that will help your students:

- come to class better prepared for your lectures
- get immediate feedback and context-sensitive help on assignments and quizzes
- track their progress throughout the course

"I just wanted to say how much this program helped me in studying... I was able to actually see my mistakes and correct them. ... I really think that other students should have the chance to use *WileyPLUS.*"

Ashlee Krisko, *Oakland University*

www.wileyplus.com

88% of students surveyed said it improved their understanding of the material.*

WileyPLUS is built around the activities you perform

Prepare & Present

Create outstanding class presentations using a wealth of resources, such as PowerPoint™ slides, image galleries, interactive simulations, and more. Plus you can easily upload any materials you have created into your course, and combine them with the resources *WileyPLUS* provides.

Create Assignments

Automate the assigning and grading of homework or quizzes by using the provided question banks, or by writing your own. Student results will be automatically graded and recorded in your gradebook. *WileyPLUS* also links homework problems to relevant sections of the online text, hints, or solutions—context-sensitive help where students need it most!

*Based upon 7,000 responses to student surveys in academic year 2006

Introduction to Information Systems

Second Edition

Introduction to
Information Systems
Second Edition

R. Kelly Rainer Jr.

Efraim Turban

John Wiley & Sons, Inc.

PUBLISHER	Don Fowley
EXECUTIVE EDITOR	Beth Golub
ASSISTANT EDITOR	Jen Devine
EXECUTIVE MARKETING MANAGER	Amy Scholz
CREATIVE DIRECTOR	Harry Nolan
DESIGNER	Michael St. Martine
SENIOR ILLUSTRATION EDITOR	Anna Melhorn
SENIOR PHOTO EDITOR	Lisa Gee
SENIOR EDITORIAL ASSISTANT	Maria Guarascio
SENIOR MEDIA EDITOR	Lauren Sapira
SENIOR PRODUCTION EDITOR	Patricia McFadden
PRODUCTION MANAGEMENT SERVICES	Ingrao Associates

This book was set in 10/12 Times Roman by GGS Book Services and printed and bound by Quebecor World Versailles. The cover was printed by Quebecor World Versailles. This book is printed on acid free paper. ∞

To order books or for customer service please, call 1-800-CALL WILEY (225-5945).

L.C. Call no.   Dewey Classification No.   L.C. Card No.
ISBN-13   978-0470-169001
ISBN-10   0470169001

Printed in the United States of America

9 8 7 6 5 4

preface

What does Information Systems have to do with business?

Rainer, Turban *Introduction to Information Systems* will answer this question for you. In every chapter, you will see how real global businesses use technology and information systems to increase their profitability, gain market share, improve their customer service, and manage their daily operations. In other words, information systems provide the foundation for business.

Our goal is to teach all business majors, especially undergraduate ones, how to use IT to master their current or future jobs and to help ensure the success of their organization. Our focus is not on merely *learning* the concepts of information technology but rather on *applying* those concepts to facilitate business processes. We concentrate on placing information systems in the context of business, so that students will more readily grasp the concepts presented in the text.

The theme of this book is What's In IT for Me? This question is asked by all students who take this course. Our book will show you that IT is the backbone of any business, whether you're in Accounting, Finance, Marketing, Human Resources, or Production/Operations Management. We also include an icon for the Management Information Systems (MIS) major.

New to This Edition

There are many exciting additions and changes in Rainer 2e. These changes make our book more interesting and readable for students of all majors, while still providing the most current information possible in the rapidly changing field of information systems.

Overall

- A new Technology Guide (Tech Guide 3) on How to Protect Your Information Assets. Our objective in this Tech Guide was to help students, in today's very dangerous environment, to protect their information assets, both by behavioral actions and computer-based actions.
- Two additional Technology Guides on Telecommunications and Networking as well as the Internet and the World Wide Web (Tech Guides 4 and 5) have been added.

- A new online Appendix to Chapter 6 on How to Build Your Own Electronic Commerce website. In this Appendix, we discuss this topic from "soup to nuts," beginning with naming and registering the Web site, continuing with constructing the Web site, and concluding with marketing the Web site.
- All new chapter opening and closing cases.
- All new IT's About Business in every chapter.
- All new examples in every chapter.
- New PowerPoint slides incorporating numerous images and video.
- New test bank with questions labeled according to difficulty: easy, medium, and hard.

Specifically

Chapters 1 and 2 have been reorganized. Chapter 1 begins with basic concepts and definitions of information systems to give students a basic vocabulary with which to work. The next section of Chapter 1, which is new, discusses the emergence of the new global, Web-based platform postulated by Thomas Friedman in his book, *The World Is Flat (3.0)*. We address Friedman's ten "flatteners" and the implications of each flattener. Our discussion of Friedman's work helps students understand today's global business environment and global information technology environment. The chapter closes with new material on why information systems are so important to all students, regardless of major.

Chapter 2 begins with a thorough description of information systems within the organization and among organizations. A new section has been added on Porter's value chain.

The structure of Chapter 3 remains the same. However, new material has been added in the section on Protecting Privacy and the section on Privacy Codes and Policies. We added a new introduction to the section on Threats to Information Security. This material discusses the factors that are contributing to the increasing vulnerability of organizational information assets. We condensed the material on software attacks into one table to make this material more readable for students.

Chapter 4 has been reorganized. First, the material on data mining has been moved to Chapter 9 where it is more appropriate. Chapter 4 now concentrates solely on data and knowledge management. Second, we added a new section on Data Governance (to include master data management), which has gained such significance to organizations that are drowning in data.

Chapter 5 has been retitled (now Network Applications) and reorganized. We moved the technical material on telecommunications and networking to our new Technology Guide 4. We also moved the introductory technical material on the Internet and the World Wide Web to our new Technology Guide 5. Moving this material means that Chapter 5 focuses only on Network Applications; i.e., how telecommunications and networks impact the organization. We also added a new section on Web 2.0 technologies and Web sites. This is exciting material because all of our students are making extensive use of Web 2.0 in their lives (blogs and social networking are just two examples). Further, organizations are using Web 2.0 technologies in many innovative ways. We present extensive examples of Web 2.0 technologies and how they are being used individually by students and by organizations.

In Chapter 7, we reorganized the material on wireless technologies to illustrate the convergence of these technologies into one device, the smart phone. We also reorganized the section on Wireless Computer Networks and Internet Access. We now discuss these networks on the basis of the size of the network. This gives students a logical progression, from small to extremely large, to aid in their understanding of this material. Throughout this chapter, we present the latest wireless technologies, such as ultrawideband, near field communications, RuBee, and others.

We have extensively rewritten Chapter 9. The second section is now entitled Business Intelligence, Multidimensional Data Analysis, Data Mining, and Decision Support Systems. This section focuses on the various data analysis tools that managers can use to access their own data and perform their own analyses to support their decisions. The next section is now entitled Digital Dashboards. We distinguish these dashboards from the tools in the previous section because dashboards typically present structured, pre-formatted information to managers. We added a new section to this chapter, called Data Visualization Technologies. This section shows how geographical information systems and virtual reality technologies can help managers visualize massive amounts of data and thus aid their decision making.

Key Features

We have been guided by the following goals that we believe will enhance the teaching and learning experience.

Cross-functional Approach

We show why IT is important by calling attention in each chapter to how that chapter's IT topic relates to students in each major. Icons guide the reader to relevant issues for their specific functional area—accounting (ACC), finance (FIN), marketing (MKT), production operations management (POM), Management Information Systems (MIS), and human resources management (HRM). In addition, chapters end with a summary of how the concepts relate to each functional area ('What's in IT for Me?').

Active Learning

We recognize the need to actively involve students in problem solving, creative thinking, and capitalizing on opportunities. Every chapter includes a variety of hands-on exercises, activities, and mini-cases, including exercises that ask students to use software application tools. Through these activities and an interactive Web site, we enable students to actually do something with the concepts they learn, such as how to improve a business through IT, to configure products, and to use spreadsheets to facilitate problem solving.

Diversified and Unique Examples from Different Industries

Extensive use of vivid examples from large corporations, small businesses, and government and not-for-profit organizations helps to enliven concepts by showing students the capabilities of IT, its cost and justification, and innovative ways that real corporations are using IT in their operations. Each chapter constantly highlights the integral connection between IT and business. This is especially evident in the 'IT's about Business' boxes. In addition to the icons noted above, other icons highlight government (GOV) and service-company (SVC) examples.

Successes and Failures

Like other textbooks, we present many examples of IT success. But, we also provide numerous examples of IT failures, in the context of lessons that can be learned from such failures. Misuse of IT can be very expensive, as we illustrate.

Innovation and Creativity

In today's rapidly changing environment, creativity and innovation are necessary for a business to operate effectively and profitably. Throughout the book we show how these concepts are facilitated by IT.

Global Focus

Since an understanding of global competition, partnerships, and trading is essential to success in business, we provide a broad selection of international cases and examples. We discuss how IT facilitates export and import, the management of multinational companies, and electronic trading around the globe. These global examples are highlighted with the global icon.

Cutting Edge Information on Wireless Technologies, e-Commerce, and Web Services

Mobile and Internet technologies have created a paradigm shift in the way that the world does business. We offer a chapter on electronic commerce (Chapter 6) and a comprehensive chapter on wireless technologies (Chapter 7). In addition, we offer examples of Web Services.

Focus on Ethics

With corporate scandals in the headlines and news daily, ethics and ethical questions have come to the forefront of business people's minds. In addition to a chapter that concentrates on ethics and security (Chapter 3), we have included examples and cases that focus on business ethics throughout the chapters. These examples are highlighted with the ethics icon.

Pedagogical Structure

Other pedagogical features provide a structured learning system that reinforces the concepts through features such as chapter-opening organizers, section reviews, frequent applications, and hands-on exercises and activities.

Chapter Opening organizers include the following pedagogical features:

- The *Learning Objectives* gives an overview of the key elements students should come away with after reading the chapter.
- *Web Resources* highlight ancillary materials available on the book companion site and within WileyPLUS for both instructors and students.
- The *Chapter Outline* lists the major concepts covered in the chapter.
- An opening *case* identifies a business problem faced by an actual company, describes the IT solution applied to the business problem, presents the results of the IT solution, and summarizes what students can learn from the case.

Study Aids are provided throughout each chapter. These include the following:

- *IT's about Business* boxes provide real-world applications, with questions that relate to concepts covered in the text. Icons relate these sections to the specific functional areas.

- Highlighted *Examples* interspersed throughout the text show the use (and misuse) of IT by real-world organizations and help illustrate the conceptual discussion.
- *Tables* list key points or summarize different concepts.
- End of section reviews (*Before You Go On . . .*) prompt students to pause and test their understanding of concepts before moving on to the next section.

End-of-Chapter Study Aids provide extensive opportunity for the reader to review and actually 'do something' with the concepts they have just studied:

- *What's in IT for Me?* is a unique chapter summary section that shows the relevance of topics for different functional areas (accounting, finance, marketing, production/operations management, and human resources management).
- The *Chapter Summary*, keyed to learning objectives that were listed at the beginning of the chapter, enables students to review the major concepts covered in the chapter.
- End of Chapter Glossary. This study tool highlights the importance of the vocabulary within the chapters and facilitates studying.
- *Discussion Questions, Problem-Solving Activities, Internet Activities*, and *Team Assignments* provide practice through active learning. These exercises are hands-on opportunities to use the concepts discussed in the chapter.
- A *Case* presents a case organized around a business problem and shows how IT helped to solve it; questions at the end of the case relate it to concepts discussed in the chapter.
- *Club IT*, as described earlier, gives the student an assignment as an intern for virtual-company Club IT. Students are referred to the Wiley Web Site for support information.

Online Supplements

www.wiley.com/college/rainer

This book also facilitates the teaching of an Introduction to IT course by providing extensive support materials for instructors and students. Go to *www.wiley.com/college/rainer* to access the Student and Instructor Web Sites.

Instructor's Manual

The *Instructor's Manual* created by Dana Newton at Eastern Michigan University includes a chapter overview, teaching tips and strategies, answers to all end-of-chapter questions, supplemental minicases with essay questions and answers, experiential exercises that relate to particular topics, and 'war stories' for each chapter. This manual also includes within each chapter a feature called 'What's Next,' which provides a glimpse of what is to come in the next chapter. Finally, also included are a Video Guide with three to five viewing questions that relate to chapter topics, relevant Web links wherever possible, and a case correlation guide that provides a correlation of each case the text authors have provided with the related chapters from the text.

Test Bank

The *Test Bank*, written by Kelly Rainer, is a comprehensive resource for test questions. It contains per chapter multiple choice, true/false, short answer, and essay questions. The multiple choice and true/false questions are labeled as to each one's difficulty: easy, medium, or hard.

PowerPoint Presentations

The Media Enriched *PowerPoint Presentations* created by Kelly Rainer consist of a series of slides for each chapter of the text that are designed around the text content, incorporating key points from the text and all text illustrations as appropriate. In addition, they include links out to relevant web sites, videos, and articles to enhance classroom discussion. The PowerPoints make extensive use of images and video clips.

Media Resource Library

The *Media Resource Library* provides instructors with a wealth of links to web sites and videos which can be used in-class to help engage students. The library is a compilation of suggestions from the author as well as many information systems instructors and comes complete with discussion questions to be used in class after viewing each resource.

Image Library

All textbook figures are available for download from the Web Site. These figures can easily be added to PowerPoint presentations.

BusinessExtra Select

This feature allows instructors to package the text with software applications, lab manuals, cases, articles, and other real-world content from sources such as INSEAD, Ivey and Harvard Business School cases, *Fortune, The Economist, The Wall Street Journal,* and much more. You can combine the book with the content you choose to create a fully customized textbook. For additional information, go to *www.wiley.com/college/bxs.*

On-line Quizzes

These practice tests for students to help prepare for class tests are provided as an online resource within the text Web site. Once students have completed a particular quiz, they can submit it electronically and receive feedback regarding any incorrect responses.

Course Management

New WebCT and Blackboard courses are available with this text. WebCT and Blackboard are tools that facilitate the organization and delivery of course materials via the Web. It provides powerful communication, loaded content, easy and flexible course administration, sophisticated online self-tests and diagnostic systems, and ease of use for both students and instructors.

Clicker Questions

Clicker questions updated by Mehmet Ulema at Manhattan College deliver a variety of multiple choice and true/false questions to use in class in order to assess students' learning throughout the course.

WileyPLUS

WileyPLUS is a powerful online tool that provides instructors and students with an integrated suite of teaching and learning resources, including an online version of the text, in one easy-to-use website. To learn more about WileyPLUS, and view a demo, please visit *www.wiley.com/college/WileyPLUS.*

WileyPLUS Tools for Instructors

WileyPLUS enables you to:

- Assign automatically graded practice questions from the Test Bank.
- Track your students' progress in an instructor's gradebook.
- Access all teaching and learning resources, including an online text, and student and instructor supplements, in one easy to use website.
- Create class presentations using Wiley-provided resources, with the ability to customize and add your own materials.

WileyPLUS Resources for Students

- ***Virtual Company*** The Web-based Virtual Company case at the end of each chapter created by Dolly Samson at Hawaii Pacific University gives students the opportunity to develop IT solutions for a simulated music venue called Club IT, which presents live music and DJs. Students are 'hired' as consultants for the club and asked to work on such projects as helping the club owners manage inventory by tracking food and beverages on spreadsheets, mining Web resources to predict music/nightclub trends, advertising through mobile devices, and streaming the DJ's shows onto the Internet. These assignments also ask students to apply their software applications skills by creating presentations in Microsoft PowerPoint and databases in Microsoft Excel and Access.
- ***Software Skills Lab Manuals*** Lab Manuals by Craig Piercy, Mark Huber, and Patrick McKeown are available in WileyPlus and online through Business Extra Select and the Wiley website (www.wiley.com/college/piercy). For further information on lab manual packaging options, please ask your Wiley representative. To find your Wiley representative, go to wiley.com/college/rep.

Acknowledgments

Creating, developing, and producing a new text for the introduction to information technology course is a formidable undertaking. Along the way, we were fortunate to receive continuous evaluation, criticism, and direction from many colleagues who regularly teach this course. We would like to acknowledge the contributions made by the following individuals.

We would like thank the Wiley team: Beth Lang Golub, Executive Editor; Jen Devine, Assistant Editor; Lauren Sapira, Media Editor; Amy Scholz, Executive Marketing Manager; and Maria Guarascio, Senior Editorial Assistant. We also thank the production team, including Dorothy Sinclair, Production Manager; Trish McFadden, Production Editor; and Suzanne Ingrao of Ingrao Associates. And thanks to Michael St. Martine, Junior Designer; Lisa Gee, Photo Editor; and Anna Melhorn, Illustrations Editor. We also would like to thank Robert Weiss for his skillful and thorough editing of the manuscript.

Reviewers

Tom Dillon, James Madison University
Efrem Mallach, University of Massachusetts, Dartmouth
Patricia McQuaid, California Polytechnic State University
Leonard Presby, William Patterson University
Eugene Rathswohl, University of San Diego
James Yao, Montclair State

Supplements Authors

We are grateful to Dolly Samson, of Hawaii Pacific University, who created the Virtual Company case that is on the book's Web Site, Dana Newton of the University of Eastern Michigan who prepared the Instructor's Manual, Mehmet Ulema of Manhattan College who prepared the Clicker Questions, and Nita Brooks of Quinnipiac University who checked all of the test bank, web quiz, and pre/post-lecture quiz questions for accuracy.

KELLY RAINER
EFRAIM TURBAN

contents

Introduction to Information Systems

Second Edition

Chapter 1

The Modern Organization in the Global, Web-Based Environment

Chapter Outline

1.1 Information Systems: Concepts and Definitions

1.2 The Global Web-Based Platform

1.3 Business Pressures, Organizational Responses, and IT Support

1.4 Why Are Information Systems Important to You?

1.5 The Plan of This Book

What's in IT for me?   ACC   FIN   MKT   POM   HRM   MIS

Google Puts Its Platform to Work

The Business Problem

When the World Wide Web needed new search methods to handle its size and complexity, Sergey Brin and Larry Page developed their PageRank algorithm (an *algorithm* is a mathematical formula) and founded Google (*www.google.com*). PageRank is a complicated mathematical formula that determines the relative importance of a Web page by analyzing the number of links to that page, along with other factors.

In June 1999, Google focused solely on algorithmic searches, and the company earned revenue by licensing its search technology to other companies. Google's own Web site had no advertising and no content other than search results. In December 1999, Google introduced paid listings, which were short text advertisements identified as "Sponsored Links" that appeared either next to, or interspersed with, search results. By mid-2001, despite having spent nothing on marketing, Google was the ninth largest U.S. Web site with 24.5 million unique monthly visitors. In mid-2004, Google had its wildly successful initial public offering (IPO).

Given Google's incredible success, you would think that the company did not have a business problem. However, the company had to consider four possibilities concerning its strategic direction. First, Google could remain a search company and continue to refine its search algorithms and targeted advertising. Second, it could become a portal like Yahoo (*www.yahoo.com*) or Microsoft Network (MSN) (*www.msn.com*). A *portal* is a Web-based, personalized gateway to a great deal of relevant information from various information systems and the Internet. Third, it could develop its role in electronic commerce (e-commerce) by facilitating transactions. *Electronic commerce* is the buying and selling of products, services, or information via computer networks, including the Internet. Fourth, it could develop products to compete with Microsoft Office. Which option would Google choose?

The IT Solution

Along the way to its IPO, Google built a platform called the GooglePlex. A **platform** consists of the hardware, software, and communications components that organizations use to process and manage information. The GooglePlex consists of:

- *Hardware*: Google has an estimated 500,000 servers that provide enormous processing power, plus massive amounts of storage. A *server* is a computer that provides access to various services available on a network, such as data and Web pages. We discuss hardware in detail in Technology Guide 1.

- *Software*: Google servers accommodate numerous types of software and applications. We discuss software in detail in Technology Guide 2.

- *Communications*: Google servers are located around the world and are connected across the Internet by high-transmission-capacity fiber-optic cables. We discuss telecommunications, networks, and the Internet in detail in Technology Guides 4 and 5 and Chapter 5.

The GooglePlex enables Google to develop applications quickly and to deliver applications and results almost instantaneously to users. Google decided to use its platform to pursue all four strategies simultaneously! The company has been developing applications at an incredible rate, expanding its domain beyond Web search.

Google continues to improve its main mission of enabling searches by introducing many new search applications. For example, Personalized Search generates and organizes search results based on analysis of the types of results a user has clicked on in past searches. Desktop Search allows users to search the contents of their own hard drives, and Vertical Search tailors searches to specific Internet sites.

Another facet of Google's main mission is targeted advertising. The company is implementing a new pricing model that lets advertisers pay for only completed actions that they define ahead of time, such as getting a lead, a sale, or a page view.

Google is also vigorously pursuing its three other strategies. Applications such as Talk and Gmail have moved Google into the domain of Web portals, such as Yahoo and Microsoft Network. Other applications, such as Base, Book Search, Maps, and Checkout, have positioned Google in the domain of electronic commerce companies, such as eBay and Amazon. Finally, Google Apps Premier Edition, which includes Desktop, Docs & Spreadsheets, Base, and Calendar, is competing with Microsoft Office in office productivity applications. Google Apps also allows businesses to create a customized home page that includes a single sign-on to all applications, as well as 10 gigabytes of free storage for each employee, all for $50 per year per employee.

As of mid-2007, every month 400 million people were going to Google as their gateway to the Web, and the company drew 56 percent of all searches. By that time, Google had a market capitalization of almost $150 billion, as well as $11 billion in cash and investments.

Despite its amazing success, Google faces intensifying competition and threats. NBC Universal and News Corporation are planning a rival to compete with Google Video (Google purchased YouTube in 2006). The rival product will run not only clips from television shows but also full-length movies on Yahoo!, AOL, MSN, and MySpace.

Perhaps even worse, Viacom is suing Google for $1 billion, charging that YouTube infringed on copyrights by allowing users to upload clips of TV shows. Copiepress, a group representing Belgian and German newspapers, won a copyright case that could impact Google if it sets a precedent.

To further complicate matters, in 2004 Google launched its Library project, in which the company began digitizing millions of books at various libraries. It did so, however, without first securing permission from book publishers. In response, in 2005 the Authors Guild and a group of publishers each filed lawsuits against the library scanning project, charging that it violates copyright protection.

The Google case illustrates how an organization can use information technologies to survive and thrive in today's environment. Google's strategies and applications illustrate the following points:

- To succeed in today's environment, it is often necessary to change business models and strategies.
- IT enables organizations to survive and thrive in the face of relentless business pressures.
- IT may require a large investment over a long period of time.
- Organizations can leverage their platforms to develop new Web-based applications, products, and services, as well as to provide superb customer service.

You are the most connected generation in history. You have grown up online. You are, quite literally, never out of touch. You use more information technologies (in the form of digital devices), for more tasks, and are bombarded with more information, than anyone in history. The *MIT Technology Review* refers to you as *Homo conexus*. Information technologies are embedded so deeply in your lives that your daily routines would be almost unrecognizable to a college student just 20 years ago.

Essentially, you are practicing *continuous computing*, whereby you are surrounded with a movable information network. Your network is created by constant cooperation between the digital devices you carry (for example, laptops, media players, and smart phones); the wired and wireless networks that you access as you move about; and Web-based tools for finding information and communicating and collaborating with other people. Your network enables you to *pull* information about virtually anything from anywhere, at any time, and *push* your own ideas back to the Web, from wherever you are, via a mobile device.

So, why study about information systems and information technology when you are already so comfortable using them? The answer is that when you graduate, you either will start your own business or will go to work for an organization, whether it is public sector, private sector, for-profit, or not-for-profit. In either case, you and your organization will have to survive and compete in an environment that has been radically changed by information technology. This environment is global, massively interconnected, intensely competitive, 24/7/365, real-time, rapidly changing, and information-intensive.

In this chapter we discuss the basic concepts of information systems in organizations. First, however, we distinguish between management information systems, also called information systems or IS, and information technology. **Management information systems (MIS)** deal with the planning for—and the development, management, and use of—information technology tools to help people perform all the tasks related to information processing and management. **Information technology (IT)** relates to any computer-based tool that people use to work with information and to support the information and information processing needs of an organization. Although these are distinct terms, in practice they are typically used interchangeably. For example, organizations refer to their MIS function as the Information Services Department, the Information Systems Department, the Information Technology Department, and other names. In keeping with this practice, we use these terms interchangeably throughout this book.

After presenting the basic concepts of information systems, we discuss today's global business environment and how businesses use information technologies to survive and prosper in this highly competitive environment. We then consider in greater detail why information systems are important to you. We finish the chapter by describing the plan of the book.

Sources: Compiled from R. Hof, "Is Google Too Powerful?" *BusinessWeek*, April 9, 2007; T. Claburn, "Google's Pay-Per-Action Model," *InformationWeek*, March 26, 2007; R. Martin, "Computer Science 101: Case Study in Google Applications," *InformationWeek*, March 26, 2007; P. McDougall, "Google Storms the Office," *InformationWeek*, February 26, 2007; J. Pallatto, "Google Apps Premier Edition Takes Aim at the Enterprise," *eWeek*, February 22, 2007; Q. Hardy, "The Google Industrial Complex," *Forbes*, October 16, 2006; T. Claburn, "Google Revealed." *InformationWeek*, August 28, 2006; J. Markoff and S. Hansell, "Google's Not-So-Very-Secret Weapon," *New York Times*, June 13, 2006; J. Markoff, "Google to Release Web-Based Spreadsheet," *New York Times*, June 5, 2006.

1.1 Information Systems: Concepts and Definitions

It has been said that the purpose of information systems is to get the right information to the right people at the right time in the right amount and in the right format. Because information systems are intended to supply useful information, we begin by defining information and two closely related terms, *data* and *knowledge*.

Data, Information, and Knowledge

One of the primary goals of information systems is to economically process data into information and knowledge. Let's take a closer look at these concepts.

Data items refer to an elementary description of things, events, activities, and transactions that are recorded, classified, and stored but are not organized to convey any specific meaning. Data items can be numbers, letters, figures, sounds, or images. Examples of data items are a student grade in a class and the number of hours an employee worked in a certain week.

Information refers to data that have been organized so that they have meaning and value to the recipient. For example, a grade point average (GPA) is data, but a student's name coupled with his or her GPA is information. The recipient interprets the meaning and draws conclusions and implications from the information.

Knowledge consists of data and/or information that have been organized and processed to convey understanding, experience, accumulated learning, and expertise as they apply to a current business problem. For example, a company recruiting at your school has found over time that students with grade point averages over 3.0 have had the most success in its management program. Based on its experience, that company may decide to interview only those students with GPAs over 3.0. Organizational knowledge, which reflects the experience and expertise of many people, has great value to all employees.

Now that we have a better idea of what information is and how it can be organized to convey knowledge, we shift our focus to the ways organizations organize and use information. To do this we must look closely at an organization's information technology architecture and information technology infrastructure. These concepts underlie all information systems within the organization.

Information Technology Architecture

An organization's **information technology (IT) architecture** is a high-level map or plan of the information assets in an organization. It is both a guide for current operations and a blueprint for future directions. The IT architecture integrates the entire organization's business needs for information, the IT infrastructure (discussed in the next section), and all applications. The IT architecture is analogous to the architecture of a house. An architecture plan describes how the house is to be constructed, including how the various components of the house, such as the plumbing and electrical systems, are to be integrated. Similarly, the IT architecture shows how all aspects of information technology in an organization fit together. Figure 1.1 illustrates the IT architecture of an online travel agency. We discuss each part of this figure in subsequent chapters.

Information Technology Infrastructure

An organization's **information technology (IT) infrastructure** consists of the physical facilities, IT components, IT services, and IT personnel that support the entire organization (see Figure 1.2). Starting from the bottom of Figure 1.2, we see that *IT components* are the computer hardware, software, and communications technologies that provide the foundation for all of an organization's information systems. As we move up the pyramid, we see that *IT personnel* use IT components to produce *IT services*, which include data management, systems development, and security concerns.

An organization's IT infrastructure should not be confused with its platform. As we can see in Figure 1.2, a firm's platform consists only of its IT components. Therefore, a platform is part of an IT infrastructure.

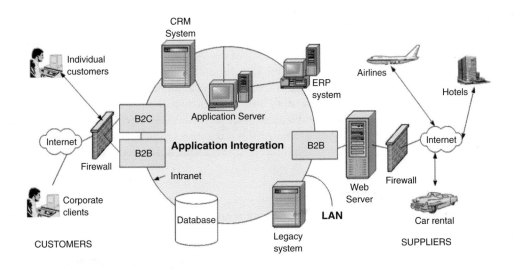

FIGURE 1.1
Architecture of an online travel agency.

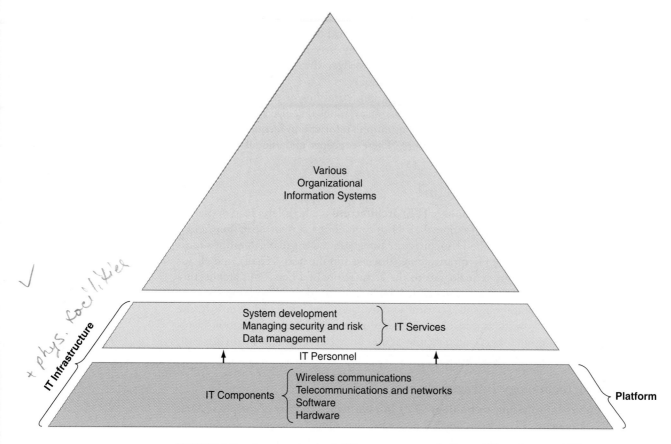

FIGURE 1.2   An organization's IT components, platform, IT services, and IT infrastructure.

The Google and Amazon cases in this chapter illustrate the vital importance of IT infrastructures and platforms to organizations in today's competitive environment. The platforms of Google and Amazon operate within a global, Web-based platform that has recently emerged (see Figure 1.3). The next section discusses this global platform.

1.2 The Global Web-Based Platform

The global, Web-based platform that has recently emerged spans the world and is best represented by the Internet and the functionality of the World Wide Web. The platform enables individuals to connect, compute, communicate, collaborate, and compete everywhere and anywhere, anytime and all the time; to access limitless amounts of information, services, and entertainment; to exchange knowledge; and to produce and sell goods and services. It operates without regard to geography, time, distance, and even language barriers. In essence, this platform enables globalization. **Globalization** is the integration and interdependence of economic, social, cultural, and ecological facets of life, enabled by rapid advances in information technology.

The Three Stages of Globalization

In his book *The World Is Flat*, Pulitzer Prize-winning author Thomas Friedman argues that the world is flat in the sense that the global competitive playing field is being leveled. Friedman identifies three eras of globalization. The first era, Globalization 1.0, lasted from 1492 to

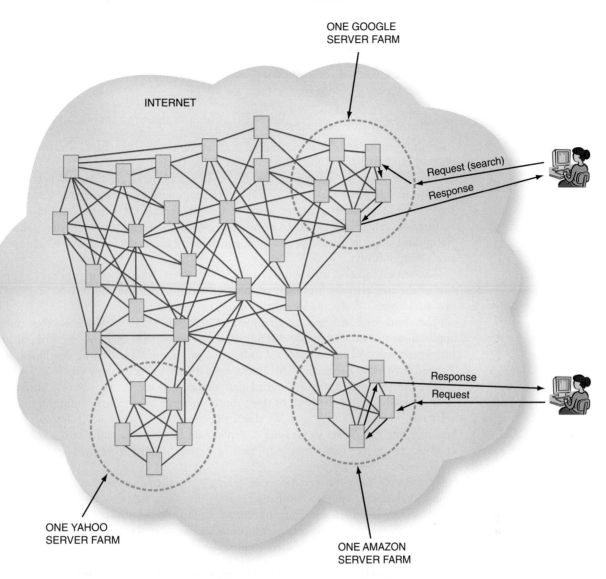

FIGURE 1.3   Organizational server farms in relation to the Internet.

1800. During this period, the force behind globalization was the amount of muscle, horsepower, wind power, or steam power a country had and could deploy.

The second era, Globalization 2.0, lasted from 1800 to 2000. In this era, the force behind globalization was multinational companies—that is, companies that had their headquarters in one country but operated in several countries. In the first half of this period, globalization was driven by falling transportation costs, generated by the development of the steam engine and the railroads. In the second half, globalization was driven by falling telecommunications costs resulting from the telegraph, telephone, computer, satellites, fiber-optic cable, and the Internet and World Wide Web. The global economy began appearing during this era.

Around the year 2000, we entered Globalization 3.0, which was driven by the convergence of ten forces that Friedman calls "flatteners" (discussed below). In era 3.0, we are witnessing the emergence of a global, Web-based platform.

Each era has been characterized by a distinctive focus: Globalization 1.0 focused on countries, Globalization 2.0 on companies, and Globalization 3.0 on groups and individuals. This observation makes our discussion all the more important for each of you, because you will be competing with people from all over a flat world when you graduate.

Friedman's Ten Flatteners

As already mentioned, Friedman noted that ten forces, or "flatteners," contributed to the emergence of era 3.0 and the flat world. (See Table 1.1.)

The first force, the collapse of the *Berlin Wall,* took place on November 9, 1989. The subsequent collapse of the Soviet Union and the communist governments of Eastern Europe in 1991 enabled these countries to move toward free-market economies and away from totalitarian, centrally planned economies. Many of these countries eventually joined the European Union, which led people to begin thinking about the world as a single market or single community.

The second force occurred on August 9, 1995, when *Netscape* went public. Netscape, the first of the user-friendly browsers, popularized the Internet and the Web by making them easy to navigate. We discuss Internet browsers in Chapter 5.

The third force was the development of *workflow software*, which enables computer applications to interoperate, or communicate and work with one another without human intervention. For workflow software to be effective, standards had to be developed, such as Extensible Markup Language (XML), which we discuss in Technology Guide 2.

The fourth force, *uploading*, means that anyone can create and upload content to the Web. Uploading takes the form of open-source software (also called community-developed software), blogging, and Wikis. We discuss open-source software in Technology Guide 2, and blogging and Wikis in Chapter 5. Uploading has led to a shift from a static, passive approach to media to an active, participatory approach. Entire communities of people now collaborate on Web content.

Outsourcing, the fifth force, involves taking a specific function that your company was doing itself, having another company perform that same function for you, and then integrating their work back into your operation. Companies outsource so that they can lower costs and concentrate on their core competencies. We discuss outsourcing in Chapter 10.

Offshoring, the sixth force, differs from outsourcing. Offshoring occurs when a company moves an entire operation, or certain tasks, to another country. An example of an entire operation would be moving an entire plant. Tasks that are likely to be offshored involve lower-value-added activities such as rendering architectural drawings and medical transcription.

Table 1.1

Friedman's Ten Flatteners

- Fall of the Berlin Wall
- Netscape now a public offering
- Development of workflow software
- Uploading
- Outsourcing
- Offshoring
- Supply chaining
- Insourcing
- Informing
- The steroids (computing, instant messaging and file sharing, wireless technologies, voice over Internet Protocol [VoIP], videoconferencing, and computer graphics)

There, the operation and/or activities are performed the same way, but with cheaper labor, lower taxes, fewer benefits, and so on. Companies also choose to offshore in order to penetrate and then serve a foreign market without having to deal with trade barriers. We discuss off-shoring in Chapter 10.

The seventh force, *supply chaining*, occurs when companies, their suppliers, and their customers collaborate and share information. Supply chaining requires common standards so that each segment of the chain can interface with the next. We discuss supply chains in Chapter 8.

The eighth force, *insourcing*, delegates operations or jobs within a business to another company, which specializes in those operations. For example, a company such as Dell will hire FedEx to analyze Dell's shipping process and then "take over" that process. FedEx employees work inside Dell but remain employed by FedEx.

The ninth force, *informing*, is your ability to search for information, and it is best illustrated by search engines. Informing also facilitates the formation of global communities, as you can now look for collaborators on any subject or project almost anywhere in the world. We discuss informing in Chapter 5.

Friedman calls the tenth force *the steroids* because they amplify the other flatteners. In essence, they enable all forms of computing and collaboration to be digital, mobile, and personal. The steroids are new and dynamic forms of information technologies: computing (including computational capability, storage, and input/output); instant messaging and file sharing; wireless technologies; voice over Internet Protocol (VoIP); videoconferencing; and advances in computer graphics. We discuss the steroids in Technology Guide 1 as well as Chapters 5 and 7.

Google and Amazon (see the closing case in this chapter) are using the global, Web-based platform to develop and deliver new applications. What is really interesting about the platform is that it is available to you as an individual. Google and Amazon (as well as other companies) provide processing, storage, and applications to anyone for free or for a very reasonable charge. Therefore, you can use their resources in the course of your daily information processing and if you want to start your own business.

In essence, you are entering a flat world that is made possible by the global, Web-based platform we have described. This platform has had an enormous impact on many industries. The following example points out that impact on the travel industry.

Do It Yourself Traveling Whatever happened to travel agencies? The answer is that the Web-based platform has heavily impacted this industry, and not for the better. Web users are planning almost all of their travel online. In 2006, for example, 80 percent of Americans who arranged trips on the Web also bought their tickets online. Now, a new generation of travel sites is making trip planning cheaper, more efficient, and more fun. Here is a quick look at the top new sites that illustrate what has happened to an entire industry.

Example

Shopping for Flights. Two-thirds of online travel planners use the big three: Expedia (*www.expedia.com*), Travelocity (*www.travelocity.com*), and Priceline (*www.priceline.com*). However, a new way to search for bargain flights is on Kayak (*www.kayak.com*). The site covers fares on some 300 airlines in any given week and saves time by letting you adjust search parameters by using a sliding dial, without having to start from scratch.

Plan Your Itinerary. Yahoo's Trip Planner (*http://travel.yahoo.com/trip*) provides a Web folder for your online research about museums, restaurants, lodging, and sights at your destination.

Organize a Group Trip. TripHub (*www.triphub.com*) allows you to book group tickets, discuss the best hotels and sights to see, or decide where you will all meet upon arrival.

Save on a Rental Car. Booking a car at an airport can cost double what you would pay online. Whether you are traveling abroad or in the United States, Bnm (*www.bnm.com*) can help you find and reserve the cheapest rentals available. If you do not care about the specific model you drive, check Bnm's prices and those at Hotwire (*www.hotwire.com*), and then go to Priceline's (*www.priceline.com*) car-rental page to bid for steeper discounts. For bidding help, go to BiddingforTravel (*www.biddingfortravel.com*).

Watch Where You Go. Reading about a place is just not the same as seeing it. Turnhere (*www.turnhere.com*) posts free short videos of popular destinations around the world to watch online.

Trip Tracking. TripStalker (*www.tripstalker.com*) constantly scans for inexpensive trips and alerts you by e-mail or text message once a flight, hotel, or rental car matching your search criteria turns up.

Sources: Compiled from *www.kayak.com, www.expedia.com, www.travelocity.com, www.bnm.com, www.hotwire.com, www.priceline.com, www.biddingfortravel.com, www.turnhere.com, www.triphub.com, www.tripstalker.com, http://travel.yahoo.com/trip*, all accessed April 15, 2007.

This book will discuss, explain, and illustrate the characteristics of the dynamic global business environment. We will also discuss how you and your organization can use the Web-based platform to survive and compete in this environment.

Before you go on . . .

1. What are the characteristics of the modern business environment?
2. Describe the Web-based, global platform.
3. Describe the platform used by Google, Amazon, and other companies.

1.3 Business Pressures, Organizational Responses, and IT Support

Modern organizations must compete in a challenging environment. Companies must react rapidly to problems and opportunities arising from extremely dynamic conditions. In this section we examine some of the major pressures confronting modern organizations, and we discuss how organizations are responding to these pressures.

Business Pressures

The *business environment* is the combination of social, legal, economic, physical, and political factors that affect business activities. Significant changes in any of these factors are likely to create business pressures on organizations. Organizations typically respond to these pressures with activities supported by IT. Figure 1.4 shows the relationships among business pressures, organizational performance and responses, and IT support. Here we focus on three types of business pressures that organizations face: market, technology, and societal pressures.

Market Pressures. Market pressures are generated by the global economy and strong competition, the changing nature of the workforce, and powerful customers. We'll look at each of these factors in turn.

Global Economy and Strong Competition. The move to a global economy has been facilitated by the emergence of the global, Web-based platform. Regional agreements such as

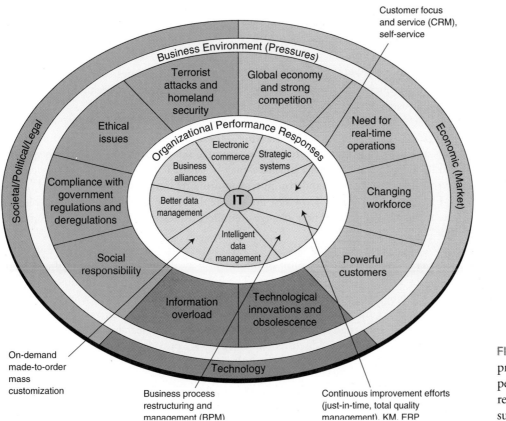

FIGURE 1.4 Business pressures, organizational performance and responses, and IT support.

the North American Free Trade Agreement (NAFTA), which includes the United States, Canada, and Mexico, and the creation of a unified European market with a single currency, the euro, have contributed to increased world trade. Furthermore, the rise of India and China as economic powerhouses has markedly increased global competition.

One important pressure that exists for businesses in a global market is the cost of labor, which varies widely among countries. In general, labor costs are higher in developed countries like the United States and Japan than in developing countries such as China and El Salvador. Also, developed countries usually offer greater benefits, such as health care, to employees, which makes the cost of doing business even higher. Therefore, many labor-intensive industries have moved their operations to countries with low labor costs. IT has made such moves much easier to implement.

The Changing Nature of the Workforce.   The workforce, particularly in developed countries, is becoming more diversified. Increasing numbers of women, single parents, minorities, and persons with disabilities now work in all types of positions. IT is easing the integration of these employees into the traditional workforce. IT is also enabling people to work from home.

Powerful Customers.   Consumer sophistication and expectations increase as customers become more knowledgeable about the availability and quality of products and services. Customers can use the Internet to find detailed information about products and services, compare prices, and purchase items at electronic auctions.

Organizations recognize the importance of customers and have increased their efforts to acquire and retain them. As a result, firms try to know as much as possible about their customers to better anticipate and serve their needs. This process, *customer intimacy*, is an important part of **customer relationship management** (CRM), an organizationwide effort toward maximizing the customer experience. We discuss CRM in Chapter 8.

Technology Pressures. The second category of business pressures consists of those pressures related to technology. Two major technology-related pressures are technological innovation and information overload.

Technological Innovation and Obsolescence. New and improved technologies rapidly create or support substitutes for products, alternative service options, and superb quality. As a result, today's state-of-the-art products may be obsolete tomorrow. For example, how fast are thin-screen televisions and computer monitors replacing the bulky TVs and monitors of just a short time ago? How fast are you replacing your old, standard cell phones with the new smart phones? These changes require businesses to keep up with consumer demands.

Information Overload. The amount of information available on the Internet doubles approximately every year, and much of it is free. The Internet and other telecommunications networks are bringing a flood of information to managers. To make decisions effectively and efficiently, managers must be able to access, navigate, and utilize these vast stores of data, information, and knowledge. Information technologies, such as search engines (discussed in Chapter 5) and data mining (discussed in Chapter 9), provide valuable support in these efforts.

Societal/Political/Legal Pressures. The third category of business pressures includes social responsibility, government regulation/deregulation, spending for social programs, spending to protect against terrorism, and ethics.

Social Responsibility. Social issues that affect businesses range from the state of the physical environment to companies' contributions to education (for example, by allowing interns to work in companies). Some corporations are willing to spend time and/or money on solving various social problems. These efforts are known as **organizational social responsibility**.

One social problem that affects modern business is the digital divide. The **digital divide** refers to the wide gap between those who have access to information and communications technology and those who do not. This gap exists both within and among countries.

According to reports by the United Nations, more than 90 percent of all Internet hosts are located in developed countries, although these countries contain only 15 percent of the world's population. Approximately 70 percent of the U.S. population has Internet access. Furthermore, this distribution is highly correlated with household income. That is, the greater a household's income, the more likely they are to have Internet access. The U.S. federal and state governments are attempting to close the digital divide within the country by encouraging training and by supporting education and infrastructure improvements.

One development that can help close the digital divide is the installation of Internet kiosks in public places and cybercafés. In addition, in the United States, computers with Internet access usually are also available at public libraries.

Cybercafés are public places in which Internet terminals are available, usually for a small fee. Cybercafés come in all shapes and sizes, ranging from a chain of cafés (*www .easyeverything.com*) that include hundreds of terminals in one location (for example, 760 in one New York setting) to a single computer in a corner of many restaurants. Computers have popped up in many other public locations: laundromats, karaoke bars, bookstores, CD stores, hotel lobbies, and convenience stores. Some facilities give free access to patrons; others charge a small fee.

Many other government and international organizations are also trying to close the digital divide around the world. As technologies develop and become less expensive, the speed at which the gap can be closed will accelerate. A well-known project is the One Laptop per Child (OLPC) project that originated from MIT's Media Lab (http://laptop.media.mit.edu). OLPC is a nonprofit association dedicated to research to develop a $100 laptop—a technology that could revolutionize how we educate the world's children. In IT's About Business 1.1, cell phones and Internet centers are helping to close the digital divide in Bangladesh.

Compliance with Government Regulations and Deregulation. Other business pressures are related to government regulations regarding health, safety, environmental control, and equal opportunity. Businesses tend to view government regulations as expensive constraints on their activities. In general, government deregulation intensifies competition.

In the wake of 9/11 and numerous corporate scandals, the U.S. government passed many new laws, including the Sarbanes-Oxley Act, the USA PATRIOT Act, the Gramm-Leach-Bliley Act, and the Health Insurance Portability and Accountability Act. Organizations must be in compliance with the regulations of these statutes. The process of becoming and remaining compliant is expensive and time-consuming. In almost all cases, organizations rely on IT support to provide the necessary controls and information for compliance, as we see in IT's About Business 1.2.

IT's About Business

1.1 The Internet Helps Bridge the Digital Divide in Bangladesh

Villages in Bangladesh, long isolated by distance and deprivation, are gaining cell-phone access to the Internet. In the process, millions of people who have no land-line telephones and who often lack electricity and running water are able to utilize services that people in developed countries consider to be basic, such as weather reports, e-mail, and a second opinion from a physician.

Bangladesh now has about 16 million cell phone subscribers—and 2 million new users each month—compared with just 1 million land-line phones to serve a population of 150 million people. About 500 Internet centers have been opened in places where there are no land lines, so the connections will be made exclusively over cell phone networks. The Internet centers are being set up by GrameenPhone (*www.grameenphone.com*), a cell phone provider partly owned by Grameen Bank (*www.initus.com*). The centers are building on a cell phone network created over the past decade by a Grameen Bank program that has helped provide more than 250,000 cell phones in villages.

People now download job applications, check news stories and crop prices, make inexpensive Internet calls, or use Web cameras to see relatives. Students from villages with few books now have access to online dictionaries and encyclopedias.

One of the most popular services is videoconferencing, which involves using a Web camera on top of a computer monitor. Entire families crowd in front of the camera to hold video conferences with relatives living overseas. Recently, one mother came in to hold up a newborn baby to give the father, working overseas, his first glimpse of his child.

Sources: Compiled from K. Sullivan, "Internet Extends Reach of Bangladeshi Villagers," *Washington Post,* November 22, 2006; D. Kirkpatrick, "Technology and the Developing World," *Fortune,* December 22, 2006; J. Elliott, "Field of Green," *Fortune,* October 2, 2006.

QUESTIONS

1. Why is accessing the Internet with cell phones such a huge advantage for countries or areas with no land lines? *Hint:* Consider costs and convenience.
2. What are some additional ways that villagers could use the Internet? Can Internet access really bridge the digital divide in these rural areas? Why or why not?
3. What is the relationship between providing cell phones to villagers and a flat world?

1.2 A Compliance Culture at Humana

Humana Inc. (*www.humana.com*) is a $14 billion healthcare company, with 9.3 million medical members in all 50 states and Puerto Rico. Compliance is a part of Humana's culture. The company has incorporated the costly and time-consuming tasks associated with regulation into its business model. Humana has also recognized the central role that its information systems function plays in all the company's compliance efforts.

Humana first faced compliance issues with the Year 2000 (Y2K) problem. To run its Y2K compliance projects, Humana appointed a "tiger team" that was comprised of relevant people from different departments to run critical projects with definite deadlines.

Another challenge confronting Humana was the Health Insurance Portability and Accountability Act (HIPAA), a broad piece of legislation designed to let Americans keep their health insurance if they change jobs or become unemployed. The act also sets standards for the healthcare industry for such concerns as patient health, data exchange, and data privacy. When the compliance deadlines of HIPAA began in 2003, Humana was ready.

The company created tiger teams to handle the development of privacy policies and practices, one team to handle information security and one team, composed of senior managers, to provide oversight for the other teams. Each tiger team had members from the company's IS department, and the oversight team included two IS vice-presidents.

Humana first reorganized its compliance division. The company already had a regulatory compliance department, a Medicare department, a department for state insurers, and various groups whose job was to ensure that the company's health plans were accredited by quality-assurance bodies. It adapted these groups into HIPAA compliance centers, making each center responsible for establishing the necessary policies for Humana to comply with the HIPAA rules that applied to that center.

Humana then revamped its information security model. The company's old security model focused only on defense against external threats. This process was not sufficient to comply with HIPAA, which required healthcare companies to protect information from internal threats as well. An example of an internal threat would be an employee losing a laptop with sensitive company information on it. Therefore, the company implemented a new security model to handle these requirements, as well as the security requirements involved with the expanding use of the Web, interactive voice systems, and wireless connectivity.

Humana's new security policies require employees to take all patient information off their desks before they go home at night. In addition, employees must memorize their passwords, and they may not write them down. Finally, Humana made annual compliance training for all employees mandatory.

Humana did not get everything right the first time. For example, it made errors by being too conservative with patient information. For instance, the company initially disclosed almost no patient health information to insurance agents and brokers, which made it difficult for these people to act on behalf of their clients. Humana also started out with a very difficult process of identifying the people who were trying to access their accounts on the Web. This system made it far too difficult to do something as simple as check the status of an insurance claim.

Humana's HIPAA compliance efforts have enhanced the company's overall operations. Being fully HIPAA compliant makes it easier for insurance companies and hospitals to communicate. This process also makes it easier for these institutions to process the vast number of healthcare transactions that occur daily.

Finally, HIPAA compliance makes Humana's customers, who are very concerned about how Humana protects their health information, feel better. In fact, being fully HIPAA compliant has become a selling point for Humana's services.

Sources: Compiled from M. Fitzgerald, "Humana Tackles Compliance Early and Often," *CIO Insight*, June 19, 2006; S. Lawrence, "Health Care Insurers Face Ranking," *eWeek*, October 10, 2006; M. Pratt, "Humana Inc.: Keeping a Watchful Eye on Patients," *Computerworld*, September 18, 2006; *www.humana.com*, accessed April 15, 2007.

QUESTIONS

1. Why is it so important for an organization to make compliance an integral part of its culture? *Hint:* Is compliance a "top down" or a "bottom up" process?
2. Why is the IS function so important to an organization's compliance efforts? Is this true of all industries, or is it true of some industries more than others? If the latter, for which industries would compliance be most critical? Why?

Protection against Terrorist Attacks. Since September 11, 2001, organizations have been under increased pressure to protect themselves against terrorist attacks. In addition, employees who are in the military reserves may be called up for active duty, creating personnel problems. Information technology can help protect businesses by providing security systems and possibly identifying patterns of behavior associated with terrorist activities that will help to prevent terrorist attacks, including cyberattacks (discussed in Chapter 3), against organizations.

An example of protection against terrorism is the Department of Homeland Security's US-VISIT program. US-VISIT is a network of biometric-screening systems, such as fingerprint and ocular (eye) scanners, that ties into government databases and watch lists to check the identities of millions of people entering the United States. The system is now operational in more than 300 locations, including major international ports of entry by air, sea, and land.

Ethical Issues. Ethics relates to general standards of right and wrong, whereas information ethics relates specifically to standards of right and wrong in information processing practices. Ethical issues are very important because, if handled poorly, they can damage an organization's image and destroy its employees' morale. The use of IT raises many ethical issues, ranging from monitoring e-mail to invading the privacy of millions of customers whose data are stored in private and public databases. Chapter 3 covers ethical issues in detail.

Clearly, then, the pressures on organizations are increasing, and organizations must be prepared to take responsive actions if they are to succeed.

Organizational Responses

Organizations are responding to these pressures by implementing IT such as strategic systems, customer focus, make-to-order and mass customization, and e-business. The Amazon case at the end of this chapter illustrates all of these responses. We discuss each type in greater detail in this section.

Strategic Systems. Strategic systems provide organizations with advantages that enable them to increase their market share and/or profits, to better negotiate with suppliers, or to prevent competitors from entering their markets. IT's About Business 1.3 provides an example of strategic systems at JPMorgan. We discuss strategic systems in detail in Chapter 2.

Customer Focus. Organizational attempts to provide superb customer service can make the difference between attracting and keeping customers on the one hand and losing them to competitors on the other. Numerous IT tools and business processes have been designed to keep customers happy. For example, consider Amazon. When you visit Amazon's Web site anytime after your first visit, the site welcomes you back by name and presents you with information on books that you might like, based on your previous purchases. In another example, Dell guides you through the process of buying a computer by providing information and choices that help you make an informed buying decision.

Make-to-Order and Mass Customization. **Make-to-order** is a strategy of producing customized products and services. The business problem is how to manufacture customized goods efficiently and at a reasonably low cost. Part of the solution is to change manufacturing processes from mass production to mass customization. In mass production, a company produces a large quantity of identical items. In **mass customization**, it also produces a large quantity of items, but it customizes them to fit the desires of each customer. Mass customization is simply an attempt to perform make-to-order on a large scale.

E-Business and E-Commerce. Doing business electronically is an essential strategy for companies competing in today's business environment. Chapter 6 will focus extensively on this topic. In addition, e-commerce applications appear throughout the book.

IT's About Business

1.3 JPMorgan Invests in IT

JPMorgan (*www.jpmorgan.com*), the third largest U.S. bank, is spending more than $2 billion to overhaul its networks, plus another $1 billion to reduce the number of its global data centers from 90 to 30. The bank's current organization is the product of many bank mergers, which led to a patchwork of out-of-date systems that speak different computer languages. These systems are decreasing the bank's efficiency, particularly on the consumer side of the business (retail banking, credit cards, and so on), which accounts for about 50 percent of the bank's profits. Of the top ten banks, JPMorgan ranks lowest both in overhead efficiency ratio and return on equity.

The bank decided to make information technology a fundamental part of its strategy. The chief information officer (CIO) is a member of the operating committee that runs the bank. The bulk of the IT spending is going to consumer banking, to perform operations as simple as enabling the network of banks to serve a customer who moves to a new city.

Retail customers are seeing technology make banking easier. JPMorgan launched the Blink credit card, which lets customers hold the card in front of a reader instead of swiping, signing, entering a PIN, or handing the card to a store employee. Also, approval for a home equity loan now takes two hours, versus days a few years ago.

On the other side of the house, investment banking is receiving an annual budget of $1 billion for technology. These monies are focusing on building sophisticated trading platforms for institutional investors and hedge fund clients who require high-end trading analysis and risk modeling.

Sources: Compiled from M. Hovanesian, "The Bank of Technology," *BusinessWeek*, June 19, 2006; C. Deutsch, "J. P. Morgan Chase: Building the Global Bank," *McKinsey Quarterly*, Fall 2006; *www.jpmorgan.com*, accessed April 10, 2007.

QUESTIONS

1. How do JPMorgan's investments in IT help the bank increase market share? increase profits? prevent competitors from entering its markets?
2. Why is it important for the CIO to sit on the bank's operating committee?
3. If you were the CIO of JPMorgan, do you think you would get a better return from your IT investments in consumer banking or in investment banking? Support your answer.

We have described the pressures that affect companies in today's business environment and the responses that organizations take to manage these pressures. To plan for the most effective responses, companies formulate strategies. In the new digital economy, these strategies rely heavily on information technology, especially strategic information systems. In Chapter 2, we discuss corporate strategy and strategic information systems.

Before you go on . . .

1. Describe some of the pressures that characterize the modern global business environment.
2. What are some of the organizational responses to these pressures? Are any of the responses specific to a particular pressure? If so, which ones?

1.4 Why Are Information Systems Important to You?

Information systems are important to you for a variety of reasons. First, information systems and information technologies are integral to your life. Second, the IS field offers many career opportunities. Finally, all functional areas in an organization utilize information systems.

Information Systems and Information Technologies Are Integral to Your Lives

There are many examples of how information systems and technologies are embedded in your lives. For example, think of all the things you can do online:

- Register for classes.
- Take classes, and not just classes from your university.
- Access class syllabi, information, PowerPoints, and lectures.
- Research class papers and presentations.
- Conduct banking.
- Pay your bills.
- Research, shop, and buy products from companies or other people.
- Sell your "stuff."
- Search for, and apply for, jobs.
- Make your travel reservations (hotel, airline, rental car).

In addition to all the activities you can perform online, there are other examples of how information systems and information technologies are essential to your daily living. For example, you may not use a regular wireline telephone. Rather, you use a smartphone that has a calendar, an address book, a calculator, a digital camera, and several types of software to download music and movies. This phone enables you to seamlessly switch between different wireless modes (Bluetooth, Wi-Fi, cellular, and/or Wi-Max) to communicate by voice, e-mail, instant messaging, and text messaging.

Going further, you have your own blog, and you post your own podcasts and videocasts to it. You have your own page on FaceBook. You make and upload videos to YouTube (now Google Video). You take, edit, and print your own digital photographs. You "burn" your own custom-music CDs and DVDs. You use RSS feeds to create your personal electronic newspaper. The list goes on. (*Note:* If a few of these terms are unfamiliar to you, don't worry. We discuss everything here in detail later in this book.)

IT Offers Career Opportunities

Becoming knowledgeable about IT can improve your chances of landing a good job. Even though computerization eliminates some jobs, it creates many more. IT also creates many opportunities to start your own business, as you will see in IT's About Business 1.4.

IT's About Business

1.4 A Startup for Used Video Games

The founder of Goozex (*www.goozex.com*) went to a used video game store with a number of Xbox games. For 17 used games, he received $34 in store credit. Out of curiosity, he went back to the store the next day. The games he had traded in were selling for prices ranging from $12.99 to $32.99. Not surprisingly, he felt that he had been ripped off.

Rather than simply becoming upset, he launched a Web site to help game fans get a better deal and to make money for himself. On Goozex, gamers can save some money by connecting with one another online and trading games through the mail. Goozex members pay $1 per transaction to use the site's matchmaking service, and they store up points that serve as a form of currency toward future trades. For example, if you send out an old Game Boy title, you might earn 100 Goozex points. If you send out a fairly recent Xbox 360 title, you might receive 850 points.

You spend the points when somebody else has a game you want. The business model is similar to such trading services as Lala (*www.lala.com*) for CDs and Peerflix (*www.peerflix.com*) for DVDs.

Experts predict that the used-game market will exceed $1.5 billion by 2008. Goozex has a few competitors that appeared quickly. However, Goozex has a reputation for having a better selection, an easy-to-use interface, and responsive customer service. One member has unloaded six old games from his collection and received five in the mail from his fellow members. He had planned to buy some of the games he got through Goozex at a retail store, but he saved about $120 by trading instead. These savings are important because some of the most avid gamers are cash-strapped college students.

Goozex has 1,500 users trading a collective library of almost 7,000 games for systems ranging from the defunct Sega Dreamcast game console to the Xbox 360. Goozex now has customers in every state and it plans to extend its business into Canada.

Sources: Compiled from M. Musgrove, "Anger from 1 Ripoff + 2 MBAs = A Game Plan," *Washington Post*, November 6, 2006; *www.goozex.com*, accessed April 15, 2007.

QUESTIONS

1. What are the advantages of having your used-game business only on the Web instead of in a "bricks-and-mortar" store? What are the disadvantages? Do the advantages outweigh the disadvantages? Why or why not?

2. Using what you have learned from the opening and closing cases of this chapter, how would you set up the computing platform for your business?

Because information technology is vital to the operation of modern businesses, it offers many employment opportunities. The demand for traditional IT staff—programmers, business analysts, systems analysts, and designers—is substantial. In addition, many well-paid jobs exist in emerging areas such as the Internet and e-commerce, mobile commerce, network security, object-oriented programming (OOP), telecommunications, and multimedia design. For details about careers in IT, see *www.computerworld.com/careertopics/careers* and *www.monster.com*. In addition, Table 1.2 provides a list of IT jobs along with a description of each one.

Since the stock market "correction" of 2000–2001, a great deal of misinformation about careers in information technology has been circulated. Let's look at four myths about IT careers.

Myth #1: There are no computing jobs. In fact, the IT job market is quite strong. The technology jobs site Dice (*www.dice.com*) listed 30,000 technology jobs in 2002, 76,000 in 2005, and almost 100,000 in 2007. See *http://news-service.stanford.edu/news/2006/november8/vardi-110806.html*.

Myth #2: There will be no IT jobs when I graduate. In fact, the four fastest growing U.S. jobs that require a bachelor's degree from 2002 through 2012 are IT-related. They are: (1) computer engineers, (2) management/computer information systems staffers, (3) computer and information systems managers, and (4) technical support specialists. Note that numbers (2) and (3) refer to MIS majors in colleges of business.

Myth #3: All IT-related jobs are moving offshore. In fact, some IT jobs are offshored (that is, sourced to areas with lower-cost labor), but the more highly skilled IT jobs will typically not be offshored. In addition, jobs related to a company's core competencies or projects will typically not be offshored, and neither will jobs requiring close business-to-customer contact.

Myth #4: Computing and IT salaries are low due to cheaper overseas labor. In fact, graduates who major in management information systems typically command among the highest starting salaries of any business major.

Information Technology Jobs

Table 1.2

Position	Job Description
Chief Information Officer	Highest-ranking IS manager; responsible for strategic planning in the organization
IS Director	Responsible for managing all systems throughout the organization and day-to-day operations of the entire IS organization
Information Center Manager	Manages IS services such as help desks, hot lines, training, and consulting
Applications Development Manager	Coordinates and manages new systems development projects
Project Manager	Manages a particular new systems development project
Systems Manager	Manages a particular existing system
Operations Manager	Supervises the day-to-day operations of the data and/or computer center
Programming Manager	Coordinates all applications programming efforts
Systems Analyst	Interfaces between users and programmers; determines information requirements and technical specifications for new applications
Business Analyst	Focuses on designing solutions for business problems; interfaces closely with users to show how IT can be used innovatively
Systems Programmer	Writes the computer code for developing new systems software or maintaining existing systems software
Applications Programmer	Writes the computer code for developing new applications or maintaining existing applications
Emerging Technologies Manager	Forecasts technology trends and evaluates and experiments with new technologies
Network Manager	Coordinates and manages the organization's voice and data networks
Database Administrator	Manages the organization's databases and oversees the use of database management software
Auditing or Computer Security Manager	Manages ethical and legal use of information systems
Webmaster	Manages the organization's World Wide Web site
Web Designer	Creates World Wide Web sites and pages

IT Is Used by All Departments

Simply put, organizations cannot operate without information technology. For this reason, every manager and professional staff member should learn about IT within his or her specialized field as well as across the entire organization and among organizations.

IT systems are integral to every functional area of an organization. In *finance* and *accounting*, for example, managers use IT systems to forecast revenues and business activity, to determine the best sources and uses of funds, and to perform audits to ensure that the organization is fundamentally sound and that all financial reports and documents are accurate.

In *sales* and *marketing*, managers use information technology to perform the following functions:

- *Product analysis:* developing new goods and services
- *Site analysis:* determining the best location for production and distribution facilities
- *Promotion analysis:* identifying the best advertising channels
- *Price analysis:* setting product prices to get the highest total revenues

Marketing managers also use IT to manage their relationships with their customers. In *manufacturing*, managers use IT to process customer orders, develop production schedules, control inventory levels, and monitor product quality. They also use IT to design and manufacture products. These processes are called computer-assisted design (CAD) and computer-assisted manufacturing (CAM).

Managers in *human resources* use IT to manage the recruiting process, analyze and screen job applicants, and hire new employees. HR managers use IT to help employees manage their careers, administer performance tests to employees, and monitor employee productivity. These managers also use IT to manage compensation and benefits packages.

These are just a few examples of the roles of information technology in the various functional areas of an organization. We think it is important for students from the different functional areas to see the value of the information systems in their fields.

Before you go on . . .

1. What are the major reasons why it is important for employees in all functional areas to become familiar with IT?
2. Why is it important to become knowledgeable about IT if you are not working as an IT employee?

1.5 The Plan of This Book

A major objective of this book is to help you understand the roles of information technologies in today's organizations. The book is also designed to help you think strategically about information systems. That is, we want you to be able to look into the future and see how these information technologies can help you, your organization, and your world. Finally, the book demonstrates how IT supports all of the functional areas of the organization.

This chapter has introduced you to the global business environment and the Web-based platform that individuals and organizations use to successfully compete in that environment. Chapter 2 will introduce you to the types of information systems in organizations and how they are used for strategic advantage. Chapter 3 addresses three critical and timely topics: ethics, security, and privacy. Corporate scandals at Enron, WorldCom, HealthSouth, Adelphia, and others emphasize the importance of ethics. The large number of massive data breaches at various institutions (see the opening case of TJX in Chapter 3) makes it essential that we keep security in mind at all times. Finally, the miniaturization and spread of surveillance technologies leads many people to wonder if they have any privacy left at all.

The amount of data available to us is increasing exponentially, which means that we have to find methods and tools to manage the deluge. Chapter 4 discusses how to manage data so that we can use them effectively to make decisions.

Chapter 5 looks at telecommunications and networks, including the Internet. Because the Internet is the foundation of the global business environment, the importance of computer networks cannot be overstated.

Electronic commerce, facilitated by the Internet, has revolutionized how businesses operate today. Chapter 6 covers this important topic. One of the newest technologies to impact organizations, wireless communications, is explored in Chapter 7. Chapter 8 provides a detailed picture of the various types of information systems used in organizations today; Chapter 9 discusses the various information systems that support managerial decision making; and Chapter 10 notes how organizations acquire or develop new applications.

Technology Guides 1 (hardware) and 2 (software) provide a detailed look at the two most fundamental IT components that are the foundation for all information systems. Technology Guide 3 provides information on how to protect your own information assets. Finally, Technology Guide 4 covers the basics of telecommunications, whereas Technology Guide 5 addresses the basics of the Internet and the World Wide Web.

What's in IT for me?

In the previous section, we discussed IT in each of the functional areas. Here, we take a brief look at the MIS function.

for the MIS major

The MIS function directly supports all other functional areas in an organization. That is, the MIS function is responsible for providing the information that each functional area needs in order to make decisions. The overall objective of MIS personnel is to help users improve performance and solve business problems using IT. To accomplish this objective, MIS personnel must understand both the information requirements and the technology of each functional area. For this reason, MIS personnel must think "business needs" first and "technology" second.

1. **Differentiate among data, information, and knowledge.**

Data items refer to an elementary description of things, events, activities, and transactions that are recorded, classified, and stored, but are not organized to convey any specific meaning. Information is data that have been organized so that they have meaning and value to the recipient. Knowledge consists of data and/or information that have been organized and processed to convey understanding, experience, accumulated learning, and expertise as they apply to a current business problem.

2. **Differentiate between information technology infrastructure and information technology architecture.**

An organization's information technology *architecture* is a high-level map or plan of the information assets in an organization. The IT architecture integrates the information requirements of the overall organization and all individual users, the IT infrastructure, and all applications. An organization's information technology *infrastructure* consists of

Summary

the physical facilities, IT components, IT services, and IT management that support the entire organization.

3. **Describe the global, Web-based platform and its relationship to today's business environment.**

The global, Web-based platform consists of the hardware, software, and communications technologies that comprise the Internet and the functionality of the World Wide Web. This platform enables individuals to connect, compute, communicate, compete, and collaborate everywhere and anywhere, anytime and all the time, and to access limitless amounts of information, services, and entertainment. This platform operates without regard to geography, time, distance, and even language barriers. The Web-based platform has created today's business environment, which is global, massively interconnected, intensely competitive, 24/7/365, real-time, rapidly changing, and information-intensive.

4. **Discuss the relationships among business pressures, organizational responses, and information systems.**

The business environment is the combination of social, legal, economic, physical, and political factors that affect business activities. Significant changes in any of these factors are likely to create business pressures. Organizations typically respond to these pressures with activities supported by IT. These activities include strategic systems, customer focus, make-to-order and mass customization, and e-business.

Chapter Glossary

customer relationship management (CRM) An enterprisewide effort to acquire and retain customers, often supported by IT.

cybercafés Public places in which Internet terminals are available, usually for a small fee.

data items An elementary description of things, events, activities, and transactions that are recorded, classified, and stored but are not organized to convey any specific meaning.

digital divide The gap between those who have access to information and communications technology and those who do not.

globalization The integration and interdependence of economic, social, cultural, and ecological facets of life, enabled by rapid advances in information technology.

information Data that have been organized so that they have meaning and value to the recipient.

information technology Technology that relates to any computer-based tool that people use to work with information and support the information and information processing needs of an organization.

information technology (IT) architecture A high-level map or plan of the information assets in an organization.

information technology (IT) infrastructure The physical facilities, IT components, IT services, and IT personnel that support the entire organization.

knowledge Data and/or information that have been organized and processed to convey understanding, experience, accumulated learning, and expertise as they apply to a current problem or activity.

make-to-order The strategy of producing customized products and services.

management information systems Systems that deal with the planning for, development, management, and use of information technology tools to help people perform all tasks related to information processing and management.

mass customization A production process in which items are produced in large quantities but are customized to fit the desires of each customer.

organizational social responsibility Efforts by organizations to solve various social problems.

platform The hardware, software, and communications components that organizations use of process and manage information.

Discussion Questions

1. Describe how IT architecture and IT infrastructure are interrelated.
2. Is the Internet an infrastructure, an architecture, or an application program? Why? If none of the above, then what is it?
3. How has the global, Web-based platform affected competition?
4. Describe Google and Amazon's new information technology infrastructure. What is the relationship between this new infrastructure and the global, Web-based platform?
5. Explain why IT is a business pressure as well as an enabler of response activities that counter business pressures.
6. What does a flat world mean to you in your choice of a major? in your choice of a career? Will you have to be a "lifelong learner"? Why or why not?
7. What impact will a flat world have on your standard of living?

Problem-Solving Activities

1. Visit some Web sites that offer employment opportunities in IT. Prominent examples are *www.dice.com, www.hotjobs.com, www.monster.com, www.collegerecruiter.com, www.careerbuilder.com, www.jobcentral.com, www.job.com, www.career.com, and www.truecareers.com*. Compare the IT salaries to salaries offered to accountants, marketing personnel, financial personnel, operations personnel, and human resources personnel. For other information on IT salaries, check *Computerworld's* annual salary survey.
2. In this chapter, we have an example of the impacts of the global, Web-based platform on the travel industry. With this as a guide, discuss the impacts of this platform on the residential real estate industry. Be specific with Web sites that you use for examples.

Web Activities

1. Enter the Web site of UPS (*www.ups.com*).
   a. Find out what information is available to customers before they send a package.
   b. Find out about the "package tracking" system.
   c. Compute the cost of delivering a $10'' \times 20'' \times 15''$ box, weighing 40 pounds, from your hometown to Long Beach, California (or to Lansing, Michigan, if you live in or near Long Beach). Compare the fastest delivery against the least cost.
2. Surf the Internet for information about Homeland Security. Examine the available information and comment on the role of information technologies in Homeland Security.
3. Access *www.digitalenterprise.org*. Prepare a report regarding the latest electronic commerce developments in the digital age.
4. Access *www.x-home.com* and find information about the home of the future.
5. Experience customization by designing your own shoes at *www.nike.com*, your car at *www.jaguar.com*, your CD at *www.easternrecording.com*, your business card at *www.iprint.com*, and your diamond ring at *www.bluenile.com*. Summarize your experiences.

Team Assignments

1. Create an online group for studying IT or a part of it that especially interests you. Each member of the group must have a Yahoo e-mail account (free). Go to Yahoo: Groups (*http://groups.yahoo.com*) and at the bottom see a section titled "Create Your Own Group."

Step 1: Click on "Start a Group Now."
Step 2: Select a category that best describes your group (use the Search Group Categories, or use Browse Group Categories tool). You must find a category.
Step 3: Describe the purposes of the group and give it a name.

Step 4: Set up an e-mail address for sending messages to all group members.

Step 5: Each member must join the group (select a "profile"); click on "Join this Group."

Step 6: Go to Word Verification Section; follow the instructions.

Step 7: Finish by clicking "Continue."

Step 8: Select a group moderator. Conduct a discussion online of at least two topics of interest to the group.

Step 9: Arrange for messages from the members to reach the moderator at least once a week.

Step 10: Find a similar group (use Yahoo's "find a group" and make a connection). Write a report for your instructor.

2. Review the *Wall Street Journal, Fortune, Business Week,* and local newspapers for the last three months to find stories about the use of Web-based technologies in organizations. Each group will prepare a report describing five applications. The reports should emphasize the role of the Web and its benefit to the organizations. Cover issues described in this chapter, such as productivity, competitive strategies, and globalization. Present and discuss your work.

CLOSING CASE   **Amazon: From Book Seller to Service Provider**   MIS

THE BUSINESS PROBLEM Many analysts wonder if Amazon (*www.amazon.com*) will ever fulfill its original promise to revolutionize retailing. Despite being the largest online retailer with annual sales in excess of $10 billion, Amazon has not shown the consistent profit growth that investors have expected. In fact, profits have fallen, and the company's operating margins (about 4.1 percent) are less than Wal-Mart's (5.9 percent).

In addition, competition is increasing, with other Web sites becoming preferred first stops on the Web. Google, for one, has replaced retail sites such as Amazon as the place where many people start their shopping (see Froogle at *http://froogle.google.com*). Other Web sites such as MySpace and YouTube (owned by Google) have become prime places for many people to gather online and eventually shop.

THE IT SOLUTIONS By 2007, Amazon had spent 12 years and some $2 billion building the infrastructure of its online store, which is among the biggest and most reliable in the world. However, Amazon uses only 10 percent of its processing capacity at any one time. As a result, the company has decided to provide a series of computing, storage, and other services that make its infrastructure available to companies and individuals to help them run the technical and logistical parts of their businesses. Three of these services are the Simple Storage Service (S3), the Elastic Compute Cloud (EC2), and the Mechanical Turk.

With S3, Amazon charges 15 cents per gigabyte per month for businesses to store data and applications on Amazon disk drives. Through EC2, Amazon rents out processing power, starting at 10 cents per hour for the equivalent of one basic server.

The Mechanical Turk service combines processing power with networks of real people who are paid to do the kind of work that machines cannot do well, such as recognizing inappropriate content in images or transcribing audio. Companies post pieces of work onto the Mechanical Turk and pay people online, for which Amazon receives a 10 percent commission.

THE RESULTS Thousands of companies are using Amazon services. For example, Webmail.us (*www.webmail.us*) is an e-mail hosting company that maintains e-mail programs, filters spam, and removes malicious software such as viruses and worms from e-mail for clients. The company uses S3 for storage, sending Amazon more than a terabyte of data per week. To host the development effort required to build and maintain its systems' interface to S3, Webmail.us uses EC2. The company also uses EC2 for processing tasks related to storage backup. Webmail.us states that Amazon cut its data backup costs by 75 percent overnight.

Another example is Startup company Powerset (*www.powerset.com*), which offers searches that use natural language rather than stilted phrases and imprecise keywords. This task requires large amounts of processing capacity. Powerset uses S3 and EC2 to keep its costs down, while handling the background work of reading, processing, and indexing the vast number of Web pages that underlie its search processes.

Since its debut, the Mechanical Turk has attracted thousands of "Turkers" working for dozens of companies. One company, Efficient Frontier (*www.efrontier.com*), uses the service to analyze tens of thousands of search keywords to see which ones best attract potential shoppers to particular Web sites. Another company, Casting Words (*www.castingwords.com*), uses Turkers to transcribe 10-minute podcast segments, assemble them into full transcriptions, and check the quality.

The jury is out on whether Amazon services will contribute significantly to the company's bottom line. However, these service offerings are a bid by Amazon to be a leading player in the next wave of the Internet. Specifically, Amazon is competing directly with Google, Microsoft, and other giants to build a Web-based, global computing platform. It remains to be seen if Amazon will be successful in this endeavor.

Sources: Compiled from R. Hof, "Jeff Bezos' Risky Bet," *Business Week*, November 13, 2006; E. Cone, "Amazon at Your Service," *CIO Insight*, January 7, 2007; D. Strom, "Five Disruptive Technologies to Watch in 2007," *Information Week*, January 13, 2007; E. Lai, "How I Cut My Data Center Costs by $700,000," *Computerworld*, March 30, 2007; *www.amazon.com*, accessed March 31, 2007.

QUESTIONS

1. What is Amazon's strategy? Is the company moving away from its core competency of being a leading online retailer? Support your answer.
2. Why is Amazon competing with Google and Microsoft? Is this a wise strategy? Compare the strategies of Amazon, Google, and Microsoft.

Web Resources   wiley.com/college/rainer

Student Web Site
- Web Quizzes
- Student Lecture Slides in PowerPoint
- Virtual Company ClubIT: Website and Assignments

WileyPLUS
- e-book
- Flash Cards
- How-To Animations for Microsoft Office

Identifying Information at Club IT

Go to the Club IT link on the *WileyPLUS* Web site. There you will find a description of your internship at this downtown music venue, as well as some assignments that will help you learn how to apply IT solutions to a virtual business.

wiley.com/college/rainer

Chapter 2

Information Systems: Concepts and Management

What's in **IT** for me? ACC FIN MKT POM HRM MIS

Chevron Corporation

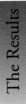

The Business Problem

Chevron Corporation (*www.chevron.com*) is huge. The company has over $200 billion in sales, and it employs 56,000 people in 180 countries. Chevron, like many giant energy companies, has an "upstream side" that deals with exploration and production, and a "downstream side" that deals with refining, marketing, transportation, and sales.

As for information technology, Chevron has 10,000 servers, handles 1 million e-mail messages every day, and has 3,500 people in its IT division. In addition, the company accumulates data at a rate of 2 terabytes per day, or 23 megabytes per second.

The IT organization had always had a reputation for innovation and technical strength, and an ability to execute huge projects. It had shown that it could deliver IT services to the company reliably and efficiently. However, top management wanted a stronger business focus and a stronger alignment between IT and the business strategy.

The IT Solutions

First, the IT executives instituted Project Everest. Everest is not an IT project in the conventional sense. Rather, it is a strategic framework for the company's biggest and most important IT projects. The purpose of Everest is to ensure that the projects with the biggest benefit to the company as a whole receive the right funding at the right time and that they get special management attention. What Everest does is make sure that the IT investments go toward projects that earn the company the most money.

Not all projects fall under the Everest umbrella. Non-Everest projects are smaller initiatives that may be important to one office or business unit but are not strategically important to the entire company.

Second, Chevron has implemented two Global Information Link (GIL) projects and is working on a third. GIL 1 standardized desktops, laptops, and operating systems, whereas GIL 2 completed the global integration of the company's network and standardized its servers, providing connectivity to operations all over the world.

GIL 3 will focus on information management. It will employ Microsoft's Vista operating system and its SharePoint product suite for communication and collaboration. SharePoint, which Microsoft says is intended to connect people, processes, and systems, will make it easier for employees, business partners, and customers to work together. Employees will be able to use SharePoint to create and manage their own Web sites and make them available to anyone at Chevron. In fact, the software will tag (or label) information so that it can be more easily found and shared in real time.

GIL 1 and GIL 2 gave users the infrastructure they needed to work with one another, and GIL 3 will give users the tools to do so. Standardizing platforms and software tools allows all relevant parties at Chevron to closely monitor operations.

The Results

Industry analysts have noted that Chevron's IT initiatives are closing the gaps that exist at some of the largest energy companies: disconnects among the scientific systems, the engineering systems, and the people involved in upstream activities; the systems and people involved in downstream activities; and the corporate-level people who have to oversee everything that happens on both sides of the company.

Therefore, Chevron's IT function is now closely aligned with the company's strategy. However, the IT group has not forgotten its responsibility to help Chevron reduce costs. In just one example, the firm's GIL 2 initiative saved Chevron $200 million in its first four years of operation.

The Chevron case illustrates the importance of information systems to organizations. The case also points out how Chevron uses its information systems to support the company's strategy more effectively by integrating its upstream component, its downstream component, and corporate management.

In this chapter, we introduce you to the basic concepts of information systems in organizations, and we explore how businesses use information systems in every facet of their operations. Information systems collect, process, store, analyze, and disseminate information for a specific purpose.

The two major determinants of IS support are the organization's structure and the functions that employees perform within the organization. As this chapter shows, information systems tend to follow the structure of organizations, and they are based on the needs of individuals and groups.

Information systems are located everywhere inside organizations, as well as among organizations. This chapter looks at the types of support that information systems provide to organizational employees. We demonstrate that any information system can be *strategic*, meaning that it can provide a competitive advantage, if it is used properly. At the same time, we provide examples of information systems that have failed, often at great cost to the enterprise. We then examine why information systems are important to organizations and society as a whole. Because these systems are so diverse, managing them can be quite difficult. Therefore, we close this chapter by taking a look at how organizations manage their IT systems.

Sources: Compiled from G. Anthes, "At Chevron Corp., Bigger Is Still Better," *Computerworld*, October 30, 2006; E. Chabrow, "Oil Companies Turn to IT to Shave Costs, Boost Efficiency, *InformationWeek*, June 5, 2006; "2006 IT Triumphs & Trip-Ups," *Baseline Magazine*, December 6, 2006; *www.chevron.com*, accessed April 12, 2007.

2.1 Types of Information Systems

Today, organizations employ many different types of information systems. Figure 2.1 illustrates the different types of information systems within organizations, and Figure 2.2 shows the different types of information systems among organizations. We discuss these interorganizational systems, which include supply chain management systems and customer relationship management systems, in Chapter 8.

Computer-Based Information Systems

The IT architecture and IT infrastructure provide the basis for all information systems in the organization. Recall that an information system (IS) collects, processes, stores, analyzes, and disseminates information for a specific purpose. A **computer-based information system (CBIS)** is an information system that uses computer technology to perform some or all of its intended tasks. Although not all information systems are computerized, today most are. For this reason the term **information system (IS)** is typically used synonymously with computer-based information system. The basic components of information systems are as follows.

- **Hardware** is a device such as the processor, monitor, keyboard, and printer. Together, these devices accept data and information, process them, and display them.
- **Software** is a program or collection of programs that enable the hardware to process data.
- A **database** is a collection of related files or tables containing data.
- A **network** is a connecting system (wireline or wireless) that permits different computers to share resources.

What We Learned from This Case

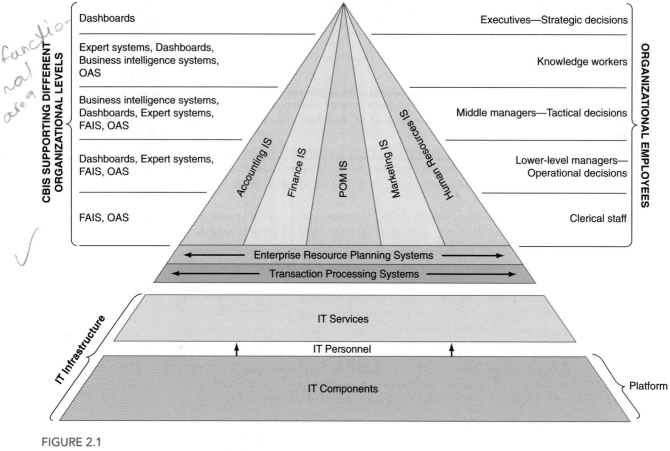

FIGURE 2.1

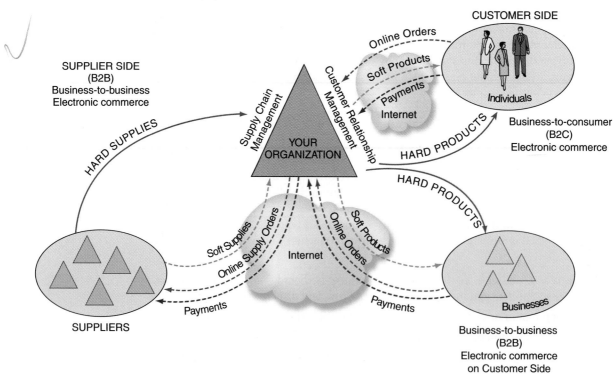

FIGURE 2.2   Information technology outside your organization (your supply chain).

Major Capabilities of Information Systems

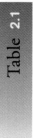

- Perform high-speed, high-volume, numerical computations.
- Provide fast, accurate communication and collaboration within and among organizations.
- Store huge amounts of information in an easy-to-access, yet small, space.
- Allow quick and inexpensive access to vast amounts of information, worldwide.
- Interpret vast amounts of data quickly and efficiently.
- Increase the effectiveness and efficiency of people working in groups in one place or in several locations, anywhere.
- Automate both semiautomatic business processes and manual tasks.

- **Procedures** are the set of instructions about how to combine the above components in order to process information and generate the desired output.

- **People** are those individuals who use the hardware and software, interface with it, or use its output.

Computer-based information systems have many capabilities. Table 2.1 summarizes the most important ones.

Application Programs

An **application program** is a computer program designed to support a specific task or business process. Each functional area or department within a business organization uses dozens of application programs. Note that application programs are synonymous with applications. For instance, the human resources department sometimes uses one application for screening job applicants and another for monitoring employee turnover. The collection of application programs in a single department is usually referred to as a *departmental information system*. For example, the collection of application programs in the human resources area is called the *human resources information system (HRIS)*. We can see in Figure 2.1 that there are collections of application programs—that is, information systems—in the other functional areas as well, such as accounting and finance. IT's About Business 2.1 shows how a variety of applications enable CarMax to successfully serve its customers.

Breadth of Support of Information Systems

Certain information systems support parts of organizations, others support entire organizations, and still others support groups of organizations.

As we have seen, each department or functional area within an organization has its own collection of application programs, or information systems. These **functional area information systems** are located at the top of Figure 2.1. Each information system supports a particular functional area in the organization. Examples are accounting IS, finance IS, production/operations management (POM) IS, marketing IS, and human resources IS.

Just below the functional area IS are two information systems that support the entire organization: enterprise resource planning systems and transaction processing systems. **Enterprise resource planning (ERP) systems** are designed to correct a lack of communication among the functional area ISs. ERP systems were an important innovation because the various functional area ISs were often developed as standalone systems and did not communicate effectively (if at all) with one another. ERP systems resolve this problem by tightly integrating the functional area ISs via a common database. In doing so, they enhance communications among the functional areas of an organization. For this reason, experts credit ERP systems with greatly increasing organizational productivity. Nearly all ERP systems are transaction processing systems, but transaction processing systems are not all ERP systems.

IT's About Business

2.1 No Haggling, No Hassle, at CarMax

CarMax (www.carmax.com) is a large, successful, retail company that sells used cars. The company's supercenters are concentrated in the U.S. Sun Belt, and they use a mix of information technology and marketing savvy to treat customers like royalty. CarMax lots are stocked with more cars than most dealerships sell in a year. Most importantly, however, CarMax has nonnegotiable sticker prices, and it pays its salespeople flat commissions. Therefore, its salespeople have no incentive to push the priciest cars. Customers go to CarMax for the wide range of choices, the nonthreatening environment, and the price.

However, it is CarMax's information systems that truly differentiate it from its competitors. In the same way that Wal-Mart revolutionized the logistics of retailing, CarMax set out to find the optimal combination of inventory and pricing through exhaustive analysis of sales data. Its proprietary software helps the company determine which models to sell and to closely track shifts in customer demand. Each car is fitted with a radio frequency identification (RFID) tag to track how long the car sits in the lot and when it is taken for a test drive. (We discuss RFID tags in Chapter 7.) Showroom computers give customers access to CarMax's nationwide catalog of 20,000 cars. Therefore, if a customer finds a car he or she wants in another location, CarMax can transfer the car for a fee.

Without its information systems, stocking CarMax lots would not be feasible. Each store carries 300 to 500 cars at any given time, and unlike Wal-Mart, the company has no vendors to replace inventory that is sold. Instead, CarMax depends on 800 car buyers, who use the company's data to appraise vehicles. CarMax acquires half of its inventory through trade-ins and the remainder via wholesale auctions.

How successful is CarMax's system? While overall used car sales have stagnated, CarMax's sales have increased dramatically. In 2006, the company sold more than 300,000 cars, totaling $6.3 billion in sales and $148 million in profit.

Sources: Compiled from M. Myser, "The Wal-Mart of Used Cars," *Business 2.0*, September 2006; "CarMax Offers Vehicle Histories," *Physorg.com*, April 24, 2006; J. Milligan, "In the Driver's Seat," *Virginia Business Magazine*, April 2006; G. Jordan, "Online, Used Car Lots that Cover the Nation," *New York Times*, October 22, 2003; D. Schell, "RFID: A Welcome Addition to the Car Sales Industry," *BusinessSolutions*, March 2002.

QUESTIONS

1. Identify the various computer-based information systems used by CarMax.
2. What is CarMax's biggest competitive advantage? Is this advantage related to information systems? Support your answer.
3. Can CarMax sustain its competitive advantage? Why or why not? *Hint:* What are the barriers to entry for a used-car dealership (see Section 2.2).

A **transaction processing system (TPS)** supports the monitoring, collection, storage, and processing of data from the organization's basic business transactions, each of which generates data. For example, when you are checking out of Wal-Mart, each time the cashier swipes an item across the bar code reader, that is one transaction. The TPS collects data continuously, typically in *real time*—that is, as soon as the data are generated—and provides the input data for the corporate databases. The TPSs are considered critical to the success of any enterprise because they support core operations. We discuss both TPSs and ERP systems in detail in Chapter 8.

Information systems that connect two or more organizations are referred to as **interorganizational information systems (IOSs)**. IOSs support many interorganizational operations, of which supply chain management is the best known. An organization's **supply chain** describes the flow of materials, information, money, and services from suppliers of raw material through factories and warehouses to the end customers.

Note that the supply chain in Figure 2.2 shows physical flows, information flows, and financial flows. Information flows, financial flows, and digitizable products (soft products) are represented with dotted lines, and physical products (hard products) as solid lines. Digitizable products are those that can be represented in electronic form, such as music and software. Information flows, financial flows, and digitizable products go through the Internet, where physical products are shipped. For example, when you order a computer from *www.dell.com*, your information goes to Dell via the Internet. When your transaction is complete (that is, your credit card is approved and your order is processed), Dell ships your computer to you.

Electronic commerce systems are another type of interorganizational information system. These systems enable organizations to conduct transactions, called business-to-business (B2B) electronic commerce, and customers to conduct transactions with businesses, called business-to-consumer (B2C) electronic commerce. All transactions are typically Internet-based. Figure 2.2 illustrates B2B and B2C electronic commerce. Electronic commerce systems are so important that we discuss them at length throughout the book.

Support for Organizational Employees

So far we have concentrated on information systems that support specific functional areas and operations. We now consider information systems that support particular employees within the organization. The right side of Figure 2.1 identifies these employees. Note that they range from clerical workers all the way up to executives.

Clerical workers, who support managers at all levels of the organization, include bookkeepers, secretaries, electronic file clerks, and insurance claim processors. *Lower-level managers* handle the day-to-day operations of the organization, making routine decisions such as assigning tasks to employees and placing purchase orders. *Middle managers* make tactical decisions, which deal with activities such as short-term planning, organizing, and control. **Knowledge workers** are professional employees such as financial and marketing analysts, engineers, lawyers, and accountants. All knowledge workers are experts in a particular subject area. They create information and knowledge, which they integrate into the business. Knowledge workers act as advisors to middle managers and executives. Finally, *executives* make decisions that can significantly change the manner in which business is done. Examples of executive decisions are introducing a new product line, acquiring other businesses, and relocating operations to a foreign country. IT support for each level of employee appears on the left side of Figure 2.1.

Office automation systems (OASs) typically support the clerical staff, lower and middle managers, and knowledge workers. These employees use OASs to develop documents (word processing and desktop publishing software), schedule resources (electronic calendars), and communicate (e-mail, voice mail, videoconferencing, and groupware).

Functional area information systems (FAISs) summarize data and prepare reports, primarily for middle managers but sometimes for lower-level managers as well. Because these reports typically concern a specific functional area, report generators (RPGs) are an important type of functional area IS.

Business intelligence (BI) systems provide computer-based support for complex, non-routine decisions, primarily for middle managers and knowledge workers. (They also support lower-level managers, though to a lesser extent.) These systems are typically used with a data warehouse and allow users to perform their own data analysis. We discuss BI systems in Chapter 9.

Expert systems (ESs) attempt to duplicate the work of human experts by applying reasoning capabilities, knowledge, and expertise within a specific domain. These systems are primarily designed to support knowledge workers. We discuss ES in Chapter 9.

Dashboards (also called **digital dashboards**) support all managers of the organization. They provide rapid access to timely information and direct access to structured information in the form of reports. Dashboards (discussed in Chapter 9) that are tailored to the information needs of executives are called *executive dashboards*. Table 2.2 provides an overview of the different types of information systems used by organizations.

Table 2.2

Types of Organizational Information Systems

Type of System	Function	Example
Functional area IS	Support the activities within a specific functional area.	System for processing payroll
Transaction processing system	Process transaction data from business events.	Wal-Mart checkout point-of-sale terminal
Enterprise resource planning system	Integrate all functional areas of the organization.	Oracle, SAP
Office automation system	Support daily work activities of individuals and groups.	Microsoft Office
Management information system	Produce reports summarized from transaction data, usually in one functional area.	Report on total sales for each customer
Decision support system	Provide access to data and analysis tools.	"What-if" analysis of changes in budget
Expert system	Mimic human expert in a particular area and make a decision.	Credit card approval analysis
Executive dashboard	Present structured, summarized information about aspects of business important to executives.	Status of sales by product
Supply chain management system	Manage flows of products, services, and information among organizations.	Wal-Mart retail link system connecting suppliers to Wal-Mart
Electronic commerce system	Enable transactions among organizations and between organizations and customers.	www.dell.com

Before you go on . . .

1. What is the difference between applications and computer-based information systems?
2. Explain how information systems provide support for knowledge workers.
3. As we move up the organization's hierarchy from clerical workers to executives, how does the type of support provided by information systems change?

2.2 Competitive Advantage and Strategic Information Systems

A competitive strategy is a statement that identifies a business's strategies to compete, its goals, and the plans and policies that will be required to carry out those goals (Porter, 1985). Through its competitive strategy, an organization seeks a **competitive advantage** in an industry. That is, it seeks to outperform its competitors in some measure such as cost, quality, or speed. Competitive advantage helps a company control a market and generate larger-than-average profits.

Competitive advantage is increasingly important in today's business environment, as we demonstrate throughout the book. In general, the *core business* of companies has remained the same. That is, information technologies simply offer the tools that can increase an organization's success through its traditional sources of competitive advantage, such as low cost, excellent customer service, and superior supply chain management. **Strategic information systems (SISs)** provide a competitive advantage by helping an organization implement its strategic goals and increase its performance and productivity. Any information system that helps an organization gain a competitive advantage, *or* reduce a competitive disadvantage, is a strategic information system.

Porter's Competitive Forces Model

The best-known framework for analyzing competitiveness is Michael Porter's **competitive forces model** (Porter, 1985). Companies use Porter's model to develop strategies to increase their competitive edge. Porter's model also demonstrates how IT can make a company more competitive.

Porter's model identifies five major forces that could either endanger or enhance a company's position in a given industry (see Figure 2.3). The Web has changed the nature of competition, and Porter (2001) concludes that the *overall* impact of the Web is to increase competition, which generally diminishes a firm's profitability. Let's examine the five forces and how the Web influences them.

1. ***The threat of entry of new competitors.*** The threat of new competitor entry is high when it is easy to enter your market and low when significant barriers to entry exist. An **entry barrier** is a product or service feature that customers have learned to expect from organizations in a certain industry. This feature must be offered by a competing organization for it to survive in the marketplace. For example, the threat of entry into automobile manufacturing is very low because the auto industry has major entry barriers, particularly the enormous capital costs for the manufacturing facility and equipment.

   For most firms, the Web *increases* the threat that new competitors will enter the market by sharply reducing traditional barriers to entry, such as the need for a sales force or a physical storefront to sell goods and services. Today, competitors frequently need only to set up a Web site. This threat is particularly acute in industries that perform an intermediation

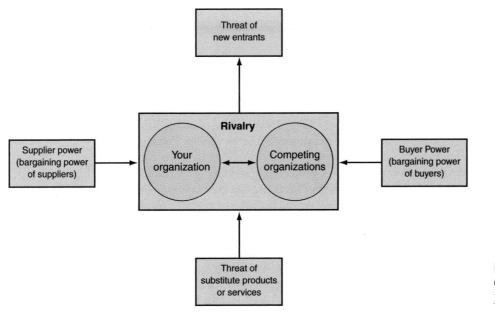

FIGURE 2.3   Porter's Competitive Forces Model.

role, which is a link between buyers and sellers (for example, stock brokers and travel agents) as well as in industries where the primary product or service is digital (for example, the music industry). In addition, the geographical reach of the Web enables distant competitors to compete more directly with an existing firm.

2. ***The bargaining power of suppliers.*** Supplier power is high when buyers have few choices from whom to buy and low when buyers have many choices. Therefore, organizations would rather have more potential suppliers to be able to better negotiate price, quality, and delivery terms.

    The Internet's impact on suppliers is mixed. On the one hand, buyers can find alternative suppliers and compare prices more easily, reducing the supplier's bargaining power. On the other hand, as companies use the Internet to integrate their supply chains, participating suppliers prosper by locking in customers.

3. ***The bargaining power of customers (buyers).*** Buyer power is high when buyers have many choices from whom to buy and low when buyers have few choices. For example, in the past, students had few places from which to buy their textbooks (typically, one or two campus bookstores). As a result, students had low buyer power. Today, students have a multitude of choices to choose from, and as a result, student buyer power has greatly increased.

    The Web also significantly increases a buyer's access to information about products and suppliers. Internet technologies can reduce customers' *switching costs*, which are the costs, in money and time, of a decision to buy elsewhere. In addition, buyers can more easily buy from other suppliers. In these ways the Internet greatly increases customers' bargaining power.

4. ***The threat of substitute products or services.*** If there are many substitutes for an organization's products or services, then the threat of substitutes is high. If there are few substitutes, then the threat is low. Today, new technologies create substitute products very rapidly. For example, customers today can purchase wireless telephones instead of land-line telephones, Internet music services instead of traditional CDs, and ethanol instead of gasoline in cars.

    Information-based industries are in the greatest danger from substitutes. Any industry in which digitized information can replace material goods (e.g., music, books, software) must view the Internet as a threat because the Internet can convey this information efficiently and at low cost.

5. ***The rivalry among existing firms in the industry.*** The threat from rivalry is high when there is intense competition among many firms in an industry. The threat is low when the competition is among fewer firms and is not as intense.

The visibility of Internet applications on the Web makes proprietary systems—systems that belong exclusively to a single organization—more difficult to keep secret. In simple terms, when I see my competitor's new system online, I will rapidly match its features in order to remain competitive. The result is fewer differences among competitors.

Internet-based systems are changing the nature of competition and even industry structure in many other ways. For example, Barnes & Noble, The Home Depot, and other companies have created independent online divisions that are competing against the parent companies' physical stores. Companies that have both online and offline sales operations are termed *click-and-mortar* firms because they combine both "brick-and-mortar" and e-commerce operations.

Competition also is being affected by the extremely low variable cost of digital products. That is, once the product has been developed, the cost of producing additional "units" approaches zero. Consider the music industry as an example. When artists record music, their songs are captured in digital format. Producing physical products, such as CDs or DVDs, with the songs on them for sale in music stores involves costs. The costs in a physical distribution channel are much higher than the costs involved in delivering the songs over the Internet in digital form.

In fact, in the future companies might give away some products for free. For example, some analysts predict that commissions for online stock trading will approach zero because investors can access the necessary information via the Internet to make their own decisions regarding buying and selling stocks. At that point, consumers will no longer need brokers to give them information that they can obtain themselves, virtually for free.

Porter's Value Chain Model

Although the Porter competitive forces model is useful for identifying general strategies, organizations use his **value chain model** (1985) to identify specific activities where they can use competitive strategies for greatest impact (see Figure 2.4). The value chain model also shows points where an organization can use information technology to achieve competitive advantage.

According to Porter's value chain model, the activities conducted in any organization can be divided into two categories: primary activities and support activities. **Primary activities** are those business activities that relate to the production and distribution of the firm's products and services, thus creating value for which customers are willing to pay. Primary activities involve purchasing materials, processing materials into products, and delivering products to customers. Typically, there are five primary activities:

1. Inbound logistics (inputs)
2. Operations (manufacturing and testing)
3. Outbound logistics (storage and distribution)

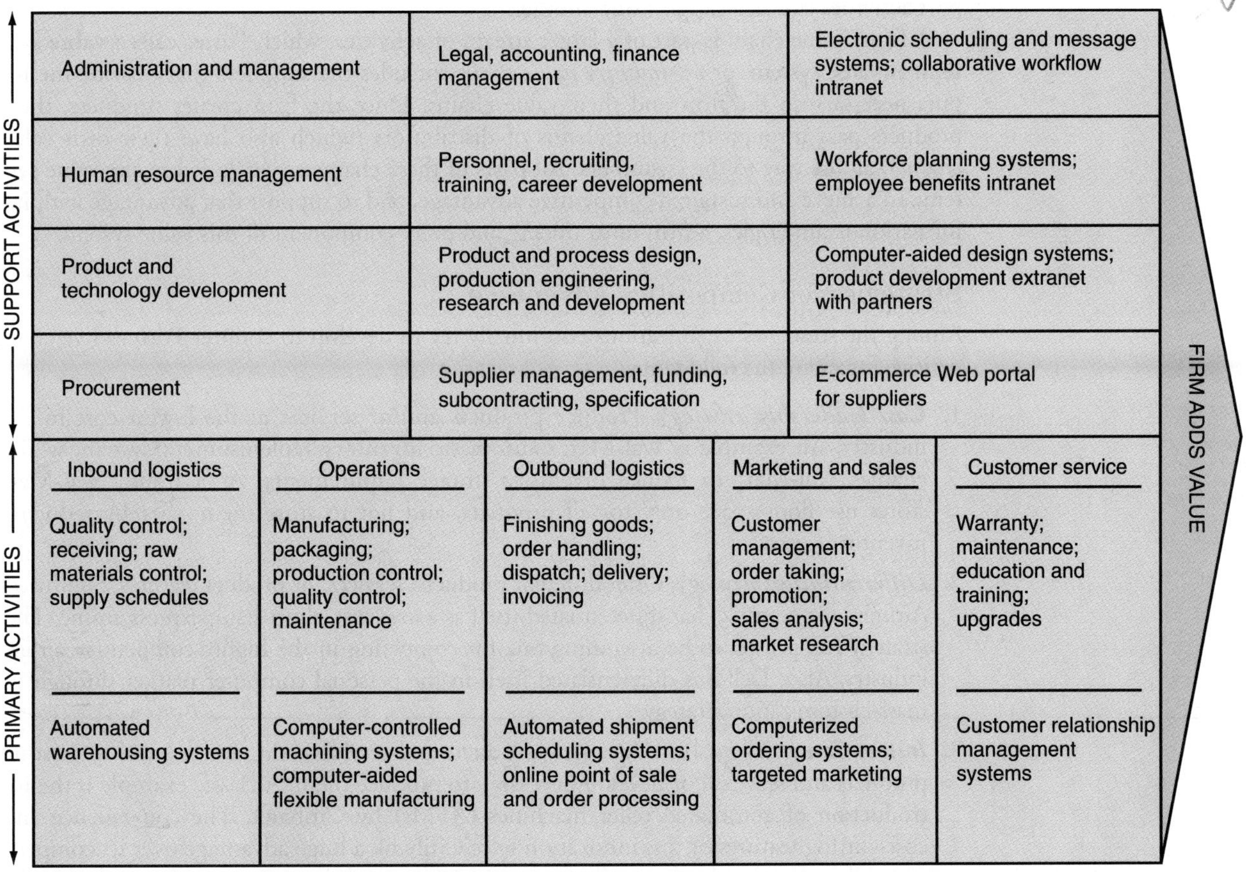

SUPPORT ACTIVITIES			FIRM ADDS VALUE
Administration and management	Legal, accounting, finance management	Electronic scheduling and message systems; collaborative workflow intranet	
Human resource management	Personnel, recruiting, training, career development	Workforce planning systems; employee benefits intranet	
Product and technology development	Product and process design, production engineering, research and development	Computer-aided design systems; product development extranet with partners	
Procurement	Supplier management, funding, subcontracting, specification	E-commerce Web portal for suppliers	

PRIMARY ACTIVITIES				
Inbound logistics	Operations	Outbound logistics	Marketing and sales	Customer service
Quality control; receiving; raw materials control; supply schedules	Manufacturing; packaging; production control; quality control; maintenance	Finishing goods; order handling; dispatch; delivery; invoicing	Customer management; order taking; promotion; sales analysis; market research	Warranty; maintenance; education and training; upgrades
Automated warehousing systems	Computer-controlled machining systems; computer-aided flexible manufacturing	Automated shipment scheduling systems; online point of sale and order processing	Computerized ordering systems; targeted marketing	Customer relationship management systems

FIGURE 2.4   Porter's Value Chain Model.

4. Marketing and sales

5. Services

Primary activities usually take place in a sequence from 1 to 5. As work progresses in the sequence, value is added to the product in each activity. Specifically, the incoming materials (1) are processed (in receiving, storage, and so on) in activities called *inbound logistics*. Next, the materials are used in *operations* (2), where value is added by turning raw materials into products. These products then need to be prepared for delivery (packaging, storing, and shipping) in the *outbound logistics* activities (3). Then *marketing and sales* (4) sell the products to customers, increasing product value by creating demand for the company's products. Finally, *after-sales service* (5), such as warranty service or upgrade notification, is performed for the customer, further adding value.

The primary activities are buttressed by **support activities**. Unlike primary activities, support activities do not add value directly to the firm's products or services. Rather, as their name suggests, they contribute to the firm's competitive advantage by supporting the primary activities. Support activities consist of:

1. The firm's infrastructure (accounting, finance, management)

2. Human resources management

3. Product and technology development (R&D)

4. Procurement

Each support activity can be applied to any or all of the primary activities. In addition, support activities can also support one another.

A firm's value chain is part of a larger stream of activities, which Porter calls a **value system**. A value system, or an *industry value chain*, includes the suppliers that provide the inputs necessary to the firm and their value chains. Once the firm creates products, these products pass through the value chains of distributors (which also have their own value chains), all the way to the customers. All parts of these chains are included in the value system. To achieve and sustain a competitive advantage, and to support that advantage with information technologies, a firm must understand every component of this value system.

Strategies for Competitive Advantage

Among the strategies organizations continually try to develop to counter Porter's five competitive forces are the following:

1. *Cost leadership strategy.* Produce products and/or services at the lowest cost in the industry. An example is Wal-Mart's automatic inventory replenishment system, which enables Wal-Mart to reduce inventory storage requirements. As a result, Wal-Mart stores use floor space only to sell products, and not to store them, thereby reducing inventory costs.

2. *Differentiation strategy.* Offer different products, services, or product features. Southwest Airlines, for example, has differentiated itself as a low-cost, short-haul, express airline. This strategy has proved to be a winning one for competing in the highly competitive airline industry. Also, Dell has differentiated itself in the personal computer market through its mass-customization strategy.

3. *Innovation strategy.* Introduce new products and services, add new features to existing products and services, or develop new ways to produce them. A classic example is the introduction of automated teller machines (ATMs) by Citibank. The convenience and cost-cutting features of this innovation gave Citibank a huge advantage over its competitors. Like many innovative products, the ATM changed the nature of competition in the banking industry. Today an ATM is a competitive *necessity* for any bank.

4. *Operational effectiveness strategy.* Improve the manner in which internal business processes are executed so that a firm performs similar activities better than its rivals. Such improvements increase quality, productivity, and employee and customer satisfaction while decreasing time to market. For example, investments in IT have given Norfolk Southern Railway a strategic advantage, as IT's About Business 2.2 shows.

5. *Customer-orientation strategy.* Concentrate on making customers happy. Web-based systems are particularly effective in this area because they can provide a personalized, one-to-one relationship with each customer.

IT's About Business

2.2 Norfolk Southern Railway

In 1955 a million people worked for the big U.S. railroads, but today there are only 160,000 rail workers. Although productivity boomed—ton-miles moved per employee increased from just 600,000 in 1955 to 11 million in 2006—the industry was unable to raise prices from 1980 to 2004. The reasons were that the industry suffered from overcapacity and bad service, and the newly deregulated trucking industry was capturing many of its customers.

Norfolk Southern Railway (*www.nscorp.com*) has approximately 14,400 miles of track in 20 states, primarily in the Southeast and Midwest. Like most railroads, Norfolk Southern used to run on an ad hoc basis. A train would leave the yard when it was ready. The company issued schedules, but they were written in pencil. If a yardmaster had a "light train," one with just 60 cars, he might let it sit in the yard for another day until another 60 cars arrived that were bound for the same location. The yardmaster assumed that he was saving the company money by not using a crew and fuel to run a light train.

Unfortunately, waiting for a long train had its own costs. Because of delays in making up a long train, locomotives and crews were bunched up in yards when they were needed elsewhere, so the company had to pay for extra crews to move the locomotives around. Even worse, the delays irritated customers whose goods were sitting in the yard.

To address these problems, Norfolk implemented a new information system to determine how it could best deliver its cars—by avoiding unnecessary stops, finding the best meeting points for cars, and making the fewest trips to switching yards. This software system reroutes trains around trouble spots that could delay delivery. It also allows Norfolk to price its service more effectively. Now sales representatives can see if a customer's cars can easily hitch onto a direct train or whether they will need to take a lengthier, and more costly, route.

The results have been excellent. Norfolk Southern spent $5.8 million on the software implementation, and by 2006 it had realized annual savings of $100 million. Carload volume had increased 14 percent since 2000, but the number of cars needed to move that volume had decreased 11 percent. Average speed was up 7 percent to 22 miles per hour, while average time in the yard, called dwell time, was down 7 percent to 23 hours. Norfolk Southern's revenues and profits have grown, and it has the best operating margins of all U.S. railroads. The company's share price rose 85 percent from the beginning of 2004 to 2006. In fact, Norfolk Southern's system was so far ahead of other railroad systems that it began to sell its software to rivals.

Sources: Compiled from "This Is How to Run a Railroad," *Forbes*, February 13, 2006; "Rail Carrier Norfolk Southern Uses Technology to Drive Big Efficiency Gains," *Supply Chain Digest*, February 2, 2006; J. O'Reilly, "Track to the Future," *www.inboundlogistics.com*, November 2005.

QUESTIONS

1. Would you classify Norfolk Southern's new system as a strategic information system? Why or why not? *Hint:* Look back at the definition of an SIS in this chapter.
2. Why did Norfolk Southern decide to sell its software to other railroads? Wouldn't this strategy diminish, rather than strengthen, the company's competitive advantage? *Hint:* What is the relationship between the railroad industry and the trucking industry?

Before you go on . . .

1. What are strategic information systems?
2. According to Porter, what are the five forces that could endanger a firm's position in its industry or marketplaces?
3. Describe Porter's value chain model. Differentiate between Porter's competitive forces model and his value chain model.
4. What strategies might companies use to gain competitive advantage?

IT's About Business

2.3 TIAA-CREF Has Problems with Upgrade

New York-based TIAA-CREF is one of the nation's largest private retirement systems, with more than 3 million members from the academic community and about 15,000 institutional investors. The company operates as both an insurance and a mutual fund company, and it is under the regulatory authority of the federal Securities and Exchange Commission (SEC) and the New York State Insurance Department.

TIAA-CREF purchased the Open Plan Solutions system from SunGard (*www.sungard.com*), a company that provides software for financial services, higher education, and public-sector organizations. TIAA-CREF bought the system (rather than develop such a system in-house) in order to provide individualized retirement options to its academic customers—institutions such as Harvard, Yale, Stanford, and many others—and their employees. The company set an aggressive timeline for migrating its 15,000 member institutions to the new system.

In addition to implementing the new system, TIAA-CREF consolidated its data network, implemented additional data security features, installed a new trading and settlement system, set up new desktop systems for customer service agents, and upgraded its financial systems.

Unfortunately, problems began to appear during the company's migration of its 30-year-old legacy system to its new Open Plan Solutions system. TIAA-CREF encountered two serious issues in the migration. First, it experienced many unanticipated problems in integrating its legacy system with the new system. Second, its customer service team was not adequately trained to handle the high number of calls from some 15,000 clients who were affected by these problems.

During the migration, tens of thousands of customers ended up with their accounts on both systems simultaneously. The results were disastrous. Customers lost access to their retirement funds, and they experienced payment delays on lump-sum annuity disbursements, systematic payments, transfer payout annuities, and individual retirement accounts. Many of the system problems dragged on for almost two years.

When these problems occurred, customers began calling TIAA-CREF with complaints, but they received no answers or help. Many customers reported that they received assistance only after they lodged formal complaints with regulatory authorities.

To resolve these problems, TIAA-CREF established a client resolution room. Now, when a complaint comes in, the company takes the issue to a room that houses a team of individuals from different functional areas in the company. In that way, the company can apply different skill sets to the problem. The company is also retraining its customer service agents and has received funding to hire more.

Sources: Compiled from R. Ferguson, "IT Issues Resurface at TIAA-CREF," *eWeek*, October 23, 2006; R. Ferguson, "TIAA-CREF Execs Speak on What Went Wrong," *eWeek*, April 14, 2006; R. Ferguson, "TIAA-CREF: Mo' Money, Mo' Problems," *eWeek*, March 13, 2006; R. Ferguson, "TIAA-CREF Plagued by Platform Upgrade," *eWeek*, January 6, 2006.

QUESTIONS

1. What are the problems (there are many) associated with the implementation of TIAA-CREF's new information system? Which problem is the most fundamental?
2. Is TIAA-CREF's new information system a strategic information system? Why or why not? *Hint:* Look back at the definition of an SIS in this chapter.

Failures of Information Systems

So far, we have introduced you to many success stories, which may cause you to ask, "Is IT all success?" The answer is, "Absolutely not." There are many failures, and we can learn as much from failures as from successes. We will provide examples of IT failures throughout the book. IT's About Business 2.3 shows how an information system upgrade caused many problems for TIAA-CREF (*www.tiaa-cref.org*).

Before you go on . . .

1. Why do SISs support many corporate strategies?
2. Besides our inability to predict the future, what are other reasons why IT projects might fail?

2.3 Why Are Information Systems So Important to Us?

Information systems have numerous impacts on organizations and on society as a whole. This section focuses on some of the more significant impacts.

IT Will Reduce the Number of Middle Managers

IT makes managers more productive and increases the number of employees who can report to a single manager, ultimately decreasing the number of managers and experts. It is reasonable to assume, then, that fewer managerial levels will exist in many organizations, and there will be fewer staff and line managers.

IT Will Change the Manager's Job

One of the manager's most important tasks is making decisions. As we will see in Chapter 9, IT can change the manner in which managers make many of their decisions. In this way IT ultimately can change managers' jobs.

Many managers have reported that IT has finally given them time to get out of the office and into the field. They also have found that they can spend more time planning activities instead of "putting out fires." Managers now can gather information for decision making much more quickly by using search engines and intranets.

IT tends to reduce the time necessary to complete any step in the decision-making process. By using IT properly, then, managers today can complete tasks more efficiently and effectively.

Another possible impact on the manager's job is a change in managerial requirements. The use of IT might lead organizations to reconsider what qualities they want in a good manager. For example, much of an employee's work is typically performed online and stored electronically. For these employees, electronic or "remote" supervision could become more common. Remote supervision places greater emphasis on completed work and less emphasis on personal contacts and office politics. Managerial supervision becomes particularly difficult when employees work in geographically dispersed locations, including homes, away from their supervisors.

Will My Job Be Eliminated?

One of the major concerns of every employee, part-time or full-time, is job security. Due to difficult economic times, increased global competition, demands for customization, and increased consumer sophistication, many companies have increased their investments in IT. As computers gain in intelligence and capabilities, the competitive advantage of replacing people with machines is increasing rapidly. For this reason, some people believe that society is heading toward higher unemployment. Others disagree.

Employees are also concerned about outsourcing and offshoring. IT's About Business 2.4 provides an interesting example of offshoring.

IT's About Business

2.4 Can Architects Be Offshored?

The overhaul of the Tropicana Casino & Resort in Las Vegas is a huge operation. When the $2 billion renovation is completed in 2010, the hotel will have more than 10,000 rooms, a new convention center and shopping mall, parking for 6,200 cars, and multiple pools. Adding to the complexity, gaming tables and sections of the hotel will remain open through the renovation. The project is a tremendous challenge for the architects who are responsible for putting all the pieces together.

In Kolkata, India, dozens of Indian architects are generating plans for the Tropicana. They work for Cadforce (www.cadforce.com), a company that is helping to bring offshoring to another sector of the U.S. workforce. Cadforce has about 150 designers and computer technicians in India, plus 41 in the United States, working on a variety of projects.

The $29 billion U.S. architecture industry ships about $100 million in work abroad each year. Some 20 percent of U.S. firms report that they offshore, while an additional 30 percent are considering doing so. They are adopting this strategy because clients are demanding shorter turnarounds, smaller fees, and better details.

Rather than developing complete designs, offshore architects tend to handle tasks such as turning schematic drawings into blueprints and making certain that doors and pipes are aligned. These are essential jobs, but they are tedious, and they can take up 60 percent of the time spent designing a building. Offshoring these time-consuming tasks frees up architects to focus on other tasks.

Another force driving the offshoring trend is digitization. More architectural firms are adopting sophisticated computer tools that allow them to render entire buildings in three dimensions, simulate stress tests, and track all construction materials. These tools, coupled with low-cost, high-bandwidth networks, make it much easier to work remotely.

Sources: Compiled from P. Engardio, "Blueprint from India," *BusinessWeek*, April 2, 2007; K. Maher, "New in Offshoring's Sights: High-Level Professionals," www.careerjournal.com, accessed April 10, 2007; www.cadforce.com, accessed April 10, 2007.

QUESTIONS

1. Has the emergence of the global, Web-based platform affected the offshoring of architectural work? If so, explain how.
2. If you were majoring in architecture, how would you prepare in order to reduce the chance that your job would be offshored? *Hint:* Think about the characteristics of work that is offshored versus the characteristics of work that "stays home." Now, extend your answer to the field of MIS.

IT Impacts Employees at Work

Many people have experienced a loss of identity because of computerization. They feel like "just another number" because computers reduce or eliminate the human element that was present in noncomputerized systems.

The Internet threatens to have an even more isolating influence than computers and television. Encouraging people to work and shop from their living rooms could produce some unfortunate psychological effects, such as depression and loneliness.

Another possible psychological impact relates to home schooling, which is much easier to conduct through the Internet (see *www.homeschool.com*). Opponents of home schooling argue that the lack of social contacts can damage the social, moral, and cognitive development of school-age children who spend long periods of time working alone on the computer.

IT Impacts Employees' Health and Safety. Computers and information systems may adversely affect one's health and safety as a result of job stress, exposure to video display terminals, and long-term use of the keyboard.

An increase in an employee's workload and/or responsibilities can trigger *job stress*. Although computerization has benefited organizations by increasing productivity, it has also created an ever-expanding workload for some employees. Some workers feel overwhelmed and have become increasingly anxious about their job performance. These feelings of stress and anxiety can diminish workers' productivity. Management's responsibility should be to help alleviate these feelings by providing training, redistributing the workload among workers, or hiring more workers.

Exposure to *video display terminals* (*VDTs*) raises the issue of radiation exposure, which has been linked to cancer and other health-related problems. For example, some experts charge that exposure to VDTs for long periods of time can damage an individual's eyesight.

Finally, the long-term use of keyboards can lead to *repetitive strain injuries* such as backaches and muscle tension in the wrists and fingers. *Carpal tunnel syndrome* is a particularly painful form of repetitive strain injury that affects the wrists and hands.

Designers, aware of the potential problems associated with prolonged use of computers, have attempted to design a better computing environment. **Ergonomics**, the science of adapting machines and work environments to people, focuses on creating an environment that is safe, well lit, and comfortable. For example, antiglare screens help alleviate problems of fatigued or damaged eyesight. Also, chairs that contour the human body help decrease backaches. Figure 2.5 displays some sample ergonomic products.

(a)

(b)

(c)

(d)

FIGURE 2.5
Ergonomic products protect computer users.
(a) Wrist support.
(b) Back support.
(c) Eye-protection filter (optically coated glass).
(d) Adjustable foot rest.
Source: (a), (b), and (d) courtesy of Ergodyne; (c) courtesy of 3M.com)

(a)   (b)   (c)

FIGURE 2.6 Enabling people with disabilities to work with computers. (a) A PC for a blind or sight-impaired user, equipped with an Oscar optical scanner and a Braille printer, both by TeleSensory. The optical scanner converts text into ASCII code or into proprietary word processing format. Files saved on disc can then be translated into Braille and sent to the printer. Visually impaired users can also enlarge the text on the screen by loading a TSR software magnification program. (b) The deaf or hearing-impaired user's PC is connected to a telephone via an Ultratec Intele-Modern Baudolt/ASCH Modem. The user is sending and receiving messages to and from someone at a remote site who is using a telecommunications device for deaf people (right). (c) This motor-disabled person is communicating with a PC using a Pointer Systems optical head pointer to access all keyboard functions on a virtual keyboard shown on the PC's display. The user can "strike" a key in one of two ways. He can focus on the desired key for a user-definable time period (which causes the key to be highlighted), or he can click an adapted switch when he chooses the desired key. (*Source:* J. J. Lazzaro, "Computers for the Disabled," *Byte,* June 1993.)

IT Provides Opportunities for People with Disabilities. Computers can create new employment opportunities for people with disabilities by integrating speech and vision recognition capabilities. For example, individuals who cannot type are able to use a voice-operated keyboard, and individuals who cannot travel can work at home.

Adaptive equipment for computers permits people with disabilities to perform tasks they would not normally be able to handle. For example, Figure 2.6 illustrates a PC for a visually challenged user, a PC for a user with a hearing impairment, and a PC for a user with a motor disability.

The Web and graphical user interfaces often still make life difficult for people with impaired vision. Audible screen tips and voice interfaces help deal with this problem. More mundane, but useful, devices that help improve quality of life for people with disabilities include a two-way writing telephone, a robotic page turner, a hair brusher, and a hospital-bedside video trip to the zoo or the museum.

IT Provides Quality-of-Life Improvements

On a broader scale, IT has significant implications for quality of life. The workplace can be expanded from the traditional 9-to-5 job at a central location to 24 hours a day at any location. IT can provide employees with flexibility that can significantly improve the quality of leisure time, even if it doesn't increase the total amount of leisure time. However, IT can also place employees on "constant call" so that they are never truly away from the office, even when they are on vacation.

Robot Revolution on the Way. Once restricted largely to science fiction movies, robots that can do practical tasks are becoming more common. "Cyberpooches," nursebots, and other mechanical beings may be our companions before we know it. Around the world, quasi-autonomous devices have become increasingly common on factory floors, in hospital corridors, and in farm fields.

In an example of precision agriculture, Carnegie Mellon University in Pittsburgh has developed self-directing tractors that harvest hundreds of acres of crops around the clock in California. These "robot tractors" use global positioning systems (GPSs) combined with video image processing that identifies rows of uncut crops.

Many robotic devices are also being developed for military purposes. For example, the Pentagon is researching self-driving vehicles and bee-like swarms of small surveillance robots, each of which would contribute a different view or angle of a combat zone. The Predator, an unmanned aerial vehicle (UAV), was used in the Gulf War and is in use in the Iraq War today.

It will likely be a long time before we see robots making decisions by themselves, handling unfamiliar situations, and interacting with people. Nevertheless, robots are extremely helpful in various environments, as we see in the following example.

Robots on the Dairy Farm   For more than 100 years, dairy farmers at Mason Dixon Farms in Pennsylvania have milked cows following the same routine several times a day, 365 days per year. Today the dairy operation has installed 10 robots to milk 500 of its 2,100 cows. The robotic system is the DeLaval Voluntary Milking System—called voluntary because cows return to the system on their own.

The system eliminates the need for farm workers to round up the animals, connect them to equipment, and manually track milking times and yields. When a cow enters the milking stall (enticed by a protein snack), the robot "recognizes" the cow by a transponder in her collar. Data about the cow, including the last time she was milked, and her expected yield, are uploaded to the robot's database. An image-processing system detects the cow's teats, which are sanitized before milking. When the equipment has finished milking the cow, it automatically detaches.

The system tracks each cow's output and records any problems involved in attaching the animal to the milking equipment. These data go into a herd-management database. Analysis tools then let farmers evaluate the status of each cow and generate reports about milk production, such as daily averages. The system contains health record software to keep track of a cow's vaccinations, breeding, and related information.

The robots have reduced the farm's labor costs by 75 percent and have raised milk production by 15 percent. Each robot does about 175 milkings per day, with the average cow producing about 100 pounds of milk.

Sources: Compiled from M. McGee, "Robots Keep Milk Moooving," *InformationWeek*, September 25, 2006; "Cows Choose Their Own Milking Times with DeLaval System," *Engineering and Technology for a Sustainable World*, June 1, 2001; *www.delaval.com*, accessed April 9, 2007.

Improvements in Health Care.   IT has brought about major improvements in health-care delivery, allowing medical personnel to make better and faster diagnoses and to monitor critically ill patients more accurately. IT also has streamlined the process of researching and developing new drugs. Expert systems now support diagnosis of diseases, and machine vision is enhancing the work of radiologists. Surgeons use virtual reality to plan complex surgeries, and some also use a surgical robot to perform long-distance surgery by controlling the robot's movements. Finally, doctors discuss complex medical cases via videoconferencing. New computer simulations re-create the sense of touch, allowing doctors-in-training to perform virtual procedures without risking harm to an actual patient.

Of the thousands of other applications related to health care, administrative systems are critically important. These systems range from detecting insurance fraud to nursing scheduling to financial and marketing management.

The Internet contains vast amounts of useful medical information (see *www.webmd.com* for example). In an interesting study, researchers at the Princess Alexandra Hospital in Brisbane, Australia, identified 26 difficult diagnostic cases published in the *New England Journal of Medicine.* They selected three to five search terms from each case and conducted a Google search. The researchers selected and recorded the three diagnoses that Google ranked most prominently and that appeared to fit the symptoms and signs. They then compared these results with the correct diagnoses as published in the journal. They discovered that their Google searches had found the correct diagnosis in 15 of the 26 cases, a success rate of 57 percent.

2.4 Managing Information Resources

Clearly, then, a modern organization possesses many information resources. *Information resources* is a general term that includes all the hardware, software (information systems and applications), data, and networks in an organization. In addition to the computing resources, numerous applications exist, and new ones are continuously being developed. Applications have enormous strategic value. Firms rely on them so heavily that, in some cases, when they are not working (even for a short time), an organization cannot function. In addition, these information systems are very expensive to acquire, operate, and maintain; therefore, it is essential to manage them properly.

Our discussion focuses on the information systems function in a large organization. Smaller firms do not have all these functions or types of jobs; in fact, in smaller firms, one person often handles several functions.

It is becoming increasingly difficult, however, to manage an organization's information resources effectively. This difficulty stems from the evolution of the MIS function in the organization. When businesses first began to use computers in the early 1950s, the *information systems department (ISD)* owned the only computing resource in the organization, the mainframe. At that time, end users did not interact directly with the mainframe.

Today, computers are located throughout the organization, and almost all employees use computers in their work. This system is known as *end-user computing.* As a result of this change, the ISD no longer owns the organization's information resources; instead, a partnership has developed between the ISD and the end users. The ISD now acts as more of a consultant to end users, viewing them as customers. Indeed, the main function of the ISD is to use IT to solve end users' business problems.

Which IT Resources Are Managed and by Whom?

As we just saw, the responsibility for managing information resources is now divided between the ISD and the end users. This arrangement raises several important questions: Which resources are managed by whom? What is the role of the ISD, its structure, and its place within the organization? What is the appropriate relationship between the ISD and the end users? In this section we provide brief answers to these questions.

There are many types of information systems resources, and their components may come from multiple vendors and be of different brands. The major categories of information resources are hardware, software, databases, networks, procedures, security facilities, and physical buildings. These resources are scattered throughout the organization, and some of them change frequently. Therefore, they can be difficult to manage.

To make things more complicated, no standard menu exists showing how to divide responsibility for developing and maintaining information resources between the ISD and the end users. Instead, that division depends on many things: the size and nature of the organization, the amount and type of IT resources, the organization's attitudes toward computing, the attitudes of top management toward computing, the maturity level of the technology, the amount and nature of outsourced IT work, and even the country in which the company operates. Generally speaking, the ISD is responsible for corporate-level and shared resources and the end users are responsible for departmental resources.

The ISD and the end users need to work closely together and to cooperate regardless of who is doing what. Let's begin by looking at the ISD's role within the organization.

The Role of the IS Department

The role of the director of the ISD is changing from a technical manager to a senior executive, who is often called the **chief information officer (CIO)**. As Table 2.3 shows, the role of the ISD is also changing from a purely technical one to a more managerial and strategic one. For example, the ISD is now responsible for managing the outsourcing of projects and for creating business alliances with vendors and IS departments in other organizations. Because its role has expanded so much, the ISD now reports directly to a senior vice president of administration or even to the chief executive officer, or CEO. (Previously, it reported to a functional department such as accounting.) In its new role, the ISD must be able to work closely with external organizations such as vendors, business partners, consultants, research institutions, and universities.

Inside the organization, the ISD and the end-user units must be close partners. The ISD has the responsibility for setting standards for hardware and software purchases, as well as for information security. The ISD also monitors user hardware and software purchases, and it serves as a gatekeeper in regard to software licensing and illegal downloads (for example, music files).

Before you go on . . .

1. How important are end users to the management of the organization's information resources?
2. Where do you think the IT staff should be located? Should they be decentralized in the functional areas? centralized at corporate level? a combination of the two? Explain your answer.

The Changing Role of the Information Systems Department

Traditional Major IS Functions

- Managing systems development and systems project management
- Managing computer operations, including the computer center
- Staffing, training, and developing IS skills
- Providing technical services
- Infrastructure planning, development, and control

New (Consultative) Major IS Functions

- Initiating and designing specific strategic information systems
- Incorporating the Internet and electronic commerce into the business
- Managing system integration, including the Internet, intranets, and extranets
- Educating non-IS managers about IT
- Educating the IS staff about the business
- Supporting end-user computing
- Partnering with the executives
- Managing outsourcing
- Proactively using business and technical knowledge to seed innovative ideas about IT
- Creating business alliances with vendors and IS departments in other organizations

Table 2.3

What's in for Me?

For the Accounting Major

Data and information are the lifeblood of accounting. Transaction processing systems—which are now Web-based—capture, organize, analyze, and disseminate data and information throughout organizations, often through corporate intranets. The Internet has vastly increased the number of transactions (especially global) in which modern businesses engage. Transactions such as billing customers, preparing payrolls, and purchasing and paying for materials provide data that the accounting department must record and track. These transactions, particularly with customers and suppliers, now usually take place online, through extranets. In addition, accounting information systems must share information with information systems in other parts of a large organization. For example, transactional information from a sales or marketing IS is now input for the accounting system as well.

For the Finance Major

The modern financial world turns on the speed, volume, and accuracy of information flow. Information systems and networks make these things possible. Finance departments use information systems to monitor world financial markets and to provide quantitative analyses (e.g., for cash flow projections and forecasting). They use decision support systems to support financial decision making (e.g., portfolio management). Financial managers now use business intelligence software to analyze information in data warehouses. Finally, large-scale information systems (e.g., enterprise resource planning packages) tightly integrate finance with all other functional areas within a wide-ranging enterprise.

For the Marketing Major

Marketing uses customer databases, decision support systems, sales automation, data warehouses, and business intelligence software to perform its functions. The Internet has created an entirely new global channel for marketing from business-to-business and business-to-consumer. It also has dramatically increased the amount of information available to customers, who can now compare prices quickly and thoroughly. As a result, shoppers have become more knowledgeable and sophisticated. In turn, marketing managers must work harder to acquire and retain customers. To accomplish this goal, they now use customer relationship management software. The Internet helps here, because it provides for much closer contact between the customer and the supplier.

For the Production/Operations Management Major

Organizations are competing on price, quality, time (speed), and customer service—all of which are concerns of production and operations management. Every process in a company's operations that adds value to a product or service (for example, purchasing inventory, quality control, receiving raw materials, and shipping products) can be enhanced by the use of Web-based information systems. Moreover, information systems have enabled the production and operations function to link the organization to other organizations in the firm's supply chain. From computer-aided design and computer-aided manufacturing through Web-based ordering systems, information systems support the production and operations function.

For the Human Resources Management Major

Information systems provide valuable support for human resources management. For example, record keeping has greatly improved in terms of speed, convenience, and accuracy as a result of technology. Furthermore, disseminating HR information throughout the company via intranets enables employees to receive consistent information and handle much of their personal business (for example, configuring their benefits) themselves, without help from HR personnel. The Internet makes a tremendous amount of information available to the job seeker, increasing the fluidity of the labor market. Finally, many careers require skills in the use of information systems. HR professionals must have an understanding of these systems and skills to support hiring, training, and retention within an organization.

For the MIS Major

Although some MIS employees actually write computer programs, more often they act as analysts, interfacing between business users on one hand and programmers on the other. For example, if a marketing manager needed to analyze data that are not in the company's data warehouse, she would forward her information requirements to an MIS analyst. The analyst would then work with MIS database personnel to obtain the needed data and input them into the data warehouse.

1. **Describe the components of computer-based information systems.**

   A computer-based information system (CBIS) uses computer technology to perform some or all of its intended tasks. The basic components of a CBIS are hardware, software, database(s), telecommunications networks, procedures, and people. Hardware is a set of devices that accept data and information, process them, and display them. Software is a set of programs that enable the hardware to process data. A database is a collection of related files, tables, relations, and so on that stores data and the associations among them. A network is a connecting system (wireline or wireless) that permits different computers to share resources. Procedures are the set of instructions about how to combine the above components in order to process information and generate the desired output. People are those individuals who work with the information system, interface with it, or use its output.

2. **Describe the various types of information systems by breadth of support.**

   The departmental information systems, also known as functional area information systems, each support a particular functional area in the organization. Two information systems support the entire organization: enterprise resource planning (ERP) systems and transaction processing systems (TPSs). ERP systems tightly integrate the functional area IS via a common database, enhancing communications among the functional areas of an organization. A TPS supports the monitoring, collection, storage, and processing of data from the organization's basic business transactions.

   Information systems that connect two or more organizations are referred to as interorganizational information systems (IOSs). IOSs support many interorganizational operations, of which supply chain management is the best known. Electronic commerce systems enable organizations to conduct business-to-business (B2B) and

Summary

business-to-consumer (B2C) electronic commerce. They are generally Internet-based.

3. Identify the major information systems that support each organizational level.

At the clerical level, employees are supported by office automation systems and functional area information systems. At the operational level, managers are supported by office automation systems, functional area information systems, dashboards, and expert systems. Middle managers are supported by office automation systems, functional area information systems, dashboards, expert systems, and business intelligence systems. At the knowledge-worker level, expert systems, dashboards, and business intelligence systems provide support. Executives are supported mainly by dashboards.

4. Describe strategic information systems (SISs) and explain their advantages.

Strategic information systems support or shape a business unit's competitive strategy. An SIS can significantly change the manner in which business is conducted to help the firm gain a competitive advantage or reduce a competitive disadvantage.

5. Describe Porter's competitive forces model and his value chain model, and explain how IT helps companies improve their competitive positions.

Companies use Porter's competitive forces model to develop strategies to gain a competitive advantage. Porter's model also demonstrates how IT can enhance a company's competitiveness. It identifies five major forces that could endanger a company's position in a given industry: (1) the threat of new competitors entering the market, (2) the bargaining power of suppliers, (3) the bargaining power of customers (buyers), (4) the threat of substitute products or services, and (5) the rivalries among existing firms in the industry.

Although the Porter competitive forces model is useful for identifying general strategies, organizations use his value chain model to identify specific activities where they can use competitive strategies for greatest impact. The value chain model also shows points where an organization can use information technology to achieve competitive advantage.

According to Porter's value chain model, the activities conducted in any organization can be divided into two categories: primary activities and support activities. Primary activities are those business activities that relate to the production and distribution of the firm's products and services. These activities are buttressed by support activities. Unlike primary activities, support activities do not add value directly to the firm's products or services. Rather, as their name suggests, they contribute to the firm's competitive advantage by supporting primary activities.

The Internet has changed the nature of competition. Porter concludes that the *overall* impact of the Internet is to increase competition, which has a negative impact on profitability.

6. Describe five strategies that companies can use to achieve competitive advantage in their industries.

The five strategies are as follows: (1) *cost leadership strategy*—produce products and/or services at the lowest cost in the industry; (2) *differentiation strategy*—offer different products, services, or product features; (3) *innovation strategy*—introduce new products and services, put new features in existing products and services, or develop new ways to produce them; (4) *operational effectiveness strategy*—improve the manner in which internal business processes are executed so that a firm performs similar activities better than rivals; and (5) *customer-orientation strategy*—concentrate on making customers happy.

7. Describe how information resources are managed, and discuss the roles of the information systems department and the end users.

Responsibility for managing information resources is divided between two organizational entities: the information systems department (ISD), which is a corporate entity, and the end users, who are located throughout the organization. Generally speaking, the ISD is responsible for corporate-level and shared resources, whereas the end users are responsible for departmental resources.

Chapter Glossary

application program (also called **program**) A computer program designed to support a specific task or business process.

business intelligence (BI) systems Information systems that provide computer-based support for complex, nonroutine decisions, primarily for middle managers and knowledge workers.

chief information officer (CIO) The executive in charge of the information systems department in an organization.

competitive advantage An advantage over competitors in some measure such as cost, quality, or speed; leads to control of a market and to larger-than-average profits.

competitive forces model A business framework devised by Michael Porter, which analyzes competitiveness by recognizing five major forces that could endanger a company's position.

computer-based information system (CBIS) An information system that uses computer technology to perform some or all of its intended tasks.

dashboards (also called **digital dashboards**) Information systems that support all managers of the organization by providing rapid access to timely information and direct access to structured information in the form of reports.

database A collection of related files, tables, relations, and so on that stores data and the associations among them.

electronic commerce systems A type of interorganizational information system that enables organizations to conduct transactions with other businesses and with customers.

enterprise resource planning (ERP) systems Systems that tightly integrate the functional area information systems via a common database.

entry barrier Product or service feature that customers expect from organizations in a certain industry; an organization trying to enter this market must provide this product or service at a minimum to be able to compete.

ergonomics The science of adapting machines and work environments to people, focusing on creating an environment that is safe, well lit, and comfortable.

expert systems (ES) Information systems that attempt to duplicate the work of human experts by applying reasoning capabilities, knowledge, and expertise within a specific domain.

functional area information systems (FAISs) Information systems designed to summarize data and prepare reports for the functional areas, such as accounting and marketing.

hardware A set of devices (for example, processor, monitor, keyboard, printer) that together accept data and information, process them, and display them.

information system (IS) A process that collects, processes, stores, analyzes, and disseminates information for a specific purpose; most ISs are computerized.

interorganizational information systems (IOSs) Information systems that connect two or more organizations.

knowledge workers Professional employees who are experts in a particular subject area and create information and knowledge.

network A connecting system (wireline or wireless) that permits different computers to share their information.

office automation systems (OASs) Information systems that typically support the clerical staff, lower and middle managers, and knowledge workers.

people Those individuals who use the hardware and software, interface with it, or use its output.

primary activities Those business activities related to the production and distribution of the firm's products and services, thus creating value.

procedures The set of instructions about how to combine components of information systems in order to process information and generate the desired output.

software A set of programs that enables the hardware to process data.

strategic information systems (SISs) Systems that help an organization gain a competitive advantage by supporting its strategic goals and/or increasing performance and productivity.

supply chain The flow of materials, information, money, and services from raw material suppliers through factories and warehouses to the end customers.

support activities Business activities that do not add value directly to a firm's product or service under consideration but support the primary activities that do add value.

transaction processing system (TPS) An information system that supports the monitoring, collection, storage, processing, and dissemination of data from the organization's basic business transactions.

value chain model Model that shows the primary activities that sequentially add value to the profit margin; also shows the support activities.

value system System that includes the producers, suppliers, distributors, and buyers, all with their value chains.

Discussion Questions

1. Discuss the logic of building information systems in accordance with the organization's hierarchical structure.
2. Knowledge workers comprise the largest segment of the workforce in U.S. business today. However, many industries need skilled workers who are not knowledge workers. What are some examples of these industries? What might replace these skilled workers? When might the U.S. economy need more skilled workers than knowledge workers?
3. Using Figure 2.2 as your guide, draw a model of a supply chain with your university as the central focus. Keep in mind that every university has suppliers and customers.
4. Explain how office automation systems, functional area information systems, and decision support systems can support multiple levels of the organization.

5. Is IT a strategic weapon or a survival tool? Discuss.
6. Why might it be difficult to justify a strategic information system?
7. Describe the five forces in Porter's competitive forces model, and explain how the Internet has affected each one.
8. Describe Porter's value chain model. What is the relationship between the competitive forces model and the value chain model?
9. Why has the Internet been called the creator of new business models?
10. Discuss the idea that an information system by itself can rarely provide a sustainable competitive advantage.
11. Discuss the reasons why some information systems fail.

Problem-Solving Activities

1. Characterize each of the following systems as one (or more) of the IT support systems:
   a. A student registration system in a university.
   b. A system that advises physicians about which antibiotics to use for a particular infection.
   c. A patient-admission system in a hospital.
   d. A system that provides a human resources manager with reports regarding employee compensation by years of service.
   e. A robotic system that paints cars in a factory.

2. Compare and contrast the two companies, Google and Amazon, with regard to their strategies, business models, IT infrastructures, service offerings, and products. After you have completed your analysis, explain why Google has such a larger market capitalization than Amazon and is more profitable.

Web Activities

1. The market for optical copiers is shrinking rapidly. It is expected that by 2008 as much as 90 percent of all duplicated documents will be done on computer printers. Can a company such as Xerox Corporation survive?

   a. Read about the problems and solutions of Xerox in 2000–2003 at *www.fortune.com, www.findarticles .com,* and *www.google.com.*

   b. Identify all the business pressures on Xerox.

   c. Find some of Xerox's response strategies (see *www .xerox.com, www.yahoo.com,* and *www.google.com*).

   d. Identify the role of IT as a contributor to the business technology pressures (e.g., obsolescence).

   e. Identify the role of IT as a facilitator of Xerox's critical response activities.

2. Enter the site of Dell.com, and find the current information systems used by the company. Explain how the systems' innovations contribute to Dell's success.

3. Access Truste (*www.truste.org*), and find the guidelines that Web sites displaying its logo must follow. What are the guidelines? Why is it important for Web sites to be able to display the Truste logo on their sites?

4. Enter *www.cio.com* and find recent information on the changing role of the CIO and the ISD. What is the role of the CIO in organizations today?

Team Assignments

1. Observe your local Wal-Mart checkout counter. Find material on the Web that describes how the scanned code is translated into the price that the customers pay. *Hint:* Look at *www.howstuffworks.com.*

   a. Identify the following components of the Wal-Mart system: inputs, processes, and outputs.

   b. What kind of a system is the scanner (TPS, dashboard, ES, etc.)? Why did you classify it as you did?

   c. Having the information electronically in the system may provide opportunities for additional managerial uses of that information. Identify such uses.

   d. Checkout systems are now being replaced by self-service checkout kiosks and scanners.

   Compare the two in terms of speed, ease of use, and problems that may arise (e.g., an item that the scanner does not recognize).

2. Assign group members to UPS (*www.ups.com*), FedEx (*www.fedex.com*), DHL (*www.dhl.com*), and the U.S. Postal Service (*www.usps.com*). Have each group study the e-commerce strategies of one organization. Then have members present the organization, explaining why it is the best.

3. Divide the class into teams. Each team will select a country government and visit its official Web site (try the United States, Australia, New Zealand, Singapore, Norway, Canada, the United Kingdom, the Netherlands, Denmark, Germany, and France). For example, the official Web portal for the U.S. government is *www.firstgov.gov.* Review and compare the services offered by each country. How does the United States stack up? Are you surprised at the number of services offered by countries through Web sites? Which country offers the most services? the least?

CLOSING CASE # Todd Pacific Shipyards Makes Effective Use of Information Systems

THE BUSINESS PROBLEM Todd Pacific Shipyards (*www.toddpacific.com*) is a large operation that builds, maintains, and repairs ships for military and commercial customers on projects that range from overhauling nuclear aircraft carriers to building new ferries. The company needed to replace its old traditional time card system—punch cards and clocks—because it was slow and inaccurate, it did not provide the kinds of information the

company needed, and it required too many clerical people to use it.

THE IT SOLUTION Todd Pacific invested $250,000 to replace its old system with personal digital assistants (PDAs), a wireless network, and a proprietary (developed in-house) software application called the Time Tracking application that securely records each employee's time and work assignment. PDAs were chosen over laptops because PDAs are smaller, lighter, and easier to move from one job to the next.

The PDAs are placed in central work areas. When a worker arrives, he takes his identification card, which includes a bar code, and runs it through the reader on a PDA. This process acts as the time stamp, recording that the employee has started work. The PDA then transmits that information via the wireless network to a server that automatically updates payroll, accounts payable, and project management records, reporting the names of the employees, arrival and departure times, and the projects they are working on.

Todd Pacific developed its Time Tracking application in-house and linked it to the company's project management application. The two applications play a key role in matching workers with assignments. Before the start of a workday, a project manager can designate how many people he needs to perform a particular task. Once the workers are hired for a particular task, the two applications automatically log their start times and charge them to the appropriate account so that clients can be charged correctly.

Todd Pacific did encounter some challenges in implementing the new system. To begin with, the PDAs had to operate in the challenging conditions of a shipyard, including dust, debris, and moisture. As a result, the PDAs had to be "hardened"—that is, they were required to survive heavy rain, dust, and being dropped onto concrete from up to 6 feet.

In addition, the Todd Pacific shipyard had many conditions that made wireless networks a problem. The 46-acre worksite includes multiple buildings and cranes, with workers often inside a ship's hull, where signals could not penetrate. To handle these problems, the shipyard set up two wireless networks—one outside the ships that connects to wireless networks inside the various ships.

The wireless network also had to meet tough security standards. Because the shipyard's customers include the U.S. Navy and Coast Guard, it has to ensure that all wireless transmissions are encrypted.

THE RESULTS The new system, which paid for itself in less than one year, allows Todd Pacific managers to better plan and execute jobs. The system helps shipyard managers determine each day if they have the right number of machinists, pipefitters, electricians, and welders to work on each project. Project managers can immediately access the schedules and activities of approximately 800 employees, and learn which skilled workers are available for a particular assignment.

Electronic collection of an employee's daily activities makes it easier to prepare payroll and bill customers for work. In fact, Todd Pacific no longer needed four data-entry clerks to review the work hours shown on a time card and then type that information into a payroll application. The company also eliminated one position in the payroll department, because the system generated electronic reports showing labor costs by project, employee, task, and other factors.

Essentially, the system gives Todd Pacific the ability to have personnel data—name, age, specialty, preferred hours, special skills and experience, assignment location, and expected completion date for current project—available instantly, as well as having a real-time report on where all workers are supposed to be and what they are supposed to be doing.

The system also helps the shipyard manage contract requirements for 11 labor unions. There are about 25 situations in which workers get paid a higher hourly wage while performing tasks that are unpleasant or dangerous, or require unusual skills. Those types of tasks warrant extra pay. The shipyard incorporated the logic for the union rules into the PDAs, so extra pay could be awarded without any paperwork.

An unexpected benefit of the system was a 50 percent reduction in workplace injuries. With the PDAs and wireless networks, an inspector or supervisor can immediately disseminate information via e-mail if he sees a hazardous condition that threatens worker safety or actually results in an injury. With the old system, an inspector or manager filled out a three-part form and filed copies with the safety department and an employee's supervisor, a process that could take as long as three days. Today, the entire process takes just minutes.

Sources: Compiled from E. Schuman, "Todd Pacific: PDAs Help Keep Shipyard on Course," *eWeek*, March 6, 2006; "Shipyard Dumps Traditional Time Card System in Favor of PDAs," *www.supplychainbrain.com*, April 19, 2006; *www.toddpacific.com*, accessed April 15, 2007.

QUESTIONS

1. If you are the CIO at Todd Pacific, to what other applications could you link the Time Tracking application?
2. Skilled union workers typically have a degree of autonomy. If you are a skilled worker at Todd Pacific, do you have any privacy concerns about being wirelessly monitored? Why or why not?
3. Would the new system at Todd Pacific improve or damage the company's relationship with its unions? Support your answer.

Web Resources   wiley.com/college/rainer

Student Web Site
- Web Quizzes
- Student Lecture Slides in PowerPoint
- Virtual Company ClubIT: Website and Assignments

WileyPLUS
- e-book
- Flash Cards
- How-To Animations for Microsoft Office

Starting Your Internship at Club IT

Go to the Club IT link on the *WileyPLUS* Web site. There you will find a description of your internship at this downtown music venue, as well as some assignments that will help you learn how to apply IT solutions to a virtual business.

wiley.com/college/rainer

Chapter 3

1. Describe the major ethical issues related to information technology and identify situations in which they occur.
2. Identify the many threats to information security.
3. Understand the various defense mechanisms used to protect information systems.
4. Explain IT auditing and planning for disaster recovery.

Ethics, Privacy, and Information Security

Student Web Site
- Web Quizzes
- Lecture Slides in PowerPoint
- Virtual Company ClubIT: Website and Assignments

WileyPLUS
- e-book
- Flash Cards
- Software Skills Tutorials: Using Microsoft Office 2007
- How-To Animations for Microsoft Office

Chapter Outline

3.1 Ethical Issues

3.2 Threats to Information Security

3.3 Protecting Information Resources

What's in IT for me?   ACC   FIN   MKT   POM   HRM   MIS

The Worst Retail Data Breach Ever?

The Business Problem

TJX (*www.tjx.com*), a $16 billion retail conglomerate, operates some 2,500 stores around the world, including T.J. Maxx, Marshalls, HomeGoods, Bob's Stores, and A.J. Wright stores in the United States, and Winners and Homesense stores in Canada. On January 17, 2007, the company reported that an intrusion into its customer transaction management systems had compromised the personal data of a number of its customers. The security breach involved systems that handle customer credit card, debit card, check, and merchandise return transactions. At first, the company did not state how many customers were affected by the incident, but later revealed that credit card information on 46 million of its customers had been compromised.

The company said that the data involved were related to individuals who shopped at its stores during 2003 and 2004, as well as between May and December 2006. TJX learned of the breach in mid-December 2006, but it did not release the information at that time at the request of law enforcement officials.

Investigators noted that TJX really had three problems. First, the company's security was originally breached and its data compromised. In fact, the intruders had the company's encryption key. (We discuss encryption later in this chapter.) Second, the company did not know about the breach for years. Finally, TJX was unable to ascertain what data were actually compromised and when.

Adding to TJX's problems, Visa notified financial institutions that issue credit cards and manage Visa transactions that TJX had stored credit and debit card data in violation of the Payment Card Industry Data Security Standard (the PCI standard) created by Visa and MasterCard. The PCI standard applies to banks, clearinghouses, and merchants that issue or accept credit cards. Merchants such as TJX are not supposed to store cardholder data because a thief can use that information to creat a counterfeit credit or debit card. Some TJX data went back to 2003, which indicated that the company had been out of compliance with the PCI standard for years.

Before the intrusion was even reported, a California credit union noticed an increase in counterfeit cards used to commit fraudulent transactions. The TJX breach resulted in financial losses to the credit union. The credit union had to issue new cards for any cardholder accounts that Visa said were affected by the TJX compromise. As an issuer of Visa cards, the credit union—not Visa or TJX—had to pay for any fraudulent transactions charged to members' accounts.

In addition, Visa encountered an increase in fraud activity on certain TJX accounts beginning in mid-November 2006. After the breach was reported, more than 60 banks in Massachusetts reported compromises of customer accounts as a result of the breach.

Also before the breach was announced, thieves used data stolen from TJX to steal $8 million in merchandise from Wal-Mart stores in Florida. The thieves created fake credit cards that they used to buy Wal-Mart gift cards, and then they used them to buy goods.

A Variety of Solutions

TJX hired General Dynamics and IBM to help investigate the intrusion, assess the volume and types of data that may have been stolen, and strengthen the company's defenses. TJX also worked with all major credit and debit card companies to help investigate any related fraud, and cooperated with law enforcement officials, including the U.S. Department of Justice and the Royal Canadian Mounted Police. The company also bought full-page newspaper ads and put a video message from its chairman on its Web site, assuring customers that rigorous steps had been taken to protect their information.

TJX identified a limited number of customers whose private information was stolen and notified them directly. TJX officials said that they did not know if they could identify the names of other customers who were at risk. The company offered additional customer support to people concerned that their data may have been compromised, and recommended that its customers carefully review their credit card and debit card statements and other account information for evidence of unauthorized use.

Basically, the company faced a stream of bad news. TJX had to record a fourth-quarter (2006) charge of about $5 million, related to the intrusion, including the costs to investigate and contain the breach, enhance information security, communicate with customers, as well as legal fees.

Several parties sued TJX over the compromise of its systems. Two class-action lawsuits, one on behalf of consumers and one on behalf of several banks impacted by the breach, alleged that TJX and one of its credit card partners, Fifth Third Bank, failed to secure the personal data of customers. The State of Massachusetts headed up a group of more than 30 states that investigated how the massive data compromise occurred. Rhode Island conducted its own probe and extended it to consider whether retailers should pay for professionals to clean up customer accounts after a breach.

Interestingly, TJX noted that the company relied on commercially available systems, software, tools, and monitoring to provide security for processing, transmission, and storage of confidential customer information. Furthermore, the company noted that the systems it used for transmission and approval of payment card transactions were determined and controlled by the payment-card industry, not by TJX.

What really worries information security experts are these questions: What if TJX did almost everything correctly? What if this massive data breach was less a case of TJX being careless and more a case of the attackers being clever, resourceful, knowledgeable, and persistent? The implication here is that modern cyberthieves can execute a breach on any retailer, regardless of the security measures in place.

The lessons that we can learn from the massive, undiscovered security breach at TJX address the three major issues discussed in this chapter: ethics, privacy, and security. Each of these issues is closely related to IT and raises significant questions. For example, is it ethical (or even necessary) for TJX to gather and keep so much information on their customers? Is this practice an invasion of their customers' privacy? By using commercially available software, did TJX show due diligence in protecting customer information? Should the blame for the breach be shared by TJX and its software suppliers? How should TJX protect its information more effectively? Does better protection involve technology, policy, or both?

The answers to these and other questions are not clear. As we discuss ethics, privacy, and security in the context of information technology, you will acquire a better understanding of these issues, their importance, their relationships, and their trade-offs.

Information technologies, properly used, can have enormous benefits for individuals, organizations, and entire societies. In the first two chapters we discussed the diverse ways in which IT has made businesses more productive, efficient, and responsive to consumers. We also have explored areas such as medicine in which IT has improved people's health and well-being. Unfortunately, information technologies can also be misused, often with devastating consequences. Consider the following:

- Individuals can have their identities stolen.
- Organizations can have customer information stolen, leading to financial losses, erosion of customer confidence, and legal action.
- Countries face the threat of cyberterrorism and cyberwarfare.

The misuse of information technologies has come to the forefront of any discussion of IT. Now that you are acquainted with the major capabilities of IT, we address the complex issues of ethics, privacy, and security.

Sources: Compiled from E. Schuman, "The Nightmare Scenario: What If TJX Did Everything Right?" *eWeek*, March 30, 2007; M. Hines, "TJX Intrusion Highlights Pursuit of Corporate Data," *eWeek*, January 18, 2007; K. Evans-Correia, "Top IT Execs Could Take Heat for TJX Breach," *SearchCIO.com*, January 18, 2007; L. Greenmeier, "Card Data, a Hack, and a Rush to Contain the Damage," *InformationWeek*, January 22, 2007; p. 28; L. Greenemeier, "Maxxed Out," *InformationWeek*, February 5, 2007, pp. 29–30; C. McCarthy, "T. J. Maxx Probe Finds Broader Hacking," *www.news.com*, February 22, 2007; E. Schuman, "Massachusetts Leads National TJX Data Probe," *eWeek*, February 7, 2007; E. Schuman, "TJX: Data Theft Began in 2005; Data Taken from 2003," *eWeek*, February 21, 2007; E. Schuman, "Stolen TJX Data Used in $8M Scheme Before Breach Discovery." *eWeek*, March 21, 2007; B. Brenner, "Mistakes to the Maxx." *Information Security*, March, 2007; L. Greenmeier, "TJX Breach Hits Wal-Mart," *InformationWeek*, March 26, 2007; E. Schuman, "TJX Intruder Had Retailer's Encryption Key," *eWeek*, March 29, 2007; E. Sutherland, "Data Breach Lawsuits Pile up on TJX," *www.internetnews.com*, February 2, 2007.

3.1 Ethical Issues

Ethics refers to the principles of right and wrong that individuals use to make choices to guide their behaviors. Deciding what is right or wrong is not always easy or clear-cut. For this reason, many companies and professional organizations develop their own codes of ethics. A **code of ethics** is a collection of principles that are intended to guide decision making by members of the organization. For example, the Association for Computing Machinery (*www.acm.org*), an organization of computing professionals, has a thoughtful code of ethics for its members (see *www.acm.org/constitution/code.html*.)

Fundamental tenets of ethics include responsibility, accountability, and liability. **Responsibility** means that you accept the consequences of your decisions and actions. **Accountability** means a determination of who is responsible for actions that were taken. **Liability** is a legal concept meaning that individuals have the right to recover the damages done to them by other individuals, organizations, or systems.

Before we go any further, it is very important that you realize that what is *unethical* is not necessarily *illegal*. In most instances, then, an individual or organization faced with an ethical decision is not considering whether to break the law. This does not mean, however, that ethical decisions do not have serious consequences for individuals, organizations, or society at large.

Unfortunately, during the last few years, we have seen a large number of extremely poor ethical decisions, not to mention outright criminal behavior. Three of the most highly publicized fiascos occurred at Enron, WorldCom, and Tyco. At each company, executives were convicted of various types of fraud using illegal accounting practices. These illegal acts resulted, at least in part, in the passage of the Sarbanes-Oxley Act in 2002. This law requires that public companies implement financial controls and that, to ensure accountability, executives must personally certify financial reports.

Improvements in information technologies are causing an increasing number of ethical problems. Computing processing power doubles about every 18 months, meaning that organizations are more dependent than ever before on their information systems. Increasing amounts of data can be stored at decreasing cost, meaning that organizations can store more data on individuals for longer amounts of time. Computer networks, particularly the Internet, enable organizations to collect, integrate, and distribute enormous amounts of information on individuals, groups, and institutions. As a result, ethical problems are arising about the appropriate use of customer information, personal privacy, and the protection of intellectual property.

All employees have a responsibility to encourage ethical uses of information and information technology. Most, if not all, of the business decisions you will face at work will have an ethical dimension. Consider these decisions you might have to make:

• Should organizations monitor employees' Web surfing and e-mail?
• Should organizations sell customer information to other companies?

- Should organizations audit employees' computers for unauthorized software or illegally downloaded music or video files?

The diversity and ever-expanding use of IT applications have created a variety of ethical issues. These issues fall into four general categories:

1. *Privacy issues* involve collecting, storing, and disseminating information about individuals.

2. *Accuracy issues* involve the authenticity, fidelity, and accuracy of information that is collected and processed.

3. *Property issues* involve the ownership and value of information.

4. *Accessibility issues* revolve around who should have access to information and whether they should have to pay for this access.

Table 3.1 lists representative questions and issues for each of these categories. In addition, Online Appendix W3.1 presents 14 ethics scenarios for you to consider. These scenarios will provide a context for you to consider situations that involve ethical or nonethical behavior.

A Framework for Ethical Issues

Privacy Issues

- □ What information about oneself should an individual be required to reveal to others?
- □ What kind of surveillance can an employer use on its employees?
- □ What types of personal information can people keep to themselves and not be forced to reveal to others?
- □ What information about individuals should be kept in databases, and how secure is the information there?

Accuracy Issues

- □ Who is responsible for the authenticity, fidelity, and accuracy of the information collected?
- □ How can we ensure that the information will be processed properly and presented accurately to users?
- □ How can we ensure that errors in databases, data transmissions, and data processing are accidental and not intentional?
- □ Who is to be held accountable for errors in information, and how should the injured parties be compensated?

Property Issues

- □ Who owns the information?
- □ What are the just and fair prices for its exchange?
- □ How should one handle software piracy (copying copyrighted software)?
- □ Under what circumstances can one use proprietary databases?
- □ Can corporate computers be used for private purposes?
- □ How should experts who contribute their knowledge to create expert systems be compensated?
- □ How should access to information channels be allocated?

Accessibility Issues

- □ Who is allowed to access information?
- □ How much should companies charge for permitting accessibility to information?
- □ How can accessibility to computers be provided for employees with disabilities?
- □ Who will be provided with equipment needed for accessing information?
- □ What information does a person or an organization have a right or a privilege to obtain, under what conditions and with what safeguards?

Table 3.1

Protecting Privacy

In general, **privacy** is the right to be left alone and to be free of unreasonable personal intrusions. *Information privacy* is the right to determine when, and to what extent, information about yourself can be gathered and/or communicated to others. Privacy rights apply to individuals, groups, and institutions.

The definition of privacy can be interpreted quite broadly. However, court decisions in many countries have followed two rules fairly closely:

1. The right of privacy is not absolute. Privacy must be balanced against the needs of society.

2. The public's right to know supersedes the individual's right of privacy.

These two rules show why it is sometimes difficult to determine and enforce privacy regulations. The right to privacy is recognized today in all U.S. states and by the federal government, either by statute or common law.

Rapid advances in information technologies have made it much easier to collect, store, and integrate data on individuals in large databases. On an average day, you generate data about yourself in many ways: surveillance cameras on toll roads, in public places, and at work; credit card transactions; telephone calls (land-line and cellular); banking transactions; queries to search engines; and government records (including police records). These data can be integrated to produce a **digital dossier**, which is an electronic description of you and your habits. The process of forming a digital dossier is called **profiling**.

Data aggregators, such as LexisNexis (*www.lexisnexis.com*), ChoicePoint (*www.choicepoint.com*), and Acxiom (*www.acxiom.com*), are good examples of profiling. These companies collect public data such as real estate records and published telephone numbers, in addition to nonpublic information such as Social Security numbers, financial data, and police, criminal, and motor vehicle records.

These companies then integrate the data to form digital dossiers, or profiles, on most adults in the United States. They sell these dossiers to law enforcement agencies and companies conducting background checks on potential employees. They also sell these dossiers to companies that want to know their customers better, a process called *customer intimacy*.

Electronic Surveillance. According to the American Civil Liberties Union (ACLU), tracking people's activities with the aid of computers has become a major privacy-related problem. The ACLU notes that this monitoring, or **electronic surveillance**, is rapidly increasing, particularly with the emergence of new technologies. Such monitoring is done by employers, the government, and other institutions.

In general, employees have very limited protection against surveillance by employers. The law supports the right of employers to read their employees' e-mail and other electronic documents and to monitor their Internet use. Today, more than three-fourths of organizations are monitoring their employees' Internet usage. In addition, two-thirds of organizations use software to block connections to inappropriate Web sites, a practice called *URL filtering*. Organizations are installing monitoring and filtering software to enhance security by stopping malicious software and to improve employee productivity by discouraging employees from wasting time.

In one organization, before deploying a URL filtering product, the chief information officer (CIO) monitored about 13,000 people for three months to determine the type of traffic they engaged in on the network. He then passed the data to the chief executive officer (CEO) and the heads of the Human Resources and Legal departments. They were shocked at the questionable Web sites the employees were visiting, as well as the amount of time employees spent on those sites. The executives quickly made the decision to implement the filtering product.

Surveillance is also a concern for private individuals regardless of whether it is conducted by corporations, government bodies, or criminals. As a nation we are still trying to determine the appropriate balance between personal privacy and electronic surveillance, especially where potential threats to national security are involved.

Personal Information in Databases.   Information about individuals is kept in many databases. Perhaps the most visible locations of such records are credit-reporting agencies. Other institutions that store personal information include banks and financial institutions; cable TV, telephone, and utilities companies; employers; mortgage companies; hospitals; schools and universities; retail establishments; government agencies (Internal Revenue Service, your state, your municipality); and many others.

The information you provide to these record keepers arouses a number of concerns, especially the following:

- Do you know where the records are?
- Are the records accurate?
- Can you change inaccurate data?
- How long will it take to make a change?
- Under what circumstances will personal data be released?
- How are the data used?
- To whom are they given or sold?
- How secure are the data against access by unauthorized people?

Information on Internet Bulletin Boards, Newsgroups, and Social Networking Sites.   Every day we see more and more *electronic bulletin boards, newsgroups, electronic discussions* such as chat rooms, and *social networking sites* (discussed in Chapter 5). These sites appear on the Internet, within corporate intranets, and on blogs. A *blog* (short for Weblog) is an informal, personal journal that is frequently updated and intended for general public reading. How does society keep owners of bulletin boards from disseminating information that may be offensive to readers or simply untrue? This is a difficult problem because it involves the conflict between freedom of speech on the one hand and privacy on the other. This conflict is a fundamental and continuing ethical issue in U.S. society.

There is no better illustration of the conflict between free speech and privacy than the Internet. Many Web sites contain anonymous, derogatory information on individuals, who typically have little recourse in the matter. Approximately one-half of U.S. firms use the Internet in examining job applications, including Googling you and searching for you on social networking sites. Derogatory information that can be found on the Internet can harm your chances for a job. The problem has become serious enough that a company called Reputation Defender (*www.reputationdefender.com*) will search for damaging content online and destroy it on behalf of clients.

Privacy Codes and Policies.   **Privacy policies** or **privacy codes** are an organization's guidelines with respect to protecting the privacy of customers, clients, and employees. In many corporations, senior management has begun to understand that when they collect vast amounts of personal information, they must protect it. Many organizations provide opt-out choices for their customers. The **opt-out model** of informed consent permits the company to collect personal information until the customer specifically requests that the data not be collected. Privacy advocates prefer the **opt-in model** of informed consent, whereby a business is prohibited from collecting any personal information unless the customer specifically authorizes it.

The Platform for Privacy Preferences (P3P) automatically communicates privacy policies between an electronic commerce Web site and visitors to that site. P3P enables visitors to determine the types of personal data that can be extracted by the Web sites they visit. It also allows visitors to compare a Web site's privacy policy to the visitors' preferences or to other standards, such as the Federal Trade Commission's (FTC) Fair Information Practices Standard or the European Directive on Data Protection.

Table 3.2 provides a sampling of privacy policy guidelines. (You can access Google's Privacy Policy at *www.google.com/privacypolicy.html*.)

Having a privacy policy in place can help organizations avoid legal problems. However, criminals do not pay any attention to privacy codes and policies, as IT's About Business 3.1 shows.

International Aspects of Privacy

As the number of online users has increased globally, governments have enacted a large number of inconsistent privacy and security laws. This highly complex global legal framework is causing regulatory problems for companies. Approximately 50 countries have some form of data protection law. Many of these laws conflict with or require specific security measures. Other countries have no privacy laws at all.

The absence of consistent or uniform standards for privacy and security obstructs the flow of information among countries. The European Union (EU), for one, has taken steps to overcome this problem. In 1998 the European Community Commission (ECC) issued guidelines to all its member countries regarding the rights of individuals to access information about themselves. The EU data protection laws are stricter than U.S. laws and

Table 3.2

Privacy Policy Guidelines: A Sampler

Data Collection

- □ Data should be collected on individuals only for the purpose of accomplishing a legitimate business objective.
- □ Data should be adequate, relevant, and not excessive in relation to the business objective.
- □ Individuals must give their consent before data pertaining to them can be gathered. Such consent may be implied from the individual's actions (e.g., applications for credit, insurance, or employment).

Data Accuracy

- □ Sensitive data gathered on individuals should be verified before they are entered into the database.
- □ Data should, where and when necessary, be kept current.
- □ The file should be made available so the individual can ensure that the data are correct.
- □ If there is disagreement about the accuracy of the data, the individual's version should be noted and included with any disclosure of the file.

Data Confidentiality

- □ Computer security procedures should be implemented to ensure against unauthorized disclosure of data. These procedures should include physical, technical, and administrative security measures.
- □ Third parties should not be given access to data without the individual's knowledge or permission, except as required by law.
- □ Disclosures of data, other than the most routine, should be noted and maintained for as long as the data are maintained.
- □ Data should not be disclosed for reasons incompatible with the business objective for which they are collected.

IT's About Business

3.1 Security Outside the Perimeter: LexisNexis

LexisNexis (*www.lexisnexis.com*), a $2 billion data aggregator, collects and integrates information on millions of people, ranging from public data such as real estate records and published telephone numbers to nonpublic information such as Social Security numbers, financial data, and criminal records. This information is very valuable, both to black-market operators who promote identity theft and to the company's 4.5 million legitimate customers, including direct marketers and law enforcement agencies.

In 2005, the personal records of 310,000 individuals, including names, Social Security numbers, and driver's license numbers, were stolen from Lexis-Nexis databases in 59 separate incidences. The theft unfolded in this manner.

A group of hackers sent out an e-mail promising an attached file of pornographic images. Someone in a police department in Florida and someone in a constable's office in Texas took the bait. By clicking on the link in the e-mail, the two victims downloaded keystroke logging software (also called keylogging software or keyloggers) onto their computers that recorded every keystroke and every click of their mouse. When they later logged into their LexisNexis accounts—which police use to obtain background information on criminal suspects—the hackers captured their passwords and user names.

LexisNexis learned of the attack weeks later, when one of the two police departments noticed an unusual amount of activity on their account and contacted the company. The company called the FBI and Secret Service, notified the press, and began an internal investigation. LexisNexis notified the people whose personal data had been stolen and provided a consolidated credit report and credit-monitoring services for each of them. The company provided credit counselors and $20,000 worth of identity theft insurance to anyone who ultimately became a victim of fraud as a result of the theft.

The real lesson learned by LexisNexis was that it is not enough to protect your own internal network. In a networked world, companies must also take responsibility for the security of their customers and business partners, both of whom can provide a point of entry for a hacker. Therefore, LexisNexis had to address the vulnerabilities on the edges of its network by making its customers more secure. This effort represented a major challenge, however, because the company's network included more than 4.5 million customers and business partners, many of whom came from government agencies.

As a result, the company implemented the LexisNexis Customer Security Program, which is designed to push more of the burden for the security of LexisNexis' information to its customers. The program consists of several action items, which include stronger login requirements, monthly user verification, and restricted access to full Social Security numbers and driver's license information.

Sources: Compiled from D. Briody, "Lexis-Nexis: Ground Zero for War vs. Data Thieves," *CIO Insight*, September 5, 2005; E. Nee, "Making Legitimate Business from Data Theft," *CIO Insight*, September 5, 2005; B. Krebs, "Five Arrested in Theft of LexisNexis Data," *Washington Post*, July 1, 2006; J. Kirk, "LexisNexis Finds Disclosure Meant Less Pain in Data Theft," *Information Security News*; April 25, 2006; "LexisNexis in the Security Hot Seat," *Baseline Magazine*, June 1, 2006.

QUESTIONS

1. Should LexisNexis be held legally liable for security breaches outside its perimeter? Support your answer.
2. Do you think that the LexisNexis Customer Security Program is sufficiently powerful to reduce security breaches that occur through its customers? Why or why not?

therefore may create problems for multinational corporations, which may face lawsuits for privacy violation.

The transfer of data in and out of a nation without the knowledge of either the authorities or the individuals involved raises a number of privacy issues. Whose laws have jurisdiction when records are stored in a different country for reprocessing or retransmission purposes? For example, if data are transmitted by a Polish company through a U.S. satellite to a British corporation, which country's privacy laws control the data, and when? Questions like these will become more complicated and frequent as time goes on. Governments must make an effort to develop laws and standards to cope with rapidly changing information technologies in order to solve some of these privacy issues.

The United States and the EU share the goal of privacy protection for their citizens, but the United States takes a different approach than the EU. To bridge the different privacy approaches, the U.S. Department of Commerce, in consultation with the EU, developed a "Safe Harbor" framework to regulate the way that U.S. companies export and handle the personal data (such as names and addresses) of European citizens. See *www.export.gov/safeharbor* and *http://ec.europa.eu/justice_home/fsj/privacy/index_en.htm.*

Before you go on . . .

1. Define ethics, and list its four categories as they apply to IT.
2. Describe the issue of privacy as it is affected by IT.
3. What does a code of ethics contain?
4. Describe the relationship between IT and privacy.

3.2 Threats to Information Security

The following factors are contributing to the increasing vulnerability of organizational information assets.

- Today's interconnected, interdependent, wirelessly networked business environment
- Governmental legislation
- Smaller, faster, cheaper computers and storage devices
- Decreasing skills necessary to be a computer hacker
- International organized crime taking over cybercrime
- Downstream liability
- Increased employee use of unmanaged devices
- Lack of management support

The first factor is the evolution of the information technology resource from mainframe-only to today's highly complex, interconnected, interdependent, wirelessly networked business environment. The Internet now enables millions of computers and computer networks to freely and seamlessly communicate with one another. Organizations and individuals are exposed to a world of untrusted networks and potential attackers. A *trusted network* is any network within your organization, whereas an *untrusted network* is any network external to your organization. In addition, wireless technologies enable employees to compute, communicate, and access the Internet anywhere and anytime. Making matters worse, wireless is an inherently nonsecure broadcast communications medium.

The second factor, governmental legislation, dictates that many types of information must be protected by law. In the United States, the Gramm-Leach-Bliley Act requires companies to notify consumers of their privacy policies and to provide opt-out provisions for consumers who do not want their personal information distributed outside the company. The Gramm-Leach-Bliley Act also protects nonpublic financial data. The Health Insurance Portability and Accountability Act (HIPAA) protects all medical records and other individually identifiable health information.

The third factor results from the fact that modern computers and storage devices (e.g., thumb drives or flash drives) continue to become smaller, faster, cheaper, and more portable, with greater storage capacity. These characteristics make it much easier to steal or lose a computer or storage device that contains huge amounts of sensitive information. Also, far more people are able to afford powerful computers and connect inexpensively to the Internet, thus raising the potential of an attack on information assets.

The fourth factor is that the computing skills necessary to be a hacker are *decreasing*. The Internet contains information and computer programs called *scripts* that users with few skills can download and use to attack any information system connected to the Internet.

The fifth factor is that international organized crime is taking over cybercrime. **Cybercrime** refers to illegal activities taking place over computer networks, particularly the Internet. iDefense (*http://labs.idefense.com*) is a company that specializes in providing security information to governments and Fortune 500 companies. The company states that groups of well-organized criminals have taken control of a global billion-dollar crime network. The network, powered by skillful hackers, targets known software security weaknesses. These crimes are typically nonviolent but quite lucrative. For example, losses from armed robberies average hundreds of dollars and those from white-collar crimes average tens of thousands of dollars. In contrast, losses from computer crimes average hundreds of thousands of dollars. Also, these crimes can be committed from anywhere in the world, at any time, effectively providing an international safe haven for cybercriminals. Computer-based crimes cause billions of dollars in damages to businesses each year, including the costs to repair information systems and the costs of lost business.

The sixth factor, *downstream liability*, occurs in this manner. If company A's information systems are compromised by a perpetrator and used to attack company B's systems, then company A can be liable for damages to company B. Note that company B is "downstream" from company A in this attack scenario. A downstream liability lawsuit would put company A's security policies and operations on trial. Under tort law, the plaintiff (the injured party or company B) would have to prove that the offending company (company A) had a duty to keep its computers secure and failed to do so, as measured against generally accepted standards and practices.

Legal experts think that it is only a matter of time before victims of computer crime start suing the owners of systems and networks used as launchpads in cyberattacks. Information security's first downstream liability lawsuit will likely come from a catastrophe. For example, an online retailer may be hit with a devastating attack that disrupts its business.

At some point, all companies will have to meet some minimal set of standards when operating information systems that connect to the Internet. The models already exist in the form of regulations and laws (e.g., Gramm-Leach-Bliley Act and HIPAA). Contractual security obligations, particularly *service-level agreements* (SLAs), which spell out very specific requirements, might also help establish a security standard. Courts or legislatures could cite typical SLA terms, such as maintaining up-to-date antivirus software, software patches, and firewalls, in crafting minimum security responsibilities.

A company being sued for downstream liability will have to convince a judge or jury that its security measures were reasonable. That is, the company would have to demonstrate that it had practiced due diligence in information security. Due diligence can be defined in part by what your competitors are doing, which defines best practices.

Verizon learned about due diligence in April 2003, when the Maine Public Utilities Commission rejected its request for relief from $62,000 in fees owed to local carriers after the SQL Slammer Worm shut down its networks. Verizon had applied for a steep break on the fees owed under its service agreement, arguing that the worm "was an event that was beyond its control" (like a lightning strike). The commission's rejection rested, in part, on comments submitted by competitors WorldCom (now MCI) and AT&T. They handled Slammer with minimal interruption, they said, because they did a better job patching their systems than Verizon did. Why should Verizon, or potentially any company, be an exception?

The seventh factor is increased employee use of unmanaged devices, which are devices outside the control of an organization's IT department. These devices include customer computers, business partners' mobile devices, computers in the business centers of hotels, and many others.

The eighth, and final, factor is management support. For the entire organization to take security policies and procedures seriously, senior managers must set the tone. Ultimately however, lower-level managers may be even more important. These managers are in close contact with employees every day and thus are in a better position to determine whether employees are following security procedures.

Before we discuss the many threats to an organization's information resources, let's look at some key terms. Organizations have many information resources (for example, computers and the information on them, information systems and applications, databases, and so on). These resources are subject to a huge number of threats. A **threat** to an information resource is any danger to which a system may be exposed. The **exposure** of an information resource is the harm, loss, or damage that can result if a threat compromises that resource. A system's **vulnerability** is the possibility that the system will suffer harm by a threat. **Risk** is the likelihood that a threat will occur. **Information systems controls** are the procedures, devices, or software aimed at preventing a compromise to the system. We discuss these controls in Section 3.3.

Information systems are vulnerable to many potential hazards or threats. Figure 3.1 illustrates the major threats to the security of an information system.

Threats to Information Systems

Whitman and Mattord (2003) classified threats into the following general categories to help us better understand the complexity of the threat problem.

1. Unintentional acts
2. Natural disasters
3. Technical failures
4. Management failures
5. Deliberate acts

Unintentional Acts.   Unintentional acts, those with no malicious intent, are of three types: human errors, deviations in the quality of service by service providers, and environmental hazards. Of these three, human errors are by far the most serious threats to information security.

Human Errors.   The first category of organizational employees is comprised of regular employees, who span the breadth and depth of the organization, ranging from mail clerks to the CEO, and in all functional areas. The higher the level of employee, the greater the threat the employee poses to information security because higher-level employees typically have greater access to corporate data and enjoy greater privileges on organizational information systems. Moreover, employees in two areas of the organization pose significant threats to information security: human resources and information systems. Human resources employees generally have access to sensitive personal information about all employees. Similarly, information systems employees not only have access to sensitive organizational data, but they often control the means to create, store, transmit, and modify that data.

The second category of organizational employees includes contract labor, consultants, and janitors and guards. Contract labor, such as temporary hires, may be overlooked in information security. However, these employees often have access to the company's network,

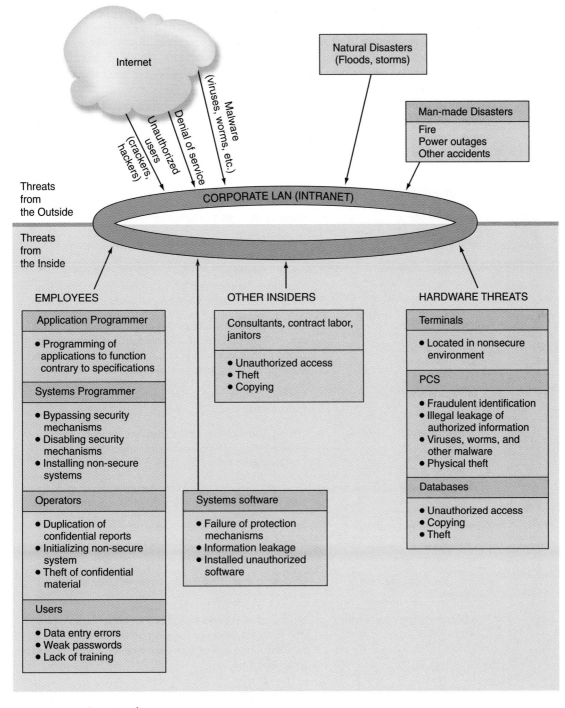

FIGURE 3.1   Security threats.

information systems, and information assets. Consultants, though technically not employees, do work for the company. Depending on the nature of their work, these people may also have access to the company's network, information systems, and information assets.

Finally, janitors and guards are the most frequently ignored people in information security. Companies might outsource their security and janitorial services. While these individuals technically are not employees, they nevertheless do work for the company. Moreover, they are usually present when most—if not all—other employees have gone home. They typically have keys to every office, and nobody questions their presence in even the most sensitive parts of the building. In fact, an article from the Winter 1994 edition of *2600: The Hacker Quarterly* described how to get a job as a janitor for the purpose of gaining physical access to an organization.

Human errors or mistakes by employees caused by laziness, carelessness, or lack of information security awareness pose a large problem for organizations. This lack of awareness comes from poor education and training efforts by the organization. Human mistakes manifest themselves in many different ways, as we see in Table 3.3.

Human Mistakes

Human Mistake	Description and Examples
Tailgating	A technique designed to allow the perpetrator to enter restricted areas that are controlled with locks or card entry. The perpetrator follows closely behind a legitimate employee and, when the employee gains entry, asks the legitimate employee to "hold the door."
Shoulder surfing	The perpetrator watches the employee's computer screen over that person's shoulder. This technique is particularly successful in public areas such as airports, commuter trains, and on airplanes.
Carelessness with laptops	Losing laptops, misplacing laptops, leaving them in taxis, and so on.
Carelessness with portable devices	Losing or misplacing these devices, or using them carelessly so that malware is introduced into an organization's network.
Opening questionable e-mails	Opening e-mails from someone unknown or clicking on links embedded in e-mails (see phishing attacks below).
Careless Internet surfing	Accessing questionable Web sites; can result in malware and/or alien software being introduced into the organization's network.
Poor password selection and use	Choosing and using weak passwords (see strong passwords below).
Carelessness with one's office	Unlocked desks and filing cabinets when employees go home at night; not logging off the company network when gone from the office for any extended period of time.
Carelessness using unmanaged devices	Unmanaged devices are those outside the control of an organization's IT department and company security procedures. These devices include computers belonging to customers and business partners, computers in the business centers of hotels, and computers in Starbucks, Paneras, and so on.
Carelessness with discarded equipment	Discarding old computer hardware and devices without completely wiping the memory; includes computers, cell phones, Blackberries, and digital copiers and printers.

Table 3.3

The human errors that we have just discussed are unintentional. However, employees can also make mistakes as a result of an attacker's deliberate actions. Such deliberate actions are called social engineering and reverse social engineering.

Social Engineering and Reverse Social Engineering.   **Social engineering** is an attack whereby the perpetrator uses social skills to trick or manipulate a legitimate employee into providing confidential company information such as passwords. The most common example of social engineering occurs when the attacker impersonates someone else on the telephone, such as a company manager or an information systems employee. The attacker says he forgot his password and asks the legitimate employee to give him a password to use. Other common exploits include posing as an exterminator, air conditioning technician, or fire marshal. Examples of social engineering abound.

In one company, a perpetrator entered a company building wearing a company ID card that looked legitimate. He walked around and put up signs on bulletin boards saying, "The help desk telephone number has been changed. The new number is 555–1234." He then exited the building and began receiving calls from legitimate employees thinking they were calling the company help desk. Naturally, the first thing the perpetrator asked for was user name and password. He now had the information necessary to access the company's information systems.

In another company, an attacker loaded a Trojan horse program (discussed later in this chapter) on 20 thumb drives. The Trojan horse was designed to collect passwords and login information from an employee's computer and then e-mail the information to the attacker. Early one morning, he scattered the thumb drives in the parking lots, designated smoking areas, and near walkways of the target company. Employees found 15 of the drives and plugged them into company computers without first scanning them with security software. The Trojan horse software transmitted their user names and passwords to the attacker and enabled him to compromise additional systems in the company.

In social engineering, the attacker approaches legitimate employees. In **reverse social engineering**, the employees approach the attacker. For example, the attacker gains employment at a company and, in informal conversations with his coworkers, lets it be known that he is "good with computers." As is often the case, the coworkers ask him for help with their computer problems. While he is helping them, he loads Trojan horses on their computers that e-mail him with their passwords and information about their machines.

Deviations in the Quality of Service by Service Providers.   This category consists of situations in which a product or service is not delivered to the organization as expected. There are many examples of such deviations in quality of service. For example, heavy equipment at a construction site cuts a fiber-optic line to your building, or your Internet service provider has availability problems. Organizations may also experience service disruptions from various providers, such as communications, electricity, telephone, water, wastewater, trash pickup, cable, and natural gas.

Environmental Hazards.   Environmental hazards include dirt, dust, humidity, and static electricity. These hazards are harmful to the safe operation of computing equipment.

Natural Disasters.   Natural disasters include floods, earthquakes, hurricanes, tornados, lightning, and, in some cases, fires. In many cases, acts of God can cause catastrophic loss of systems and data. To avoid such losses, companies must engage in proper planning for backup and recovery of information systems and data, a topic we discuss later in this chapter.

Technical Failures.   Technical failures include problems with hardware and software. The most common hardware problem is a crash of a hard disk drive. A notable hardware problem occurred when Intel released a Pentium chip with a defect that caused the chip to perform some mathematical calculations incorrectly.

The most common software problem is errors—called bugs—in computer programs. Software bugs are so common that entire Web sites are dedicated to documenting them (e.g., see *www.bug-track.com* and *www.bugaware.com*).

Management Failures.   Management failures involve a lack of funding for information security efforts and a lack of interest in those efforts. Such lack of leadership will cause the information security of the organization to suffer.

Deliberate Acts.   Deliberate acts by organizational employees (i.e., insiders) account for a large number of information security breaches. Here is a brief list to guide our discussion of these widespread acts.

- Espionage or trespass
- Information extortion
- Sabotage or vandalism
- Theft of equipment or information
- Identity theft
- Compromises to intellectual property
- Software attacks
- Supervisory control and data acquisition (SCADA) attacks
- Cyberterrorism and cyberwarfare

Espionage or Trespass.   Espionage or trespass occurs when an unauthorized individual attempts to gain illegal access to organizational information. When we discuss trespass, it is important that we distinguish between competitive intelligence and industrial espionage. *Competitive intelligence* consists of legal information-gathering techniques, such as studying a company's Web site and press releases, attending trade shows, and so on. In contrast, *industrial espionage* crosses the legal boundary.

Information Extortion.   Information extortion occurs when an attacker either threatens to steal, or actually steals, information from a company. The perpetrator demands payment for not stealing the information, for returning stolen information, or for agreeing not to disclose the information.

Sabotage or Vandalism.   Sabotage and vandalism are deliberate acts that involve defacing an organization's Web site, possibly causing the organization to lose its image and experience a loss of customer confidence. One form of online vandalism is a hacktivist or cyberactivist operation. These are cases of high-tech civil disobedience to protest the operations, policies, or actions of an organization or government agency.

Web site defacement occurs for varying reasons. One recent survey listed these reasons: just for fun, to be the best defacer, political reasons, and patriotism. For example, in May 2007, John McCain was a candidate for president and his MySpace page was defaced. For details see: *http://mike.newsvine.com/_news/2007/03/27/633799-hacking-john-mccain.*

Theft of Equipment and Information.   Computing devices and storage devices are becoming smaller, yet more powerful, with vastly increased storage (for example, laptops, Blackberries, personal digital assistants, smart phones, digital cameras, thumb drives, and iPods). As a result, these devices are becoming easier to steal and easier for attackers to use to steal information.

The uncontrolled proliferation of portable devices in companies has led to a type of attack called pod slurping. In *pod slurping*, perpetrators plug portable devices into a USB port on a computer and download huge amounts of information very quickly and easily. An iPod, for example, contains 60 gigabytes of storage and can download most of a computer's hard drive in a matter of minutes.

Another form of theft, known as *dumpster diving*, involves the practice of rummaging through commercial or residential trash to find information that has been discarded. Files, letters, memos, photographs, IDs, passwords, credit cards, and other forms of information can be found in dumpsters. Unfortunately, many people never consider that the sensitive items they throw in the trash may be recovered. Such information, when recovered, can be used for fraudulent purposes.

Dumpster diving is possible theft, because the legality of this act varies. Because dumpsters are usually located on private premises, dumpster diving is illegal in some parts of the United States, although the law is enforced with varying degrees of rigor.

Identity Theft.   **Identity theft** is the deliberate assumption of another person's identity, usually to gain access to his or her financial information or to frame him or her for a crime. Techniques for obtaining information include:

- Stealing mail or dumpster diving
- Stealing personal information in computer databases
- Infiltrating organizations that store large amounts of personal information (e.g., data aggregators such as Acxiom) (*www.acxiom.com*)
- Impersonating a trusted organization in an electronic communication (phishing).

Recovering from identity theft is costly, time-consuming, and difficult. A survey by the Identity Theft Resource Center (*www.idtheftcenter.org*) found that victims spent 330 hours repairing the damage. Victims also reported difficulties in obtaining credit and obtaining or holding a job, as well as adverse effects on insurance or credit rates. In addition, victims stated that it was difficult to remove negative information from their records, such as their credit reports.

Your personal information can be compromised in other ways. For example, AOL released detailed keyword search data for approximately 658,000 anonymized users. AOL said that the release of the data, which amounted to about 20 million search queries, was an innocent attempt to help academic researchers interested in search queries. The data, which were mirrored on multiple Web sites, represented a random selection of searches conducted over a three-month period. They included User ID, the actual query, the time of the search, and the destination domain visited. In some cases, the data included personal names, addresses, and Social Security numbers.

Although AOL apologized for the error and withdrew the site, the damage was done. The ability to analyze all searches by a single user can enable a criminal to identify who the user is and what he or she is doing. As just one example, the *New York Times* tracked down a particular person based solely on her AOL searches.

Once criminals have stolen personal information, they can use it in a variety of nefarious activities. One such activity, illustrated in IT's About Business 3.2, is the "hack, pump, and dump" scheme.

Compromises to Intellectual Property.   Protecting intellectual property is a vital issue for people who make their livelihood in knowledge fields. **Intellectual property** is the property created by individuals or corporations that is protected under *trade secret*, *patent*, and *copyright* laws.

A **trade secret** is an intellectual work, such as a business plan, that is a company secret and is not based on public information. An example is a corporate strategic plan. A **patent**

IT's About Business

3.2 The "Hack, Pump, and Dump" Scheme

Criminals have discovered yet another way to steal money. They are combining phishing attacks, Trojan horses, and keyloggers to steal identities for use in investment fraud. The scheme works like this. Hackers first gain the personal information of legitimate investors, including names, account numbers, passwords, and PINs. These criminals then hack into the accounts of unsuspecting investors, selling off their holdings in various companies to purchase shares in penny stocks. As they buy the penny stocks, the share price increases. (A penny stock is a low-priced, speculative stock of a small company.) After a short time, the hackers sell the penny stocks for a profit and transfer the money to offshore accounts.

Aleksey Karmardin, for example, used this scheme 14 times to defraud investors of more than $80,000. He and his accomplices allegedly hacked into four legitimate online trading accounts, sold their holdings, and purchased shares in a penny stock. The stock's price went from 26 cents to 80 cents in less than one day. The hackers promptly sold the shares and moved the profits to an offshore account.

The fraud affects not only investors, but also companies whose stocks are pumped and then dumped. One firm had its stock price go from 88 cents to $1.28 in one day. The following day, the stock fell to 13 cents, where it remained. TD Ameritrade, an online broker, restricted online trade on the company's stock. The company's owner had planned to make a large acquisition, but the declining stock price canceled the purchase.

Sources: Compiled from E. Nakashima, "Hack, Pump, and Dump," *Washington Post,* January 26, 2007; R. Naraine, "Pump and Dump Spam Surge Linked to Russian Bot Herders," *eWeek,* November 16, 2006; J. Libbenga, "Pump and Dump Blues," *The Register;* November 21, 2006; E. Sutherland, "Fraudsters Update Pump and Dump," *Internet News,* January 31, 2007.

QUESTIONS

1. How can investors protect themselves from hack, pump, and dump schemes?
2. How can companies protect themselves from hack, pump, and dump schemes?
3. Should online brokers be held liable for hack, pump, and dump schemes? Why or why not?

is a document that grants the holder exclusive rights on an invention or process for 20 years. **Copyright** is a statutory grant that provides the creators of intellectual property with ownership of the property for the life of the creator plus 70 years. Owners are entitled to collect fees from anyone who wants to copy the property.

The most common intellectual property related to IT deals with software. The U.S. Federal Computer Software Copyright Act (1980) provides protection for *source* and *object code* of computer software, but the law does not clearly identify what is eligible for protection. For example, copyright law does not protect similar concepts, functions, and general features such as pull-down menus, colors, and icons. However, copying a software program without making payment to the owner—including giving a disc to a friend to install on his or her computer—is a copyright violation. Not surprisingly, this practice, called **piracy**, is a major problem for software vendors. The global trade in pirated software amounts to hundreds of billions of dollars.

The Business Software Alliance (BSA), an organization representing the world's commercial software industry, promotes legal software and conducts research on software piracy in an attempt to eliminate it. The BSA (*www.bsa.org*) has identified Vietnam, China, Indonesia, Ukraine, and Russia as the countries with the highest percentages of illegal software. More than 85 percent of the software used in these countries consists of illegal copies.

Software Attacks.   Software attacks have evolved from the outbreak era, where malicious software tried to infect as many computers worldwide as possible, to the profit-driven, Web-based attacks of today. Cybercriminals are heavily involved with malware attacks to make money, and they use sophisticated, blended attacks typically via the Web. Table 3.4 shows a variety of software attacks.

Types of Software Attacks	Description
Virus	Segment of computer code that performs malicious actions by attaching to another computer program.
Worm	Segment of computer code that performs malicious actions and will replicate, or spread, by itself (without requiring another computer program).
Trojan Horse	Software programs that hide in other computer programs and reveal their designed behavior only when they are activated.
Back Door	Typically a password, known only to the attacker, that allows him or her to access a computer system at will, without having to go through any security procedures (also called trap door).
Logic Bomb	Segment of computer code that is embedded with an organization's existing computer programs and is designed to activate and perform a destructive action at a certain time or date.
Password Attack Dictionary Attack	Attacks that try combinations of letters and numbers that are most likely to succeed, such as all words from a dictionary.
Brute Force Attack	Attacks that use massive computing resources to try every possible combination of password options to uncover a password.
Denial-of-Service Attack	Attacker sends so many information requests to a target computer system that the target cannot handle them successfully and typically crashes (i.e., ceases to function).
Distributed Denial-of-Service Attack	An attacker first takes over many computers, typically by using malicious software. These computers are called *zombies*, or *bots*. The attacker uses these bots (which form a *botnet*) to deliver a coordinated stream of information requests to a target computer, causing it to crash.
Phishing Attack	Phishing attacks use deception to acquire sensitive personal information by masquerading as official-looking e-mails or instant messages.
Zero-day Attack	A zero-day attack takes advantage of a newly discovered, previously unknown vulnerability in a software product. Perpetrators attack the vulnerability before the software vendor can prepare a patch for the vulnerability.

Table 3.4

Alien Software.   Many personal computers have alien software (also called *pestware*) running on them that the owners do not know about. **Alien software** is clandestine software that is installed on your computer through duplicitous methods. Alien software is typically not as malicious as viruses, worms, or Trojan horses, but it does use up valuable system resources. In addition, it can report on your Web surfing habits and other personal behavior.

One clear indication that software is pestware is that it does not come with an uninstaller program. An *uninstaller* is an automated program that removes a particular software package systematically and entirely. The different types of alien software include adware, spyware, spamware, and cookies.

The vast majority of pestware is **adware**—software that is designed to help pop-up advertisements appear on your screen. Adware is so common because it works. According to advertising agencies, for every 100 people who delete such an ad, 3 click on it. This "hit rate" is extremely high for Internet advertising.

Spyware is software that collects personal information about users without their consent. Two types of spyware are: keystroke loggers and screen scrapers. **Keystroke loggers** (also called **keyloggers**) record your keystrokes and your Internet Web browsing history. The purposes range from criminal (e.g., theft of passwords and sensitive personal information such as credit card numbers) to annoying (e.g., recording your Internet search history for targeted advertising). Companies have attempted to counter keyloggers by switching to other forms of input for authentication. For example, rather than typing in a password, the user has to accurately select each character in turn from a series of boxes, using a mouse. As a result, attackers have turned to **screen scrapers** (or screen grabbers). This software records a continuous "movie" of a screen's contents rather than simply recording keystrokes.

Spamware is pestware that is designed to use your computer as a launchpad for spammers. **Spam** is unsolicited e-mail, usually for the purpose of advertising for products and services. When your computer is used in this way, e-mails from spammers appear to come from you. Even worse, spam will be sent to everyone in your e-mail address book.

Not only is spam a nuisance, but it wastes time and money. Spam costs U.S. companies more than $20 billion per year. These costs come from productivity losses, clogged e-mail systems, additional storage, user support, and antispam software. Spam can also carry viruses and worms, making it even more dangerous.

Cookies are small amounts of information that Web sites store on your computer, temporarily or more-or-less permanently. In many cases, cookies are useful and innocuous. For example, some cookies are passwords and user IDs that you do not have to retype every time you load a new page at the Web site that issued the cookie. Cookies are also necessary if you want to shop online, because they are used for your shopping carts at various online merchants.

Tracking cookies, however, can be used to track your path through a Web site, the time you spend there, what links you click on, and other details that the company wants to record, usually for marketing purposes. Tracking cookies can also combine this information with your name, purchases, credit card information, and other personal data, to develop an intrusive profile of your spending habits.

Most cookies can be read only by the party that created them. However, some companies that manage online banner advertising are, in essence, cookie-sharing rings. These companies can track information such as which pages you load and which ads you click on. They then share this information with their client Web sites (which may number in the thousands). For a cookie demonstration, see *http://privacy.net/track/*.

Supervisory Control and Data Acquisition (SCADA) Attacks.   SCADA refers to a large-scale, distributed, measurement and control system. SCADA systems are used to monitor or to control chemical, physical, or transport processes such as oil refineries, water and sewage treatment plants, electrical generators, and nuclear power plants.

SCADA systems consist of multiple sensors, a master computer, and communications infrastructure. The sensors connect to physical equipment. They read status data such as the open/closed status of a switch or a valve, as well as measurements such as pressure, flow, voltage, and current. By sending signals to equipment, sensors control that equipment, such as opening or closing a switch or valve or setting the speed of a pump.

The sensors are connected in a network, and each sensor typically has an Internet (Internet Protocol, or IP) address. (We discuss IP addresses in Technology Guide 5.) If an attacker can gain access to the network, he or she can disrupt the power grid over a large area or disrupt the operations of a large chemical plant. Such actions could have catastrophic results.

Although experts see little chance of a SCADA system being attacked, at least one such event has already occurred. In Australia in 2000, a disgruntled sewage-treatment plant job reject hacked the sewage plant's pump control systems. He repeatedly sent torrents of effluent into nearby rivers and parks and at least one hotel.

Cyberterrorism and Cyberwarfare. Through both **cyberterrorism** and **cyberwarfare**, attackers use a target's computer systems, particularly via the Internet, to cause physical, real-world harm or severe disruption, usually with a political agenda. Cyberterrorism and cyberwarfare range from gathering data to attacking critical infrastructure (via SCADA systems). We treat the two interchangeably here, even though cyberterrorism typically involves individuals or groups, whereas cyberwarfare involves nations.

The director of the U.S. Cyber Consequences Unit, a Department of the Homeland Security advisory group, believes that cyberattacks on U.S. information technology infrastructure are poised to escalate to full-scale disasters that could bring down companies and kill people. He warns that intelligence "chatter" increasingly points to possible plans to use SCADA systems to destroy or disrupt physical infrastructure, such as gas, electricity, telecommunications, and water companies.

Other types of attack involve altering process control systems to produce defective products or altering quality control systems so that defects will not be detected. The pharmaceutical and automotive industries are potential targets in these types of attack.

Terrorist groups around the world have expanded their activities on the Internet, increasing the sophistication and volume of their videos and messages, in an effort to recruit new members and raise money. In response, the U.S. military is expanding its offensive capabilities to attack terrorists' Web sites rather than just monitor them.

The United States has already undergone coordinated attacks on its information technology infrastructure. One series of attacks began in 1999. The U.S. government traced the attacks to Russia, but it has not been confirmed that the attack originated there.

What Companies Are Doing. Why is it so difficult to stop cybercriminals? One reason is that the online commerce industry is not particularly willing to install safeguards that would make it harder to complete transactions. It would be possible, for example, to demand passwords or personal identification numbers for all credit card transactions. However, these requirements might discourage people from shopping online. Also, there is little incentive for companies like AOL to share leads on criminal activity either with one another or with the FBI. For credit card companies, it is cheaper to block a stolen credit card and move on than to invest time and money on a prosecution.

Despite these difficulties, the information security industry is battling back. Companies are developing software and services that deliver early warnings of trouble on the Internet. Unlike traditional antivirus software, which is reactive, early-warning systems are proactive, scanning the Web for new viruses and alerting companies to the danger.

The new systems are emerging in response to ever more effective virus writers. As virus writers become more expert, the gap between the time when they learn of vulnerabilities and when they exploit them is closing quickly. Hackers are now producing new viruses and worms in a matter of hours (see zero-day attacks).

Technicians at TruSecure (*www.cybertrust.com*) and Symantec (*www.symantec.com*) are working around the clock to monitor Web traffic. Symantec's team taps into 20,000 sensors placed at Internet hubs in 180 countries to spot e-mail and other data packets that seem to be carrying viruses. TruSecure sends technicians posing as hackers into online virus-writer chat rooms to find out what they are planning. TruSecure boasts that it even contributed to the arrests of the authors of the Melissa, Anna Kournikova, and Love Letter viruses.

In addition, many companies hire information security experts to attack their own systems. These surprise attacks are called penetration tests. A **penetration test** is a method of evaluating the security of an information system by simulating an attack by a malicious perpetrator. The idea is to proactively discover weaknesses before real attackers exploit them.

Despite the difficulties involved in defending against attacks, organizations spend a great deal of time and money protecting their information resources. We discuss these methods of protection in the next section.

Before you go on . . .

1. Give an example of one type of unintentional threat to a computer system.
2. Describe the various types of software attacks.
3. Describe the issue of intellectual property protection.

3.3 Protecting Information Resources

Before spending money to apply controls, organizations must perform risk management. As we discussed earlier in the chapter, a risk is the probability that a threat will impact an information resource. The goal of **risk management** is to identify, control, and minimize the impact of threats. In other words, risk management seeks to reduce risk to acceptable levels. Risk management involves three processes: risk analysis, risk mitigation, and controls evaluation.

Risk analysis is the process by which an organization assesses the value of each asset being protected, estimates the probability that each asset will be compromised, and compares the probable costs of the asset's being compromised with the costs of protecting that asset. Organizations perform risk analysis to ensure that their information systems' security programs are cost effective. The risk analysis process prioritizes the assets to be protected based on each asset's value, its probability of being compromised, and the estimated cost of its protection. The organization then considers how to mitigate the risk.

In **risk mitigation**, the organization takes concrete actions against risks. Risk mitigation has two functions: (1) implementing controls to prevent identified threats from occurring and (2) developing a means of recovery should the threat become a reality. Organizations may adopt several risk mitigation strategies; the three most common strategies are:

- **Risk acceptance**: Accept the potential risk, continue operating with no controls, and absorb any damages that occur.
- **Risk limitation**: Limit the risk by implementing controls that minimize the impact of the threat.
- **Risk transference**: Transfer the risk by using other means to compensate for the loss, such as by purchasing insurance.

In **controls evaluation**, the organization identifies security deficiencies and calculates the costs of implementing adequate control measures. If the costs of implementing a control are greater than the value of the asset being protected, then control is not cost effective. For example, an organization's mainframe computers are too valuable for risk acceptance. As a result, organizations limit the risk to mainframes through controls, such as access controls. Organizations also use risk transference for their mainframes by purchasing insurance and having off-site backups.

In another example, suppose that the old car you are driving is worth $2,000. Also suppose that you think the probability of an accident or other damage happening to your car is 0.01. The amount of your probable loss would be $20 ($2,000 × 0.01). If you live in a state that allows it, you might decide not to carry any insurance on your car. In this way, you are practicing risk acceptance. Or you might try to limit your risk by driving carefully. Finally, you could transfer the risk by purchasing insurance, but you would try to keep the cost of the insurance below $20, which is the amount you assigned to your probable loss.

Controls

Organizations protect their systems in many ways. One major strategy is to join with the FBI to form the *National Infrastructure Protection Center (NIPC)*. This partnership between government and private industry is designed to protect the nation's infrastructure—its telecommunications, energy, transportation, banking and finance, emergency, and governmental operations. The FBI has also established *Regional Computer Intrusion Squads*, which focus on intrusions into telephone and computer networks, privacy violations, industrial espionage, pirated computer software, and other cybercrimes. Yet another national organization is the *Computer Emergency Response Team* (*CERT*) at Carnegie Mellon University (*www.cert.org*).

Table 3.5 lists the major difficulties involved in protecting information. Because it is so important to the entire enterprise, organizing an appropriate defense system is one of the major activities of any prudent CIO and of the functional managers who control information resources. As a matter of fact, IT security is the business of *everyone* in an organization.

To protect their information assets, organizations implement **controls**, or defense mechanisms (also called *countermeasures*). *Security controls* are designed to protect all of the components of an information system, including data, software, hardware, and networks. Because there are so many diverse threats, organizations utilize layers of controls, or defense-in-depth.

Controls are intended to prevent accidental hazards, deter intentional acts, detect problems as early as possible, enhance damage recovery, and correct problems. Before we discuss

The Difficulties in Protecting Information Resources

- Hundreds of potential threats exist.
- Computing resources may be situated in many locations.
- Many individuals control information assets.
- Computer networks can be located outside the organization and are difficult to protect.
- Rapid technological changes make some controls obsolete as soon as they are installed.
- Many computer crimes are undetected for a long period of time, so it is difficult to learn from experience.
- People tend to violate security procedures because the procedures are inconvenient.
- The amount of computer knowledge necessary to commit computer crimes is usually minimal. As a matter of fact, one can learn hacking, for free, on the Internet.
- The cost of preventing hazards can be very high. Therefore, most organizations simply cannot afford to protect against all possible hazards.
- It is difficult to conduct a cost-benefit justification for controls before an attack occurs because it is difficult to assess the value of a hypothetical attack.

Table 3.5

controls in more detail, we emphasize that the single most effective control is user education and training, leading to increased awareness of the vital importance of information security on the part of every organizational employee.

The four major categories of controls are physical, access, communications, and application controls (see Figure 3.2).

Physical Controls. **Physical controls** prevent unauthorized individuals from gaining access to a company's facilities. Common physical controls include walls, doors, fencing, gates, locks, badges, guards, and alarm systems. More sophisticated physical controls include pressure sensors, temperature sensors, and motion detectors. One weakness of physical controls is that they can be inconvenient to employees.

Guards deserve special mention because they have very difficult jobs. First, their jobs are boring and repetitive, and they are typically not highly paid. Second, if they do their jobs thoroughly, other employees harass them, particularly if their conscientiousness slows up the process of entering a facility.

Organizations also put other physical security considerations in place. Such controls limit users to acceptable login times and acceptable login locations. These controls also limit the number of unsuccessful login attempts, and they require everyone to log off their computers when they leave for the day. In addition, computers are set to automatically log the user off after a certain period of disuse.

Access Controls. **Access controls** restrict unauthorized individuals from using information resources. These controls involve two major functions: authentication and authorization.

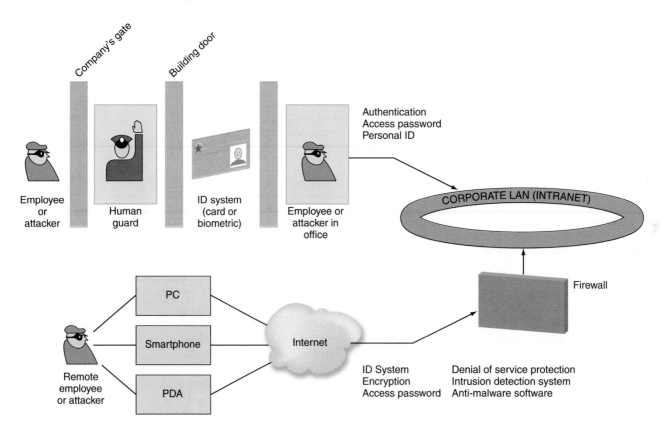

FIGURE 3.2   Where defense mechanisms are located.

Authentication determines the identity of the person requiring access, and **authorization** determines which actions, rights, or privileges the person has, based on verified identity. Organizations use many methods to identify authorized personnel (i.e., authenticate someone): something the user is, something the user has, something the user does, and something the user knows.

Something the User Is.   Also known as **biometrics**, these authentication methods examine a person's innate physical characteristics. Common biometric applications are fingerprint scans, palm scans, retina scans, iris recognition, and facial recognition. Of these applications, fingerprints, retina scans, and iris recognition provide the most definitive identification.

Something the User Has.   These authentication mechanisms include regular identification (ID) cards, smart ID cards, and tokens. **Regular ID cards**, or *dumb cards*, typically have the person's picture, and often, his or her signature. **Smart ID cards** have a chip embedded in them with pertinent information about the user. (Smart ID cards used for identification differ from smart cards used in electronic commerce—see Chapter 6. Both types of card have embedded chips, but they are used for different purposes.) **Tokens** have embedded chips and a digital display that presents a login number used by the employees to access the organization's network. The number changes with each login.

Something the User Does.   These authentication mechanisms include voice and signature recognition. In **voice recognition**, the user speaks a phrase (e.g., his or her name and department) that has been previously recorded under controlled, monitored conditions. The voice recognition system matches the two voice signals.

In **signature recognition**, the user signs his or her name, and the system matches this signature with one previously recorded under controlled, monitored conditions. Signature recognition systems also match the speed of the signature and the pressure of the signature.

Something the User Knows.   These authentication mechanisms include passwords and passphrases. **Passwords** present a huge information security problem in all organizations. All users should use strong passwords so that the password cannot be broken by a password attack, which we discussed earlier. **Strong passwords** have the following characteristics:

- They should be difficult to guess.
- They should be longer rather than shorter.
- They should have uppercase letters, lowercase letters, numbers, and special characters.
- They should not be a recognizable word.
- They should not be the name of anything or anyone familiar, such as family names or names of pets.
- They should not be a recognizable string of numbers, such as a Social Security number or birthday.

Unfortunately, strong passwords are irritating. If the organization mandates longer (stronger) passwords and/or frequent password changes, they become more difficult to remember, causing employees to write them down. What is needed is a way for a user to create a strong password that is easy to remember. A passphrase can help, either by being a password itself or by helping you create a strong password.

A **passphrase** is a series of characters that is longer than a password but can be memorized easily. Examples of passphrases include "maytheforcebewithyoualways," "goahead-makemyday," "livelongandprosper," and "aman'sgottoknowhislimitations." A user can turn a passphrase into a strong password in this manner. Start with the last passphrase above and use the first letter of each word. You will have amgtkhl. Then capitalize every other letter, to have AmGtKhL. Then add special characters and numbers, to have 9AmGtKhL//*. Now you have a strong password that you can remember.

Multifactor Authentication. Many organizations are using multifactor authentication to identify authorized users more efficiently and effectively. This type of authentication is particularly important when users are logging in from remote locations.

Single-factor authentication, which is notoriously weak, commonly consists simply of a password. Two-factor authentication consists of a password plus one type of biometric identification (e.g., a fingerprint). Three-factor authentication is any combination of three authentication methods. We should keep in mind that stronger authentication is more expensive, and can be irritating to users as well.

Once users have been properly authenticated, then the rights and privileges that they have on the organization's systems are established, a process called authorization. Companies use the principle of least privilege for authorization purposes. A **privilege** is a collection of

---

IT's About Business

3.3 Providing Least Privilege at UPS

Just before Christmas each year, UPS hires 50,000 to 60,000 temporary workers to help sort, load, and deliver packages. Keeping track of these employees, in addition to 350,000 regular employees, as well as each person's access to business applications, is a major business problem for UPS.

To address this problem, UPS uses the IBM Tivoli Identity Manager to automate some processes involved with giving employees a digital identity and a password for access to the UPS corporate portal or other applications. (The UPS Enterprise Portal allows employees to communicate with other employees, update their personal information, and access links to healthcare and other benefit information.)

The identity manager provides a central, companywide catalog of UPS employees, and it details the systems and applications each one can access. When someone is hired, his or her name, job title, and responsibilities are entered into the company's PeopleSoft human resources application, which feeds information to the identity manager.

The identity manager has provided several benefits for UPS. Employees are now able to change or reset their own passwords when they forget them without having to rely on the technical staff for help. The number of calls to the help desk has decreased by 60 percent.

UPS has also improved security and is better able to comply with the Sarbanes-Oxley Act. Providing employees with access only to the applications they need to do their jobs has increased security. The identity manager denies access to UPS servers that house financial data. This policy helps ensure that UPS complies with Sarbanes-Oxley. In another benefit linked to Sarbanes-Oxley compliance and security, UPS uses the identity manager to immediately turn off access when a worker is terminated or voluntarily leaves the company.

UPS has seen cost savings beyond the savings on its help desk. Prior to implementing the identity manager, UPS relied on a time-consuming process for granting and denying access to applications. The technical staff had to manually allow, or delete, privileges across numerous systems when someone was hired, fired, or quit. The identity manager has largely automated this process.

Sources: Compiled from B. Violino, "Tracking Digital Identities: No Holiday for UPS," *Baseline Magazine*, December 20, 2006; B. Violino, "Identity Management and Access: A Smarter Gatekeeper," *Baseline Magazine*, December 22, 2006; K. J. Higgins, "Company Cuts Privileges to Cut Malware," *Dark Reading*, January 19, 2007; S. Gates, "Identity Management: Controlling the Costs of Continuous Compliance," *Sarbanes-Oxley Compliance Journal*, February 3, 2005.

QUESTIONS

1. Why is it so important for organizations to provide least privilege to employees?
2. What are the possible disadvantages of least privilege?

related computer system operations that can be performed by users of the system. **Least privilege** is a principle that users be granted the privilege for some activity only if there is a justifiable need to grant this authorization. As IT's About Business 3.3 shows, granting least privilege in organizations can be complicated.

Communications Controls. **Communications (network) controls** secure the movement of data across networks. Communications controls consist of firewalls, anti-malware systems, intrusion detection systems, encryption, virtual private networking (VPN), and vulnerability management systems. Firewalls, anti-malware systems, intrusion detection systems, encryption, and VPNs are reactive. Only vulnerability management systems provide a proactive approach, identifying network and device vulnerabilities before networks are compromised.

Firewalls. A **firewall** is a system that prevents a specific type of information from moving between untrusted networks, such as the Internet, and private networks, such as your company's network. Put simply, firewalls prevent unauthorized Internet users from accessing private networks. Firewalls can consist of hardware, software, or a combination of both. All messages entering or leaving your company's network pass through a firewall. The firewall examines each message and blocks those that do not meet specified security rules.

Firewalls range from simple, for home use, to very complex for organizational use. Figure 3.3a shows a basic firewall for a home computer. In this case, the firewall is implemented as software on the home computer. Figure 3.3b shows an organization that has implemented an external firewall, which faces the Internet, and an internal firewall, which faces the company network. A **demilitarized zone (DMZ)** is located between the two firewalls. Messages from the Internet must first pass through the external firewall. If they conform to the defined security rules, then they are sent to company servers located in the DMZ. These servers typically handle Web page requests and e-mail. Any messages designated for the company's internal network (for example, its intranet) must pass through the internal firewall, again with its own defined security rules, to gain access to the company's private network.

The danger from viruses and worms is so severe that many organizations are placing firewalls at strategic points *inside* their private networks. In this way, if a virus or worm does get through both the external and internal firewalls, then the internal damage may be contained.

Anti-**malware** *systems.* **Anti-malware systems**, also called AV, or **antivirus software**, are software packages that attempt to identify and eliminate viruses, worms, and other malicious

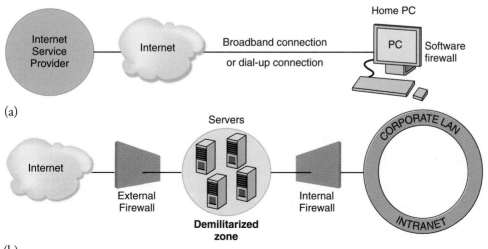

FIGURE 3.3 (a) Basic firewall for home computer.
(b) Organization with two firewalls and demilitarized zone.

software. This software is implemented at the organizational level by the Information Systems department. Currently, hundreds of AV software packages are available. Among the best known are Norton Antivirus (*www.symantec.com*), McAfee Virusscan (*www.mcafee.com*), and Trend Micro PC-cillin (*www.trendmicro.com*).

As already mentioned, anti-malware systems are generally reactive. These products work by creating definitions, or signatures, of various types of malware and then updating these signatures in their products. The anti-malware software then examines suspicious computer code to see if it matches a known signature. If it does, then the anti-malware software will remove it. This is the reason organizations update their malware definitions so often.

Because malware is such a serious problem, the leading vendors are rapidly developing anti-malware systems that function proactively as well as reactively. These systems evaluate behavior rather than relying on signature matching. In theory, therefore, it is possible to catch malware before it can infect systems. Cisco, for example, has released a product called Cisco Security Agent. This product functions proactively by analyzing computer code to see if it functions like malware (see *www.cisilion.com/cisco-security-agent.htm*). Prevx is another vendor offering this proactive type of anti-malware system (*www.prevx.com*).

Whitelisting and Blacklisting. A recent report by the Yankee Group (*www.yankeegroup.com*), a technology research and consulting firm, stated that 99 percent of organizations had anti-malware systems installed, but 62 percent of companies still suffered successful malware attacks. As we have discussed, anti-malware systems are usually reactive, and malware continues to infect companies.

One solution to this problem is **whitelisting**, a process in which a company identifies the software that it will allow to run and does not try to recognize malware. Whitelisting permits acceptable software to run and either prevents anything else from running or lets new software run in a quarantined environment until the company can verify its validity.

Where whitelisting allows nothing to run unless it is on the whitelist, blacklisting allows everything to run unless it is on the blacklist. **Blacklisting**, then, includes certain types of software that are not allowed to run in the company environment. For example, a company might blacklist peer-to-peer file sharing on its systems. In addition to software, people, devices, and Web sites can also be whitelisted and blacklisted.

Intrusion Detection Systems. **Intrusion detection systems** are designed to detect all types of malicious network traffic and computer usage that cannot be detected by a firewall. These systems capture all network traffic flows and examine the contents of each packet for malicious traffic. An example of this type of malicious traffic is a denial-of-service attack (discussed earlier).

Encryption. When organizations do not have a secure channel for sending information, they use encryption to stop unauthorized eavesdroppers. **Encryption** is the process of converting an original message into a form that cannot be read by anyone except the intended receiver.

All encryption systems use a key, which is the code that scrambles, and then decodes, the messages. The majority of encryption systems use public-key encryption. **Public-key encryption**—also known as *asymmetric encryption*—uses two different keys: a public key and a private key (see Figure 3.4). The public key and the private key are created simultaneously using the same mathematical formula or algorithm. Because the two keys are mathematically related, the data encrypted with one key can be decrypted by using the other key. The public key is publicly available in a directory that all parties can access. The private key is kept secret, never shared with anyone, and never sent across the Internet. In this system, if Alice wants to send a message to Bob, she first obtains Bob's public key, which she uses to

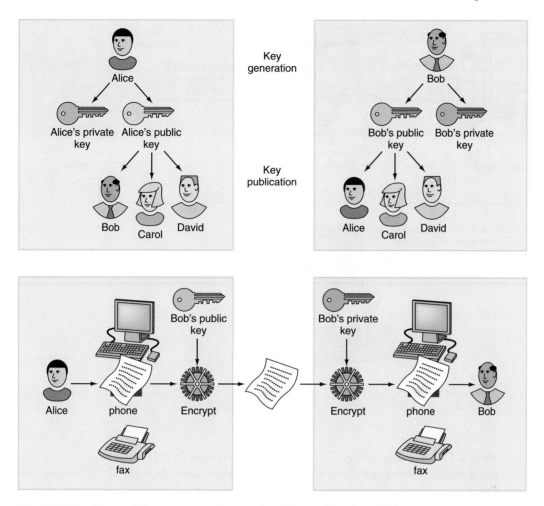

FIGURE 3.4 How public-key encryption works. (*Source*: Omnisec AG.)

encrypt (scramble) her message. When Bob receives Alice's message, he uses his private key to decrypt (unscramble) it.

Public-key systems also show that a message is authentic. That is, if you encrypt a message using your private key, you have electronically "signed" it. A recipient can verify that the message came from you by using your public key to decrypt it.

Although this system is adequate for personal information, organizations doing business over the Internet require a more complex system. In such cases, a third party, called a **certificate authority**, acts as a trusted intermediary between companies. As such, the certificate authority issues digital certificates and verifies the worth and integrity of the certificates. A **digital certificate** is an electronic document attached to a file certifying that the file is from the organization it claims to be from and has not been modified from its original format. As you can see in Figure 3.5, Sony requests a digital certificate from Verisign, a certificate authority, and uses this certificate when doing business with Dell. Note that the digital certificate contains an identification number, the issuer, validity dates, and the requester's public key. For examples of certificate authorities, see *www.entrust.com, www.verisign.com, www.cybertrust.com, www.secude.com,* and *www.thawte.com.* IT's About Business 3.4 provides an example of a health maintenance organization that uses encryption for added security of sensitive information.

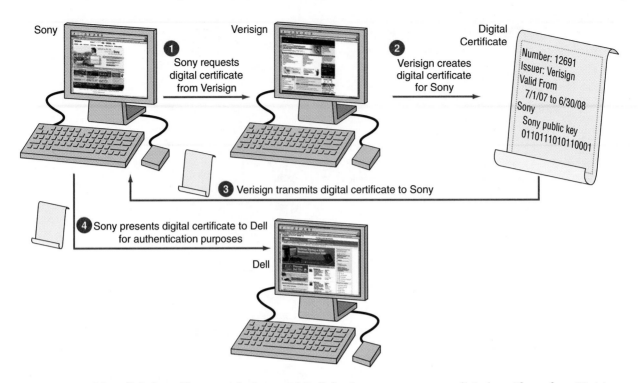

FIGURE 3.5   How digital certificates work. Sony and Dell, business partners, use a digital certificate from Verisign for authentication.

Virtual Private Networking.   A **virtual private network (VPN)** is a private network that uses a public network (usually the Internet) to connect users. As such, VPNs integrate the global connectivity of the Internet with the security of a private network and thereby extend the reach of the organization's networks.

VPNs are labeled "virtual" because the connections (among organizations, between remote sites of one organization, or between an organization and its off-site employees) are created when a transmission needs to be made and terminated when the transmission has been sent. VPNs are handled by common carriers (i.e., telephone service providers).

VPNs have several advantages. First, they allow remote users to access the company network. Second, they allow flexibility. That is, without being constrained by the need for dedicated connections, mobile users can access the organization's network from properly configured remote devices. Third, organizations can impose their security policies through VPNs. For example, an organization may dictate that only corporate e-mail applications are available to users when they connect from unmanaged devices.

To provide secure transmissions, VPNs use a process called tunneling. **Tunneling** encrypts each data packet to be sent and places each encrypted packet inside another packet. In this manner, the packet can travel across the Internet with confidentiality, authentication, and integrity. Figure 3.6 shows a VPN and tunneling.

Secure Socket Layer.   **Secure socket layer (SSL)**, now called **transport layer security (TLS)**, is an encryption standard used for secure transactions such as credit card purchases and online banking. TLS is indicated by a URL that begins with https rather than http, and it often has a small padlock icon in the browser's status bar. TLS encrypts and decrypts data between a Web server and a browser end to end.

IT's About Business

3.4   Using Encryption to Reduce E-Mail Security Risks at Harvard Pilgrim

Harvard Pilgrim Health Care (*www.harvardpilgrim.org*) is a health maintenance organization (HMO) with 975,000 members. The nonprofit company exchanges data on its members each day with employers, insurance companies, and a network of more than 130 hospitals and 22,000 physicians across New England.

In light of the large number of information security debacles that occurred during 2006, the HMO decided that it had to secure its information infrastructure to prevent the unauthorized disclosure of confidential data on its members. However, the organization works with numerous third parties. Therefore, the information security staff worried that Harvard Pilgrim could not effectively control the data when they left the organization's domain.

Gartner, an information technology consulting company, estimates that the direct costs associated with a data breach would be about $90 per customer account involved. This number would include legal fees, communications to the affected parties, and other services. In addition, Harvard Pilgrim assumed that a large-scale disclosure of private data would result in a mass defection of customers, which would be far more devastating than the costs associated with recovering from a single security breach. In the healthcare industry, a large breach could result in a 20 percent loss of the total customer base from people either canceling their accounts or deciding not to do business with the organization. For Harvard Pilgrim, which had $2.3 billion in annual revenue for 2005, a breach could result in losing almost 200,000 customers and $500 million in revenue.

To reduce its risk, Harvard Pilgrim implemented three e-mail security projects in 2006: e-mail encryption, file-based encryption, and outbound e-mail content filtering. These three projects cost the company less than $500,000.

Under the new e-mail policy, whenever employees send out an e-mail containing confidential data,

such as a Social Security number, they have to click on a button that says "PGP Send." That click tells the PGP server to encrypt the contents of that e-mail. An outside user who receives a PGP-encrypted message sees instructions for downloading a certificate from a Harvard Pilgrim Web server, which allows the e-mail program to decrypt the contents of the message.

In addition to e-mail encryption, the company implemented file-encryption software, which automatically encrypts all of the data on its laptop and desktop computers. Therefore, if any of those machines were stolen, the data on them would be meaningless to a thief without the correct digital key for decryption.

Prior to implementing e-mail content filtering software, Harvard Pilgrim assessed the risk of its e-mail system for 21 days. The company found that in some cases, employees were sending out confidential data without realizing it. For example, they might have received a form as an attachment, such as a Word document, from an outside provider. They then replied to, or forwarded, the original e-mail but did not properly apply PGP encryption, thereby violating the policy. The e-mail content filtering software tracked and enforced the company's encryption policy by automatically encrypting every e-mail message and attachment.

Sources: Compiled from T. Spangler, "E-Mail Security Case: Sealing Cracks at Harvard Pilgrim," *Baseline Magazine*, February 14, 2007; "Harvard Pilgrim Membership Grows," *Boston Business Journal*, March 1, 2007; "Harvard Pilgrim Health Care," *www.pgp.com*, accessed March 5, 2007.

QUESTIONS

1. Is e-mail encryption likely to be as important to organizations in other industries as it is in healthcare organizations? Why or why not?
2. Why was it necessary for Harvard Pilgrim to implement outbound e-mail content filtering?

FIGURE 3.6 Virtual private network and tunneling.

Vulnerability Management Systems. Users need access to their organization's network from anywhere and at any time. To accommodate these needs, **vulnerability management systems**, also called *security on demand*, extends the security perimeter that exists for the organization's managed devices. That is, vulnerability management systems handle security vulnerabilities on unmanaged, remote devices. Recall that we discussed the dangers inherent in using unmanaged devices earlier. Vendors of vulnerability management software include Symantec (*www.symantec.com*), Trend Micro (*www.trendmicro.com*), McAfee (*www.mcafee.com*), and Qualys (*www.qualys.com*).

Vulnerability management systems scan the remote system and decide whether to allow the user to access it. These systems allow the user to download anti-malware software to the remote computer for the user's protection. The systems will also implement virtual user sessions on the remote computer. These sessions separate and encrypt data, applications, and networks from the main system of the unmanaged computer. After the user is finished, the vulnerability management system cleans the unmanaged computer's browser cache and temporary files.

Employee Monitoring Systems. Many companies are taking a proactive approach to protecting their networks from what they view as one of their major security threats, namely, employee mistakes. These companies are implementing **employee monitoring systems**, which monitor their employees' computers, e-mail activities, and Internet surfing activities. These products are useful to identify employees who spend too much time surfing on the Internet for personal reasons, who visit questionable Web sites, or who download music illegally. Vendors that provide monitoring software include SpectorSoft (*www.spectorsoft.com*) and Websense (*www.websense.com*).

Application Controls. **Application controls**, as their name suggests, are security countermeasures that protect specific applications. The three major categories of these controls are input, processing, and output controls. Input controls are programmed routines that are performed to edit input data for errors before they are processed. For example, Social Security numbers should not contain any alphabetic characters. Processing controls, for example, might match employee time cards with a master payroll file and report missing or duplicate time cards. Processing controls also balance the total number of transactions processed with the total number of transactions input or output. An example of output controls is documentation specifying that authorized recipients have received their reports, paychecks, or other critical documents.

Business Continuity Planning, Backup, and Recovery

An important strategy for organizations is to be prepared for any eventuality. A critical element in any security system is a business continuity plan, also known as a disaster recovery plan.

Business continuity is the chain of events linking planning to protection and to recovery. The purpose of the business continuity plan is to keep the business operating after a disaster occurs. The plan prepares for, reacts to, and recovers from events that affect the security of information assets and the subsequent restoration to normal business operations. The plan ensures that critical business functions continue.

In the event of a major disaster, organizations can employ several strategies for business continuity, including hot sites, warm sites, cold sites, and off-site data storage. A **hot site** is a fully configured computer facility, with all services, communications links, and physical plant operations. A hot site duplicates computing resources, peripherals, telephone systems, applications, and workstations. A **warm site** provides many of the same services and options of the hot site, but it typically does not include the actual applications the company needs. A warm site does include computing equipment such as servers, but it often does not include user workstations. A **cold site** provides only rudimentary services and facilities and so does not supply computer hardware or user workstations. Hot sites reduce risk to the greatest extent, but they are the most expensive option. Conversely, cold sites reduce risk the least, but they are the least expensive option.

In addition to hot, warm, and cold sites, organizations also use *off-site data storage*. IT's About Business 3.5 shows how the National Football League's Baltimore Ravens plan for business continuity in case of disaster with off-site data storage.

IT's About Business

3.5   The Baltimore Ravens Plan for Business Continuity

As a result of Hurricane Katrina, the National Football League (NFL) offered a workshop on disaster preparedness for its teams after the 2005 season. The NFL recommended that each team update its disaster contingency and recovery plans with data replication and off-site data storage. The Baltimore Ravens decided that the club would no longer handle any of its data on-site.

The Ravens decided to outsource the care and keeping of all its business information, including customer, sales, human resources, accounting, e-mail, and document data—everything except the videotapes the coaches use to evaluate talent and prepare for future opponents.

The Ravens entrusted their information to AmeriVault (*www.amerivault.com*), an online storage and security specialist. The team no longer relies on tape backup machines that were used to archive in-house information until an armored truck would come and transport tape cassettes to a secure off-site location. The Ravens now pay a monthly fee for the service based on the number of gigabytes being stored.

None of the digital data is physically housed in the Ravens' headquarters, where the team maintains its executive offices and practice facility. Nevertheless, nothing has changed for the people who work with the data every day. Staff members and coaches still use their desktop and laptop computers to sign up new season-ticket holders, deal with the media, communicate with potential draft choices, produce payroll, pay contractors, and handle operations for a professional football franchise.

Each evening after the close of business, all new information that came into the Ravens' office during the previous 24 hours is backed up through the AmeriVault system at one of the company's server farms, which are under 24-hour high security.

Dealing with tape backup and archiving was time consuming and resource intensive for the Ravens. The retrieval process from AmeriVault is almost instantaneous because all data are stored on disk, not tape.

AmeriVault's system is completely automated, and the company redundantly backs up all its data and spreads them around to various locations within its own storage network. This means that AmeriVault backs itself up, and a client's data are never located all in one place.

Sources: Compiled from C. Preimesberger, "Team Scores with Data Handoff," *Baseline Magazine*, January 28, 2007; B. Watson, "Disaster Recovery Software: Make a Copy, Stay in Business," *Baseline Magazine*, August 7, 2006; *www.amerivault.com*, accessed March 9, 2007.

QUESTIONS

1. Does outsourcing data management increase risk for the Ravens? If so, how?
2. What is the relationship between outsourcing data management and business continuity planning for the Ravens?

Information Systems Auditing

Companies implement security controls to ensure that information systems work properly. These controls can be installed in the original system, or they can be added after a system is in operation. Installing controls is necessary but not sufficient to provide adequate security. In addition, people responsible for security need to answer questions such as: Are all controls installed as intended? Are they effective? Has any breach of security occurred? If so, what actions are required to prevent future breaches?

These questions must be answered by independent and unbiased observers. Such observers perform the task of *information systems auditing*. In an IS environment, an **audit** is an examination of information systems, their inputs, outputs, and processing.

Types of Auditors and Audits. There are two types of auditors and audits: internal and external. IS auditing is usually part of accounting *internal auditing*, and it is frequently performed by corporate internal auditors. An *external auditor* reviews the findings of the internal audit as well as the inputs, processing, and outputs of information systems. The external audit of information systems is frequently a part of the overall external auditing performed by a certified public accounting (CPA) firm.

Because IS auditing is a broad topic, we present only its essentials here. Auditing considers all potential hazards and controls in information systems. It focuses on topics such as operations, data integrity, software applications, security and privacy, budgets and expenditures, cost control, and productivity. Guidelines are available to assist auditors in their jobs, such as those from the Institute of Internal Auditors (*www.theiia.org*).

How Is Auditing Executed? IS auditing procedures fall into three categories: (1) auditing around the computer, (2) auditing through the computer, and (3) auditing with the computer.

Auditing around the computer means verifying processing by checking for known outputs using specific inputs. This approach is best used in systems with limited outputs. In *auditing through the computer*, inputs, outputs, and processing are checked. Auditors review program logic and test data. *Auditing with the computer* means using a combination of client data, auditor software, and client and auditor hardware. This approach allows the auditor to perform tasks such as simulating payroll program logic using live data.

Before you go on . . .

1. Describe the two major types of controls for information systems.
2. What is information system auditing?
3. What is the purpose of a disaster recovery plan?

What's in **IT** for me?

For the Accounting Major

Public companies, their accountants, and their auditors now have significant information security responsibilities. Accountants are now being held professionally responsible for reducing risk, assuring compliance, eliminating fraud, and increasing the transparency of transactions according to Generally Accepted Accounting Principles (GAAP). The Securities and Exchange Commission (SEC) and the Public Company Accounting Oversight Board (PCAOB), among other regulatory agencies, require information security, fraud prevention and detection, and internal controls over financial reporting. Forensic accounting, a combination of accounting and information security, is one of the most rapidly growing areas in accounting today.

For the Finance Major

Because information security is essential to the success of organizations today, it is no longer just the concern of the CIO. As a result of global regulatory requirements and the passage of Sarbanes-Oxley, responsibility for information security lies with the CEO and chief financial officer (CFO). Consequently, all aspects of the security audit, including the security of information and information systems, are a key concern for financial managers.

In addition, CFOs and treasurers are increasingly involved with investments in information technology. They know that a security breach of any kind can have devastating financial effects on a company. Banking and financial institutions are prime targets for computer criminals. A related problem is fraud involving stocks and bonds that are sold over the Internet. Finance personnel must be aware of both the hazards and the available controls associated with these activities.

For the Marketing Major

Marketing professionals have new opportunities to collect data on their customers, for example, through business-to-consumer electronic commerce. Business ethics clearly state that these data should be used internally in the company and should not be sold to anyone else. Marketers clearly do not want to be sued because of invasion of privacy concerning data collected for the marketing database.

Customers expect their data to be properly secured. Profit-motivated criminals want that data. Therefore, marketing managers must analyze the risk of their operations. Failure to protect corporate and customer data will cause significant public relations problems and make customers very angry. CRM operations and tracking customers' online buying habits can expose data to misuse (if they are not encrypted) or result in privacy violations.

For the Production/Operations Management Major

Every process in a company's operations—inventory purchasing, receiving, quality control, production, and shipping—can be disrupted by an information technology security breach or an IT security breach at a business partner. Any weak link in supply chain management or enterprise resource management systems puts the entire chain at risk. Companies may be held liable for IT security failures that impact other companies.

POM professionals decide whether to outsource (or offshore) manufacturing operations. In some cases, these operations are sent overseas to countries that do not have strict labor laws. This situation raises serious ethical questions. For example, is it ethical to hire people as employees in countries with poor working conditions in order to reduce labor costs? POM managers must answer other difficult questions: To what extent do security efforts reduce productivity? Are incremental improvements in security worth the additional costs?

For the Human Resources Management Major

Ethics is critically important to HR managers. HR policies describe the appropriate use of information technologies in the workplace. Questions arise such as: Can employees use the Internet, e-mail, or chat systems for personal purposes while at work? Is it ethical to monitor employees? If so, how? How much? How often? HR managers must formulate and enforce such policies while at the same time maintaining trusting relationships between employees and management.

HR managers also have responsibilities to secure confidential employee data and provide a nonhostile work environment. In addition, they must ensure that all employees explicitly verify that they understand the company's information security policies and procedures.

For the MIS Major

Ethics might be more important for MIS personnel than for anyone else in the organization because they have control of the information assets. They also have control over a huge amount of personal information on all employees. As a result, the MIS function must be held to the highest ethical standards.

The MIS function provides the security infrastructure that protects the organization's information assets. This function is critical to the success of the organization, even though it is almost invisible until an attack succeeds. All application development, network deployment, and introduction of new information technologies have to be guided by IT security considerations. MIS personnel must customize the risk exposure security model to help the company identify security risks and prepare responses to security incidents and disasters.

Senior executives look to the MIS function for help in meeting Sarbanes-Oxley requirements, particularly in detecting "significant deficiencies" or "material weaknesses" in internal controls and remediating them. Other functional areas also look to the MIS function to help them meet their security responsibilities.

Summary

1. Describe the major ethical issues related to information technology, and identify situations in which they occur.

The major ethical issues related to IT are privacy, accuracy, property (including intellectual property), and accessibility to information. Privacy may be violated when data are held in databases or are transmitted over networks. Privacy policies that address issues of data collection, data accuracy, and data confidentiality can help organizations avoid legal problems. Intellectual property is the intangible property created by individuals or corporations that is protected under trade secret, patent, and copyright laws. The most common intellectual property related to IT deals with software. Copying software without paying the owner is a copyright violation, and it is a major problem for software vendors.

2. Describe the many threats to information security.

There are numerous threats to information security, which fall into the general categories of unintentional and intentional. Unintentional threats include human errors, environmental hazards, and computer system failures. Intentional failures include espionage, extortion, vandalism, theft, software attacks, and compromises to intellectual property. Software attacks include viruses, worms, Trojan horses, logic bombs, back doors, denial of service, alien software, and phishing. A growing threat is cybercrime, which often utilizes identity theft and phishing attacks.

3. Understand the various defense mechanisms used to protect information systems.

Information systems are protected with a wide variety of controls such as security procedures, physical guards, and detection software. These can be classified as controls used for prevention, deterrence, detection, damage control, recovery, and correction of information systems. The major types of general controls include physical controls, access controls, administrative controls, and communications controls. Application controls include input, processing, and output controls.

4. Explain IT auditing and planning for disaster recovery.

Information systems auditing is done in a similar manner to accounting/finance auditing, around, through, and with the computer. A detailed internal and external IT audit may involve hundreds of issues and can be supported by both software and checklists. Related to IT auditing is the preparation for disaster recovery, which specifically addresses how to avoid, plan for, and quickly recover from a disaster.

Chapter Glossary

access controls Controls that restrict unauthorized individuals from using information resources and are concerned with user identification.

accountability A term that means a determination of who is responsible for actions that were taken.

adware Alien software designed to help pop-up advertisements appear on your screen.

alien software Clandestine software that is installed on your computer through duplicitous methods.

anti-anti-malware systems (antivirus software) Software packages that attempt to identify and eliminate viruses, worms, and other malicious software.

application controls Controls that protect specific applications.

audit An examination of information systems, their inputs, outputs, and processing.

authentication A process that determines the identity of the person requiring access.

authorization A process that determines which actions, rights, or privileges the person has, based on verified identity.

back door Typically a password, known only to the attacker, that allows the attacker to access the system without having to go through any security procedures.

biometrics The science and technology of authentication (i.e., establishing the identity of an individual) by measuring the subject's physiologic or behavioral characteristics.

blacklisting A process in which a company identifies certain types of software that are not allowed to run in the company environment.

brute force attack Attacks that use massive computing resources to try every possible combination of password options to uncover a password.

certificate authority A third party that acts as a trusted intermediary between computers (and companies) by issuing digital certificates and verifying the worth and integrity of the certificates.

code of ethics A collection of principles that are intended to guide decision making by members of the organization.

cold site A backup location that provides only rudimentary services and facilities.

communications controls (see also **network controls**) Controls that deal with the movement of data across networks.

controls Defense mechanisms, also called countermeasures, employed by organizations to protect their information assets.

controls evaluation A process in which the organization identifies security deficiencies and calculates the costs of implementing adequate control measures.

cookies Small amounts of information that Web sites store on your computer, temporarily or more or less permanently.

copyright A grant that provides the creator of intellectual property with ownership of it for the life of the creator plus 70 years.

cybercrime Illegal activities executed on the Internet.

cyberterrorism A premeditated, politically motivated attack against information, computer systems, computer programs, and data that results in violence against noncombatant targets by subnational groups or clandestine agents.

cyberwarfare War in which a country's information systems could be paralyzed from a massive attack by destructive software.

demilitarized zone (DMZ) A separate organizational local area network that is located between an organization's internal network and an external network, usually the Internet.

denial-of-service attack A cyberattack in which an attacker sends a flood of data packets to the target computer, with the aim of overloading its resources.

dictionary attack Attacks that try combinations of letters and numbers that are most likely to succeed, such as all words from a dictionary.

digital certificate An electronic document attached to a file certifying that this file is from the organization it claims to be from and has not been modified from its original format or content.

digital dossier An electronic description of a user and his or her habits.

distributed denial-of-service attack A denial-of-service attack that sends a flood of data packets from many compromised computers simultaneously.

electronic surveillance Monitoring or tracking people's activities with the aid of computers.

employee monitoring systems Systems that monitor employees' computers, e-mail activities, and Internet surfing activities.

encryption The process of converting an original message into a form that cannot be read by anyone except the intended receiver.

ethics A term that refers to the principles of right and wrong that individuals use to make choices to guide their behaviors.

exposure The harm, loss, or damage that can result if a threat compromises an information resource.

firewall A system (either hardware, software, or a combination of both) that prevents a specific type of information from moving between untrusted networks, such as the Internet, and private networks, such as your company's network.

hot sites A fully configured computer facility, with all information resources and services, communications links, and physical plant operations, that duplicate your company's computing resources and provide near real-time recovery of IT operations.

identity theft Crime in which someone steals the personal information of others to create a false identity and then uses it for some fraud.

information systems controls The procedures, devices, or software aimed at preventing a compromise to a system.

intellectual property The intangible property created by individuals or corporations, which is protected under trade secret, patent, and copyright laws.

intrusion detection system A system designed to detect all types of malicious network traffic and computer usage that cannot be detected by a firewall.

keystroke loggers (keyloggers) Hardware or software that can detect all keystrokes made on a compromised computer.

least privilege A principle that users be granted the privilege for some activity only if there is a justifiable need to grant this authorization.

liability A legal concept meaning that individuals have the right to recover the damages done to them by other individuals, organizations, or systems.

logic bombs Segments of computer code embedded within an organization's existing computer programs.

malware Malicious software such as viruses and worms.

network controls (see **communications controls**)

opt-in model A model informed consent, where a business is prohibited from collecting any personal information unless the customer specifically authorizes it.

opt-out model A model of informed consent that permits the company to collect personal information until the customer specifically requests that the data not be collected.

password attack (see **brute force attack** and **dictionary attack**)

passphrase A series of characters that is longer than a password but that can be memorized easily.

password A private combination of characters that only the user should know.

patent A document that grants the holder exclusive rights on an invention or process for 20 years.

penetration test A method of evaluating the security of an information system by simulating an attack by a malicious perpetrator.

phishing attack An attack that uses deception to fraudulently acquire sensitive personal information by masquerading as an official-looking e-mail.

physical controls Controls that restrict unauthorized individuals from gaining access to a company's computer facilities.

piracy Copying a software program without making payment to the owner.

privacy The right to be left alone and to be free of unreasonable personal intrusion.

privacy codes (see **privacy policies**)

privacy policies An organization's guidelines with respect to protecting the privacy of customers, clients, and employees.

privilege A collection of related computer system operations that can be performed by users of the system profiling.

profiling The process of compiling a digital dossier on a person.

public-key encryption (also called **asymmetric encryption**) A type of encryption that uses two different keys, a public key and a private key.

regular ID card An identification card that typically has the person's picture and, often, his or her signature.

responsibility A term that means you accept the consequences of your decisions and actions.

reverse social engineering A type of attack in which employees approach the attacker.

risk The likelihood that a threat will occur.

risk acceptance A strategy in which the organization accepts the potential risk, continues to operate with no controls, and absorbs any damages that occur.

risk analysis The process by which an organization assesses the value of each asset being protected, estimates the probability that each asset might be compromised, and compares the probable costs of each being compromised with the costs of protecting it.

risk limitation A strategy in which the organization limits its risk by implementing controls that minimize the impact of a threat.

risk management A process that identifies, controls, and minimizes the impact of threats, in an effort to reduce risk to manageable levels.

risk mitigation A process whereby the organization takes concrete actions against risks, such as implementing controls and developing a disaster recovery plan.

risk transference A process in which the organization transfers the risk by using other means to compensate for a loss, such as by purchasing insurance.

screen scraper Software that records a continuous "movie" of a screen's contents rather than simply recording keystrokes.

secure socket layer (SSL) (see also **transport layer security**) An encryption standard used for secure transactions such as credit card purchases and online banking.

signature recognition The user signs his or her name, and the system matches this signature with one previously recorded under controlled, monitored conditions.

smart ID cards Cards with a chip embedded in them with pertinent information about the user.

social engineering Getting around security systems by tricking computer users inside a company into revealing sensitive information or gaining unauthorized access privileges.

spam Unsolicited e-mail.

spamware Alien software that uses your computer as a launch platform for spammers.

spyware Alien software that can record your keystrokes and/or capture your passwords.

strong passwords A password that is difficult to guess, longer rather than shorter, contains upper and lower case letters, numbers, and special characters, and is not a recognizable word or string of numbers.

threat Any danger to which an information resource may be exposed.

tokens Devices with embedded chips and a digital display that presents a login number that the employees use to access the organization's network.

trade secret Intellectual work, such as a business plan, that is a company secret and is not based on public information.

transport layer security (TLS) (see **secure socket layer**)

trap doors (see **back door**)

Trojan horses A software program containing a hidden function that presents a security risk.

tunneling A process that encrypts each data packet to be sent and places each encrypted packet inside another packet.

virtual private network (VPN) A private network that uses a public network (usually the Internet) to securely connect users by using encryption.

virus Malicious software that can attach itself to (or "infect") other computer programs without the owner of the program being aware of the infection.

voice recognition System whereby the user speaks a phrase that has been previously recorded under controlled, monitored conditions, and the voice recognition system matches the two voice signals.

vulnerability The possibility that an information resource will suffer harm by a threat.

vulnerability management system A system that handles security vulnerabilities on unmanaged, remote devices and, in doing so, extends the security perimeter that exists for the organization's managed devices.

warm site A site that provides many of the same services and options of the hot site, but does not include the company's applications.

whitelisting A process in which a company identifies acceptable software and permits it to run, and either prevents anything else from running or lets new software run in a quarantine environment until the company can verify its validity.

worms Destructive programs that replicate themselves without requiring another program to provide a safe environment for replication.

zero-day attack An attack that takes advantage of a newly discovered, previously unknown vulnerability in a particular software product; perpetrators attack the vulnerability before the software vendor can prepare a patch for it, or sometimes before the vendor is even aware of the vulnerability.

Discussion Questions

1. Why are computer systems so vulnerable?
2. Why should information security be of prime concern to management?
3. Compare information security in an organization with insuring a house.
4. Why are authentication and authorization important to e-commerce?
5. Why is cross-border cybercrime expanding rapidly? Discuss possible solutions.
6. Discuss why the Sarbanes-Oxley Act is having an impact on information security.

Problem-Solving Activities

1. An information security manager routinely monitored the Web surfing among her company's employees. She discovered that many employees were visiting the "sinful six" Web sites. (*Note:* The sinful six are Web sites with material related to pornography, gambling, hate, illegal activities, tastelessness, and violence.) She then prepared a list of the employees and their surfing histories and gave the list to management. Some managers punished their employees. Some employees, in turn, objected to the monitoring, claiming that they should have a right to privacy.
   a. Is monitoring of Web surfing by managers ethical? (It is legal.) Support your answer.
   b. Is employee Web surfing on the "sinful six" ethical? Support your answer.
   c. Is the security manager's submission of the list of abusers to management ethical? Why or why not?
   d. Is punishing the abusers ethical? Why or why not? If yes, then what types of punishment are acceptable?
   e. What should the company do in order to rectify the situation?

2. Frank Abignale, the criminal played by Leonardo di Caprio in the motion picture *Catch Me If You Can*, ended up in prison. However, when he left prison, he went to work as a consultant to many companies on matters of fraud. Why do so many companies not report computer crimes? Why do these companies hire the perpetrators (if caught) as consultants? Is this a good idea?

3. A critical problem is assessing how far a company is legally obligated to go in order to secure personal data. Because there is no such thing as perfect security (i.e., there is always more that you can do), resolving this question can significantly affect cost.
   a. When are a company's security measures sufficient to comply with its obligations?
   b. Is there any way for a company to know if its security measures are sufficient? Can you devise a method for any organization to determine if its security measures are sufficient?

4. Complete the computer ethics quiz at *http://web.cs .bgsu.edu/maner/xxicee/html/welcome.htm.*

Web Activities

1. Enter *www.scambusters.org*. Find out what the organization does. Learn about e-mail scams and Web site scams. Report your findings.
2. Visit *www.junkbusters.com* and learn how to prohibit unsolicited e-mail (spam). Describe how your privacy is protected.
3. Visit *www.dhs.gov/dhspublic* (Department of Homeland Security). Search the site for "National Strategy to Secure Cyberspace" and write a report on their agenda and accomplishments to date.
4. Enter *www.biopay.com* and other vendors of biometrics. Find the devices they make that can be used to control access into information systems. Prepare a list of products and major capabilities of each.
5. Access the Computer Ethics Institute's Web site at *www.cpsr.org/issues/ethics/cei*. The site offers the "Ten Commandments of Computer Ethics." Study these 10 and decide if any should be added.
6. Software piracy is a global problem. Access the following Web sites: *www.bsa.org* and *www.microsoft.com/piracy/*. What can organizations do to mitigate this problem? Are some organizations dealing with the problem better than others?

Team Assignments

1. Access *www.consumer.gov/sentinel* to learn more about how law enforcement agencies around the world work together to fight consumer fraud. Each team should obtain current statistics on one of the top five consumer complaint categories and prepare a report. Are any categories growing faster than others? Are any categories more prevalent in certain parts of the world?
2. Read In the Matter of BJ's Wholesale Club, Inc., Agreement containing Consent Order, FTC File No. 042 3160, June 16, 2005, at *www.ftc.gov/opa/2005/06/bjswholesale.htm*. Describe the security breach at BJ's Wholesale Club. What was the reason for this agreement? Identify some of the causes of the security breach and how BJ's can better defend itself against hackers and legal liability.

CLOSING CASE **Click Fraud**

THE BUSINESS PROBLEM Spending on Internet ads is growing faster than any other sector of the advertising industry and is projected to reach $29 billion in the United States alone by 2010. About half of these dollars are paid by the click. Google and Yahoo are making billions of dollars once collected by traditional print and broadcast outlets, based on the assumption that clicks are a reliable, quantifiable measure of consumer interest.

MostChoice.com (*www.mostchoice.com*) offers consumers rate quotes and other information on insurance and mortgages. In 2006, the company paid Yahoo and Google $2 million in advertising fees. The company is required to pay such fees only when prospective customers click on its ads.

Over the past three years, however, MostChoice has seen an increasing number of clicks coming from such places as Botswana, Mongolia, and Syria. This was strange, because MostChoice steers customers to insurance and mortgage brokers only in the United States. The validity of clicks on its ads is critically important to MostChoice, because the company pays up to $8 for each click.

The company is a victim of click fraud. Click fraud occurs in pay-per-click online advertising when a person or automated computer program imitates a legitimate user clicking on an ad for the purpose of generating a fee per click without having any interest in the company of the advertisement. MostChoice estimates that click fraud has cost it more than $100,000 since 2003.

The problem is magnified when large Internet companies (e.g., Yahoo and Google) boost their profits by recycling ads to millions of other Web sites, ranging from the familiar, such as *www.cnn.com*, to dummy Web addresses that display lists of ads and very little else. When someone clicks on these recycled ads, companies such as MostChoice are billed. Google or Yahoo then share the revenue with a chain of Web site hosts and operators. About one penny trickles down to the actual people who click on the ads.

"Paid to read" rings pay hundreds of thousands of individuals for clicking on ads. One couple set up dummy Web sites filled with only recycled Google and Yahoo advertisements. They paid others small amounts to visit the sites, where they would click on the ads.

In other cases, "clickbot" software generates ad hits automatically and anonymously. Clickbots use proxy, or anonymous, servers to disguise a computer's Internet Protocol address (discussed in Chapter 5), and they can space clicks minutes apart to make them less conspicuous. Some criminals are creating botnets with thousands of zombie computers, each with clickbot software clicking away on ads.

THE SOLUTION Google and Yahoo say they filter out most questionable clicks and either do not charge for them, or reimburse advertisers who have been incorrectly billed. The two companies maintain that they use sophisticated mathematical formulas and intelligence from advertisers to identify the vast majority of fake clicks. However, they will not release their specific methods, because criminals would exploit the information.

MostChoice assigned an in-house programmer to design a system for analyzing every click on a company ad: the Web page where the ad appeared, the clicker's country, the length of the clicker's visit to the MostChoice Web site, and whether the visitor became a customer. Using these data, the company continues to demand recompense from Google and Yahoo, noting that they have received refunds from the two Internet giants totaling about $35,000 out of the $100,000 they think they are owed.

THE RESULTS The industry simply does not know exactly how widespread click fraud is. The practice skews statistics on the popularity of an ad, drains marketing budgets, and enriches the criminals behind it. Both Google and Yahoo have been targeted by class-action lawsuits accusing the two companies of (1) a lack of transparency in methods used to detect click fraud and (2) conflict of interest in that both companies can profit from the click fraud that they are supposed to be filtering out.

If the click fraud problem is not fixed, then it will present a major obstacle to the further development of the Internet as an advertising medium. In fact, some analysts are questioning the value of Google and Yahoo stock because they see click fraud as a tangible risk to the profits of the two firms.

Sources: Compiled from B. Helm, "Click Fraud Gets Smarter," *BusinessWeek Online*, February 27, 2007; B. Helm, "How Do You Clock the Clicks?" *BusinessWeek*, March 13, 2006; B. Grow and B. Elgin, "Click Fraud," *BusinessWeek*, October 2, 2006; D. Vise, "Clicking to Steal," *Washington Post*, April 17, 2005.

QUESTIONS

1. How would Yahoo and Google find people who are committing click fraud?
2. Is it a stretch to think that the value of Yahoo and Google can be decreased as a result of undetected click fraud? Support your answer.

Web Resources wiley.com/college/rainer

Student Web Site
- Web Quizzes
- Student Lecture Slides in PowerPoint
- Virtual Company ClubIT: Website and Assignments

WileyPLUS
- e-book
- Flash Cards
- How-To Animations for Microsoft Office

Information and Ethics at Club IT

Go to the Club IT link on the *WileyPLUS* Web site. On the Web site, you will find some assigments that will help you learn how to apply IT solutions to a business.

wiley.com/college/rainer

Chapter 4

Learning Objectives

1. Recognize the importance of data, the issues involved in managing these data, and the data life cycle.

2. Describe the sources of data and explain how data are collected.

3. Explain the advantages of the database approach.

4. Explain the operation of data warehousing and its role in decision support.

5. Explain data governance and how it helps to produce high-quality data.

6. Define knowledge and describe the different types of knowledge.

Data and Knowledge Management

What's in IT for me?   ACC   FIN   MKT   POM   HRM   MIS

A Single Version of the Truth

The Business Problem

Panasonic (*www.panasonic.com*), one of the world's leading electronics manufacturers, makes plasma TVs, DVD players, mobile phones, and many other products. The company has implemented a long-term plan to double its profit margins. However, consumers have come to expect Panasonic to continually lower the prices of its products. In the face of fierce competition, the company cannot raise prices, even though it is, for example, the market-share leader in plasma TVs. Therefore, the company has to concentrate on reducing costs and increasing sales to improve its profit margins. However, to accomplish these goals, Panasonic had to improve its system for collecting and utilizing data and information.

Panasonic has the ability to create, store, share, and analyze data about products, customers, and suppliers in ways that were not even feasible just a few decades ago. Nevertheless, the company noted that it had lost a consistent and accurate single view of those products, customers, and suppliers. Furthermore, it had developed numerous duplicative, inconsistent, and incomplete records stored in multiple isolated databases across the enterprise.

Such inconsistent and incorrect business information caused the company to botch product shipments, confuse billings, and alienate customers. It also prevented the company from making timely decisions, which diminished the company's flexibility and agility. Product launches were delayed, and customer satisfaction and service declined. In essence, poor information was costing Panasonic a great deal of money.

Consider the introduction of a single product at Panasonic. With multiple sales subsidiaries, manufacturing facilities, research and development centers, and administrative centers, the task of procuring the right materials—photos, product specifications, manuals, pricing, and point-of-sale marketing information—from the right sources and getting them into the right hands and in the right language had become incredibly complex. In addition, the amount of time required to modify product materials for regional or national purposes has made it almost impossible for Panasonic to have a simultaneous product launch in one of its regions, much less across the world. This problem made Panasonic more vulnerable to its competitors, who could enter markets before Panasonic could. This "timeliness" problem is particularly acute in the electronics industry, where being first-to-market with new products is absolutely essential.

The IT Solution

Panasonic set the goal of vastly improving its data management, the "single version of the truth," by implementing a master data management process. (We discuss master data management in Section 4.5.) The company used IBM's master data management software. Panasonic's overall goal was to gain control over all internal information.

The company replaced what was largely a "pull" model, in which marketing and sales had to request both structured and unstructured information (from product specifications to photos) from numerous sources, with a "push" approach, in which information is centralized and delivered automatically to everyone who needs it, simultaneously. Necessary information, from product introduction to product phaseout, is delivered to retail partners, electronic commerce systems (e.g., direct-to-consumer Internet sales), and Panasonic employees, when and where they need it.

The Results

The master data management system enabled Panasonic to save millions of dollars per year. Perhaps most significantly, the system improved Panasonic's time-to-market. It reduced the time required to bring a product to market from six months to one month. It similarly reduced the amount of time required for creating and maintaining product information by 50 percent.

In addition, the system allowed Panasonic to move away from its "push" inventory model, in which the company would push products to retailers such as Best Buy and Circuit City, toward a "pull" model, where vendors order products on an as-needed basis. The pull model reduces vendors' inventory levels and reduces their costs. For example, retailers used to stock 35 days of inventory of large-size plasma TVs. With the new data management system, Panasonic has improved its response to retailers' orders so that its retailers have been able to cut inventory to seven days.

The Panasonic case illustrates the importance of high-quality data and information to today's organizations. The case also shows how Panasonic realized many benefits from implementing a process to produce high-quality data. In this chapter, we explain the process of managing data, transforming the data into usable information, and using the information in context to produce knowledge.

Between 2006 and 2010, the amount of digital information created, captured, and replicated each year will add about 18 million times as much information as currently exists in all the books ever written. Images captured by more than 1 billion devices around the world, from digital cameras and camera phones to medical scanners and security cameras, comprise the largest component of this digital information.

We are accumulating data and information at a frenzied pace from such diverse sources as e-mails, Web pages, credit card swipes, phone messages, stock trades, memos, address books, and radiology scans. New sources of data and information include blogs, podcasts, videocasts (think of YouTube), digital video surveillance, and radio frequency identification (RFID) tags and other wireless sensors (discussed in Chapter 7). We are awash in data, and yet we have to manage it and make sense of it. To deal with the growth and the diverse nature of digital data, organizations must employ sophisticated techniques for information management.

Information technologies and systems support organizations in managing—that is, acquiring, organizing, storing, accessing, analyzing, and interpreting—data. When these data are managed properly, they become *information* and then *knowledge*. As we have seen, information and knowledge are valuable organizational resources that can provide a competitive advantage. In this chapter, we explore the process whereby data are transformed first into information and then into knowledge.

Few business professionals are comfortable making or justifying business decisions that are not based on solid information. This is especially true today, when modern information systems make access to that information quick and easy. For example, we have technology that puts data in a form that managers and analysts can easily understand. These professionals can then access the data themselves and analyze these data according to their needs with a variety of tools, thereby producing information. They can then apply their experience to use this information to address a business problem, thus producing knowledge. Knowledge management, enabled by information technology, captures and stores knowledge in forms that all organizational employees can access and apply, creating the flexible, powerful "learning organization."

But why should you learn about data management? You will have an important role in the development of database applications. The structure and content of your organization's database depends on how the users look at their business activities. For example, when database developers in the firm's MIS group build a database, they use a tool called entity-relationship (ER) modeling. This tool creates a model of how users view a business activity. You must understand how to interpret an ER model so that you can examine whether the developers have captured your business activity correctly.

We begin this chapter by discussing the multiple problems involved in managing data and the database approach that organizations use to solve those problems. We then show how database management systems enable organizations to access and use the data in databases. Data warehouses have become increasingly important because they provide the data that managers need in order to make decisions. We close the chapter with a look at knowledge management.

Sources: Compiled from D. McDonald, "Panasonic Searches the Master Data for a Single Version of the Truth," *CIO Insight,* May 22, 2006; D. Bartholomew, "Master Data Management: How Mentor Graphics Mastered the Data Monster," *Baseline Magazine,* September 8, 2006; S. Schwartz, "Out of Many, One," *DB2 Magazine,* October, 2006; *www.panasonic.com,* accessed April 16, 2007.

4.1 Managing Data

As we have seen throughout this textbook, IT applications require data. Data should be of high quality, meaning that they should be accurate, complete, timely, consistent, accessible, relevant, and concise. Unfortunately, however, the process of acquiring, keeping, and managing data is becoming increasingly difficult.

The Difficulties of Managing Data

Because data are processed in several stages and often in several places, they may be subject to problems and difficulties. Managing data in organizations is difficult for many reasons.

The amount of data increases exponentially with time. Much historical data must be kept for a long time, and new data are added rapidly. For example, to support some 40 million people who play fantasy football, Web sites such as ESPN.com, NFL.com, and CBSSportsLine.com have to manage terabytes of sports data.

Data are scattered throughout organizations and are collected by many individuals using various methods and devices. Data are frequently stored in numerous servers and locations and in different computing systems, databases, formats, and human and computer languages.

Data come from internal sources (e.g., corporate databases), personal sources (e.g., personal thoughts, opinions, and experiences), and external sources (e.g., commercial databases, government reports, and corporate Web sites). Data also come from the Web, in the form of clickstream data. **Clickstream data** are those data that visitors and customers produce when they visit a Web site and click on hyperlinks (described in Chapter 5). Clickstream data provide a trail of the users' activities in the Web site, including user behavior and browsing patterns.

New sources of data, such as blogs, podcasts, videocasts, and RFID tags and other wireless sensors are constantly being developed. Much of these new data are unstructured, meaning that their content cannot be truly represented in a computer record. Examples of unstructured data are digital images, digital video, voice packets, and musical notes in an MP3 file.

Data decays over time. For example, customers move to new addresses or change their names, companies go out of business or are bought, new products are developed, employees are hired or fired, companies expand into new countries, and so on.

Data security, quality, and integrity are critical, yet they are easily jeopardized. In addition, legal requirements relating to data differ among both countries and industries, and they change frequently.

Because of these problems, data are difficult to manage. As a result, organizations are using databases and data warehouses to manage their data more efficiently and effectively. We discuss the data life cycle in the next section, which shows you how organizations process and manage data to make decisions, generate knowledge, and utilize this knowledge in a variety of applications.

The Data Life Cycle

Businesses run on data that have been processed into information and knowledge. Managers then apply this knowledge to business problems and opportunities. Businesses transform data into knowledge and solutions in several ways; the general process is illustrated in Figure 4.1. It starts with the collection of data from various sources and the storage of data in a database(s). Selected data from the organization's databases are then processed to fit the format of a data warehouse or data mart. Next, users access the data in the warehouse or data mart for analysis.

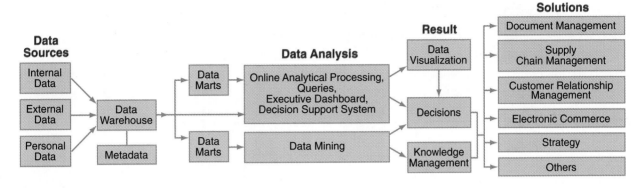

FIGURE 4.1   Data life cycle.

The analysis is done with data analysis tools, which look for patterns, and with intelligent systems, which support data interpretation. We discuss each of these concepts in this chapter.

These activities ultimately generate knowledge that can be used to support decision making. Both the data (at various times during the process) and the knowledge (derived at the end of the process) must be presented to users. This presentation can be accomplished by using different visualization tools. The knowledge created can also be stored in an organizational knowledge base and then used, together with decision support tools, to provide solutions to organizational problems. The remaining sections of this chapter will examine the elements and the process shown in Figure 4.1 in greater detail.

Before you go on . . .

1. What are some of the difficulties involved in managing data?
2. Describe the data life cycle.
3. What are the various sources for data?

4.2 The Database Approach

Using databases eliminates many problems that arose from previous methods of storing and accessing data. Databases are arranged so that one set of software programs—the *database management system*—provides all users with access to all the data. This system minimizes the following problems:

- *Data redundancy:* The same data are stored in many places.
- *Data isolation:* Applications cannot access data associated with other applications.
- *Data inconsistency:* Various copies of the data do not agree.

In addition, database systems maximize the following issues:

- Data security.
- Data integrity: Data meet certain constraints, such as no alphabetic characters in a Social Security number field.
- Data independence: Applications and data are independent of one another (i.e., applications and data are not linked to each other, meaning that all applications are able to access the same data).

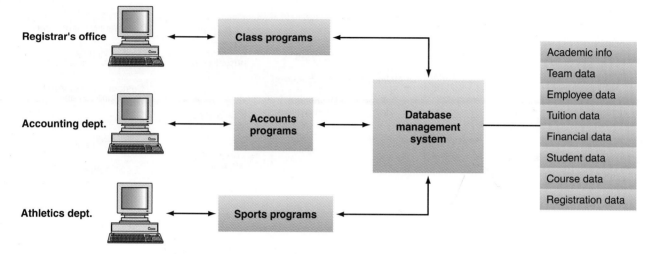

FIGURE 4.2 A database management system (DBMS) provide access to all data in the database.

Figure 4.2 illustrates a university database. Note that university applications from the Registrar's office, the Accounting department, and the Athletics department access data through the database management system.

In the next section, we discuss the data hierarchy, after which we turn our attention to how databases are designed.

The Data Hierarchy

Data are organized in a hierarchy that begins with bits and proceeds all the way to databases (see Figure 4.3). A **bit** (*b*inary dig*it*) represents the smallest unit of data a computer can process. The term *binary* means that a bit can consist only of a 0 or a 1. A group of eight bits, called a **byte**, represents a single character. A byte can be a letter, a number, or a symbol. A logical grouping of characters into a word, a small group of words, or an identification number is called a **field**. For example, a student's name in a university's computer files would appear in the "name" field, and her or his Social Security number would appear in the "Social Security number" field. Fields can also contain data other than text and numbers. A field can contain an image, or any other type of multimedia. For example, a motor vehicle department's licensing database could contain a person's photograph. A logical grouping of related fields, such as the student's name, the courses taken, the date, and the grade, comprise a **record**. A logical grouping of related records is called a **file** or **table**. For example, the records from a particular course, consisting of course number, professor, and students' grades, would constitute a data file for that course. A logical grouping of related files would constitute a **database**. Using the same example, the student course file could be grouped with files on students' personal histories and financial backgrounds to create a student database.

The next section discusses designing the database in today's organizations. We focus on entity-relationship modeling and normalization procedures.

Designing the Database

Data must be organized so that users can retrieve, analyze, and understand them. A key to effectively designing a database is the data model. A **data model** is a diagram that represents entities in the database and their relationships. An **entity** is a person, place, thing, or event—such as a customer, an employee, or a product—about which information is maintained. Entities can typically be identified in the user's work environment. A record generally describes an entity. Each characteristic or quality of a particular entity is called an **attribute**. Using the above examples, we would consider customer name, employee number, and product color attributes.

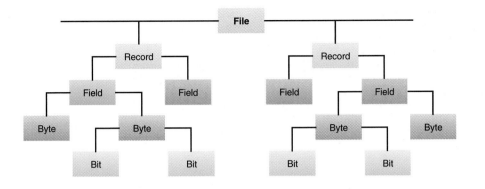

FIGURE 4.3
Hierarchy of data for a
computer-based file.

Every record in a file must contain at least one field that uniquely identifies that record so that it can be retrieved, updated, and sorted. This identifier field is called the **primary key**. For example, a student record in a U.S. college would probably use the Social Security number as its primary key. In some cases, locating a particular record requires the use of secondary keys. **Secondary keys** are other fields that have some identifying information but typically do not identify the file with complete accuracy. For example, the student's major might be a secondary key if a user wanted to find all students in a particular major field of study. It should not be the primary key, however, because many students can have the same major.

Entity-Relationship Modeling. Database designers plan the database design in a process called **entity-relationship (ER) modeling**, using an **entity-relationship diagram**. ER diagrams consist of entities, attributes, and relationships. Entities are pictured in boxes, and relationships are shown in diamonds. The attributes for each entity are listed next to the entity, and the primary key is underlined. Figures 4.4a and 4.4b show an entity-relationship diagram.

As defined earlier, an *entity* can be identified in the users' work environment. For example, consider student registration at a university. Students register for courses and register their cars for parking permits. In this example, STUDENT, PARKING PERMIT, CLASS, and PROFESSOR are entities, as shown in Figure 4.4.

Entities of a given type are grouped in **entity classes**. In our example, STUDENT, PARKING PERMIT, CLASS, and PROFESSOR are entity classes. An **instance** of an entity class is the representation of a particular entity. Therefore, a particular STUDENT (James Smythe, 145-89-7123) is an instance of the STUDENT entity class; a particular parking permit (91778) is an instance of the PARKING PERMIT entity class; a particular class (76890) is an instance of the CLASS entity class; and a particular professor (Margaret Wilson, 115-65-7632) is an instance of the PROFESSOR entity class.

Entity instances have **identifiers**, which are attributes that are unique to that entity instance. For example, STUDENT instances can be identified with StudentIdentificationNumber; PARKING PERMIT instances can be identified with PermitNumber; CLASS instances can be identified with ClassNumber; and PROFESSOR instances can be identified with Professor IdentificationNumber. These identifiers (or primary keys) are underlined on ER diagrams, as in part (b) of Figure 4.4.

Entities have attributes, or properties, that describe the entity's characteristics. In our example, examples of attributes for STUDENT would be StudentIdentificationNumber, StudentName, and StudentAddress. Examples of attributes for PARKING PERMIT would be PermitNumber, StudentIdentificationNumber, and CarType. Examples of attributes for CLASS would be ClassNumber, ClassName, ClassTime, and ClassPlace. Examples of attributes for PROFESSOR would be ProfessorIdentificationNumber, ProfessorName, and ProfessorDepartment. (Note that each course at this university has one professor—no team teaching.)

Why is StudentIdentificationNumber an attribute of both the STUDENT and PARKING PERMIT entity classes? That is, why do we need the PARKING PERMIT entity

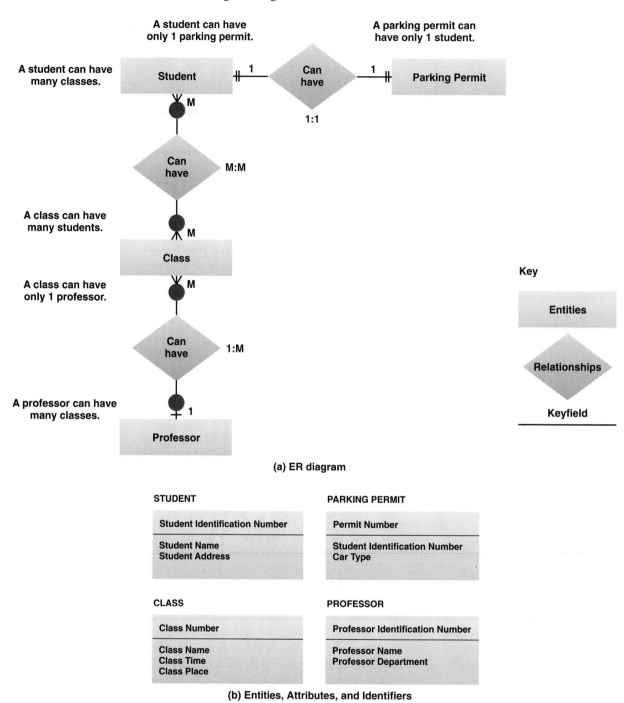

A student can have only 1 parking permit.

A parking permit can have only 1 student.

A student can have many classes.

A class can have many students.

A class can have only 1 professor.

A professor can have many classes.

1:1

M:M

1:M

Key

Entities

Relationships

Keyfield

(a) ER diagram

STUDENT

Student Identification Number

Student Name
Student Address

PARKING PERMIT

Permit Number

Student Identification Number
Car Type

CLASS

Class Number

Class Name
Class Time
Class Place

PROFESSOR

Professor Identification Number

Professor Name
Professor Department

(b) Entities, Attributes, and Identifiers

FIGURE 4.4   Entity-relationship diagram model.

class? If you consider all interlinked university systems, the PARKING PERMIT entity class is needed for other applications, such as fee payments, parking tickets, and external links to the state Department of Motor Vehicles.

Entities are associated with one another in relationships, which can include many entities. (Remember that relationships are noted by diamonds on ER diagrams.) The number of entities in a relationship is the degree of the relationship. Relationships between two items are called *binary relationships*. The three types of binary relationships are one-to-one, one-to-many, and many-to-many.

In a *one-to-one* (*1:1*) relationship, a single-entity instance of one type is related to a single-entity instance of another type. Figure 4.4 shows STUDENT-PARKING PERMIT as a 1:1 relationship that relates a single STUDENT with a single PARKING PERMIT. That is, no student has more than one parking permit, and no parking permit is issued for more than one student.

The second type of relationship, *one-to-many* (*1:M*), is represented by the CLASS-PROFESSOR relationship in Figure 4.4. This relationship means that a professor can have many courses, but each course can have only one professor.

The third type of relationship, *many-to-many* (*M:M*), is represented by the STUDENT-CLASS relationship. This M:M relationship means that a student can have many courses, and a course can have many students.

Entity-relationship modeling is valuable because it allows database designers to talk with users throughout the organization to ensure that all entities and the relationships among them are represented. This process underscores the importance of taking all users into account in designing organizational databases. Notice that all entities and relationships in our example are labeled in terms that users can understand. Now that we understand how a database is designed, we turn our attention to database management systems.

Before you go on . . .

1. What is a data model?
2. What is a primary key? a secondary key?
3. What is an entity? a relationship?

4.3 Database Management Systems

A **database management system (DBMS)** is a set of programs that provide users with tools to add, delete, access, and analyze data stored in one location. An organization can access the data by using query and reporting tools that are part of the DBMS or by using application programs specifically written to access the data. DBMSs also provide the mechanisms for maintaining the integrity of stored data, managing security and user access, and recovering information if the system fails. Because databases and DBMSs are essential to all areas of business, they must be carefully managed.

There are a number of different database architectures, but we focus on the relational database model because it is popular and easy to use. Other database models (e.g., the hierarchical and network models) are the responsibility of the MIS function and are not used by organizational employees. Popular examples of relational databases are Microsoft Access and Oracle.

The Relational Database Model

Most business data—especially accounting and financial data—traditionally were organized into simple tables consisting of columns and rows. Tables allow people to compare information quickly by row or column. In addition, items are easy to retrieve by finding the point of intersection of a particular row and column.

The **relational database model** is based on the concept of two-dimensional tables. A relational database is not always one big table—usually called a *flat file*—that contains all of the records and attributes. Such a design would entail far too much data redundancy. Instead, a relational database is usually designed with a number of related tables. Each of these tables contains records (listed in rows) and attributes (listed in columns).

These related tables can be joined when they contain common columns. The uniqueness of the primary key tells the DBMS which records are joined with others in related tables.

This feature allows users great flexibility in the variety of queries they can make. Despite these features, this model has some disadvantages. Because large-scale databases can be composed of many interrelated tables, the overall design can be complex and therefore have slow search and access times.

Consider the relational database example about students shown in Figure 4.5. The table contains data about the entity called students. Attributes of the entity are name, undergraduate major, and grade point average. The rows are the records on Sally Adams, John Jones, Jane Lee, Kevin Durham, Juan Rodriguez, Stella Zubnicki, and Ben Jones. Of course, your university keeps much more data on you than our example shows. In fact, your university's student database probably keeps hundreds of attributes on each student.

Query Languages. Requesting information from a database is the most commonly performed operation. **Structured query language (SQL)** is the most popular query language used to request information. It allows people to perform complicated searches by using relatively simple statements or keywords. Typical keywords are SELECT (to specify a desired attribute), FROM (to specify the table to be used), and WHERE (to specify conditions to apply in the query).

To understand how SQL works, imagine that a university wants to know the names of students who will graduate with honors in May 2009. The university IS staff would query the student relational database with an SQL statement such as SELECT Student Name, FROM Student Database, WHERE Grade Point Average > 3.40 and Grade Point Average < 3.59. The SQL query would return John Jones and Juan Rodriguez.

Another way to find information in a database is to use **query by example (QBE)**. In QBE, the user fills out a grid or template (also known as a *form*) to construct a sample or description of the data he or she wants. Users can construct a query quickly and easily by using drag-and-drop features in a DBMS such as Microsoft Access. Conducting queries in this manner is simpler than keying in SQL commands.

Student Name	Student ID	Major	GPA	Graduation Date
Sally Adams	111-12-4321	Finance	2.94	5/12/2005
John Jones	420-33-9834	Accounting	3.45	12/5/2005
Jane Lee	241-35-7432	MIS	3.17	5/12/2005
Kevin Durham	021-79-6679	Economics	2.77	5/12/2005
Juan Rodriguez	335-77-5124	Marketing	3.52	12/5/2005
Stella Zubnicki	408-99-5798	Operations Man	3.37	8/5/2005
Ben Jones	422-89-0011	Finance	3.11	5/12/2005

FIGURE 4.5 Student database example.

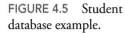

Data Dictionary. When a relational model is created, the **data dictionary** defines the format necessary to enter the data into the database. The data dictionary provides information on each attribute, such as its name, whether it is a key or part of a key, the type of data expected (alphanumeric, numeric, dates, and so on), and valid values. Data dictionaries can also provide information on how often the attribute should be updated, why it is needed in the database, and which business functions, applications, forms, and reports use the attribute.

Data dictionaries provide many advantages to the organization. Because they provide names and standard definitions for all attributes, they reduce the chances that the same attribute will be used in different applications but with a different name. In addition, data dictionaries enable programmers to develop programs more quickly because they don't have to create new data names.

Normalization. In order to use a relational database management system effectively, the data must be analyzed to eliminate redundant data elements. **Normalization** is a method for analyzing and reducing a relational database to its most streamlined form for minimum redundancy, maximum data integrity, and best processing performance. When data are *normalized*, attributes in the table depend only on the primary key.

As an example of normalization, consider an automotive repair garage. This business takes orders from customers who want to have their cars repaired. In this example, ORDER, PART, SUPPLIER, and CUSTOMER are entities. There can be many PARTS in an ORDER, but each PART can come from only one SUPPLIER. In a nonnormalized relation called ORDER (see Figure 4.6), each ORDER would have to repeat the name, description, and price of each PART needed to complete the ORDER, as well as the name and address of each SUPPLIER. This relation contains repeating groups and describes multiple entities.

The normalization process, illustrated in Figure 4.7, breaks down the relation, ORDER, into smaller relations: ORDER, SUPPLIER, and CUSTOMER (Figure 4.7a) and ORDERED-PARTS and PART (Figure 4.7b). Each of these relations describes a single entity. This process is conceptually simpler, and it eliminates repeating groups. For example,

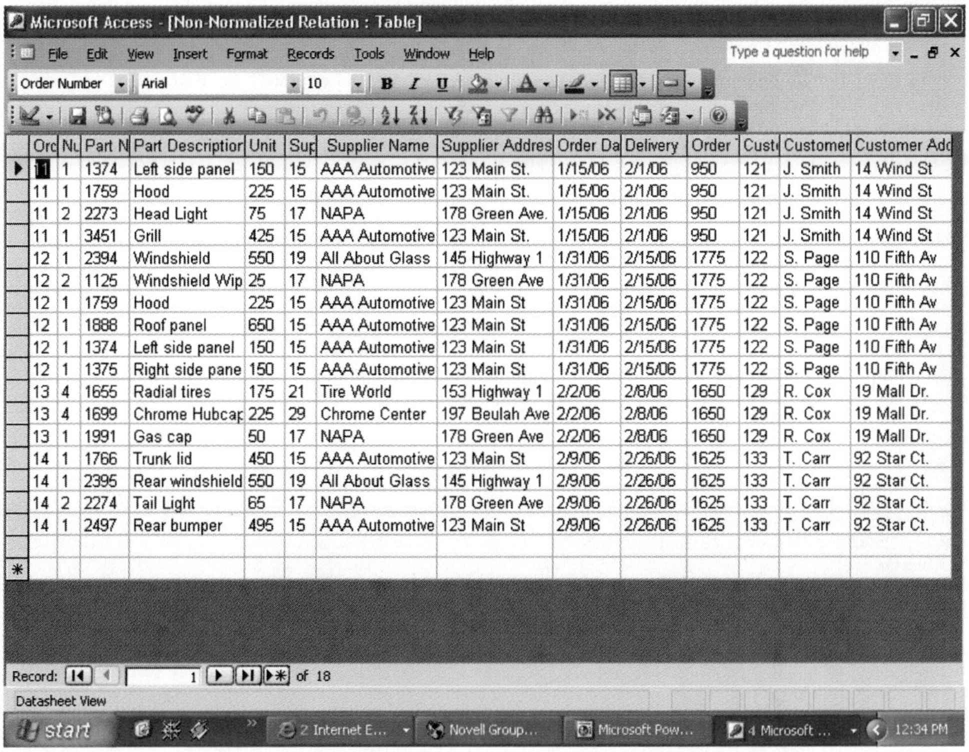

Orc	Nu	Part N	Part Descriptior	Unit	Sup	Supplier Name	Supplier Addres	Order Da	Delivery	Order	Custo	Customer	Customer Add
11	1	1374	Left side panel	150	15	AAA Automotive	123 Main St.	1/15/06	2/1/06	950	121	J. Smith	14 Wind St
11	1	1759	Hood	225	15	AAA Automotive	123 Main St.	1/15/06	2/1/06	950	121	J. Smith	14 Wind St
11	2	2273	Head Light	75	17	NAPA	178 Green Ave.	1/15/06	2/1/06	950	121	J. Smith	14 Wind St
11	1	3451	Grill	425	15	AAA Automotive	123 Main St.	1/15/06	2/1/06	950	121	J. Smith	14 Wind St
12	1	2394	Windshield	550	19	All About Glass	145 Highway 1	1/31/06	2/15/06	1775	122	S. Page	110 Fifth Av
12	2	1125	Windshield Wip	25	17	NAPA	178 Green Ave	1/31/06	2/15/06	1775	122	S. Page	110 Fifth Av
12	1	1759	Hood	225	15	AAA Automotive	123 Main St	1/31/06	2/15/06	1775	122	S. Page	110 Fifth Av
12	1	1888	Roof panel	650	15	AAA Automotive	123 Main St	1/31/06	2/15/06	1775	122	S. Page	110 Fifth Av
12	1	1374	Left side panel	150	15	AAA Automotive	123 Main St	1/31/06	2/15/06	1775	122	S. Page	110 Fifth Av
12	1	1375	Right side pane	150	15	AAA Automotive	123 Main St	1/31/06	2/15/06	1775	122	S. Page	110 Fifth Av
13	4	1655	Radial tires	175	21	Tire World	153 Highway 1	2/2/06	2/8/06	1650	129	R. Cox	19 Mall Dr.
13	4	1699	Chrome Hubcap	225	29	Chrome Center	197 Beulah Ave	2/2/06	2/8/06	1650	129	R. Cox	19 Mall Dr.
13	1	1991	Gas cap	50	17	NAPA	178 Green Ave	2/2/06	2/8/06	1650	129	R. Cox	19 Mall Dr.
14	1	1766	Trunk lid	450	15	AAA Automotive	123 Main St	2/9/06	2/26/06	1625	133	T. Carr	92 Star Ct.
14	1	2395	Rear windshield	550	19	All About Glass	145 Highway 1	2/9/06	2/26/06	1625	133	T. Carr	92 Star Ct.
14	2	2274	Tail Light	65	17	NAPA	178 Green Ave	2/9/06	2/26/06	1625	133	T. Carr	92 Star Ct.
14	1	2497	Rear bumper	495	15	AAA Automotive	123 Main St	2/9/06	2/26/06	1625	133	T. Carr	92 Star Ct.

FIGURE 4.6 Nonnormalized relation.

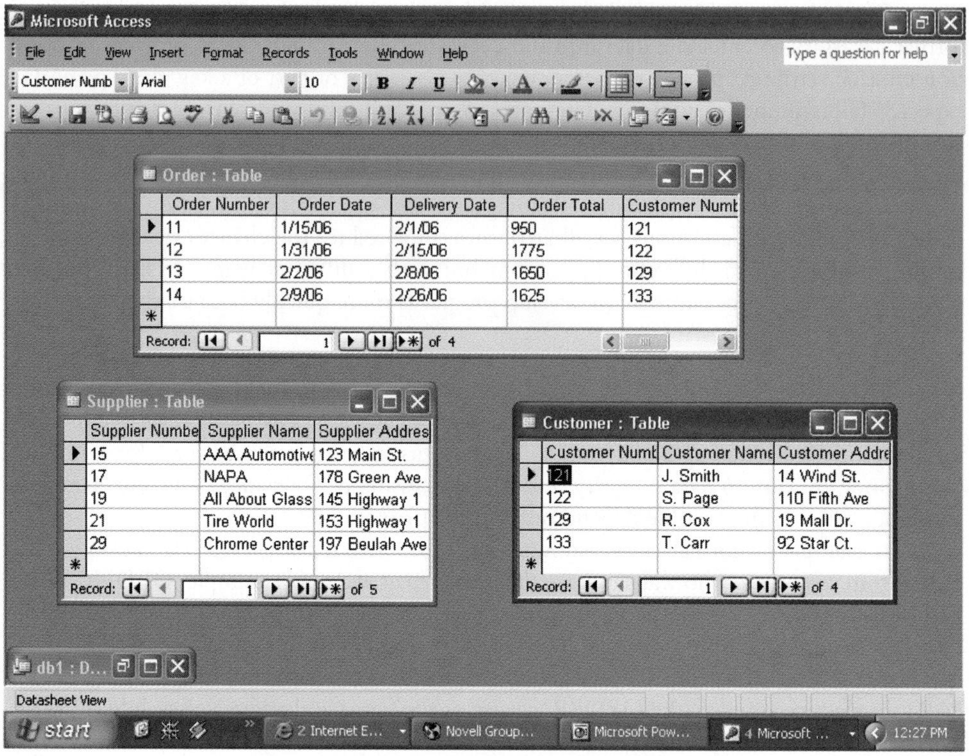

Order Number	Order Date	Delivery Date	Order Total	Customer Numb
11	1/15/06	2/1/06	950	121
12	1/31/06	2/15/06	1775	122
13	2/2/06	2/8/06	1650	129
14	2/9/06	2/26/06	1625	133

Supplier Numbe	Supplier Name	Supplier Addres
15	AAA Automotive	123 Main St.
17	NAPA	178 Green Ave.
19	All About Glass	145 Highway 1
21	Tire World	153 Highway 1
29	Chrome Center	197 Beulah Ave

Customer Numb	Customer Name	Customer Addre
121	J. Smith	14 Wind St.
122	S. Page	110 Fifth Ave
129	R. Cox	19 Mall Dr.
133	T. Carr	92 Star Ct.

(a)

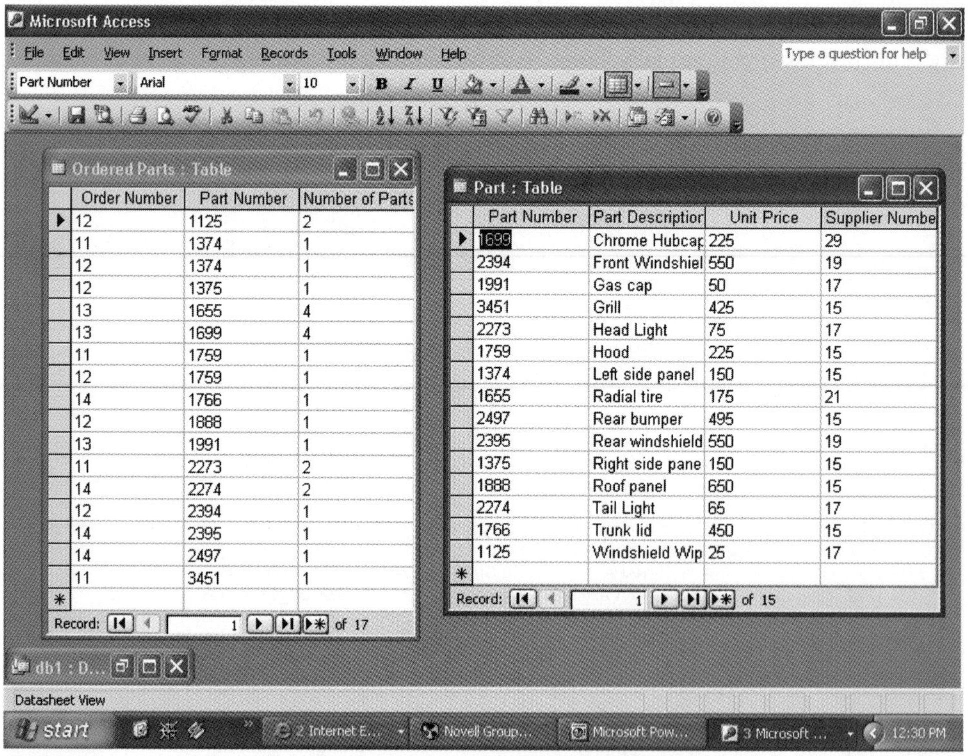

Order Number	Part Number	Number of Parts
12	1125	2
11	1374	1
12	1374	1
12	1375	1
13	1655	4
13	1699	4
11	1759	1
12	1759	1
14	1766	1
12	1888	1
13	1991	1
11	2273	2
14	2274	2
12	2394	1
14	2395	1
14	2497	1
11	3451	1

Part Number	Part Descriptior	Unit Price	Supplier Numbe
1699	Chrome Hubcap	225	29
2394	Front Windshiel	550	19
1991	Gas cap	50	17
3451	Grill	425	15
2273	Head Light	75	17
1759	Hood	225	15
1374	Left side panel	150	15
1655	Radial tire	175	21
2497	Rear bumper	495	15
2395	Rear windshield	550	19
1375	Right side pane	150	15
1888	Roof panel	650	15
2274	Tail Light	65	17
1766	Trunk lid	450	15
1125	Windshield Wip	25	17

(b)

FIGURE 4.7 Smaller relationships broken down from the nonnormal relations. (a) Order, Supplier, Customer. (b) Ordered Parts, Part.

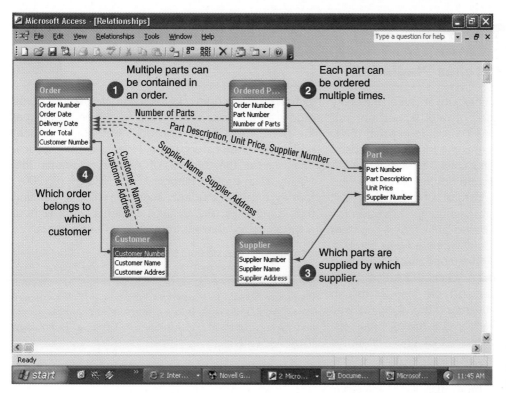

FIGURE 4.8 How normalized relations produce the order.

consider an order at the automobile repair shop. The normalized relations can produce the order in the following manner (see Figure 4.8).

1. The ORDER relation provides the Order Number (the primary key), Order Date, Delivery Date, Order Total, and Customer Number.

2. The primary key of the ORDER relation (Order Number) provides a link to the ORDERED PARTS relation (the link numbered 1 in Figure 4.8).

3. The ORDERED PARTS relation supplies the Number of Parts information to ORDER.

4. The primary key of the ORDERED PARTS relation (Part Number) provides a link to the PART relation (the link numbered 2 in Figure 4.8).

5. The PART relation supplies the Part Description, Unit Price, and Supplier Number to ORDER.

6. The Supplier Number in the PART relation provides a link to the SUPPLIER relation (the link numbered 3 in Figure 4.8).

7. The SUPPLIER relation provides the Supplier Name and Supplier Address to ORDER.

8. The Customer Number in ORDER provides a link to the CUSTOMER relation (the link numbered 4 in Figure 4.8).

9. The CUSTOMER relation supplies the Customer Name and Customer Address to ORDER.

Databases in Action

It is safe to say that almost all organizations have one or more databases. Furthermore, there are a large number of interesting database applications. IT's About Business 4.1 shows us how databases can be used to catch plagiarists.

IT's About Business

4.1 Database Catches Plagiarists

The Center for Academic Integrity at Duke University surveyed 18,000 public and private high school students from 2002 through 2006 and found that more than 60 percent admitted to some form of plagiarism. Now, when high school and university students write class papers, their teachers are not the only ones who examine those papers. Instead, their papers will be checked for plagiarism by Turnitin (*www.turnitin.com*). Turnitin is a Web-based anti-cheating system designed by iParadigms (*www.iparadigms.com*), a California-based company that specializes in tracking digital information. Turnitin checks student work against a database containing more than 22 million papers written by students around the world, as well as online sources and electronic archives of journals. School administrators maintain that the service is meant to deter plagiarism at a time when the Internet makes it easy to copy other students' work.

Turnitin is now used by more than 7,000 academic institutions in 90 countries. The service adds thousands of student assignments to its database every day.

Students can submit rough drafts to Turnitin. They receive an "originality report" that identifies similarities to other sources and alerts both the student and his or her teacher. In many schools, students are allowed to submit unlimited numbers of drafts to the service to catch intentional or accidental overlaps.

Although many instructors value this service, some students are rebelling against it. They object to Turnitin's practice of automatically adding their papers to the database, calling it an infringement of their intel-

lectual property rights. In response, lawyers for iParadigms and various universities have concluded that the paper-checking system does not violate student rights. Many educators agree. However, some educators accuse the system of making students feel "guilty, until proven innocent." On March 19, 2007, four high school students sued iParadigms, claiming that Turnitin illegally archives students' work without payment to, or consent from, the student authors.

Sources: Compiled from M. Glod, "Students Rebel Against Database Designed to Thwart Plagiarists," *Washington Post*, September 22, 2006; K. Jones, "Students Sue Turnitin Anti-Plagairism Service for Copyright Infringement," *Information-Week*, April 3, 2007; L. Briggs, "Turnitin: Fighting Plagiarism and Saving Time at Fresno State," *Campus Technology*, March 14, 2007.

QUESTIONS

1. Explain the two sides to this issue. Take one side or the other, and defend your position.
2. What will be the outcome for iParadigms if it loses the lawsuit?
3. If iParadigms wins the lawsuit, student papers will continue to be added to the database. Is it possible that, once the database is large enough, any paper submitted will have "suspect passages"? That is, what will happen if 500,000 papers already have been written on your topic and stored in the database? Is database technology itself the culprit here?

Before you go on . . .

1. What are the advantages and disadvantages of relational databases?
2. What are the benefits of data dictionaries?
3. Describe how structured query language works.

4.4 Data Warehousing

Today, the most successful companies are those that can respond quickly and flexibly to market changes and opportunities. A key to this response is the effective and efficient use of data and information by analysts and managers, as shown in the Continental Airlines case at the end of the chapter. The problem is providing users with access to corporate data so that they can analyze it. Let's look at an example.

If the manager of a local bookstore wanted to know the profit margin on used books at her store, she could find out from her database, using SQL or QBE. However, if she needed to know the trend in the profit margins on used books over the last 10 years, she would have a very difficult query to construct in SQL or QBE.

The bookstore manager's problem shows us two reasons why organizations are building data warehouses. First, the organization's databases have the necessary information to answer her query, but it is not organized in a way that makes it easy for her to search for needed information and insight. Also, the organization's databases are designed to process millions of transactions per day. Therefore, complicated queries might take a long time to answer and also might degrade the performance of the databases. As a result of these problems, companies are using data warehousing and data mining tools to make it easier and faster for users to access, analyze, and query data. Data mining tools (discussed in Chapter 9) allow users to search for valuable business information in a large database or data warehouse.

Describing the Data Warehouse

A **data warehouse** is a repository of historical data that are organized by subject to support decision makers in the organization. Data warehouses facilitate business intelligence activities, such as data mining, decision support, and querying applications (discussed in Chapter 9). The basic characteristics of a data warehouse include:

- *Organized by business dimension or subject*. Data are organized by subject (e.g., by customer, vendor, product, price level, and region) and contain information relevant for decision support and data analysis.

- *Consistent*. Data in different databases may be encoded differently. For example, gender data may be encoded 0 and 1 in one operational system and "m" and "f" in another. In the data warehouse, though, all data must be coded in a consistent manner.

- *Historical*. The data are kept for many years so that they can be used for identifying trends, forecasting, and making comparisons over time.

- *Nonvolatile*. Data are not updated after they are entered into the warehouse.

- *Use online analytical processing*. Typically, organizational databases are oriented toward handling transactions. That is, databases use **online transaction processing (OLTP)**, where business transactions are processed online as soon as they occur. The objectives are speed and efficiency, which are critical to a successful Internet-based business operation. Data warehouses, which are not designed to support OLTP but to support decision makers, use online analytical processing. **Online analytical processing (OLAP)** involves the analysis of accumulated data by end users.

- *Multidimensional*. Typically, the data warehouse uses a multidimensional data structure. Recall that relational databases store data in two-dimensional tables. In contrast, data warehouses store data in more than two dimensions. For this reason, the data are said to be stored in a **multidimensional structure**. A common representation for this multidimensional structure is the *data cube*.

  The data in the data warehouse are organized by *business dimensions*, which are the edges of the data cube and are subjects such as functional area, vendor, product, geographic area, or time period (look ahead briefly to Figure 4.11). Users can view and analyze data from the perspective of the various business dimensions. This analysis is intuitive because the dimensions are in business terms, easily understood by users.

- *Relationship with relational databases*. The data in data warehouses come from the company's operational databases, which can be relational databases. Figure 4.9 illustrates the process of building and using a data warehouse. The organization's data are stored in operational systems (left side of the figure). Using special software called extract, transform, and load (ETL), the system processes data and then stores them in a data warehouse. Not

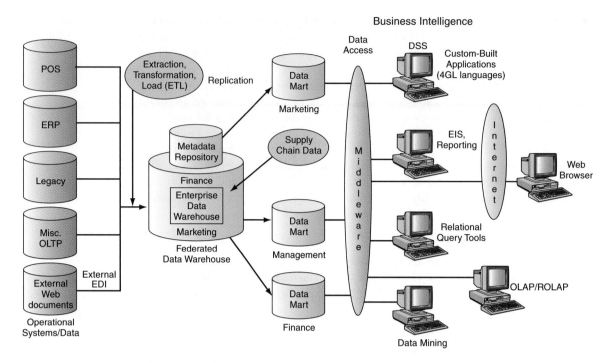

FIGURE 4.9 Data warehouse framework and views.

all data are necessarily transferred to the data warehouse; frequently, only a summary of the data is transferred. Within the warehouse the data are organized in a form that is easy for end users to access.

To differentiate between relational and multidimensional databases, suppose your company has four products—nuts, screws, bolts, and washers—which have been sold in three territories—East, West, and Central—for the previous three years—2006, 2007, and 2008. In a relational database, these sales data would look like Figures 4.10a, b, and c. In a multidimensional data-

(a) 2006

Product	Region	Sales
Nuts	East	50
Nuts	West	60
Nuts	Central	100
Screws	East	40
Screws	West	70
Screws	Central	80
Bolts	East	90
Bolts	West	120
Bolts	Central	140
Washers	East	20
Washers	West	10
Washers	Central	30

(b) 2007

Product	Region	Sales
Nuts	East	60
Nuts	West	70
Nuts	Central	110
Screws	East	50
Screws	West	80
Screws	Central	90
Bolts	East	100
Bolts	West	130
Bolts	Central	150
Washers	East	30
Washers	West	20
Washers	Central	40

(c) 2008

Product	Region	Sales
Nuts	East	70
Nuts	West	80
Nuts	Central	120
Screws	East	60
Screws	West	90
Screws	Central	100
Bolts	East	110
Bolts	West	140
Bolts	Central	160
Washers	East	40
Washers	West	30
Washers	Central	50

FIGURE 4.10 Relational databases.

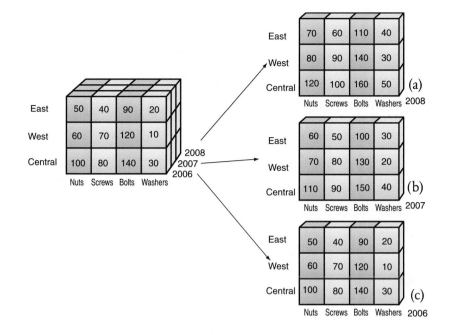

FIGURE 4.11
Multidimensional
database.

base, these data would be represented by a three-dimensional matrix (or data cube), as shown in Figure 4.11. We would say that this matrix represents sales *dimensioned by* products and regions and year. Notice that in Figure 4.10a we can see only sales for 2006. Therefore, sales for 2007 and 2008 are shown in Figures 4.10b and 4.10c, respectively. Figure 4.12 shows the equivalence between these relational and multidimensional databases.

Companies have reported hundreds of successful data-warehousing applications. For example, you can read client success stories and case studies at the Web sites of vendors such as NCR Corp. (*www.ncr.com*) and Oracle (*www.oracle.com*). For a more detailed discussion, visit the Data Warehouse Institute (*www.tdwi.org*). Some of the benefits of data warehousing include the following:

- End users can access needed data quickly and easily via Web browsers because they are located in one place.
- End users can conduct extensive analysis with data in ways that may not have been possible before.
- End users can have a consolidated view of organizational data.

These benefits can improve business knowledge, provide competitive advantage, enhance customer service and satisfaction, facilitate decision making, and streamline business processes. IT's about Business 4.2 demonstrates the benefits of data warehousing at the New York Police Department.

Data warehouses do have problems. First, they can be very expensive to build and to maintain. Second, incorporating data from obsolete mainframe systems may be difficult and inexpensive. Finally, people in one department might be reluctant to share data with other departments.

Data Marts

Because data warehouses are so expensive, they are used primarily by large companies. Many other firms employ a lower-cost, scaled-down version of a data warehouse called a data mart. A **data mart** is a small data warehouse that is designed for end-user needs in a strategic business unit (SBU) or a department.

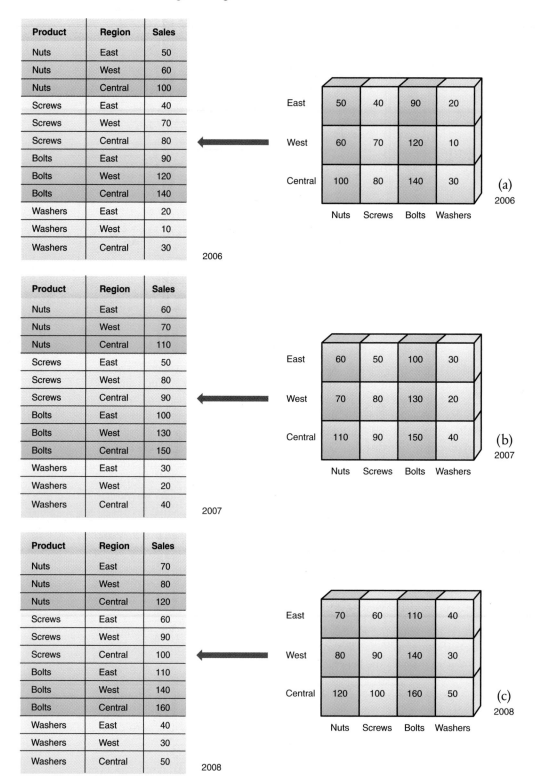

FIGURE 4.12 Equivalence between relational and multidimensional databases.

IT's About Business

4.2 Using a Data Warehouse to Help Solve Crimes

"We're in a war, so we need to give our guys in the front lines the best tools possible," said the CIO of the New York Police Department (NYPD). The NYPD has spent $300 million for those tools, one of which is the Real-Time Crime Center (RTCC). The RTCC is essentially a centralized help desk tasked with providing quick data to the department's 8,000 detectives. The underlying technology of the RTCC is a data warehouse.

To build the data warehouse, the NYPD first uploaded years of historical data, including complaints, arrests, stops, "questions and frisks," criminal summons, shootings, and homicides. It also included detectives' free text notes in the arrest records. The NYPD obtained these internal data from 55 databases scattered in various locations, many of which used older technologies such as FoxPro and Microsoft Access. Data from 911 emergency calls also were added. Finally, the data warehouse contains additional data from outside agencies. One source of these external data is the fingerprint databases operated by New York State and the FBI.

The police department is seeing many benefits from the data warehouse. Detectives can search on items such as a "silver gun" or a name on a tattoo, as well as search on a person's name. The fingerprint matching process, which once took up to three weeks, can now be completed in seconds. The system also generates an alert when a "stop and frisk" report matches a name in an outstanding warrant in the data warehouse. Precincts can generate crime-trend reports in weekly, daily, or near real-time fashion via dashboards that commanding officers can monitor.

The NYPD envisions many future applications for the system as well. For example, New York is planning to set up thousands of cameras at major intersections around the city to scan license plates in real time. The data warehouse will be able to match those license plates and generate alerts if matches to outstanding warrants are found. The city also plans for the data warehouse to serve as a central information hub for as many as 30 local government agencies, the district attorney's office, and police departments in neighboring Nassau and Westchester counties. The data warehouse will also take over the CompStat tool, which uses a geographic information system to display crime locations on a map.

Finally, to speed up reports that are still mostly written primarily with pen on paper, the NYPD is testing wireless pens and pads from IBM that let officers continue to handwrite reports in the field while the data are being simultaneously uploaded digitally into the system.

The ultimate benefit? NYPD detectives solved three-fourths of all homicides in 2005.

Sources: Compiled from E. Lai, "NYPD Boosts Data Warehouse to Snare Bad Guys Faster," *Computerworld*, September 1, 2006; B. Johnson, "NYPD Fights Crime in Real Time," *CIO Insight*, July 15, 2005; E. Lai, "NYPD Launches Third Phase of Data Warehouse," *Computerworld*, September 4, 2006; "NYPD Real Time Crime Center Expands," *www.govtech.com/digitalcommunities*, February 11, 2006; "NYPD Tackles Crime in Real Time," *Government Technology*, August 29, 2006; *www.nyc.gov/nypd*, accessed April 17, 2007.

QUESTIONS

1. As the NYPD data warehouse continues to expand in size and sophistication, is there a question of privacy for citizens? Support your answer.
2. What other types of data would you include in the data warehouse? *Hint*: Think about national security matters.

As previously stated, data marts are far less costly than data warehouses. A typical data mart costs less than $100,000, compared with $1 million or more for a data warehouse. Also, data marts can be implemented more quickly, often in less than 90 days. Furthermore, because they contain less information than a data warehouse, they have a more rapid response and are easier to learn and navigate. Finally, they support local rather than central control by conferring power on the using group. They also empower an SBU to build its own decision support systems without relying on a centralized IS department.

We have discussed databases, data warehouses, and data marts as systems for managing organizational data. However, companies are finding that, over time, their data have developed problems. To address these problems, companies must develop an enterprisewide approach to managing their data. This approach, which we discuss in the next section, is called data governance.

4.5 Data Governance

At the beginning of this chapter, we discussed the many reasons why managing data is so difficult. In addition to those problems, over time organizations have developed information systems for specific business processes, such as transaction processing, supply chain management, customer relationship management (all discussed in Chapter 8), and other processes. Information systems that specifically support these processes impose unique requirements on data, which results in repetition and conflicts across an organization. For example, the marketing function might maintain information on customers, sales territories, and markets that duplicates data within the billing or customer service functions. This situation produces inconsistent data in the enterprise. Inconsistent data prevents a company from developing a unified view of core business information—data concerning customers, products, finances, and so on—across the organization and its information systems.

Two other factors complicate data management. First, federal regulations (for example, Sarbanes-Oxley) have made it a top priority for companies to better account for how information is being managed with their organizations. Sarbanes-Oxley requires that public companies evaluate and disclose the effectiveness of their internal financial controls and that independent auditors for these companies agree to this disclosure. Furthermore, CEOs and CFOs are now held personally responsible for such disclosure.

Federal regulations place intense pressure on corporate executives. If their companies lack satisfactory data management policies, and fraud or a security breach occurs, they could be held personally responsible and face prosecution. Second, companies are drowning in data, much of which are unstructured.

For all these reasons, organizations are turning to data governance. **Data governance** is an approach to managing information across an entire organization. It involves a formal set of business processes and policies that are designed to ensure that data are handled in a well-defined fashion. That is, the organization follows unambiguous rules for the creation, collection, handling, and protection of information. The objective is to make information available, transparent, and useful for the people authorized to access it, from the moment it enters an organization, until it is outdated and deleted.

One method used to implement data governance is master data management. **Master data management** is a process that spans all organizational business processes and applications. It provides companies with the ability to store, maintain, exchange, and synchronize a consistent, accurate, and timely "single version of the truth" for the company's core master data.

Master data are a set of core data, such as customer, product, employee, vendor, and geographic location, that span the enterprise information systems. It is important to distinguish between master data and transaction data. *Transaction data* (discussed in detail in Chapter 8), which are generated and captured by operational systems, describes the activities, or transactions of the business. In contrast, master data are applied to multiple transactions and are used to categorize, aggregate, and evaluate the transaction data.

Let's look at an example of a transaction. The transaction is: You (Mary Jones) purchase one Samsung 42-inch plasma television, part number 6345, from Bill Roberts at Circuit City, for $2000, on April 20, 2007. In this example, the master data are "product sold," "vendor," "salesperson," "store," "part number," "purchase price," and "date." When specific values are applied to the master data, then a transaction is represented.

The opening case of this chapter showed how Panasonic implemented a master data management plan. Another example is the city of Dallas, Texas, which is implementing a master data management plan for digitizing public and private records, such as paper documents, images, drawings, and video and audio content, that are maintained by the city. The master database can be accessed by any of the 38 government departments that have appropriate access. The city is integrating its financial and billing processes with its customer relationship management program.

How will Dallas utilize this system? Imagine that the city experiences a water-main break. Before it implemented the system, repair crews had to search City Hall for records that were filed haphazardly. Once the workers found the hard-copy blueprints, they would take the blueprints to the site and, after going over the documents manually, would decide on a plan of action. Now, the blueprints are delivered wirelessly to the laptops of crews in the field, who can magnify or highlight areas of concern to generate a quick response. This process is reducing the time it takes to respond to an emergency by several hours.

4.6 Knowledge Management

As we have discussed throughout the book, data and information are critically important organizational assets. Knowledge is a vital asset as well. Successful managers have always used intellectual assets and recognized their value. But these efforts were not systematic, and they did not ensure that knowledge was shared and dispersed in a way that benefited the overall organization. Moreover, industry analysts estimate that most of a company's knowledge assets are not housed in relational databases. Instead, they are dispersed in e-mail, Word documents, spreadsheets, and presentations on individual computers. This arrangement makes it extremely difficult for companies to access and integrate this knowledge. The result frequently is less effective decision making.

Concepts and Definitions

Knowledge management (KM) is a process that helps organizations manipulate important knowledge that is part of the organization's memory, usually in an unstructured format. For an organization to be successful, knowledge, as a form of capital, must exist in a format that can be exchanged among persons. In addition, it must be able to grow.

Knowledge.   In the information technology context, knowledge is distinct from data and information. As we discussed in Chapter 1, data are a collection of facts, measurements, and statistics; information is organized or processed data that are timely and accurate. **Knowledge** is information that is *contextual*, *relevant*, and *actionable*. Simply put, knowledge is *information in action*. **Intellectual capital** (or **intellectual assets**) is another term for knowledge.

To illustrate with an example, a bulletin listing all the courses offered by your university during one semester would be considered data. When you register, you process the data from the bulletin to create your schedule for the semester. Your schedule would be considered information. Awareness of your work schedule, your major, your desired social schedule, and characteristics of different faculty members could be construed as knowledge, because it can affect the way you build your schedule. We see that this awareness is contextual and relevant (to developing an optimal schedule of classes), as well as actionable (it can lead to changes in your schedule). The implication is that knowledge has strong experiential and reflective elements that distinguish it from information in a given context. Unlike information, knowledge can be exercised to solve a problem.

Explicit and Tacit Knowledge. **Explicit knowledge** deals with more objective, rational, and technical knowledge. In an organization, explicit knowledge consists of the policies, procedural guides, reports, products, strategies, goals, core competencies of the enterprise, and the IT infrastructure. In other words, explicit knowledge is the knowledge that has been codified (documented) in a form that can be distributed to others or transformed into a process or strategy. A description of how to process a job application that is documented in a firm's human resources policy manual is an example of explicit knowledge.

In contrast, **tacit knowledge** is the cumulative store of subjective or experiential learning. In an organization, tacit knowledge consists of an organization's experiences, insights, expertise, know-how, trade secrets, skill sets, understanding, and learning. It also includes the organizational culture, which reflects the past and present experiences of the organization's people and processes, as well as the prevailing values. Tacit knowledge is generally slow, imprecise, and costly to transfer. It is also highly personal. Finally, because it is unstructured, it is difficult to formalize or codify. For example, salespersons who have worked with particular customers over time know the needs of those customers quite well. This knowledge is typically not recorded. In fact, it might be difficult for the salesperson to put into writing.

Knowledge Management Systems

The goal of knowledge management is to help an organization make the most effective use of the knowledge it has. Historically, management information systems have focused on capturing, storing, managing, and reporting explicit knowledge. Organizations now recognize the need to integrate both explicit and tacit knowledge in formal information systems. **Knowledge management systems (KMSs)** refer to the use of modern information technologies—the Internet, intranets, extranets, LotusNotes, data warehouses—to systematize, enhance, and expedite intrafirm and interfirm knowledge management. KMSs are intended to help an organization cope with turnover, rapid change, and downsizing by making the expertise of the organization's human capital widely accessible. IT's About Business 4.3 describes a knowledge management system used by Wipro Technologies.

IT's About Business

4.3 Knowledge Management Portal at Wipro

Wipro Technologies (*www.wipro.com*) is an information technology company that provides comprehensive IT solutions and services to corporations around the world. Wipro needed to gather and integrate the knowledge gained by its 30,000 employees so that other employees could access this information easily.

To accomplish this task, Wipro implemented a Web-based knowledge portal called KNET to gather employee knowledge on their experiences, clients, projects, processes, best practices, documentation, and presentations. Another important goal of the portal was to make it easy to search for, and find, people with the right knowledge and domain expertise. A *portal* offers a single point of access to critical

business information. We discuss portals in more detail in Chapter 5.

KNET has five components: DocKNet, KoNnEcT, KNetworks, Reusable Components, and War Rooms. DocKNet is a comprehensive document portal that contains knowledge that is relevant to all employees. One section of DocKNet contains general and technical information for all employees, while another section contains sensitive sales support material such as pricing and proposals, which has restricted access.

KoNnEcT is a directory of employees who are experts in various technologies. Employees who need guidance can find an expert here, and then post a query to that person. If an employee cannot find an expert, then he or she sends a query in an e-mail message to the entire company. Replies are captured in a database for future reference.

KNetworks are online discussion forums that enable employees to discuss or exchange information on a particular project or technology. Any employee can start a new query or participate in existing discussions.

Reusable Components saves users a significant amount of time in all aspects of their work. Here, employees can find items such as ready-to-use templates for systems development (discussed in Chapter 10), best practices, reusable computer code, and IS tools and methodologies.

The War Rooms component is designed for workgroup members situated at different physical locations. It is an invitation-only area and is used for large-scale projects. Prior to KNET, multiple workgroups would have to come together at one location. With War Rooms, all collaboration is now done online.

The Project Data Bank contains detailed information about completed projects. All employees have access to and can refer to the data bank for knowledge and experience gained from previous projects. The data bank's greatest value is in training new employees.

KNET has become a significant strategic tool for Wipro. Productivity and knowledge sharing have increased, leading to faster time-to-market with solutions. At the same time, costs related to the creation and delivery of proposals and projects have been reduced.

Sources: Compiled from "Knowledge Management Portal Saves Time and Money, Improves Productivity at Wipro," *www.techrepublic.com*, November 23, 2006; *www.wipro.com* and *www.microsoft.com/servers/default.mspx*, accessed April 17, 2007.

QUESTIONS

1. If Wipro is so successful with its knowledge management portal, why don't other companies implement the same type of portal? *Hint*: Consider corporate culture and the type of industry in which Wipro competes.
2. If you were the Wipro CEO, what other components would you add to KNET? Support your answer.

Organizations can realize many benefits with KMSs. Most importantly, they make **best practices**, which are the most effective and efficient ways of doing things, readily available to a wide range of employees. Enhanced access to best-practice knowledge improves overall organizational performance. For example, account managers can now make available their tacit knowledge about how best to handle large accounts. This knowledge can then be used to train new account managers. Other benefits include better customer service, more efficient product development, and improved employee morale and retention.

At the same time, implementing effective KMSs presents some challenges. First, employees must be willing to share their personal tacit knowledge. To encourage this behavior, organizations must create a "knowledge management" culture that rewards employees who add their expertise to the knowledge base. Second, the knowledge base must be continually maintained and updated. New knowledge must be added, and old, outdated knowledge must be deleted. Companies must be willing to invest in the resources needed to carry out these operations.

The Knowledge Management System Cycle

A functioning KMS follows a cycle that consists of six steps (see Figure 4.13). The reason the system is cyclical is that knowledge is dynamically refined over time. The knowledge in an effective KMS is never finalized because the environment changes over time, and knowledge must be updated to reflect these changes. The cycle works as follows:

1. *Create knowledge.* Knowledge is created as people determine new ways of doing things or develop know-how. Sometimes external knowledge is brought in.
2. *Capture knowledge.* New knowledge must be identified as valuable and be represented in a reasonable way.

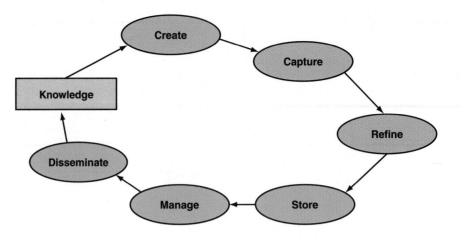

FIGURE 4.13
The knowledge
management cycle.

3. **Refine knowledge.** New knowledge must be placed in context so that it is actionable. This is where tacit qualities (human insights) must be captured along with explicit facts.

4. **Store knowledge.** Useful knowledge must then be stored in a reasonable format in a knowledge repository so that others in the organization can access it.

5. **Manage knowledge.** Like a library, the knowledge must be kept current. It must be reviewed regularly to verify that it is relevant and accurate.

6. **Disseminate knowledge.** Knowledge must be made available in a useful format to anyone in the organization who needs it, anywhere and anytime.

Before you go on . . .

1. What is knowledge management?
2. What is the difference between tacit knowledge and explicit knowledge?
3. Describe the knowledge management system cycle.

What's in IT for Me?

ACC

For the Accounting Major

The accounting function is intimately concerned with keeping track of the transactions and internal controls of an organization. Modern data warehouses enable accountants to perform these functions more effectively. Data warehouses help accountants manage the flood of data in today's organizations so that they can keep their firms in compliance with the new standards imposed by Sarbanes-Oxley.

Accountants also play a role in cost-justifying the creation of a knowledge base and then auditing its cost-effectiveness. In addition, if you work for a large CPA company that provides management services or sells knowledge, you will most likely use some of your company's best practices that are stored in a knowledge base.

For the Finance Major

Financial managers make extensive use of computerized databases that are external to the organization, such as CompuStat or Dow Jones, to obtain financial data on organizations in their industry. They can use these data to determine if their organization meets industry benchmarks in return on investment, cash management, and other financial ratios.

Financial managers, who produce the organization's financial status reports, are also closely involved with Sarbanes-Oxley. Data warehouses help these managers comply with the new standards.

For the Marketing Major

Data warehouses help marketing managers access data from the organization's marketing transactions (for example, customer purchases) to plan targeted marketing campaigns and to evaluate the success of previous campaigns. Knowledge about customers can make the difference between success and failure. In many data warehouses and knowledge bases, the vast majority of information and knowledge concerns customers, products, sales, and marketing. Marketing managers certainly use an organization's knowledge base, and they often participate in its creation.

For the Production/Operations Management Major

Production/operations personnel access organizational data to determine optimum inventory levels for parts in a production process. Past production data enable POM personnel to determine the optimum configuration for assembly lines. Firms also keep quality data that inform them not only about the quality of finished products but also about quality issues with incoming raw materials, production irregularities, shipping and logistics, and after-sale use and maintenance of the product.

Knowledge management is extremely important for running complex operations. The accumulated knowledge regarding scheduling, logistics, maintenance, and other functions is very valuable. Innovative ideas are necessary for improving operations and can be supported by knowledge management.

For the Human Resources Management Major

Organizations keep extensive data on employees, including gender, age, race, current and past job descriptions, and performance evaluations. Human resources personnel access these data to provide reports to government agencies regarding compliance with federal equal opportunity guidelines. HR managers also use these data to evaluate hiring practices and salary structures and to manage any discrimination grievances or lawsuits brought against the firm.

Data warehouses help HR managers provide assistance to all employees as companies turn over more and more decisions about health care and retirement planning to the employees themselves. The employees can use the data warehouses for help in selecting the optimal mix among these critical choices.

Human resources managers also need to use a knowledge base frequently to find out how past cases were handled. Consistency in how employees are treated not only is important, but it protects the company against legal actions. Also, training for building, maintaining, and using the knowledge system sometimes is the responsibility of the HR department. Finally, the HR department might be responsible for compensating employees who contribute their knowledge to the knowledge base.

For the MIS Major

The MIS function manages the organization's data and the databases, data warehouses, and data marts where they are stored. MIS database administrators standardize data names by using the data dictionary. This process ensures that all users understand which data are in the database. Database personnel also provide data for the data warehouse to help users access needed data. MIS personnel—and users as well—can now generate reports with query tools much more quickly than was possible using old mainframe systems written in COBOL.

Summary

1. Recognize the importance of data, issues involved in managing these data, and their life cycle.

IT applications cannot be performed without using data. Data should be accurate, complete, timely, consistent, accessible, relevant, and concise. Managing data in organizations is difficult for various reasons: (1) the amount of data increases with time; (2) data are stored in various systems, databases, formats, and languages; and (3) data security, quality, and integrity are often compromised.

The data life cycle starts with data collection. The data are stored in a database(s) and then preprocessed to fit the format of a data warehouse or data marts. Users then access data from the warehouse or data mart for analysis. The result of all these activities is the generation of decision support and knowledge.

2. Describe the sources of data and explain how data are collected.

Data sources can be internal, personal, clickstream (from your company's Web transactions), and external (particularly the Internet). Internal data are usually located in corporate databases and are usually accessible via an organization's intranet. IS users create personal data by documenting their own expertise. These data can reside on the user's PC, or they can be placed on corporate databases or on corporate knowledge bases. Sources of external data range from commercial databases to sensors and satellites. Government reports constitute a major source of external data. Many thousands of databases all over the world are accessible through the Internet.

3. Explain the advantages of the database approach.

In a database, which is a group of logically related files, data are integrated and related so that one set of software programs provides access to all the data. Therefore, data redundancy, data isolation, and data inconsistency are minimized, and data can be shared among all users of the data. In addition, data security and data integrity are increased, and applications and data are independent of one another.

4. Explain the operation of data warehousing and its role in decision support.

A data warehouse is a repository of subject-oriented historical data that are organized to be accessible in a form readily acceptable for analytical processing activities. End users can access needed data in a data warehouse quickly and easily via Web browsers. They can conduct extensive analysis with data and can have a consolidated view of organizational data. These benefits can improve business knowledge, provide competitive advantage, enhance customer service and satisfaction, facilitate decision making, and help in streamlining business processes.

5. Describe data governance and how it helps produce high-quality data.

Data governance is an approach to managing information across an entire organization. Data governance ensures that data are handled in a certain, well-defined fashion. That is, the organization follows unambiguous rules for the creation, collection, handling, and protection of information.

6. Define knowledge and describe the different types of knowledge.

Knowledge is information that is contextual, relevant, and actionable. Explicit knowledge deals with more objective, rational, and technical knowledge. Tacit knowledge is usually in the domain of subjective, cognitive, and experiential learning. It is highly personal and difficult to formalize.

Chapter Glossary

attribute Each characteristic or quality describing a particular entity.

best practices The most effective and efficient ways to do things.

bit A binary digit; that is, a 0 or a 1.

byte A group of eight bits that represents a single character.

clickstream data Data collected about user behavior and browsing patterns by monitoring users' activities when they visit a Web site.

database A group of logically related files that stores data and the associations among them.

database management system (DBMS) The software program (or group of programs) that provides access to a database.

data dictionary Collection of definitions of data elements, data characteristics that use the data elements, and the individuals, business functions, applications, and reports that use this data element.

data governance An approach to managing information across an entire organization.

data mart A small data warehouse designed for a strategic business unit (SBU) or a department.

data model Definition of the way data in a DBMS are conceptually structured.

data warehouse A repository of subject-oriented historical data that are organized to be accessible in a form readily acceptable for analytical processing.

entity A person, place, thing, or event about which information is maintained in a record.

entity classes A grouping of entities of a given type.

entity-relationship (ER) diagram Document that shows data entities and attributes and relationships among them.

entity-relationship (ER) modeling The process of designing a database by organizing data entities to be used and identifying the relationships among them.

explicit knowledge The more objective, rational, and technical types of knowledge.

field A grouping of logically related characters into a word, a small group of words, or a complete number.

file A grouping of logically related records.

identifier An attribute that identifies an entity instance.

instance A particular entity within an entity class.

intellectual capital (intellectual assets) Other terms for knowledge.

knowledge Information that is contextual, relevant, and actionable.

knowledge management (KM) A process that helps organizations identify, select, organize, disseminate, transfer, and apply information and expertise that are part of the organization's memory and that typically reside within the organization in an unstructured manner.

knowledge management systems (KMSs) Information technologies used to systematize, enhance, and expedite intra- and interfirm knowledge management.

master data A set of core data, such as customer, product, employee, vendor, geographic location, and so on that span the enterprise information systems.

master data management A process that provides companies with the ability to store, maintain, exchange, and synchronize a consistent, accurate, and timely "single version of the truth" for the company's core master data.

multidimensional structure The manner in which data are structured in a data warehouse so that they can be analyzed by different views or perspectives, which are called dimensions.

normalization A method for analyzing and reducing a relational database to its most streamlined form for minimum redundancy, maximum data integrity, and best processing performance.

online analytical processing (OLAP) The analysis of accumulated data by end users.

online transaction processing (OLTP) Online processing of business transactions as soon as they occur.

primary key The identifier field or attribute that uniquely identifies a record.

query by example (QBE) Database language that enables the user to fill out a grid (form) to construct a sample or description of the data wanted.

record A grouping of logically related fields.

relational database model Data model based on the simple concept of tables in order to capitalize on characteristics of rows and columns of data.

secondary keys An identifier field or attribute that has some identifying information, but typically does not identify the file with complete accuracy.

structured query language (SQL) Popular relational database language that enables users to perform complicated searches with relatively simple instructions.

table A grouping of logically related records.

tacit knowledge The cumulative store of subjective or experiential learning; highly personal and hard to formalize knowledge.

Discussion Questions

1. Explain the difficulties involved in managing data.
2. What are the problems associated with poor-quality data?
3. What is master data management? What does it have to do with high-quality data?
4. Describe the advantages of relational databases.
5. Discuss the benefits of data warehousing to end users.
6. What is the relationship between a company's databases and its data warehouse?
7. Distinguish between data warehouses and data marts.
8. Explain why it is important to capture and manage knowledge.
9. Compare and contrast tacit knowledge and explicit knowledge.

Problem-Solving Activities

1. Access various employment Web sites (e.g., *www.monster.com* and *www.dice.com*) and find several job descriptions for a database administrator. Are the job descriptions similar? What are the salaries offered in these positions?
2. Access the Web sites of several real estate companies. Find the sites that take you through a step-by-step process for buying a home, that provide virtual reality tours of homes in your price range and location, that provide mortgage and interest rate calculators, and that offer financing for your home. Do the sites require that you register to access their services? Can you request that an e-mail be sent to you when properties in which you might be interested become available?
3. It is possible to find many Web sites that provide demographic information. Access several of these sites and see what they offer. Do the sites differ in the types of demographic information they offer? If so, how? Do the sites require a fee for the information they offer? Would demographic information be useful to you if you wanted to start a new business? If so, how and why?
4. The Internet contains many Web sites that provide information on financial aid resources for students. Access several of these sites. Do you have to register to access the information? Can you apply for financial aid on the sites, or do you have to request paper applications that you must complete and return?

5. Draw an entity-relationship diagram for a small retail store. You wish to keep track of the product name, description, unit price, and number of items of that product sold to each customer. You also wish to record customer name, mailing address, and billing address. You must track each transaction (sale), as to date, product purchased, unit price, number of units, tax, and total amount of the sale.

Web Activities

1. Access the Web sites of IBM (*www.ibm.com*), Sybase (*www.sybase.com*), and Oracle (*www.oracle.com*) and trace the capabilities of their latest products, including Web connections.
2. Access the Web sites of two of the major data warehouse vendors, such as NCR (*www.ncr.com*) and SAS (*www.sas.com*). Describe their products and how they are related to the Web.
3. Enter the Web site of the Gartner Group (*www.gartner.com*). Examine their research studies pertaining to data management and data warehousing. Prepare a report on the state of the art.
4. Access *www.teradatastudentnetwork.com*, read and answer the questions of the assignment entitled: "Data Warehouse Failures." Choose one of the cases and discuss the failure and the potential remedy.

Team Assignments

1. Each team will select an online database to explore, such as AOL Music (*http://music.aol.com*), iGo (*www.igo.com*), or the Internet Movie Database (*www.imdb.com*). Explore these Web sites to see what information they provide for you. List the entities and the attributes that the Web sites must track in their databases. Diagram the relationship between the entities you have identified.
2. In groups, create a data model for a pet store to include:
   • Customer data
   • Product data
   • Employee data
   • Financial data
   • Vendor data
   • Sales data
   • Inventory data
   • Building data
   • Other data (specify)

Create attributes (four or more) for each entity. Create relationships between the entities, name the relationships, and create an entity-relationship diagram for the pet store.

Continental Airlines: Flying High with Its Data Warehouse

THE BUSINESS PROBLEM The airlines were very profitable during the late 1990s, when travel was up and fuel costs were down. Today, soaring oil prices, an antiquated air traffic control system, the 9/11 attacks, and the success of low-cost carriers have changed the entire airline industry. Several of the biggest airlines either have gone bankrupt or have barely avoided it. In addition, while most of the older airlines continue to confuse and annoy customers with restrictions, delays, and poor customer service, passengers are increasingly opting to fly with regional, no-frills carriers that have straightforward policies and still-affordable rates.

However, one of the major airlines has not decreased service. Continental Airlines (*www.continental.com*), the fourth-largest airline in the United States, has invested in customer service improvements, increased the number of routes it flies, and kept prices steady. The company's strategy is simple. Identify and increase the loyalty of its most valuable customers while luring new, more profitable customers—many of whom do not live in the United States—with top-notch customer service. Continental decided to concentrate on attracting a loyal group of frequent fliers who would be willing to pay more for superior customer service.

THE IT SOLUTION To accomplish its strategy, Continental is going beyond the typical airline technology such as on-line check-in and electronic ticketing. The company is relying on an IT department that is creating automated tools, boosting efficiency, and sharpening business intelligence to increase the airline's profits and make it a favorite with the flying public.

In the late 1990s, Continental's information systems did not communicate with each other. In fact, it was impossible to track a customer whose itinerary included more than one stop. To compound this problem, the airline did not have a system to identify its most important customers. A big part of the problem was the company's old IBM mainframe system, called the Transaction Processing Facility (TPF). It was very inflexible and was not designed for customer service.

To rectify its information problems, Continental's IT team got rid of the old mainframe. The team consolidated the airline's disparate customer management relationship (CRM) systems into one integrated system, saving the company roughly $6 million annually. Then the company partnered with Teradata (*www.teradata.com*), a division of NCR Corporation, to create an enterprisewide data warehouse that is fed by more than 25 enterprise systems.

The warehouse includes schedules, reservations, customer profiles and demographics, airline maintenance records and schedules, employee and crew payroll, and customer care. It provides a single, 360-degree view of each customer, including the 31 million who are members of Continental's OnePass or Elite frequent-flier programs.

The warehouse has allowed Continental executives to establish the Customer Value Metric (CVM), which takes into account the amount of money a customer spends with Continental and how much it costs the company to fly that passenger. The CVM for every passenger is calculated each month on a scale of 1 to 100, and is used for designating frequent fliers and placing them into tiers of profitability. For example, if an airplane is more than 90 minutes late, the company sends an automated e-mail to its top customers (highest CVMs) on that flight, apologizing for the delay and awarding frequent-flier miles as compensation for the inconvenience. High-CVM customers are also granted privileges such as access to private lounges, head-of-the-line boarding, and first-off-the-carousel baggage handling.

Continental maintains that much of its IT success can be attributed to the fact that the company's IT staff of 350, including 150 software developers, handles just about everything. Furthermore, Continental's executives value technology, and they view the IT function as a strategic investment, as opposed to a function used only to cut costs.

THE RESULTS Continental has seen many signs of success. The company has expanded its routes to the extent that it serves more destinations from its hubs in Newark, Houston, Cleveland, and Guam than any other airline in the world. It is also one of the few airlines that still serves meals on every flight. In addition, Continental is profitable, and it has won numerous awards for its superior customer service and passenger experience. The airline was the top-ranked airline in *Fortune* magazine's most admired companies of 2007.

Sources: Compiled from D. D'Agostino, "Continental Airline's Tech Strategy Takes Off," *CIO Insight*, July 14, 2006; "Continental Airlines Provides Frequent Fliers with Better Self-Service through Innovative Speech Technologies," *www.tmc.net*, November 28, 2006; K. Ferrell, "Continental Airlines: Landing the Right Data," *www.teradata.com*, June 2005; *www.continental.com*, accessed April 11, 2007.

QUESTIONS

1. Why have other airlines not adopted a program similar to Continental's?
2. How can IT be used to improve customer service and satisfaction?

Web Resources wiley.com/college/rainer

Student Web Site
• Web Quizzes
• Student Lecture Slides in PowerPoint
• Virtual Company ClubIT: Website and Assignments

WileyPLUS
• e-book
• Flash Cards
• How-To Animations for Microsoft Office

Databases at Club IT

Go to the Club IT link on the *WileyPLUS* Web site. There you will find assignments that will ask you to advise the club owners on how they can use databases to track information for their business.

wiley.com/college/rainer

Chapter 5

Learning Objectives

1. Describe the four major network applications.
2. Discuss the various technologies, applications, and Web sites that fall under the umbrella of Web 2.0.
3. Differentiate between e-learning and distance learning.
4. Understand the advantages and disadvantages of telecommuting for both employers and employees.

Network Applications

Chapter Outline

5.1 Network Applications
5.2 Web 2.0
5.3 E-Learning and Distance Learning
5.4 Telecommuting

What's in IT for me?   ACC   FIN   MKT   POM   HRM   MIS

The Business Problem

POM

The Business Problem

Hannaford Bros. (*www.hannaford.com*) has 26,000 employees and operates more than 150 supermarkets and combination food and drug stores in the northeastern United States. Several years ago, the company was a good example of a poorly planned, poorly performing network.

Inventory and order data were decentralized in its stores, and there was little or no standardization across stores of operating systems, networks, data protocols, and transmission channels. The company was using four different transmission protocols and was transmitting data via satellite, telephone dial-up, and telephone leased lines. Transmission was extremely slow (19.2 kilobits per second), and the network was very unreliable. In fact, in heavy rain the satellite connections went down. The company estimated that its unstable network was costing it millions of dollars per year in lost sales and expenses.

Each store maintained four or five servers containing that store's inventory and order data to compensate for unpredictable connections with headquarters. The company often would lose network contact with stores, in the process losing data and also losing synchronization between store data and data at headquarters. The overall system was so inefficient that the data were essentially useless.

At that time, managers would discount aging meat by posting a sign in the meat case with the reduced price. The cashier would use this lower price at the cash register, but the only information that was transmitted to headquarters was that meat was on sale. Headquarters did not know which type of meat, and they often did not know the exact price of the meat. Furthermore, managing the network was a huge problem because every technical problem required a store visit by IT personnel. In essence, Hannaford had no technology strategy.

The IT Solution

To improve its poor, expensive network performance, Hannaford designed and built a new network. The network was composed of T1 transmission lines from Verizon, an asynchronous transfer mode (ATM) system (from Cisco Systems) that transferred data in packets over the network, and a mainframe computer (from IBM) at headquarters to house data from all stores. (We discuss the ATM system in Technology Guide 4.)

The Results

Today, the Hannaford network is more than 80 times faster than its old one (1.5 megabits per second), and it uses only one protocol, the Transmission Control Protocol/Internet Protocol (TCP/IP), which is the protocol of the Internet. All Hannaford stores are connected to its new network.

Hannaford's growth, in terms of both store locations and sales, has doubled since the mid-1990s. The company attributes at least some of this growth to the faster, more reliable network. The new network has made it possible for Hannaford to eliminate 1,000 servers across the company, with only one or two remaining in each store.

Not only is the new network much more efficient than the old one, but it also costs less to support. For example, despite its rapid growth, the technology staff has actually decreased by 10 percent. In addition, whereas the old network required in-store servicing, the new network can be maintained with remote management tools that can diagnose problems and repair equipment over the network. Furthermore, the network seldom goes down.

One major benefit of the upgrade is that Hannaford now knows that it is working with current and accurate data. Store managers use handheld wireless devices (discussed in Chapter 7) to look up inventory, order more products, adjust prices, and produce the coupon stickers that are processed at the register. All of this activity is transmitted back to headquarters.

The new network has also made a difference at the cash register. Linux-based cash registers, which connect to the central mainframe, have cut 4 to 5 seconds off the time it takes to verify credit card information. This faster process results in higher customer satisfaction. Perhaps 80 percent of that speed increase can be attributed to the network.

And the most important benefit? Now that Wal-Mart has entered the grocery business, Hannaford feels that its new network makes it possible for the company to compete with the giant retailer.

The opening case about Hannaford illustrates three fundamental points about network computing. First, computers do not work in isolation in modern organizations. Rather, they constantly exchange data. Second, this exchange of data—facilitated by telecommunications technologies—provides companies with a number of very significant advantages. Third, this exchange can take place over any distance and over networks of any size. In addition, the case illustrates how networks enable discovery, communications, and collaboration within Hannaford. In fact, with Wal-Mart's entry into the grocery business, the network may have saved Hannaford entirely. Networks in general, and the Internet in particular, have fundamentally altered the ways we do business and the way we live.

Without networks, the computer on your desk would be merely another productivity-enhancement tool, just as the typewriter once was. The power of networks, however, turns your computer into an amazingly effective tool for discovery, communication, and collaboration, vastly increasing your productivity and your organization's competitive advantage. Regardless of the type of organization (profit/not-for-profit, large/small, global/local) or industry (manufacturing, financial services, health care), networks have transformed the way we do business.

Networks support new ways of doing business, from marketing to supply chain management to customer service to human resources management. In particular, the Internet and its private organizational counterpart, intranets, have an enormous impact on our lives, both professionally and personally. For all organizations, having an Internet strategy is no longer just a source of competitive advantage; rather, it is necessary for survival.

In this chapter we discuss network applications (that is, what networks help us to do). We then take a look at the variety of network applications that fall under the umbrella of Web 2.0. We conclude the chapter with a brief look at e-learning and telecommuting.

In Technology Guide 4, we discuss how networks function. First, we describe the basic telecommunications system. Understanding this system is important because it is the way all networks function, regardless of size. We then discuss the various types of networks, and we continue with a look at network protocols and types of network processing.

In Technology Guide 5, we discuss the basics of the Internet and the World Wide Web. We describe how we can access the Internet and then define the World Wide Web and differentiate it from the Internet.

Sources: Compiled from E. Bennett, "Hannaford Bros. Is a Cut Above," *Baseline Magazine,* October 2, 2006; P. Hochmuth, "Linux Makes Gains, Sees Challenges, in Retail IT," *Network World,* May 15, 2006; J. Mears, "Network Support Key as Mainframe Evolves," *Network World,* June 26, 2006; T. Hoffman, "Grocer Rings Up Savings with Linux Cash Registers," *Computerworld,* January 31, 2005; P. Thibodeau, "Mixed IT Environments Remain King with Large Users," *Computerworld,* December 5, 2005; *www.hannaford.com* and *www.delhaize.com,* accessed April 19, 2007.

What We Learned from This Case

5.1 Network Applications

If you have read this chapter's opening case and Technology Guide 4, you now have a working knowledge of what a network is and how you can access it. At this point, the key question is: How do businesses use networks to improve their operations? This section addresses that question. Stated in general terms, networks support businesses and other organizations in all types of functions. These functions fall into the following major categories: discovery, communication, collaboration, and Web services. We discuss the first three of these categories in the following sections, and we discuss Web services in the section on Web 2.0.

Discovery

The Internet permits users to access information located in databases all over the world. By browsing and searching data sources on the Web, users can apply the Internet's discovery capability to areas ranging from education to government services to entertainment to commerce. It is critically important for everyone to realize that there is no quality assurance on information on the Web. *Anyone* can post information to the Web. For example, as we see later in this chapter, anyone can edit a Wikipedia page (with some exceptions in controversial areas). The rule about information on the Web is: User Beware!

In addition, the Web's major strength is also a challenge. The amount of information on the Web can be overwhelming, and it doubles approximately each year. As a result, navigating through the Web and gaining access to necessary information are becoming more and more difficult. To accomplish these tasks, people increasingly are using search engines, directories, and portals.

Search Engines and Metasearch Engines. A **search engine** is a computer program that searches for specific information by keywords and reports the results. A search engine maintains an index of billions of Web pages. It uses that index to find pages that match a set of user-specified keywords. Such indexes are created and updated by *webcrawlers,* which are computer programs that browse the Web and create a copy of all visited pages. Search engines then index these pages to provide fast searches.

People actually use four main search engines for almost all their searches: Google (*www.google.com*), Yahoo (*www.yahoo.com*), Microsoft Network (*www.msn.com*), and Ask (*www.ask.com*). However, there are an incredible number of other search engines that are quite useful, with many providing very specific searches (see *http://www.readwriteweb .com/archives/top_100_alternative_search_engines.php.*)

For an even more thorough search, you can use a metasearch engine. **Metasearch engines** search several engines at once and integrate the findings of the various search engines to answer queries posted by users. Examples are Surf-wax (*www.sufwax.com*), Metacrawler (*www.metacrawler.com*), Mamma (*www.mamma.com*), Ungoogle (*www.ungoogle.com*), KartOO (*www.kartoo.com*), and Dogpile (*www.dogpile.com*). Figure 5.1 shows the KartOO home page.

Publication of Material in Foreign Languages. Not only is there a huge amount of information on the Internet, but it is written in many different languages. How, then, do you access this information? The answer is that you use an *automatic translation* of Web pages. Such translation is available, to and from all major languages, and its quality is improving with time. Some major translation products are Altavista (*http://babelfish .altavista.com*) (see Figure 5.2) and Google (*www.google.com/language_tools*) as well as products and services available at Trados (*www.trados.com*).

Should companies care about providing their Web sites in multiple languages? The answer is, absolutely. Multilingual Web sites are now a competitive necessity because of the global nature of the business environment, which we discussed in Chapter 1. Companies increasingly are looking outside their home markets to grow revenues and attract new customers. When companies are disseminating information around the world, getting that information correct is essential. It is not enough for companies to translate Web content.

FIGURE 5.1   The KartOO Home Page www.kartoo.com

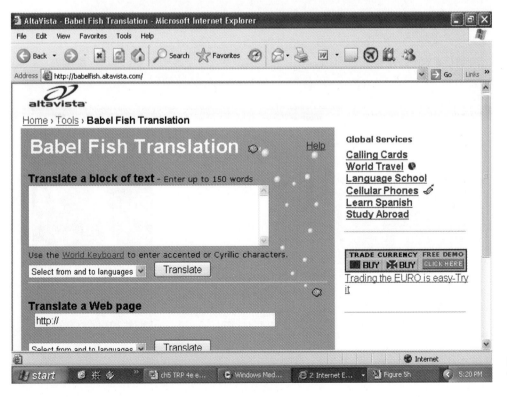

FIGURE 5.2   Alta-Vista translator.

They must also localize that content and be sensitive to the needs of the people in local markets.

To reach 80 percent of the world's Internet users, a Web site needs to support a minimum of 10 languages: English, Chinese, Spanish, Japanese, German, Korean, French, Italian, Russian, and Portuguese. At 20 cents and more per word, translation services are expensive. Companies supporting 10 languages can spend $200,000 annually to localize information and another $50,000 to maintain the Web sites. Translation budgets for big multinational companies can run in the millions of dollars. Many large companies use Systran S.A. (*www.systransoft.com*) for high-quality machine translation services.

Portals.   Most organizations and their managers encounter information overload. Information is scattered across numerous documents, e-mail messages, and databases at different locations and systems. Finding relevant and accurate information is often time consuming and may require access to multiple systems.

One solution to this problem is to use portals. A **portal** is a Web-based, personalized gateway to information and knowledge that provides relevant information from different IT systems and the Internet using advanced search and indexing techniques. We distinguish among four types of portals: commercial, affinity, corporate, and industrywide.

Commercial (public) portals offer content for diverse communities, and they are the most popular portals on the Internet. They are intended for broad audiences, and they offer fairly routine content, some in real time (for example, a stock ticker). Examples are Lycos (*www.lycos.com*) and Microsoft Network (*www.msn.com*).

Affinity portals support communities such as a hobby group or a political party. They offer a single point of entry to an entire community of affiliated interests. For example, your university most likely has an affinity portal for its alumni. Figure 5.3 shows the affinity portal

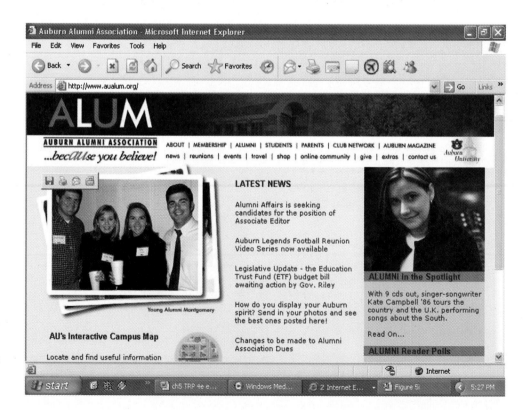

FIGURE 5.3   Auburn University affinity portal.

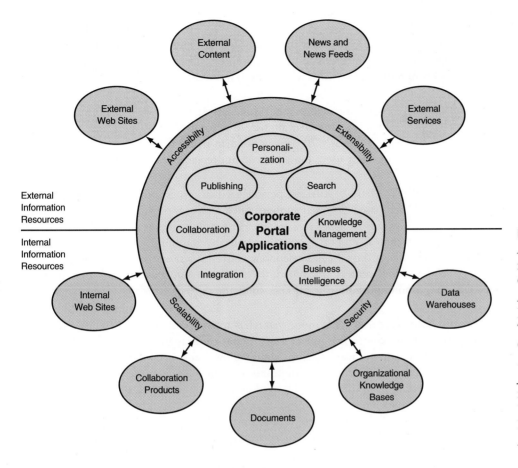

FIGURE 5.4

A corporate portal framework.(*Sources:* Compiled from A. Aneja et al.,"Corporate Portal Framework for Transforming Content Chaos on Intranets," *Intel Technology Journal,* Q1, 2000, and from T. Kounandis, "How to Pick the Best Portal," *e-Business Advisor,* August 2000).

for the Auburn University Alumni Association. Other examples include *www.techweb.com* and *www.zdnet.com.*

Corporate portals offer a personalized, single point of access through a Web browser to critical business information located inside and outside an organization. They are also known as *enterprise portals, information portals*, or *enterprise information portals*. In addition to making it easier to find needed information, corporate portals offer customers and employees self-service opportunities. Figure 5.4 provides a framework for corporate portals.

In addition to single-company portals, there are also **industrywide portals**. An example is TruckNet (*www.truck.net*), which is the portal for the trucking industry and the trucking community, including professional drivers, owner/operators, and trucking companies. TruckNet provides drivers with personalized Web-based e-mail, access to applications to leading trucking companies in the United States and Canada, and access to the Drivers RoundTable, a forum where drivers can discuss issues of interest. The portal also provides a large database of trucking jobs and general information related to the trucking industry.

These four portals are differentiated by the audience they serve. Another type of portal, the mobile portal, is distinguished by its technology. **Mobile portals** are portals that are accessible from mobile devices. Any of the four portals above can be accessed by mobile devices. These mobile devices are typically wireless, so we discuss mobile portals in detail in Chapter 7.

Communication

The second major category of network applications is communication. There are many types of communications, including e-mail, call centers, chat rooms, and voice. Blogging is also a type of communication, which we discuss in the section on Web 2.0.

Electronic Mail. Electronic mail (e-mail) is the largest-volume application running over the Internet. A recent study found that almost 90 percent of companies conduct business transactions via e-mail, and nearly 70 percent confirm that e-mail is tied to their means of generating revenue. For many users, e-mail has all but replaced the telephone.

Web-Based Call Centers. Effective personalized customer contact is becoming an important aspect of Web-based customer support. Such service is provided through *Web-based call centers*, also known as *customer care centers*. For example, if you need to contact a software vendor for technical support, you will usually be communicating with the vendor's Web-based call center, using e-mail, a telephone conversation, or a simultaneous voice/Web session. Web-based call centers are sometimes located in foreign countries such as India. Such *offshoring* is an important issue for U.S. companies.

Electronic Chat Rooms. *Electronic chat* refers to an arrangement whereby participants exchange conversational messages in real time. A **chat room** is a virtual meeting place where groups of regulars come to "gab." Chat programs allow you to send messages to people who are connected to the same channel of communication at the same time. Anyone can join in the online conversation. Messages are displayed on your screen as they arrive, even if you are in the middle of typing a message.

Two major types of chat programs exist. The first type is a Web-based chat program, which allows you to send messages to Internet users by using a Web browser and visiting a Web chat site (e.g., *http://chat.yahoo.com*). The second type is an e-mail-based (text-only) program called *Internet Relay Chat (IRC)*. A business can use IRC to interact with customers, provide online experts' answers to questions, and so on.

Voice Communication. When people need to communicate with one another from a distance, they use the telephone more frequently than any other communication device. With the plain old telephone service (POTS), every call opened up a dedicated circuit for the duration of the call. (A dedicated circuit connects you to the person you are talking with and is devoted only to your call.) In contrast, as we discuss in Technology Guide 5, the Internet divides data into packets, which traverse the Internet in random order and are reassembled at their destination.

With **Internet telephony**, also known as **voice-over Internet protocol or VoIP**, phone calls are treated as just another kind of data. That is, your analog voice signals are digitized, sectioned into packets, and then sent over the Internet. VoIP significantly reduces your monthly phone bills.

In the past, VoIP required a computer with a sound card and a microphone. Today, however, you do not need special phones or headsets for your computer. Vonage sells do-it-yourself kits through retailers such as Best Buy and Radio Shack.

Skype (*www.skype.com*) provides several voice-over IP services for free: calling other people on Skype, video calls on Skype, one-to-one and group chats, and conference calls with up to nine people (see Figure 5.5). Skype offers other functions for which users pay. Skype-Out allows you to make calls to land-line phones and mobile phones. SkypeIn is a number that your friends can call from any phone, and you pick up the call in Skype. Other functions include Skype Voicemail and Skype Short Message Service. IT's About Business 5.1 provides examples of businesses that have implemented VoIP systems.

FIGURE 5.5 Skype Interface *http://blogews .net/uploaded_images/sk pe_796446.bmp*

Collaboration

The third major category of network applications is collaboration. An important feature of modern organizations is that people collaborate to perform work. **Collaboration** refers to efforts by two or more entities (that is, individuals, teams, groups, or organizations) who work together to accomplish certain tasks. The term **work group** refers specifically to two or more individuals who act together to perform some task. If group members are in different locations, they constitute a **virtual group (team)**. Virtual groups conduct *virtual meetings*, that is, they "meet" electronically. **Virtual collaboration** (or *e-collaboration*) refers to the use of digital technologies that enable organizations or individuals to collaboratively plan, design, develop, manage, and research products, services, and innovative applications.

As one example of virtual collaboration, organizations interact with customers, suppliers, and other business partners to improve productivity and competitiveness. As we discussed earlier, a variety of tools are available to support collaboration. In this section we consider two of them: workflow technologies and groupware tools. Wikis are another type of virtual collaboration, and we discuss them in the section on Web 2.0.

Workflow Technologies. **Workflow** is the movement of information as it flows through the sequence of steps that make up an organization's work procedures. Workflow management makes it possible to pass documents, information, and tasks from one participant to another in a way that is governed by the organization's rules or procedures. Workflow systems are tools for automating business processes. One key benefit of these tools is that they place system controls in the hands of user departments.

Groupware. **Groupware** refers to software products that support groups of people who collaborate to accomplish a common task or goal. Groupware uses networks to connect people, even if the people are in the same room. In this section we will describe some of the most common groupware products.

IT's About Business

POM

5.1 Businesses Use Voice over Internet Protocol

Businesses of all kinds are discovering new functionality with VoIP technology that they did not have with POTS. Let's take a look at companies that have implemented VoIP systems.

One Coldwell Banker franchise, which sells about $1 billion of real estate each year, spends 85 percent of its advertising budget on print ads. However, 75 percent of home buyers begin their searches online. The franchise CEO suspected for several years that his firm was wasting advertising dollars. When the franchise installed its VoIP system, he found the evidence he was looking for. The franchise developed an application for its VoIP system that tracked inquiries from every ad. The firm uses a different phone number on each ad, and because calls come in as IP data packets, the software can analyze each call. The franchise now has the ability to gauge how effective its ads are, and it expects to shift ad spending to the Internet now that it has hard data showing that buyers respond better to online ads.

Similarly, when law firm Kenwick & West moved to new offices, it upgraded its voice systems to a VoIP system. The law firm quickly discovered the anytime, anywhere nature of VoIP. Where traditional phone systems are based on a single location per telephone number, with VoIP a user's location is irrelevant. The firm's attorneys were outfitted with wireless VoIP phones so that they could take calls when they were away from their desks. Traveling attorneys have software on their laptops that enables them to make and receive calls from wireless hot spots (discussed in Chapter 7) as if they were in the office. The mobility also proved convenient and cost effective for teams of attorneys who needed to work in a courthouse or at a client site for extended periods of time.

Muzak (*www.muzak.com*) has 50 offices spread across the United States and had 46 separate phone systems, nearly all with their own receptionist. The company also worked with multiple-service providers. Getting even basic things accomplished like adding a new employee to the system could take days. Since installing a VoIP system, however, Muzak has reduced the number of telephone receptionists to just a few at the main office. VoIP also saved the company money by allowing it to centralize its entire system, discarding 35 maintenance contracts for its PBXs. Muzak has tied its VoIP phone directory into Microsoft Outlook so employees can click on a name in their directory to make a call.

Cambridge Health Alliance (*www.cha.harvard.edu*), a healthcare organization, also benefited from VoIP's location independence. The organization, with 3 hospitals and 20 clinics, serves the Boston, Massachusetts, area, where people speak 40 languages. The company thus employs many interpreters, who could be at any facility at any time and therefore hard to locate. The VoIP system enabled the company to create a virtual call center, grouping interpreters on the network. Today, if a doctor needs a particular translator, he or she dials an extension to reach a dispatcher who can see which interpreter is available and where that person is. The call is then routed appropriately.

Sources: Compiled from T. Spangler, "VoIP: Grandpa Bell Meets the Future," *Baseline Magazine*, October 2, 2006; M. Gimein, "The Phone Companies Don't Get It," *BusinessWeek*, July 31, 2006; J. Hoover, "Five Things You Must Know about VoIP," *InformationWeek*, July 3, 2006; E. Horwitt, "ROI Insider: VoIP Helps Company Trim Costs, Response Time," *www.calliwave.com*, May 24, 2006; J. Rendon, "Making Strides with VoIP," *CIO Decisions*, July, 2005.

QUESTIONS

1. Look over these examples. Use the VoIP advantages to propose a VoIP system for your university. Which advantages would be most applicable to your university? What VoIP disadvantages would be most applicable to your university?
2. If you were the CEO of a traditional telephone company, what strategies would you implement to counter the threat of VoIP?

Groupware technologies are often integrated with other computer-based technologies to create *groupware suites*. (A *software suite* is created when several products are integrated into one system.) Lotus Notes/Domino is one of the most popular groupware suites.

The Lotus Notes/Domino suite (*www.ibm.com*) provides online collaboration capabilities, workgroup e-mail, distributed databases, bulletin whiteboards, text editing (electronic), document management, workflow capabilities, instant virtual meetings, application sharing, instant messaging, consensus building, voting, ranking, and various application development tools. All of these capabilities are integrated into one environment with a graphic, menu-based user interface. Two types of groupware technologies are electronic teleconferencing and real-time collaboration tools.

Electronic Teleconferencing. **Teleconferencing** is the use of electronic communication that allows two or more people at different locations to hold a simultaneous conference. There are several types of teleconferencing. The oldest and simplest is a telephone conference call, where several people talk to one another from multiple locations. The biggest disadvantage of conference calls is that they do not allow face-to-face communication. Also, participants in one location cannot see graphs, charts, and pictures at other locations. One solution is video teleconferencing, in which participants can see one another as well as the documents.

In a **videoconference**, participants in one location can see participants at other locations. The latest version of videoconferencing, called *telepresence*, enables participants to seamlessly share data, voice, pictures, graphics, and animation by electronic means. Conferees can also transmit data along with voice and video, which allows them to work on documents together and to exchange computer files.

Several companies are offering high-end telepresence systems. Hewlett-Packard's Halo system (*www.hp.com*), Cisco's TelePresence 3000 (*www.cisco.com*), and Polycom's HDX (*www.polycom.com*) use massive high-definition screens up to 8 feet wide to show people sitting around conference tables (see Figure 5.6). Telepresence systems also have advanced audio capabilities that let everyone talk at once without canceling out any voices. Telepresence systems can cost up to $400,000 for a room, with network management fees ranging up to $18,000 per month. Financial and consulting firms are quickly adopting telepresence systems. For example, the Blackstone Group (*www.blackstone.com*), a private equity

FIGURE 5.6
Telepresence System.
Sources: PRNewsFoto/
Polycom, Inc./
NewsCom

firm, has 40 telepresence rooms around the world, and Deloitte & Touche is installing 12 telepresence rooms.

Real-Time Collaboration Tools. The Internet, intranets, and extranets offer tremendous potential for people working in groups to interact synchronously and in real time. Real-time collaboration (RTC) tools help companies bridge time and space to make decisions and to collaborate on projects. RTC tools support synchronous communication of graphical and text-based information. These tools are being used in distance training, product demonstrations, customer support, and sales applications.

For example, computer-based **whiteboards** enable all participants to join in. During meetings, each user can view and draw on a single document "pasted" onto the electronic whiteboard on a computer screen. Computer-based whiteboards can be used by participants in the same room or across the world. Digital whiteboarding sessions can also be saved for later reference or other use.

Google

We mention Google in its own section because the company is developing and deploying applications that span discovery, communications, and collaboration (see Table W5.1 on this book's Web site). As you recall, the opening case of Chapter 1 discussed how Google is using its platform to enable its various strategies. The company's applications fall into five categories: (1) search applications; (2) "communicate, show, and share" applications; (3) mobile applications; (4) applications to "make your computer work better"; and (5) applications to "make your Web site work better." This link provides a look at the number and variety of Google applications: *www.google.com/intl/en/options/*.

Before you go on . . .

1. Describe the three network applications that we discussed in this section and the tools and technologies that support each one.
2. What are the business conditions that are leading to the increased importance of videoconferencing?

5.2 Web 2.0

Web 1.0 (discussed in Technology Guide 5) was the first generation of the Web. Key developments of Web 1.0 were the creation of Web sites and the commercialization of the Web. Users typically have minimal interaction with Web 1.0 sites, which provide information that users receive passively.

Web 2.0 is a popular term that has proved difficult to define. According to Tim O'Reilly, a noted blogger (see *www.oreillynet.com/lpt/a/6228*), **Web 2.0** is a loose collection of information technologies and applications, and of the Web sites that use them. These Web sites enrich the user experience by encouraging user participation, social interaction, and collaboration. Unlike Web 1.0 sites, Web 2.0 sites are not so much online places to visit as services to get something done, usually with other people. Web 2.0 is often referred to as the Live Web or the Next Web. Web 2.0 sites harness collective intelligence (e.g., Wikis); deliver functionality as services, rather than packaged software (e.g., Web services); and feature remixable applications and data (e.g., mashups).

We begin our exploration of Web 2.0 by examining the various Web 2.0 information technologies and applications. We then look at the categories of Web 2.0 sites, and we provide examples for each category.

Web 2.0 Information Technologies and Applications

The foundation for Web 2.0 is the global, Web-based platform that we discussed in Chapter 1. Information technologies and applications used by Web 2.0 sites include XML, AJAX, tagging, blogs, wikis, Really Simple Syndication, podcasting, and videocasting. Let's take a closer look at each of these technologies.

AJAX.   **AJAX** is a Web development technique that allows portions of Web pages to reload with fresh data instead of requiring the entire Web page to reload. This process speeds up response time and increases user satisfaction.

Tagging.   A **tag** is a keyword or term that describes a piece of information (e.g., blog, picture, article, video clip). Users typically choose tags that are meaningful to them. Tagging allows users to place information in multiple, overlapping associations rather than in rigid categories. For example, a photo of a car might be tagged with "Corvette," "sports car," and "Chevrolet." Tagging is the basis of *folksonomies*, which are user-generated classifications used to categorize and retrieve Web pages, photos, videos, and other Web content using tags.

Web site del.icio.us (*http://del.icio.us*) provides a system for organizing not just individuals' information but the entire Web. Del.icio.us is basically a tagging system, or a place to store all those links that do not fit in a "Favorites" folder. It not only collects your links in one place, but it organizes them as well. The Web site has no rules governing how its users create and use tags. Although each person makes his or her own tags, the product of all those individual decisions is well organized. That is, if you do a search on del.icio.us for all the pages that are tagged with a particular word, you are likely to come up with a very good selection of related Web sources.

Blogs and Blogging.   A **weblog** (**blog** for short) is a personal Web site, open to the public, in which the site creator expresses his or her feelings or opinions. *Bloggers*—people who create and maintain blogs—write stories, tell news, and provide links to other articles and Web sites that are of interest to them. The simplest method to create a blog is to sign up with a blogging service provider, such as *www.blogger.com* (now owned by Google; see Figure 5.7), *www.pitas.com*, and *www.sixapart.com*. The **blogosphere** is the term for the millions of blogs on the Web.

Companies are using blogs in different ways. Some companies listen to the blogosphere for marketing purposes, whereas others open themselves up to the public for input into their processes and products. Let's take a look at examples.

Boeing (*www.boeing.com*) is embracing the power of blogging, meaning that the company is ceding some control and exposing itself to criticism in exchange for a potentially more constructive dialog with the public, customers, and employees. Boeing's Flight Test Journal (*www.boeing.com/commercial/777family/200LR/flight_test/*) gave the public a look at the process the company and federal regulators went through to certify the firm's newest airplane, the Boeing 777. The company received positive feedback from bloggers, one of whom attested that it gave him assurance that the 777 would be a "good airplane."

Many companies are listening to consumers in the blogosphere who are offering their views on products. In marketing, these views are called consumer-generated media. Two companies, Cymfony (*www.cymfony.com*) and BuzzMetrics (*www.nielsenbuzzmetrics.com*), "mine the blogosphere" for their clients to provide information in several areas. They help their clients find ways to serve potential markets, from broad-based to niche markets. They also help their clients detect false rumors before they appear in the mainstream press, and they gauge the potency of a marketing push or the popularity of a new product.

Wikis.   A **wiki** is a Web site on which anyone can post material and make changes to other material. Wikis have an "edit" link on each page that allows anyone to add, change, or delete material, fostering easy collaboration.

FIGURE 5.7
Blogger.com

Wikis harness the collective intelligence of Internet users, meaning that the collective input of many individuals can produce outstanding results. Consider this example. Amazon and Barnes and Noble sell the same products, and they receive the same product descriptions and editorial content from their vendors. However, Amazon has led all bookstores in soliciting user input in the form of user editorial reviews. As a result, most Amazon users go directly to the user reviews when they are deciding whether to buy a book.

Wikipedia (*www.wikipedia.org*), the online encyclopedia, is the largest wiki in existence (see Figure 5.8). It contains almost 2 million articles in English, which are viewed almost 400 million times every day. The question is: How reliable are the articles? Many educators do not allow students to cite references from Wikipedia because content can be provided by anyone at any time. This process leads to questions about the authenticity of the content.

Consider, for example, the Wikipedia article on McDonald's Corporation. One anonymous contributor removed a link to Eric Schlosser's *Fast Food Nation*, a critique of McDonald's. He or she replaced it with a link to *McDonald's: Behind the Arches*, a book covering the history of the company. The Internet address of the person who made this change belonged to McDonald's, indicating that he or she was a company employee.

Wikipedia's volunteer administrators enforce a neutral point of view and encourage users to delete copy displaying clear bias. On the McDonald's page, the link to *Fast Food Nation* was quickly restored by users. In 2006, Wikipedia administrators barred the entire staff of Congress for a time for sabotaging one another's profiles.

Organizations use wikis in several ways. In project management, for example, wikis provide a central repository for capturing constantly updated product features and specifications, issue tracking and resolving problems, and maintaining project histories. In addition, wikis enable companies to collaborate with customers, suppliers, and other business partners on projects. Wikis are also useful in knowledge management. For example, companies use

FIGURE 5.8
Wikipedia
www.wikipedia.org

wikis to keep enterprisewide documents, such as guidelines and frequently asked questions, accurate and current.

Dresdner Kleinwort Wasserstein (*www.dresdnerkleinwort.com*), the international investment bank, uses a wiki to create meeting agendas and to post training videos for new hires. Participants in a project can avoid endless e-mail exchanges and instead post documents, schedules, and other materials on the wiki, which anyone else on the project can then append with changes or comments. Six months after the bank launched the wiki, the number of e-mails on projects using the wiki had declined by 75 percent.

Really Simple Syndication. **Really Simple Syndication (RSS)** allows users to receive the information they want (customized information), when they want it, without having to surf thousands of Web sites. RSS allows anyone to syndicate (publish) his or her blog, or any other content, to anyone who has an interest in subscribing. When changes to the content are made, subscribers receive a notification of the changes and an idea of what the new content contains. Subscribers can click on a link that will take them to the full text of the new content. You can find thousands of Web sites that offer RSS feeds at Syndic8 (*www.syndic8.com*) and NewsIsFree (*www.newsisfree.com*). Figure 5.9 shows an example of how an RSS can be searched and RSS feeds located.

To start using RSS, you need a special news reader that displays RSS content feeds from Web sites you select. There are many such readers available, several of which are free. Examples of readers are AmphetaDesk (*www.disobey.com/amphetadesk*) and Pluck (*www.pluck.com*). For an excellent tutorial of RSS, visit *www.mnot.net/rss/tutorial.*

Podcasts and Videocasts.   A **podcast** is a digital audio file that is distributed over the Web using RSS for playback on portable media players or personal computers. A **videocast** is the same as a podcast, except that it is a digital video file. IT's About Business 5.2 shows how Cheerios uses podcasts to develop a closer relationship with its customers.

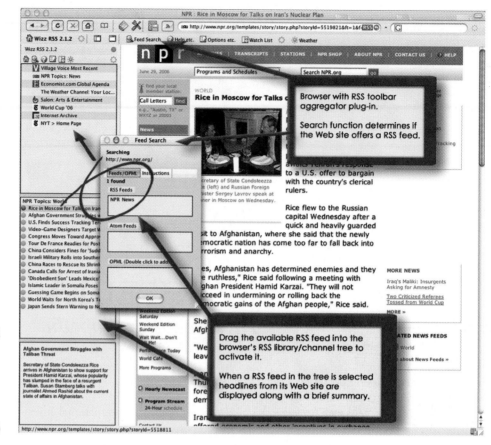

FIGURE 5.9 National Public Radio's (NPR) Web site with RSS toolbar aggregator and search function. (Courtesy of NPR. Used with permission.)

Categories of Web 2.0 Sites

Web 2.0 sites that use some or all of the technologies and applications we have just discussed can be grouped into several categories: social media, aggregators, and mashups. In this section, we discuss these categories, and we examine the various ways in which business utilize them.

Social Networking. **Social networking** Web sites allow users to upload their content to the Web, in the form of text (for example, blogs), voice (for example, podcasts), images, and videos (for example, videocasts). Social networking sites provide an easy, interactive way to communicate and collaborate with others on the Web. These sites can be a useful way to find like-minded people online, either to pursue an interest or a goal or just to help establish a sense of community among people who may never meet in the real world. Well-known social networking sites include:

- MySpace (*www.myspace.com*) and FaceBook (*www.facebook.com*): popular social networking Web sites
- Flickr (*www.flickr.com*): a photo-sharing Web site, widely used by bloggers as a photo repository
- Last.fm (*www.last.fm*): a personalized streaming Web-based radio station based on a profile of your musical tastes

IT's About Business

5.2   Cheerios: Building the Customer Relationship with Podcasting

Cheerios cereal is a brand of the Consumer Packaged Goods (CPG) division of General Mills (*www .generalmills.com*). In keeping with an important characteristic of Web 2.0, CPG decided to supplement its marketing efforts in television (a passive medium) with user-generated content (an interactive medium).

To accomplish this goal, Cheerios launched a Web site (*www.cheerios.com*) to provide more content to consumers than just information about cereal. One theme for the site was "stories from parents," giving users a place to share proud parenting moments through both photos and narratives. Over the years, Cheerios had received many stories, some of which it used as the basis for its advertising.

Cheerios, aware that many parents go online to seek out knowledge and answers to questions on raising their children, decided to use multiple delivery mechanisms to deliver the Web site's content. One of the mechanisms they chose is podcasting because it reflects the lifestyle of modern parents, who rely on multitasking. Podcasting provides the content whenever and wherever parents want it. The Cheerios podcasts utilized rich content from a partnership with KidsHealth (*www.kidshealth.org*)—a

Web site that provides health information about children—and they made the broadcasts relatively brief so as not to impose on busy parents.

Cheerios also implemented a wiki for parents to share their collective wisdom. Parents may share their experiences with text, voice (podcasts), and video (videocasts). Reaction to the Cheerios Web site has been very positive.

Sources: Compiled from J. Havens, "Leveraging Emotion and Interactivity for True Consumer Value," *http://podcasting .about.com/od/corporatecasestudies/a/cheerioscstudy.htm*, accessed April 20, 2007; S. Baker, "Electronic Paper Could Put Blogs on Cheerios," *BusinessWeek*, December 16, 2005; *www.generalmills.com* and *www.cheerios.com*, accessed April 20, 2007.

QUESTIONS

1. What is the relationship between Cheerios' use of blogs and 1:1, or personalized, marketing?
2. What are the advantages of Cheerios' strategy of relying on user-generated content rather than television advertising? What are the disadvantages? Will this strategy be successful in the long run? Why or why not? Be specific.

- LinkedIn (*www.linkedin.com*): a business-oriented social networking site that is valuable for recruiting, sales, and investment. The company makes money from advertising and services. People—mainly the site's 60,000 recruiters—pay an average of $3,600 per year for premium features such as sending messages to LinkedIn members outside their own networks. Corporate members pay fees of up to six figures for access to the network.
- Tagworld (*www.tagworld.com*): a Web site that people utilize for sharing blogs, photos, and music, as well as for online dating. All of the site's content can be tagged for easy searching.
- Twitter (*http://twitter.com*): a site that allows users to post short updates on their lives (no more than 160 characters) via the Web site, instant messaging, or mobile devices;
- YouTube (*www.youtube.com*): a social networking site for video uploads.

Social networking is also being used to help small businesses around the world. An excellent example is Kiva (*www.kiva.org*), a Web site through which people can loan money to small businesses in the developing world. Kiva's objective is to help poor working people in those countries achieve economic independence. Loans usually last from 6 to 12 months. During that time, lenders receive e-mail updates from the businesses they have sponsored. Kiva posts profiles of people who need capital to start or expand their businesses. Potential lenders read through pages of business ideas and then grant loans in increments as tiny as $25. PayPal processes the transactions for free, and lenders receive monthly repayments.

Aggregators. **Aggregators** are Web sites that provide collections of content from the Web. Well-known aggregator Web sites include:

- Bloglines (*www.bloglines.com*): collect blogs and news from all over the Web and present it in one, consistent, updated format;
- Digg (*www.digg.com*): is part news site, part blog, and part forum. Users suggest and rate news stories, which are then ranked based on this feedback.
- Simply Hired (*www.simplyhired.com*): searches some 4.5 million listings on job and corporate Web sites and contacts subscribers via an RSS feed or an e-mail alert when a job that meets their parameters is listed.
- Technorati (*www.technorati.com*): contains information on all blogs in the blogosphere. It shows how many other blogs link to a particular blog, and it ranks blogs by topic.

Mashups. Mashup means to "mix and match" content from other parts of the Web. A **mashup** is a Web site that takes content from a number of other Web sites and mixes them together to create a new kind of content. The launch of Google Maps is credited with providing the start for mashups. You can take a map from Google, add your own data, and then display a map mashup on your Web site that plots crime scenes, cars for sale, or virtually any other subject.

New tools are emerging to build location mashups. For example, Pipes from Yahoo (*http://pipes.yahoo.com*) is a service that lets users visually remix data feeds and create mashups, using drag-and-drop features to connect multiple Web data sources. IT's About Business 5.3 provides several illustrations of organizations that are creating mashups.

IT's About Business

5.3 Businesses Use Mashups

SkiBonk (*www.skibonk.com*) is a business that utilizes a mashup to provide a clearinghouse for ski information (see Figure 5.10). Skibonk overlays Google Maps with slope conditions, trail maps, live Webcams, ski area locations, and local weather reports. The Web site also integrates information on lodging, gear, and food. A skier icon marks slope locations worldwide on the map, and a click brings up a multitude of information. Users can submit additional or edited data. Together, SkiBonk, and its sister site, WeatherBonk (*www.weatherbonk.com*), pull information from more than 20 sources.

Another business that relies on a mashup is John L. Scott Real Estate. This firm integrated Microsoft's Virtual Earth (*http://maps.live.com*) services into its Web site, letting potential clients search for properties in the northwestern United States using three-dimensional aerial views and interactive maps (see *www.johnlscott.com/SearchInteractive.aspx*). The company's property search mashup boosted online visits, with return visits increasing 46 percent.

Starbucks (*www.starbucks.com*) integrated Map-Point (the Microsoft mapping product that competes with Google Maps) into its Web site to make it easier for customers to find its locations, both domestic and international. When consumers click on one of the stores identified by Starbucks' locator, they receive information on the store's facilities and the option to request driving directions and a route map. Starbucks customers can search for stores that have

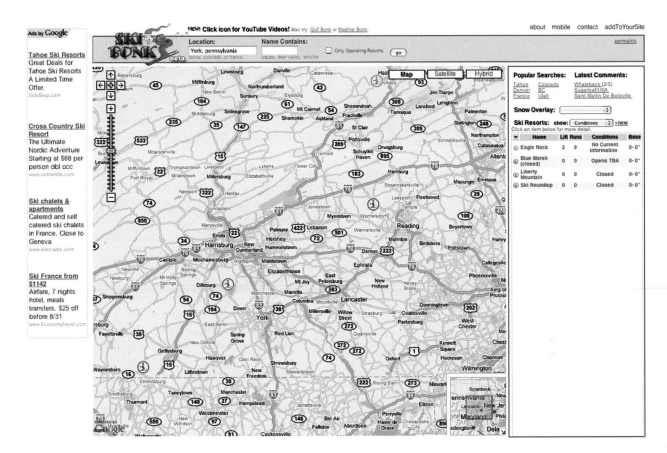

FIGURE 5.10   A skibonk page for York, Pennsylvania.

Wi-Fi hot spots, offer drive-through windows, or serve lunch.

Choice Hotels International (*www.choicehotels.com*), operator of eight hotel chains, including Comfort Inn and Clarion, uses MapPoint to let visitors search for a place to stop for the night. Its mashup includes trip-planning tools.

Liaison Canada/U.S., a transportation and logistics company, has created a location mashup for internal use. The company's dispatchers use the site to track trucks, monitor traffic, reroute vehicles, and decrease delivery times. The mashup integrates radio frequency identification tracking data, aerial photography, and interactive maps from Microsoft's Virtual Earth. Additional data is presented below the map in a table. If a dispatcher wants to know more about one of the trucks, he can click on the driver's ID to bring up that information.

Healthmap (*www.healthmap.org*) is a mashup that integrates data sources to present a unified view of infectious diseases around the world and their effects on people and animals. Among the sources it pulls together are Google News, global electronic reporting systems that track disease outbreaks, and official alerts from the World Health Organization. These data are categorized by disease type and displayed on a map. Visitors can link to the original alerts from the map. The mashup is widely used by both public health officials and international travelers.

ChicagoCrime (*www.chicagocrime.org*) is a mashup that combines the Chicago Police Department's publicly available Web site of crime-report information with Google Maps to create an easy-to-use guide to crime in Chicago.

Sources: Compiled from E. Malykhina, "Maps Meet Mashups," *InformationWeek*, March 19, 2007; T. Claburn, "Google Maps Bring Mashups to the Masses," *Information-Week*, April 7, 2007; S. Wellman, "Do It Yourself Map Mashups Now on Google Maps," *InformationWeek*, April 5, 2007; G. Gruman, "Enterprise Mashups," *InfoWorld*, July 28, 2006; E. Lai, "Microsoft Seeks Mashups for Live Search in Bid to Best Google," *Computerworld*, March 14, 2007; *www.skibonk.com*, *www.starbucks.com*, *www.choicehotel.com*, *www.healthmap.org*, *www.chicagocrime.org*, *www.johnlscott.com/SearchInteractive.aspx*, *http://maps.live.com*, accessed April 21, 2007.

QUESTIONS

1. Apply the IT applications that these examples illustrate to your university. Give an example of a mashup that would be useful to your university. Describe your mashup, its functions, and its target audience. What data sources would you access, mix, and match?
2. You are an entrepreneur and would like to start a mashup (e.g., like SkiBonk). Describe the mashup that you would create. List several ways that you could make money with your mashup.

Web Services and Service-Oriented Architecture

Web services are applications, delivered over the Internet, that users can select and combine through almost any device, from personal computers to mobile phones. By using a set of shared protocols and standards, these applications permit different systems to "talk" with one another—that is, to share data and services—without requiring human beings to translate the conversations.

Web services have great potential because they can be used in a variety of environments: over the Internet, on an intranet inside a corporate firewall, on an extranet set up by business partners. Web services perform a wide variety of tasks, from automating business processes to integrating components of an enterprisewide system to streamlining online buying and selling.

Web services are based on four key standards, or protocols: XML, SOAP, WSDL, and UDDI.

Extensible Markup Language (*XML*) makes it easier to exchange data among a variety of applications and to validate and interpret such data. An XML document describes a Web service, and it includes information detailing exactly how the Web service can be run. (We describe XML in more detail in Technology Guide 2.)

Simple Object Access Protocol (*SOAP*) is a set of rules that define how messages can be exchanged among different network systems and applications through the use of XML. These rules establish a common standard, or protocol, that allows different Web services to interoperate. For example, Visual Basic clients can use SOAP to access a Java server. SOAP runs on all hardware and software systems.

The *Web Services Description Language* (*WSDL*) is used to create the XML document that describes the tasks performed by various Web services. Tools such as VisualStudio.Net automate the process of accessing the WSDL, reading it, and coding the application to reference the specific Web service.

Universal Description, Discovery, and Integration (*UDDI*) allows users to search for needed Web services by creating public or private searchable directories of these services. In other words, it is the registry of descriptions of Web services.

An interesting Web service, called a widget, is being used by many companies for advertising. IT's About Business 5.4 shows how widgets are being used.

IT's About Business

5.4   Widgets on the Web

Online advertisement creators are pushing a new idea. They are putting a brand on a "Web service" that is so useful or entertaining—a video game, a calculator, or a live sports update—that people will download it; paste it onto their personal blogs, social networking sites, or personal computers; use it again and again; and share it with their friends. These Web services are called widgets. On the screen, most widgets resemble a small window on the user's desktop or Web page, similar to picture-in-picture television sets. What the widgets do, and how they promote their clients vary.

For example, Purina has created a widget that alerts pet owners about good dog-walking weather. Hewlett-Packard offered a downloadable March Madness scoreboard that continuously pulled down the results of the college basketball tournament. Finally, 20th Century Fox promoted *Live Free or Die Hard* with an iTunes player that also blurts out quotes from the movie.

These promotions offer multiple advantages to advertisers. To begin with, once these widgets are placed onto personal Web pages, they tend to live longer than traditional ads. This is not necessarily because users care about the brand, but because they like the interactive feature they downloaded it for. Furthermore, friends who see the widget on someone else's blog or MySpace profile might want to copy it for themselves.

Clearspring (*www.clearspring.com*) and Freewebs (*http://members.freewebs.com*) are two companies that make widgets. Freewebs created a Reebok widget that lets you design your own sneaker and a zombie-killing video game to promote the movie *Ghost Rider*. In addition to making widgets, Clearspring

tracks wigets as they spread across the Internet, providing its clients with information about a potential customer base.

Yahoo now has more than 4,300 widgets in its gallery, including one from Target that counts down the days until Christmas and others that show live webcam views of Hong Kong traffic, Australian beaches, and New York City's Greenwich Village. Apple and Microsoft have implemented desktop tools such as constantly updating stock tickers, news feeds, and airline schedules.

Despite all these benefits, widgets present certain problems. For one thing, they utilize computer resources, which slows down page loads. In addition, advertisers are reluctant to pay top prices for widgets because their influence on consumers is unknown. Also, the longer a popular widget lives online, the less incentive there is for an advertiser to pay for a new one.

Sources: Compiled from K. Hart, "Wave of Widgets Spreads on the Web," *Washington Post*, April 9, 2007; T. Claburn, "Yahoo Updates Widget Platform," *Information-Week*, March 22, 2007; U. Hedquist, "Widgets: A Wedge into Your System?" *Computerworld*, January 22, 2007; M. Elgan, "Go Wild With Widgets," *Computerworld*, October 27, 2006.

QUESTIONS

1. What types of widgets would you propose for your university to develop? What would their target audience be? What would these widgets provide for your university?
2. Are widgets a viable advertising strategy? Why or why not?

A **service-oriented architecture** (SOA) is an IT architecture that makes it possible to construct business applications using Web services. The Web services can be reused across an organization in other applications. So, a Web service that checks a consumer's credit could be used with a service that processes a mortgage application or a service that processes a credit card application. The closing case in this chapter illustrates the use of SOA in a large regional bank.

Before you go on . . .

1. Describe the underlying technologies, applications, and types of Web sites that comprise Web 2.0.
2. Describe the function of Web services.
3. Describe the function of service-oriented architectures.

5.3 E-Learning and Distance Learning

E-learning and distance learning are not the same thing, but they do overlap. **E-learning** refers to learning supported by the Web. It can take place inside classrooms as a support to conventional teaching, such as when students work on the Web during class. It also can take place in virtual classrooms, in which all coursework is done online and classes do not meet face to face. In these cases, e-learning is a part of distance learning. **Distance learning (DL)** refers to any learning situation in which teachers and students do not meet face to face.

Today, the Web provides a multimedia interactive environment for self-study. Web-enabled systems make knowledge accessible to those who need it, when they need it, any time, anywhere. For this reason, E-learning and DL can be useful for both formal education and corporate training.

For example, Gap (*www.gap.com*) used a combination of classroom and e-learning instruction to school its information technology managers in leadership skills. Gap employed an interactive e-learning course to help its leaders develop the management and coaching tools they need to assess and enhance their employees' skills and competencies. The company placed the e-learning course between an in-person, three-hour kickoff program that included a demonstration of the software and a two-day classroom course designed to reinforce the material presented in the e-learning program.

Using simulation and interactive scenarios, the course instructs students on how to assess staffers' skills and competencies, identify the best management approach in assisting and directing people based on their competencies, and partner with individuals to help them be more productive and self-sufficient.

The Benefits and Drawbacks of E-Learning

E-learning has many benefits. For example, online materials can deliver very current content that is of high quality (created by content experts) and consistent (presented the same way every time). It also gives students the flexibility to learn from any place, at any time, and at their own pace. In corporate training centers that use e-learning, learning time generally is shorter, which means that more people can be trained within a given timeframe. This system reduces training costs as well as the expense of renting facility space.

Despite these benefits, e-learning has some drawbacks. To begin with, students must be computer literate. Also, they may miss the face-to-face interaction with instructors. Finally, assessing students' work can be problematic because instructors really do not know who completed the assignments.

E-learning does not usually replace the classroom setting. Rather, it enhances it by taking advantage of new content and delivery technologies. Advanced e-learning support environments, such as Blackboard (*www.blackboard.com*), add value to traditional learning in higher education.

Virtual Universities

Virtual universities are online universities from which students take classes from home or at an off-site location, via the Internet. A large number of existing universities offer online education of some form. Some universities, such as the University of Phoenix (*www.phoenix.edu*), California Virtual Campus (*www.cvc.edu*), and the University of Maryland (*www.umuc.edu/gen/virtuniv.shtml*), offer thousands of courses and dozens of degrees to students worldwide, all online. Other universities offer limited online courses and degrees but use innovative teaching methods and multimedia support in the traditional classroom.

Before you go on . . .

1. Differentiate between e-learning and distance learning.
2. Describe virtual universities.

5.4 Telecommuting

Knowledge workers are being called the distributed workforce. This group of highly prized workers is now able to work anywhere and anytime, a process called **telecommuting**. Distributed workers are those who have no permanent office at their companies, preferring to work at home offices, in airport lounges or client conference rooms, or on a high school stadium bleacher. The growth of the distributed workforce is driven by globalization, extremely long commutes to work, rising gasoline prices, ubiquitous broadband communications links (wireline and wireless), and powerful laptop computers and computing devices.

Currently, about 12 percent of the U.S. workforce qualifies as distributed. At IBM, 40 percent of the workforce has no office at the company; at AT&T, more than 30 percent of its managers are distributed; and at Sun Microsystems, nearly 50 percent of employees are distributed, saving the company $300 million in real estate costs. Sun also notes that its distributed workers are 15 percent more productive than their coworkers in offices.

Telecommuting has a number of potential advantages for employees, employers, and society. For employees, the benefits include reduced stress and improved family life. In addition, telecommuting offers employment opportunities for housebound people such as single parents and persons with disabilities. Employer benefits include increased productivity, the ability to retain skilled employees, and the ability to attract employees who don't live within commuting distance.

Telecommuting also has some potential disadvantages, however. For employees, the major disadvantages are increased feelings of isolation, possible loss of fringe benefits, lower pay (in some cases), no workplace visibility, the potential for slower promotions, and lack of socialization. The major disadvantages to employers are difficulties in supervising work, potential data security problems, and training costs.

Before you go on . . .

1. What is telecommuting? Do you think you would like to telecommute?
2. What are the advantages and disadvantages of telecommuting from the viewpoint of the employee? from the viewpoint of the organization?

What's in [IT] for Me?

For the Accounting Major

Accounting personnel use corporate intranets and portals to consolidate transaction data from legacy systems to provide an overall view of internal projects. This view contains the current costs charged to each project, the number of hours spent on each project by individual employees, and an analysis of how actual costs compare to projected costs. Finally, accounting personnel use Internet access to government and professional Web sites to stay informed on legal and other changes affecting their profession.

For the Finance Major

Corporate intranets and portals can provide a model to evaluate the risks of a project or an investment. Financial analysts use two types of data in the model: historical transaction data from corporate databases via the intranet, and industry data obtained via the Internet. In addition, financial services firms can use the Web for marketing and to provide services.

For the Marketing Major

Marketing managers use corporate intranets and portals to coordinate the activities of the sales force. Sales personnel access corporate portals via the intranet to discover updates on pricing, promotion, rebates, customer information, and information about competitors. Sales staff can also download and customize presentations for their customers. The Internet, particularly the Web, opens a completely new marketing channel for many industries. Just how advertising, purchasing, and information dispensation should occur appears to vary from industry to industry, product to product, and service to service.

For the Production/Operations Management Major

Companies are using intranets and portals to speed product development by providing the development team with three-dimensional models and animation. All team members can access the models for faster exploration of ideas and enhanced feedback. Corporate portals, accessed via intranets, enable managers to carefully supervise their inventories as well as real-time production on assembly lines. Extranets are also proving valuable as communication formats for joint research and design efforts among companies. The Internet is also a great source of cutting-edge information for POM managers.

For the Human Resources Management Major

Human resources personnel use portals and intranets to publish corporate policy manuals, job postings, company telephone directories, and training classes. Many companies deliver online training obtained from the Internet to employees through their intranets. Human resources departments use intranets to offer employees healthcare, savings, and benefit plans, as well as the opportunity to take competency tests online. The Internet supports worldwide recruiting efforts, and it can also be the communications platform for supporting geographically dispersed work teams.

For the MIS Major

As important as the networking technology infrastructure is, it is invisible to users (unless something goes wrong). The MIS function is responsible for keeping all organizational networks up and running all the time. MIS personnel, therefore, provide all users with an "eye to the world" and the ability to compute, communicate, and collaborate anytime, anywhere. For example, organizations have access to experts at remote locations without having to duplicate that expertise in multiple areas of the firm. Virtual teaming allows experts physically located in different cities to work on projects as though they were in the same office.

1. **Describe the four major network applications.**

   Networks support discovery, communication, collaboration, and Web services. Discovery involves browsing and information retrieval, and provides users the ability to view information in databases, download it, and/or process it. Discovery tools include search engines, directories, and portals. Networks provide fast, inexpensive communications, via e-mail, call centers, chat rooms, voice communications, and blogs. Collaboration refers to mutual efforts by two or more entities (individuals, groups, or companies) who work together to accomplish tasks. Collaboration is enabled by workflow systems and groupware. We discuss Web services in the next summary.

2. **Discuss the various technologies, applications, and Web sites that fall under the umbrella of Web 2.0.**

   Information technologies and applications used by Web 2.0 sites include XML (discussed in Technology Guide 2), AJAX, tagging, blogs, Wikis, Really Simple Syndication, podcasting, and videocasting. AJAX is a Web development technique that allows portions of Web pages to reload with fresh data instead of requiring the entire Web page to reload. This process speeds up response time and increases user satisfaction. A tag is a keyword or term that describes a piece of information. Users typically choose tags that are meaningful to them. A weblog (blog for short) is a personal Web site, open to the public, in which the site creator expresses his or her feelings or opinions. A wiki is a Web site on which anyone can post material and make changes to other material.

   Really Simple Syndication (RSS) allows anyone to syndicate (publish) his or her blog, or any other content, to anyone who has an interest in subscribing. When changes to the content are made, the subscribers get a notification of the changes and an idea of what the new content contains. The subscriber can click on a link that will take them to the full text of the new content.

   A podcast is a digital audio file that is distributed over the Web using Really Simple Syndication for playback on portable media players or personal computers. A videocast is the same as a podcast, except that it is a digital video file.

   Web 2.0 Web sites that use some or all of these technologies and applications may be grouped into several categories: social media, aggregators, and mashups. Social networking Web sites allow users to upload their content to the Web, in the form of text (e.g., blogs), voice (e.g., podcasts), images, and videos (e.g., videocasts). Social networking sites provide an easy, interactive way to communicate and collaborate with others on the Web. Aggregators are Web sites that provide collections of content from the Web. A mashup is a Web site that takes content from a number of other Web sites and mixes them together to create a new kind of content. Web services are self-contained, self-describing applications, delivered over the Internet, that users can select and combine through almost any device (from personal computers to mobile phones). By using a set of shared protocols and standards, these applications permit different systems to talk with one another—that is, to share data and services—without requiring human beings to translate the conversations.

3. **Differentiate between e-learning and distance learning.**

   E-learning refers to learning supported by the Web. It can take place inside classrooms as a support to conventional teaching, such as when students work on the Web during class. It also can take place in *virtual classrooms*, in which all coursework is done online and classes do not meet face to face. In these cases, e-learning is a part of distance learning. Distance learning refers to any learning situation in which teachers and students do not meet face to face.

4. **Understand the advantages and disadvantages of telecommuting for both employers and employees.**

   The benefits of telecommuting for employees include less stress, improved family life, and employment opportunities for housebound people. Telecommuting can provide the organization with increased productivity, the ability to retain skilled employees, and the ability to tap the remote labor pool.

The major disadvantages for employees are increased feelings of isolation, possible loss of fringe benefits, lower pay (in some cases), no workplace visibility, the potential for slower promotions, and lack of socialization. The major disadvantages to employers are difficulties in supervising work, potential data security problems, training costs, and the high cost of equipping and maintaining telecommuters' homes.

Chapter Glossary

affinity portal A Web site that offers a single point of entry to an entire community of affiliated interests.

aggregators Web sites that provide collections of content from the Web.

AJAX A Web development technique that allows portions of Web pages to reload with fresh data instead of requiring the entire Web page to reload.

blog (short for Weblog) A personal Web site, open to the public, in which the site creator expresses his or her feelings or opinions.

blogosphere The term for the millions of blogs on the Web.

chat room A virtual meeting place where groups of regulars come to "gab" electronically.

collaboration Mutual efforts by two or more individuals who perform activities in order to accomplish certain tasks.

commercial (public) portal A Web site that offers fairly routine content for diverse audiences; offers customization only at the user interface.

corporate portal A Web site that provides a single point of access to critical business information located inside and outside of an organization.

distance learning (DL) Learning situations in which teachers and students do not meet face to face.

e-learning Learning supported by the Web; can be done inside traditional classrooms or in virtual classrooms.

groupware Software products that support groups of people who collaborate on a common task or goal and that provide a way for groups to share resources.

industrywide portal A Web-based gateway to information and knowledge for an entire industry.

Internet telephony (voice-over Internet protocol or VoIP) Use of the Internet as the transmission medium for telephone calls.

mashup A Web site that takes content from a number of other Web sites and mixes them together to create a new kind of content.

metasearch engine A computer program that searches several engines at once and integrates the findings of the various search engines to answer queries posted by users.

mobile portal A Web site that is accessible from mobile devices.

podcast A digital audio file that is distributed over the Web using Really Simple Syndication for playback on portable media players or personal computers.

portal A Web-based personalized gateway to information and knowledge that provides information from disparate information systems and the Internet, using advanced search and indexing techniques.

Really Simple Syndication (RSS) Allows anyone to syndicate (publish) his or her blog, or any other content, to anyone who has an interest in subscribing.

search engine A computer program that searches for specific information by keywords and reports the results.

service-oriented architecture (SOA) An IT architecture that makes it possible to construct business applications using Web services, which can be reused across an organization in other applications.

social networking Web sites that allow users to upload their content to the Web, in the form of text (for example, blogs), voice (for example, podcasts), images, and videos (for example, videocasts).

tag A keyword or term, chosen by users, that describes a piece of information (for example, a blog, a picture, an article, or a video clip).

telecommuting A work arrangement whereby employees work at home, at the customer's premises, in special workplaces, or while traveling, usually using a computer linked to their place of employment.

teleconferencing The use of electronic communication that allows two or more people at different locations to have a simultaneous conference.

topology The physical layout and connectivity of a network.

videocast A digital video file that is distributed over the Web using Really Simple Syndication for playback on portable media players or personal computers.

videoconference A virtual meeting in which participants in one location can see and hear participants at other locations and can share data and graphics by electronic means.

virtual collaboration The use of digital technologies that enable organizations or individuals to collaboratively plan, design, develop, manage, and research products, services, and innovative information systems and electronic commerce applications.

virtual group (team) A work group whose members are in different locations and who meet electronically.

virtual universities Online universities from which students take classes from home or an off-site location, via the Internet.

voice over Internet Protocol (VoIP; also Internet telephony) A communications system in which analog voice signals are digitized, sectioned into packets, and then sent over the Internet.

Web 2.0 A loose collection of information technologies and applications, and the Web sites that use them; the

Web sites enrich the user experience by encouraging user participation, social interaction, and collaboration.

Web services Self-contained business/consumer modular applications delivered over the Internet.

weblog A personal Web site, open to the public, in which the site owner expresses his or her feelings or opinions.

whiteboard An area on a computer display screen on which multiple users can write or draw; multiple users can use a single document "pasted" onto the screen.

wiki A Web site on which anyone can post material and make changes quickly, without using difficult commands.

work group Two or more individuals who act together to perform some task, on either a permanent or temporary basis.

workflow The movement of information as it flows through the sequence of steps that make up an organization's work procedures.

Discussion Questions

1. Apply Porter's competitive forces model, which we discussed in Chapter 2, to Google. Address each component of the model as it pertains to Google. Can Google maintain its competitive advantage? If so, how? If not, why not?
2. How would you describe Web 2.0 to someone who has not taken a course in information systems?
3. If you were the CEO of a company, would you pay any attention to blogs about your company? Why or why not? If yes, would you consider some blogs to be more important or reliable than others? If so, which ones? How would you find blogs relating to your company?
4. Is it a good idea for a business major to join LinkedIn as a student? Why or why not?
5. How are the network applications of communication and collaboration related? Do communication tools also support collaboration? Give examples.

Problem-Solving Activities

1. You plan to take a two-week vacation in Australia this year. Using the Internet, find information that will help you plan the trip. Such information includes, *but is not limited to*, the following:
   a. Geographical location and weather conditions at the time of your trip.
   b. Major tourist attractions and recreational facilities.
   c. Travel arrangements (airlines, approximate fares).
   d. Car rental; local tours.
   e. Alternatives for accommodation (within a moderate budget) and food.
   f. Estimated cost of the vacation (travel, lodging, food, recreation, shopping, etc.).
   g. Country regulations regarding the entrance of your dog which you would like to take with you.
   h. Shopping.
   i. Passport information (either to obtain one or to renew one).

   j. Information on the country's language and culture.
   k. What else do you think you should research before going to Australia?
2. From your own experience or from the vendor's information, list the major capabilities of Lotus Notes/Domino. Do the same for Microsoft Exchange. Compare and contrast the products. Explain how the products can be used to support knowledge workers and managers.
3. Visit Web sites of companies that manufacture telepresence products for the Internet. Prepare a report. Differentiate between telepresence products and videoconferencing products.
4. Access the Web site of your university. Does the Web site provide high-quality information (right amount, clear, accurate, etc.)? Do you think a high school student who is thinking of attending your university would feel the same way?

Web Activities

1. Access the Web site of the Recording Industry Association of America (*www.riaa.com*). Discuss what you find there regarding copyright infringement (that is, downloading music files). How do you feel about the RIAA's efforts to stop music downloads? Debate this issue from your point of view and from the RIAA's point of view.

2. Visit *www.cdt.org*. Find what technologies are available to track users' activities on the Internet.

3. Research the companies involved in Internet telephony (voice-over IP). Compare their offerings as to price, necessary technologies, ease of installation, and so on. Which company is the most attractive to you? Which company might be the most attractive for a large company?

4. Access some of the alternative search engines at *www.readwriteweb.com/archives/top_100_alternative_search_ engines.php*. Search for the same terms on several of the alternative search engines and on Google. Compare the results on breadth (number of results found) and precision (results are what you were looking for).

5. Second Life (www.secondlife.com) is a three-dimensional, online world built and owned by its residents. Residents of Second Life are avatars who have been created by real-world people. Access Second Life, learn about it, and create your own avatar to explore this world. Learn about the thousands of people who are making "real-world" money from operations in Second Life.

Team Assignments

1. Assign each group member to an integrated group support tool kit (Lotus Notes, Exceloncorp, Group-Wise, etc.). Have each member visit the Web site of the commercial developer and obtain information about this product. As a group, prepare a comparative table of the major similarities and differences among the kits.

2. Have each team download a free copy of Groove from *www.groove.net*. Install the software on the members' PCs and arrange collaborative sessions. What can the free software do for you? What are its limitations?

3. Each team should pick a subject that needs aggregation. Set up the plans for an aggregator Web site to accomplish this mission. Present to the class.

4. Enter *www.podcasting-tools.com*. Explain how to record a podcast and make it available on the Web. Each team will create a podcast on some idea in this course and make it available online.

CLOSING CASE | **Service-Oriented Architecture at TD Banknorth**   MKT POM

THE BUSINESS PROBLEM   The bank of a decade ago has changed. It is no longer a place where customers primarily cash checks, pay bills, and update balance books. Instead, customers are much more likely to walk in seeking advice on how to invest, establish lines of credit, buy a home or life and auto insurance, or sign up for a credit card with loyalty rewards. Many people predicted that ATMs, online banking, and telephone banking would replace the bank branch. However, these predictions have not materialized. Instead, these have supplemented, but not replaced, the branch. In fact, over the past few years, the nation's banks have been rapidly building new branches. In addition, banks have been struggling to find a way to cut through information systems silos, where information systems supporting individual functional areas of the business do not communicate with one another.

TD Banknorth (*www.tdbanknorth.com*), a Maine-based bank with $40 billion in assets and 600 branches, followed the expansion trend. The bank pursued an aggressive acquisition program and was experiencing problems integrating the information systems of banks it acquired with its own systems.

To compound this problem, one of TD Banknorth's key technology suppliers announced that they would no longer support a crucial information system at the bank. TD Banknorth depended on this information system to integrate a new Internet banking application with the bank's transaction processing systems and databases (that is, its back-end systems). The bank had to quickly implement a new information systems to accomplish this integration task.

THE IT SOLUTION   TD Banknorth decided to implement a service-oriented architecture (SOA), which is an

IT architecture that allows an organization to make its applications and computing resources, such as databases, available as services that can be called upon when necessary. The bank knew where it wanted to go with SOA over the long term, but it started with a small project.

TD Banknorth first implemented a Web service to help employs input customer address changes much more efficiently. The service allows a call center agent or branch employee to initiate an address change, which then automatically updates all of the customer's accounts or products within the bank. The next two projects developed Web services to originate small-business loans and to handle project requests.

TD Banknorth then moved to a larger project, namely, its online banking system. The IT group implemented an SOA-based system with no major problems, but they learned some lessons along the way. The biggest challenge was figuring out the right granularity of each service, that is, how basic each service should be. The bank could create a service, for example, that allowed its employees to look up customer bank accounts. As an alternative, the bank could create that service with more functionality so that employees could look up all accounts, such as mortgages, insurance products, and credit cards. However, if the bank wanted to reuse the more functional service in other applications, then employees probably would receive more information than they need. The bottom line with services is that services should have a high reuse factor.

THE RESULTS The initial development costs for the SOA were $467,000. The payback over a 10-year period was estimated to be almost $11 million, with most of the savings coming from reduced mainframe usage. In addition, application development time was because the bank could reuse the services in other applications.

Sources: Compiled from A. Bernard, "SOA Taking Hold in Banking," *CIO Update*, February 2, 2007; M. Duvall, "SOA: TD Banknorth Is Banking on It," *Baseline Magazine*, October 2, 2006; C. Martens, "Users Offer SOA Advice: Start Small," *Computerworld*, November 13, 2006; P. Roberts, "Financial Services, High Pressure, High Performance," *www.techworld.com*, August 25, 2006; *www.tdbanknorth.com*, accessed April 25, 2007.

QUESTIONS

1. Why did TD Banknorth implement a service-oriented architecture?
2. Given the advantages discussed in this case, discuss potential disadvantages of TD Banknorth's use of SOA.

Web Resources   wiley.com/college/rainer

Student Web Site
- Web Quizzes
- Student Lecture Slides in PowerPoint
- Virtual Company ClubIT: Website and Assignments

WileyPLUS
- e-book
- Flash Cards
- How-To Animations for Microsoft Office

Telecommunications at Club IT

Go to the Club IT link on the *WileyPLUS* Web site. There you will find assignments that will ask you to advise the club owners on how they can use databases to track information for their business.

wiley.com/college/rainer

Chapter 6

E-Business and E-Commerce

Student Web Site
- Web Quizzes
- Lecture Slides in PowerPoint
- Virtual Company ClubIT: Website and Assignments

WileyPLUS
- e-book
- Flash Cards
- Software Skills Tutorials: Using Microsoft Office 2007
- How-To Animations for Microsoft Office

What's in [IT] for me? ACC FIN MKT POM HRM MIS

Electronic Commerce Provides Another Channel to the Customer

MKT

The Business Problem

In 1998, J&R Electronics (*www.jr.com*) was a bricks-and-mortar, family-owned business, selling a large variety of consumer electronics products from its 250,000-square-foot store in lower Manhattan, and also via catalog orders. The company featured highly competitive pricing and an enormous inventory. In addition, it was a "first-stop" showcase for manufacturers' products, meaning that vendors would offer the most recent release of an MP3 player or the latest version of a video game before it appeared anywhere else. J&R was also quick to pick up on technology trends. For example, the store created a separate Apple room at a time when most consumer electronics stores were concentrating almost exclusively on personal computers. J&R was also at the forefront in recognizing that DVDs would replace VHS tapes.

Equally important, J&R's sales staff had the well-earned reputation of excelling at explaining the workings of the latest high-tech products to customers who ranged from technology neophytes to Wall Street analysts.

Although J&R enjoyed great success in its one location, the company realized that it would always be limited by geography. To overcome this limitation, J&R had two options: (1) expand its bricks-and-mortar operations by building more stores, or (2) turn to the Internet and electronic commerce.

The IT Solutions

J&R decided to make a commitment to electronic commerce. The company developed its first Web site (*www.jr.com*) using an electronic commerce product from InterWorld Corporation. At that time, the InterWorld product represented the best practices in online merchandising, order processing, and customer service. The product also enabled businesses to extend their existing business processes onto the Web. Unfortunately, InterWorld failed in 2001 during the dot-com crash.

After InterWorld's demise, J&R had no support for the product, so the company customized it themselves. J&R's technology staff created an e-commerce solution that supported the company's 400,000 stock-keeping units (SKUs). However, the platform lacked key capabilities such as the ability to collect and display customer reviews. The platform also could not provide supporting information, for example, inventory statistics and shipping time. This information was a mainstay of large retail Web sites like Amazon.

Despite these limitations, in 2006 *www.jr.com* was ranked among the nation's 50 top e-tailers by *Internet Retailer* magazine, based on factors such as success in adapting new technologies and functions, as well as metrics such as the time needed to fully download the site.

In 2007, after J&R's technology staff had done all it could with the old product, the company decided to completely revamp its Web site. The company adopted an e-commerce platform from Blue Martini, now a part of Escalate Retail (*www.escalateretail.com*), an on-demand customer-relationship management product from Loyalty Lab (*www.loyaltylab.com*), a relationship and retention-marketing vendor; and various features of Web 2.0.

J&R intended to leverage the store's most important assets and competitive differentiators by making a commitment to its e-commerce channel. For example, the site's Guided Selling application leads users through an interactive product recommendation and selection process, incorporating user input on needs and preferences to present a targeted view of the product catalog. For example, if a customer is looking for a new plasma television, he or she can shop based on a number of criteria: brand, price, top sellers, screen type and size, and models on which special offers, price specials, and rebates are available. For a retailer like J&R that offers hundreds of thousands of products, many of them new to the market, guided selling and an interactive product recommendation-and-selection process make it easier for customers to understand and compare features.

The new Web site also offered product pages with extensive details as well as comparison grids to make the selection process even simpler for customers. Customers told J&R that deep content, such as customer reviews, alternative product reviews, and comprehensive product descriptions, helps them make their purchase decisions. The new site also allows users to see where the customers are on its site, what they have in their shopping baskets, where they have been on the site during the current session, and everything they have purchased in the past.

Furthermore, the new Web site provides online videos that emphasize the communication skills of the tech-savvy sales staff. The videos feature J&R's salespeople explaining the intricacies of a particular product. J&R notes that some customers learn from oral presentations, whereas others learn from written presentations.

In conjunction with the makeover of its Web site, J&R launched an online national loyalty program to motivate customers to come directly to its Web site rather than arrive via another site. This program provided customers with incentives equal to 2 percent of their purchase. The goal was to increase the number of unique visitors from the 745,000 it had in 2006. The program was designed to counter the intense engine-driven price comparison shopping that is common in the consumer electronics business. By having customers go directly to *www.jr.com* and offering them incentives, J&R hoped to minimize customer defections and draw new buyers as well.

As of mid-2007, the new Web site is only two months old, so results are not yet in. However, it is interesting to note that about 30 percent of the company's $400 million in annual revenue comes from its online, Web-based channel. In fact, J&R now sees electronic commerce as the key to its future.

The Results

The J&R case points out two important advantages of electronic commerce. First, electronic commerce increases an organization's reach, or the number of potential customers to whom the company can market its products. Second, rather than replace traditional bricks-and-mortar retailing operations, electronic commerce integrates very well with these operations. In fact, J&R moved from being solely a bricks-and-mortar operation to being a "clicks-and-mortar" company. In addition, this case illustrates the incredible richness of information that organizations can put on their Web sites for the benefit of their customers.

One of the most profound changes in the modern world of business is electronic commerce, also known as e-commerce (EC). E-commerce is changing all business functional areas and their important tasks, from advertising to paying bills. Its impact is so widespread that it is affecting almost every organization. In addition, it is drastically changing the nature of competition, due to new online companies, new business models, and the diversity of EC-related products and services. E-commerce provides unparalleled opportunities for companies to expand worldwide at a small cost, to increase market share, and to reduce costs. E-commerce also offers unparalleled opportunities for you to open your own business by developing an e-commerce Web site.

In this chapter we explain the major applications of e-business and we identify the services that are necessary for its support. We then look at the major types of electronic commerce: business-to-consumer (B2C), business-to-business (B2B), consumer-to-consumer (C2C), business-to employee (B2E), and government-to-citizen (G2C). We conclude by examining several legal and ethical issues that have arisen as a result of the rapid growth of e-commerce. Before we examine these specifics, however, we begin with a general overview of e-commerce and e-business.

What We Learned from This Case

Sources: Compiled from L. McCartney, "J&R Electronics Pumps Up the Volume," *Baseline Magazine*, March 13, 2007; T. Claburn, "Jellyfish.com's Smack Shopping Makes Paying into Play," *InformationWeek*, February 26, 2007; E. Schuman, "What Retailers Don't Tell Consumers," *eWeek*, May 29, 2006; *www.jr.com*, accessed May 12, 2007.

6.1 Overview of E-Business and E-Commerce

This section examines the basics of e-business and e-commerce. We define these two concepts as well as pure and partial electronic commerce; describe the various types of electronic commerce; note e-commerce mechanisms, which are the ways that businesses and people buy and sell over the Internet; and discuss the benefits and limitations of e-commerce.

Definitions and Concepts

Electronic commerce (EC or e-commerce) describes the process of buying, selling, transferring, or exchanging products, services, or information via computer networks, including the Internet. **E-business** is a somewhat broader concept. In addition to the buying and selling of goods and services, e-business also refers to servicing customers, collaborating with business partners, and performing electronic transactions within an organization. However, because e-commerce and e-business are so similar, we use the two terms interchangeably throughout the book.

Pure versus Partial EC. Electronic commerce can take several forms depending on the degree of digitization involved. The *degree of digitization* refers to the extent to which the commerce has been transformed from physical to digital. It can relate to: (1) the product or service being sold, (2) the process by which the product or service is produced, or (3) the delivery agent or intermediary. In other words, the product can be physical or digital; the process can be physical or digital; and the delivery agent can be physical or digital.

In traditional commerce all three dimensions are physical. Purely physical organizations are referred to as **bricks-and-mortar organizations**. In *pure EC* all dimensions are digital. Companies engaged only in EC are considered **virtual** (or *pure-play*) **organizations**. All other combinations that include a mix of digital and physical dimensions are considered *partial* EC (but not pure EC). **Clicks-and-mortar organizations** are those that conduct some e-commerce activities, yet their primary business is done in the physical world. Therefore, clicks-and-mortar organizations are examples of partial EC. E-commerce is now so well established that people increasingly expect companies to offer e-commerce in some form.

For example, buying a shirt at Wal-Mart Online or a book from Amazon.com is *partial EC*, because the merchandise is physically delivered by FedEx. However, buying an e-book from Amazon.com or a software product from Buy.com is pure EC, because the product as well as its delivery, payment, and transfer are all conducted online. To avoid confusion, in this book we use the term EC to denote either pure or partial EC. IT's About Business 6.1 illustrates how one clicks-and-mortar online grocer thrives.

Types of E-Commerce

E-commerce can be conducted between and among various parties.

- **Business-to-consumer (B2C)** In B2C, the sellers are organizations, and the buyers are individuals. We discuss B2C electronic commerce in Section 6.2. (Recall that Figure 2.2 illustrated B2C electronic commerce.)

- **Business-to-business (B2B)** In B2B transactions, both the sellers and the buyers are business organizations. The vast majority of EC volume is of this type. We discuss B2B electronic commerce in Section 6.3. (Recall that Figure 2.2 illustrated B2B electronic commerce.)

- **Consumer-to-consumer (C2C)** In C2C, an individual sells products or services to other individuals. (You also will see the term *C2C* used as "customer-to-customer." The terms

IT's About Business

6.1 FreshDirect Defies the Critics

Critics have been dubious about the potential for online grocers since the demise of Webvan, one of the first online grocers, in 2001. FreshDirect (*www.freshdirect.com*), an online grocer, has been catering to time-pressed and finicky gourmets since its trucks began rolling through the streets of New York City in 2002. The company now sells $200 million worth of food every year. It shipped 2 million orders of 60 million items packed into 8 million boxes in 2006. One-quarter of its 10,000 items are customizable (for example, pick your steak's thickness). The company assembles each day's orders between 11 P.M. and 11 A.M., and most of the trucks must depart by 1 P.M. to meet delivery schedules.

So, how does FreshDirect survive? The answer is through relentless attention to logistics and costs. FreshDirect is one of a very few online grocers to have survived the dot-com collapse, along with Peapod (*www.peapod.com*), now a unit of Dutch grocer Royal Ahold, and SimonDelivers (*www.simondelivers.com*) in the Minneapolis area.

FreshDirect is constantly cutting costs. Since its inception, the company has increased its item accuracy by three-tenths of a point, to 99.9 percent. Item accuracy refers to the number of correct items that the grocer delivers to its customers. That figure represents $1.1 million in savings. In another example, a telephone ringing at FreshDirect means that a customer has received the wrong order, does not like the look of his salmon filets, or is angry because the order arrived late. Every time that one of FreshDirect's customer-service representatives picks up the phone, it costs the company $3.50, plus the cost of crediting wrong items.

The company's early days were a struggle. It took FreshDirect three years to sufficiently tune its software and sorting systems so that it could make its first deliveries. Finally, in 2005, FreshDirect turned its first profit.

FreshDirect's continued success depends on product quality, logistics, and continued cost-cutting. The company worries about things as minuscule as the number of times an item is scanned before it gets to the packing station. There, workers take items off a conveyor, scan them, and put them in a cardboard box. If the wrong item gets sent to the packers by mistake, a runner exchanges it, holding up the order and possibly the entire refrigerated truck. The company has invested in additional scanners so that items are scanned three times before they reach the box, providing extra opportunities to catch mistakes. The additional 50 cents it costs to find an error is much less than the $6 or so it would cost if the error slipped through.

FreshDirect's 150 drivers must meet the two-hour window the company promises customers. Manhattan-bound drivers have to know the intricacies of service elevators, parking spots, and difficult building superintendents. That's why new drivers deliver 35 percent fewer orders than experienced ones.

The company's software helps its drivers accomplish these goals. The software places more orders on experienced drivers' trucks and places orders in adjacent locations on the same truck for added efficiency. During rush hour, the FreshDirect software limits the number of delivery slots it offers, instead dispatching a bigger truck to serve as a base for deliverymen pushing handcarts to customers' apartments.

Sources: Compiled from C. Schoenberger, "Will Work with Food," *Forbes*, September 18, 2006; "NetTracker Web Analytics Software Delivers Web Site Marketing, Merchandising, and Usability Analysis to FreshDirect," *www.zdnet.com*, May 4, 2006; L. Dignan, "FreshDirect: Ready to Deliver," *Baseline Magazine*, February, 2004; *www.freshdirect.com*, accessed May 13, 2007.

QUESTIONS

1. Look up articles on Webvan and find the various reasons for its failure. Compare and contrast Webvan and FreshDirect to determine the reasons for FreshDirect's success. Speculate as to whether FreshDirect can continue to thrive.
2. Apply Porter's competitive forces model to FreshDirect. Discuss each of the five forces as it applies to FreshDirect.
3. What else could FreshDirect do with its Web site to attract and retain customers? *Hint:* Consider Web 2.0 technologies.

are interchangeable, and we use both in this book.) The major ways that C2C is conducted on the Internet are auctions and classified ads.

In dozens of countries, C2C selling and buying on auction sites is exploding. Most auctions are conducted by intermediaries, like eBay (*www.ebay.com*). Consumers can select general sites such as *www.auctionanything.com*. In addition, many individuals are conducting their own auctions. For example, *www.greatshop.com* provides software to create online C2C reverse auction communities.

The major categories of online classified ads are similar to those found in print ads: vehicles, real estate, employment, pets, tickets, and travel. Classified ads are available through most Internet service providers (AOL, MSN, etc.), at some portals (Yahoo, etc.), and from Internet directories and online newspapers. On many of these sites, shoppers can use search engines to narrow their searches.

Internet-based classified ads have one big advantage over traditional types of classified ads: They offer an international, rather than a local, audience. This wider audience greatly increases both the supply of goods and services and the number of potential buyers.

- **Business-to-employee (B2E)** In B2E, an organization uses EC internally to provide information and services to its employees. Companies allow employees to manage their benefits and to take training classes electronically. In addition, employees can buy discounted insurance, travel packages, and tickets to events on the corporate intranet. They also can order supplies and materials electronically. Finally, many companies have electronic corporate stores that sell the company's products to its employees, usually at a discount.

- **E-government** E-government is the use of Internet technology in general and e-commerce in particular to deliver information and public services to citizens (called government-to-citizen or G2C EC) and business partners and suppliers (called government-to-business or G2B EC). It is also an efficient way of conducting business transactions with citizens and businesses and within the governments themselves. E-government makes government more efficient and effective, especially in the delivery of public services. An example of G2C electronic commerce is electronics benefits transfer, in which governments transfer benefits, such as Social Security and pension payments, directly to recipients' bank accounts.

- **Mobile commerce (m-commerce)** The term *m-commerce* refers to e-commerce that is conducted entirely in a wireless environment. An example is using cell phones to shop over the Internet. We discuss m-commerce in Chapter 7.

Each of the above types of EC is executed in one or more business models. A **business model** is the method by which a company generates revenue to sustain itself. Table 6.1 summarizes the major EC business models.

E-Commerce and Search

The development of e-commerce has proceeded in phases. Offline and online brands were initially kept distinct and then were awkwardly merged. Initial e-commerce efforts were flashy brochure sites, with rudimentary shopping carts and checkout systems. They were replaced with systems that tried to anticipate customer needs and accelerate checkout.

From Google's perspective, however, one of the biggest changes has been the growing importance of search. Google managers point to a huge number of purchases that follow successful Web searches as well as abandoned shopping carts that immediately followed a nonproductive search. Here is a classic example: A visitor searches a retail site for "video camera" or "movie camera," finds nothing, and leaves. What was the problem? The Web site categorizes these items under "camcorder" and would have shown the customer 20 models had he used the magic word.

Google is confident that in the future retailers will post tremendous amounts of additional details. Merchants will pour continuous structured feeds of data—including SKU listings,

E-Commerce Business Models

Table 6.1

EC Model	Description
Online direct marketing	Manufacturers or retailers sell directly to customers. Very efficient for digital products and services. Can allow for product or service customization. (*www.dell.com*)
Electronic tendering system	Businesses request quotes from suppliers. Uses B2B with a reverse auction mechanism.
Name-your-own-price	Customers decide how much they are willing to pay. An intermediary (e.g., *www.priceline.com*) tries to match a provider.
Find-the-best-price	Customers specify a need; an intermediary (e.g., *www.hotwire.com*) compares providers and shows the lowest price. Customers must accept the offer in a short time or may lose the deal.
Affiliate marketing	Vendors ask partners to place logos (or banners) on partner's site. If customers click on logo, go to vendor's site, and buy, then vendor pays commissions to partners.
Viral marketing	Receivers send information about your product to their friends.
Group purchasing (e-coops)	Small buyers aggregate demand to get a large volume; then the group conducts tendering or negotiates a low price.
Online auctions	Companies run auctions of various types on the Internet. Are very popular in C2C, but gaining ground in other types of EC. (*www.ebay.com*)
Product customization	Customers use the Internet to self-configure products or services. Sellers then price them and fulfill them quickly (*build-to-order*). (*www.jaguar.com*)
Electronic marketplaces and exchanges	Transactions are conducted efficiently (more information to buyers and sellers, less transaction cost) in electronic marketplaces (private or public).
Bartering online	Intermediary administers online exchange of surplus products and/or company receives "points" for its contribution, and the points can be used to purchase other needed items. (*www.bbu.com*)
Deep discounters	Company (e.g., *www.half.com*) offers deep price discounts. Appeals to customers who consider only price in their purchasing decisions.
Membership	Only members can use the services provided, including access to certain information, conducting trades, etc. (*www.egreetings.com*)

daily inventory, and hours of operation—into public search engines such as Google. Google is currently using Google Base, the company's online database, to work on this process.

This process will allow customers to access much more specific and relevant search results. For example, not only will a customer seeking a particular model of electric drill find retailers who claim to sell it, but they will also find the closest merchants who are open and have the drills in stock.

Major E-Commerce Mechanisms

There are a number of mechanisms through which businesses and customers can buy and sell on the Internet. The most widely used ones are electronic catalogs, electronic auctions, e-storefronts, e-malls, and e-marketplaces.

Catalogs have been printed on paper for generations. Today, however, they are available on CD-ROM and the Internet. Electronic catalogs consist of a product database, directory and search capabilities, and a presentation function. They are the backbone of most e-commerce sites.

An **auction** is a competitive process in which either a seller solicits consecutive bids from buyers or a buyer solicits bids from sellers. The primary characteristic of auctions is that prices are determined dynamically by competitive bidding. Electronic auctions (e-auctions) generally increase revenues for sellers by broadening the customer base and shortening the cycle time of the auction. Buyers generally benefit from e-auctions because they can bargain for lower prices. In addition, they don't have to travel to an auction at a physical location.

The Internet provides an efficient infrastructure for conducting auctions at lower administrative costs and with many more involved sellers and buyers. Individual consumers and corporations alike can participate in auctions. There are two major types of auctions: forward and reverse.

Forward auctions are auctions that sellers use as a channel to many potential buyers. Usually, sellers place items at sites for auction, and buyers bid continuously for them. The highest bidder wins the items. Both sellers and buyers can be individuals or businesses. The popular auction site eBay.com is a forward auction.

In **reverse auctions**, one buyer, usually an organization, wants to buy a product or a service. The buyer posts a request for quotation (RFQ) on its Web site or on a third-party Web site. The RFQ provides detailed information on the desired purchase. The suppliers study the RFQ and then submit bids electronically. Everything else being equal, the lowest-price bidder wins the auction. The buyer notifies the winning supplier electronically. The reverse auction is the most common auction model for large purchases (in terms of either quantities or price). Governments and large corporations frequently use this approach, which may provide considerable savings for the buyer.

Auctions can be conducted from the seller's site, the buyer's site, or a third party's site. For example, eBay, the best-known third-party site, offers hundreds of thousands of different items in several types of auctions. Overall, more than 300 major companies, including Amazon.com and Dellauction.com, offer online auctions.

An *electronic storefront* is a Web site on the Internet that represents a single store. An *electronic mall*, also known as a *cybermall* or *e-mall*, is a collection of individual shops under one Internet address. Electronic storefronts and electronic malls are closely associated with B2C electronic commerce. We discuss each one in more detail in Section 6.2.

An *electronic marketplace* (e-marketplace) is a central, virtual market space on the Web where many buyers and many sellers can conduct electronic commerce and electronic business activities. Electronic marketplaces are associated with B2B electronic commerce. We discuss this topic in Section 6.3.

Benefits and Limitations of E-Commerce

Few innovations in human history have provided as many benefits to organizations, individuals, and society as e-commerce has. E-commerce benefits organizations by making national and international markets more accessible and by lowering the costs of processing, distributing, and retrieving information. Customers benefit by being able to access a vast number of products and services, around the clock. The major benefit to society is the ability to easily and conveniently deliver information, services, and products to people in cities, rural areas, and developing countries.

Despite all these benefits, EC has some limitations, both technological and nontechnological, that have slowed its growth and acceptance. Technological limitations include the lack of universally accepted security standards, insufficient telecommunications bandwidth, and expensive accessibility. Nontechnological limitations include the perceptions that EC is insecure, has unresolved legal issues, and lacks a critical mass of sellers and buyers. As time passes, the limitations, especially the technological ones, will lessen or be overcome.

Before you go on . . .

1. Define e-commerce, and distinguish it from e-business.
2. Differentiate among B2C, B2B, C2C, and B2E electronic commerce.
3. Define e-government.
4. Describe forward and reverse auctions.
5. List some benefits and limitations of e-commerce.

6.2 Business-to-Consumer (B2C) Electronic Commerce

B2B EC is much larger than B2C EC by volume, but B2C EC is more complex because B2C involves a large number of buyers making millions of diverse transactions per day with a relatively small number of sellers. As an illustration, consider Amazon, an online retailer (e-tailer) that offers thousands of products to its customers. Each customer purchase is relatively small, but Amazon must manage that transaction as if that customer were its most important one. Each order must be processed quickly and efficiently, and the products must be shipped to the customer in a timely manner. In addition, returns must be managed. Multiply this simple example by millions, and you get an idea of the complexity of B2C EC.

This section addresses the more important issues in B2C EC. We begin by discussing the two basic mechanisms for customers to access companies on the Web: electronic storefronts and electronic malls. In addition to purchasing products over the Web, customers also access online services. Our next section covers several online services, such as banking, securities trading, job search, travel, and real estate. The complexity of B2C EC creates two major challenges for sellers: channel conflict and order fulfillment. We examine these two topics in detail. Finally, companies engaged in B2C EC must "get the word out" to prospective customers. Therefore, we conclude this section with a look at online advertising.

Electronic Storefronts and Malls

For several generations, home shopping from catalogs, and later from television shopping channels, has attracted millions of customers. Today, shopping online offers an alternative to catalog and television shopping. **Electronic retailing (e-tailing)** is the direct sale of products and services through electronic storefronts or electronic malls, usually designed around an electronic catalog format and/or auctions.

Like any mail-order shopping experience, e-commerce enables you to buy from home and to do so 24 hours a day, 7 days a week. However, EC offers a wider variety of products and services, including the most unique items, often at lower prices. Furthermore, within seconds, shoppers can access very detailed supplementary information on products. In addition, they can easily locate and compare competitors' products and prices. Finally, buyers can find hundreds of thousands of sellers. Two popular online shopping mechanisms are electronic storefronts and electronic malls.

Electronic Storefronts.   As we discussed earlier, an **electronic storefront** is a Web site that represents a single store. Hundreds of thousands of electronic storefronts can be found on the

Internet. Each one has its own uniform resource locator (URL), or Internet address, at which buyers can place orders. Some electronic storefronts are extensions of physical stores such as Hermes, The Sharper Image, and Wal-Mart. Others are new businesses started by entrepreneurs who saw a niche on the Web. Examples are Restaurant.com and Alloy.com. Manufacturers (for example, *www.dell.com*) as well as retailers (for example, *www.officedepot.com*) also use storefronts.

Electronic Malls.   Whereas an electronic storefront represents a single store, an **electronic mall**, also known as a cybermall or e-mall, is a collection of individual shops under a single Internet address. The basic idea of an electronic mall is the same as that of a regular shopping mall—to provide a one-stop shopping place that offers many products and services. Each cybermall may include thousands of vendors. For example, *http://eshop.msn.com* includes tens of thousands of products from thousands of vendors (see Figure 6.1).

There are two types of cybermalls. In the first type, known as *referral malls* (e.g., *www.hawaii.com*), you cannot buy anything. Instead, you are transferred from the mall to a participating storefront. In the second type of mall (e.g., *http://shopping.yahoo.com*), you can actually make a purchase. At this type of mall, you might shop from several stores, but you make only one purchase transaction at the end. An *electronic shopping cart* enables you to gather items from various vendors and pay for them all together in one transaction. (The mall organizer, such as Yahoo, takes a commission from the sellers for this service.)

Online Service Industries

In addition to purchasing products, customers can also access needed services via the Web. Selling books, toys, computers, and most other products on the Internet can reduce vendors' selling costs by 20 to 40 percent. Further reduction is difficult to achieve because the products must be delivered physically. Only a few products (such as software or music) can be digitized to be delivered online for additional savings. In contrast, services, such as buying an airline

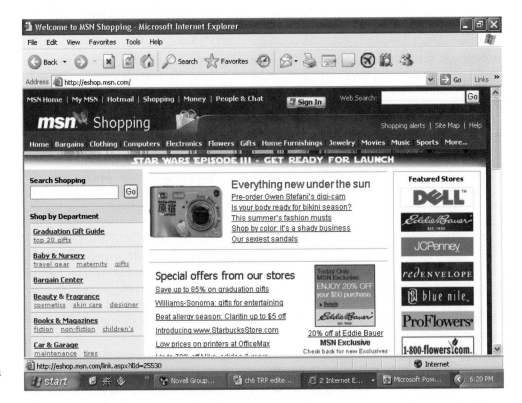

FIGURE 6.1
Electronic malls
include products from
thousands of vendors.

ticket or purchasing stocks or insurance, can be delivered entirely through e-commerce, often with considerable cost reduction. Not surprisingly, then, online delivery of services is growing very rapidly, with millions of new customers being added each year.

One of the most pressing EC issues relating to online services (as well as in marketing tangible products) is disintermediation. Intermediaries, also known as middlemen, have two functions: (1) They provide information, and (2) they perform value-added services such as consulting. The first function can be fully automated and will most likely be assumed by e-marketplaces and portals that provide information for free. When this occurs, the intermediaries who perform only (or mainly) this function are likely to be eliminated. This process is called **disintermediation**.

In contrast, performing value-added services requires expertise. Unlike the information function, then, it can be only partially automated. Thus, intermediaries who provide value-added services not only are likely to survive, but they may actually prosper. The Web helps these employees in two situations: (1) when the number of participants is enormous, as with job searches, and (2) when the information that must be exchanged is complex.

In this section, we examine the leading online service industries: real estate, banking, trading of securities (stocks, bonds), job matching, and travel services.

Cyberbanking. *Electronic banking*, also known as **cyberbanking**, involves conducting various banking activities from home, at a place of business, or on the road instead of at a physical bank location. Electronic banking has capabilities ranging from paying bills to applying for a loan. For customers, it saves time and is convenient. For banks, it offers an inexpensive alternative to branch banking (for example, about 2 cents cost per transaction versus $1.07 at a physical branch). It also enables banks to attract remote customers. In addition to regular banks with added online services, we are seeing the emergence of **virtual banks**, which are dedicated solely to Internet transactions. An example of a virtual bank is NetBank (*www.netbank.com*) (see Figure 6.2).

International banking and the ability to handle trading in multiple currencies are critical for international trade. Transfers of electronic funds and electronic letters of credit are important

FIGURE 6.2 Virtual banks are devoted to online transactions. www.netbank.com

services in international banking. An example of support for EC global trade is provided by TradeCard, in conjunction with MasterCard. TradeCard is an international company that provides a secure method for buyers and sellers to make digital payments anywhere on the globe (see the demo at *www.tradecard.com*). In another example, banks and companies such as Oanda (*www.oanda.com*) provide conversions of more than 160 currencies.

Online Securities Trading.   Emarketer.com estimates that some 40 million people in the United States use computers to trade stocks, bonds, and other financial instruments. In Korea, more than half of stock traders are already using the Internet for that purpose. Why? Because it is cheaper than a full-service or discount broker. On the Web, investors can find a considerable amount of information regarding specific companies or mutual funds in which to invest (e.g., *http://money.cnn.com* and *www.bloomberg.com*).

For example, let's say you have an account with Charles Schwab. You access Schwab's Web site (*www.schwab.com*) from your personal computer or your Internet-enabled mobile device, enter your account number and password to access your personalized Web page, and then click on "stock trading." Using a menu, you enter the details of your order (buy or sell, margin or cash, price limit, market order, and so on). The computer tells you the current "ask" and "bid" prices, much as a broker would do over the telephone. You can then approve or reject the transaction. Some well-known companies that offer only online trading are E*Trade, Ameritrade, and Suretrade.

The Online Job Market.   The Internet offers a promising new environment for job seekers and for companies searching for hard-to-find employees. Thousands of companies and government agencies advertise available positions, accept resumes, and take applications via the Internet.

Job seekers use the online job market to reply online to employment ads, to place resumes on various sites, and to use recruiting firms (e.g., *www.monster.com* and *www.truecareers.com*). Companies that have jobs to offer advertise openings on their Web sites, and they search the bulletin boards of recruiting firms. In many countries, governments must advertise job openings on the Internet.

Travel Services.   The Internet is an ideal place to plan, explore, and arrange almost any trip economically. Online travel services allow you to purchase airline tickets, reserve hotel rooms, and rent cars. Most sites also offer a fare-tracker feature that sends you e-mail messages about low-cost flights. Examples of comprehensive online travel services are Expedia.com, Travelocity.com, and Orbitz.com. Online services are also provided by all major airline vacation services, large conventional travel agencies, car rental agencies, hotels (e.g., *www.hotels.com*), and tour companies. In a variation of this process, Priceline.com allows you to set a price you are willing to pay for an airline ticket or hotel accommodations. It then attempts to find a vendor that will match your price.

An interesting problem that e-commerce can cause is "mistake fares" in the airline industry. For example, United Airlines offered a $1,221 fare for a United States to New Zealand round trip in business class. This fare was available for about 48 hours over the weekend of May 4–6, 2007. Hundreds of tickets were sold at the wrong price, thanks in part to online travel discussion groups, before United noticed the mistake and pulled the fare.

Issues in E-Tailing

Despite e-tailing's increasing popularity, many e-tailers continue to face serious issues that can restrict their growth. Perhaps the two major issues are channel conflict and order fulfillment.

Clicks-and-mortar companies may face a conflict with their regular distributors when they sell directly to customers online. This situation, known as **channel conflict**, can alienate the distributors. Channel conflict has forced some companies (for example, Ford Motor

Company) to avoid direct online sales. An alternative approach for Ford allows customers to configure a car online but requires them to pick up the car from a dealer, where they arrange financing, warranties, and service.

Channel conflict can arise in areas such as pricing of products and services and resource allocation (for example, how much to spend on advertising). Another potential source of conflict involves logistics services provided by the offline activities to the online activities. For example, how should a company handle returns of items bought online? Some companies have completely separated the "clicks" (the online portion of the organization) from the "mortar" or "bricks" (the traditional bricks-and-mortar part of the organization). However, this approach can increase expenses and reduce the synergy between the two organizational channels. As a result, many companies are integrating their online and offline channels, a process known as **multichanneling**. IT's About Business 6.2 illustrates problems that some companies may have with the process of multichanneling.

IT's About Business

6.2   Best Buy Makes Mistake with Multiple Channels

As Best Buy (www.bestbuy.com) tries to integrate the multiple channels it uses to reach its customers, company officials are conceding that human error and employee confusion were the reasons that customers were shown a Web site displaying higher bricks-and-mortar prices while incorrectly being told that the displayed Web site was showing online prices. The confusion stemmed from two visually identical Web sites that Best Buy employees can show customers. The sites have only a few minor functionality differences, with the key difference being that the prices are sometimes different.

The issue has come to haunt the $31 billion retail chain—which owns more than 900 stores in the United States and Canada—after the Connecticut Attorney General's Office launched an investigation into the chain, trying to establish whether employees had deliberately conned customers with the almost-duplicate Web site. Best Buy says that the matter was not one of deception, but more a matter of employees' not recognizing the differences between the sites.

The intrastore version is showcased in store kiosks using Internet Explorer. It is intended to provide customers with information about products that are available in the store, along with their official prices. The problem came from Best Buy's price-matching policy, which promises to match the price of other retailers. This policy explicitly includes www.bestbuy.com.

The problem developed when customers saw a low Web price and went into a Best Buy physical store to trigger the price match and obtain that low price. Employees would agree to match the price and would say they were calling up the Web site to verify the claim. Instead of calling up the Web site, though, employees would access the intrastore version of the site, which looked identical (other than its prices) to www.bestbuy.com. They then used the intrastore site to "prove" that the online pricing was not correct.

The obvious question is: Why do the two Web sites look identical? Best Buy claims that it created the mirror designs to save money and not to deceive customers. The company maintains that the online kiosk differs from the intrastore site in the following ways: (1) Unlike the Web site, checkout on the kiosk does not require an e-mail address; (2) pop-up payment information forms time out faster on the kiosk version to make it more difficult for another customer to read a credit card number; and (3) the kiosk version can view only sites owned by Best Buy. Best Buy imposed this browsing restriction to prevent customers from using these very publicly displayed kiosks to visit price-comparison sites or competitors' Web sites.

Best Buy officials claim that the Web site uses extensive customization, meaning that one customer visiting the site and looking at a certain product might be presented with a lower overall purchase price than another customer looking at the identical product at the same time. The difference in price is based on each customer's buying history and other factors. In addition, Best Buy maintains that it has a complex multichannel pricing situation, in which prices can change based on inventory and supplier changes. These price changes automatically feed into the pricing system.

Connecticut officials are unswayed by Best Buy's arguments. They "seek full and complete answers that address the potential consumer rights issues raised by the apparent practice of advertising one price and charging another." On May 24, 2007, after months of investigation, the State of Connecticut sued Best Buy, accusing the company of tricking its customers with two identical-looking Web sites, with the only difference being that one had higher prices.

Sources: Compiled from E. Schuman, "Connecticut Sues Best Buy for Deceiving Customers," *PC Magazine*, May 25, 2007; G. Gombossy, "Best Buy Confirms It Has Secret Web

Site," *Connecticut News*, March 2, 2007; E. Schuman, "Connecticut Investigating Best Buy's Intrastore Web Site," *eWeek*, March 4, 2007; E. Schuman, "Best Buy Officials Concede Dual-Site System Caused by 'Human Error,' 'Employee Confusion,'" *eWeek*, March 6, 2007; B. Krasnov, "Is Best Buy Playing Web Games?" *InformationWeek*, March 5, 2007; *www.bestbuy.com*, accessed May 11, 2007.

QUESTIONS

1. First, take the position of Best Buy and defend its actions. Then take the position of the Connecticut Attorney General's Office and argue the case from the other viewpoint.
2. Redesign the kiosk Web site so that it complements the Best Buy Web site.

The second major issue is order fulfillment, which can also be a source of problems for e-tailers. Any time a company sells directly to customers, it is involved in various order-fulfillment activities. It must perform the following activities: quickly find the products to be shipped; pack them; arrange for the packages to be delivered speedily to the customer's door; collect the money from every customer, either in advance, by COD, or by individual bill; and handle the return of unwanted or defective products.

It is very difficult to accomplish these activities both effectively and efficiently in B2C, because a company has to ship small packages to many customers and do it quickly. For this reason, companies involved in B2C activities often have difficulties in their supply chains.

In addition to providing customers with the products they ordered and doing it on time, order fulfillment also provides all related customer services. For example, the customer must receive assembly and operation instructions for a new appliance. In addition, if the customer is not happy with a product, an exchange or return must be arranged. (Visit *www.fedex.com* to see how returns are handled via FedEx.)

In the late 1990s, e-tailers faced continuous problems in order fulfillment, especially during the holiday season. These problems included late deliveries, delivery of wrong items, high delivery costs, and compensation to unhappy customers. For e-tailers, taking orders over the Internet is the easy part of B2C e-commerce; delivering orders to customers' doors is the hard part. In contrast, order fulfillment is less complicated in B2B. These transactions are much larger, but they are fewer in number. In addition, these companies have had order-fulfillment mechanisms in place for many years.

Online Advertising

Advertising is the practice of disseminating information in an attempt to influence a buyer–seller transaction. Traditional advertising on TV or in newspapers is impersonal, one-way mass communication. Direct-response marketing, or telemarketing, contacts individuals by direct mail or telephone and requires them to respond in order to make a purchase. The direct-response approach personalizes advertising and marketing, but it can be expensive, slow, and ineffective. It can also be extremely annoying to the consumer.

Internet advertising redefines the advertising process, making it media-rich, dynamic, and interactive. It improves on traditional forms of advertising in a number of ways. First, Internet ads can be updated any time at minimal cost and therefore can be kept current. In addition, Internet ads can reach very large numbers of potential buyers all over the world. Furthermore, these ads are generally cheaper than radio, television, and print ads. Finally, Internet ads can be interactive and targeted to specific interest groups and/or individuals. Despite all these advantages, it is difficult to measure the effectiveness of online ads. For this reason, there are no concrete standards to evaluate whether the results of Internet ads justify their costs.

Advertising Methods.   The most common online advertising methods are banners, pop-ups, and e-mail. **Banners** are simply electronic billboards. Typically, a banner contains a short text or graphical message to promote a product or a vendor. It may even contain video clips and sound. When customers click on a banner, they are transferred to the advertiser's home page. Banner advertising is the most commonly used form of advertising on the Internet (see Figure 6.3).

A major advantage of banners is that they can be customized to the target audience. If the computer system knows who you are or what your profile is, you may be sent a banner that is supposed to match your interests. A major disadvantage of banners is that they can convey only limited information due to their small size. Another drawback is that many viewers simply ignore them.

Pop-up and pop-under ads are contained in a new browser window that is automatically launched when you enter or exit a Web site. A **pop-up ad** appears in front of the current browser window. A **pop-under ad** appears underneath the active window: when users close the active window, they see the ad. Many users strongly object to these ads, which they consider intrusive. Modern browsers let users block pop-up ads, but this feature must be used with caution because some Web sites depend on them to function correctly.

E-mail is emerging as an Internet advertising and marketing channel. It is generally cost-effective to implement, and it provides a better and quicker response rate than other advertising channels. Marketers develop or purchase a list of e-mail addresses, place them in a customer database, and then send advertisements via e-mail. A list of e-mail addresses can be a very powerful tool because the marketer can target a group of people or even individuals.

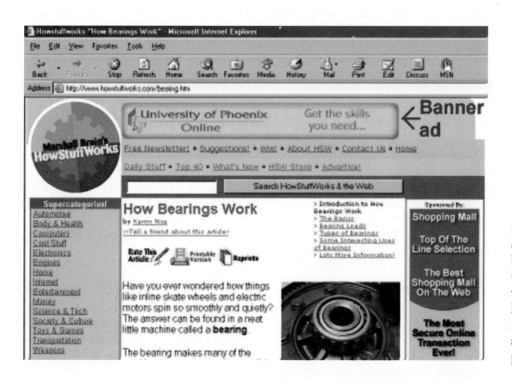

FIGURE 6.3   When customers click on a banner ad, they are transfered to the vendor's homepage. http://images.encarta .msn.com/xrefmedia/ sharemed/taracts/images/ pho/0007faba.jpg

As you have probably concluded by now, there is a potential for misuse of e-mail advertising. In fact, some consumers receive a flood of unsolicited e-mail, or *spam*. **Spamming** is the indiscriminate distribution of electronic ads without the permission of the receiver. Unfortunately, spamming is becoming worse over time.

Two important responses to spamming are permission marketing and viral marketing. **Permission marketing** asks consumers to give their permission to voluntarily accept online advertising and e-mail. Typically, consumers are asked to complete an electronic form that asks what they are interested in and requests permission to send related marketing information. Sometimes, consumers are offered incentives to receive advertising.

Permission marketing is the basis of many Internet marketing strategies. For example, millions of users receive e-mails periodically from airlines such as American and Southwest. Users of this marketing service can ask to be notified of low fares from their hometown or to their favorite destinations. Users can easily unsubscribe at any time. Permission marketing is also extremely important for market research (for example, see Media Metrix at *www.comscore.com*).

In one particularly interesting form of permission marketing, companies such as Clickdough.com, ExpressPaid Surveys.com, and CashSurfers.com have built customer lists of millions of people who are happy to receive advertising messages whenever they are on the Web. These customers are paid $0.25 to $0.50 an hour to view messages while they do their normal surfing.

Viral marketing refers to online "word-of-mouth" marketing. The idea behind viral marketing is to have people forward messages to friends, suggesting that they "check this out." For example, a marketer can distribute a small game program embedded with a sponsor's e-mail that is easy to forward. By releasing a few thousand copies, vendors hope to reach many more thousands of potential customers via friends, family, and other acquaintances. Viral marketing allows companies to build brand awareness at a minimal cost.

Before you go on . . .

1. Describe electronic storefronts and malls.
2. Discuss various types of online services (for example, cyberbanking, securities trading, job searches, travel services).
3. List the major issues relating to e-tailing.
4. Describe online advertising, its methods, and its benefits.
5. What are spamming, permission marketing, and viral marketing?

6.3 Business-to-Business (B2B) Electronic Commerce

In *business-to-business (B2B)* e-commerce, the buyers and sellers are business organizations. B2B comprises about 85 percent of EC volume. It covers a broad spectrum of applications that enable an enterprise to form electronic relationships with its distributors, resellers, suppliers, customers, and other partners. Organizations can use B2B to restructure their supply chains and their partner relationships.

There are several business models for B2B applications. The major ones are sell-side marketplaces, buy-side marketplaces, and electronic exchanges.

Sell-Side Marketplaces

In the **sell-side marketplace** model, organizations attempt to sell their products or services to other organizations electronically from their own private e-marketplace Web site and/or from a third-party Web site. This model is similar to the B2C model in which the buyer is expected to come to the seller's site, view catalogs, and place an order. In the B2B sell-side marketplace, however, the buyer is an organization.

The key mechanisms in the sell-side model are electronic catalogs that can be customized for each large buyer and forward auctions. Sellers such as Dell Computer (*www.dellauction.com*) use auctions extensively. In addition to auctions from their own Web sites, organizations can use third-party auction sites, such as eBay, to liquidate items. Companies such as Ariba (*www.ariba.com*) are helping organizations to auction old assets and inventories.

The sell-side model is used by hundreds of thousands of companies and is especially powerful for companies with superb reputations. The seller can be either a manufacturer (e.g., Dell or IBM), a distributor (e.g., *www.avnet.com*), or a retailer (e.g., *www.bigboxx.com*). The seller uses EC to increase sales, reduce selling and advertising expenditures, increase delivery speed, and reduce administrative costs. The sell-side model is especially suitable to customization. Many companies allow their customers to configure their orders online. For example, at Dell (*www.dell.com*), you can determine the exact type of computer that you want. You can choose the type of chip (e.g., Itanium 2), the size of the hard drive (e.g., 300 gigabytes), the type of monitor (e.g., 21-inch flat screen), and so on. Similarly, the Jaguar Web site (*www.jaguar.com*) allows you to customize the Jaguar you want. Self-customization generates fewer misunderstandings about what customers want, and it encourages businesses to fill orders more quickly.

Buy-Side Marketplaces

The **buy-side marketplace** is a model in which organizations attempt to buy needed products or services from other organizations electronically. A major method of buying goods and services in the buy-side model is the reverse auction.

The buy-side model uses EC technology to streamline the purchasing process. The goal is to reduce both the costs of items purchased and the administrative expenses involved in purchasing them. In addition, EC technology can shorten the purchasing cycle time. Procurement includes purchasing goods and materials as well as sourcing, negotiating with suppliers, paying for goods, and making delivery arrangements. Organizations now use the Internet to accomplish all these functions.

Purchasing by using electronic support is referred to as **e-procurement**. E-procurement uses reverse auctions, particularly group purchasing. In **group purchasing**, multiple buyers combine their orders so that they constitute a large volume and therefore attract more seller attention. In addition, when buyers place their combined orders on a reverse auction, they can negotiate a volume discount. Typically, the orders of small buyers are aggregated by a third-party vendor, such as the United Sourcing Alliance (*www.usa-llc.com*).

Electronic Exchanges

Private exchanges have one buyer and many sellers. E-marketplaces, in which there are many sellers and many buyers, are called **public exchanges**, or just **exchanges**. Public exchanges are open to all business organizations. They frequently are owned and operated by a third party. Public exchange managers provide all the necessary information systems to the participants. Thus, buyers and sellers merely have to "plug in" in order to trade. B2B public exchanges are often the initial point for contacts between business partners. Once they make contact, the partners may move to a private exchange or to the private trading rooms provided by many public exchanges to conduct their subsequent trading activities.

Some electronic exchanges are for direct materials, and others are for indirect materials. *Direct materials* are inputs to the manufacturing process, such as safety glass used in automobile windshields and windows. *Indirect materials* are those items, such as office supplies, that are needed for maintenance, operations, and repairs (MRO). There are three basic types of public exchanges: vertical, horizontal, and functional.

Vertical exchanges connect buyers and sellers in a given industry. Examples of vertical exchanges are *www.plasticsnet.com* in the plastics industry, *www.papersite.com* in the paper industry, *www.chemconnect.com* in the chemical industry, and *www.isteelasia.com* in the steel industry.

Horizontal exchanges connect buyers and sellers across many industries and are used mainly for MRO materials. Examples of horizontal exchanges are EcEurope (*www.eceurope.com*), Globalsources (*www.globalsources.com*), and Alibaba (*www.alibaba.com*).

In **functional exchanges**, needed services such as temporary help or extra office space are traded on an "as-needed" basis. For example, Employease (*www.employease.com*) can find temporary labor using employers in its Employease Network.

All types of exchanges offer diversified support services, ranging from payments to logistics. Vertical exchanges are frequently owned and managed by a *consortium*, a term for a group of big players in an industry. For example, Marriott and Hyatt own a procurement consortium for the hotel industry, and ChevronTexaco owns an energy e-marketplace. The vertical e-marketplaces offer services that are particularly suited to the community they serve.

Before you go on . . .

1. Briefly differentiate between the sell-side marketplace and the buy-side marketplace.
2. Briefly differentiate among vertical exchanges, horizontal exchanges, and functional exchanges.

6.4 Electronic Payments

Implementing EC typically requires electronic payments. **Electronic payment systems** enable you to pay for goods and services electronically, rather than writing a check or using cash. Electronic payment systems include electronic checks, electronic credit cards, purchasing cards, and electronic cash. Payments are an integral part of doing business, whether in the traditional manner or online. Traditional payment systems have typically involved cash and/or checks.

In most cases, traditional payment systems are not effective for EC, especially for B2B. Cash cannot be used because there is no face-to-face contact between buyer and seller. Not everyone accepts credit cards or checks, and some buyers do not have credit cards or checking accounts. Finally, contrary to what many people believe, it may be *less* secure for the buyer to use the telephone or mail to arrange or send payments, especially from another country, than to complete a secured transaction on a computer. For all of these reasons, a better way is needed to pay for goods and services in cyberspace. This better method is electronic payment systems. We now take a closer look at four types of electronic payment: electronic checks, electronic credit cards, purchasing cards, and electronic cash.

Electronic Checks

Electronic checks (e-checks) are similar to regular paper checks. They are used mostly in B2B. A customer who wishes to use e-checks must first establish a checking account with a bank. Then, when the customer buys a product or a service, he or she e-mails an encrypted electronic check to the seller. The seller deposits the check in a bank account, and funds are transferred from the buyer's account into the seller's account.

Like regular checks, e-checks carry a signature (in digital form) that can be verified (see *www.authorize.net*). Properly signed and endorsed e-checks are exchanged between financial institutions through electronic clearinghouses (see *www.eccho.org* and *www.troygroup.com* for details).

Electronic Credit Cards

Electronic credit (e-credit) cards allow customers to charge online payments to their credit card account (see Figure 6.4). Here is how e-credit cards work. When you buy a book from Amazon, for example, your credit card information and purchase amount are encrypted in

FIGURE 6.4
Electronic credit card.

your browser. This way the information is safe while it is "traveling" on the Internet. Furthermore, when this information arrives at Amazon, it is not opened. Rather, it is transferred automatically (in encrypted form) to a clearinghouse, where the information is decrypted for verification and authorization. The complete process of how e-credit cards work is shown in Figure 6.5. Electronic credit cards are used primarily in B2C and in shopping by small-to-medium enterprises (SMEs).

Several major credit card issuers are offering customers the option of shopping online with *virtual, single-use credit card numbers.* The goal is to thwart criminals by using a different, random card number every time you shop online. A virtual number is only good on the Web site where you make your purchase. An online purchase made with a virtual card number shows up on a customer's bill just like any other purchase.

Purchasing Cards

The B2B equivalent of electronic credit cards is *purchasing cards* (see Figure 6.6). In some countries companies pay other companies primarily by means of purchasing cards rather than by paper checks. Unlike credit cards, where credit is provided for 30 to 60 days (for

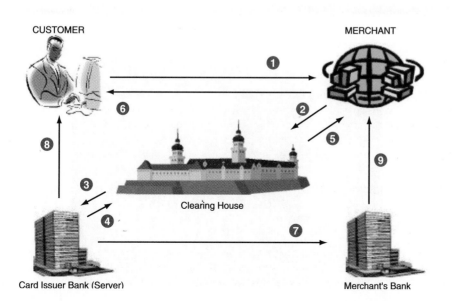

FIGURE 6.5   How e-credit cards work. (The numbers 1–9 indicate the sequence of activities.)
Source: Drawn by E. Turban

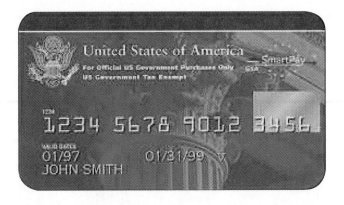

FIGURE 6.6
Purchasing card.

free) before payment is made to the merchant, payments made with purchasing cards are settled within a week.

Purchasing cards typically are used for unplanned B2B purchases, and corporations generally limit the amount per purchase (usually $1,000 to $2,000). Purchasing cards can be used on the Internet, much like regular credit cards.

Electronic Cash

Despite the growth of credit cards, cash remains the most common mode of payment in offline transactions. However, many EC sellers, and some buyers, prefer electronic cash. *Electronic cash* (*e-cash*) appears in four major forms: stored-value money cards, smart cards, person-to-person payments, and digital wallets.

Stored-Value Money Cards. Although they resemble credit cards, **stored-value money cards** actually are a form of e-cash. The cards that you use to pay for photocopies in your library, for transportation, and for telephone calls are stored-value money cards. They are called stored-value because they allow you to store a fixed amount of prepaid money and then spend it as necessary. Each time you use the card, the amount is reduced by the amount you spent.

Smart Cards. Although some people refer to stored-value money cards as "smart cards," they are not really the same. True **smart cards** contain a chip that can store a considerable amount of information (more than 100 times that of a stored-value money card) (see Figure 6.7). Smart

FIGURE 6.7 Smart cards are frequently multipurpose.

FIGURE 6.8   Visa Cash Card.

cards are frequently *multipurpose*; that is, you can use them as a credit card, a debit card, or a stored-value money card. In addition, when you use a smart card in department store chains as a *loyalty card*, it may contain your purchasing information.

Advanced smart cards can help customers transfer funds, pay bills, and purchase items from vending machines. Consumers can also use them to pay for services such as those offered on television or personal computers. For example, the VISA Cash Card (see Figure 6.8) allows you to buy goods or services at participating gas stations, fast-food outlets, pay phones, discount stores, post offices, convenience stores, coffee shops, and even movie theaters. You can load money values onto advanced smart cards at ATMs and kiosks as well as from your personal computer. Smart cards are ideal for *micropayments*, which are small payments of a few dollars or less. However, they have additional functions. In Hong Kong, for example, the transportation card called Octopus is a stored-value money card that can be used for trains and buses (see Figure 6.9). However, as its capabilities have expanded so that it can be used in stores and vending machines, it is being transformed to a smart card.

Person-to-Person Payments.   **Person-to-person payments** are a form of e-cash that enables two individuals or an individual and a business to transfer funds without using a credit card. They are one of the newest and fastest-growing payment mechanisms. Person-to-person payments can be used for a variety of purposes, such as sending money to students at college, paying for an item purchased at an online auction, or sending a gift to a family member.

FIGURE 6.9   Hong Kong's Octopus card is a stored-value money card for transportation.

One of the first companies to offer this service was PayPal (an eBay company). Today, AOL QuickCash, One's Bank eMoneyMail, Yahoo PayDirect, and WebCertificate (*www. webcertificate.com*) all compete with PayPal.

Virtually all of these person-to-person payment services work in a similar way. First, you select a service and open up an account. Basically, this process entails creating a user name, selecting a password, and providing the service with a credit card or bank account number. Next, you transfer funds from your credit card or bank account to your new account. Now you're ready to send money to someone over the Internet. You access the service (e.g., Pay-Pal) with your user name and password, and you specify the e-mail address of the person to receive the money, along with the dollar amount that you want to send. The service then sends an e-mail to the payee's e-mail address. The e-mail will contain a link back to the service's Web site. When the recipient clicks on the link, he or she will be taken to the service. The recipient will be asked to set up an account to which the money that you sent will be credited. The recipient can then credit the money from this account to either a credit card or a bank account. The service charges the payer a small amount, generally around $1 per transaction.

Digital Wallets. **Digital wallets** (or **e-wallets**) are software mechanisms that provide security measures, combined with convenience, to EC purchasing. The wallet stores the financial information of the buyer, such as credit card number and shipping information. Thus, the buyer does not need to reenter sensitive information for each purchase. If the wallet is stored at the vendor's Web site, it does not have to travel on the Internet for each purchase, making the information more secure.

The major shortcoming of this system is that you need to set up a separate e-wallet with each merchant. One solution to this problem is to install a wallet on your computer (e.g., MasterCard Wallet or AOL Wallet). In that case, though, you cannot use the e-wallet to make a purchase from another computer. Moreover, it is not a totally secured system.

Before you go on . . .

1. List the various electronic payment mechanisms. Which of these mechanisms are most often used for B2B payments?
2. What are micropayments?

6.5 Ethical and Legal Issues in E-Business

Technological innovation often forces a society to reexamine and modify its ethical standards. In many cases the new standards are incorporated into law. In this section, we discuss two important ethical issues: privacy and job loss. We then turn our attention to various legal issues arising from the practice of e-business.

Ethical Issues

Many of the ethical and global issues related to IT also apply to e-business. By making it easier to store and transfer personal information, e-business presents some threats to privacy. To begin with, most electronic payment systems know who the buyers are. It may be necessary, then, to protect the buyers' identities. Businesses frequently use encryption to provide this protection.

Another major privacy issue is tracking. For example, individuals' activities on the Internet can be tracked by cookies, discussed in Chapter 3. Programs such as cookies raise privacy concerns. Cookies store your tracking history on your personal computer's hard drive, and any time you revisit a certain Web site, the computer knows it (see *http://netinsight.unica.com/*). In response, some users install programs to exercise some control over cookies and thus restore their online privacy.

In addition to compromising employees' privacy, the use of EC may eliminate the need for some of a company's employees, as well as brokers and agents. The manner in which these unneeded workers, especially employees, are treated can raise ethical issues: How should the company handle the layoffs? Should companies be required to retrain employees for new positions? If not, how should the company compensate or otherwise assist the displaced workers?

Legal Issues Specific to E-Commerce

Many legal issues are related specifically to e-commerce. When buyers and sellers do not know one another and cannot even see one another, there is a chance that dishonest people will commit fraud and other crimes. During the first few years of EC, the public witnessed many such crimes. These illegal actions ranged from creating a virtual bank that disappeared along with the investors' deposits, to manipulating stock prices on the Internet. Unfortunately, fraudulent activities on the Internet are increasing. In the following section we examine some of the major legal issues that are specific to e-commerce.

Fraud on the Internet.   Internet fraud has grown even faster than Internet use itself. In one case, stock promoters falsely spread positive rumors about the prospects of the companies they touted in order to boost the stock price. In other cases, the information provided might have been true, but the promoters did not disclose that they were paid to talk up the companies. Stock promoters specifically target small investors who are lured by the promise of fast profits.

Stocks are only one of many areas where swindlers are active. Auctions are especially conducive to fraud, by both sellers and buyers. Other types of fraud include selling bogus investments and setting up phantom business opportunities. Thanks to the growing use of e-mail, financial criminals now have access to many more people. The U.S. Federal Trade Commission (*www.ftc.gov*) regularly publishes examples of scams that are most likely to be spread via e-mail or to be found on the Web. Later in this section we discuss some ways in which consumers and sellers can protect themselves from online fraud.

Domain Names.   Another legal issue is competition over domain names. Domain names are assigned by central nonprofit organizations that check for conflicts and possible infringement of trademarks. Obviously, companies that sell goods and services over the Internet want customers to be able to find them easily. This is most likely when the domain name matches the company's name.

Problems arise when several companies with similar names compete over a domain name. Several cases of disputed names are already in court. IT's About Business 6.3 provides an example of legal, but perhaps unethical, use of domain names.

Cybersquatting.   **Cybersquatting** refers to the practice of registering or using domain names for the purpose of profiting from the goodwill or trademark belonging to someone else. For example, domain tasting could be considered cybersquatting. The practice is legal but certainly can be thought of as unethical. The Anti-Cybersquatting Consumer Protection Act (1999) lets trademark owners in the United States sue for damages.

A domain name is considered to be legal when the person or business who owns the name has had a legitimate business under that name for some period of time.

IT's About Business

6.3 Domain Tasting

A Verizon Communications (*www.verizon.com*) attorney regularly scours the Web and finds hundreds of new Web sites that use variations of Verizon's name. Examples include verizonpicture.com, vorizonrington.com, and varizoncellularphone.com. Significantly, none of these sites has anything to do with Verizon. The use of such similar but not identical names reflects a rapidly growing activity called "domain tasting."

Domain tasting, which is perfectly legal, lets registrars profit from the complex money trail of pay-per-click advertising. The practice can be traced back to the policies of the organization responsible for regulating Web names, the Internet Corporation for Assigned Names and Numbers (ICANN) (*www.icann.org*). In 2000, ICANN established the "create grace period," a five-day period when a company or person can claim a domain name and then return it for a full refund of the $6 registry fee. ICANN implemented this policy to allow someone who mistyped a domain to return it without cost.

"Domain tasters" exploit this policy by claiming Internet domains for five days at no cost. As we saw above, these domain names frequently resemble those of prominent companies and organizations. The tasters then jam these domains full of advertisements that come from Google and Yahoo. This means that the taster vorizonrington.com, for example, receives cash every time a visitor clicks on an ad like the one for Cingular found on that site at the end of 2006. With zero risk and 100 percent profit margins, tasters are now registering mass quantities of domain names every day—some of them over and over again. The Verizon attorney asserts that these individuals are purposely exploiting trademarks and misleading consumers.

In late 2004, roughly 100,000 domain names were being sampled on any given day. By mid-2007, that number exceeded 4 million. Experts estimate that registrants ultimately purchase less than 2 percent of the sites that they try out for a few days. In addition, with more than 250 suffixes besides ".com" to choose from, there is no end in sight to this practice.

Executives at domain tasting companies maintain that they provide a legitimate service. For example, if a Web surfer mistypes a Web address and lands on one of their sites, the companies can post an ad that redirects the surfer to the proper site. Other powerful forces oppose changing the system. For example, VeriSign, Inc. (*www.verisign.com*), which existed before ICANN, has made an agreement with ICANN that gives VeriSign control over both the .com and .net names until 2012. VeriSign can therefore sell .com and .net names to various companies. VeriSign claims that it is against any abuse of domain tasting, but it does not advocate the elimination of the five-day grace period, because it can sometimes be legitimate. Critics contend that VeriSign supports the status quo because the company makes so much money from its control of the .com and .net names.

Sources: Compiled from M. Herbst, "See Anything Odd about 'Vorizon'?" *BusinessWeek*, January 8, 2007; P. Thibodeau, "Cybersquatters Bank on 'A Good Typo'," *Computerworld*, April 16, 2007; L. Seltzer, "How Can We Take Domains Down Faster?" *eWeek*, April 5, 2007; *www.icann.org*, accessed May 11, 2007.

QUESTIONS

1. Should domain tasting be outlawed? Why or why not? Consider your answer from the viewpoint of a company with a strong brand presence on the Web. Then, consider your answer from the viewpoint of a domain taster.
2. Defend VeriSign's position in the domain tasting debate. Then oppose its position.

Companies such as Christian Dior, Nike, Deutsche Bank, and even Microsoft have had to fight or pay to get the domain name that corresponds to their company's name away from cybersquatters.

In an example that is *not* cybersquatting, Delta Air Lines originally could not obtain the Internet domain delta.com because Delta Faucet had purchased it first. Delta Faucet, in business under that name since 1954, had a legitimate business interest in it. Delta Air Lines had to settle for delta-airlines.com until it bought the domain name from Delta Faucet. Delta Faucet is now at deltafaucet.com.

Taxes and Other Fees. In offline sales, most states and localities tax business transactions that are conducted within their jurisdiction. The most obvious example is sales taxes. Federal, state, and local authorities now are scrambling to figure out how to extend these policies to e-business. This problem is particularly complex for interstate and international e-commerce. For example, some people claim that the state in which the *seller* is located deserves the entire sales tax (or in some countries, value-added tax, VAT). Others contend that the state in which the *server* is located also should receive some of the tax revenues.

In addition to the sales tax, there is a question about where (and in some cases, whether) electronic sellers should pay business license taxes, franchise fees, gross-receipts taxes, excise taxes, privilege taxes, and utility taxes. Furthermore, how should tax collection be controlled? Legislative efforts to impose taxes on e-commerce are opposed by an organization named the Internet Freedom Fighters. So far, their efforts have been successful. As of mid-2007, the United States and several other countries had imposed a ban on imposing a sales tax on business conducted on the Internet. In addition, buyers were exempt from tax on Internet access.

Copyright. Recall from Chapter 3 that intellectual property is protected by copyright laws and cannot be used freely. Protecting intellectual property in e-commerce is very difficult, however. Hundreds of millions of people in some 200 countries with differing copyright laws having access to billions of Web pages makes it far too difficult to protect intellectual property rights. For example, some people mistakenly believe that once they purchase a piece of software, they have the right to share it with others. In fact, what they have bought is the right to *use* the software, not the right to *distribute* it. That right remains with the copyright holder. Similarly, copying material from Web sites without permission is a violation of copyright laws.

Before you go on . . .

1. List some ethical issues in EC.
2. List the major legal issues of EC.
3. Describe buyer protection in EC.
4. Describe seller protection in EC.

What's in IT for Me?

For the Accounting Major

Accounting personnel are involved in several EC activities. Designing the ordering system and its relationship with inventory management requires accounting attention. Billing and payments are also accounting activities, as are determining cost and profit allocation. Replacing paper documents by electronic means will affect many of the accountant's tasks, especially the auditing of EC activities and systems. Finally, building a cost-benefit and cost-justification system of which products/

services to take online and creating a chargeback system are critical to the success of EC.

For the Finance Major

The worlds of banking, securities and commodities markets, and other financial services are being reengineered due to EC. Online securities trading and its supporting infrastructure are growing more rapidly than any other EC activity. Many innovations already in place are changing the rules of economic and financial incentives for financial analysts and managers. Online banking, for example, does not recognize state boundaries, and it may create a new framework for financing global trades. Public financial information is now accessible in seconds. These innovations will dramatically change the manner in which finance personnel operate.

For the Marketing Major

A major revolution in marketing and sales is taking place due to EC. Perhaps its most obvious feature is the transition from a physical to a virtual marketplace. Equally important, though, is the radical transformation to one-on-one advertising and sales and to customized and interactive marketing. Marketing channels are being combined, eliminated, or re-created. The EC revolution is creating new products and markets and significantly altering others. Digitization of products and services also has implications for marketing and sales. The direct producer-to-consumer channel is expanding rapidly and is fundamentally changing the nature of customer service. As the battle for customers intensifies, marketing and sales personnel are becoming the most critical success factor in many organizations. Online marketing can be a blessing to one company and a curse to another.

For the Production/Operations Management Major

EC is changing the manufacturing system from product-push mass production to order-pull mass customization. This change requires a robust supply chain, information support, and reengineering of processes that involve suppliers and other business partners. Using extranets, suppliers can monitor and replenish inventories without the need for constant reorders. In addition, the Internet and intranets help reduce cycle times. Many production/operations problems that have persisted for years, such as complex scheduling and excess inventories, are being solved rapidly with the use of Web technologies. Companies can now use external and internal networks to find and manage manufacturing operations in other countries much more easily. Also, the Web is reengineering procurement by helping companies conduct electronic bids for parts and subassemblies, thus reducing cost. All in all, the job of the progressive production/operations manager is closely tied in with e-commerce.

For the Human Resources Management Major

HR majors need to understand the new labor markets and the impacts of EC on old labor markets. Also, the HRM department may use EC tools for such functions as procuring office supplies. Also, becoming knowledgeable about new government online initiatives and online training is critical. Finally, HR personnel must be familiar with the major legal issues related to EC and employment.

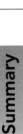

Summary

1. Describe electronic commerce, its scope, benefits, limitations, and types.

E-commerce can be conducted on the Web and on other networks. It is divided into the following major types: business-to-consumer, business-to-business, consumer-to-consumer, business-to-employee, and government-to-citizen. E-commerce offers many benefits to organizations, consumers, and society, but it also has limitations (technological and nontechnological). The current technological limitations are expected to lessen with time.

2. Distinguish between pure and partial electronic commerce.

In pure EC, the product or service, the process by which the product or service is produced, and the delivery agent are all digital. All other combinations that include a mix of digital and physical dimensions are considered partial EC.

3. Understand the basics of how online auctions work.

A major mechanism in EC is auctions. The Internet provides an infrastructure for executing auctions at lower cost, and with many more involved sellers and buyers, including both individual consumers and corporations. Two major types of auctions exist: forward auctions and reverse auctions. Forward auctions are used in the traditional process of *selling* to the highest bidder. Reverse auctions are used for *buying*, using a tendering system to buy at the lowest bid.

4. Differentiate among business-to-consumer (B2C), business-to-business (B2B), consumer-to-consumer (C2C), business-to-employee (B2E), and government-to-citizen (G2C) electronic commerce.

B2C (e-tailing) can be pure or part of a clicks-and-mortar organization. Direct marketing is done via solo storefronts, in malls, through electronic catalogs, or by using electronic auctions. The leading online B2C service industries are banking, securities trading, job markets, travel, and real estate. The major B2B applications are selling from catalogs and by forward auctions (the sell-side marketplace), buying in reverse auctions and in group and desktop purchasing (the buy-side marketplace), and trading in electronic exchanges and hubs. EC also can be done between consumers (C2C) but should be undertaken with caution. Auctions are the most popular C2C mechanism. C2C also can be done by use of online classified ads. B2E provides services to employees, typically over the company's intranet. G2C takes place between government and citizens, making government operations more effective and efficient.

5. Describe the major e-commerce support services, specifically payments and logistics.

New electronic payment systems are needed to complete transactions on the Internet. Electronic payments can be made by e-checks, e-credit cards, purchasing cards, e-cash, stored-value money cards, smart cards, person-to-person payments via services like Pay-Pal, electronic bill presentment and payment, and e-wallets. Order fulfillment is especially difficult and expensive in B2C, because of the need to ship relatively small orders to many customers.

6. Discuss some ethical and legal issues relating to e-commerce.

There is increasing fraud and unethical behavior on the Internet, including invasion of privacy by sellers and misuse of domain names. The value of domain names, taxation of online business, and how to handle legal issues in a multicountry environment are major legal concerns. Protection of customers, sellers, and intellectual property is also important.

Chapter Glossary

auction A competitive process in which either a seller solicits consecutive bids from buyers or a buyer solicits bids from sellers, and prices are determined dynamically by competitive bidding.

banners Electronic billboards, which typically contain a short text or graphical message to promote a product or a vendor.

bricks-and-mortar organizations Organizations in which the product, the process, and the delivery agent are all physical.

business-to-business (B2B) Electronic commerce in which both the sellers and the buyers are business organizations.

business-to-consumer (B2C) Electronic commerce in which the sellers are organizations and the buyers are individuals; also known as e-tailing.

business-to-employee (B2E) An organization using electronic commerce internally to provide information and services to its employees.

business model The method by which a company generates revenue to sustain itself.

buy-side marketplace B2B model in which organizations buy needed products or services from other organizations electronically, often through a reverse auction.

channel conflict The alienation of existing distributors when a company decides to sell to customers directly online.

clicks-and-mortar organizations Organizations that do business in both physical and digital dimensions.

consumer-to-consumer (C2C) Electronic commerce in which both the buyer and the seller are individuals (not businesses).

cyberbanking Various banking activities conducted electronically from home, a business, or on the road instead of at a physical bank location.

cybersquatting Registering domain names in the hope of selling them later at a higher price.

digital wallet (e-wallet) A software component in which a user stores secured personal and credit card information for one-click reuse.

disintermediation Elimination of intermediaries in electronic commerce.

e-business A broader definition of electronic commerce, including buying and selling of goods and services, as well as servicing customers, collaborating with business partners, conducting e-learning, and conducting electronic transactions within an organization.

e-government The use of electronic commerce to deliver information and public services to citizens, business partners, and suppliers of government entities, and those working in the public sector.

e-procurement Purchasing by using electronic support.

e-wallet (see **digital wallet**)

electronic commerce (e-commerce) The process of buying, selling, transferring, or exchanging products, services, or information via computer networks, including the Internet.

electronic mall A collection of individual shops under one Internet address.

electronic marketplace A virtual market space on the Web where many buyers and many sellers conduct electronic business activities.

electronic payment systems Computer-based systems that allow customers to pay for goods and services electronically, rather than writing a check or using cash.

electronic retailing (e-tailing) The direct sale of products and services through storefronts or electronic malls, usually designed around an electronic catalog format and/or auctions.

electronic storefront The Web site of a single company, with its own Internet address, at which orders can be placed.

exchange (see **public exchange**)

forward auction An auction that sellers use as a selling channel to many potential buyers; the highest bidder wins the items.

functional exchanges Electronic marketplaces where needed services such as temporary help or extra office space are traded on an "as-needed" basis.

group purchasing The aggregation of purchasing orders from many buyers so that a volume discount can be obtained.

horizontal exchanges Electronic marketplaces that connect buyers and sellers across many industries, used mainly for MRO materials.

mobile commerce (m-commerce) Electronic commerce conducted in a wireless environment.

multichanneling A process through which a company integrates its online and offline channels.

permission marketing Method of marketing that asks consumers to give their permission to voluntarily accept online advertising and e-mail.

person-to-person payments A form of electronic cash that enables the transfer of funds between two individuals, or between an individual and a business, without the use of a credit card.

pop-up ad An advertisement that is automatically launched by some trigger and appears in front of the active window.

pop-under ad An advertisement that is automatically launched by some trigger and appears underneath the active window.

public exchange (or exchange) Electronic marketplace in which there are many sellers and many buyers, and entry is open to all; it is frequently owned and operated by a third party.

reverse auction An auction in which one buyer, usually an organization, seeks to buy a product or a service, and suppliers submit bids; the lowest bidder wins.

sell-side marketplace B2B model in which organizations sell to other organizations from their own private e-marketplace and/or from a third-party site.

smart card A card that contains a microprocessor (chip) that enables the card to store a considerable amount of information (including stored funds) and to conduct processing.

spamming Indiscriminate distribution of e-mail without the receiver's permission.

stored-value money card A form of electronic cash on which a fixed amount of prepaid money is stored; the amount is reduced each time the card is used.

vertical exchanges Electronic marketplaces that connect buyers and sellers in a given industry.

viral marketing Online word-of-mouth marketing.

virtual bank A banking institution dedicated solely to Internet transactions.

virtual organizations Organizations in which the product, the process, and the delivery agent are all digital; also called pure-play organizations.

Discussion Questions

1. Discuss the major limitations of e-commerce. Which of these limitations are likely to disappear? Why?
2. Discuss the reasons for having multiple EC business models.
3. Distinguish between business-to-business forward auctions and buyers' bids for RFQs.
4. Discuss the benefits to sellers and buyers of a B2B exchange.

5. What are the major benefits of G2C electronic commerce?
6. Discuss the various ways to pay online in B2C. Which one(s) would you prefer and why?
7. Why is order fulfillment in B2C considered difficult?
8. Discuss the reasons for EC failures.
9. Should Mr. Coffee sell coffee makers online? *Hint*: Take a look at the discussion of channel conflict in this chapter.

Problem-Solving Activities

1. Assume you are interested in buying a car. You can find information about cars at numerous Web sites. Access five of them for information about new and used cars, financing, and insurance. Decide what car you want to buy. Configure your car by going to the car manufacturer's Web site. Finally, try to find the car from *www.autobytel.com*. What information is most supportive of your decision-making process? Write a report about your experience.
2. Compare the various electronic payment methods. Specifically, collect information from the vendors cited in the chapter and find more with google.com.

Pay attention to security level, speed, cost, and convenience.

3. Conduct a study on selling diamonds and gems online. Access such sites as *www.bluenile.com*, *www.diamond.com*, *www.thaigem.com*, *www.tiffany.com*, and *www.jewelryexchange.com*.
   a. What features are used in these sites to educate buyers about gemstones?
   b. How do these sites attract buyers?
   c. How do these sites increase trust for online purchasing?
   d. What customer service features do these sites provide?

4. Access *www.nacha.org*. What is NACHA? What is its role? What is the ACH? Who are the key participants in an ACH e-payment? Describe the "pilot" projects currently underway at ACH.

5. Access *www.espn.com*. Identify at least five different ways it generates revenue.

6. Access *www.queendom.com*. Examine its offerings and try some of them. What type of electronic commerce is this? How does this Web site generate revenue?

7. Access *www.ediets.com*. Prepare a list of all the services the company provides. Identify its revenue model.

8. Access *www.theknot.com*. Identify its revenue sources.

Web Activities

1. Access the Stock Market Game Worldwide (*www.smgww.org*). You will be bankrolled with $100,000 in a trading account every month. Play the game and relate your experiences with regard to information technology.

2. Access *www.realtor.com*. Prepare a list of services available on this site. Then prepare a list of advantages derived by the users and advantages to realtors. Are there any disadvantages? to whom?

3. Enter *www.alibaba.com*. Identify the site's capabilities. Look at the site's private trading room. Write a report. How can such a site help a person who is making a purchase?

4. Enter *www.campusfood.com*. Explore the site. Why is the site so successful? Could you start a competing one? Why or why not?

5. Enter *www.dell.com*, go to "desktops," and configure a system. Register to "my cart" (no obligation). What calculators are used there? What are the advantages of this process as compared with buying a computer in a physical store? What are the disadvantages?

6. Enter *www.checkfree.com* and *www.lmlpayment.com* to find their services. Prepare a report.

7. Access various travel sites such as *www.travelocity.com*, *www.orbitz.com*, *www.expedia.com*, *www.sidestep.com*, and *www.pinpoint.com*. Compare these Web sites for ease of use and usefulness. Note differences among the sites. If you ask each site for the itinerary, which one gives you the best information and the best deals?

8. Access *www.outofservice.com* and answer the musical taste and personality survey. When you have finished, click on Results and see what your musical tastes say about your personality. How accurate are the findings about you?

Team Assignments

1. Have each team study a major bank with extensive EC strategy. For examples, look at Wells Fargo Bank (*www.wellsfargo.com*), Citicorp (*www.citicorp.com*), NetBank (*www.netbank.com*), and HSBC (*www.hsbc.com*) in Hong Kong. Each team should attempt to convince the class that its e-bank activities are the best.

2. Assign each team to one industry vertical. An industry vertical is a group of industries in the "same" business, such as financial services, insurance, health care, manufacturing, retail, telecommunications, pharmaceuticals, and chemicals. Each team will find five real-world applications of the major business-to-business models listed in the chapter. (Try success stories of vendors and EC-related magazines.) Examine the problems they solve or the opportunities they exploit.

3. Have teams investigate how B2B payments are made in global trade. Consider instruments such as electronic letters of credit and e-checks. Visit *www.tradecard.com* and examine their services to small and medium-size enterprises (SMEs). Also, investigate what Visa and MasterCard are offering. Finally, check Citicorp and some German and Japanese banks.

Just How Predictable Are You?

THE BUSINESS PROBLEM In a time of giant, impersonal retailers and self-checkout stations, independent retailers compete by attempting to know you almost better than you know yourself. Why is this important? By knowing you this well, retailers can recommend products to you that you are likely to purchase.

We do not simply *buy* products; rather, our products are an extension of who we *are*. We put ourselves on display through our purchases, wearing our personalities on our sleeves, literally and figuratively, for the world to see. In the real world, we use apparent information, coupled with context, experience, and stereotypes, to size up one another. This sort of intuition is useful and often accurate, but it is also fallible.

In the online world, the picture becomes clearer. Consumers now routinely rank experiences on the Web—four stars on IMDb (*www.imdb.com*) for *The Departed*, three stars on Epinions (*www.epinions.com*) for a Roomba vacuum, a positive eBay or Amazon rating, a Flickr tag. Each time you leave such a mark, you provide valuable information for other people, but you also leave a trail. For the company that can decipher all that information, the opportunities are amazing. That company will know you better than anyone. It will pinpoint your tastes and determine the likelihood that you will buy a given product.

Companies in the recommendation business, from newcomers like MyStrands (*www.mystrands.com*) and StumbleUpon (*www.stumbleupon.com*) to titans like Yahoo and Amazon, maintain that the Web is leaving the era of search and entering the era of discovery. Search is what you do when you are looking for something. Discovery is when something great that you did not know exists, or did not know how to ask for, finds you.

When it comes to search, Google is the clear winner. But there is not yet a go-to discovery site. Building a personalized discovery mechanism will mean tapping into all the manners of expression, categorization, and opinions that exist on the Web today. If a company can do this and make the formula portable so that it works on your mobile device, such a tool could change not just marketing, but all of commerce.

POTENTIAL IT SOLUTIONS Amazon realized early on how powerful a recommender system could be, and to this day it remains the prime example of such a system. The company uses a series of collaborative filtering algorithms (mathematical formulas) to compare your purchasing patterns with everyone else's and thus narrow its vast inventory to products it predicts you will buy.

However, the new generation of recommenders will do it better than Amazon. For example, Pandora (*www.pandora.com*) has an incredibly efficient new-music discovery mechanism. Consider the alternatives: scouring magazines for reviews, flipping through DVDs in the record store, listening to radio stations. At Pandora, you type in the name of a band or song and immediately begin hearing similar tunes that the site's recommendation system—the Music Genome Project—has determined that you will enjoy. By rating songs and artists, you can refine the suggestions, allowing Pandora to create a truly personalized music collection for you.

Unlike collaborative filtering engines, Pandora understands each song in its database. Forty-five analysts, many with music degrees, rank 15,000 songs every month on 400 characteristics (or descriptors), on a scale from 1 to 10. When a user chooses the first song, the algorithm searches for songs with similar characteristics. Each time the user rates a song with a thumbs-up or a thumbs-down, the algorithm changes the weighting of the descriptors to better reflect the tastes of the user. Four million people now use Pandora.

Pandora's Music Genome Project combs through hundreds of thousands of songs and millions of pieces of user feedback. This analysis has serious implications. If Pandora knows your musical preferences intimately, and your musical tastes are an intimate expression of who you are, then Pandora could introduce you to a lot more than music.

Pandora's founder and a psychology professor have conducted research studies on the links between musical taste and personality. They discovered that music turns out to be a poor predictor of emotional stability, courage, and ambition. However, it accurately predicts extroversion, agreeableness, conscientiousness, openness, imagination, and even intellect. An ongoing study at *www.outofservice.com*, where 90,000 people have taken a music/personality quiz, pushes the point even further, tying musical taste to political leanings, demographics, lifestyle, favorite authors, and movies.

THE RESULTS As of mid-2007, as Pandora and other recommender companies (for example, What to Rent, *www.whattorent.com*) were still in the startup stage. Therefore, the results of these efforts to get to know customers intimately through their musical tastes are not in. However, the big question at this time is: Where is Google? Google refuses to comment on whether the company has a recommendation application in the works. Interestingly, however,

Google's director of research, Peter Norvig, is an advisor to CleverSet (*www.cleverset.com*), a recommender company.

Recommender connections have broad implications for businesses of all kinds. The most fundamental implication is rather simple: Goodbye, context-based advertising. Hello, personality-based advertising.

Sources: Compiled from D. DeJean, "Copyright Board Puts Internet Radio on Death Watch," *InformationWeek*, April 17, 2007; D. DeJean, "Now Hear This: More on Internet Radio," *InformationWeek*, April 16, 2007; D. DeJean, "6 Internet Radio Sites Help You Discover New Music," *InformationWeek*, April 15, 2007; R. Martin, "Outrageous Royalty Ruling to Be Reviewed," *InformationWeek*, March 23, 2007; Y. Adegoke, "Slacker Personalizes Internet Radio with iPod Rival,"

Reuters, March 16, 2007; P. Sloan, "The Quest for the Perfect Online Ad," *Business 2.0*, March 2007; J. O'Brien, "You're Sooooooooooo Predictable," *Fortune*, November 27, 2006; *www.pandora.com*, *www.whattorent.com*, *www.cleverset.com*, accessed May 11, 2007.

QUESTIONS

1. What are the implications of recommenders? What is the relationship between your privacy and recommendation engines? Are recommendation engines the ultimate form of 1:1, or personalized, marketing?
2. What are the implications for a recommender like Pandora with regard to copyright violations?

Web Resources   wiley.com/college/rainer

Student Web Site
- Web Quizzes
- Student Lecture Slides in PowerPoint
- Virtual Company ClubIT: Website and Assignments

WileyPLUS
- e-book
- Flash Cards
- How-To Animations for Microsoft Office

E-commerce at Club IT

Go to the Club IT link on the *WileyPLUS* Web site to find assignments that will ask you to help Club IT's owner's leverage e-commerce.

wiley.com/college/rainer

How-To Appendix

Tips for Safe Electronic Shopping
- Look for reliable brand names at sites like *Wal-Mart Online, Disney Online*, and Amazon.com. Before purchasing, make sure that the site is authentic by entering the site directly and not from an unverified link.

- Search any unfamiliar selling site for the company's address and phone and fax numbers. Call up and quiz the employees about the seller.

- Check out the vendor with the local Chamber of Commerce or Better Business Bureau (bbbonline.org). Look for seals of authenticity such as TRUSTe.

- Investigate how secure the seller's site is by examining the security procedures and by reading the posted privacy policy.

- Examine the money-back guarantees, warranties, and service agreements.

- Compare prices with those in regular stores. Too-low prices are too good to be true, and some catch is probably involved.

- Ask friends what they know. Find testimonials and endorsements in community sites and well-known bulletin boards.

- Find out what your rights are in case of a dispute. Consult consumer protection agencies and the National Fraud Information Center (fraud.org).

- Check consumerworld.org for a listing of useful resources.

Chapter 7

Wireless, Mobile Computing, and Mobile Commerce

Student Web Site

- Web Quizzes
- Lecture Slides in PowerPoint
- Virtual Company ClubIT: Website and Assignments

WileyPLUS

- e-book
- Flash Cards
- Software Skills Tutorials: Using Microsoft Office 2007
- How-To Animations for Microsoft Office

What's in IT for me?   ACC   FIN   MKT   POM   HRM   MIS

RFID Shows Disconnect between Manufacturers and Retailers

The Business Problem

Gillette (*www.pg.com/en_US/gillette/index.jhtml*), purchased by Procter & Gamble (P&G), is the market leader in razors. Gillette was aware that consumer goods manufacturers, like the retailers they supply, are still in the learning phase of how to use electronic product codes, the product information stored on radio frequency identification (RFID) tags. RFID technology allows manufacturers to attach tags with antennas and computer chips on goods and then track their movement through radio signals.

In fact, RFID has many problems. RFID readers get crushed by forklifts and clumsy warehouse employees. Many RFID tags are rendered unreadable by product packaging or poor placement on products. Metal, such as aluminum foil packaging, can block RFID signals. In addition, little of the data generated by RFID systems is being utilized effectively.

As a result, Gillette took a careful, measured approach to RFID during the launch of its new Fusion brand, a five-bladed razor with a trimmer on the back. The company used RFID to track the pallets, cases, and displays in order to test the display compliance—that is, whether stores were setting up displays on time and according to directions—at just two of its retail partners. Only 400 stores and 4 distribution centers were involved in the test.

Gillette had conducted RFID trials in the past. One such trial, which tracked displays of the company's Venus line of razors for women, pointed out a major problem. More than 30 percent of the Venus displays were not getting set up on the sales floor in time. A similar trial with Gillette's Braun CruZer electric shavers revealed equally poor results.

In the retail business, promotional display compliance rates are not what they should be. Manufacturers are lucky if 60 percent of their displays make it out on the sales floor within three days of a launch or promotion. Sales typically spike during promotions. Therefore, if a promotion is not successful, then the lost sales are especially large.

In the case of Fusion, the launch had to be successful for P&G, in part to justify the $57 billion the company spent to acquire Gillette. To ensure success, P&G planned to spend a reported $200 million to support the launch. The marketing campaign included two Super Bowl ads, at a total cost of $6 million, and ads in every major men's magazine, from *Sports Illustrated* to *Esquire*. A critical part of the launch was making certain that the product was available and visible in stores when the launch began. In the first week alone, P&G sent out 180,000 promotional Fusion displays to participating stores.

The IT Solution

Given the high stakes, Gillette executives took RFID into account two years before the launch, after the product had been developed but before the packaging was designed. Gillette put its RFID engineers together with its packaging engineers to make sure that the packaging would not interfere with the function of the RFID system. From the type of aluminum foil used in the packaging to the placement of the tags on pallets and displays, Gillette's engineers looked for what is known as the "sweet spot." This spot provides the most consistent reading from the RFID tags.

The Results

One of the goals of tagging the Fusion displays was to boost sales at the 400 stores participating in the RFID program. More importantly, though, was what P&G learned from the launch. The company received data from the tags at a number of spots along the supply chain: leaving P&G's distribution center, arriving at the retailer's distribution center, leaving the retailer's distribution center, entering the retail store's stockroom, entering the sales floor, and finally, entering the retail store's box crusher.

As soon as the data began flowing back to P&G, the inefficiencies in the supply chain became apparent. Some stores were getting too much product, while others received none at all. Some displays never even made it to the retail floor. In response, Gillette representatives were able to notify their retailers and redirect product shipments, usually within 24 hours. Stock clerks used handheld devices to detect RFID transmissions in order to find Fusion displays that were buried behind other merchandise. Finally, P&G merchandising employees were dispatched to stores that were not in compliance with the schedule to correct these problems.

By the third day of the launch, the RFID-enabled stores involved in the test had achieved a compliance rate of 92 percent, a level that exceeded expectations. They also achieved significantly higher sales numbers, which P&G claimed more than covered the costs of applying the tags. The overall launch was also successful. In its first four weeks on the market, Fusion gained 55 percent of the razor market. Sales slowed down considerably after that, perhaps because consumers were not buying refills as quickly as predicted.

P&G conceded that some problems emerged at each location because of radio interference and because some RFID tag readers were turned off or were run over by forklifts. Overall, however, the RFID data from the Fusion launch highlighted a significant disconnect between manufacturers and retailers, one that RFID is designed to address.

Basically, compliance does not mean the same thing to the manufacturer as it does to the retailer. Some retailers allow store managers to make decisions about which products they will sell to their particular customers. This policy places the manufacturers at a disadvantage because they do not have control over what store managers do. There is also the issue of when and how RFID is implemented along the supply chain. Manufacturers want to implement RFID one product at a time, whereas retail stores want to install the physical infrastructure for RFID systems store by store.

P&G has developed a timetable for tagging its thousands of products, called the EPC (Electronic Product Code) Advanced Strategy. This strategy places P&G products into three categories: EPC Advantaged, EPC Testable, and EPC Challenged. Fusion was in the Advantaged category because the product has high volume and can be easily tagged. Swiffer sweepers are in the Testable category, for which P&G is still determining the business case for tagging. Challenged products include low-value items or items with packaging that makes RFID impossible, such as Cascade dishwasher detergent, which uses a foil liner.

The eventual goal at both P&G (a manufacturer) and Wal-Mart (a retailer) is to tag all their products. That goal will have to wait, however, until the costs of both the RFID tags themselves and the infrastructure needed to read them drop significantly. In the meantime, tracking product-display compliance is a practical, cost-effective way for manufacturers to enter the RFID arena.

Wireless is a term used to describe telecommunications in which electromagnetic waves, rather than some form of wire or cable, carry the signal between communicating devices (e.g., computers, personal digital assistants, and cell phones). The opening case is an example of the use of a wireless technology (RFID) that provided valuable information about a problem between P&G and its retailers. P&G's problem also applies to any company with a supply chain (e.g., Wal-Mart). Going further, the case also demonstrates that wireless technology is in its beginning stages, with exciting potential but currently high costs.

In many situations, the traditional working environment that requires users to come to a wired computer is either ineffective or inefficient. In these situations, the solution is to build computers small enough to carry or wear, which can communicate via wireless networks. The ability to communicate anytime and anywhere provides organizations with strategic advantage by increasing productivity and speed and improving customer service.

Wireless technologies enable mobile computing, mobile commerce, and pervasive computing. **Mobile computing** refers to a real-time, wireless connection between a mobile device and other computing environments, such as the Internet or an intranet. **Mobile commerce**—also

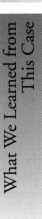
What We Learned from This Case

known as **m-commerce**—refers to e-commerce (EC) transactions that are conducted in a wireless environment, especially via the Internet. **Pervasive computing**, also called **ubiquitous computing**, means that virtually every object has processing power with wireless or wired connections to a global network.

Wireless technologies and mobile commerce are spreading rapidly, replacing or supplementing wired computing. In some cases, wireless technologies are allowing countries to build a communications infrastructure from scratch. For example, in India's Orissa State, an Indian nongovernmental organization is providing bus-powered Wi-Fi service. The buses use short-range radio that pick up electronic messages three or four times per day from Wi-Fi-enabled computers placed in kiosks. This combination of wireless technology and old-fashioned "bus technology" makes communications affordable to people with no previous access to the Internet.

The wireless infrastructure on which mobile computing is built may reshape the entire IT field. The technologies, applications, and limitations of mobile computing and mobile commerce are the main focus of this chapter. We begin the chapter with a discussion of wireless devices and wireless transmission media. We continue by examining wireless computer networks and wireless Internet access. We then look at mobile computing and mobile commerce, which are made possible by wireless technologies. Next, we turn our attention to pervasive computing, and we conclude the chapter by discussing wireless security.

Sources: Compiled from D. Briody, "Gillette's Fusion Launch Makes a Good Business Case for RFID," *CIO Insight*, August 11, 2006; E. Schuman, "P&G's End-to-End RFID Plan," *Baseline Magazine*, June 28, 2006; M. O'Connor, "Gillette Fuses RFID with Product Launch," *RFID Journal*, March 27, 2006; C. Sliwa, "Gillette Shaves Costs with RFID," *TechWorld*, January 5, 2005; *www.pg.com/en_US/gillette/index.jhtml*, accessed April 27, 2007.

7.1 Wireless Technologies

Wireless technologies include both wireless devices, such as smart phones, and wireless transmission media, such as microwave, satellite, and radio. These technologies are fundamentally changing the ways organizations operate and do business.

Wireless Devices

Individuals are finding it convenient and productive to use wireless devices for several reasons. First, they can make productive use of time that was formerly wasted (for example, while commuting to work on public transportation). Second, because they can take these devices with them, their work locations are becoming much more flexible. Third, wireless technology enables them to allocate their working time around personal and professional obligations.

The **Wireless Application Protocol (WAP)** is the standard that enables wireless devices to access Web-based information and services. WAP-compliant devices contain **microbrowsers**, which are Internet browsers with a small file size that can work within the confines of small screen sizes on wireless devices and the relatively low bandwidths of wireless networks. Figure 7.1A shows the full-function browser on Amazon's Web page, and Figure 7.1B shows the microbrowser on the screen of a cell phone accessing Amazon.com. As wireless devices become increasingly powerful, the trend is for these devices to have browsers with more functionality. For example, the Apple iPhone (*www.apple.com/iphone*) runs the Safari browser.

Wireless devices are small enough to easily carry or wear, have sufficient computing power to perform productive tasks, and can communicate wirelessly with the Internet and other devices. In the past we have discussed these devices in separate categories, such as pagers, e-mail handhelds, personal digital assistants (PDAs), and cellular telephones. Today, however, new devices, generally called *smart phones*, combine the functions of these devices.

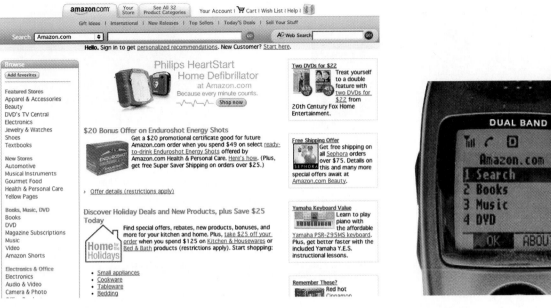

FIGURE 7.1A   Amazon Web page browser. *Source: www.amazon.com*

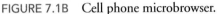

FIGURE 7.1B   Cell phone microbrowser.

The capabilities of these new devices include cellular telephony, Bluetooth, Wi-Fi, a digital camera, global positioning system (GPS), an organizer, a scheduler, an address book, a calculator, access to e-mail and **short message service** (sending and receiving short text messages up to 160 characters in length), instant messaging, text messaging, an MP3 music-player, a video-player, Internet access with a full-function browser, and a QWERTY keyboard. Not all of these new devices have all these capabilities, but they are heading rapidly in that direction. Examples of new devices include:

- The BlackBerry 8800 (see *www.rim.com* and *www.blackberry8800.com*) (see Figure 7.2)
- The Treo 750 (see *www.palm.com*)
- The Motorola Q (see *www.motorola.com*)
- The Helio Ocean (see *www.helio.com*) (see Figure 7.3)
- The Apple iPhone (see *www.apple.com/iphone*) (see Figure 7.4)
- The Sony Mylo (see *www.sony.com/mylo*) (see Figure 7.5)

One downside of smart phones is that people can use them to copy and pass on confidential information. For example, if you were an executive at Intel, would you want workers snapping pictures of their colleagues with your secret new technology in the background? Unfortunately, managers think of these devices as phones, not as digital cameras that can transmit wirelessly. New jamming devices are being developed to counter the threat. For example, Iceberg Systems (*www.iceberg-ip.com*) provides technology that deactivates the imaging systems in camera phones after they enter specific locations. Some companies, such as Samsung (*www.samsung.com*), have recognized the danger and have banned the devices altogether.

FIGURE 7.2
BlackBerry 8800.
Source: Courtesy
Research in Motion
Limited.

Wireless Transmission Media

Wireless media, or broadcast media, transmit signals without wires over the air or in space. The major types of wireless media are microwave, satellite, radio, and infrared. Table 7.1 lists the advantages and disadvantages of wireless media.

FIGURE 7.3   Helio Ocean. *Source:* Courtesy HELIO, LLC.

FIGURE 7.4   Apple iPhone. *Source:* © Edward A. Ornelas/ San-Antonio Express-News/ Zuma Press.

FIGURE 7.5   Sony Mylo. *Source:* Used by permission of Sony Electronics, Inc.

Microwave.   **Microwave transmission** systems are widely used for high-volume, long-distance, line-of-sight communication. Line of sight means that the transmitter and receiver must be in view of each other. The fact that adjacent microwave towers must be in view of each other creates problems because the earth's surface is curved and not flat. For this reason, microwave towers usually cannot be spaced more than 30 miles apart.

This requirement severely limits the usefulness of microwave transmissions as a solution to data communications needs, especially over very long distances. In addition, microwave transmissions are susceptible to environmental interference during severe weather such as heavy rain or snowstorms. Although long-distance microwave data communications systems are still widely used, they are being replaced by satellite communications systems.

Satellite.   **Satellite transmission** systems make use of communication satellites. Currently, there are three types of satellites around the earth: geostationary (GEO), medium earth orbit (MEO), and low earth orbit (LEO). Each type has a different orbit, with GEO being

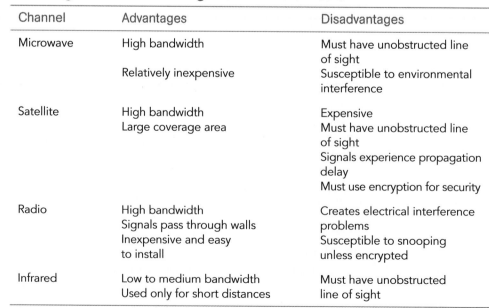

Table 7.1

Advantages and Disadvantages of Wireless Media

Channel	Advantages	Disadvantages
Microwave	High bandwidth	Must have unobstructed line of sight
	Relatively inexpensive	Susceptible to environmental interference
Satellite	High bandwidth	Expensive
	Large coverage area	Must have unobstructed line of sight
		Signals experience propagation delay
		Must use encryption for security
Radio	High bandwidth	Creates electrical interference problems
	Signals pass through walls	Susceptible to snooping unless encrypted
	Inexpensive and easy to install	
Infrared	Low to medium bandwidth	Must have unobstructed line of sight
	Used only for short distances	

farthest from the earth and LEO the closest. Table 7.2 compares and contrasts the three types of satellites.

As with microwave transmission, satellites must receive and transmit data via line of sight. However, the enormous *footprint*—the area of the earth's surface reached by a satellite's transmission—overcomes the limitations of microwave data relay stations. The most basic rule governing footprint size is simple: The higher a satellite orbits, the larger its footprint. Thus, middle-earth-orbit satellites have a smaller footprint than geostationary satellites, and low-earth-orbit satellites have the smallest footprint of all. Figure 7.6 compares the footprints of the three types of satellite.

In contrast to line-of-sight transmission with microwave, satellites use *broadcast* transmission, which sends signals to many receivers at one time. So, even though satellites are line-of-sight like microwave, they are high enough for broadcast transmission, thus overcoming the limitations of microwave.

Types of Orbits. *Geostationary earth orbit (GEO)* satellites orbit 22,300 miles directly above the equator. These satellites maintain a fixed position above the earth's surface because at their altitude, their orbital period matches the 24-hour rotational period of the earth. For this reason, receivers on the earth do not have to track GEO satellites. GEO satellites are excellent for sending television programs to cable operators and broadcasting directly to homes.

Three Basic Types of Telecommunications Satellites

Table 7.2

Type	Characteristics	Orbit	Number	Use
GEO	• Satellites remain stationary relative to point on earth • Few satellites needed for global coverage • Transmission delay (approximately 0.25 second) • Most expensive to build and launch • Longest orbital life (many years)	22,300 miles	8	TV signal
MEO	• Satellites move relative to point on earth • Moderate number needed for global coverage • Requires medium-powered transmitters • Negligible transmission delay • Less expensive to build and launch • Moderate orbital life (6–12 years)	6,434 miles	10–12	GPS
LEO	• Satellites move rapidly relative to point on earth • Large number needed for global coverage • Requires only low-power transmitters • Negligible transmission delay • Least expensive to build and launch • Shortest orbital life (as low as 5 years)	400–700 miles	Many	Telephone

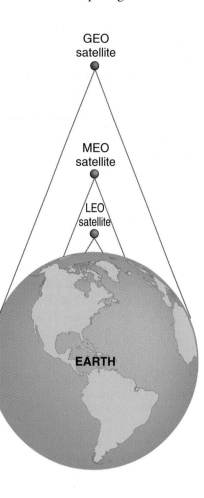

FIGURE 7.6
Comparison of satellite
footprints.
Source: Drawn by Kelly
Rainer.

One major limitation of GEO satellites is that their transmissions take a quarter of a second to send and return. This brief pause, called **propagation delay**, makes two-way telephone conversations difficult. Also, GEO satellites are large and expensive, and require large amounts of power to launch.

Medium-earth-orbit (MEO) satellites are located about 6,000 miles above the earth's surface. MEO orbits require more satellites to cover the earth than GEO orbits, because MEO footprints are smaller. MEO satellites have two advantages over GEO satellites: They are less expensive, and they do not have an appreciable propagation delay. However, because MEO satellites move with respect to a point on the earth's surface, receivers must track these satellites. (Think of a satellite dish slowly turning to remain oriented to a MEO satellite.)

Low-earth-orbit (LEO) satellites are located 400 to 700 miles above the earth's surface. Because LEO satellites are much closer to the earth, they have little, if any, propagation delay. Like MEO satellites, however, LEO satellites move with respect to a point on the earth's surface and therefore must be tracked by receivers. Tracking LEO satellites is more difficult than tracking MEO satellites, because LEO satellites move much more quickly than MEO satellites relative to a point on the earth.

Unlike GEO and MEO satellites, LEO satellites can pick up signals from weak transmitters. This is important because handheld telephones that operate via LEO satellites need less power and can use smaller batteries. Another advantage of LEO satellites is that they consume less power and cost less to launch than GEO and MEO satellites.

At the same time, however, the footprints of LEO satellites are small, which means that many of them are required to cover the earth. For this reason a single organization often produces multiple LEO satellites, known as *LEO constellations.* Two examples are Iridium and Globalstar.

Iridium (*www.iridium.com*) has placed a LEO constellation in orbit that consists of 66 satellites and 12 in-orbit spare satellites. The company maintains that it provides complete satellite communications coverage of the earth's surface, including the polar regions. Globalstar (*www.globalstar.com*) also has a LEO constellation in orbit.

Global Positioning Systems. The **global positioning system (GPS)** is a wireless system that uses satellites to enable users to determine their position anywhere on the earth. GPS is supported by 24 satellites that are shared worldwide. As of mid-2007, the only GPS is owned and operated by the U.S. Department of Defense.

The exact position of each satellite is always known because the satellite continuously broadcasts its position along with a time signal. By using the known speed of the signals and the distance from three satellites (for two-dimensional location) or four satellites (for three-dimensional location), it is possible to find the location of any receiving station or user within a range of 10 feet. GPS software can also convert the user's latitude and longitude to an electronic map. Figure 7.7 shows a smart phone giving directions obtained from a GPS system.

Commercial use of GPS has become widespread, including for navigation, mapping, and surveying, particularly in remote areas. Cell phones in the United States now must have a GPS embedded in them so that the location of a person making an emergency call (for example, 911 in the United States) can be detected immediately. For a GPS tutorial, see *www.trimble.com/gps.*

FIGURE 7.7 Smart phone and GPS system. *Source:* ©AP/Wide World Photos.

Internet over Satellite (IoS). In many regions of the world, IoS is the only option available for Internet connections because installing the necessary cables is either too expensive or is physically impossible. *Internet over Satellite* allows users to access the Internet via GEO satellites from a dish mounted on the side of their homes. Although IoS makes the Internet available to many people who otherwise could not access it, it has its drawbacks. As we have seen, GEO satellite transmissions entail a propagation delay, and they can be disrupted by environmental influences such as thunderstorms.

Radio. **Radio transmission** uses radio-wave frequencies to send data directly between transmitters and receivers. Radio transmission has several advantages. To begin with, radio waves travel easily through normal office walls. In addition, radio devices are fairly inexpensive and easy to install. Finally, radio waves can transmit data at high speeds. For these reasons, radio increasingly is being used to connect computers to both peripheral equipment and local area networks.

As with other technologies, however, radio transmission has its drawbacks as well. Radio media can create electrical interference problems, and radio transmissions are susceptible to snooping by anyone who has similar equipment that operates on the same frequency.

Satellite Radio. One problem with radio transmission is that when you travel too far away from the source station, the signal breaks up and fades into static. Most radio signals can travel only about 30 or 40 miles from their source. However, **satellite radio**, also called **digital radio**, overcomes this problem. Satellite radio offers uninterrupted, near CD-quality music that is beamed to your radio, either at home or in your car, from space. In addition, satellite radio offers a broad spectrum of stations, types of music, news, and talk.

XM Satellite Radio (*www.xmradio.com*) and Sirius Satellite Radio (*www.sirius.com*) were competitors who launched satellite radio services. XM broadcast its signals from GEO satellites, and Sirius used MEO satellites. The two companies merged in 2007. Listeners subscribe to the service for a monthly fee.

Infrared.   The final type of wireless transmission is infrared transmission. **Infrared** light is red light that is not commonly visible to human eyes. Common applications of infrared light are in remote control units for televisions, VCRs, DVDs, and CD players. In addition, like radio transmission, infrared transceivers are used for short-distance connections between computers and peripheral equipment and local area networks. A *transceiver* is a device that can transmit and receive signals. Many portable PCs have infrared ports, which are handy when cable connections with a peripheral (such as a printer or modem) are not practical.

Before you go on . . .

1. Describe today's wireless devices.
2. Describe the various types of transmission media.

7.2 Wireless Computer Networks and Internet Access

Wireless devices typically form wireless computer networks, which provide wireless Internet access.

Short-Range Wireless Networks

Short-range wireless networks simplify the task of connecting one device to another, eliminating wires and enabling users to move around while they use the devices. In general, short-range wireless networks have a range of 100 feet or less.

Bluetooth.   **Bluetooth** (*www.bluetooth.com*) is an industry specification used to create small personal area networks. A **personal area network** is a computer network used for communication among computer devices (for example, telephones, personal digital assistants, and smart phones) close to one person. Bluetooth can link up to eight devices within a 10-meter area (about 30 feet) using low-power, radio-based communication. It can transmit up to 2.1 Mbps (megabits per second). Ericsson, the Scandinavian mobile handset company that developed this standard, called it Bluetooth, after the tenth-century Danish King Harald Blatan, who was known as Bluetooth.

Common applications for Bluetooth are wireless handsets for cell phones and portable music players. The advantages of Bluetooth include its low power consumption and its use of omnidirectional radio waves. This means that you do not have to point one Bluetooth device at another for a connection to occur.

Ultra-Wideband.   **Ultra-wideband (UWB)** is a high-bandwidth wireless technology with transmission speeds in excess of 100 Mbps. This very high speed makes UWB a good choice for applications such as streaming multimedia from, say, a personal computer to a television. Developers of Bluetooth and UWB are now collaborating so that the two technologies will work together seamlessly.

Near-Field Communications.   **Near-field communications (NFC)** has the smallest range of any short-range wireless networks. It is designed to be embedded in mobile devices such as cell phones and credit cards. Using NFC, you can swipe your device or card within a few centimeters of point-of-sale terminals to pay for items.

Medium-Range Wireless Networks

Medium-range wireless networks are the familiar wireless local area networks (WLANs). The most common type of medium-range wireless network is Wireless Fidelity or Wi-Fi.

Wireless Fidelity (Wi-Fi).   **Wireless Fidelity (or Wi-Fi)** is a medium-range **wireless local area network (WLAN)**, which is basically a wired LAN but without the cables. In a typical configuration, a transmitter with an antenna, called a **wireless access point**, connects to a wired LAN or to satellite dishes that provide an Internet connection. Figure 7.8 shows a wireless access point. A wireless access point provides service to a number of users within a small geographical perimeter (up to a couple of hundred feet), known as a **hotspot**. To support a larger number of users across a larger geographical area, several wireless access points are needed. To communicate wirelessly, mobile devices, such as laptop PCs, typically have a built-in **wireless network interface card (WNIC)**.

FIGURE 7.8   Wireless access point.
Source: D-Link systems.

Wi-Fi provides fast and easy Internet or intranet broadband access from public hotspots located at airports, hotels, Internet cafés, universities, conference centers, offices, and homes. Figure 7.9 shows people computing wirelessly at Starbucks. Broadband means high bandwidth. Users can access the Internet while walking across the campus, in their office, or throughout their homes (see *www.weca.net*). In addition, users can access Wi-Fi with their laptops, desktops, or PDAs by adding a wireless network card. Most PC and laptop manufacturers incorporate these cards directly in their PCs (as an option).

The Institute of Electrical and Electronics Engineers (IEEE) has established a set of standards for wireless computer networks. The IEEE standard for Wi-Fi is the 802.11 family. There are four standards in this family: 802.11a, 802.11b, 802.11g, and 802.11n.

Today, most WLANs use the 802.11g standard, which can transmit up to 54 Mbps and has a range of about 300 feet. As of mid-2007, the 802.11n standard is still under development. This standard is designed to have wireless transmission speeds between 250 and 300 Mbps, and a range double that of 802.11g, or some 600 feet.

Many vendors offer equipment that can boost wireless transmission speeds. For example, Netgear (*www.netgear.com*) states that its Super G wireless router can provide a transmission speed of 108 Mbps.

The major benefits of Wi-Fi are its low cost and its ability to provide simple Internet access. It is the greatest facilitator of the *wireless Internet*, that is, the ability to connect to the Internet wirelessly. Significantly, laptop PCs are equipped with chips that can send and receive Wi-Fi signals.

Corporations are using Wi-Fi to provide a broad range of services. For example, Starbucks, McDonald's, Borders, Panera, and Barnes & Noble are offering customers Wi-Fi in many of their stores, mainly for Internet access. They receive some revenue from their fees for Wi-Fi services, but their strategy is to encourage customers to spend more time in their stores and to choose their stores over those of competitors.

FIGURE 7.9
Starbucks' patrons using Wi-Fi.
Source: © Marianna Day Massey/Zuma Press.

Although Wi-Fi has become extremely popular, it is not without problems. Three factors are preventing the commercial Wi-Fi market from expanding even further: roaming, security, and cost. Regarding the first factor, at this time users cannot roam from hotspot to hotspot if the hotspots use different Wi-Fi network services. Unless the service is free, users have to log on to separate accounts and pay a separate fee for each service. Keep in mind that some Wi-Fi hotspots offer free service, while others charge a fee.

Security is the second barrier to greater acceptance of Wi-Fi. Because Wi-Fi uses radio waves, it is difficult to shield from intruders. We discuss Wi-Fi security in the last section of this chapter.

The final limitation to greater Wi-Fi expansion is cost. Even though Wi-Fi services are relatively inexpensive, many experts question whether commercial Wi-Fi services can survive when so many free hotspots are available to users. For example, Freenetworks (*www.freenetworks.org*) is an organization that supports the creation of free community wireless network projects around the globe.

In some places, Wi-Fi Internet hubs are marked by symbols on sidewalks and walls. This practice is called *war chalking*. Certain war chalking symbols indicate that there is an accessible Wi-Fi hotspot in the vicinity of a building. Therefore, if your laptop has a wireless network interface card, you can access the Internet for free. You could also access the wireless network of a company located in the building. Other symbols indicate that the Wi-Fi hotspot around the building is closed; you can access it only if you are authorized.

Wireless Mesh Networks. **Mesh networks** use multiple Wi-Fi access points to create a wide-area network that can be as large as, for instance, the 135-square-mile network being developed in Philadelphia. Mesh networks could have been included in the long-range wireless section, but they are placed here because they are essentially a series of interconnected local area networks.

Wide-Area Wireless Networks

Wide-area wireless networks connect users to the Internet over geographically dispersed territory. These networks typically operate over the licensed spectrum. That is, they use portions of the wireless spectrum that are regulated by the government. In contrast, Bluetooth and Wi-Fi operate over the unlicensed spectrum and are therefore more prone to interference and security problems.

In general, wide-area wireless network technologies fall into two categories: cellular radio and wireless broadband.

Cellular Radio. **Cellular telephones** use radio waves to provide two-way communication. The cell phone communicates with radio antennas (towers) placed within adjacent geographic areas called *cells* (see Figure 7.10). A telephone message is transmitted to the local cell (antenna) by the cell phone and then is passed from cell to cell until it reaches the cell of its destination. At this final cell, the message is either transmitted to the receiving cell phone or is transferred to the public switched telephone system to be transmitted to a wireline telephone. This is why you can use a cell phone to call both other cell phones and standard wireline phones.

Cellular technology is quickly evolving, moving toward higher transmission speeds and richer features. The technology has progressed through several stages. *First generation (1G)* cellular used analog signals and had low bandwidth (capacity). *Second generation (2G)* uses digital signals primarily for voice communication; it provides data communication up to 10 Kbps. *2.5 G* uses digital signals and provides voice and data communication up to 144 Kbps.

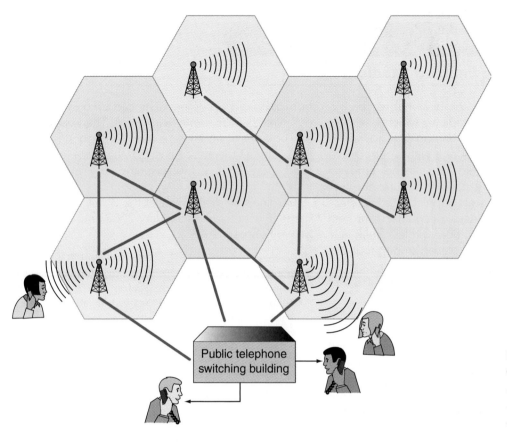

FIGURE 7.10
Cellular network.
Source: Adapted from
*http://people.bu.edu/
storo/iml.gif*

Third generation (3G) uses digital signals and can transmit voice and data up to 384 Kbps when the device is moving at a walking pace, 128 Kbps when moving in a car, and up to 2 Mbps when the device is in a fixed location. 3G supports video, Web browsing, and instant messaging.

Fourth generation (4G) is still under development and is not a single defined technology or standard. The Wireless World Research Forum defines 4G as a network that operates on Internet technology, combines this technology with other applications and technologies such as Wi-Fi and WiMax (discussed next), and operates at speeds ranging from 100 Mbps in cell phone networks to 1 Gbps in local Wi-Fi networks.

Third-generation cellular service does have disadvantages. Perhaps the most fundamental problem is that cellular companies in North America use two separate technologies: Verizon and Sprint use Code Division Multiple Access (CDMA), and Cingular and others use Global System for Mobile Communications (GSM). CDMA companies are currently using *Evolution-Data Optimized* (*EV-DO*) technology, which is a wireless broadband cellular radio standard.

In addition, 3G is relatively expensive, and most carriers limit how much you can download and what the service can be used for. For instance, some carriers prohibit downloading or streaming audio or video. If you go beyond the limits, the carriers reserve the right to cut off your service.

Many organizations have wireless networks that combine cellular service and Wi-Fi service. IT's About Business 7.1 shows how the Arizona Cardinals of the National Football League are using this combination in their new stadium.

IT's About Business

7.1 A Wirelessly Enabled Stadium

The Arizona Cardinals play professional football in the University of Phoenix Stadium, which is widely considered to be the most technologically advanced sports facility in the world. Along with a retractable roof and a sliding grass field that can be removed for nonfootball events, the stadium features the National Football League's most sophisticated wireless network. This network uses a distributed antenna system, which consists of multiple wireless, relatively low-power antennas that are placed throughout the facility rather than a few high-powered antennas. The multiple antennas provide better coverage and have minimal "dead zones."

There are four primary users of the network: fans, stadium workers, public safety personnel, and the media. The network offers both cellular voice and Wi-Fi coverage to all of the stadium's 63,400 seats as well as luxury suites, corridors, concessions, press areas, locker rooms, and team and tenant offices. The network also provides full coverage for public-safety radios throughout the 1.7-million-square-foot facility.

By utilizing the network, sports photographers can instantly upload their images to company networks from the field and journalists can upload their stories directly from the locker rooms. The luxury boxes are equipped with interactive VoIP phones, which have digital touch screens, so that fans can order food, play fantasy football, and buy merchandise instantly.

Cardinals Stadium will host the BCS Championship game (Fiesta Bowl) in January 2008 and Super Bowl XLII in February 2008.

Sources: Compiled from R. Martin, "Wireless Win for NFL," *Unstrung*, September 26, 2006; C. Lynch, "Arizona Cardinals Stadium Goes High Tech with Wireless," *CIO*, October 15, 2006; "New Cardinals Stadium Creates Ultimate Wireless Experience for Fans, Media and Staff," *www.mobileaccess.com*, accessed April 28, 2007.

QUESTIONS

1. Given that the National Football League sells out most of its games, why is wireless access so important to the Arizona Cardinals? What is their overall strategy?
2. Which wireless applications are the most important in this case? Support your answer.

Wireless Broadband or WiMax. Worldwide Interoperability for Microwave Access, popularly known as WiMax, is the name for IEEE Standard 802.16. WiMax has a wireless access range of up to 31 miles, compared to 300 feet for Wi-Fi and 30 feet for Bluetooth. WiMax also has a data-transfer rate of up to 75 Mbps. It is a secure system, and it offers features such as voice and video.

WiMax is not yet mobile; rather, it is currently a point-to-point technology. WiMax antennas can transmit broadband Internet connections to antennas on homes and businesses miles away. The technology can therefore provide long-distance broadband wireless access to rural areas and other locations that are not currently being served, as we see in IT's About Business 7.2.

IT's About Business

7.2 Wireless Coverage for an Entire State

America's smallest state is on its way to becoming the first state to offer a wireless broadband network from border to border. Rhode Island's $20 million project is intended to improve state services and make the state a testing ground for new business technologies. The project is being funded by public and private sources. When it becomes fully operational, users will pay either $20 per month or a membership fee based on annual usage. Rhode Island's capital, Providence, is trying to lure business from Boston, a moderate drive away.

The Rhode Island network is a hybrid of WiMax and Wi-Fi technologies that deliver real-time connections at a minimum speed of 1 Mbps. The system will be supported by 120 base antennas (wireless access points) placed throughout the state.

The network will support public and private services, including business, education, emergency, health care, and port security. For example, it will enable state health inspectors to enter data from restaurant visits into laptops and send the information to the health department. Emergency workers will use the network to send patient information from an ambulance while en route to a hospital. Finally, graduate students from Brown University will utilize the system when they are teaching public school students. The system will also provide a secure broadband network for waterborne first responders (police, firemen, and emergency personnel) for transmission of sensitive text, voice, data, and video information during daily operations and in emergency situations.

Although the system is not intended specifically for consumers, state officials claim that it could have daily applications, such as retrieving real-time information on surf conditions and crowd sizes at beaches or accessing traffic information while driving. The prime benefit, however, is to draw businesses that are looking to use Rhode Island as a laboratory to test-market new technologies on a statewide, demographically diverse population.

Sources: Compiled from R. Lewis, "Rhode Island Embarks on Wireless Network," *Reuters*, May 1, 2006; "Rhode Island Wireless Innovation Networks," *Rhode Island Economic Development Corporation*, www.riedc.com/riedc/blue_sky/32/429/, accessed April 28, 2007; "Rhode Island Wireless Innovation Networks," Business Innovation Factory, www.businessinnovationfactory.com/ri-wins, accessed April 28, 2007; www.state.ri.us, accessed April 28, 2007.

QUESTIONS

1. Go to *www.wimatex.com*, and learn about what this company is doing in the Netherlands. Compare the Wimatex wireless project with the wireless project in Rhode Island.
2. What does Rhode Island mean when it says it wants businesses to test new technologies in a diverse population? What types of technologies would businesses test?

Before you go on . . .

1. What is Bluetooth? What is a WLAN?
2. Describe Wi-Fi, cellular service, and WiMax.

7.3 Mobile Computing and Mobile Commerce

In the traditional computing environment, users come to a computer, which is connected with wires to other computers and to networks. The need to be linked by wires makes it difficult or impossible for people on the move to use them. In particular, salespeople, repair people, service employees, law enforcement agents, and utility workers can be more effective if they can use IT while in the field or in transit. Thus, mobile computing was designed for workers who travel outside the boundaries of their organizations or for anyone traveling outside his or her home.

Recall that mobile computing refers to a real-time, wireless connection between a mobile device and other computing environments, such as the Internet or an intranet. This innovation is revolutionizing how people use computers. It is spreading at work and at home, in education, health care, and entertainment, and in many other areas.

Mobile computing has two major characteristics that differentiate it from other forms of computing: mobility and broad reach. *Mobility* is based on the fact that users carry a mobile device with them and can initiate a real-time contact with other systems from wherever they happen to be. *Broad reach* refers to the fact that when users carry an open mobile device, they can be reached instantly.

These two characteristics, mobility and broad reach, create five value-added attributes that break the barriers of geography and time: ubiquity, convenience, instant connectivity, personalization, and localization of products and services. A mobile device can provide information and communication regardless of the user's location (*ubiquity*). With an Internet-enabled mobile device, it is easy and fast to access the Web, intranets, and other mobile devices without booting up a PC or placing a call via a modem (*convenience* and *instant connectivity*). Information can be customized and sent to individual consumers as an SMS (*customization*). Finally, knowing a user's physical location helps a company advertise its products and services (*localization*). Mobile computing provides the foundation for mobile commerce (m-commerce), which we discuss next.

Mobile Commerce

In addition to affecting our everyday lives, mobile computing is also transforming the way we conduct business by allowing businesses and individuals to engage in mobile commerce. As we saw at the beginning of the chapter, mobile commerce (or m-commerce) refers to e-commerce (EC) transactions that are conducted in a wireless environment, especially via the Internet. Like regular EC applications, m-commerce can be transacted via the Internet, private communication lines, smart cards, and other infrastructures. M-commerce creates opportunities for businesses to deliver new services to existing customers and to attract new customers. To see how m-commerce applications are classified by industry, see *www.nordicwirelesswatch.com/wireless/* and *www.mobiforum.org*.

The development of m-commerce is driven by the following factors:

- *Widespread availability of mobile devices* According to estimates, approximately 2.6 billion cell phones will be in use throughout the world in 2009. Experts further estimate that within a few years about 70 percent of cell phones in the developed countries will have Internet access. Thus, a potential mass market is developing for mobile computing and m-commerce. Cell phones are also spreading quickly in developing countries. In China, for example, the number of cell phones will approach 500 million in 2009. This growth enables developing countries to leapfrog to m-commerce.

- *No need for a PC* Because users can access the Internet via a smart phone or other wireless device, they do not need a PC to go online. Even though the cost of a PC that is used primarily for Internet access can be less than $300, that amount is still a major expense for the vast majority of people in the world, particularly in developing countries.

- *The "cell phone culture"* The widespread use of cell phones is a social phenomenon, especially among young people. The use of SMS and instant messaging has increased enormously in European and Asian countries. The members of the "cell phone culture" will constitute a major force of online buyers once they begin to make and spend more money.

- *Declining prices* The price of wireless devices is declining and will continue to decline.

- *Bandwidth improvement* To properly conduct m-commerce, you need sufficient bandwidth for transmitting text, voice, video, and multimedia. Wi-Fi, 3G cellular technology, and WiMax provide the necessary bandwidth.

Mobile computing and m-commerce include many applications that result from the capabilities of various technologies.

Mobile Commerce Applications

There are a large variety of mobile commerce applications. The most popular applications include financial services, intrabusiness applications, accessing information, location-based applications, telemedicine, and telemetry.

Financial Services.   Mobile financial applications include banking, wireless payments and micropayments, money transfers, wireless wallets, and bill-payment services. The bottom line for mobile financial applications is to make it more convenient for customers to transact business regardless of where they are or what time it is. Harried customers are demanding such convenience.

Mobile Banking.   In many countries, banks increasingly offer mobile access to financial and account information. For example, Citibank (*www.citibank.com*) alerts customers on their digital cell phones about changes in account information.

Wireless Electronic Payment Systems.   Wireless payment systems transform mobile phones into secure, self-contained purchasing tools capable of instantly authorizing payments over the cellular network. In the United States, CPNI (*www.cpni-inc.com/index.php*) allows people to transfer money instantly to individuals and make payments to businesses anywhere in the world with any wireline or mobile phone.

At Atlanta's Philips Arena, for example, season-ticket holders with Chase-issued Visa credit accounts and Cingular wireless accounts can make contactless payments at concession stands throughout the arena using near-field communication-enabled Nokia cell phones. Customers wave the phone within an inch or two of a radio frequency reader without the need for a PIN or a signature. This process speeds up customer flow and frees up workers to help other customers.

Micropayments.   If you took a taxi ride in Frankfurt, Germany, you could use your cell phone to pay the taxi driver. Electronic payments for small-purchase amounts (generally less than $10) are called *micropayments*.

Web shoppers have historically preferred to pay with credit cards. But because credit card companies charge fees on every transaction, credit cards are an inefficient way of making a very small purchase. The growth of digital content, such as music (for example, iTunes), ring tones, and downloadable games, is driving the growth of micropayments, as customers want to avoid credit card fees on small transactions.

The success of micropayment applications, however, ultimately depends on the costs of the transactions. Transaction costs will be small only when the volume of transactions is large. One technology that can increase the volume of transactions is wireless e-wallets.

Mobile (Wireless) Wallets.   Various companies offer **mobile wallet** (*m-wallet,* also known as *wireless wallet*) technologies that enable cardholders to make purchases with a single click from their mobile devices. One example is the Nokia wallet. This application securely stores information (such as credit card numbers) in the customer's Nokia phone for use in making mobile payments. People can also use this information to authenticate transactions by signing them digitally. Microsoft also offers an m-wallet, Passport, for use in a wireless environment.

Wireless Bill Payments.   A number of companies are now providing their customers with the option of paying their bills directly from a cell phone. For example, HDFC Bank of India (*www.hdfcbank.com*) allows customers to pay their utility bills through SMS.

In China, SmartPay allows users to use their mobile phones to pay their phone bills and utility bills, purchase lottery tickets and airline tickets, and make other purchases. SmartPay launched *www.172.com,* a portal that centralizes SmartPay's mobile, telephone, and Internet-based payment services for consumers. The portal is designed to provide a convenient, centralized source of information for all these transactions.

Intrabusiness Applications.   Although B2C m-commerce gets considerable publicity, most of today's m-commerce applications actually are used *within* organizations. In this section we will look at how companies use mobile computing to support their employees.

Mobile devices increasingly are becoming an integral part of workflow applications. For example, companies can use nonvoice mobile services to assist in dispatch functions, that is, to assign jobs to mobile employees, along with detailed information about the job. Target areas for mobile delivery and dispatch services include transportation (delivery of food, oil, newspapers, cargo, courier services, tow trucks, and taxis), utilities (gas, electricity, phone, water), field service (computer, office equipment, home repair), health care (visiting nurses, doctors, social services), and security (patrols, alarm installation). We now provide several examples of intrabusiness applications.

AirIQ (*www.airiq.com*) provides telematics applications for owners and managers of rental vehicle, commercial transport, and heavy equipment fleets. *Telematics* refers to the wireless communication of location-based information and control messages to and from vehicles and other mobile assets. AirIQ's applications combine Internet, wireless, GPS, and digital mapping. A device in each of the vehicles being tracked collects vital information about a vehicle's direction, speed, and location. Managers can view and access information about the fleet on digital maps. They can also monitor the location of their vehicles on the Internet. Companies using AirIQ applications can, for example, receive daily location reports on fleet vehicles; locate overdue and stolen vehicles; disable stolen and overdue vehicles on demand; and know when a vehicle is traveling at an unsafe speed.

At Kemper Insurance Company (*www.kemperinsurance.com*), property adjusters use a wireless digital camera in their smart phones to take pictures at the scene of an accident and transmit them to a processing center database. These applications eliminate delays in obtaining information and in processing film that exist with conventional methods.

Like many national franchises, Taco Bell (*www.tacobell.com*) employs "mystery customers" who visit restaurants to conduct a survey, unknown to the managers. Taco Bell provides these customers with handheld computers so that they can communicate their reports more quickly to the company's headquarters. The mystery customers answer 35 questions, ranging from the speed of the service to the quality of their food. Before they had these devices, they had to fill out paper forms and then send them to headquarters via overnight mail. The information was then scanned into computers for processing. The information flow using the handhelds is faster, more accurate, and less expensive.

Accessing Information.   Mobile portals and voice portals are designed to aggregate and deliver content in a form that will work with the limited space available on mobile devices. These portals provide users with information anywhere and anytime.

Mobile Portals.   A **mobile portal** aggregates and provides content and services for mobile users. These services include news, sports, and e-mail; entertainment, travel, and restaurant information; community services; and stock trading.

The field of mobile portals is increasingly being dominated by a few big companies. The world's best known mobile portal—i-mode from NTT DoCoMo—has more than 40 million subscribers, mostly in Japan. Major players in Europe are Vodafone, O2, and T-Mobile. Some traditional portals—for example, Yahoo, AOL, and MSN—have mobile portals as well.

Voice Portals.   A **voice portal** is a Web site with an audio interface. Voice portals are not Web sites in the normal sense because they can also be accessed through a standard or a cell phone. A certain phone number connects you to a Web site, where you can request information verbally. The system finds the information, translates it into a computer-generated voice reply, and tells you what you want to know. Most airlines provide real-time information on flight status this way.

An example of a voice portal is the voice-activated 511 travel-information line developed by Tellme.com. It enables callers to inquire about weather, local restaurants, current traffic, and other handy information. In addition to retrieving information, some sites provide true interaction. For example, iPing (*www.iping.com*) is a reminder and notification service that allows users to enter information via the Web and receive reminder calls. This service can even call a group of people to notify them of a meeting or conference call.

Location-Based Applications.   As in e-commerce, m-commerce B2C applications are concentrated in three major areas—retail shopping, advertising, and providing customer service. Location-based mobile commerce is called **location-based commerce** or **L-commerce**.

Shopping from Wireless Devices.   An increasing number of online vendors allow customers to shop from wireless devices. For example, customers who use Internet-ready cell phones can shop at certain sites such as *http://mobile.yahoo.com* and *www.amazon.com.*

Cell phone users can also participate in online auctions. For example, eBay offers "anywhere wireless" services. Account holders at eBay can access their accounts, browse, search, bid, and rebid on items from any Internet-enabled phone or PDA. The same is true for participants in Amazon.com auctions.

Location-Based Services.   Location-based services provide information specific to a location. For example, a mobile user can request the nearest business or service, such as an ATM or a restaurant; can receive alerts, such as a warning of a traffic jam or an accident; or can find a friend. Wireless carriers can provide location-based services such as locating taxis, service personnel, doctors, and rental equipment; scheduling fleets; tracking objects such as packages and train boxcars; finding information such as navigation, weather, traffic, and room schedules; targeting advertising; and automating airport check-in.

Location-Based Advertising.   One type of location-based service is location-based advertising. When marketers know the current locations and preferences of mobile users, they can send user-specific advertising messages to wireless devices about nearby shops, malls, and restaurants. Let's look at an example.

The Cell Phone Becomes a Sell Phone   Joanne Smith from Auburn, New York, has two boys, and she recently vacationed in Las Vegas. She sent a text message to a number she saw on a billboard there, giving Adidas all the information the company needed to advertise basketball shoes to her over her phone. Adidas knew she was in Las Vegas because she responded to a billboard ad that offered information about National Basketball Association All-Star Game events in that city. Adidas sent her a text message about the sale of 200 pairs of limited-edition All-Star basketball shoes. Tipped off, she lined up outside an Adidas store in Las Vegas with hundreds of other people. She bought two pairs of shoes for her boys.

A chain of Subway restaurants has a history of using coupons for free food to entice customers to try a specific location or a particular sandwich. When Subway sent the coupons by direct mail, the response rate was between 2 and 4 percent. When the chain recently sent the same coupons to people's cell phones, the response rate was 50 percent.

Mobile services use area codes, Zip codes, and even GPS data to return results for nearby businesses in response to a search for, say, coffee shops. They then serve an ad for a Mocha Latte on cell phones just as the user passes a Starbucks. Early results on cell phone ads indicate that about 5 percent of consumers who see targeted ads respond to them. That seems to be a small percentage, but it is far higher than the 1 percent of people who click on conventional Web ads.

Example

Sources: Compiled from C. Holahan, "The Sell-Phone Revolution," *BusinessWeek*, April 23, 2007; E. Schuman, "The Age of Sell Phones," *eWeek*, August 2, 2006.

Wireless Telemedicine. *Telemedicine* is the use of modern telecommunications and information technologies to provide clinical care to individuals located at a distance and to transmit the information that clinicians need in order to provide that care. Three different kinds of technology are used for telemedicine applications. The first involves storing digital images and then transferring them from one location to another. The second allows a patient in one location to consult with a medical specialist in another location in real time through videoconferencing. The third type uses robots to perform remote surgery. In most of these applications, the patient is in a rural area, and the specialist is in an urban location.

Wireless technology is also transforming the ways in which prescriptions are filled. Traditionally, physicians wrote out a prescription and you took it to the pharmacy, where you either waited on line or returned later. Today, mobile systems allow physicians to enter a prescription onto a PDA. That information then goes by cellular modem (or Wi-Fi) to a company such as Med-i-nets (*www.med-i-nets.com*). There, employees make certain that the prescription conforms to the insurance company's regulations. If everything checks out, then the prescription is transferred electronically to the appropriate pharmacy. For refills, the system notifies physicians when it is time for the patient to reorder. The doctor can then renew the prescription with a few clicks on the modem.

Another valuable application involves emergency situations that arise during airplane flights. In-flight medical emergencies occur more frequently than you might think. Alaska Airlines, for example, deals with about 10 medical emergencies every day. Many companies now use mobile communications to attend to these situations. For example, MedLink, a service of MedAire (*www.medaire.com*), provides around-the-clock access to board-certified physicians. These mobile services can also remotely control medical equipment, like defibrillators, that are located on the plane.

Telemetry Applications. **Telemetry**, the wireless transmission and receipt of data gathered from remote sensors, has numerous mobile computing applications. For example, technicians can use *telemetry* to identify maintenance problems in equipment. Also, as we just saw, doctors can monitor patients and control medical equipment from a distance.

Car manufacturers use telemetry applications for remote vehicle diagnosis and preventive maintenance. For instance, drivers of many General Motors cars use its OnStar system (*www.onstar.com*) in numerous ways. As one example, OnStar automatically alerts an On-Star operator when an air bag deploys. In another example, drivers can call OnStar with questions about a warning light that appears on their dashboard. There are many other examples of telemetry, as IT's About Business 7.3 shows.

IT's About Business

7.3 A Rolling Wireless Network

Trucking companies have to manage geographically dispersed mobile trucks and drivers. These companies also have to comply with a number of regulations relating to the transportation industry. These regulations include the number of continuous hours that drivers can operate their vehicles, locations where trucks carrying certain dangerous goods (for example, nuclear fuel) can operate, the speeds at which the trucks can travel, and many others.

As a result, trucking companies are installing driver management systems in their trucks. These systems include wireless computers, GPS-enabled phones, and wireless sensors. The sensors collect diagnostic data, including warnings of certain conditions that may indicate problems somewhere on a truck. These messages are sent to a vehicle-component database, which lets fleet managers and maintenance staff determine whether the truck needs to be pulled from its route for maintenance. These driver management systems are much cheaper (on the order of several hundred dollars) than the $3,000 satellite terminals that earlier driver management systems used.

International Truck and Engine's (*www.internationaldelivers.com*) Vehicle Intelligence application—known as Aware—manages sensor information, ranging from moving parts in the engine and transmission to the number of times the tailgate is opened. The application transmits the vehicle's location every 15 to 20 minutes with a time stamp, making it possible for managers to map the sequence of stops a vehicle makes—when, where, and for how long. This system helps keep drivers on track and make deliveries on time. The vehicles are equipped with GPS-based telematics or wireless connectivity via Verizon's cellular network. Vehicle time and location reports can be displayed on a map, indicating where the truck has been. Summaries of on-board information can be automatically transmitted to a Web site, where owners log in and view information even while their trucks are moving.

International's Aware application also lets managers define a set of boundaries, called geofencing, that a driver is expected to stay within as well as others to be avoided. A propane truck driver, for example, must not try to go through a tunnel or into congested downtown neighborhoods. An alert is triggered at headquarters if the vehicle goes off course.

In one example, the transportation director of one school district used the Aware system to check on the whereabouts of his fleet's buses and discovered that one was 45 miles outside the district in another city. When he called the dispatcher, who was not using the Aware system, he was told that the bus was in a nearby parking lot. Further investigation revealed that a substitute driver had taken the wrong bus on a field trip.

International's Aware system offers many benefits. For one thing, it allows trucking companies to do a better job of tracking their most expensive assets—drivers and vehicles. In addition, the detailed reports on service stops and deliveries that Aware provides have benefited the companies both by increasing customer satisfaction and by making it easier for the companies to handle customer disputes. Finally, by enabling these companies to control drivers' activities, including speed and location boundaries, the system has reduced their fuel, maintenance, and insurance costs.

Sources: Compiled from C. Babcock, "Trucks Morph into High-Tech Networks on 18 Wheels," *InformationWeek*, September 25, 2006; B. Charny, "Big Boss Is Watching," *CNET News.com*, September 24, 2004; E. Schwartz, "Geofencing May Keep Employees in Check, But They Might Not Stick Around," *InfoWorld*, October 24, 2003; *www.internationaldelivers.com*, accessed April 27, 2007.

QUESTIONS

1. As a driver, how would you feel about a driver management system reporting your every location, and with a time stamp? Would privacy considerations outweigh the benefits? Discuss the pros and cons of these systems from the driver's point of view.
2. You are the owner of a trucking company. Discuss the pros and cons of these systems from your point of view.

Before you go on . . .

1. What are the major drivers of mobile computing?
2. Describe mobile portals and voice portals.
3. Describe wireless financial services.
4. List some of the major intrabusiness wireless applications.

7.4 Pervasive Computing

A world in which virtually every object has processing power with wireless or wired connections to a global network is the world of pervasive computing, also called ubiquitous computing. Pervasive computing is invisible "everywhere computing" that is embedded in the objects around us—the floor, the lights, our cars, the washing machine, our cell phones, our clothes, and so on.

For example, in a *smart home*, your home computer, television, lighting and heating controls, home security system, and many appliances can communicate with one another via a home network. These linked systems can be controlled through various devices, including your pager, cellular phone, television, home computer, PDA, or even your automobile. One of the key elements of a smart home is the *smart appliance*, an Internet-ready appliance that can be controlled by a small handheld device or a desktop computer via a home network (wireline or wireless) or the public Internet (see *www.internethomealliance.com*). Two technologies provide the infrastructure for pervasive computing: radio frequency identification (RFID) and wireless sensor networks (WSNs).

Radio Frequency Identification

Radio frequency identification (RFID) technology allows manufacturers to attach tags with antennas and computer chips on goods and then track their movement through radio signals. RFID was developed to replace bar codes. A typical bar code, known as the *Universal Product Code (UPC)*, is made up of 12 digits, in various groups. The first digit identifies the item type, the next 5 digits identify the manufacturer, and the next 5 identify the product. The last digit is a check digit for error detection. Bar codes have worked well, but they have limitations. First, they require line of sight to the scanning device. This is fine in a store, but it can pose substantial problems in a manufacturing plant or a warehouse or on a shipping/receiving dock. Second, because bar codes are printed on paper, they can be ripped, soiled, or lost. Third, the bar code identifies the manufacturer and product, but not the actual item.

RFID systems use tags with embedded microchips, which contain data, and antennas to transmit radio signals over a short distance to RFID readers. The readers pass the data over a network to a computer for processing. The chip in the RFID tag is programmed with information that uniquely identifies an item. It also contains information about the item such as its location and where and when it was made. Figure 7.11 shows an RFID reader and an RFID tag on a pallet.

One problem with RFID has been the expense. Tags remain expensive, which makes them unusable for low-priced items. To alleviate this problem, a California company called Alien Technology (*www.alientechnology.com*) has invented a way to mass-produce RFID tags for less than 10 cents apiece for large production runs.

Another problem with RFID has been the size of the tags. However, this problem may have been solved. Hitachi's mu chip was 0.4 mm by 0.4 mm, but the company now has released its "RFID powder" chips, which are 0.05 mm by 0.05 mm, some 60 times smaller than the mu chips.

RuBee, a wireless networking protocol that relies on magnetic rather than electrical energy, gives retailers and manufacturers an alternative to RFID for some applications. RuBee works in harsh environments, near metal and water, and in the presence of electromagnetic noise. Environments such as these have been a major impediment to the widespread, cost-effective deployment of RFID. RuBee is an alternative to, and not a replacement for, RFID. RuBee technology is being used in smart shelf environments, where specially designed shelves can read RuBee transmissions. The shelves alert store employees when inventory of a product is running low.

As opposed to RuBee, an alternative to RFID, the Memory Spot by Hewlett-Packard is a competitor to RFID. The Memory Spot, the size of a tomato seed, stores up to 4 megabits of data and has a transfer rate of 10 Mbps.

Despite the expense of RFID tags, a Dutch bookseller is successfully using them. IT's About Business 7.4 shows how the tags more than pay for themselves.

Wireless Sensor Networks (WSNs)

Wireless sensor networks are networks of interconnected, battery-powered, wireless sensors called *motes* (analogous to nodes) that are placed into the physical environment. The

FIGURE 7.11   Small RFID reader and RFID tag. *Source:* Kruell/laif/Redux Pictures.

IT's About Business

7.4 An RFID Tag for Every Book

While U.S. retailers are still struggling to put RFID tags on boxes and pallets (see the chapter opening case), Dutch bookseller Selexyz may be the first merchant to tag every single item on its shelves with RFID technology. Selexyz, the Netherlands' largest book chain, has been testing an RFID inventory management system at one of its stores. Here is how the RFID system works.

Selexyz's distributor places an RFID tag, usually the size of a strip of tape, on every book being shipped to the store. The tag contains a bar code, and it also functions as an antitheft device. Each tag costs about 25 cents. At the store, each box of books goes through an RFID scanning tunnel, which takes five seconds per box to compare the contents with what was ordered and then enter every book into the inventory system. Three times per week, employees roll an RFID scanning cart through the store to check the inventory. They wave a wand over each shelf, and the books and their locations are noted in the system. It takes two employees two and one-half hours to scan 38,000 books.

Three kiosks let shoppers pinpoint within seconds the exact location of any book in the store. Customers can search for books using the same inventory system that the employees use. The kiosks tell shoppers not only whether a book is in stock but also what bookcase it is on. If a book is not in stock, the shopper can order it online at the kiosk for either home or store delivery the following day. The kiosk also suggests other books that the customers might want, based on his or her searches. About half of the people who use the kiosks end up buying something. At checkout, scanners remove books from inventory and disable the RFID tags.

Before Selexyz implemented the RFID system, the company could conduct only spot checks of incoming boxes, and it had to scan each book's bar code by hand. Furthermore, the company could conduct a complete inventory only once per year. At that time it had to shut down its stores for an entire day, at a cost of about $800,000 in labor expenses and lost sales.

Sources: Compiled from E. Schonfeld, "Tagged for Growth," *Business 2.0*, December, 2006; B. Trebilcock, "Selexyz Implements Item-Level RFID Tagging," *Modern Materials Handling*, May 17, 2006; R. Mitchell, "Getting a Read on Book Inventories," *Computerworld*, August 14, 2006; R. Malone, "Smart Store," *Forbes*, October 24, 2006.

QUESTIONS

1. If Selexyz has been so successful using RFID tags on individual books, why aren't all book stores doing the same thing? What are the problems associated with starting up an RFID system at a huge bookstore chain? Is it as simple as it seems?
2. What are other benefits of this RFID system that are not mentioned in the case?

motes collect data from many points over an extended space. Each mote contains processing, storage, and radio frequency sensors and antennas. Each mote "wakes up" or activates for a fraction of a second when it has data to transmit and then relays that data to its nearest neighbor. So, instead of every mote transmitting its information to a remote computer at a base station, the data are moved mote by mote until they reach a central computer where it can be stored and analyzed. An advantage of a wireless sensor network is that, if one mote fails, another one can pick up the data. This process makes WSNs very efficient and reliable. Also, if more bandwidth is needed, it is easy to boost performance by placing new motes when and where they are required.

The motes provide information that enables a central computer to integrate reports of the same activity from different angles within the network. Therefore, the network can determine with much greater accuracy information such as the direction in which a person is moving, the weight of a vehicle, or the amount of rainfall over a field of crops. There are many diverse uses for WSNs, and IT's About Business 7.5 provides an example.

IT's About Business

7.5   A Real-Time Traffic System

Inrix (*www.inrix.com*) has developed the first real-time traffic system based on data from vehicles and mobile devices with global positioning technology. The company uses navigation equipment already installed in motor vehicles to collect data about their users' locations, how fast they are traveling, and how long it takes them to reach their destinations. The company has signed contracts to collect this data from more than 500,000 devices embedded in fleets of taxis, shuttles, trucks, and delivery vehicles. Inrix also gathers data from toll booth sensors, as well as from the Department of Transportation's wireless sensor networks.

Inrix covers 73 U.S. markets and more than 47,000 miles of road by providing up-to-the-minute information about traffic conditions. This information includes:

- Incident data (e.g., accidents)
- Flow data (how traffic is moving and at what average speed)
- Predictions (current accident should be cleared by 5 P.M.)
- Real-time and predictive travel times (current travel time to your destination is 56 minutes; travel time at 9 A.M. is predicted to be 37 minutes).
- Predictive dynamic routing (the fastest path to your destination at 7 A.M. is Interstate 40, exiting at Exit 38).
- Dynamic fuel prices (which gas station along your route has the cheapest gas).
- National average speeds (average speed per road segment by hour of day and day of week).

- National reference speeds (free-flow speed by road segment to replace "speed limits" as new reference speed).

The company's database contains hundreds of variables that affect traffic. It automatically collects data on those variables, which include weather reports and forecasts, special events, school schedules, construction, and traffic information, and it combines them with the data it collects from the vehicle fleets.

The company's customers include Microsoft, which uses traffic information on its MSN Web site, cell phone carrier AT&T, and Tom Tom (*www.tomtom.com*), a provider of portable GPS navigation systems. These companies integrate Inrix's traffic information into their consumer applications.

Sources: Compiled from "Clear Channel Expands Total Traffic Network with Inrix Real-Time Traffic," *Reuters*, January 31, 2007; "Traffic Jams, Not," *Red Herring*, May 29, 2006; "Inrix Expands Real-Time Traffic Flow Coverage," *Intelligent Transportation Systems* (*www.itsa.org*), December 6, 2006; *www.inrix.com*, accessed April 17, 2007.

QUESTIONS

1. Is it possible for a driver to receive so much information from a service like Inrix that it becomes a distraction? If so, what are some possible solutions to this problem?
2. Are wireless networks fast enough to allow Inrix to provide real-time information to drivers? Would drivers be able to use real-time information?

One kind of wireless sensor network is ZigBee (*www.ZigBee.org*). ZigBee is a set of wireless communications protocols that target applications requiring low data-transmission rates and low power consumption. ZigBee can handle hundreds of devices at once. Its current focus is on wirelessly linking sensors that are embedded into industrial controls, medical devices, smoke and intruder alarms, and building and home automation.

A promising application of ZigBee is reading utility meters, such as electricity. ZigBee sensors embedded in these meters would send wireless signals that could be picked up by utility employees driving by your house. The employees would not even have to get out of their trucks to read your meter.

Before you go on . . .

1. Define pervasive computing, RFID, and wireless sensor networks.
2. Differentiate between RFID and RuBee and include the benefits of each.

7.5 Wireless Security

Clearly, wireless networks provide numerous benefits for businesses. However, they also present a huge challenge to management, namely, their inherent lack of security. Wireless is a broadcast medium, and transmissions can be intercepted by anyone who is close enough and has access to the appropriate equipment. There are four major threats to wireless networks: rogue access points, war driving, eavesdropping, and RF jamming.

A *rogue access point* is an unauthorized access point to a wireless network. The rogue could be someone in your organization who sets up an access point meaning no harm but fails to tell the IT department. In more serious cases the rogue is an "evil twin," someone who wishes to access a wireless network for malicious purposes.

In an evil twin attack, the attacker is in the vicinity with a Wi-Fi-enabled computer and a separate connection to the Internet. Using a hotspotter—a device that detects wireless networks and provides information on them (see *www.canarywireless.com*)—the attacker simulates a wireless access point with the same wireless network name, or SSID, as the one that authorized users expect. If the signal is strong enough, users will connect to the attacker's system instead of the real access point. The attacker can then serve them a Web page, asking them to provide confidential information such as user names, passwords, and account numbers. In other cases the attacker simply captures wireless transmissions. These attacks are more effective with public hotspots (for example, McDonald's or Starbucks) than in corporate networks.

War driving is the act of locating WLANs while driving (or walking) around a city or elsewhere (see *www.wardriving.com*). To war drive or walk, you simply need a Wi-Fi detector and a wirelessly enabled computer. If a WLAN has a range that extends beyond the building in which it is located, then an unauthorized user might be able to intrude into the network. The intruder can then obtain a free Internet connection and possibly gain access to important data and other resources.

Eavesdropping refers to efforts by unauthorized users to access data that are traveling over wireless networks. Finally, in *radio frequency (RF) jamming* a person or a device intentionally or unintentionally interferes with your wireless network transmissions.

In Technology Guide 3, we discuss a variety of techniques and technologies that you should implement to help you avoid these threats.

Before you go on . . .

1. Describe the four major threats to the security of wireless networks.
2. Which of these threats is the most dangerous for a business? Which is the most dangerous for an individual? Support your answers.

What's in **IT** for Me?

For the Accounting Major

Wireless applications help the accountants to count and audit inventory. They also expedite the flow of information for cost control. Price management, inventory control, and other accounting-related activities can be improved by use of wireless technologies.

For the Finance Major

Wireless services can provide banks and other financial institutions with a competitive advantage. For example, wireless electronic payments, including micropayments, are more convenient (any place, any time) than traditional means of payment, and they are also less expensive. Electronic bill payment from mobile devices is becoming more popular, increasing security and accuracy, expediting cycle time, and reducing processing costs.

For the Marketing Major

Imagine a whole new world of marketing, advertising, and selling, with the potential to increase sales dramatically. Such is the promise of mobile computing. Of special interest for marketing are location-based advertising as well as the new opportunities resulting from pervasive computing and RFIDs. Finally, wireless technology also provides new opportunities in sales force automation (SFA), enabling faster and better communications with both customers (CRM) and corporate services.

For the Production/Operations Management Major

Wireless technologies offer many opportunities to support mobile employees of all kinds. Wearable computers enable off-site employees and repair personnel working in the field to service customers faster, better, and less expensively. Wireless devices can also increase productivity within factories by enhancing communication and collaboration as well as managerial planning and control. In addition, mobile computing technologies can improve safety by providing quicker warning signs and instant messaging to isolated employees.

For the Human Resources Management Major

Mobile computing can improve HR training and extend it to any place at any time. Payroll notices can be delivered as SMSs. Finally, wireless devices can make it even more convenient for employees to select their own benefits and update their personal data.

For the MIS Major

MIS personnel provide the wireless infrastructure that enables all organizational employees to compute and communicate any time, anywhere. This convenience provides exciting, creative, new applications for organizations to cut costs and improve the efficiency and effectiveness of operations (for example, to gain transparency in supply chains). Unfortunately, as we discussed earlier, wireless applications are inherently insecure. This lack of security is a serious problem confronting MIS personnel.

Summary

1. Discuss today's wireless devices and wireless transmission media.

In the past we have discussed these devices in separate categories, such as pagers, e-mail handhelds, personal digital assistants (PDAs), cellular telephones, and smart phones. Today, however, new devices, generally called *smart phones*, combine the functions of these devices. The capabilities of these new devices include cellular telephony, Bluetooth, Wi-Fi, a digital camera, global positioning system (GPS), an organizer, a scheduler, an address book, a calculator, access to e-mail and short message service, instant messaging, text messaging, an MP3 music-player, a video-player, Internet access with a full-function browser, and a QWERTY keyboard.

Microwave transmission systems are widely used for high-volume, long-distance, point-to-point communication. Communication *satellites* are used in satellite transmission systems. The three types of satellite are geostationary earth orbit (GEO), medium earth orbit (MEO), and low earth orbit (LEO). *Radio* transmission uses radio-wave frequencies to send data directly between transmitters and receivers. *Infrared* light is red light not commonly visible to human eyes. The most common application of infrared light is in remote-control units for televisions and VCRs. Infrared transceivers are being used for short-distance connections between computers and peripheral equipment and LANs. Many portable PCs have infrared ports, which are handy when cable connections with a peripheral are not practical.

2. Describe wireless networks, according to their effective distance.

Wireless networks can be grouped by their effective distance, short range, medium range, and wide area. Short-range wireless networks simplify the task of connecting one device to another, eliminating wires and enabling users to move around while they use the devices. In general, short range wireless networks have a range of 100 feet or less, and include Bluetooth, ultra-wideband (UWB), and near-field communications (NFC).

Medium-range wireless networks are the familiar wireless local area networks (WLANs). The most common type of medium-range wireless network is Wireless Fidelity or Wi-Fi. Another type of medium-range wireless network is the mesh network, which uses multiple Wi-Fi access points to create a wide-area network. Mesh networks are essentially a series of interconnected local area networks.

Wide-area wireless networks connect users to the Internet over geographically dispersed territory. These networks typically operate over the licensed spectrum. That is, they use portions of the wireless spectrum that are regulated by the government. In contrast, Bluetooth and Wi-Fi operate over the unlicensed spectrum and are therefore more prone to interference and security problems. In general, wide-area wireless network technologies include cellular radio and wireless broadband, or WiMax.

3. Define mobile computing and mobile commerce.

Mobile computing is a computing model designed for people who travel frequently. *Mobile commerce* (*m-commerce*) is any e-commerce conducted in a wireless environment, especially via the Internet.

4. Discuss the major m-commerce applications.

Mobile financial applications include banking, wireless payments and micropayments, wireless wallets, and bill-payment services. Job dispatch is a major intrabusiness application. *Voice portals* and *mobile portals* provide access to information. Location-based applications include retail shopping, advertising, and customer service. Other major m-commerce applications include wireless *telemedicine* and *telemetry*.

5. Define pervasive computing and describe two technologies underlying this technology.

Pervasive computing is invisible, everywhere computing that is embedded in the objects around us. Two technologies provide the infrastructure for pervasive computing: *radio frequency identification (RFID)* and *wireless sensor networks (WSNs)*.

RFID is the term for technologies that use radio waves to automatically identify the location of individual items equipped with tags that contain embedded microchips. WSNs are networks of interconnected, battery-powered, wireless devices placed in the physical environment to collect data from many points over an extended space.

6. Discuss the four major threats to wireless networks.

The four major threats to wireless networks are rogue access points, war driving, eavesdropping, and radio frequency jamming. A rogue access point is an unauthorized access point to a wireless network; war driving is the act of locating WLANs while driving around a city or elsewhere; and eavesdropping refers to efforts by unauthorized users to access data that are traveling over wireless networks. Radio frequency jamming occurs when a person or a device intentionally or unintentionally interferes with wireless network transmissions.

Chapter Glossary

Bluetooth Chip technology that enables short-range connection (data and voice) between wireless devices.

cellular telephones (also called cell phones); telephones that use radio waves to provide two-way communications.

digital radio (see **satellite radio**)

global positioning system (GPS) A wireless system that uses satellites to enable users to determine their position anywhere on earth.

hotspot A small geographical perimeter within which a wireless access point provides service to a number of users.

infrared A type of wireless transmission that uses red light not commonly visible to human eyes.

location-based commerce (L-commerce) Mobile commerce transactions targeted to individuals in specific locations, at specific times.

mesh network A network composed of motes in the physical environment that "wake up" at intervals to transmit data to their nearest neighbor mote.

microbrowser Internet browsers with a small file size that can work within the low-memory constraints of wireless devices and the low bandwidths of wireless networks.

microwave transmission A wireless system that uses 226 microwaves for high-volume, long-distance, point-to-point communication.

mobile commerce (m-commerce) Electronic commerce transactions that are conducted in a wireless environment, especially via the Internet.

mobile computing A real-time, wireless connection between a mobile device and other computing environments, such as the Internet or an intranet.

mobile portal A portal that aggregates and provides content and services for mobile users.

mobile wallet A technology that allows users to make purchases with a single click from their mobile devices.

near-field communications (NFC) The smallest of the short-range wireless networks that is designed to be embedded in mobile devices such as cell phones and credit cards.

personal area network A computer network used for communication among computer devices close to one person.

pervasive computing (also called ubiquitous computing) A computer environment in which virtually every object has processing power with wireless or wired connections to a global network.

propagation delay The one-quarter second transmission delay in communication to and from GEO satellites.

radio frequency identification (RFID) technology A wireless technology that allows manufacturers to attach tags with antennas and computer chips on goods and then track their movement through radio signals.

radio transmission System that uses radio-wave frequencies to send data directly between transmitters and receivers.

satellite radio (also called digital radio) A wireless system that offers uninterrupted, near CD-quality music that is beamed to your radio from satellites.

satellite transmission A wireless transmission system that uses satellites for broadcast communications.

short message service (SMS) A service provided by digital cell phones that can send and receive short text messages (up to 160 characters in length).

telemetry The wireless transmission and receipt of data gathered from remote sensors.

ubiquitous computing (see **pervasive computing**)

ultra-wideband (UWB) A high-bandwidth wireless technology with transmission speeds in excess of 100 Mbps that can be used for applications such as streaming multimedia from, say, a personal computer to a television.

voice portal A Web site with an audio interface.

wireless Telecommunications in which electromagnetic waves carry the signal between communicating devices.

wireless access point An antenna connecting a mobile device to a wired local area network.

wireless application protocol (WAP) The standard that enables wireless devices with tiny display screens, low-bandwidth connections, and minimal memory to access Web-based information and services.

wireless fidelity (Wi-Fi) A set of standards for wireless local area networks based on the IEEE 802.11 standard.

wireless local area network (WLAN) A computer network in a limited geographical area that uses wireless transmission for communication.

wireless network interface card (NIC) A device that has a built-in radio and antenna and is essential to enable a computer to have wireless communication capabilities.

wireless sensor networks (WSN) Networks of interconnected, battery-powered, wireless sensors placed in the physical environment.

Discussion Questions

1. Discuss how m-commerce can expand the reach of e-business.
2. Discuss how mobile computing can solve some of the problems of the digital divide.
3. List three to four major advantages of wireless commerce to consumers, and explain what benefits they provide to consumers.
4. Discuss the ways in which Wi-Fi is being used to support mobile computing and m-commerce. Describe the ways in which Wi-Fi is affecting the use of cellular phones for m-commerce.
5. You can use location-based tools to help you find your car or the closest gas station. However, some people see location-based tools as an invasion of privacy. Discuss the pros and cons of location-based tools.
6. Discuss the benefits of telemetry in health care for the elderly.
7. Discuss how wireless devices can help people with disabilities.
8. Some experts say that Wi-Fi is winning the battle with 3G cellular service; others disagree. Discuss both sides of the argument, and support each one.
9. Which of the applications of pervasive computing do you think are likely to gain the greatest market acceptance over the next few years? Why?

Problem-Solving Activities

1. Enter *www.kyocera-wireless.com* and view the demos. What is a smart phone? What are its capabilities? How does it differ from a regular cell phone?
2. Investigate commercial applications of voice portals. Visit several vendors (e.g., *www.tellme.com*, *www.bevocal.com*, and so on). What capabilities and applications are offered by the various vendors?
3. Using a search engine, try to determine whether there are any commercial Wi-Fi hotspots in your area. (*Hint:* Access *www.wifinder.com*.) Enter *www.wardriving.com*. Based on information provided at this site, what sorts of equipment and procedures could you use to locate hotspots in your area?
4. Examine how new data capture devices such as RFID tags help organizations accurately identify and segment their customers for activities such as targeted marketing. Browse the Web and develop five potential new applications for RFID technology not listed in this chapter. What issues would arise if a country's laws mandated that such devices be embedded in everyone's body as a national identification system?
5. Investigate commercial uses of GPS. Start with *http://gpshome.ssc.nasa.gov*; then go to *www.gpsstore.com*. Can some of the consumer-oriented products be used in industry? Prepare a report on your findings.

Web Activities

1. Explore *www.nokia.com*. Prepare a summary of the types of mobile services and applications Nokia currently supports and plans to support in the future.
2. Enter *www.ibm.com*. Search for *wireless e-business*. Research the resulting stories to determine the types of wireless capabilities and applications IBM's software and hardware supports. Describe some of the ways these applications have helped specific businesses and industries.
3. Research the status of 3G and 4G cellular service by visiting *www.itu.int*, *www.4g.co.uk*, and *www.3gnewsroom.com*. Prepare a report on the status of 3G and 4G based on your findings.
4. Enter *www.mapinfo.com* and look for the location-based services demos. Try all the demos. Find all of the wireless services. Summarize your findings.

5. Enter *www.packetvideo.com* and *www.microsoft.com/mobile/pocketpc*. Examine their demos and products and list their capabilities.

6. Enter *www.onstar.com*. What types of *fleet* services does OnStar provide? Are these any different from the services OnStar provides to individual car owners? (Play the movie.)

7. Access *www.itu.int/osg/spu/publications/internetofthings/InternetofThings_summary.pdf*. Read about the Internet of Things. What is it? What types of technologies are necessary to support it? Why is it important?

Team Assignments

1. Each team should examine a major vendor of mobile devices (Nokia, Kyocera, Motorola, Palm, BlackBerry, and so on). Each team will research the capabilities and prices of the devices offered by each company and then make a class presentation, the objective of which is to convince the rest of the class why one should buy that company's products.

2. Each team should explore the commercial applications of m-commerce in one of the following areas: financial services, including banking, stocks, and insurance; marketing and advertising; manufacturing; travel and transportation; human resources management; public services; and health care. Each team will present a report to the class based on their findings. (Start at *www.mobiforum.org*.)

3. Each team should take one of the following areas—homes, cars, appliances, or other consumer goods like clothing—and investigate how embedded microprocessors are currently being used and will be used in the future to support consumer-centric services. Each team will present a report to the class based on their findings.

CLOSING CASE **Webster Forest Nursery Goes Wireless**

THE BUSINESS PROBLEM The Webster Forest Nursery (*http://www3.wadnr.gov/dnrapp3/webster/*) grows seedlings to reforest lands depleted by logging. The nursery gathers seeds from around the State of Washington and operates as a tree factory that produces between 8 and 10 million seedlings per year. The nursery pays close attention to the needs of different plant species, their regions of origin, and the early care required for the seedlings to thrive.

The nursery's 18-person staff works hard to collect distinguishing data on every seedling. For example, you cannot plant a Douglas fir seedling that came from a tree on Mount St. Helens on coastal land at sea level, because the DNA of the fir tree would not be suited for that environment. To avoid this sort of problem, the nursery staff keeps extensive records of all its millions of seedlings, categorizing them not just by the 42 different species it grows, but by additional details such as seed zone and elevation of origin.

In the past, the Webster Nursery was a very low-tech operation, where employees spent most of their time outside and haphazardly kept records on paper. Seedling information and plant orders were typically written down on a clipboard, transferred to index cards, and kept in the desk drawer of the office manager, who maintained a system that resembled an old-fashioned library card catalog.

The most obvious problem with this system was that it was impossible to get an accurate count of plants spread across the nursery's 276 acres and 30,000 square feet of greenhouse space. The best that workers could do was to make estimates based on square footage. In addition, the paper-based inventory tracking system was full of errors, created by workers who failed to update tracking data or misread other workers' handwriting. Those errors often caused workers to under- or overwater plants, and to misidentify plant species. These errors sometimes led workers to transfer mature seedlings to inappropriate environments.

The nursery reached a point where the paper-based inventory tracking system placed demands on the staff that could not be tolerated. The nursery estimated that employees' workloads would decrease by 33 percent if the inventory system were automated. Furthermore, there was one person in the office who kept all the records on paper and knew where to find everything, and she was about to retire.

THE IT SOLUTION The nursery installed an inventory tracking system called Reforestation Information Management System (RIMS), consisting of an Oracle database and wireless handheld computers, which were linked to both the database and the personal computers in the nursery office.

THE RESULTS The inventory tracking system was an immediate success. Workers now enter data in real time, from the field, reducing errors in seedling data. As a result, the seedlings are more likely to be planted in appropriate locations, take root, and fulfill the nursery's mission of reforestation. The system has also freed up staff at the nursery, enabling the nursery to expand its operation by adding more greenhouses for young seedlings. In addition, the nursery recently incorporated all its sales data into RIMS, making it easier to track the nursery's performance and to project future revenues.

Sources: Compiled from A. Pettis, "Reforesting System Takes Root," *eWeek,* January 8, 2007; T. Wark et al., "Transforming Agriculture through Pervasive Wireless Sensor Networks," *IEEE Pervasive Computing,* April–June 2007; *http://www3.wadnr.gov/dnrapp3/webster/,* accessed April 28, 2007.

QUESTIONS

1. Now that the nursery is using wireless handheld computers to enter accurate seedling data, what would you recommend as the next technological step? *Hint:* Refer to the section on wireless sensor networks in this chapter.
2. What are other advantages that wireless handheld technology can provide for the nursery?

Web Resources wiley.com/college/rainer

Student Web Site
- Web Quizzes
- Student Lecture Slides in PowerPoint
- Virtual Company ClubIT: Website and Assignments

WileyPLUS
- e-book
- Flash Cards
- How-To Animations for Microsoft Office

Pervasive Computing at Club IT

Go to the Club IT section of the *WileyPLUS* Web site to find assignments about using wireless technologies at Club IT.

wiley.com/college/rainer

Chapter 8

Organizational Information Systems

Web Resources wiley.com/college/rainer

Student Web Site
- Web Quizzes
- Lecture Slides in PowerPoint
- Virtual Company ClubIT: Website and Assignments

WileyPLUS
- e-book
- Flash Cards
- Software Skills Tutorials: Using Microsoft Office 2007
- How-To Animations for Microsoft Office

Chapter Outline

8.1 Transaction Processing Systems

8.2 Functional Area Information Systems

8.3 Enterprise Resource Planning Systems

8.4 Customer Relationship Management Systems

8.5 Supply Chain Management Systems

8.6 Electronic Data Interchange and Extranets

What's in IT for me? ACC FIN MKT POM HRM MIS

Toyota Uses Information Systems in Drive for 1

POM

The Business Problem

In Toyota Motor's (*www.toyota.com*) largest manufacturing facility in North America, located in Kentucky, a new Toyota rolls off the assembly line every 55 seconds. Some 7,000 employees at this plant know that they have just 55 seconds to install engine components, brakes, dashboards, windows, doors, or some other component before the car is transported to the next stage of the assembly line on the overhead conveyor. Driverless carts take parts to assembly stations just as they are needed so that inventory does not pile up. This production process is called just-in-time manufacturing.

The Toyota Production System (TPS) is behind this precision. The TPS is a set of principles, philosophies, and business processes that make the manufacturing process as efficient as possible. The TPS helps Toyota to eliminate waste, to operate with virtually no inventory, and to continually improve production. The TPS is enabled and supported by information technology.

The TPS has enabled Toyota to implement a pull system in which it purchases parts and supplies only when they are needed and only in the quantities necessary to satisfy production requirements. In addition, the company now can match production as closely as possible with consumer demand. This process limits the amount of money that Toyota must commit to inventory. It also allows Toyota to respond quickly to defects or changes in demand.

The IT Solution

Information systems are essential to the TPS. One such IS is Toyota's proprietary Assembly Line Control System (ALCS) software, which controls the sequencing of parts in the assembly process. For example, when a car comes out of the paint shop, the ALCS sends the seat supplier an electronic message detailing the exact configuration of the seats required. The seat supplier has four hours to ship those seats to the plant in the exact sequence required.

The ALCS also controls the most time-intensive part of the vehicle assembly process, the paint shop. In the past, Toyota had difficulty painting different colored cars back to back. Every drop of the previous paint color had to be removed from the tubes of the paint-spraying robots with solvents before the next car could be painted. Now when a car enters the paint shop, the ALCS tells the painting robot the exact color required, and cleaning with solvents is no longer necessary. This process saves about $29 per vehicle and reduces the time needed to produce a car by two hours. In addition, because this process is more efficient, Toyota was able to close one of the three painting booths at the plant.

At every stage of the assembly line, Toyota employs devices that allow workers to stop production to correct defects. In some cases, the device may be as simple as a handle to pull; in other cases this "device" is sophisticated monitoring software that alerts operators to problems with equipment or robots in real time.

Where possible, Toyota uses visual controls, such as overhead displays, plasma screens, and electronic dashboards to quickly convey the status of work. On the assembly-line floor, overhead displays inform supervisors with one glance whether the station is functioning smoothly (green light), whether there is a problem being investigated (yellow light), or whether the assembly line has stopped (red light). Some displays provide even more information, such as which machine malfunctioned, the machine operator, and the exact conditions (for example, speed, temperature) when it broke down.

Toyota uses other devices throughout plant operations to prevent defects. One type of device is a light curtain, which is a beam of light that sends a signal to a computer when a hand or some other object interrupts its flow. The light curtain can signal a warning if, for instance, a worker fails to pick up a bolt, nut, or some other required part.

Toyota consistently produces high-quality cars, with low inventory and few defects. In 2003, Toyota overtook Ford Motor Company to become the world's second largest automaker. Experts predict that Toyota will unseat General Motors as the world's largest automaker before 2010. In fact, Toyota long ago replaced Detroit's Big Three automakers as the world's most profitable automobile manufacturer.

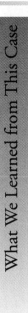

The opening case provides a timely illustration of many of the information systems discussed in this chapter. Toyota has developed information systems to support its operations and its global supply chain. It has implemented many different information systems and integrated them successfully, with outstanding corporate results.

In this chapter we discuss the various systems that support organizations. We begin our discussion with transaction processing systems (TPSs), the most fundamental information systems within organizations. We continue our discussion by following a progression: information systems that support part of an organization (the functional area management information systems), information systems that support an entire organization (enterprise resource planning systems and customer relationship management systems), and, finally, information systems that span multiple organizations (supply chain management systems). We conclude by looking at the technologies that support interorganizational systems.

You will notice that we briefly introduced the systems in this chapter in Chapter 2. Here in Chapter 8 we are going into greater detail on how organizations use these systems.

Sources: Compiled from J. Teresko, "Toyota's Real Secret: Hint, It's Not TPS," *Industry Week*, February 1, 2007; M. Duvall, "What's Driving Toyota?" *Baseline Magazine*, September 5, 2006; Y. Sheffi, "Book excerpt: The Resilient Enterprise," *CIO*, March 1, 2006; E. Pearlman, "Robert I. Sutton: Making a Case for Evidence-Based Management" *CIO Insight*, February 6, 2006; T. Siems, "Supply Chain Management: The Science of Better, Faster, Cheaper," *Federal Reserve Bank of Dallas Publication*, March/April 2005; D. Drickhammer, "Lean Manufacturing: The 3rd Generation," *Industry Week*, December 1, 2004; P. Strassmann, "Why IT Will Continue to Matter," *Computerworld*, September 6, 2004; *www.toyota.com*, accessed April 30, 2007.

8.1 Transaction Processing Systems

Millions (sometimes billions) of transactions occur in every organization every day. A **transaction** is any business event that generates data worthy of being captured and stored in a database. Examples of transactions are a product manufactured, a service sold, a person hired, a payroll check generated, and so on. When you check out at Wal-Mart, every time one of your purchases is swiped over the bar code reader, that is one transaction.

Transaction processing systems (TPSs) monitor, collect, store, and process data generated from all business transactions. These data are inputs to the organization's database. In the modern business world, they also are inputs to the functional information systems, decision support systems, customer relationship management, knowledge management, and e-commerce. TPSs have to handle high volume and large variations in volume (for example, during peak times) efficiently, avoid errors and downtime, record results accurately and securely, and maintain privacy and security. Avoiding errors is particularly critical, because data from the TPSs are input into the organization's database and must be correct (remember: "garbage in, garbage out"). Figure 8.1 shows how TPSs manage data.

Regardless of the specific data processed by a TPS, a fairly standard process occurs, whether in a manufacturing firm, a service firm, or a government organization. First, data are collected by people or sensors and are entered into the computer via any input device. Generally speaking, organizations try to automate the TPS data entry as much as possible because of the large volume involved, a process called *source-data automation*.

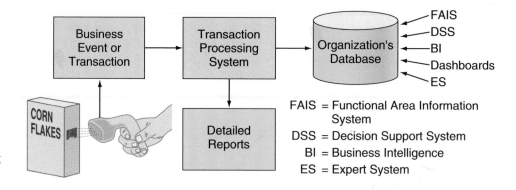

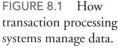

FIGURE 8.1 How transaction processing systems manage data.

Next, the system processes data in one of two basic ways: batch processing or online processing. In **batch processing**, the firm collects data from transactions as they occur, placing them in groups or *batches*. The system then prepares and processes the batches periodically (say, every night).

Traditional TPSs are centralized and run on a mainframe. In **online transaction processing (OLTP)**, business transactions are processed online as soon as they occur. For example, when you pay for an item at a store, the system records the sale by reducing the inventory on hand by a unit, increasing the store's cash position by the amount you paid, and increasing sales figures for the item by one unit—by means of online technologies and in real time.

Before you go on . . .

1. Define TPS.
2. List the key objectives of a TPS.

8.2 Functional Area Information Systems

Functional area information systems (FAISs) provide information mainly to lower- and middle-level managers in the functional areas. They use this information to help them plan, organize, and control operations. The information is provided in a variety of reports. As shown in Figure 8.1, the FAISs access data from the corporate databases. However, to create management reports the FAISs also use data from external databases.

Functional Area Information Systems Reports

As we just discussed, each FAIS generates reports in its functional area. The FAIS also sends information to the corporate data warehouse and can be used for decision support. An FAIS produces primarily three types of reports: routine, ad hoc (on-demand), and exception.

Routine reports are produced at scheduled intervals. They range from hourly quality control reports to daily reports on absenteeism rates. Although routine reports are extremely valuable to an organization, managers frequently need special information that is not included in these reports. Other times they need the information but at different times ("I need the report today, for the last three days, not for one week"). Such out-of-the routine reports are called **ad-hoc (on-demand) reports**. Ad-hoc reports also can include requests for the following types of information:

- **Drill-down reports** show a greater level of detail. For example, a manager might examine sales by region and decide to "drill down to more detail" to look at sales by store and then by salesperson.

- **Key-indicator reports** summarize the performance of critical activities. For example, a chief financial officer might want to monitor cash flow and cash on hand.

- **Comparative reports** compare, for example, the performances of different business units or time periods.

Finally, some managers prefer **exception reports**. Exception reports include only information that falls outside certain threshold standards. To implement *management by exception*, management first creates performance standards. The company then sets up systems to monitor performance (via the incoming data about business transactions such as expenditures), compare actual performance to the standards, and identify predefined exceptions. Managers are alerted to the exceptions via exception reports.

Let's use sales as an example. First, management establishes sales quotas. The company then implements an FAIS that collects and analyzes all sales data. An exception report would identify only those cases where sales fell outside an established threshold—for example, more than 20 percent short of the quota. It would *not* report expenditures that fell *within* the accepted range of standards. By leaving out all "acceptable" performances, exception reports save managers time and help them focus on problem areas.

Information Systems for Specific Functional Areas

Traditionally, information systems were designed within each functional area, to support the area by increasing its internal effectiveness and efficiency. Typical function-specific systems are accounting, finance, marketing, production/operations (POM), and human resources management. Table 8.1 provides an overview of the activities that the functional area information systems support. Figure 8.2 diagrams many of the information systems that support these five functional areas.

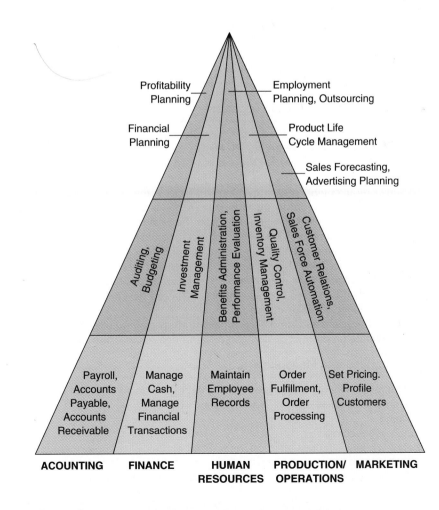

FIGURE 8.2
Examples of information systems supporting the functional areas.

Historically, the functional area information systems were developed independently of one another, resulting in "information silos." These silos did not communicate with one another, and this lack of integration made organizations less efficient. This inefficiency was particularly evident in business processes that crossed the boundaries of functional areas. For example, developing new products involves all functional areas. To understand this point, consider an automobile manufacturer. Developing a new automobile involves every functional area in the company, including design, engineering, production/operations, marketing, finance,

Table 8.1

Activities Supported by Functional Area Information Systems

Accounting and Finance

Financial planning—availability and cost of money
Budgeting—allocates financial resources among participants and activities
Capital budgeting—financing of asset acquisitions
Managing financial transactions
Handling multiple currencies
Virtual close—ability to close books at any time on short notice
Investment management—managing organizational investments in stocks, bonds, real estate, and other investment vehicles
Budgetary control—monitoring expenditures and comparing against budget
Auditing—ensuring the accuracy and condition of financial health of organization
Payroll

Marketing and Sales

Customer relations—know who customers are and treat them like royalty
Customer profiles and preferences
Sales force automation—using software to automate the business tasks of sales, thereby improving the productivity of salespeople

Production/Operations and Logistics

Inventory management—how much inventory to order, how much inventory to keep, and when to order new inventory
Quality control—controlling for defects in incoming material and defects in goods produced
Materials requirements planning—planning process that integrates production, purchasing, and inventory management of interdependent items (MRP)
Manufacturing resource planning—planning process that integrates an enterprise's production, inventory management, purchasing, financing, and labor activities (MRP II)
Just-in-time systems—principle of production and inventory control in which materials and parts arrive precisely when and where needed for production (JIT)
Computer-integrated manufacturing—manufacturing approach that integrates several computerized systems, such as computer-assisted design (CAD), computer-assisted manufacturing (CAM), MRP, and JIT
Product life-cycle management—business strategy that enables manufacturers to collaborate on product design and development efforts, using the Web

Human Resource Management

Recruitment—finding employees, testing them, and deciding which ones to hire
Performance evaluation—periodic evaluation by superiors
Training
Employee records
Benefits administration—medical, retirement, disability, unemployment, etc.

accounting, and human resources. To solve their integration problems, companies developed enterprise resource planning systems. We discuss these systems in the next section.

Before you go on . . .

1. What is a functional area information system? List its major characteristics.

2. How does an FAIS support management by exception? How does it support on-demand reports?

8.3 Enterprise Resource Planning Systems

Enterprise resource planning (ERP) systems integrate the planning, management, and use of all of an organization's resources. The major objectives of ERP systems are to tightly integrate the functional areas of the organization and to enable information to flow seamlessly across the functional areas. Tight integration means that changes in one functional area are immediately reflected in all other pertinent functional areas. The advantages of an ERP system are demonstrated at International Game Technology in IT's About Business 8.1.

уместный

IT's About Business

8.1 Gaming Company Bets on ERP

International Game Technology (IGT) (*www.igt.com*) manufactures slot machines and lottery machines in factories in Reno, Las Vegas, and Manchester, England. Until 2002 the company depended on several different information systems to manage its sales, customer orders, manufacturing, and accounting. When an executive, a sales manager, or a production manager wanted to learn the status of a particular order, there was no single system he or she could access. Instead, each functional area had its own system that contained a different piece of information about that order. Across IGT, different functional groups depended on different applications. Keeping all the applications communicating with one another was a difficult task for the IS department.

IGT, therefore, had a huge amount of useful business information contained in applications that were not integrated. IGT desperately needed more cohesive information systems that would help the company grow. For example, the company's accounting department complained about having multiple types of software in their functional area. It wanted one information system that would handle all of its accounting functions, if only to achieve greater efficiency in closing the books, which took about two weeks.

The problem was, if accounting bought a new system on its own, then manufacturing and engineering would want to do the same thing. As a result, IGT decided to implement an enterprise resource planning (ERP) system.

Following a two-year implementation effort, IGT installed the SAP R/3 system, which is produced by software vendor SAP. The SAP system produced many benefits for the company. Perhaps most importantly, it enabled the company to integrate its three major business functions—finance, manufacturing, and product development—through a common information platform. In addition, the new system connected the company's worldwide operations.

The SAP system contains product configuration software that gives IGT additional flexibility in manufacturing products. This software is very important for IGT, because the company's products are made on a build-to-order basis.

There were benefits on the plant floor as well. Operations employees are now able to access manufacturing process details online at their workstations.

Therefore, at each step of the manufacturing process, the SAP system makes the process more efficient and effective through the discipline it enforces. That is, the system forces the workers to do things the right way. The end results are fewer errors and higher yields.

On the factory floor, IGT uses its proprietary factory control system. This system coordinates the delivery of materials to the production line at the proper location and time. Integrating this system with SAP allows IGT's customer order staff to find out exactly which machines were built and at which plant locations. IGT also uses SAP's project management system to monitor costs and to design changes in developing and launching new products, such as its EZ Pay "cashless" feature—where winners are paid off in redeemable or reusable tickets.

IGT experienced other operational benefits from the SAP system. The company's inventory records have become more accurate, and inventory turns are up as well. Inventory turns are a measure of how fast a company is selling its inventory. Customer order-to-delivery lead times have been reduced from 10 to 8 weeks. The company also was able to establish a quick turnaround process in which rush orders are filled in 4 weeks instead of 7 or 8 weeks in the old system.

IGT did experience some challenges during the implementation process. SAP is a very structured software product with very structured processes. For this reason, IGT had to change some of its business processes to accommodate the SAP system. For example, the company had to revamp its order process to accommodate the way the software works. The company was not able to release a sales order to the production department until two weeks before manufacturing was scheduled to begin.

Another challenge involved customizing some of the SAP software. For example, the company had to assemble a team of people from the order group and the engineering department. Their mission was to customize the SAP system to handle the company's complex bill of materials for its various product lines.

Sources: Compiled from M. Songini, "New Slot Machines Promise More Options for Gamblers," *Computerworld*, March 28, 2007; D. Bartholomew, "ERP: Gaming Company Hits Jackpot," *Baseline Magazine*, October 2, 2006; D. Bartholomew, "Leaders Supporting Growth with IT," *Industry Week*, November 1, 2005; www.igt.com, accessed May 1, 2007.

QUESTIONS

1. Why did so many companies develop nonintegrated functional information systems ("silos"), which necessitated the typically long, expensive implementation of ERP systems?
2. Users have usually been able to readily adapt software to their needs. ERP systems, though, are notoriously difficult and expensive to customize. Organizations often have to adapt their business processes to the ERP software, rather than customizing the software. Discuss the implications of changing your organization's business processes while, at the same time, implementing an ERP system.

ERP systems provide the information necessary to control the business processes of the organization. A **business process** is a set of related steps or procedures designed to produce a specific outcome. Business processes can be located entirely within one functional area, such as approving a credit card application or hiring a new employee. They can also span multiple functional areas, such as fulfilling a large order from a new customer.

ERP software includes a set of interdependent software modules, linked to a common database, that provide support for the internal business processes in the following functional areas: finance and accounting, sales and marketing, manufacturing and production, and human resources. The modules are built around predefined business processes, and users access them through a single interface. Table 8.2 provides examples of the predefined business processes.

The business processes in ERP software are often predefined by the best practices that the ERP vendor has developed. **Best practices** are the most successful solutions or problem-solving methods for achieving a business objective.

Business Processes Supported by ERP Modules

Table 8.2

- *Financial and accounting processes:* general ledger, accounts payable, accounts receivable, fixed assets, cash management and forecasting, product-cost accounting, cost-center accounting, asset accounting, tax accounting, credit management, financial reporting
- *Sales and marketing processes:* order processing, quotations, contracts, product configuration, pricing, billing, credit checking, incentive and commission management, sales planning
- *Manufacturing and production processes:* procurement, inventory management, purchasing, shipping, production planning, production scheduling, material requirements planning, quality control, distribution, transportation, plant and equipment maintenance
- *Human resources processes:* personnel administration, time accounting, payroll, personnel planning and development, benefits accounting, applicant tracking, compensation, workforce planning, performance management

Although some companies have developed their own ERP systems, most organizations use commercially available ERP software. The leading ERP software vendor is SAP (*www.sap.com*), with its SAP R/3 package (the one adopted by IGT). Other major vendors include Oracle (*www.oracle.com*) and PeopleSoft (*www.peoplesoft.com*), now an Oracle company. (With more than 700 customers, PeopleSoft is the market leader in higher education.) For up-to-date information on ERP software, visit *http://erp.ittoolbox.com.*

Despite all of their benefits, ERP systems have drawbacks. To begin with, they can be extremely complex, expensive, and time consuming to implement. Also, as we saw in the IGT case, companies may need to change existing business processes to fit the predefined business processes of the software. For companies with well-established procedures, this requirement can be a huge problem. Finally, companies must purchase the entire software package even if they require only a few of the modules. For these reasons, ERP software is not attractive to everyone.

During the late 1990s, companies began to extend ERP systems along the supply chain to suppliers and customers. These extended systems add functions to help companies manage customer interactions and relationships with suppliers and vendors. We discuss supply chain management systems in Section 8.5.

Before you go on . . .

1. Define ERP, and describe its functionalities.
2. List some drawbacks of ERP software.

8.4 Customer Relationship Management Systems

Customer relationship management (CRM) is an enterprisewide effort to acquire and retain customers. CRM recognizes that customers are the core of a business and that a company's success depends on effectively managing its relationships with them. CRM focuses on building long-term and sustainable customer relationships that add value for both the customer and the company. For additional information on CRM products, visit *www.mycustomer.com* and *http://crm.ittoolbox.com.*

CRM includes a *one-to-one* relationship between a customer and a seller. To be a genuine one-to-one marketer, a company must be willing and able to change its behavior toward a specific customer, based on what it knows about that customer. In essence, CRM is based on a simple idea: *Treat different customers differently.* For example, "good" customers account for about 80 percent of a company's profits, but they comprise only 20 percent of its customers.

Acquiring a new customer can cost many times more than retaining an existing customer. Therefore, CRM helps organizations to keep profitable customers and to maximize lifetime revenue from them.

Because a firm must be able to modify its products and services based on the needs of individual customers, CRM involves much more than just sales and marketing. Rather, as we saw in the section on Web 2.0 in Chapter 5, smart companies encourage customers to participate in the development of products, services, and solutions. In order to build enduring one-to-one relationships in a CRM initiative, a company must continuously interact with customers *individually*. One reason so many firms are beginning to focus on CRM is that this kind of marketing can create high customer loyalty, which will increase the firm's profits. Significantly, for CRM to be effective, almost all other functional areas must become involved. IT's About Business 8.2 illustrates how three companies use on-demand CRM to improve customer relations.

Customer Relationship Management Applications

In the past, customer data were located in many isolated systems in various functional areas, such as finance, distribution, sales, service, and marketing. In addition, e-commerce generated huge amounts of customer data that were not integrated with the data in the functional area ISs.

CRM systems were designed to address these problems by providing information and tools to deliver a superior customer experience and to maximize the lifetime customer value for a firm. CRM systems integrate customer data from various organizational sources, analyze these data, and then provide the results to both employees and customer touch points. A **customer touch point** is a method of interaction with a customer, such as telephone, e-mail, a customer service or help desk, conventional mail, a Web site, and a store.

Properly designed CRM systems provide a single, enterprisewide view of each customer. These systems also provide customers with a single point of contact within the enterprise as well as a unified view of the enterprise.

CRM systems provide applications in three major areas: sales, marketing, and customer service. Let's take a look at each one.

Sales. *Sales force automation (SFA)* functions in CRM systems make salespeople more productive by helping them focus on the most profitable customers. SFA functions provide data such as sales prospect and contact information, product information, product configurations, and sales quotes. SFA software can integrate all the information about a particular customer so that the salesperson can put together a personalized presentation for that customer.

Marketing. CRM systems support marketing campaigns by providing prospect and customer data, product and service information, qualified sales leads, and tools for analyzing marketing and customer data. In addition, they enhance opportunities for cross-selling, up-selling, and bundling.

Cross-selling refers to the marketing of complementary products to customers. For example, a bank customer with a large balance in his or her checking account might be directed toward CDs or money market funds. **Up-selling** is the marketing of higher-value products or services to new or existing customers. For example, if you are in the market for a television, a salesperson will show you a plasma-screen TV next to a conventional TV, in hopes that you will pay extra for a clearer picture. Finally, **bundling** is a type of cross-selling in which a vendor sells a combination of products together at a lower price than the combined costs of the individual products. For example, your cable company might offer a

IT's About Business

8.2 Software as a Service for Customer Relationship Management

Customer relationship management (CRM) software covers a broad spectrum of service issues, from tracking sales leads to fielding customer complaints. Historically, CRM software was sold as proprietary vendor software (for example, Siebel Systems, now owned by Oracle). Customers purchased the software and implemented it in their organizations.

The market changed in the late 1990s with the arrival of firms like Salesforce.com (1999), which offered CRM in the "software as a service," or SaaS, model (discussed in Technology Guide 2). Current SaaS products are called on-demand CRM software. We now discuss two examples of companies employing this software.

The first example involves Shaklee (*www.shaklee.com*), the health food and personal-care product company. When Shaklee came under new management in 2004, the company had no apparatus for tracking the kinds of questions its customers were asking its call-center representatives. It also had no online self-service tools such as a frequently asked questions (FAQ) page. Instead, the company tabulated questions and complaints using pen and paper. It also performed follow-ups manually, and its representatives kept records in separate files.

Seeking a solution that could be deployed quickly, the company chose on-demand CRM software from RightNow (*www.rightnow.com*). RightNow could be implemented in 3 months, as opposed to an enterprise system, which could take up to 18 months.

In the second example, the salespeople in the Capita Group (*www.capita.co.uk*), a London-based management consulting firm, managed their own accounts on individual laptops, and managers aggregated the data by business unit on spreadsheets.

Integrating the individually kept records required 4 hours per month each from 15 staffers, which meant that managers were spending a total of 60 hours just on reporting.

In 2006, Capita became the first European customer for SAP's on-demand CRM software. By selecting this software, the company spent almost $300,000 less than it would have spent to purchase an enterprise solution. Sales representatives now are able to enter sales figures directly into the SAP system, which automatically aggregates these data across the company's units, producing reports instantly. Obtaining these reports so quickly not only helps Capita's operations, but it enhances its collaboration with clients.

Sources: Compiled from J. Blau, "SAP Chief Developer Heads for the 'Clouds'," *Computerworld*, March 9, 2007; B. Watson, "Software as a Service: Handling Customers, Hands-Free," *Baseline Magazine*, March 8, 2007; R. Ferguson, "SAP Outlines Q4, Full Year '06 Earnings, Looks Forward," *eWeek*, January 24, 2007; C. Finch, "The Benefits of the Software-as-a-Service Model," *Computerworld*, January 2, 2006.

QUESTIONS

1. Why would a company use an on-demand CRM product rather than a traditional enterprisewide CRM product? Wouldn't the on-demand product lend itself to fragmented views of a customer across the enterprise? After all, CRM software is supposed to repair such a problem, not cause it.

2. How would an organization control the use of on-demand CRM software across an enterprise to eliminate such a fragmented view of a customer?

package that includes basic cable TV, all the movie channels, and broadband Internet access for a lower price than these services would cost individually. As another example, computer manufacturers or retailers often bundle a computer, monitor, and printer at a reduced cost.

Customer Service.   Customer service functions in CRM systems provide information and tools to make call centers, help desks, and customer support staff more efficient. These functions often include Web-based self-service capabilities. Customer service can take many forms, as we see below.

CRM systems can personalize interactive experiences to induce a consumer to commit to a purchase or to remain loyal to a company. For example, General Electric's Web site (*www.ge.com*) provides detailed technical and maintenance information. In addition, it sells replacement parts for discontinued models. These types of parts and information are quite difficult to find offline. The ability to download manuals and solutions to common problems at any time is another innovation of Web-based customer service. Finally, customized information—such as product and warranty information—can be efficiently delivered when the customer logs on to the vendor's Web site. Not only can the customer pull (search and find) information as needed, but the vendor also can push (send) information to the customer.

Dell Computer revolutionized the purchasing of computers by letting customers configure their own systems. Many other online vendors now offer this type of mass customization. Consumers are shown prepackaged specials and are then given the option to custom-build products using product configurators.

Customers can view their account balances or check the shipping status of their orders at any time from their computers or cell phones. If you order books from Amazon, for example, you can find the anticipated arrival date. Many companies follow this model and provide similar services (see *www.fedex.com* and *www.ups.com*).

Many companies allow customers to create their own individual Web pages. These pages can be used to record purchases and preferences, as well as problems and requests. For example, you can create your own personalized Google Web page by visiting *www.google.com/ig*.

FAQs are the simplest and least expensive tool for dealing with repetitive customer questions. Customers use this tool by themselves, which makes the delivery cost minimal. However, nonstandard questions still require an individual e-mail.

E-mail has become the most popular tool of customer service. Inexpensive and fast, e-mail is used primarily to answer inquiries from customers. However, firms also rely on e-mail to disseminate product and other information (for example, confirmations) and to conduct correspondence regarding any topic.

One of the most important tools of customer service is the *call center*. Call centers are typically the "face" of the organization to its customers, and they handle incoming product support and customer inquiries.

8.5 Supply Chain Management Systems

A **supply chain** refers to the flow of materials, information, money, and services from raw material suppliers, through factories and warehouses to the end customers. A supply chain also includes the *organizations* and *processes* that create and deliver products, information, and services to end customers.

The function of **supply chain management (SCM)** is to plan, organize, and optimize the supply chain's activities. Like other functional areas, SCM utilizes information systems. The goal of SCM systems is to reduce friction along the supply chain. Friction can involve increased time, costs, and inventories as well as decreased customer satisfaction. SCM systems, then, reduce uncertainty and risks by decreasing inventory levels and cycle time and improving business processes and customer service. All of these benefits contribute to increased profitability and competitiveness.

Significantly, SCM systems are a type of interorganizational information system. An **interorganizational information system (IOS)** involves information flows among two or more organizations. By connecting the information systems of business partners, IOSs enable the partners to perform a number of tasks:

- Reduce the costs of routine business transactions.
- Improve the quality of the information flow by reducing or eliminating errors.

- Compress the cycle time involved in fulfilling business transactions.
- Eliminate paper processing and its associated inefficiencies and costs.
- Make the transfer and processing of information easier for users.

IT's About Business 8.3 illustrates these advantages as they apply to a supply chain that manages digital, rather than physical, goods.

IT's About Business

POM

8.3 The Digital Supply Chain at Warner Brothers

The Warner Home Entertainment Group, a division of Warner Bros. Entertainment (*www.warnerbros.com*), is responsible for all business units involved in the digital delivery of entertainment to consumers. The entertainment business is in transition because the consumer, empowered by new technologies, has an active role in the entertainment process instead of being a passive recipient.

Warner is transforming itself into a digital end-to-end business. This change has been driven by a dispersion of how customers want to consume content. As customers have turned to digital media, the Warner production systems have done so as well. At the front (production) end, filmmakers are increasingly using digital cameras. At the back (distribution) end, Warner is implementing digital distribution through broadband communications links, DVD, and high-definition television (HDTV). Warner's digital transformation enables the studio to deliver product electronically worldwide over existing and new digital platforms.

In some ways, the film industry resembles a cottage or boutique industry. Companies are formed for production of one film, or a few films, and then are dissolved. Therefore, the film industry revolves around very short-term production and is very expensive.

Until recently, there was a comfortable period of time—several months—between the time a film was released in theaters and the time a studio had to stamp and distribute the DVD version. DVDs, the Internet, broadband, and cheaper, high-volume storage have changed all that. Now, the industry must handle three different types of DVDs (DVD, HD DVD, and Blu-ray Disc), Apple iTunes and other mobile devices, plus more aggressive demand from video-on-demand (VOD). These technologies put pressure on studios to create alternative content very close to the initial release date of a film.

Warner Bros. has made the earliest and most far-reaching commitment to new technology in the industry. Currently, it is partnering with Hewlett-Packard to transform the studio's entire film production and distribution process to an all-digital, file-based system, and to create an information technology architecture to make this process possible. Hewlett-Packard is providing a digital media platform, consisting of software, hardware, and services. The platform manages rich digital content and relies on service-oriented architecture.

To see the huge scale of Warner's project, consider that in 2006 the company produced more than 2,500 different DVDs, delivered more than 180 hours of video programming weekly over its global digital media exchange, produced and/or distributed more than 50 television series, is in the process of digitizing more than 6,000 feature films in its storage vaults for DVD release, and released numerous films, three of which earned more than $200 million—a studio and industry record for a single year.

For all of its films, Warner now has a film version plus a digital version. Both versions, as well as additional information regarding rights, royalties, and so on, make up what Warner calls an "E-master" and are stored on servers at Warner Bros. Warner tried to leverage existing techniques for database management to handle the large E-master files that the company was creating. However, the communications links that interconnected the storage servers could not manage such huge files. Therefore, files could not be moved in and out of Warner's repository in a timely fashion; nor could they be quickly found.

To resolve this problem, Warner worked with Hewlett-Packard to develop high-performance storage systems that permit Warner to manipulate the files at the speed the company must have. At the same time, the two companies were able to manage the different forms of distribution, which have varying requirements. As an example, VOD requires bandwidth of 3 to 4 Mbps, whereas high-definition broadcasts require 10 to 20 Mbps.

When Warner first began to operate its digital supply chain, the company was able to process only one or two films at a time. After one year, Warner has the capability of simultaneously working on ten motion picture projects. The creation of E-masters is critical, because it enables Warner to utilize any channel to reach the consumer.

Warner is also digitizing the 6,000 or so motion pictures—many of them made in the late 1930s—in its film library, using digital technology to restore the original quality of the Technicolor photography. The company also has an online Web initiative that will enable fans of various cartoon shows such as Looney Tunes to download new, interactive content, related games, and flash animations of Bugs Bunny, Daffy Duck, and other popular characters. The company found that customers wanted to use Warner content

to create content of their own and post it on their own Web sites.

Sources: Compiled from M. Perenson, "CES: Warner Home Video Back Dual-DVD Format," *Computerworld,* January 11, 2007; L. McCartney, "Digital Supply Chain: Warner Bros.' Next Big Release," *Baseline Magazine,* October 2, 2006; "Warner Bros: Digital Supply Chain Transformation," *www.accenture.com,* accessed April 30, 2007; M. Perenson, "Format Wars Redux: Blu-Ray Disc versus HD DVD," *Computerworld,* February 20, 2005.

QUESTIONS

1. Differentiate between supply chains for digital content and supply chains for physical goods. Use Warner Bros. for an example of a digital supply chain and Wal-Mart for a physical supply chain.
2. Draw the supply chain for Warner Bros. Label the upstream and downstream components (discussed in the next section), with Warner Bros. in the middle.

The Structure and Components of Supply Chains

The term *supply chain* comes from a picture of how the partnering organizations are linked together. A typical supply chain, which links a company with its suppliers and its distributors and customers, is shown in Figure 8.3. Recall that Figure 2.2 also illustrated a supply chain in a slightly different way than Figure 8.3. Note that the supply chain involves three segments:

1. *Upstream,* where sourcing or procurement from external suppliers occurs
2. *Internal,* where packaging, assembly, or manufacturing takes place
3. *Downstream,* where distribution takes place, frequently by external distributors

The flow of information and goods can be bidirectional. For example, damaged or unwanted products can be returned, a process known as *reverse logistics.* Using the retail clothing

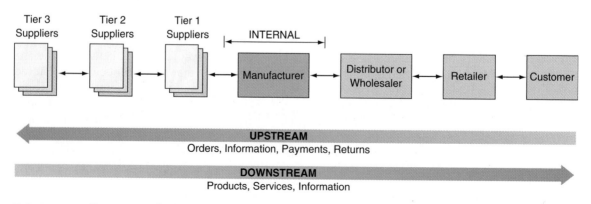

FIGURE 8.3   Generic supply chain.

industry as an example, we see that reverse logistics would involve clothing that customers return, either because the item had defects or because the customer did not like the item.

Tiers of Suppliers.   If you look closely at Figure 8.3, you will notice that there are several tiers of suppliers. As the diagram shows, a supplier may have one or more subsuppliers, and the subsupplier may have its own subsupplier(s), and so on. For example, with an automobile manufacturer, Tier 3 suppliers produce basic products such as glass, plastic, and rubber. Tier 2 suppliers use these inputs to make windshields, tires, and plastic moldings. Tier 1 suppliers produce integrated components such as dashboards and seat assemblies.

The Flows in the Supply Chain.   There are typically three flows in the supply chain: materials, information, and financial. *Material flows* are the physical products, raw materials, supplies, and so forth that flow along the chain. Material flows also include *reverse* flows—returned products, recycled products, and disposal of materials or products. A supply chain thus involves a *product life-cycle* approach, from "dirt to dust."

Information flows consist of data that are related to demand, shipments, orders, returns, and schedules, as well as changes in any of these data. Finally, *financial flows* involve money transfers, payments, credit card information and authorization, payment schedules, e-payments, and credit-related data.

All supply chains do not have the same number and types of flows. For example, in service industries there may be no physical flow of materials, but frequently there is a flow of information, often in the form of documents (physical or electronic copies). The digitization of software, music, and other content may create a supply chain without any physical flow. Notice, however, that in such a case, there are two types of information flows: one that replaces materials flow (for example, digitized software) and one that provides the supporting information (orders, billing, and so on). To manage the supply chain, an organization must coordinate all the above flows among all of the parties involved in the chain.

Problems along the Supply Chain

As we discussed earlier, problems, or friction, can develop within a supply chain. One major symptom of ineffective supply chains is poor customer service. In some cases, supply chains don't deliver products or services when and where customers—either individuals or businesses—need them. In other cases the supply chain provides poor-quality products. Other problems are high inventory costs and loss of revenues.

The problems along the supply chain stem primarily from two sources: (1) uncertainties, and (2) the need to coordinate several activities, internal units, and business partners. A major source of supply chain uncertainties is the *demand forecast*. Demand for a product can be influenced by numerous factors such as competition, prices, weather conditions, technological developments, and customers' general confidence. Another uncertainty is delivery times, which depend on factors ranging from production machine failures to road construction and traffic jams. In addition, quality problems in materials and parts can create production delays, which also lead to supply chain problems.

One of the major difficulties in properly setting inventory levels in various parts of the supply chain is known as the bullwhip effect. The **bullwhip effect** refers to erratic shifts in orders up and down the supply chain. Basically, customer demand variables can become magnified when they are viewed through the eyes of managers at each link in the supply chain. If each distinct entity that makes ordering and inventory decisions places its own interests above those of the chain, then stockpiling can occur at as many as seven or eight locations along the supply chain. Research has shown that in some cases such hoarding has led to as many as 100 days of inventory that is waiting "just in case" (versus 10–20 days in the normal case).

Solutions to Supply Chain Problems

Supply chain problems can be very costly for companies. Therefore, organizations are motivated to find innovative solutions. During the oil crises of the 1970s, for example, Ryder Systems, a large trucking company, purchased a refinery to control the upstream part of the supply chain and ensure timely availability of gasoline for its trucks. Such a strategy is known as vertical integration. A general definition of **vertical integration** is a business strategy in which a company buys its suppliers. (Ryder sold the refinery later, because (1) it could not manage a business it did not know and (2) oil became more plentiful.) In the remaining portion of this section, we will look at some of the possible solutions to supply chain problems, many of which are supported by IT.

Using Inventories to Solve Supply Chain Problems. Undoubtedly, the most common solution is *building inventories* as insurance against supply chain uncertainties. The main problem with this approach is that it is very difficult to correctly determine inventory levels for each product and part. If inventory levels are set too high, the costs of keeping the inventory will greatly increase. (Also, as we have seen, excessive inventories at multiple points in the supply chain can result in the bullwhip effect.) If the inventory is too low, there is no insurance against high demand or slow delivery times. In such cases, customers don't receive what they want, when they want or need it. The result is lost customers and revenues. In either event, the total cost—including the costs of maintaining inventories, the costs of lost sales opportunities, and the costs of developing a bad reputation—can be very high. Thus, companies make major attempts to optimize and control inventories.

Information Sharing. Another common way to solve supply chain problems, and especially to improve demand forecasts, is *sharing information* along the supply chain. Such sharing can be facilitated by electronic data interchange and extranets, topics we discuss in the next section.

One of the most notable examples of information sharing occurs between large manufacturers and retailers. For example, Wal-Mart provides Procter & Gamble with access to daily sales information from every store for every item P&G makes for Wal-Mart. This access enables P&G to manage the *inventory replenishment* for Wal-Mart's stores. By monitoring inventory levels, P&G knows when inventories fall below the threshold for each product at any Wal-Mart store. These data trigger an immediate shipment.

Such information sharing between Wal-Mart and P&G is done automatically. It is part of a vendor-managed inventory strategy. **Vendor-managed inventory (VMI)** occurs when a retailer does not manage the inventory for a particular product or group of products. Instead, the supplier manages the entire inventory process. P&G has similar agreements with other major retailers. The benefit for P&G is accurate and timely information on consumer demand for its products. Thus, P&G can plan production more accurately, minimizing the bullwhip effect.

Issues in Global IOS Design

Interorganizational systems that connect companies located in two or more countries are referred to as **global information systems**. Regardless of its structure, a company with global operations relies heavily on IT. The major benefits of global information systems for such organizations are effective communication at a reasonable cost and effective collaboration that overcomes differences in distance, time, language, and culture.

The task of designing any effective IOS is complicated. It is even more complex when the IOS is a global system, because of differences in cultures, economies, and politics among parties in different countries. Some countries are erecting artificial borders through local language preference, local regulation, and access limitations. Some issues to consider in designing global IOSs are cultural differences, localization, economic and political differences, and legal issues.

Cultural Differences.   *Culture* consists of the objects, values, and other characteristics of a particular society. It includes many different elements ranging from tradition to legal and ethical issues to what types of information are considered offensive. When companies plan to do business in countries other than their own, they must consider the cultural environment.

Localization.   Many companies use different names, colors, sizes, and packaging for their overseas products and services. This practice is referred to as *localization*, which means that products and services are modified for each locality. In order to maximize the benefits of global information systems, the localization approach also should be used in the design and operation of such systems. For example, many Web sites offer different language and/or currency options, as well as special content.

Economic and Political Differences.   Countries also differ considerably in their economic and political environments. One result of such variations is that IT infrastructures often differ from country to country. For example, many countries own the telephone services or control communications systems very tightly. For example, France insisted for years that French should be the sole language on French Web sites. The country now permits Web sites to use other languages, but French still must appear in every site. China goes even further. The Chinese government controls the content of the Internet and blocks some Web sites from being viewed in the country.

Legal Issues.   Legal systems differ considerably among countries. As a result, laws and rules concerning copyrights, patents, computer crimes, file sharing, privacy, and data transfer vary from country to country. All of these issues can affect what information is transmitted via global systems. For this reason, companies must consider these issues when they establish a global IS.

The impact of legal, economic, and political differences on the design and use of global information systems can be clearly seen in the issue of cross-border data transfer. The term **trans-border data flow** refers to the flow of corporate data across national borders. Several countries, such as Canada and Brazil, impose strict laws to control this transfer. These countries usually justify their laws as protecting the privacy of their citizens, because corporate data frequently contain personal information. Other justifications are protecting intellectual property and keeping jobs within the country by requiring that data processing be done there.

Before you go on . . .

1. Define a supply chain and supply chain management (SCM).
2. List the major components of supply chains.
3. What is the bullwhip effect?
4. Describe solutions to supply chain problems.

8.6 Electronic Data Interchange and Extranets

Clearly, SCM systems are essential to the successful operation of many businesses. As we discussed, these systems—and IOSs in general—rely on various forms of IT to resolve problems. Three technologies in particular provide support for IOSs and SCM systems: electronic data interchange, extranets, and Web services. (Web services was discussed in Chapter 5.)

Electronic Data Interchange (EDI)

Electronic data interchange (EDI) is a communication standard that enables business partners to exchange routine documents, such as purchasing orders, electronically. EDI formats these documents according to agreed-upon standards (for example, data formats) and then transmits messages using a converter, called a translator. The message travels over either a value-added network (VAN) or the Internet.

EDI provides many benefits compared with a manual delivery system (see Figure 8.4). To begin with, it minimizes data entry errors because each entry is checked by the computer. In

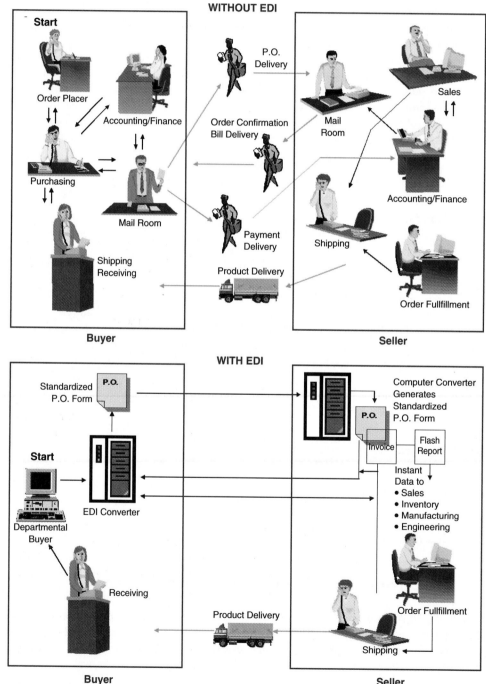

FIGURE 8.4
Comparing purchase order (PO) fulfillment with and without EDI. *Source:* Drawn by E. Turban.

addition, the length of the message can be shorter, and the messages are secured. EDI also reduces cycle time, increases productivity, enhances customer service, and minimizes paper usage and storage.

Despite all of EDI'S advantages, various factors prevented it from being more widely used. To begin with, implementing an EDI system involves a significant initial investment. In addition, the ongoing operating costs also are high, due to the use of expensive, private VANs. Another major issue for some companies is that the traditional EDI system is inflexible. For example, it is difficult to make quick changes, such as adding business partners. In addition, an EDI system requires a long startup period. Furthermore, business processes must sometimes be restructured to fit EDI requirements. Finally, many EDI standards are in use today. As a result, one company might have to use several standards in order to communicate with different business partners.

Despite these complications, EDI remains popular, particularly among major business partners, though it is being replaced by XML-based Web services. Many EDI service providers offer secure, lower-cost EDI services over the Internet, as IT's About Business 8.4 shows.

Extranets

In building IOSs and SCM systems, it is necessary to connect the intranets of different business partners to build extranets. As we have discussed in previous chapters, extranets link business partners to one another over the Internet by providing access to certain areas of each other's corporate intranets (see Figure 8.5).

The main goal of extranets is to foster collaboration between and among business partners. An extranet is open to selected B2B suppliers, customers, and other business partners. These individuals access the extranet through the Internet. Extranets enable people who are located outside a company to work together with the company's internally located employees. An extranet also enables external business partners to enter the corporate intranet, via the Internet, to access data, place orders, check status, communicate, and collaborate. It also enables partners to perform self-service activities such as checking the status of orders or inventory levels.

Extranets use virtual private network (VPN) technology to make communication over the Internet more secure. The Internet-based extranet is far less costly than proprietary networks. It is a nonproprietary technical tool that can support the rapid evolution of electronic communication and commerce. The major benefits of extranets are faster processes and information flow, improved order entry and customer service, lower costs (for example, for communications, travel, and administrative overhead), and an overall improvement in business effectiveness.

Types of Extranets. Depending on the business partners involved and the purpose, there are three major types of extranets, as follows.

A Company and Its Dealers, Customers, or Suppliers. Such an extranet is centered around one company. An example is the FedEx extranet that allows customers to track the status of a package. To do so, customers use the Internet to access a database on the FedEx intranet. By enabling a customer to check the location of a package, FedEx saves the cost of having a human operator perform that task over the phone.

An Industry's Extranet. The major players in an industry may team up to create an extranet that will benefit all of them. For example, ANXeBusiness (*www.anx.com*) enables companies to collaborate effectively through a network that provides a secure global medium for B2B information exchange. The ANX Network is used for mission-critical business transactions by leading international organizations in aerospace, automotive,

IT's About Business

ACC

8.4 EDI at the Memorial Sloan-Kettering Cancer Center

Accounts payable traditionally has been a time-consuming, routine process of matching purchase orders with invoices, confirming that shipments or services were received, and then producing and mailing a check. This laborious process lasted so long because many companies used it to their advantage. They held off on paying suppliers for up to 60 or 70 days from receipt of the invoice. The idea was that they could earn money by investing the funds for as many days as possible in short-term investment before having to pay the suppliers.

Memorial Sloan-Kettering Cancer Center (MSKCC) (*www.mskcc.org*) was searching for a better way to process the nearly half-million invoices it received annually from its suppliers. The center decided to utilize Xign (*www.xign.net*), which offers a hosted online payments service. Xign provides a network that enables companies to issue purchase orders, receive invoices, and make electronic payments to suppliers. An online payment service acts as an intermediary between a company's accounts payable department and the supplier, speeding up the payment process while eliminating paper invoicing and most of the labor-intensive invoice-purchase order matching function. To participate in the Xign network, MSKCC suppliers had to provide Xign with the bank information that Xign needed to process electronic payments from MSKCC to its suppliers.

MSKCC was already a big user of electronic data interchange (EDI) and chose to use standard EDI protocols for data transactions. Before moving to Xign, MSKCC had already automated about half of its payables, with 53 percent of invoices being transmitted via EDI to its dozen largest suppliers. However, with a total of 10,000 suppliers, a huge number of paper invoices remained.

In most cases, suppliers elect to sign onto Xign's payment network and simply "flip" MSKCC's purchase order, automatically convert it into an invoice, and submit it for approval by MSKCC. Payments are made through Xign's payment process, and MSKCC pays a per-transaction fee to Xign.

By moving to Xign, MSKCC increased the percentage of invoices it processed electronically from roughly 60 percent in 2003 to about 85 percent in 2006. MSKCC saved so much time on the volume of invoices it had been processing manually that it reduced its full-time staff from six to four, saving about $120,000 annually. At the same time, the department processed a higher total volume of invoices, and on-time payments increased from 15 percent before MSKCC started using Xign to more than 95 percent by 2007. In addition, the cost per transaction with Xign is lower than MSKCC was paying for its all-EDI-based transactions.

MSKCC has enjoyed even larger savings as a result of supplier discounts. A typical discounted pricing arrangement is the "2%–10–net 30." This means the vendor agrees to give MSKCC a 2 percent reduction for invoices paid in 10 days that are due in 30 days. These discounts amount to approximately $500,000 annually.

In addition, many of MSKCC's smaller suppliers (and there are thousands of them) who would not use EDI due to its expense signed on to Xign. This process simplified MSKCC's accounts payable process even more. Interestingly, a few of MSKCC's largest suppliers chose not to use Xign for various reasons. Some did not want to learn new technology, others did not want to change their business processes, and still others were not willing to divulge their banking information.

Sources: Compiled from D. Bartholomew, "E-Payment Portal: When Time Is Money," *Baseline Magazine*, March 13, 2007.

QUESTIONS

1. What is the difference between MSKCC's use of Xign and its use of EDI?
2. If you were the CIO at MSKCC, would you demand that all of your suppliers use Xign? Why or why not? *Could* you demand that all of your suppliers use Xign? Why or why not?

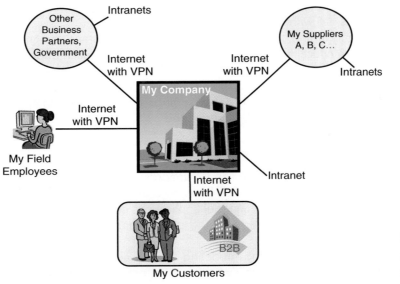

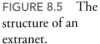

FIGURE 8.5   The structure of an extranet.

chemical, electronics, financial services, healthcare, logistics, manufacturing, transportation, and related industries. The ANX Network offers customers a reliable extranet and VPN services.

Joint Ventures and Other Business Partnerships.   In this type of extranet, the partners in a joint venture use the extranet as a vehicle for communications and collaboration. An example is Bank of America's extranet for commercial loans. The partners involved in making such loans include a lender, a loan broker, an escrow company, and a title company. The extranet connects lenders, loan applicants, and the loan organizer, Bank of America. A similar case is Lending Tree (*www.lendingtree.com*), a company that provides mortgage quotes for your home and also sells mortgages online. Lending Tree uses an extranet for its business partners (for example, the lenders).

Before you go on . . .

1. Define EDI, and list its major benefits and limitations.
2. Define an extranet, and explain its infrastructure.
3. List and briefly define the major types of extranets.

What's in **IT** for Me?

For the Accounting Major

Understanding the functions and outputs of TPSs effectively is a major concern of any accountant. It is also necessary to understand the various activities of all functional areas and how they are interconnected. Accounting information systems are a central component in any ERP package. In fact, all large CPA firms actively consult with clients on ERP implementations, using thousands of specially trained accounting majors. Also, many supply chain issues, ranging from inventory management to risk analysis, fall within the realm of accounting.

Going further, accounting rules and regulations and the cross-border transfer of data are critical for global trade. IOSs can facilitate such trade. Other issues that are important for accountants are taxation and government reports. In addition, creating information systems that rely on EDI requires the attention of accountants. Finally, fraud detection in global settings (for example, transfers of funds) can be facilitated by appropriate controls and auditing.

For the Finance Major

IT helps financial analysts and managers perform their tasks better. Of particular importance is analyzing cash flows and securing the financing required for smooth operations. In addition, financial applications can support such activities as risk analysis, investment management, and global transactions involving different currencies and fiscal regulations.

Finance activities and modeling are key components of ERP systems. Flows of funds (payments), at the core of most supply chains, must be done efficiently and effectively. Financial arrangements are especially important along global supply chains, where currency conventions and financial regulations must be considered.

Many finance-related issues exist in implementing IOSs. For one thing, establishing EDI and extranet relationships involves structuring payment agreements. Global supply chains may involve complex financial arrangements, which may have legal implications.

For the Marketing Major

Marketing and sales expenses are usually targets in a cost-reduction program. Also, sales force automation improves not only salespeople's productivity (and thus reduces costs), but also customer service.

The downstream segment of supply chains is where marketing, distribution channels, and customer service are conducted. An understanding of how downstream activities are related to the other segments is critical. Supply chain problems can reduce customer satisfaction and negate marketing efforts. It is essential, then, that marketing professionals understand the nature of such problems and their solutions. Also, learning about CRM, its options, and its implementation is important for designing effective customer services and advertising.

As competition intensifies globally, finding new global markets becomes critical. Use of IOSs provides an opportunity to improve marketing and sales. Understanding the capabilities of these technologies and their implementation issues will enable the marketing department to excel.

For the Production/Operations Management Major

Managing production tasks, materials handling, and inventories in short time intervals, at a low cost, and with high quality is critical for competitiveness. These activities can be achieved only if they are properly supported by IT. In addition, IT can greatly enhance interaction with other functional areas, especially sales. SCM is usually the responsibility of the POM department because it involves activities such as materials handling, inventory control, and logistics. Because they are in charge of procurement, production/operations managers must understand how their supporting information systems interface with those of their business partners. In addition, collaboration in design, manufacturing, and logistics requires knowledge of how modern information systems can be connected. Finally, supply chain collaboration frequently requires EDI agreements on data formats.

For the Human Resources Management Major

Human resources managers can increase their efficiency and effectiveness by using IT for some of their routine functions. Human resources personnel need to understand how information flows between the HR department and the other functional areas. Finally, the integration of functional areas via ERP systems has a major impact on skill requirements and scarcity of employees, which are related to the tasks performed by the HRM department.

Interactions among employees along the supply chain, especially between business partners from different countries, are important for supply chain effectiveness. It is necessary, therefore, for the HRM expert to understand the flows of information and the collaboration issues in SCM. In addition, the HRM manager is usually actively involved in setting up the CRM program, which may serve employees as well.

Preparing and training employees to work with business partners (frequently in foreign countries) requires knowledge about how IOSs operate. Sensitivity to cultural differences and extensive communication and collaboration can be facilitated with IT.

For the MIS Major

The MIS function is responsible for the most fundamental information systems in organizations, the transaction processing systems. The TPSs provide the data for the databases. In turn, all other information systems use these data. MIS personnel develop applications that support all levels of the organization (from clerical to executive) and all functional areas. The applications also enable the firm to do business with its partners.

1. **Describe transaction processing systems.**

   The backbone of most information systems applications is the transaction processing system. TPSs monitor, store, collect, and process data generated from all business transactions. These data provide the inputs into the organization's database.

2. **Describe functional area information systems and the support they provide for each functional area of the organization.**

   The major business functional areas are production/operations management, marketing, accounting/finance, and human resources management. A functional area information system (FAIS) is designed to support lower- and midlevel managers in functional areas. FAISs generate reports (routine, ad hoc, and exception) and provide information to managers regardless of their functional areas. Table 8.1 provides an overview of the many activities in each functional area supported by FAISs.

3. **Describe enterprise resource planning systems.**

   Enterprise resource planning (ERP) systems integrate the planning, management, and use of all of the organization's resources. The major objective of ERP systems is to tightly integrate the organization's functional areas. This integration enables information to flow seamlessly across the various functional areas. ERP software includes a set of interdependent software modules, linked to a common database, that provide support for internal business processes.

Summary

4. Describe customer relationship management systems.

Customer relationship management (CRM) is an enterprisewide activity through which an organization takes care of its customers and their needs. It is based on the idea of one-to-one relationships with customers. CRM is conducted through many services, most of which are IT-supported and many of which are delivered on the Web.

5. Describe supply chain management systems.

A supply chain refers to the flow of materials, information, money, and services from raw material suppliers, through factories and warehouses, to the end customers. A supply chain also includes the *organizations* and *processes* that create and deliver products, information, and services to end customers. The function of supply chain management (SCM) is to plan, organize, and optimize the supply chain's activities. A typical supply chain, which links a company with its suppliers and its distributors and customers, involves three segments: upstream, internal, and downstream.

6. Describe EDI and extranets.

EDI is a communication standard that enables the electronic transfer of routine documents, such as purchasing orders, between business partners. It formats these documents according to agreed-upon standards, and it reduces costs, delays, and errors inherent in a manual document-delivery system.

Extranets are networks that link business partners to one another over the Internet by providing access to certain areas of one another's corporate intranets. The term *extranet* comes from "extended intranet." The main goal of extranets is to foster collaboration among business partners. The major benefits of extranets include faster processes and information flow, improved order entry and customer service, lower costs (for example, for communications, travel, and administrative overhead), and overall improvement in business effectiveness.

Chapter Glossary

ad-hoc (on-demand) reports Nonroutine reports.

batch processing TPS that processes data in batches at fixed periodic intervals.

best practices The most successful solutions or problem-solving methods for achieving a business outcome.

bullwhip effect Erratic shifts in orders up and down the supply chain.

bundling A type of cross-selling in which a combination of products is sold together at a lower price than the combined costs of the individual products.

business process A set of related steps or procedures designed to produce a specific outcome.

comparative reports Reports that compare performances of different business units or time periods.

cross-selling The marketing of complementary products to customers.

customer relationship management (CRM) An enterprisewide effort to acquire and retain customers, often supported by IT.

customer touch point Any method of interaction with a customer.

drill-down reports Reports that show a greater level of detail than is included in routine reports.

electronic data interchange (EDI) A communication standard that enables the electronic transfer of routine documents between business partners.

enterprise resource planning (ERP) systems Software that integrates the planning, management, and use of all resources in the entire enterprise.

exception reports Reports that include only information that exceeds certain threshold standards.

functional area information systems (FAISs) A system that provides information to managers (usually midlevel) in the functional areas, in order to support managerial tasks of planning, organizing, and controlling operations.

global information systems Interorganizational systems that connect companies located in two or more countries.

interorganizational information system (IOS) An information system that supports information flow among two or more organizations.

key-indicator reports Reports that summarize the performance of critical activities.

online transaction processing (OLTP) TPS that processes data after transactions occur, frequently in real time.

routine reports Reports produced at scheduled intervals.

supply chain The flow of materials, information, money, and services from raw material suppliers through factories and warehouses to the end customers; includes the organizations and processes involved.

supply chain management (SCM) The planning, organizing, and optimization of one or more of the supply chain's activities.

trans-border data flow The flow of corporate data across nations' borders.

transaction Any business event that generates data worth capturing and storing in a database.

transaction processing systems (TPSs) Information system that supports routine, core business transactions.

up-selling The marketing of higher-value products and services to new or existing customers.

vendor-managed inventory (VMI) Strategy in which the supplier monitors a vendor's inventory levels and replenishes products when needed.

vertical integration Strategy of integrating the upstream part of the supply chain with the internal part, typically by purchasing upstream suppliers, in order to ensure the timely availability of supplies.

Discussion Questions

1. Why is it logical to organize IT applications by functional areas?
2. Describe the role of a TPS in a service organization.
3. Discuss the benefits of online self-service by employees and customers. How can these activities be facilitated by IT?
4. Distinguish between ERP and SCM software. In what ways do they complement each other? Relate them to system integration.
5. It is said that supply chains are essentially "a series of linked suppliers and customers; every customer is in turn a supplier to the next downstream organization, until the ultimate end-user." Explain. Use of a diagram is recommended.
6. Explain the bullwhip effect. In which type of business is it most likely to occur? How can the effect be controlled?
7. Discuss why Web-based call centers are critical for a successful CRM.
8. Compare an EDI to an extranet and discuss the major differences.
9. Discuss the manner in which trans-border data flow can be a limitation to a company that has manufacturing plants in other countries.

Problem-Solving Activities

1. Go to a bank and find out the process and steps of obtaining a mortgage for a house. Draw the supply chain in this case. Explain how such a database can shorten the loan approval time. Compare your bank with *www.ditech.com* and *www.lendingtree.com*.
2. Enter *www.bluenile.com, www.bluenile.ca,* and *www.bluenile.co.uk*. Observe the differences in the three Web sites and identify the features of localization. Does Blue Nile need these three Web sites, or could the company just use one Web site?
3. General Electric Information Systems is the largest provider of EDI services. Investigate what services GEIS and other EDI vendors provide. If you were to evaluate their services for your company, how would you plan to approach the evaluation? Prepare a report.

Web Activities

1. Examine the capabilities of the following (and similar) financial software packages: Financial Analyzer (from Oracle) and CFO Vision (from SAS Institute). Prepare a report comparing the capabilities of the software packages.
2. Access *www.aberdeen.com* and observe its "online supply chain community" (go to supply chain and logistics research channel). Most of the information there is free. Prepare a report on the major resources available on the Web site.
3. Enter *www.ups.com* and *www.fedex.com*. Examine some of the IT-supported customer services and tools provided by the company. Write a report on how UPS and FedEx contribute to supply chain improvements.
4. Enter *www.sdcexec.com* and *www.supplychaintoday.com*. Find information on the bullwhip effect and on the strategies and tools used to lessen the effect.
5. Access *www.oracle.com/crmondemand/index.html*. Describe the Oracle On-Demand CRM product.
6. Enter *www.anntaylor.com* and identify the customer service activities offered there.

Team Assignments

1. The class is divided into groups. Each group member represents a major functional area: accounting/finance, sales/marketing, production/operations management, and human resources. Find and describe several examples of processes that require the integration of functional information systems in a company of your choice. Each group will also show the interfaces to the other functional areas.
2. Each group is to investigate an HRM software vendor (Oracle, Peoplesoft—now owned by Oracle), SAP, Lawson Software, and others). The group should prepare a list of all HRM functionalities supported by the software. Then each of the groups makes a presentation to convince the class that its vendor is the best.
3. Each group in the class will be assigned to a major ERP/SCM vendor such as SAP, Oracle, or Lawson Software. Members of the groups will investigate topics such as: (a) Web connections, (b) use of business intelligence tools, (c) relationship to CRM and to EC, and (d) major capabilities by the specific vendor. Each group will prepare a presentation for the class, trying to convince the class why the group's software is best for a local company known to the students (for example, a supermarket chain).
4. Create groups to investigate the major CRM software vendors, their products, and the capabilities of those products in the following categories. (Each group represents a topical area or several companies.)

   - Salesforce automation (Oracle, Onyx, Sage CRM Solutions, Pivotal)
   - Call centers (LivePerson, Cisco, Oracle)
   - Marketing automation (Oracle, Pivotal)
   - Customer service (Oracle, Broadvision, ATG)

   Start with *www.searchcrm.com* and *www.customerthink.com* (to ask questions about CRM solutions). Each group must present arguments to the class to convince class members to use the product(s) the group investigated.
5. Have each team locate several organizations that use IOSs, including one with a global reach. Students should contact the companies to find what IOS technology support they use (for example, an EDI, extranet, etc.). Then find out what issues they faced in implementation. Prepare a report.

CLOSING CASE # Meltdown at JetBlue

THE BUSINESS PROBLEM Until the Valentine's Day storm of 2007, JetBlue Airways (*www.jetblue.com*) had been a success story. Although the company had been in operation only since 2000, by the end of 2006 it had posted $2.4 billion in revenue, and it operated 500 daily flights to 50 cities.

On that day, freezing rain and sleet virtually shut down northeastern airports. While most other airlines canceled dozens of flights in preparation for the storm, JetBlue management opted to wait out the bad weather. The airline's policy was to do whatever it could to ensure that a flight was completed, even if it meant waiting for several hours. Consequently, the airline sent outbound flights to the runway at John F. Kennedy (JFK) Airport in New York City at about 8:00 A.M., to be ready to take off as soon as the weather permitted, while incoming flights arrived and filled up the gates. But instead of improving, the bad weather continued. Under federal aviation guidelines, planes cannot take off in icy conditions. Very soon, planes and equipment were literally freezing to the tarmac.

By 3:00 P.M., JetBlue gave up hope of getting the planes sitting on the runway off the ground, and it began calling in buses to bring passengers back to the terminal. By then, however, the damage was done. Airport terminals, particularly at JFK, were filled with passengers who still expected to get on their flights. They were now being joined by hundreds of infuriated passengers who were getting off their planes. Some JetBlue passengers were left stranded on planes for as long as 11 hours.

THE IT PROBLEMS As passengers were bumped off planes or arrived at JFK and other East Coast airports to find that their JetBlue flights had been canceled, they had only one option for rebooking their flights: call the JetBlue reservation office. JetBlue does not offer its customers the option to rebook their flights via its Web site, nor can passengers rebook using airport kiosks. As a result, the Salt Lake City reservation agents were suddenly deluged with calls from irate passengers looking to get on another flight or to find out what compensation was available.

JetBlue reservation agents primarily work from home, using an Internet-based communications system to access the company's Navitaire Open Skies reservation system. However, the Navitaire system was configured for JetBlue to accommodate up to only 650 agents at one time, a number that more than met its requirements under normal circumstances.

As customers' wait times on phones began to exceed one hour—if they could get through at all—JetBlue urgently called Navitaire to see if anything could be done to increase the number of agents using the system. Navitaire was able to boost the system to accommodate up to 950 agents at one time, but it could not add more agents without degrading the performance of the system.

Even with the 950 agents, JetBlue was having difficulty finding enough people to staff the phones. Managers with JetBlue's reservation office began calling in off-duty agents to assist with the unexpectedly high volume of calls. Off-duty crews and airport personnel volunteered to staff phones, but they were not trained in how to use the system.

As passengers struggled to get through to reservations, their bags piled up in huge mounds at airports. Surprisingly, JetBlue did not have a computerized system in place for recording and tracking lost bags.

The airline does have a data warehouse that stores reservation and check-in information, such as the number of bags checked in by a passenger and the bag tag identification numbers. What was missing was an information systems component to record which bags had not been picked up and their location. There was no way for a passenger agent, for example, to look up by computer if a lost bag for a particular passenger was among the pile of unclaimed bags in New York. Not having that functionality had not been a problem in the past. If bags were left over at the end of a flight, airport personnel figured out ownership by looking up a passenger record.

JetBlue dispatched a technology team to JFK to help with the problem of bags. The team ended up hauling most of the bags to another location where the bags could be sorted and identified. Over three days, programmers cobbled together an application that would permit personnel using a handheld device to scan a bag tag and identify the passenger. Agents could then access the database to provide passengers with information on the location of their lost luggage.

The airline used a planning application to help figure out the best way to emerge from flight disruptions. The application allows operations planners to enter a number of scenarios in order to determine which actions will get operations back on track in the quickest amount of time while minimizing passenger disruptions. However, the planners were unable to transfer the planning application's solutions into the company's flight operations applications. The vendor of the planning application was able to come up with a fix within a matter of hours, but the damage was done. JetBlue had reached a virtual gridlock.

Even if the airline had been able to work out a plan to bring a quick end to the disruption, there was no guarantee that it could have gotten flight crews to the redirected planes. Normally during disruptions, off-duty crews call into headquarters to give their location and availability to work. However, because of the huge number of flights affected—more than 1,000 were canceled due to the storm—phone lines were busy, calls could not get through, and information had to be recorded with pen and paper. JetBlue did not have a database system to keep track of off-duty crews in such a situation. Once again, JetBlue's technology team created a database in 24 hours to keep track of crew locations and their contact information.

THE PROPOSED SOLUTIONS JetBlue experienced an operational and, more importantly, a public relations nightmare. The company learned an expensive lesson (at least $30 million) about what happens when a company does not adequately prepare for disaster. The most damaging outcome, however, was the blow to its reputation.

JetBlue took several measures to restore its reputation as well as consumer confidence. First, the company introduced a JetBlue Customer Bill of Rights that offered various forms of compensation to customers whose flights have been canceled or who are left sitting too long on planes. It also offered compensation to the thousands of its passengers who were inconvenienced during the storm and into the next week.

Second, JetBlue addressed its information systems failures with a number of new initiatives.

- Work with Navitaire to add a feature to JetBlue .com that will allow passengers to rebook canceled flights at the airport at kiosks without having to call reservations.

- Work with Navitaire to double the number of agents that can be accommodated on the reservation system.

- Enhance the lost-bag tracking system (developed in the emergency in 24 hours).

- Implement new information systems that will allow Jet-Blue to notify passengers by e-mail, phone, or its Web site of canceled or changed flights as soon as possible to prevent lines at airports.

- Implement a new system that allows JetBlue to figure out the best alternative to a canceled flight for an individual passenger and automatically rebook that passenger on the new flight.

- Cross-train staff on reservation, flight, and crew scheduling applications.

In other words, JetBlue is implementing new information systems so that it can offer many of the features that its major airline competitors already provide.

ONE RESULT On May 10, 2007, JetBlue's CEO David Neeleman was relieved of his operational responsibilities. This outcome was widely seen as a result of the problems discussed in this case.

Sources: Compiled from D. Bartholomew and M. Duvall, "What Really Happened at JetBlue," *Baseline Magazine*, April 5, 2007; S. Overby, "What JetBlue's CIO Learned about Customer Satisfaction," *CIO*, April 5, 2007; M. Hugos, "JetBlue and the Lessons of Business Agility," *CIO*, March 5, 2007; "An Extraordinary Stumble at JetBlue," *BusinessWeek*, March 5, 2007; L. Rosencrance, "Overwhelmed IT Systems Partly to Blame for JetBlue Meltdown," *Computerworld*, February 20, 2007; *www.jetblue.com*, accessed April 30, 2007.

QUESTIONS

1. Was the main cause of JetBlue's meltdown: managerial, technological, or some combination of both? Explain your answer.
2. Critique JetBlue's actions in this crisis, both managerial and technological. What could the airline have done better in both areas? Keep in mind that we are not asking about what the airline decided to do after the crisis, but what it could have done better during the crisis.

Web Resources   wiley.com/college/rainer

Student Web Site
- Web Quizzes
- Student Lecture Slides in PowerPoint
- Virtual Company ClubIT: Website and Assignments

WileyPLUS
- e-book
- Flash Cards
- How-To Animations for Microsoft Office

Functional Systems at Club IT

Go to the Club IT section of the *WileyPLUS* Web site to find out how you can help the owners compile dollar and volume numbers more efficiently.

wiley.com/college/rainer

Chapter 9

Learning Objectives

1. Describe the concepts of management, decision making, and computerized support for decision making.
2. Describe multidimensional data analysis and data mining.
3. Describe digital dashboards.
4. Describe data visualization, and explain geographical information systems and virtual reality.
5. Describe artificial intelligence (AI).
6. Define an expert system and identify its components.
7. Describe natural language processing, natural language generation, and neural networks.

Managerial Support Systems

Chapter Outline

What's in IT for me?   ACC   FIN   MKT   POM   HRM   MIS

Eastern Mountain Sports Uses Web 2.0 for Business Intelligence and Dashboards

The Business Problem

Eastern Mountain Sports (EMS) (*www.ems.com*) is an outdoor specialty retailer founded in 1967 by two rock climbers who were dissatisfied with the poor selection of climbing equipment they found in existing stores. From the first small store, the company has grown into a large company with more than $200 million in annual revenue, more than 80 retail stores, and formidable Web site offerings. The company designs and sells a wide variety of equipment and clothing for outdoor enthusiasts.

The overall strategy of EMS is customer satisfaction. The company wants to ensure that it always has the products its customers need in stock. EMS wanted to use new technologies to engage customers and business partners to make it easier to do business with the company.

The IT Solution

Eastern Mountain Sports felt that Web 2.0 technologies would help the company achieve its overall strategy and business goals. (Recall that we discussed Web 2.0 in Chapter 5.) EMS first developed a digital dashboard and then integrated Web 2.0 technologies with the dashboard.

The dashboard enables EMS decision makers to quickly access a unified, high-level view of key performance indicators such as sales, inventory, and margin levels. They can also drill down to more detail to analyze specific data and transactions. The company enhanced the basic dashboard so that it contains all the information relevant to corporate goals, integrated with productivity tools and role-based content customized to each individual user. Next, EMS integrated Web 2.0 technologies for collaboration among employees, business partners, and customers.

EMS uses some 20 operational metrics to govern the fundamental health of the business. For example, merchandising managers must keep abreast of inventory positions and stock turns. E-commerce managers monitor hour-by-hour Web traffic and customer conversion rates. Each area of the business relies on the dashboard to learn when certain key performance indicators are out of the tolerance range. The dashboard has made such situations easy to recognize by implementing a color-coded system of red (metrics are out of tolerance, and the condition must be addressed), yellow (metrics are trending to out of tolerance and the condition should be monitored), and green (metrics are within tolerance).

For example, if certain items sell better than others, it should be easy to analyze the transaction characteristics and selling behaviors that produce these results and then cascade that knowledge throughout the organization. One EMS buyer accessed the dashboard and noticed an upward spike in footwear sales at a particular store. Investigating further, she learned that employees there had perfected a multistep sales technique that included recommending socks designed for specific uses, such as hiking or running, along with an inner sole that could be custom fitted to each customer. The dashboard made it easy to analyze the data to see what was selling and then drill down to see why. Not only did the buyer discover what prompted the growth in sales, but she suggested that EMS formalize the practice across the chain.

EMS wanted to encourage such interactions throughout the company and make them almost automatic. Their goal was to let any dashboard user pose a hypothesis and invite commentary. For example, the dashboard examines Web visitors and sales by the hour. EMS has successfully tied that data to an Really Simple Syndication (RSS) feed so that managers do not have to visit a Web page to view the latest numbers. Instead, the information pops up on their desktops automatically.

EMS also implemented a wiki that lets users test and refine hypotheses. In particular, EMS wants its employees to share tips and best practices and to initiate discussions with one another. Wikis will make this process much easier.

EMS also has created blogs for its employees around a particular piece of data or a key metric. Blogs are useful to post information on a Web site on a regular basis and invite comments. For example, if sales per payroll hour hover at $125 for several months and suddenly drop to $75, a store manager might want to post an explanation or inquiry concerning the anomaly. A blog attached to a metric might reveal that payroll hours were higher that week to handle additional back-office work. Keeping comments in a blog lets readers put data in context.

EMS is including its extended organization in this new information system as well. The company allows its suppliers to see authorized portions of the dashboard so that they can keep track of data such as product sales, product returns, and average cost per order. Some of EMS's e-commerce suppliers ship directly to customers. In these cases, EMS does not own the inventory. Rather, it just passes the orders to these suppliers. EMS shares sales plans and progress toward those plans with this category of suppliers.

For example, one section of the dashboard focuses on camping equipment. All pertinent camping vendors can access this part of the dashboard to view top-line sales information and post comments to a blog or a wiki. The camping equipment product manager keeps up with the blogs and wikis to better integrate EMS with these suppliers. The product manager can also pose questions to EMS suppliers, such as soliciting their ideas for innovative ways to increase sales in the next quarter or year.

Some EMS customers and business partners subscribe to an RSS feed on the EMS Web site called Extreme Deals, which refers to products that are marked down significantly. RSS provides an efficient means of keeping interested parties apprised of this information.

Because use of the dashboard and the Web 2.0 technologies is so new, the results were unknown as of mid-2007. However, there are two interesting results for EMS. Related to the buyer who noticed and then investigated the spike in footware sales, EMS had a 57 percent increase in same-store sales in the footwear category and a 61 percent increase in the gross margin for that category. In addition, after the dashboard was implemented, EMS observed a noticeable decrease in calls to customer service, which is saving company staffers at the home office approximately 40 hours per week.

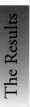

The Results

The Eastern Mountain Sports case illustrates the importance and far-reaching nature of digital dashboards. Digital dashboards enable decision makers to quickly ascertain the status of a business enterprise by looking at key performance indicators. EMS managers needed current, timely, accurate information that they were not receiving prior to implementing the dashboard. Implementing the dashboard produced significant benefits throughout the company. The dashboard supported important decisions in several functional areas. Another interesting facet of the case is the value of integrating Web 2.0 technologies with the dashboard to increase participation, collaboration, and discussion among EMS employees, business partners, and customers.

Business intelligence systems encompass two types of information systems: (1) those that provide data analysis tools (that is, data mining, online analytical processing, and predictive analytics) and (2) those that provide easily accessible information in a structured format (that is, digital dashboards). A third type of information system, intelligent systems, can actually make a decision (that is, expert systems), as well as provide support for decision making.

This chapter describes information systems that support *managerial decision makers.* We begin by reviewing the manager's job and the nature of today's decisions. This discussion will help you to understand why managers need computerized support. We then present the

What We Learned from This Case

concepts of business intelligence for supporting individuals, groups, and whole organizations. Finally, we introduce several types of intelligent systems, and we consider their role in supporting managerial decision making.

Sources: Compiled from J. Neville, "Web 2.0's Wild Blue Yonder," *InformationWeek*, January 1/8, 2007; B. Beal, "Diving into Dashboards," *CIO Decisions*, June 1, 2006; R. Mitchell, "Where Real Time Dashboards Fit," *Computerworld*, June 26, 2006; D. Robb, "Eastern Mountain Sports: Getting Smarter with Each Sale," *Computerworld*, September 18, 2006; H. Havenstein, "Users Embrace 'BI for the Masses'," *Computerworld*, May 1, 2006; *www.ems.com*, accessed April 29, 2007.

9.1 Managers and Decision Making

Management is a process by which organizational goals are achieved through the use of resources (people, money, energy, materials, space, and time). These resources are considered to be *inputs*. The attainment of the organization's goals is the *output* of the process. Managers oversee this process in an attempt to optimize it. A manager's success is often measured by the ratio between inputs and outputs for which he or she is responsible. This ratio is an indication of the organization's **productivity**.

The Manager's Job and Decision Making

To appreciate how information systems support managers, we must first understand the manager's job. Managers do many things, depending on their position in the organization, the type and size of the organization, organizational policies and culture, and the personalities of the managers themselves. Despite this variety, all managers have three basic roles (Mintzberg, 1973):

1. *Interpersonal roles:* figurehead, leader, liaison
2. *Informational roles:* monitor, disseminator, spokesperson, analyzer
3. *Decisional roles:* entrepreneur, disturbance handler, resource allocator, negotiator

Early information systems primarily supported the informational roles. In recent years, information systems have been developed that support all three roles. In this chapter, we focus on the support that IT can provide for decisional roles.

A *decision* refers to a choice that individuals and groups make among two or more alternatives. Decisions are diverse and are made continuously. Decision making is a systematic process. Simon (1977) described the process as composed of three major phases: *intelligence*, *design*, and *choice*. A fourth phase, *implementation*, was added later. Figure 9.1 illustrates this four-stage process, indicating which tasks are included in each phase. Note that there is a continuous flow of information from intelligence to design to choice (bold lines), but at any phase there may be a return to a previous phase (broken lines).

The decision-making process starts with the *intelligence phase*, in which managers examine a situation and identify and define the problem. In the *design phase*, decision makers construct a model that simplifies the problem. They do this by making assumptions that simplify reality and by expressing the relationships among all the relevant variables. Managers then validate the model by using test data. Finally, decision makers set criteria for evaluating all potential solutions that are proposed. The *choice phase* involves selecting a solution, which is tested "on paper." Once this proposed solution seems to be feasible, decision making enters the last phase—*implementation*. Implementation is successful if the proposed solution actually resolves the problem. Failure leads to a return to the previous phases. Computer-based decision support attempts to automate several tasks in the decision-making process, in which modeling is the core.

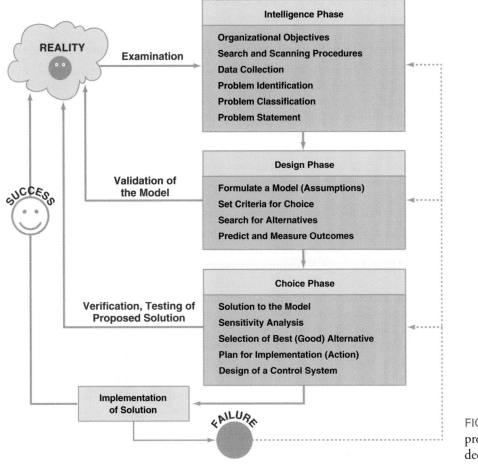

FIGURE 9.1   The process and phases in decision making.

Why Managers Need IT Support

It is difficult to make good decisions without valid and relevant information. Information is vital for each phase and activity in the decision-making process. Despite the widespread availability of information, making decisions is becoming increasingly difficult owing to the following trends:

- The *number of alternatives* to be considered is constantly *increasing*, due to innovations in technology, improved communications, the development of global markets, and the use of the Internet and e-business. A key to good decision making is to explore and compare many relevant alternatives. The more alternatives that exist, the more computer-assisted search and comparisons are needed.

- Typically, decisions must be made *under time pressure.* Frequently, it is not possible to process information manually fast enough to be effective.

- Due to increased uncertainty in the decision environment, decisions are becoming more complex. It is usually necessary to *conduct a sophisticated analysis* in order to make a good decision. Such analysis requires the use of modeling.

- It is often necessary to access remote information rapidly, consult with experts, or conduct a group decision-making session, all without incurring large expenses. Decision makers can be in different locations, as can the information. Bringing them all together quickly and inexpensively may be a difficult task.

These trends create major difficulties in decision making. Fortunately, as we will see throughout this chapter, a computerized analysis can be of enormous help.

What Information Technologies Are Available to Support Managers?

In addition to discovery, communication, and collaboration tools (Chapter 5) that provide indirect support to decision making, several other information technologies have been successfully used to support managers. As we noted earlier, they are collectively referred to as business intelligence (BI) systems and intelligent systems. These systems and their variants can be used independently, or they can be combined, each providing a different capability. They are frequently related to data warehousing. We now address additional aspects of decision making to put our discussion of these systems in context. We look first at the different types of decisions that managers face.

A Framework for Computerized Decision Analysis

To better understand BI and intelligent systems, it helps if we classify decisions along two major dimensions: problem structure and the nature of the decision (Gorry and Scott Morton, 1971). Figure 9.2 gives an overview of decision making along these two dimensions.

Problem Structure. The first dimension is *problem structure*, where decision-making processes fall along a continuum ranging from highly structured to highly unstructured decisions. (See the left column in Figure 9.2.) *Structured decisions* refer to routine and repetitive problems for which standard solutions exist, such as inventory control. In a structured problem, the first three of the decision process phases—intelligence, design, and choice—are laid out in a particular sequence, and the procedures for obtaining the best (or at least a good enough) solution are known. Two basic criteria that are used to evaluate proposed solutions are minimizing costs and maximizing profits.

Type of Decision	Nature of Decision			Support Needed
	Operational Control	**Management Control**	**Strategic Planning**	**Support Needed**
Structured	Accounts receivable, order entry [1]	Budget analysis, short-term forecasting, personnel reports, make-or-buy analysis [2]	Financial management (investment), warehouse location, distribution systems [3]	MIS, management science models, financial and statistical models
Semistructured	Production scheduling, inventory control [4]	Credit evaluation, budget preparation, plant layout, project scheduling, reward systems design [5]	Building new plant, mergers and acquisitions, new product planning, compensation planning, quality assurance planning [6]	DSS
Unstructured	Selecting a cover for a magazine, buying software, approving loans [7]	Negotiating, recruiting an executive, buying hardware, lobbying [8]	R & D planning, new technology development, social responsibility planning [9]	DSS ES neural networks
Support Needed	MIS, management science	Management science, DSS, EIS, ES	EIS, ES, neural networks	

FIGURE 9.2 Decision support framework. Technology is used to support the decisions shown in the column at the far right and in the bottom row.

At the other extreme of problem complexity are *unstructured decisions*. These are "fuzzy," complex problems for which there are no cut-and-dried solutions. An unstructured problem is one in which intelligence, design, and choice are not organized in a particular sequence. In such a problem, human intuition often plays an important role in making the decision. Typical unstructured problems include planning new service offerings, hiring an executive, and choosing a set of research and development (R&D) projects for the coming year.

Located between structured and unstructured problems are *semistructured* problems, in which only some of the decision process phases are structured. Semistructured problems require a combination of standard solution procedures and individual judgment. Examples of semistructured problems are evaluating employees, setting marketing budgets for consumer products, performing capital acquisition analysis, and trading bonds.

The Nature of Decisions.   The second dimension of decision support deals with the *nature of decisions*. We can define three broad categories that encompass all managerial decisions:

1. *Operational control*—executing specific tasks efficiently and effectively
2. *Management control*—acquiring and using resources efficiently in accomplishing organizational goals
3. *Strategic planning*—setting the long-range goals and policies for growth and resource allocation

These categories are shown along the top row of Figure 9.2.

The Decision Matrix.   The three primary classes of problem structure and the three broad categories of the nature of decisions can be combined in a decision support matrix that consists of nine cells, as shown in Figure 9.2. Lower-level managers usually perform the structured and operational control-oriented tasks (cells 1, 2, and 4). The tasks in cells 3, 5, and 7 are usually the responsibility of middle managers and professional staff. Finally, tasks in cells 6, 8, and 9 are generally the responsibility of senior executives.

Computer Support for Structured Decisions.   Computer support for the nine cells in the matrix is shown in the right-hand column and the bottom row of Figure 9.2. Structured and some semistructured decisions, especially of the operational and management control type, have been supported by computers since the 1950s. Decisions of this type are made in all functional areas, but particularly in finance and operations management.

Problems that lower-level managers encounter on a regular basis typically have a high level of structure. Examples are capital budgeting (for example, replacement of equipment), allocating resources, distributing merchandise, and controlling inventory. For each type of structured decision, prescribed solutions have been developed through the use of mathematical formulas. This approach is called *management science* or *operations research*, and it is also executed with the aid of computers.

As we have noted, business intelligence systems support managerial decision making. There are a variety of BI systems, and we discuss them in detail in the next two sections.

Before you go on . . .

1. Describe the decision-making process proposed by Simon.
2. Why do managers need IT support?
3. Describe the decision matrix.

9.2 Business Intelligence, Multidimensional Data Analysis, Data Mining, and Decision Support Systems

Once an organization has captured data and organized them into databases, data warehouses, and data marts, it can use them for further analysis (see Figure 9.3). **Business intelligence (BI)** refers to applications and technologies for consolidating, analyzing, and providing access to vast amounts of data to help users make better business and strategic decisions. Business intelligence systems encompass two types of information systems: (1) those that provide data analysis tools (that is, multidimensional data analysis or online analytical processing, data mining, and decision support systems) and (2) those that provide easily accessible information in a structured format (that is, digital dashboards).

Many vendors offer integrated packages of these tools, under the overall name of business intelligence (BI) software. Major BI vendors include SAS (*www.sas.com*), Hyperion (*www.hyperion.com*), Business Objects (*www.businessobjects.com*), Cognos Corp. (*www.cognos.com*), Information Builders (*www.informationbuilders.com*), and SPSS (*www.spss.com*).

Multidimensional Data Analysis

Multidimensional analysis provides users with an excellent view of what is happening or what has happened. To accomplish this, multidimensional analysis tools allow users to "slice and dice" the data in any desired way. In the data warehouse, relational tables can be linked, forming multidimensional data structures, or *cubes*. This process looks like rotating the cube as users view it from different perspectives. Statistical tools provide users with mathematical models that can be applied to the data to gain answers to their queries.

We can refer back to Figure 4.11 for an example of slice and dice. Assume that a business has organized its sales force by regions—say Eastern, Western, and Central. These three regions might then be broken down into states. The VP of sales could slice and dice the data cube to see the sales figures for each region (that is, the sales of nuts, screws, bolts, and washers). The VP might then want to see the Eastern region broken down by state so that he

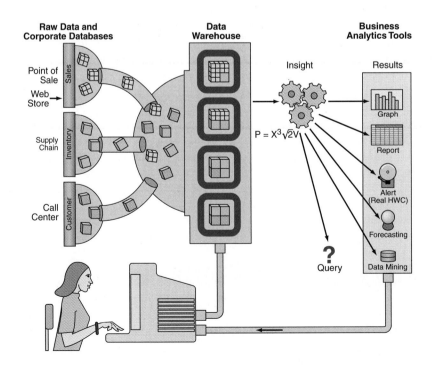

FIGURE 9.3 How business intelligence works.

could evaluate the performance of individual state sales managers. Note that the business organization is reflected in the multidimensional data structure.

The power of multidimensional analysis lies in its ability to analyze the data in such a way as to allow users to quickly answer business questions. "How many bolts were sold in the Eastern region in 2005?" "What is the trend in sales of washers in the Western region over the past three years?" "Are any of the four products typically purchased together?" IT's About Business 9.1 shows how companies can use multidimensional data analysis to analyze employee travel and entertainment expenses.

Data Mining

Data mining derives its name from searching for valuable business information in a large database, data warehouse, or data mart. Data mining can perform two basic operations: predicting trends and behaviors and identifying previously unknown patterns. We emphasize that multidimensional analysis provides users with a view of what is happening. Data mining addresses why it is happening and provides predictions of what will happen in the future.

Regarding the first operation, data mining automates the process of finding predictive information in large databases. Questions that traditionally required extensive hands-on analysis can now be answered directly and quickly from the data. A typical example of a predictive problem is *targeted marketing*. Data mining can use data from past promotional mailings to identify people who are most likely to respond favorably to future mailings. Another example of a predictive problem is forecasting bankruptcy and other forms of default.

Data mining can also identify previously hidden patterns in a single step. For example, it can analyze retail sales data to discover seemingly unrelated products that are often purchased together.

One interesting pattern-discovery problem is detecting fraudulent credit card transactions. After you use your credit card for a time, a pattern emerges of the typical ways you use your card (for example, places you use your card, the amount you spend, and so on). If your card is stolen and used fraudulently, this usage is often different from your pattern of use. Data mining tools can distinguish the difference in the two patterns of use and bring this issue to your attention.

Numerous data mining applications are used in business and in other fields. According to a Gartner report (*www.gartner.com*), most of the Fortune 1000 companies worldwide currently use data mining, as the following representative examples illustrate. Note that in most cases the intent of data mining is to identify a business opportunity in order to create a sustainable competitive advantage.

- *Retailing and sales* Predicting sales, preventing theft and fraud, and determining correct inventory levels and distribution schedules among outlets. For example, retailers such as AAFES (stores on military bases) use Fraud Watch from Triversity (*www.triversity.com*) to combat fraud by employees in their 1,400 stores.

- *Banking* Forecasting levels of bad loans and fraudulent credit card use, predicting credit card spending by new customers, and determining which kinds of customers will best respond to (and qualify for) new loan offers.

- *Manufacturing and production* Predicting machinery failures and finding key factors that help optimize manufacturing capacity.

- *Insurance* Forecasting claim amounts and medical coverage costs, classifying the most important elements that affect medical coverage, and predicting which customers will buy new insurance policies.

- *Policework* Tracking crime patterns, locations, and criminal behavior; identifying attributes to assist in solving criminal cases.

- *Health care* Correlating the demographics of patients with critical illnesses and developing better insights on how to identify and treat symptoms and their causes.
- *Marketing* Classifying customer demographics that can be used to predict which customers will respond to a mailing or buy a particular product.

IT's About Business

9.1 Don't Pad Your Expense Account!

Business travel has finally met or exceeded the volume that existed before 9/11, but the fat expense account is quickly becoming obsolete. Covansys Corporation (www.covansys.com) is a technology services company whose 7,300 employees accrue almost $15 million in travel and entertainment (T&E) expenses every year. This does not come as a big surprise to the company, given that India is a necessary destination. Covansys' consultants go on some 100 trips every quarter. To make the 15-hour flight less unpleasant, Covansys allows its consultants to fly business class. However, the company's largess ends there. Covansys has auditors who look over both companywide expense reports and upcoming itineraries every night.

Corporate auditors have identified employee T&E as a promising area for cost control. In the past, it was easier to "game" the system. Employees padded accounts by filing bogus charges, extending business trips for vacations, and taking family members along. For example, one old trick was to file reimbursement requests for fictional expenses just under the amount for which receipts would be required. It could take six months or longer before an auditor would even have the requests on his or her desk.

Today, auditors are using multidimensional data analysis tools and monitoring technologies to keep T&E under constant scrutiny. To obtain the data they need for analysis, companies are turning to credit card providers, who are making additional information accessible to auditors. American Express now produces reports that highlight gaps between company-approved compact car rentals (what the traveler reserved) and prohibited upgrades to luxury cars (what the traveler actually drove and paid for). American Express can also aggregate which items were paid for in cash and how often receipts fall under the company's daily cash threshold. Along the same lines, MasterCard totals commercial transactions daily and sends the data directly to companies.

Using these data, companies can curb costs even before employees get on a plane or make that unauthorized stay at a five-star hotel. Companies track petty cash expenses, red flag upgrades on planes and rental cars, spot trends in suspect spending patterns, and require explanations from employees about extravagant expenses as soon as they are booked rather than after the company has reimbursed its employees.

Most companies now make employees pay out of pocket for unapproved T&E expenditures that deviate from company policy. In addition, e-mail alerts about overdue expense reports are copied to supervisors if employees do not respond.

Morgan Stanley has adopted a creative approach to the T&E issue. The company has implemented an incentive that bases T&E expenses on employee behavior. The company increased its T&E budget to help its brokers wine and dine wealthy clients. However, brokers must qualify for the added T&E budget. Specifically, when they bring in $250,000 to $400,000 in new business, they receive $1,000 to help foot the T&E bill.

Sources: Compiled from M. Hovanesian, "Eagle Eye on Your T&E," *BusinessWeek*, May 8, 2006; "The Risky Business of Padding T&E," *BusinessWeek*, May 4, 2006; www.covansys .com, accessed May 2, 2007.

QUESTIONS

1. Why is business travel so necessary? What impact do you think telepresence systems will have on business travel? Support your answer. Can telepresence systems replace business travel? Why or why not? (See the discussion on telepresence systems in Chapter 5.)
2. Refer to the section on Ethics in Chapter 3. Discuss the ethics of padding an expense account. Is the use of sophisticated data mining tools to examine T&E reports just another invasion of employee privacy? Or is it justifiable? Consider these questions from the standpoint of both the employees and company shareholders.

We can see that there are myriad opportunities to use data mining in organizations. IT's About Business 9.2 shows how a large vacation company uses data mining to increase occupancy rates at its numerous properties.

Decision Support Systems

Decision support systems (DSSs) combine models and data in an attempt to solve semistructured and some unstructured problems with extensive user involvement. **Models** are simplified representations, or abstractions, of reality. The DSS is designed to enable interactive access to

---

IT's About Business

9.2   Center Parcs Uses Data Mining for Prediction

Center Parcs Europe (*www.centerparcs.com*) wants to stimulate traffic to its 16 short-stay vacation villages in the Netherlands, Belgium, Germany, and France. Center Parcs' primary marketing effort had always lacked targeting accuracy. Twice each year, the company would blanket Europe with 5 million brochures. The strategy worked, but the company spent a great deal of money on printing and mailing costs.

Center Parcs attracts more than 3 million visitors per year and generates revenues of more than $600 million. Its 10,000 or so bungalows enjoy an average occupancy rate of about 90 percent. However, the company believed that a more targeted campaign could raise occupancy rates even higher while reducing marketing costs.

The company's plan was to shift away from the bulk mailings to many smaller and more targeted campaigns. To be effective, the company had to segment customers so that they received the right brochures at the right time. For example, customers are loyal to their home countries and prefer not to drive long distances. Families with children prefer parks with many activities, whereas older people seek out quieter surroundings. Also, mailings must be timed to coincide with the period when people typically make vacation plans—not too early and not too late.

These criteria, and others, were rather obvious. The company knew what drove customers to one of its parks. The problem was more fundamental. The company could not find a way to take all the criteria into account and come up with a rating that would indicate which brochures to send to which customers and when.

To solve its problem, Center Parcs utilized a predictive-analytics product from SPSS, Inc. (*www.spss.com*). Predictive-analysis software uses statistical

algorithms (formulas) to find patterns that can be used to predict future actions. These predictions, often expressed in the form of a ranking or score, can predict consumer behavior, market trends, the likelihood that a customer will make a repeat purchase, the effectiveness of products or services, and so on.

The SPSS application uses data from Center Parcs' customer database to rank prospects by the likelihood that they will be receptive to a particular marketing campaign. Now, when the company wants to mail a brochure about a facility, the predictive-analytics application produces a list of prospects who are most likely to respond. The results have been outstanding. In Germany alone, the number of Center Parcs' mailings dropped from 2 million to 450,000, while occupancy increased by 10 percent.

Sources: Compiled from "What Does Predictive Analytics Do for My Organization?" *Predictive Analytics Insight* (*www.predictiveanalyticsinsight.com/successes.htm*), May 3, 2007; L. Stevens, "Technology: Predictive Analytics Lets Companies See into the Future," *PC Magazine*, August 23, 2006; *www.centerparcs.com*, accessed April 30, 2007.

QUESTIONS

1. You are the CIO of Center Parcs, and you want to find an alternative method to reach customers. Design a Web site to do this. *Hint:* You may want to design a mashup that includes several data sources. Which data sources would you include? Should you include a customer blog? Why or why not?

2. Why is Center Parcs still using mailed brochures? Consider the market segment(s) that the company is trying to reach versus the market penetration of the Internet (and television) in Europe.

data, to enable manipulation of these data, and to provide business managers and analysts the ability to conduct appropriate analyses.

Decision support systems can manipulate data, enhance learning, and contribute to all levels of decision making. DSSs also employ mathematical models. Finally, they have the related capabilities of sensitivity analysis, what-if analysis, and goal-seeking analysis.

Sensitivity Analysis.   **Sensitivity analysis** is the study of the impact that changes in one (or more) parts of a decision-making model have on other parts. Most sensitivity analyses examine the impact that changes in input variables have on output variables.

Sensitivity analysis is extremely valuable because it enables the system to adapt to changing conditions and to the varying requirements of different decision-making situations. It provides a better understanding of the model and the problem it purports to describe. It also may increase the users' confidence in the model, especially if it indicates that the model is not very sensitive to changes. A *sensitive model* means that small changes in conditions dictate a different solution. In a *nonsensitive model*, changes in conditions do not significantly change the recommended solution. For this reason the chances for a solution to succeed are much higher in a nonsensitive model than in a sensitive one.

What-If Analysis.   A model builder must make predictions and assumptions regarding the input data, many of which are based on the assessment of uncertain futures. The results depend on the accuracy of these assumptions, which can be highly subjective. **What-if analysis** attempts to predict the impact of a change in the assumptions (input data) on the proposed solution. For example, what will happen to the total inventory cost *if* the originally assumed cost of carrying inventories is not 10 percent but 12 percent? In a well-designed BI system, managers themselves can interactively ask the computer these types of questions as many times as they need to.

Goal-Seeking Analysis.   **Goal-seeking analysis** represents a "backward" solution approach. It attempts to find the value of the inputs necessary to achieve a desired level of output. For example, let's say that an initial solution of a BI system yielded a profit of $2 million. Management may want to know what sales volume and additional advertising would be necessary to generate a profit of $3 million. To find out they would perform a goal-seeking analysis.

Group Decision Support Systems.   Continuing our discussion of DSS, we turn our attention to group decision support systems. As their name suggests, these systems are designed specifically to support decision making by groups.

Decision making is frequently a shared process. Electronic support for a decision-making group is referred to as *group decision support*. Two types of groups may be supported electronically: a "one-room" group, whose members are in one place (for example, a meeting room); and a virtual group, whose members are in different locations. (We discussed virtual groups, or teams, in Chapter 5.)

A **group decision support system (GDSS)** is an interactive, computer-based system that facilitates a group's efforts to find solutions to semistructured and unstructured problems. The objective of these systems is to support the *process* of arriving at a decision. The first generation of GDSSs was designed to support face-to-face meetings in what is called a **decision room**—a face-to-face setting for a group DSS in which terminals are made available to the participants.

Organizational Decision Support System.   In contrast to a GDSS, which assists a particular group within an organization, an **organizational decision support system (ODSS)** focuses on an *organizational* task or activity that involves a *sequence* of operations and decision makers. Examples of organizational tasks are capital budgeting and developing a divisional marketing plan. To complete an organizational task successfully, each individual's activities must mesh closely with other people's work. In these tasks, computer support serves primarily as a vehicle for improving communication, coordination, and problem solving.

Before you go on . . .

1. Describe the capabilities of data mining.
2. What are the major differences between a GDSS and an ODSS?

9.3 Digital Dashboards

Digital dashboards evolved from executive information systems, which were information systems designed specifically for the information needs of top executives. As we saw in this chapter's opening case, however, today all employees, business partners, and customers can use digital dashboards.

A **digital dashboard** (also called an executive dashboard or a management cockpit) provides rapid access to timely information and direct access to management reports. It is very user friendly and is supported by graphics. Of special importance, it enables managers to examine exception reports and drill-down reports (discussed in Chapter 8). Table 9.1 summarizes the capabilities common to many digital dashboards. In addition, some of the capabilities discussed in this section are now part of many business intelligence products, as shown in Figure 9.4.

Digital dashboards can have shortcomings. Consider the case of Del Monte Foods, a $3 billion food producer. Although Del Monte had installed digital dashboards, the company's business managers practically ignored them. For example, a dashboard was tracking the

The Capabilities of Digital Dashboards

Capability	Description
Drill-down	Ability to go to details, at several levels; can be done by a series of menus or by direct queries (using intelligent agents and natural language processing).
Critical success factors (CSFs)	The factors most critical for the success of business. These can be organizational, industry, departmental, etc.
Key performance indicators (KPIs)	The specific measures of CSFs.
Status access	The latest data available on KPI or some other metric, ideally in real time.
Trend analysis	Short-, medium-, and long-term trend of KPIs or metrics, which are projected using forecasting methods.
Ad-hoc analysis	Analyses made any time, upon demands and with any desired factors and relationships.
Exception reporting	Reports that highlight deviations larger than certain thresholds. Reports may include only deviations.

Table 9.1

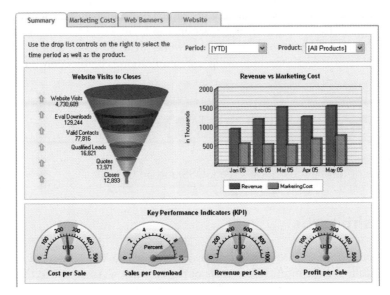

FIGURE 9.4 Sample performance dashboard. *Source:* Dundas Software, demos1 .dundas.com/Dundas Gauge/Marketing-Dashboard/Summary .aspx

fill-rate, an important measure of how the company was filling customer orders. However, few managers even looked at the results. The CIO eventually recognized the problem. The dashboard alerted managers when the targets for the fill-rates were not being met, but it did not tell them why these targets were not being met. Thus, managers did not know whether a target was missed due to bad forecasting, issues with Del Monte's distribution channels, or some other reason. To make the dashboard more useful, the CIO applied data mining tools to analyze potential causes. At that point the business came to realize the dashboard's value. Requests for dashboard projects increased by 30 percent in less than one year.

One outstanding example of a digital dashboard is the "Bloomberg." Bloomberg LLP (*www.bloomberg.com*), a privately held company, provides a subscription service that sells financial data, analytic software to leverage the usefulness of these data, trading tools, and news (electronic, print, TV, and radio). All of this information is accessible through a color-coded Bloomberg keyboard that displays the desired information on a computer screen, either your own or one that Bloomberg provides. Users can also set up their own computers to use the service without a Bloomberg keyboard. The subscription service plus the keyboard is called the "Bloomberg," and it literally represents a do-it-yourself digital dashboard, because users can customize their information feeds as well as the look and feel of those feeds. See Figure 9.5.

The Management Cockpit

One important application of digital dashboards to support the informational needs of executives is the Management Cockpit. Essentially, a Management Cockpit is a strategic management room containing an elaborate set of digital dashboards that enables top-level decision makers to pilot their businesses better. The aim is to create an environment that encourages more efficient management meetings and boosts team performance via effective communication. To help achieve this goal, key performance indicators and information relating to critical success factors are displayed graphically on the walls of a meeting room, called the Management Cockpit Room (see Figure 9.6). The cockpit-like arrangement of instrument panels and displays helps managers to grasp how all the different factors in the business interrelate.

Within the room, the four walls are designated by color: Black, Red, Blue, and White. The Black Wall shows the principal success factors and financial indicators; the Red Wall measures market performance; the Blue Wall projects the performance of internal processes and

FIGURE 9.5
A Bloomberg terminal.
Source: Carlos
Osorio/Toronto
Star/Zuma Press.

employees; and finally, the White Wall indicates the status of strategic projects. The Flight Deck, a six-screen, high-end PC, enables executives to drill down to detailed information. External information needed for competitive analysis can easily be imported into the room.

Board members and other executives hold meetings in the Cockpit Room. Managers also meet there with the comptroller to discuss current business issues. For this purpose, the Management Cockpit can implement various what-if scenarios. It also provides a common basis for information and communication. Finally, it supports efforts to translate a corporate strategy into concrete activities by identifying performance indicators.

FIGURE 9.6
Management Cockpit.
The Management
Cockpit is a registered
trademark of SAP,
created by Professor
Patrick M. Georges.

Before you go on . . .

1. What are some of the capabilities of digital dashboards?
2. What is a management cockpit?

9.4 Data Visualization Technologies

After data have been processed, they can be presented to users in visual formats such as text, graphics, and tables. This process, known as data visualization, makes IT applications more attractive and understandable to users. Data visualization is becoming more and more popular

---

IT's About Business

POM

9.3 Halliburton's CyberWell

With gasoline prices rising and equipment to drill new wells becoming backlogged, oil producers want to find every drop of oil in existing wells. Halliburton (*www.halliburton.com*) is a company that manages the entire life cycle of oil and gas reservoirs, including exploration, development, production, operations, maintenance, and refining.

Halliburton scientists first look at wells in which production was very high initially but then decreased rapidly. These reservoirs could have gotten clogged somehow, but they possibly could be kick-started back into production. However, wading through data to examine these sites is a difficult and time-consuming process that involves comparing many thousands of variables. The scientists use internal and public well data and seismic readings, but they have to look through these data one spreadsheet at a time.

To streamline this process, Halliburton's energy services group uses a data visualization tool. By creating a "picture" of the data—a process that entails rendering multiple variables into a graphical presentation—Halliburton analysts have found ways to see deep into the earth, spotting patterns, trends, and anomalies in the data.

Halliburton calls its data visualization tool Cyber-Well. The company can use CyberWell to virtually design, test, and integrate the systems needed to kick-start older wells before it physically installs them. CyberWell has a very easy-to-use format. In addition, its all-inclusive screens allow Halliburton personnel to share data visualization with others over the company's networks. As CyberWell completes the design for a well, it automatically provides access to the bill of material (BOM) for each assembly component. The BOM contains a description of each component of the assembly as well as an illustration of that component, showing all of its parts.

CyberWell has helped Halliburton to secure more contracts. Specifically, it has provided the company with these advantages:

- CyberWell reduces risk and improves service quality. Well equipment and the blueprint for the entire well can be visualized before the system is built, which ensures that problems can be solved before the equipment is actually installed in a well.
- CyberWell provides clear technology transfer. Halliburton clients can virtually see the company's well equipment operations and therefore understand the purpose of the equipment before Halliburton delivers it to them.
- CyberWell can be used by any Halliburton employee.

Sources: Compiled from C. Winkler, "Get the Picture," *Computerworld*, January 9, 2006; "Modeling and Visualization Tool Provides Virtual Platform that Advances Completion and Work String Design and Reduces Cost of Poor Quality," *Halliburton Knowledge Central*, November, 2005; *www.halliburton.com*, accessed April 30, 2007.

QUESTIONS

1. Why is it important that CyberWell can be used by all Halliburton employees?
2. Discuss possible ways that Halliburton could use CyberWell to generate an income stream.
3. Discuss how CyberWell addresses Porter's five forces as they apply to Halliburton.

on the Web not only for entertainment but also for decision support. A variety of visualization methods and software packages that support decision making are available. The most popular technologies include geographic information systems and virtual reality. IT's About Business 9.3 illustrates the use of data visualization at Halliburton.

Geographic Information Systems

A **geographic information system (GIS)** is a computer-based system for capturing, integrating, manipulating, and displaying data using digitized maps. Its most distinguishing characteristic is that every record or digital object has an identified geographical location. This process, called *geocoding*, enables users to generate information for planning, problem solving, and decision making. In addition, the graphical format makes it easy for managers to visualize the data.

Today, relatively inexpensive, fully functional PC-based GIS packages are readily available. Representative GIS software vendors are ESRI (*www.esri.com*), Intergraph (*www.intergraph.com*), and Mapinfo (*www.mapinfo.com*), now owned by Pitney-Bowes. GIS data are available from a wide variety of sources. Both government sources and private vendors provide diversified commercial data. Some of these packages are free—for example, CD-ROMs from Mapinfo and downloadable material from *www.esri.com* and *http://data.geocomm.com*.

There are countless applications of GISs to improve decision making in both the public and private sectors. An important trend is the integration of GISs and global positioning systems (GPSs), discussed in Chapter 7. Using GISs and GPSs together can help restructure and redesign many industries, as we see in IT's About Business 9.4.

Virtual Reality

There is no standard definition of virtual reality. The most common definitions usually imply that **virtual reality (VR)** is interactive, computer-generated, three-dimensional graphics delivered to the user through a head-mounted display. In VR, a person "believes" that what he or she is doing is real even though it is artificially created.

IT's About Business

9.4 GPS and GIS

Geographic information systems (GISs) and the global positioning system (GPS) are becoming strategic components in a variety of industries, from construction and trucking to marketing and health care. When GISs and GPSs are used together, they are called *geospatial technology*. In this feature we examine some examples of organizations using geospatial technology.

Loma Linda University Medical Center (LLUMC) (*www.llu.edu*) uses geospatial technology to locate and dispatch ambulances and rescue helicopters and to plot the fastest routes to area trauma centers. In some cases, geospatial technology reduces response and transport time from a half-hour or more to a lifesaving few minutes. All emergency responders in Southern California can access LLUMC's Advanced Emergency Geographic Information System (AEGIS) via the Web. LLUMC also feeds traffic and weather data into AEGIS, enabling ambulance dispatchers to quickly evaluate road conditions and alternate routes. It also receives live GPS data from fire and police departments, hospitals, and emergency medical services providers so that it can identify the closest responder in an emergency and determine which hospital emergency rooms can accept more patients.

Caterpillar Inc. (*www.caterpillar.com*), an equipment manufacturer for mining, construction, and agriculture, offers its GPS AccuGrade technology as a feature in its bulldozers, graders, and other construction vehicles. AccuGrade tracks a machine's blade location and tells it where to move next based on preprogrammed coordinates. In the past, an operator would base blade movements on measurements written on wooden stakes in the ground. The improved precision of AccuGrade translates into higher productivity at construction sites. AccuGrade has increased productivity in construction projects by 40 percent or more, because operators now get accurate measurements more quickly.

The Dover, New Hampshire, Police Department (*www.ci.dover.nh.us*) uses GIS software to map crime trends and schedule police beats. Incident reports appear in real time on a map viewed by dispatchers, along with the locations and status of police vehicles. Later, the department uses a geographical analysis of the calls—including the times, locations, and nature of the incidents, as well as other details—to forecast criminal trends and schedule patrols to help prevent crime and respond to incidents more quickly.

GreenLeaf, a food distributor in San Francisco, uses GIS route-mapping functionality and GPS devices on its trucks to help it plan routes. The company can monitor how its drivers actually drive their routes, which allows it to tell its customers where

their deliveries are at any moment. However, GPS technology is accurate to a few yards, and Green-Leaf's system gets confused when delivery sites are close together. For example, if there are two or three restaurants in the same block, the system will not show the deliveries for all of them.

Sources: Compiled from S. Hildreth, "GPS and GIS: On the Corporate Radar," *Computerworld*, April 2, 2007; E. Malykhina, "Maps Meet Mashups," *InformationWeek*, March 17, 2007; J. Francica, "Location, Location, Location," *InformationWeek*, April 1, 2006; *www.llu.edu, www.caterpillar.com, www.ci.dover .nh.us*, accessed April 29, 2007.

QUESTIONS

1. How would you use Google Earth (*http://earth .google.com*) or Microsoft Virtual Earth (*www .microsoft.com/virtualearth*) in each of the examples above?
2. What geospatial applications can you devise for your university?

Examples of Virtual Reality Applications

Table 9.2

Applications in Manufacturing	Applications in Business
Training Design testing and interpretation of results Safety analysis Virtual prototyping Engineering analysis Ergonomic analysis Virtual simulation of assembly, production, and maintenance	Real estate presentation and evaluation Advertising Presentation in e-commerce Presentation of financial data
Applications in Medicine	Applications in Research Applications and Education
Training surgeons (with simulators) Interpretation of medical data Planning surgeries Physical therapy	Virtual physics lab Representation of complex mathematics Galaxy configurations
Applications in Amusement	Applications in Architecture
Virtual museums Three-dimensional racecar games (on PCs) Air combat simulation (on PCs) Virtual reality arcades and parks Ski simulator	Design of buildings and other structures

More than one person and even a large group can share and interact in the same artificial environment. For this reason, VR can be a powerful medium for communication, entertainment, and learning. Instead of looking at a flat computer screen, the VR user interacts with a three-dimensional, computer-generated environment. To see and hear the environment, the user wears stereo goggles and a headset. To interact with the environment, control objects in it, or move around within it, the user wears a computerized display and hand-position sensors (gloves). VR displays achieve the illusion of a surrounding medium by updating the display in real time. The user can grasp and move virtual objects. Table 9.2 provides examples of the many different types of VR applications.

Before you go on . . .

1. Why is data visualization important?
2. What is a geographical information system?
3. What is virtual reality, and how does it contribute to data visualization?

9.5 Intelligent Systems

In the first three sections of this chapter, we have discussed a variety of information systems that support managerial decision making. In this section, we turn our attention to information systems that can make a decision themselves. These systems are called intelligent systems.

Intelligent systems is a term that describes the various commercial applications of artificial intelligence. **Artificial intelligence (AI)**, a subfield of computer science, is concerned with studying the thought processes of humans and re-creating the effects of those processes via machines, such as computers and robots.

AI is generally defined as "behavior by a machine that, if performed by a human being, would be considered *intelligent*." This definition raises the question, What is *intelligent behavior*? The following capabilities are considered to be signs of intelligence: learning or understanding from experience, making sense of ambiguous or contradictory messages, and responding quickly and successfully to new situations.

AI's ultimate goal is to build machines that will mimic human intelligence. An interesting test to determine whether a computer exhibits intelligent behavior was designed by Alan Turing, a British AI pioneer. The **Turing test** proposes that a man and a computer both pretend to be women (or men), and the human interviewer has to decide which is which. Based on this standard, the intelligent systems exemplified in commercial AI products are far from exhibiting any significant intelligence.

The potential value of AI can be better understood by contrasting it with natural (human) intelligence. AI has several important commercial advantages over natural intelligence, but also some limitations, as shown in Table 9.3.

The major intelligent systems are expert systems, natural language processing, speech recognition, and artificial neural networks. We discuss each of these systems in this section. In addition, two or more of the above can be combined into a *hybrid* intelligent system. We also discuss fuzzy logic, a branch of mathematics often useful in AI applications.

Expert Systems

When an organization has a complex decision to make or a problem to solve, it often turns to experts for advice. These experts have specific knowledge and experience in the problem area. They are aware of alternative solutions as well as the chances that the proposed solutions will succeed. At the same time, they can calculate the costs that the organization may incur if it doesn't resolve the problem. Companies engage experts for advice on such matters

Table 9.3

Comparison of the Capabilities of Natural vs. Artificial Intelligence

Capabilities	Natural Intelligence	Artificial Intelligence
Preservation of knowledge	Perishable from an organizational point of view	Permanent
Duplication and dissemination of knowledge	Difficult, expensive, takes time	Easy, fast, and inexpensive once in a computer
Total cost of knowledge	Can be erratic and inconsistent, incomplete at times	Consistent and thorough
Documentability of process and knowledge	Difficult, expensive	Fairly easy, inexpensive
Creativity	Can be very high	Low, uninspired
Use of sensory experiences	Direct and rich in possibilities	Must be interpreted first; limited
Recognizing patterns and relationships	Fast, easy to explain	Machine learning still not as good as people in most cases, but in some cases can do better than people
Reasoning	Making use of wide context of experiences	Good only in narrow, focused, and stable domains

as mergers and acquisitions, advertising strategy, and purchasing equipment. The more unstructured the situation, the more specialized and expensive is the advice.

Expertise refers to the extensive, task-specific knowledge acquired from training, reading, and experience. This knowledge enables experts to make better and faster decisions than nonexperts in solving complex problems. Expertise takes a long time (possibly years) to acquire, and it is distributed in organizations in an uneven manner.

Expert systems (ESs) are computer systems that attempt to mimic human experts by applying expertise in a specific domain. Expert systems can either *support* decision makers or completely *replace* them. Expert systems are the most widely applied and commercially successful AI technology.

Typically, an ES is decision-making software that can reach a level of performance comparable to a human expert in certain specialized problem areas. Essentially, an ES transfers expertise from an expert (or other source) to the computer. This knowledge is then stored in the computer. Users can call on the computer for specific advice as needed. The computer can make inferences and arrive at conclusions. Then, like a human expert, it offers advice or recommendations. In addition, it can explain the logic behind the advice. Because ESs can integrate and manipulate so much data, they sometimes perform better than any single expert can.

An often overlooked benefit of expert systems is as components embedded in larger systems. Rule-driven technology has become pervasive in numerous applications. For example, credit card issuers use rule-driven technology to process credit card applications.

The transfer of expertise from an expert to a computer and then to the user involves four activities:

1. *Knowledge acquisition.* Knowledge is acquired from experts or from documented sources.
2. *Knowledge representation.* Acquired knowledge is organized as rules or frames (object-oriented) and stored electronically in a knowledge base.

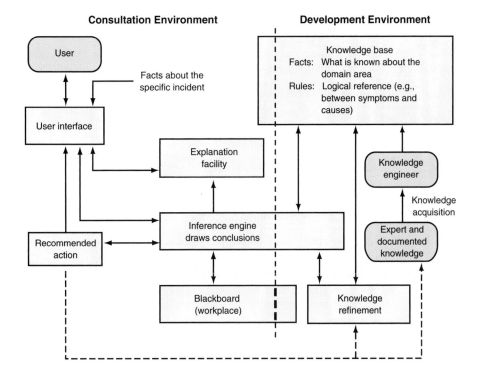

Consultation Environment

Development Environment

FIGURE 9.7   Structure
and process of an
expert system.

3. **Knowledge inferencing.** The computer is programmed so that it can make inferences based on the stored knowledge.

4. **Knowledge transfer.** The inferenced expertise is transferred to the user in the form of a recommendation.

The Components of Expert Systems.   An expert system contains the following components: knowledge base, inference engine, user interface, blackboard (workplace), and explanation subsystem (justifier). In the future, systems will include a knowledge-refining component. Figure 9.7 diagrams the relationships among these components.

The *knowledge base* contains knowledge necessary for understanding, formulating, and solving problems. It includes two basic elements: (1) *facts,* such as the problem situation and (2) *rules* that direct the use of knowledge to solve specific problems in a particular domain.

The *inference engine* is essentially a computer program that provides a methodology for reasoning and formulating conclusions. It enables the system to make inferences based on the stored knowledge. The inference engine is considered the brain of the ES.

The *user interface* enables users to communicate with the computer. That communication can best be carried out in a natural language, usually in a question-and-answer format. In some cases it is supplemented by graphics. The dialogue between the user and the computer triggers the inference engine to match the problem symptoms with the knowledge in the knowledge base and then generate advice.

The *blackboard* is an area of working memory set aside for the description of a current problem, as specified by the input data. It is a kind of database.

A unique feature of an ES is its ability to *explain* its recommendations. It performs this function in a subsystem called the *explanation subsystem* or *justifier.* The explanation subsystem interactively answers questions such as the following: *Why* did the ES ask a certain question? *How* did the ES reach a particular conclusion? *What* is the plan to reach the solution?

Human experts have a *knowledge-refining* system; that is, they can analyze their own performance, learn from it, and improve it for future consultations. This type of evaluation is also

Table 9.4

Ten Generic Categories of Expert Systems

Category	Problem Addressed
Interpretation	Inferring situation descriptions from observations
Prediction	Inferring likely consequences of given situations
Diagnosis	Inferring system malfunctions from observations
Design	Configuring objects under constraints
Planning	Developing plans to achieve goal(s)
Monitoring	Comparing observations to plans, flagging exceptions
Debugging	Prescribing remedies for malfunctions
Repair	Executing a plan to administer a prescribed remedy
Instruction	Diagnosing, debugging, and correcting student performance
Control	Interpreting, predicting, repairing, and monitoring systems behavior

necessary in computerized learning so that the program will be able to improve by analyzing the reasons for its success or failure. Unfortunately, such a component is not yet available in commercial expert systems but it is being developed in experimental systems.

Applications, Benefits, and Limitations of Expert Systems. Today, expert systems are found in all types of organizations. They are especially useful in 10 generic categories, displayed in Table 9.4.

During the past few years, thousands of organizations worldwide have successfully applied ES technology to problems ranging from AIDS research to the analysis of dust in mines. Why have ESs become so popular? The answer lies in the large number of capabilities and benefits they provide. Table 9.5 lists the major benefits of ESs.

Natural Language Processing and Voice Technologies

Natural language processing (NLP) refers to communicating with a computer in the user's native language. To understand a natural language inquiry, a computer must have the knowledge to analyze and then interpret the input. This knowledge may include linguistic knowledge about words, domain knowledge (knowledge of a narrowly defined, specific area, such as student registration or air travel), commonsense knowledge, and even knowledge about the users and their goals. Once the computer understands the input, it can perform the desired action.

In this section we briefly discuss two types of NLP: natural language (NL) understanding and natural language (NL) generation. NL understanding is the input side, and NL generation is the output side of NLP.

Natural Language Understanding. **Natural language understanding**, or **speech (voice) recognition**, allows a computer to comprehend spoken instructions given in the user's everyday language. Speech recognition is deployed today in wireless smart phones as well as in many applications in stores and warehouses.

Natural language understanding offers several advantages. First, it is easy to use. Many more people can speak than can type. As long as communication with a computer depends on typing skills, many people will not be able to use computers effectively. In addition, voice recognition is faster than typing. Even the most competent typists can speak more quickly than they can type. It is estimated that the average person can speak twice as quickly as a proficient typist can type.

Benefits of Expert Systems

Table 9.5

Benefit	Description
Increased output and productivity	ESs can configure components for each custom order, increasing production capabilities.
Increased quality	ESs can provide consistent advice and reduce error rates.
Capture and dissemination of scarce expertise	Expertise from anywhere in the world can be obtained and used.
Operation in hazardous environments	Sensors can collect information that an ES interprets, enabling human workers to avoid hot, humid, or toxic environments.
Accessibility to knowledge and help desks	ESs can increase the productivity of help-desk employees, or even automate this function.
Reliability	ESs do not become tired or bored, call in sick, or go on strike. They consistently pay attention to details.
Ability to work with incomplete or uncertain information	Even with an answer of "don't know," ES can produce an answer, although it may not be a definite one.
Provision of training	The explanation facility of an ES can serve as a teaching device and knowledge base for novices.
Enhancement of decision-making and problem-solving capabilities	ESs allow the integration of expert judgment into analysis (for example, diagnosis of machine and problem malfunction and even medical diagnosis).
Decreased decision-making time	ESs usually can make faster decisions than humans working alone.
Reduced downtime	ESs can quickly diagnose machine malfunctions and prescribe repairs.

A final advantage is manual freedom. Obviously, communicating with a computer through typing occupies your hands. In many situations computers might be useful to people whose hands are otherwise engaged, such as product assemblers, airplane pilots, and busy executives. Speech recognition also enables people with hand-related physical disabilities to use computers.

However, certain limitations of NL understanding restrict its use. The major limitation is its inability to recognize long sentences. Also, the better the system is at speech recognition, the higher its cost.

Natural Language Generation.   **Natural language generation**, or **voice synthesis**, enables computers to produce everyday languages—either by "voice" or on the screen—so that people can understand computers more easily. As the term *synthesis* implies, sounds that make up words and phrases are electronically constructed from basic sound components. Significantly, these sounds can be made to form any desired voice pattern.

The current quality of synthesized voice is very good, but the technology remains somewhat expensive. Anticipated lower costs and improved performance should encourage more widespread commercial *interactive voice response (IVR)* applications, especially on the Web. Theoretically, IVR can be used in almost all applications that can provide an automated response to a user, such as inquiries by employees pertaining to the payroll and benefits. A number of banks and credit card companies already offer voice service to their customers to provide information on balances, payments, and so on. For a list of other voice synthesis and voice recognition applications, see Table 9.6.

Table 9.6

Examples of Voice Technology Applications

Types of Applications	Companies	Devices Used
Answering inquiries about reservations, schedules, lost baggage, etc.	Scandinavian Airlines, other airlines,	Output
Informing credit card holders about balances and credits, providing bank account balances and other information to customers	Citibank, many other banks	Output
Verifying coverage information	Delta Dental Plan (CA)	Output
Requesting pickups, ordering supplies	Federal Express	Input
Giving information about services, receiving orders	Illinois Bell, other telephone companies	Output and Input
Enabling stores to order supplies, providing price information	Domino's Pizza	Output and Input
Allowing inspectors to report results of quality assurance tests	General Electric, Rockwell International, Austin Rover, Westpoint Pepperell, Eastman Kodak	Input
Allowing receivers of shipments to report weights and inventory levels of various meats and cheeses	Cara Donna Provisions	Input
Conducting market research and telemarketing	Weidner Insurance, AT&T	Input
Notifying people of emergencies detected by sensors	U.S. Department of Energy, Idaho National Engineering Lab, Honeywell	Output
Notifying parents about cancellation of classes and about where students are	New Jersey Department of Education	Output
Calling patients to remind them of appointments, summarizing and reporting results of tests	Kaiser-Permanente HMO	Output
Activating radios, heaters, etc. by voice	Car manufacturers	Input
Logging in and out to payroll department by voice	Taxoma Medical Center	Input
Prompting doctors in the emergency room to conduct all necessary tests, reporting of results by doctors	St. Elizabeth's Hospital	Output and Input
Sending and receiving patient data by voice, searching for doctors, preparing schedules and medical records	Hospital Corporation of America	Output and Input

Neural Networks

A **neural network** is a system of programs and data structures that simulates the underlying concepts of the human brain. A neural network usually involves a large number of processors operating in parallel, each with its own small sphere of knowledge and access to data in its local memory (see Figure 9.8). Typically, a neural network is initially "trained" or fed large amounts of data and rules about data relationships.

Neural networks are particularly good at recognizing subtle, hidden, and newly emerging patterns within complex data, as well as interpreting incomplete inputs. Neural networks can help users solve a wide range of problems, from airline security to infectious disease control. They have become the standard for combating fraud in the credit card, healthcare, and telecom industries, and they're playing an increasingly important role in today's stepped-up international efforts to prevent money laundering. The following example shows neural networks in action against fraud.

Let's look at an example of mortgage applications as shown in Figure 9.8. The figure illustrates a neural network, which has three levels of interconnected nodes (similar to the human brain): an input layer of nodes, a middle or hidden layer, and an output layer. As you train the neural network, the strengths (or weights) of the connections change. In our example, the input nodes would be age, income, occupation, marital status, employer, length of time with that employer, amount of mortgage desired, current interest rate, and many more. The neural network has already been trained with data input from many successful and unsuccessful mortgage applications. That is, the neural network has established a pattern as to which input variables are necessary for a successful mortgage application. Interestingly, the neural network can adjust as mortgage amounts increase or decrease and interest rates increase or decrease.

Fuzzy Logic

Fuzzy logic is a branch of mathematics that deals with uncertainties by simulating the process of human reasoning. The rationale behind fuzzy logic is that decision making is not always a matter of black and white, true or false. It often involves gray areas where the term *maybe* is more appropriate.

A computer programmed to use fuzzy logic precisely handles subjective concepts that humans do not define precisely. A term such as "warm" is related, via precisely defined formulas, to an imprecise concept. For example, where the concept is "income," "high" could have values ranging over $200,000 per year and "moderate" could have values ranging from $75,000 to $150,000 per year. A loan officer at a bank might use fuzzy values such as high and moderate when considering a loan application.

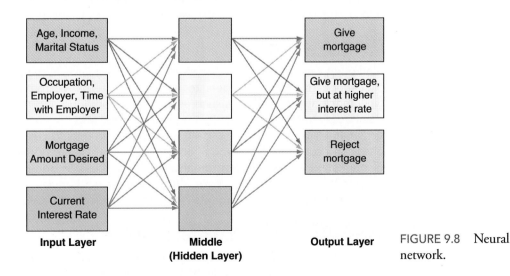

FIGURE 9.8 Neural network.

Fuzzy logic has also been used in financial analysis and in the manufacture of antilock brakes. In accounting and finance, fuzzy logic allows you to analyze information with imprecise values, such as an intangible asset like goodwill.

Before you go on . . .

1. Describe what is meant by intelligent behavior.
2. Compare artificial and natural intelligence.
3. Describe the transfer of expertise from human expert(s) to a computer and then to a user.
4. What are the benefits and limitations of expert systems?
5. What are the advantages and disadvantages of natural language understanding?
6. What are the advantages and disadvantages of artificial neural networks?
7. What is fuzzy logic?

What's in IT for Me?

For the Accounting Major

BI systems, dashboards, and intelligent systems are used extensively in auditing to uncover irregularities. They are also used to uncover and prevent fraud. Today's CPAs use BI and intelligent systems for many of their duties, ranging from risk analysis to cost control. Accounting personnel also use intelligent agents for mundane tasks such as managing accounts and monitoring employees' Internet use.

For the Finance Major

People have been using computers for decades to solve financial problems. Innovative BI applications exist for activities such as making stock market decisions, refinancing bonds, assessing debt risks, analyzing financial conditions, predicting business failures, forecasting financial trends, and investing in global markets. In many cases, intelligent systems can facilitate the use of spreadsheets and other computerized systems used in finance. Finally, intelligent systems can help to reduce fraud in credit cards, stocks, and other financial services.

For the Marketing Major

Marketing personnel utilize BI systems and dashboards in many applications, from allocating advertising budgets to evaluating alternative routings of salespeople. New marketing approaches such as targeted marketing and marketing transaction databases are heavily dependent on IT in general and on intelligent systems in particular. Intelligent systems are particularly useful in mining customer databases and predicting customer behavior. Successful applications are noted in almost any area of marketing and sales, from analyzing the success of one-to-one advertising to supporting customer help desks. With the increased importance of customer service, the use of intelligent agents is becoming critical for providing fast response.

For the Production/Operations Management Major

BI systems and dashboards support complex operations and production decisions ranging from inventory to production planning. Many of the early ESs were developed in the production/operations management field for tasks ranging from diagnosis of machine failures and prescription of repairs to complex production scheduling and inventory control. Some companies, such as DuPont and Kodak, have deployed hundreds of ESs in the planning, organizing, and control of their operational systems.

For the Human Resources Management Major

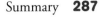

Human resources personnel use BI systems, dashboards, and intelligent systems for many applications. For example, these systems can find resumes of applicants posted on the Web and sort them to match needed skills. Expert systems are used in evaluating candidates (tests, interviews). Intelligent systems are used to facilitate training and to support self-management of fringe benefits. Neural computing is used to predict employee performance on the job as well as to predict labor needs. Voice recognition systems provide benefits information to employees.

For the MIS Major

The MIS function provides the data and models that managers use in BI systems and the structured information used in dashboards. MIS personnel are also responsible for the information on each screen of digital dashboards. MIS employees have the difficult task of interacting with subject-area experts to develop expert systems.

1. **Describe the concepts of management, decision making, and computerized support for decision making.**

   Management is a process by which organizational goals are achieved through the use of resources (people, money, energy, materials, space, time). Managers have three basic roles: interpersonal, informational, and decisional. When making a decision, either organizational or personal, the decision maker goes through a four-step process: intelligence, design, choice, and implementation. Several information technologies have been successfully used to directly support managers. Collectively, they are referred to as business intelligence information systems and intelligent systems.

2. **Describe multidimensional data analysis and data mining.**

   Multidimensional data analysis provides users with a view of what is happening or what has happened by allowing users to "slice and dice" the data in any desired way. Data mining searches for valuable business information in a large database, data warehouse, or data mart. It can perform two basic operations: predicting trends and behaviors and identifying previously unknown patterns.

3. **Describe digital dashboards.**

   Digital dashboards provide rapid access to timely, structured information and direct access to management reports. Digital dashboards are very user friendly, are supported by graphics, and allow users to examine various structured reports.

4. **Describe data visualization and explain geographical information systems and virtual reality.**

   Data visualization involves presenting data by technologies such as geographical information systems and virtual reality. A geographical information system (GIS) is a computer-based system for manipulating and displaying data using digitized maps. Virtual reality refers to interactive, computer-generated, three-dimensional graphics delivered to the user through a head-mounted display.

5. **Describe artificial intelligence (AI).**

   Artificial intelligence involves studying the thought processes of humans and attempting to represent those processes in machines (computers, robots, and so on). AI's ultimate goal is to build machines that will mimic human intelligence.

Summary

6. **Define an expert system and identify its components.**

   Expert systems (ESs) are an attempt to mimic the reasoning abilities of human experts. An ES is decision-making software that can reach a level of performance comparable to a human expert in some specialized and usually narrow problem area.

   The components of expert systems include the knowledge base, the inference engine, the user interface, the blackboard (an area of working memory), and the explanation subsystem. It is expected that in the future ESs will also have a knowledge-refining system that can analyze performance and improve on it.

7. **Describe natural language processing and natural language generation and neural networks.**

   Natural language understanding or speech (voice) recognition allows certain applications to comprehend instructions given in ordinary language so that they can understand people. Natural language generation or voice synthesis strives to allow computer applications to produce ordinary language, on the screen or by voice, so that people can understand computers more easily.

   A neural network is a system of programs and data structures that approximates the operation of the human brain. A neural network usually involves a large number of processors operating in parallel, each with its own small sphere of knowledge and access to data in its local memory. Typically, a neural network is initially "trained" or fed large amounts of data and rules about data relationships.

Chapter Glossary

artificial intelligence (AI) A subfield of computer science concerned with studying the thought processes of humans and representing the effects of those processes via machines.

business intelligence Applications and technologies for consolidating, analyzing, and providing access to vast amounts of data to help users make better business and strategic decisions.

data mining The process of searching for valuable business information in a large database, data warehouse, or data mart.

decision room A face-to-face setting for a group DSS, in which terminals are available to the participants.

decision support system (DSS) Business intelligence systems that evolved from decision support systems; they combine models and data in an attempt to solve semi-structured and some unstructured problems with extensive user involvement.

digital dashboard A business intelligence system that provides rapid access to timely information and direct access to management reports.

expert system (ES) A computer system that attempts to mimic human experts by applying reasoning methodologies or knowledge in a specific domain.

geographic information system A computer-based system for capturing, integrating, manipulating, and displaying data using digitized maps.

goal-seeking analysis Study that attempts to find the value of the inputs necessary to achieve a desired level of output.

group decision support system (GDSS) An interactive computer-based system that supports the process of finding solutions by a group of decision makers.

intelligent systems A term that describes the various commercial applications of artificial intelligence.

management A process by which organizational goals are achieved through the use of resources.

model (in decision making) A simplified representation, or abstraction, of reality.

natural language generation (also **voice synthesis**) Technology that enables computers to produce ordinary language, by "voice" or on the screen, so that people can understand computers more easily.

natural language processing (NLP) Communicating with a computer in the user's native language.

natural language understanding (also **speech or voice recognition**) The ability of a computer to comprehend instructions given in ordinary language, via the keyboard or by voice.

neural network A system of programs and data structures that approximates the operation of the human brain.

organizational decision support system (ODSS) A DSS-BI system that focuses on an organizational task or activity involving a sequence of operations and decision makers.

productivity The ratio between the inputs to a process and the outputs from that process.

sensitivity analysis The study of the impact that changes in one (or more) parts of a model have on other parts.

Turing test A test for artificial intelligence in which a human interviewer, conversing with both an unseen human being and an unseen computer, cannot determine which is which; named for English mathematician Alan Turing.

virtual reality Interactive, computer-generated, three-dimensional graphics delivered to the user through a head-mounted display.

what-if analysis The study of the impact of a change in the assumptions (input data) on the proposed solution.

Discussion Questions

1. Your company is considering opening a new factory in China. List several typical activities involved in each phase of the decision (intelligence, design, choice, and implementation).

2. American Can Company announced that it was interested in acquiring a company in the health maintenance organization (HMO) field. Two decisions were involved in this act: (1) the decision to acquire an HMO and (2) the decision of which HMO to acquire. How can the company use DSS-BI systems, expert systems, and digital dashboards to assist it in this endeavor?

3. A major difference between a conventional DSS-BI system and an expert system is that the former can explain a *how* question, whereas the latter can also explain a *why* question. Discuss the implications of this statement.

4. Discuss the strategic benefits of BI systems.

5. Will BI systems replace business analysts? (*Hint*: See W. McKnight, "Business Intelligence: Will Business Intelligence Replace the Business Analyst?" *DMReview*, February 2005).

6. Why is the combination of GIS and GPS becoming so popular? Examine some applications of GIS/GPS combinations related to data management.

Problem-Solving Activities

1. The city of London (U.K.) has an entrance fee for automobiles and trucks into the central city district. About 1,000 digital cameras photograph the license plate of every vehicle passing by. Computers read the plate numbers and match them against records in a database of cars for which the fee has been paid for that day. If the computer does not find a match, the car owner receives a citation by mail. Examine the issues pertaining to how this process is accomplished, the mistakes that can be made, and the consequences of those mistakes. Also examine how well the system is working by checking press reports. Finally, relate the process to business intelligence.

2. Enter *www.applix.com* and go to the Executive Viewer demo. Take the guided tour and interact with each feature.

3. Enter *www.fairisaac.com* and find products for fraud detection and risk analysis. Prepare a report.

4. Enter *www.spss.com* and find a demo on predictive analytics. Write a summary on the usability and benefits of the technology.

5. Enter *www.microsoft.com/office/dataanalyzer/evaluation/tour* and take the four-part tour. Summarize the system's major capabilities in a report.

Web Activities

1. Enter *www.teradatastudentnetwork.com* (TSN) (you will need a password) and find the paper titled "Data Warehousing Supports Corporate Strategy at First American Corporation" (by Watson, Wixom, and Goodhue). Read the paper and answer the following questions:
   a. What were the drivers for the data warehouse/business intelligence project in the company?
   b. What strategic advantages were realized?
   c. What were the critical success factors for the project?

2. Enter *www.teradatastudentnetwork.com* and find the Web seminar titled: "Enterprise Business Intelligence: Strategies and Technologies for Deploying BI on Large Scale" (by Eckerson and Howson). View the Web seminar and answer the following questions:
   a. What are the benefits of deploying BI to many employees?
   b. Who are the potential users of BI? What does each type of user attempt to achieve?

c. What BI implementation lessons did you learn from the seminar?

3. Enter *www.gapminder.org*. Access *www.ted.com/index .php/talks/view/id/92* to find the video of Hans Rosling's presentation. Comment on his data visualization techniques. Note further that Google has purchased Gapminder's TrendAnalyzer software. Relate this latest Google acquisition to our discussion of Google's strategy in Chapter 1.

4. Enter *www.visualmining.com*. Explore the relationship between visualization and business intelligence. See how business intelligence is related to dashboards.

5. Access *http://businessintelligence.ittoolbox.com*. Identify all types of business intelligence software. Join a discussion group about topics discussed in this chapter. Prepare a report.

6. Visit the sites of some GIS vendors (such as *www .mapinfo.com*, *www.esri.com*, *www.autodesk.com*, or *www.bently.com*). Join a newsgroup and discuss new applications in marketing, banking, and transportation. Download a demo. What are some of the most important capabilities and applications?

Team Assignments

1. Access *www.dmreview.com/resources/demos.cfm*. Examine the list of demos, and identify software with analytical capabilities. Each group prepares a report on five companies.

2. Using data mining, it is possible not only to capture information that has been buried in distant courthouses but also to manipulate and index it. This process can benefit law enforcement but invade privacy. In 1996, Lexis-Nexis, the online information service, was accused of permitting access to sensitive information on individuals. The company argued that it was unfairly targeted because it provided only basic residential data for lawyers and law enforcement personnel. Should Lexis-Nexis be prohibited from allowing access to such information? Debate the issue.

3. Use Google to find combined GIS/GPS applications. Also, look at various vendor sites to find success stories. For GPS vendors, look at *http://biz.yahoo.com* (directory) and Google. Each group will make a presentation of five applications and their benefits.

4. Each group will access a leading business intelligence vendor's Web site (for example, MicroStrategy, Oracle, Hyperion, Microsoft, SAS, SPSS, Cognos, Applix, and Business Objects). Each group will present a report on a vendor, highlighting each vendor's BI capabilities.

CLOSING CASE

GPS and Business Intelligence Combine for Precision Agriculture

THE BUSINESS PROBLEM The United States grows $200 billion of agricultural products each year, of which it exports $68 billion. Rubenacker Farms in Dahlgren, Illinois, has more than 9,300 acres of corn, wheat, and soybeans. As recently as ten years ago, a grain farmer would walk the fields and run his fingers through the soil to measure its moisture and depth. He would then use pencil and paper to record the date he seeded his fields and how much fertilizer he sprayed. Today, "precision farmers" supplement their farming knowledge with business intelligence software and statistical analysis to help decide which crops to plant, how to grow them, and when to sell them.

THE IT SOLUTION Precision farmers plow and plant with auto-steer, driverless tractors equipped with global positioning systems that guide the machines over fields by themselves. They fertilize with sprayers loaded with GIS maps and computerized instructions to vary the amounts of nitrogen applied to different spots on a field, down to 4-inch patches. In addition, when farmers harvest their crops, weight and force sensors attached to 15-ton combines record the volume of corn or soybeans pulled from each plant at two-second intervals, associating the data with specific locations on field maps.

Precision farmers upload these data points via wireless networks into business intelligence software in their offices. There, they combine these data with business information such as the price of seed, the cost of fertilizer, weather records, and current market pricing. Farmers analyze costs and income related to specific physical locations in the field so that they can calculate crop profitability, row by row.

At the same time, the U.S. Department of Agriculture and various universities offer data and analysis tools for free, for monitoring crop prices, predicting weather, and comparing infestation treatments. Further, farmers buy and sell grain over the Internet at sites such as Farmstech.com (*www.farmstech.com*).

THE RESULTS Purdue University estimates that 20 percent of U.S. grain is planted using tractors with auto-guidance systems and custom-fertilized with computerized sprayers. Moreover, half of all U.S. grain is harvested by combines with yield monitors. In 1950, American farmers planted 83 million acres of corn, which produced 38 bushels per acre. In 2004, farmers planted 81 million acres of corn, with each acre yielding 160 bushels, an increase of more than 300 percent. Not all of this increase is attributable to precision agriculture, but quite a bit of it is.

In addition to greater yields, precision agriculture has also generated financial benefits. As one example, when fertilizing was done by hand, a farmer pulling a sprayer behind his tractor would usually overlap up to 10 percent of the ground to be certain that he covered everything. In contrast, a tractor with auto-steer and a variable-rate sprayer overlaps just 1 to 2 percent. More accurate spraying requires less labor and results in less wear on machinery. It also means spending less on expensive diesel fuel and fertilizer, both of which (being petroleum based) tend to increase in price every year.

Given all of these benefits, why hasn't everyone turned to precision farming? The biggest impediment is cost. GPS systems and on-board computers for a tractor cost about $25,000. A GPS base station with an antenna to relay signals to orbiting satellites costs another $20,000. Business intelligence systems can cost an additional $1,000. Another factor is the lack of integration between vendors' technologies, meaning that farmers must select one proprietary system and cannot mix and match components from different vendors in order to save money.

Sources: Compiled from K. Nash, "GPS and Business Intelligence: Rubenacker Farms Makes Hay with I.T.," *Baseline Magazine,* October 2, 2006; C. Ambrosio, "Understanding Adoption of Precision Agriculture Technologies," *Proceedings of the APEN International Conference,* March 2006; J. Cox, "Bring on the WiMax Apps," *Network World,* November 5, 2005; "Precision Agriculture: GPS, Apps, and Algorithms," *CIO,* August 15, 2003.

QUESTIONS

1. Compare precision farmers in the United States as shown in this case with e-choupals in India (see for example, *www.itcportal.com/ruraldevp_philosophy/echoupal .htm*). What are the similarities and differences between precision farming in the United States and e-choupals in India? What are the similarities and differences in the technologies used in both types of farming?

2. Create a plan for a mashup that would allow farmers to obtain the information they need without having to buy proprietary systems. Be sure to describe your data sources and how you would mix and match them for the farmer.

Web Resources   wiley.com/college/rainer

Student Web Site
- Web Quizzes
- Student Lecture Slides in PowerPoint
- Virtual Company ClubIT: Website and Assignments

WileyPLUS
- e-book
- Flash Cards
- How-To Animations for Microsoft Office

Future Planning At Club IT

The assignments on the *WileyPLUS* Web site will ask you to help the club owners make decisions about staffing, pricing, and ordering.

wiley.com/college/rainer

Chapter 10

Acquiring Information Systems and Applications

What's in IT for me? ACC FIN MKT POM HRM MIS

Zappos Uses Open-Source Software to Build Applications

MKT

POM

The Business Problem

Zappos (*www.zappos.com*), an online retailer founded in 1999, began by selling shoes. The online store had $1.6 million in gross sales in 2000, grew rapidly to $597 million in 2006, and projects sales of $800 million in 2007. The company has added handbags, eyeglasses, and other accessories to its products.

Zappos offers its customers three promises: fast and free shipping (including returns); 24/7 live customer support; and a 110-percent price guarantee. This guarantee says that if you find a better price on an item, the company will refund 110 percent of the difference to you. Customers also have an inventory advantage at Zappos, compared to traditional brick-and-mortar retail stores. The company has more than 100,000 styles, 900 brands, and 3 million items in stock.

This case is different from the previous chapter-opening cases. Those cases introduced a business problem and then examined how the affected company used information systems to resolve the problem. In contrast, this case focuses on how IS contributed to Zappos' incredible growth and enabled the company to fulfill its promises to its customers.

The IT Solutions

Zappos has built the majority of its information systems largely using open-source software. These systems include the company's Web site itself, its warehouse management system, customer service and merchandising planning applications, and the extranet available to the company's vendors. The company develops or builds its own applications primarily for flexibility because Zappos systems developers want to be able to make changes on a daily basis.

Zappos feels that open-source software provides other advantages as well. For one thing, the company can solve coding problems faster than they would be able to using commercial software. They simply do a Google search or go to a message board and obtain an answer instantly, rather than waiting for a vendor representative to call. Furthermore, with the company growing so fast, they can add servers and people without having to worry about buying additional licenses for commercial software use.

All departments in the company use a central database, and Zappos has built a wide variety of applications that are specifically tailored to the needs of each department and the ways in which that department interacts with customers. For example, if the company begins to sell a new category of product, its systems developers can set up a simple Web report in a single day that shows inventory levels and sales levels for each day. If someone wants to see a detailed breakdown of sales on a given day, the developers will create a report for that function and link it to the first report. This process has generated a very rich set of applications that has grown as employee needs have grown.

Zappos' IS also includes an extranet that allows the company's suppliers to view almost all of the information that the company's employees can see: inventory; sales over the past 24 hours, week, or month; products on sale; products that are or are not selling well at that exact instant; and so on. Similarly, vendors can use a Web-based interface to log into Zappos' Web site to find an array of reports that provide analyses of how their products are selling. Zappos uses standard protocols such as XML and EDI to exchange information with vendors. Zappos is also prepared to adapt to whatever particular protocols and applications a vendor has already implemented.

Zappos produces a report every morning that shows which brands customers searched for the previous day. If Zappos has not heard of a brand, the company's merchandising team follows up.

The company also has a direct link between its customer service representatives and the systems development team. In this way, the development team hears directly what customers are saying. In addition, Zappos holds weekly meetings between actual programmers and frontline customer-service supervisors. A wiki collaboration tool lets all company employees post any information they think is worth sharing—from the addition of new products to good places to eat near the office.

Zappos keeps its warehouse open 24 hours, 7 days per week. That way, a customer can order shoes as late as 11:00 P.M. and still have the option of next-day delivery. Short of "next-day" shipping, Zappos promises customers that their shoes will arrive in four to five business days, free of charge. For repeat customers, the company's order-management system randomly selects customers for upgrades to second-day shipping, or sometimes even next-day-air shipping.

Zappos also enables its customers to track the status of their orders on the Zappos Web site or on its shippers' Web sites. The company works with its shippers, such as UPS, to monitor and improve communications between Zappos systems and shipper systems.

The company's warehouse management system provides for an average turnaround of eight hours from the time a customer places an order to the time it goes out the door. To make sure that customers find what they need, Zappos stocks every shoe that is listed on its Web site. A pair of shoes will not show up for sale until warehouse workers scan a bar code on a shoebox and a sticker on a warehouse shelf to log the shoes' location, thus guaranteeing that every shoe shown online is in stock.

Zappos' customers can talk to live representatives around the clock—the 1-800 number is on every Web page. They can also submit questions or requests through the Web site itself.

The Results

Zappos now has more than 4 million paying customers, meaning that more than 1 percent of the U.S. population has purchased something from the company. Approximately 60 percent of Zappos' sales come from repeat customers.

With such a large number of customers, an examination of how a new product sells on the company's Web site can be an indication for how that new product will sell in general. This process helps Zappos' vendors to see trends quickly and to gather invaluable information for product planning. One vendor praises Zappos for giving his company far more dynamic and comprehensive access to how his company's shoes are selling than any other retailer. This vendor uses real-time data from Zappos to gather information on shoes down to specific sizes and widths. He further maintains that Zappos built an algorithm that uses past and predicted sales trends to help him order appropriately.

Zappos pays close attention to its return policy. Although the company's free shipping policy has resulted in very high customer satisfaction, Zappos' return rate is about 25 percent, well above the 5 percent of a typical retailer. However, the company has found that customers who return 25 to 50 percent of their orders are more profitable than those who return less. They buy more frequently, choose higher-priced items, and spend more dollars per order.

What We Learned from This Case

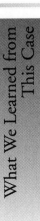

The Zappos case demonstrates that a company (albeit a startup) can build its own information systems in-house. Zappos used open-source software to build its own systems for flexibility as opposed to acquiring systems in some other way.

Competitive organizations move as quickly as they can to acquire new information technologies (or modify existing ones) when they need to improve efficiencies and gain strategic advantage. Today, however, acquisition goes beyond building new systems in-house, and IT resources go beyond software and hardware. The old model in which firms built their own systems is being replaced with a broader perspective of IT resource acquisition that provides companies with a number of options. Companies now must decide which IT tasks will remain in-house, and even whether the entire IT resource should be provided and managed by other organizations.

In this chapter we describe the process of acquiring IT resources from a managerial perspective. This means from your perspective, because you will be closely involved in all aspects of acquiring information systems and applications in your organization. In fact, when we mention "users" in this chapter, we are talking about you.

We pay special attention to the available options for acquiring IT resources and how to evaluate them. We also take a close look at planning and justifying the need for information systems.

Sources: Compiled from "Zappos.com Adds Bill Me Later Payments," *www.paymentsnews.com*, April 24, 2007; E. Schuman, "Beauty Killed the Beast and Slowed Its Download Speed," *eWeek*, October 18, 2006; D. McDonald, "Fast, Simple Open-Source IT," *CIO Insight*, November 10, 2006; L. Walker, "Surf's Up on Web Shopping," *Washington Post*, July 17, 2005; "Spotlight on BBBOnline Participant Zappos.com," *BBBOnline Update*, June, 2005; Associated Press, "Small Internet Retailers Prosper," *CBS News*, February 5, 2004; *www.zappos.com*, accessed May 5, 2007.

10.1 Planning for and Justifying IT Applications

Organizations must analyze the need for applications and then justify each application in terms of cost and benefits. The need for information systems is usually related to organizational planning and to the analysis of its performance vis-à-vis its competitors. The cost-benefit justification must look at the wisdom of investing in a specific IT application versus spending the funds on alternative projects.

When a company examines its needs and performance, it generates a prioritized list of both existing and potential IT applications, called the **application portfolio**. These are the applications that have to be added, or modified if they already exist.

IT Planning

The planning process for new IT applications begins with analysis of the *organizational strategic plan*, as shown in Figure 10.1. The organization's strategic plan states the firm's overall mission, the goals that follow from that mission, and the broad steps necessary to reach these goals. The strategic planning process modifies the organization's objectives and resources to meet its changing markets and opportunities.

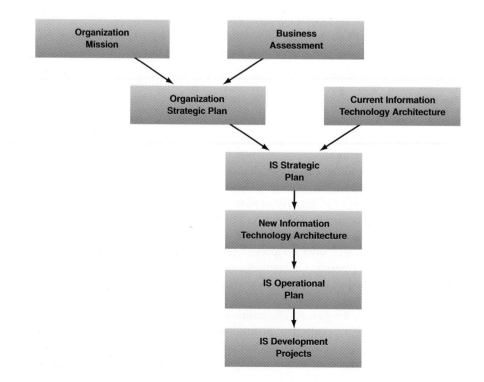

FIGURE 10.1   The information systems planning process.

The organizational strategic plan and the existing IT architecture provide the inputs in developing the IT strategic plan. As we discussed in Chapter 1, the *IT architecture* delineates the way an organization's information resources should be used to accomplish its mission. It encompasses both technical and managerial aspects of information resources. The technical aspects include hardware and operating systems, networking, data management systems, and applications software. The managerial aspects specify how managing the IT department will be accomplished, how functional area managers will be involved, and how IT decisions will be made.

The **IT strategic plan** is a set of long-range goals that describe the IT infrastructure and identify the major IT initiatives needed to achieve the goals of the organization. The IT strategic plan must meet three objectives:

1. It must be aligned with the organization's strategic plan.

2. It must provide for an IT architecture that enables users, applications, and databases to be seamlessly networked and integrated.

3. It must efficiently allocate IS development resources among competing projects so that the projects can be completed on time and within budget and have the required functionality.

The **IT steering committee** is very important in organizations. This committee, comprised of a group of managers and staff representing various organizational units, is set up to establish IT priorities and to ensure that the MIS function is meeting the needs of the enterprise. The committee's major tasks are to link corporate strategy and IT strategy, approve the allocation of resources for the MIS function, and establish performance measures for the MIS function and see that they are met. The IT steering committee is important to you because it ensures that you get the information systems and applications that you need to do your job.

After a company has agreed on an IT strategic plan, it next develops the *IS operational plan*. This plan consists of a clear set of projects that the IS department and the functional area managers will execute in support of the IT strategic plan. A typical IS operational plan contains the following elements:

- *Mission* The mission of the IS function (derived from the IT strategy).

- *IS environment* A summary of the information needs of the functional areas and of the organization as a whole.

- *Objectives of the IS function* The best current estimate of the goals of the IS function.

- *Constraints on the IS function* Technological, financial, personnel, and other resource limitations on the IS function.

- *The application portfolio* A prioritized inventory of present applications and a detailed plan of projects to be developed or continued during the current year.

- *Resource allocation and project management* A listing of who is going to do what, how, and when.

Evaluating and Justifying IT Investment: Benefits, Costs, and Issues

As we already discussed, developing an IT plan is the first step in the acquisition process. All companies have a limited amount of resources available to them. For this reason they must justify investing resources in some areas, including IT, rather than in others. Essentially, justifying IT investment involves assessing the costs and the benefits (values), and comparing the two. This comparison is frequently referred to as cost-benefit analysis. This analysis is not a simple task.

Assessing the Costs.   Placing a dollar value on the cost of IT investments may not be as simple as it sounds. One of the major challenges that companies face is to allocate fixed costs among different IT projects. *Fixed costs* are those costs that remain the same regardless of any change in the activity level. For IT, fixed costs include infrastructure cost, cost of IT services, and IT management cost. For example, the salary of the IT director is fixed, and adding one more application will not change it.

Another complication is that the cost of a system does not end when the system is installed. Costs for maintaining, debugging, and improving the system can accumulate over many years. In some cases the company does not even anticipate them when it makes the investment.

An example is the cost of the Year 2000 (Y2K) reprogramming projects that cost organizations worldwide billions of dollars at the end of the twentieth century. In the 1960s, computer memory was very expensive. To save money, programmers coded the "year" in the date field 19_ _, instead of _ _ _ _. With the "1" and the "9" hard-coded in the computer program, only the last two digits varied and computer programs needed less memory. However, this process meant that when we reached the year 2000, computers would have 1900 as the year, instead of 2000. This programming technique could have caused serious problems with, for example, financial and insurance applications.

Assessing the Benefits.   Typically, evaluating the benefits of IT projects is even more complex than calculating their costs. Benefits may be harder to quantify, especially because many of them are intangible (for example, improved customer or partner relations or improved decision making). You will probably be asked for input about the intangible benefits that an information system provides for you.

The fact that organizations use IT for several different purposes further complicates benefit analysis. In addition, to obtain a return from an IT investment, the company must implement the technology successfully. In reality, many systems are not implemented on time, within budget, or with all the features originally envisioned for them. Finally, the proposed system may be "cutting edge." In these cases there may be no previous evidence of what sort of financial payback the company can expect.

Conducting Cost-Benefit Analysis.   After a company has assessed the costs and benefits of IT investments, it must compare the two. There is no uniform strategy to conduct this analysis. Rather, it can be performed in several ways. Here we discuss four common approaches: (1) net present value, (2) return on investment, (3) breakdown analysis, and (4) the business case approach.

Organizations often use *net present value (NPV)* calculations for cost-benefit analyses. Using the NPV method, analysts convert future values of benefits to their present-value equivalent by "discounting" them at the organization's cost of funds. They then can compare the present value of the future benefits to the cost required to achieve those benefits and determine whether the benefits exceed the costs. NPV analysis works well in situations where the costs and benefits are well defined or "tangible" enough to be converted into monetary values.

Another traditional tool for evaluating capital investment is *return on investment (ROI)*. ROI measures management's effectiveness in generating profits with its available assets. The ROI measure is a percentage, and the higher the percentage return, the better. ROI is calculated by dividing net income attributable to a project by the average assets invested in the project. In the case of IT, then, the company would divide the income generated by an IT investment by the costs of that investment. The greater the value of ROI, the more likely the company is to approve the investment.

Breakeven analysis determines the point at which the cumulative dollar value of the benefits from a project equals the investment made in the project. Breakeven analysis is attractive for its simplicity, but is flawed because it ignores the value of system benefits after the breakeven point.

One final method used to justify investments in projects is the *business case approach*. A business case is a written document that managers use to justify funding one or more specific applications or projects. You will be a major source of input when business cases are developed because these cases describe what you do, how you do it, and how a new system could better support you.

In addition, a business case provides the bridge between the initial plan and its execution. Its purpose is not only to get approval and funding but also to provide the foundation for tactical decision making and technology risk management. The business case approach is usually employed in existing organizations that want to embark on new IT projects. The business case helps to clarify how the organization can best use its resources to accomplish its IT strategy. It helps the organization to concentrate on justifying the investment. It also focuses on risk management and on how an IT project corresponds with the organization's mission.

IT's About Business 10.1 shows how British Telecom justifies its information systems applications.

IT's About Business

10.1 British Telecom Justifies Its Applications

British Telecom (*www.bt.com*) had a problem. In 2005, when the United Kingdom's $34 billion telecommunications giant transformed itself from a provider of traditional telephone services to a leader in network-centric information technology solutions, it discovered that its own IS function was a problem. The company had no central IS department or global control. Instead, each business unit had its own CIO and IS staff, as well as thousands of technology initiatives, each operating by itself.

BT needed a new approach to reshape its IS efforts and unify the company's global technology strategy. The first step was to identify and consolidate all technology initiatives underway at that time. It turned out that BT had 4,300 technology initiatives across the company, all with random delivery dates. Only about 20 percent of these initiatives had a definitive business purpose, and none was being tracked in any way.

BT evaluated each project, prioritizing strategic initiatives and killing any project that had little or no value to the company's overall strategic mission. In addition, BT killed any project that had no return on investment (ROI). In one year, BT reduced the number of IS initiatives from 4,300 projects to 29. At the same time, the company standardized its information systems, closed down some 700 of its 3,000 older existing systems, and settled on a service-oriented architecture that gave the company a new platform from which to launch its own Web-based services.

BT also instituted a project management system to continually monitor progress and ensure return on investment. The system runs on 90-day cycles, meaning that projects have to deliver on a set of metrics, such as customer satisfaction and ROI every 90 days. At the beginning of each new cycle, IS staffers and business partners brainstorm ideas and set goals and deadlines for the coming cycle. Ninety days later, each project team reviews how well the team performed against its goals. If the team's goals are met and the project meets its objective for the cycle, staffers receive a bonus for their work.

In one year, BT achieved 100 percent business coverage, which means that everything the company does now has an ROI. The company's IS costs decreased by almost 20 percent, and the IS group doubled the amount of work it completes every year. Furthermore, customer satisfaction increased from 65 to 80 percent, and, most importantly, the credibility of the IS function has significantly increased across the company.

Sources: Compiled from D. D'Agostino, "British Telecom's Tech Transformation," *CIO Insight*, February 6, 2007; L. Meadows and S. Hanly, "Agile Coaching in British Telecom," *Agile Journal*, November 9, 2006; E. Knorr, "SOA: Under Construction," *CIO*, December 12, 2006; *www.bt.com*, accessed May 11, 2007.

QUESTIONS

1. Explain how British Telecom ended up with 4,300 information systems initiatives across the company.
2. Detail how the company went from 4,300 initiatives to 29.

Before you go on . . .

1. What are some problems associated with assessing the costs of IT?
2. What difficulties accompany the intangible benefits from IT?
3. Describe the NPV, ROI, breakeven analysis, and business case approaches.

10.2 Strategies for Acquiring IT Applications

If a company has successfully justified an IT investment, it must then decide how to pursue it. Companies have several options for acquiring IT applications, including buying the applications, leasing them, using open-source software, using software-as-a-service, developing them in-house, or outsourcing them. In this section we discuss the first five options and one particular type of leasing—application service providers—along with outsourcing in Section 10.5.

Buy the Applications (Off-the-Shelf Approach)

The standard features required by IT applications can be found in many commercial software packages. Buying an existing package can be a cost-effective and time-saving strategy compared with developing the application in-house. Nevertheless, the buy option should be carefully considered and planned to ensure that the selected package contains all of the features necessary to address the company's current and future needs. Otherwise such packages can quickly become obsolete. You will decide the features that a selected package must have to be suitable.

In reality, a single software package can rarely satisfy all of an organization's needs. For this reason a company sometimes must purchase multiple packages to fulfill different needs. It then must integrate these packages with one another as well as with existing software.

The buy option is especially attractive if the software vendor allows the company to modify the technology to meet its needs. However, this option may not be attractive in cases where customization is the only method of providing the necessary flexibility to address the company's needs. It also is not the best strategy when the software is very expensive or is likely to become obsolete in a short time. The advantages and limitations of the buy option are summarized in Table 10.1. When the buy option is not appropriate, organizations consider leasing.

Lease the Applications

Compared with the buy option and the option to develop applications in-house, the "lease" option can save a company both time and money. Of course, leased packages (such as purchased packages) may not always exactly fit the company's application requirements. However, vendor software generally includes the features that are most commonly needed by organizations in a given industry. Again, you will decide the features that are necessary.

It is common for interested companies to apply the 80/20 rule when evaluating vendor software. Put simply, if the software meets 80 percent of the company's needs, then the company should seriously consider changing its business processes to resolve the remaining 20 percent. This is often a better long-term solution than modifying vendor software. Otherwise, the company will have to customize the software every time the vendor releases an updated version.

Leasing can be especially attractive to small-to-medium-sized enterprises (SMEs) that cannot afford major investments in IT software. Large companies may also prefer to lease packages in order to test potential IT solutions before committing to heavy investments. Also, because there is a shortage of IT personnel with appropriate skills for developing custom IT applications, many companies choose to lease instead of developing software in-house. Even those companies that employ in-house experts may not be able to afford the long wait needed for strategic applications to be developed in-house. Therefore, they lease (or buy) applications from external resources to establish a quicker presence in the market.

Advantages and Limitations of the "Buy" Option

Table 10.1

Advantages

☐ Many different types of off-the-shelf software are available.
☐ Software can be tried out.
☐ Much time can be saved by buying rather than building.
☐ The company can know what it is getting before it invests in the product.
☐ The company is not the first and only user.
☐ Purchased software may avoid the need to hire personnel specifically dedicated to a project.

Disadvantages

☐ Software may not exactly meet the company's needs.
☐ Software may be difficult or impossible to modify, or it may require huge business process changes to implement.
☐ The company will not have control over software improvements and new versions.
☐ Purchased software can be difficult to integrate with existing systems.
☐ Vendors may drop a product or go out of business.
☐ Software is controlled by another company with its own priorities and business considerations.
☐ The purchasing company does not have intimate knowledge of how the software works and why it works that way.

Leasing can be done in one of three ways. The first way is to lease the application from a software developer and install it on the company's premises. The vendor can help with the installation and frequently will offer to contract for the support and maintenance of the system. Many conventional applications are leased this way. The second way, using an application service provider (ASP), is becoming more popular (see Section 10.5). The third way is to utilize software-as-a-service.

Use Open-Source Software

As we saw in the chapter's opening case, Zappos customized open-source software (which we discuss in Technology Guide 2) to develop its applications in-house. An organization can obtain a license to use an open-source software product and either use it as is, or customize it, to develop applications.

Utilize Software-as-a-Service

Software-as-a-Service (SaaS) refers to a method of delivering software in which a vendor hosts the applications. Customers access these applications over a network, typically the Internet, and have no control over the applications. Customers do not own the software but pay for using it.

Develop the Applications In-House

Although building applications in-house is usually more time-consuming and may be more costly than buying or leasing, it often leads to a better fit with the specific organizational requirements.

In-house development can make use of various methodologies. The basic, backbone methodology is the systems development life cycle (SDLC), which we discuss in the next section. In Section 10.4, we discuss the methodologies that complement the SDLC: prototyping, joint application development, rapid application development, and integrated computer-assisted systems development tools. We also discuss three other methodologies: agile development, end-user development, and component-based development.

10.3 The Traditional Systems Development Life Cycle

The **systems development life cycle (SDLC)** is the traditional systems development method that organizations use for large-scale IT projects. The SDLC is a structured framework that consists of sequential processes by which information systems are developed. For our purposes (see Figure 10.2), these processes are systems investigation, systems analysis, systems design, programming, testing, implementation, operation, and maintenance. Each process in turn consists of well-defined tasks. We consider all eight processes in this section.

Other models for the SDLC may contain more or fewer than the eight stages we present here. The flow of tasks, however, remains largely the same. In the past, developers used the **waterfall approach** to the SDLC; that is, tasks in one stage were completed before the work proceeded to the next stage. If we look at Figure 10.2, we see that the stages "flow" down and to the right, as if in a waterfall. Today, however, design tools allow for greater flexibility than was true of the traditional approach.

Systems development projects produce desired results through team efforts. Development teams typically include users, systems analysts, programmers, and technical specialists. *Users* are employees from all functional areas and levels of the organization who interact with the system, either directly or indirectly. **Systems analysts** are IS professionals who specialize in analyzing and designing information systems. *Programmers* are IS professionals who modify existing computer programs or write new computer programs to satisfy user requirements. **Technical specialists** are experts on a certain type of technology, such as databases or telecommunications. All people who are affected by changes in information systems (users and managers, for example) are known as **systems stakeholders**. All stakeholders are typically involved in varying degrees and at various times in systems development.

The SDLC has three major advantages: control, accountability, and error detection. An important issue in systems development is that the later in the development process that errors are detected, the more expensive they are to correct. Thus, the structured sequence of tasks and milestones in the SDLC makes error prevention and detection easier and saves money in the long run.

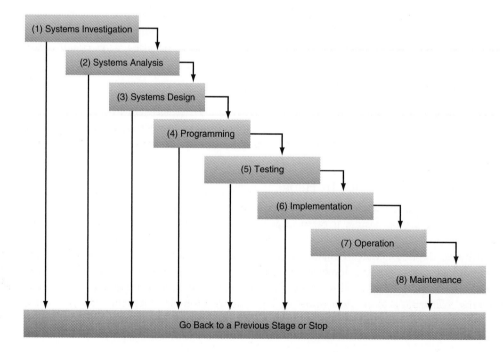

FIGURE 10.2 An eight-stage systems development life cycle (SDLC).

The SDLC does have disadvantages, however. Because of its structured nature, it is relatively inflexible. It is also time-consuming and expensive, and it discourages changes to user requirements once they have been established. Development managers who must develop large, enterprisewide applications must consider these disadvantages carefully.

Systems Investigation

The initial stage in a traditional SDLC is systems investigation. Systems development professionals agree that the more time they invest in (a) understanding the business problem to be solved, (b) the technical options for systems, and (c) the problems that are likely to occur during development, the greater the chances of success. For these reasons, systems investigation begins with *the business problem* (or business opportunity), followed by the feasibility analysis.

Feasibility Study. The main task in the systems investigation stage is the feasibility study. Organizations have three basic solutions to any business problem relating to an information system: (1) do nothing and continue to use the existing system unchanged, (2) modify or enhance the existing system, or (3) develop a new system. The **feasibility study** analyzes which of these three solutions best fits the particular business problem. This study determines the probability that the proposed systems development project will succeed. It also provides a rough assessment of the project's technical, economic, behavioral, and organizational feasibility, as we discuss below. The feasibility study is critically important to the systems development process because it can prevent organizations from making costly mistakes.

Technical feasibility determines if the hardware, software, and communications components can be developed and/or acquired to solve the business problem. Technical feasibility also determines if the organization's existing technology can be used to achieve the project's performance objectives.

Economic feasibility determines if the project is an acceptable financial risk and if the organization can afford the expenses and time needed to complete the project. Economic feasibility addresses two primary questions: (1) Do the benefits outweigh the costs of the project? (2) Can the company afford the project? We have already discussed the commonly used methods to determine economic feasibility: NPV, ROI, breakeven analysis, and the business case approach.

You will be heavily involved in the behavioral aspect of the feasibility study because *behavioral feasibility* addresses the human issues of the project. All systems development projects introduce change into the organization, and people generally fear change. Overt resistance from employees may take the form of sabotaging the new system (for example, entering data incorrectly) or deriding the new system to anyone who will listen. Covert resistance typically occurs when employees simply continue to use the old system.

Organizational feasibility refers to an organization's ability to accept the proposed project. Sometimes, for example, organizations cannot accept an affordable project due to legal or other constraints. In checking organizational feasibility, the firm should consider if the proposed project meets the criteria stated in the company's strategic plan.

Go/No-Go Decision. After the feasibility analysis is considered, a "Go/No-Go" decision is reached by the steering committee if there is one, or by top management in the absence of a committee. The Go/No Go decision does not depend solely on the feasibility analysis. Organizations often have more feasible projects than they can fund. Therefore, the firm must prioritize the feasible projects, pursuing those with the highest priority. Unfunded feasible projects may not be presented to the IT department at all. These projects therefore contribute to the *hidden backlog*, which are projects of which the IT department is not aware.

If the decision is "No-Go," then the project either is put on the shelf until conditions are more favorable or is discarded. If the decision is "Go," then the project proceeds, and the systems analysis phase begins.

Systems Analysis

Once a development project has the necessary approvals from all participants, the systems analysis stage begins. **Systems analysis** is the examination of the business problem that the organization plans to solve with an information system. This stage defines the business problem in more detail, identifies its causes, specifies the solution, and identifies the information requirements that the solution must satisfy. Understanding the business problem requires understanding the various processes involved. These processes are often complicated and interdependent.

The main purpose of the systems analysis stage is to gather information about the existing system in order to determine the requirements for an enhanced or new system. The end product of this stage, known as the "deliverable," is a set of *system requirements*.

Arguably the most difficult task in systems analysis is to identify the specific requirements that the system must satisfy. These requirements are often called *user requirements*, because users (meaning you) provide them. In this phase, the team must outline what information is needed, how much is needed, for whom, when, and in what format. Systems analysts use many different techniques to identify the information requirements for the new system. These techniques include interviews with users, surveys of users, direct observation, and document analysis ("follow the paper"). With direct observation, analysts observe users interacting with the existing system.

You can see that you will have a great deal of input into these processes. The closer your involvement, the better the chance that you will get an information system or application that meets your needs.

There are problems associated with eliciting information requirements, regardless of the method used. First, the business problem may be poorly defined. Second, the users may not know exactly what the problem is, what they want, or what they need. Third, users may disagree with one another about business procedures or even about the business problem. Finally, the problem may not be information related. Instead, it might require other solutions, such as a change in management or organizational structure.

The systems analysis stage produces the following information: (1) strengths and weaknesses of the existing system, (2) functions that the new system must have in order to solve the business problem, and (3) user information requirements for the new system. Armed with this information, systems developers can proceed to the systems design stage.

Systems Design

Systems design describes how the system will accomplish this task. The deliverable of the systems design phase is the *technical design*, which specifies the following:

- System outputs, inputs, and user interfaces
- Hardware, software, databases, telecommunications, personnel, and procedures
- A blueprint of how these components are integrated

This output represents the set of *system specifications*.

Systems design encompasses two major aspects of the new system: logical and physical system design. **Logical system design** states *what* the system will do, using abstract specifications, whereas **physical system design** states *how* the system will perform its functions, with actual physical specifications. Logical design specifications include the design of outputs, inputs, processing, databases, telecommunications, controls, security, and IS jobs. Physical design specifications include the design of hardware, software, database, telecommunications, and procedures. For example, the logical telecommunications design may call for a wide area network that connects the company's plants. The physical telecommunications design will specify the types of communications hardware (computers and routers), software (the network operating system), media (fiber optics and satellite), and bandwidth (100 Mbps).

When both aspects of system specifications are approved by all participants, they are "frozen." That is, once the specifications are agreed upon, they should not be changed. Adding functions after the project has been initiated causes **scope creep**, which endangers the budget and schedule of a project. Scope creep occurs during development when users add to or change the information requirements of a system after those requirements have been "frozen." Scope creep occurs for two reasons. First, as users more clearly understand how the system will work and what their needs are, they request that additional functions be incorporated into the system. Second, after the design specifications are frozen, business conditions often change, leading users to request additional functions. Because scope creep is expensive, successful project managers place controls on changes requested by users. These controls help to prevent *runaway projects*—systems development projects that are so far over budget and past deadline that they must be abandoned, typically with large monetary loss.

Programming

Systems developers utilize the design specifications to acquire the software needed for the system to meet its functional objectives and solve the business problem. Although many organizations tend to purchase packaged software, many other firms continue to develop custom software in-house. For example, Wal-Mart and Eli Lilly design practically all of their software in-house.

If the organization decides to construct the software in-house, then programming begins. **Programming** involves translating the design specifications into computer code. This process can be lengthy and time-consuming, because writing computer code is as much an art as a science. Large systems development projects can require hundreds of thousands of lines of computer code and hundreds of computer programmers. These large-scale projects employ programming teams, which often include functional area users, who help the programmers focus on the business problem.

Testing

Thorough and continuous testing occurs throughout the programming stage. Testing is the process that checks to see if the computer code will produce the expected and desired results under certain conditions. Proper testing requires a large amount of time, effort, and expense. However, the costs of improper testing, which could result in a company's implementing a system that does not meet its objectives, are enormous.

Testing is designed to detect errors, or bugs, in the computer code. These errors are of two types: syntax and logic. *Syntax errors* (for example, a misspelled word or a misplaced comma) are easier to find and will not permit the program to run. *Logic errors* permit the program to run, but they cause it to generate incorrect output. Logic errors are more difficult to detect, because the cause is not obvious. The programmer must follow the flow of logic in the program to determine the source of the error in the output.

As software becomes more complex, the number of errors increases, until it is almost impossible to find them all. This situation has led to the idea of *"good-enough" software*, defined as software that developers believe will meet its functional objectives, although it contains errors in the code. That is, developers are convinced they have found all the "show-stopper" bugs. These bugs are the serious errors that will cause catastrophic loss or corruption of data and perhaps will shut down the system completely. In contrast, the errors that remain embedded in good-enough software should not affect the system's performance in any significant way.

Implementation

Implementation (or *deployment*) is the process of converting from the old system to the new system. Organizations use three major conversion strategies: direct, pilot, and phased.

In a **direct conversion**, the old system is cut off and the new system is turned on at a certain point in time. This type of conversion is the least expensive. It is also the most risky if the new system doesn't work as planned. Because of these risks, few systems are implemented using direct conversion.

A **pilot conversion** introduces the new system in one part of the organization, such as in one plant or in one functional area. The new system runs for a period of time and is then assessed. If the assessment confirms that it is working properly, then it is introduced in other parts of the organization.

Finally, a **phased conversion** introduces components of the new system, such as individual modules, in stages. Each module is assessed. If it works properly, then other modules are introduced until the entire new system is operational.

A fourth strategy, parallel conversion, whereby the old and new systems operate simultaneously for a time, is hardly used today. For example, parallel conversion is totally impractical when both the old and new systems are online. Imagine that you are finishing an order on Amazon.com, only to be told, "Before your order can be entered here, you must provide all the same information again, in a different form, and on a different set of screens." The results would be disastrous for Amazon.

Operation and Maintenance

After the new system is implemented, it will operate for a period of time, until (like the old system it replaced) it no longer meets its objectives. Once the new system's operations are stabilized, the company performs *audits* to assess the system's capabilities and to determine if it is being used correctly.

Systems need several types of maintenance. The first type is *debugging* the program, a process that continues throughout the life of the system. The second type is *updating* the system to accommodate changes in business conditions. An example is adjusting to new governmental regulations, such as changes in tax rates. These corrections and upgrades usually do not add any new functions. Instead, they simply help the system to continue meeting its objectives. In contrast, the third type of maintenance *adds new functions* to the existing system without disturbing its operation.

Before you go on . . .

1. Describe the feasibility study.
2. What is the difference between systems analysis and systems design?
3. Describe structured programming.
4. What are the four conversion methods?

10.4 Alternative Methods and Tools for Systems Development

A number of tools are used in conjunction with the traditional systems development life cycle (SDLC). The first four tools that we discuss in this section are designed to supplement the SDLC and make various functions of the SDLC easier and faster to perform. These tools are prototyping, joint application design, computer-aided software engineering, and rapid application development.

The alternative methods to developing systems are used instead of the SDLC. These methods include agile development, end-user development, and component-based development.

Prototyping

The **prototyping** approach defines an initial list of user requirements, builds a prototype system, and then improves the system in several iterations based on users' feedback. Developers do not try to obtain a complete set of user specifications for the system at the outset, and they do not plan to develop the system all at once. Instead, they quickly develop a smaller version of the system known as a *prototype*. A prototype can take two forms. In some cases it contains only the components of the new system that are of most interest to the users. In other cases it is a small-scale working model of the entire system.

Users make suggestions for improving the prototype, based on their experiences with it. The developers then review the prototype with the users and use their suggestions to refine the prototype. This process continues through several iterations until either the users approve the system or it becomes apparent that the system cannot meet the users' needs. If the system is viable, then the developers can use the prototype on which to build the full system. Developing screens that a user will see and interact with is a typical use of prototyping.

The main advantage of prototyping is that it speeds up the development process. In addition, prototyping gives users the opportunity to clarify their information requirements as they review iterations of the new system.

Prototyping also has disadvantages. The first disadvantage is that users, seeing screens that appear to behave like the completed system, will not realize the amount of work that still must be done behind the scenes to provide an operational system with a database, error checking, security precautions, and all the other functions that a prototype does not have (and does not need). This situation can lead to users having unrealistic expectations about when the finished application will be delivered.

Furthermore, because it can largely replace the analysis and design stages of the SDLC in some projects, systems analysts may not produce adequate documentation for the programmers. This lack of documentation can lead to problems after the system becomes operational and needs maintenance. Prototyping can also generate an excess number of iterations. These iterations can actually consume the time that prototyping should be saving. Another drawback is the risk of *idiosyncratic design*. That is, the prototype may be revised based on the feedback of only a small group of users who are not necessarily representative of the entire user population.

Joint Application Design

Joint application design (JAD) is a group-based tool for collecting user requirements and creating system designs. JAD is most often used within the systems analysis and systems design stages of the SDLC. JAD involves a group meeting in which all users meet simultaneously with the analysts. It is basically a group decision-making process that can be done manually or on the computer. During this meeting, all users jointly define and agree on systems requirements. This process saves a tremendous amount of time.

The JAD approach to systems development has several advantages. First, the group process involves many users in the development process while still saving time. This involvement leads to greater support for the new system. In addition, it can improve the quality of the new system and make it easier to implement. In turn, this will reduce training costs.

The JAD approach also has disadvantages. First, it is very difficult to get all users to attend the JAD meeting. For example, in large organizations the users might literally be scattered all over the world. Second, the JAD approach has all the problems associated with any group process (for example, one person can dominate the meeting, some participants may not contribute in a group setting, and so on). To alleviate these problems, JAD sessions usually have a facilitator who is skilled in systems analysis and design as well as in managing group meetings and processes. Also, the use of groupware (such as GDSS) can help facilitate the meeting.

Integrated Computer-Assisted Software Engineering Tools

Computer-aided software engineering (CASE) is a development approach that uses specialized tools to automate many of the tasks in the SDLC. The tools used to automate the early stages of the SDLC (systems investigation, analysis, and design) are called upper CASE tools. The tools used to automate later stages in the SDLC (programming, testing, operation, and maintenance) are called lower CASE tools. CASE tools that provide links between upper CASE and lower CASE tools are called **integrated CASE (ICASE) tools**.

CASE tools provide advantages for systems developers. These tools can produce systems with a longer effective operational life that more closely meet user requirements. They can also speed up the development process. Furthermore, they help produce systems that are more flexible and adaptable to changing business conditions. Finally, systems produced using CASE tools typically have excellent documentation.

At the same time, initial systems produced by CASE tools are often more expensive to build and maintain. In addition, CASE tools require more extensive and accurate definitions of user needs and requirements. Finally, CASE tools are difficult to customize. For this reason, they are sometimes difficult to use with existing systems.

Rapid Application Development

Rapid application development (RAD) is a systems development method that can combine JAD, prototyping, and integrated CASE tools to rapidly produce a high-quality system. In the first RAD stage, JAD sessions are used to collect system requirements, so that users are intensively involved early on. The development process in RAD is iterative, similar to prototyping. That is, requirements, designs, and the system itself are developed and then undergo a series, or sequence, of improvements. RAD uses ICASE tools to quickly structure requirements and develop prototypes. As the prototypes are developed and refined, users review them in additional JAD sessions. RAD produces functional components of a final system, rather than limited-scale versions. To understand how RAD functions and how it differs from SDLC, see Figure 10.3.

RAD methodologies and tools make it possible to develop systems faster, especially systems where the user interface is an important component. RAD can also improve the process of rewriting legacy applications.

Agile Development

Agile development is a software development methodology that delivers functionality in rapid iterations—measured in weeks—requiring frequent communication, development, testing, and delivery. Agile development focuses on rapid development and frequent user contact to create software that is highly relevant to business users. This software does not have to include every possible feature the user will require. Rather, it must meet only the

FIGURE 10.3
A rapid prototyping development process versus SDLC.
Source: datawarehouse-training.com/ Methodologies/ rapid-application-development

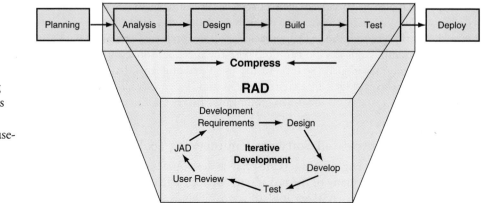

user's more important and immediate needs. The software can be updated later to introduce further functionality. Agile's core tenet is to do only what you have to do to be successful right now.

Agile development uses small (5 to 9 people) teams, which are located with users and are cross-functional. The teams deliver project features about every two to four weeks. They schedule a demonstration with users in order to receive feedback. After each demo, the development team meets to decide which aspects of the project are going well and which aspects need improvement. The team then selects the next three top priorities and adjusts the upcoming schedule accordingly.

A "very present" user is critical to the success of agile development. For example, consider a system with an initial requirement to handle electronic payments. The development team discovers that using PayPal will be much easier than trying to write new computer code to integrate with credit card processors. If the user agrees that PayPal is sufficient, then the development team can quickly implement the solution.

End-User Development

Over the years, computers have become cheaper, smaller, and more widely dispersed throughout organizations. Today, almost everybody who works at a desk or in the field has a computer. One result of these developments is that many computer-related activities have shifted out into the work area. For example, end users now handle most of their own data entry. They create many of their own reports and print them locally, instead of waiting for them to arrive in the interoffice mail after a computer operator has run them at a remote data center. Users also provide unofficial training and support to other workers in their area. Finally, they design and develop an increasing number of their own applications, sometimes even relatively large and complex systems.

As beneficial as end-user development is to both workers and the organization as a whole, it has some limitations. To begin with, end users may not be skilled enough in computers. This lack of skill can jeopardize quality and cost unless the organization installs proper controls. Also, many end users do not take enough time to document their work. In addition, they sometimes fail to take proper security measures. Finally, users often develop databases that cannot efficiently manage all of their production data.

Component-Based Development

Component-based development uses standard components to build applications. Components are reusable applications in their own right, generally with one specific function, such as a shopping-cart component, a user-authentication component, or a catalog component. Component-based development is closely linked with the idea of Web services and service-oriented architectures, which we discussed in Chapter 5.

Many startup companies are pursuing the idea of component-based application development, or less programming and more assembly. Examples of these companies are as follows.

- Ning (*www.ning.com*) allows you to create, customize, and share your own social network.
- Coghead (*www.coghead.com*) allows you to quickly develop custom applications and share them with coworkers in real time. You can use pre-built applications from Coghead or build your own.
- Teqlo (*www.teqlo.com*) lets you use a simple drag-and-drop interface to weave Web services together and build applications. For example, you could take data from your shipping company, mash it up with real-time manufacturing data from your supplier, and then integrate both sets of data into a sales report from an eBay store.

Web services can also be used in conjunction with legacy applications on mainframes, which IT's About Business 10.2 illustrates at Merrill Lynch.

IT's About Business

10.2 Web Services and Mainframes

Merrill Lynch (*www.ml.com*) is one of the world's leading wealth management, capital markets, and advisory companies, with offices in 37 countries and total client assets of approximately $1.6 trillion. The company has a huge IBM mainframe installation—one of the largest in the world—with 1,200 programmers supporting some 2,300 mainframe programs that handle more than 80 million transactions per day.

As reliable and robust as Merrill's mainframe infrastructure was, it also had limitations. As new Web-based applications, such as self-help credit card balance checks, were being developed, programmers needed to access mainframe data. It was difficult to access those data using non-mainframe-based software. Merrill had been copying mainframe data into Oracle databases, which could more easily integrate with Web-based applications. But the copying process was unreliable, and the data became out-of-date as soon as they were copied. For example, a client making several trades would have to wait until the following day to see an accurate balance in his account. As a result, the client might make a trade believing he possessed adequate funds, only to have the trade rejected because, in fact, the funds were not available.

Merrill decided to employ Web services to modernize the firm's multibillion dollar investment in mainframe technology. The company chose to develop and implement Web services on its own, without using an outside vendor, because the firm would have had to retrain many of its 1,200 mainframe programmers.

The Merrill initiative was named X4ML for "XML for Modernizing Legacy." The most vital aspect of the X4ML project was that the platform would not require changing application code on the mainframe or impede mainframe performance in any way. Consequently, new applications request data directly from the mainframe. For example, a Merrill financial adviser may submit a request from her desktop application to find all of her clients with shares in ExxonMobil, perhaps due to a sudden dip in the stock. The request is submitted directly to the mainframe, and the results are returned to the adviser's desktop application.

Merrill has developed more than 420 Web services. In the process, X4ML has helped Merrill save some $42 million in application development by enabling the company to directly use applications and data on the mainframe, thereby making new hardware purchases unnecessary.

X4ML was really tested when Merrill launched a $1 billion effort to create new applications for wealth management that are available for use by the company's 14,000 financial advisers. The wealth management project provides these advisers with access to research, tools, and account information to help them serve clients via a wide range of new programs.

Sources: Compiled from L. Alexander, "Oh, SOLA mio," *Application Development Trends*, July 5, 2006; M. Duvall, "Merrill Lynch & Co.: Web Services, Millions of Transactions, All Good," *Baseline Magazine*, February 7, 2006; E. Malykhina, "Merrill Lynch Embraces SOA," *InformationWeek*, November 8, 2005; C. Babcock, "Merrill Lynch Sells Its Web Services Vendor a Web Services Tool," *InformationWeek*, December 6, 2005.

QUESTIONS

1. Why are mainframe applications and data so important to organizations today?
2. Why do mainframe applications and data pose such an impediment to modern IS applications?

Before you go on . . .

1. Describe the tools that augment the traditional SDLC.
2. Describe the alternate methods that can be used for systems development, other than the SDLC.

10.5 Outsourcing and Application Service Providers

Small or medium-sized companies with few IT staff and limited budgets are best served by outside contractors. Acquiring IT applications from outside contractors or external organizations is called **outsourcing**. Large companies may also choose this strategy in certain circumstances. For example, they might want to experiment with new IT technologies without making a substantial up-front investment. They also might use outsourcing to protect their internal networks and to gain access to outside experts. Outsourcers can perform any or all of the tasks involved in IT development. IT's About Business 10.3 shows how General Motors has changed its outsourcing strategy.

IT's About Business

POM

10.3 General Motors Turns to Multisourcing

General Motors (*www.gm.com*), which produces about 8 million vehicles a year worldwide, has been moving toward a global operational model where any car for any market can be designed and built anywhere in the world. Collaboration on a project may occur among different design groups in different locations. GM's long-term survival depends on a flexible manufacturing network, deployed globally, that can change production extremely rapidly.

In 2003, GM's Brazilian e-commerce site, which generates 80,000 online car sales annually, crashed. GM immediately convened a meeting of the vendors involved, including Oracle, AT&T, Microsoft, Cisco Systems, EDS, and IBM. While these vendors blamed each other for the crash, GM only knew that it was not selling cars and trucks on the Web site and that its existing IS strategy was not meeting the company's needs.

From 1996 to 2006, GM outsourced most of its information systems operations to Electronic Data Systems (EDS; *www.eds.com*), while retaining 2,000 employees who handle strategic management of information systems. In 2006, GM concluded its 10-year outsourcing agreement with EDS, divided up the work, and awarded approximately $7.5 billion in new five-year contracts to a small group of service firms that included EDS, IBM, Capgemini, Covisint, and Wipro. In 2007, GM awarded AT&T a $1 billion contract to manage its global data network. AT&T will help GM deploy and manage a standard set of compatible voice, video, and data applications that will be available for use by GM employees regardless

of location. The network incorporates local and long-distance services, global voice mail, conferencing, and high-speed Internet access.

In effect, GM moved from outsourcing to multisourcing. These changes were driven by the need for cost savings and greater flexibility and the need to re-engineer the way the company operates information systems globally.

GM has worked with its vendors to develop 44 process standards, 29 of which affect suppliers. All vendors must now conform not only to GM standards, but to common technology standards as well. Moreover, GM has consolidated 10,000 information systems into 2,500 systems. The results have been encouraging and GM has realized financial savings.

Sources: Compiled from "GM Taps AT&T for 'Anywhere, Anytime' Application Support," *InformationWeek*, February 26, 2007; D. Bartholomew, "GM Outsourcing Overhaul, 1 Year Later," *Baseline Magazine*, January 7, 2007; R. Mitchell, "Driving Economies of Scale in IT," *Computerworld*, October 30, 2006; "GM's IT Overhaul Takes Off," *InformationWeek*, September 18, 2006; S. Hamm, "GM's Way or the Highway," *BusinessWeek*, December 19, 2005.

QUESTIONS

1. Why is it so important that GM hold its vendors to common technology standards?
2. What functions do GM's IS employees perform? What skills or knowledge do they bring to the table? Why doesn't GM outsource these people as well?

Several types of vendors offer services for creating and operating IT systems including e-commerce applications. Many software companies, from IBM to Oracle, offer a range of outsourcing services for developing, operating, and maintaining IT applications. IT outsourcers, such as EDS, offer a variety of services. Also, the large CPA companies and management consultants (for example, Accenture) offer some outsourcing services. As the trend to outsource is rising, so is the trend to relocate these operations offshore, particularly in India and China. Offshoring can save money, but it includes risks as well, such as sending sensitive corporate data overseas.

In the past, companies could also use application service providers. An **application service provider (ASP)** is an agent or a vendor who assembles the software needed by enterprises and packages the software with services such as development, operations, and maintenance. The customer then accesses these applications via the Internet or VANs through a standard Web browser interface.

Today, however, companies are using vendors who provide hosting services to acquire applications (see, for example, Google and Amazon, the opening and closing cases in Chapter 1). For hardware resources, these vendors provide utility computing (discussed in Technology Guide 1). For software resources, these vendors provide software-as-a-service (discussed in Technology Guide 2). These vendors also provide high-speed communications links to connect with client.

Using hosting vendors is a particularly desirable option for SME businesses. Simply put, developing and operating IT applications in-house can be time-consuming and expensive for these entities. Leasing from ASPs offers such companies several advantages. First, it saves various expenses (such as labor costs) in the initial development stage. It also helps reduce the costs of software maintenance and upgrading and user training over the long run. In addition, the company can select another software product from the vendor to meet its changing needs. This option saves the company the costs of upgrading the existing software. It also makes the company more competitive by enhancing the company's ability to adapt to changing market conditions.

We have discussed many methods that can be used to acquire new systems. Table 10.2 provides an overview of the advantages and disadvantages of these methods.

Table 10.2

Advantages and Disadvantages of System Acquisition Methods

Traditional Systems Development (SDLC)

Advantages

- Forces staff to systematically go through every step in a structured process.
- Enforces quality by maintaining standards.
- Has lower probability of missing important issues in collecting user requirements.

Disadvantages

- May produce excessive documentation.
- Users may be unwilling or unable to study the specifications they approve.
- Takes too long to go from the original ideas to a working system.
- Users have trouble describing requirements for a proposed system.

Prototyping

Advantages

- Helps clarify user requirements.
- Helps verify the feasibility of the design.
- Promotes genuine user participation.
- Promotes close working relationship between systems developers and users.
- Works well for ill-defined problems.
- May produce part of the final system.

Disadvantages

- May encourage inadequate problem analysis.
- Not practical with large number of users.
- User may not give up the prototype when the system is completed.
- May generate confusion about whether the system is complete and maintainable.
- System may be built quickly, which may result in lower quality.

Joint Application Design

Advantages

- Involves many users in the development process.
- Saves time.
- Greater user support for new system.
- Improved quality of the new system.
- New system easier to implement.
- New system has lower training costs.

Disadvantages

- Difficult to get all users to attend JAD meeting.
- JAD approach has all the problems associated with any group meeting.

Integrated Computer-Assisted Software Engineering

Advantages

- Can produce systems with a longer effective operational life.
- Can produce systems that closely meet user requirements.
- Can speed up the development process.
- Can produce systems that are more flexible and adaptable to changing business conditions.
- Can produce excellent documentation.

Disadvantages

- Systems often more expensive to build and maintain.
- Require more extensive and accurate definition of user requirements.
- Difficult to customize.

Rapid Application Development

Advantages

- Can speed up systems development.
- Users intensively involved from the start.
- Improves the process of rewriting legacy applications.

Disadvantages

- Produces functional components of final systems, but not final systems.

End-User Development

Advantages

- Bypasses the IS department and avoids delays.
- User controls the application and can change it as needed.
- Directly meets user requirements.

(continued)

Advantages and Disadvantages of System Acquisition Methods (Continued)

- Increased user acceptance of new system.
- Frees up IT resources.
- May create lower-quality systems.

Disadvantages

- May eventually require maintenance from IS department.
- Documentation may be inadequate.
- Poor quality control.
- System may not have adequate interfaces to existing systems.

Outsourcing

Advantages

- Saves costs.
- Relies on experts.
- Experiments with new information technologies.

Disadvantages

- Valuable corporate data in another company's control.
- During system development, programmers in another company could put malicious computer code (for example, back doors) in applications.

Application Service Providers

Advantages

- Save costs.
- Reduce software maintenance and upgrades.
- Reduce user training.
- Make the company more competitive by reducing time-to-market and enhance the company's ability to adapt to changing market conditions.

Disadvantages

- ASPs might not offer adequate security protection.
- Software might not be a perfect fit for the desired application.
- Company must make certain that the speed of the Internet connection between the customer and the ASP is adequate to handle the requirements of the application.

Before you go on . . .

1. What types of companies provide outsourcing service?
2. Define ASPs, and discuss their advantages to companies using them.
3. List some disadvantages of ASPs.

10.6 Vendor and Software Selection

Few organizations, especially SMEs, have the time, financial resources, or technical expertise required to develop today's complex IT or e-business systems. As a result, business firms are increasingly relying on outside vendors to provide software, hardware, and technical expertise.

As a result, selecting and managing these vendors and their software offerings has become a major aspect of developing an IT application. The following six steps in selecting a software vendor and an application package are useful.

Step 1: Identify Potential Vendors. Companies can identify potential software application vendors through various sources:

- Software catalogs
- Lists provided by hardware vendors
- Technical and trade journals
- Consultants and industry analysts experienced in the application area
- Peers in other companies
- Web searches

These sources often yield so many vendors and packages that the company must use some evaluation criteria to eliminate all but the most promising ones from further consideration. For example, it can eliminate vendors that are too small or have a questionable reputation. Also, it can eliminate packages that do not have the required features or are not compatible with the company's existing hardware and/or software.

Step 2: Determine the Evaluation Criteria. The most difficult and crucial task in evaluating a vendor and a software package is to select a detailed set of evaluation criteria. Some areas in which a customer should develop detailed criteria are:

- Characteristics of the vendor
- Functional requirements of the system
- Technical requirements that the software must satisfy
- Amount and quality of documentation provided
- Vendor support of the package

These criteria should be set out in a **request for proposal (RFP)**. An RFP is a document that is sent to potential vendors inviting them to submit a proposal that describes their software package and explains how it would meet the company's needs. The RFP provides the vendors with information about the objectives and requirements of the system. Specifically, it describes the environment in which the system will be used, the general criteria that the company will use to evaluate the proposals, and the conditions for submitting proposals. The RFP may also request a list of current users of the package whom the company may contact. Finally, it can require the vendor to demonstrate the package at the company's facilities using specified inputs and data files.

Step 3: Evaluate Vendors and Packages. The responses to an RFP generate massive volumes of information that the company must evaluate. The goal of this evaluation is to determine the gaps between the company's needs (as specified by the requirements) and the capabilities of the vendors and their application packages. Often, the company gives the vendors and packages an overall score by (1) assigning an importance weight to each of the criteria, (2) ranking the vendors on each of the weighted criteria (say 1 to 10), and then (3) multiplying the ranks by the associated weights. The company can then shorten the list of potential suppliers to include only those vendors who achieved the highest overall scores.

Step 4: Choose the Vendor and Package. Once the company has shortened the list of potential suppliers, it can begin negotiations with these vendors to determine how their packages might be modified to remove any discrepancies with the company's IT needs. Thus, one of the most important factors in the decision is the additional development effort

Table 10.3

Criteria for Selecting a Software Application Package

Functionality (Does the package do what the organization needs?)
Cost and financial terms
Upgrade policy and cost
Vendor's reputation and availability for help
Vendor's success stories (visit their Web site, contact clients)
System flexibility
Ease of Internet interface
Availability and quality of documentation
Necessary hardware and networking resources
Required training (check if provided by vendor)
Security
Learning (speed of) for developers and users
Graphical presentation
Data handling
System-required hardware

that may be required to tailor the system to the company's needs or to integrate it into the company's computing environment. The company must also consider the opinions of both the users and the IT personnel who will have to support the system.

Several software selection methods exist. For a list of general criteria, see Table 10.3.

Step 5: Negotiate a Contract. The contract with the software vendor is very important. It specifies both the price of the software and the type and amount of support that the vendor agrees to provide. The contract will be the only recourse if either the system or the vendor does not perform as expected. It is essential, then, that the contract directly reference the proposal, because this is the vehicle that the vendor used to document the functionality supported in their system. Furthermore, if the vendor is modifying the software to tailor it to the company's needs, the contract must include detailed specifications (essentially the requirements) of the modifications. Finally, the contract should describe in detail the acceptance tests that the software package must pass.

Contracts are legal documents, and they can be quite tricky. For this reason, companies might need the services of experienced contract negotiators and lawyers. Many organizations employ software-purchasing specialists who assist in negotiations and write or approve the contract. These specialists should be involved in the selection process from the start.

Step 6: Establish a Service Level Agreement. Service level agreements (SLAs) are formal agreements that specify how work is to be divided between the company and its vendors. These divisions are based on a set of agreed-upon milestones, quality checks, and what-if situations. They describe how quality checks will be made and what is to be done in case of disputes. SLAs accomplish these goals by (1) defining the responsibilities of both partners, (2) providing a framework for designing support services, and (3) allowing the company to retain as much control as possible over its own systems. SLAs include such issues as performance, availability, backup and recovery, upgrades, and hardware and software ownership. For example, the SLA might specify that the ASP have its system available to the customer 99.9 percent of the time.

Before you go on . . .

1. List the major steps of selection of a vendor and a software package.
2. Describe a request for proposal (RFP).
3. Describe SLAs.

What's in IT for Me?

For the Accounting Major

Accounting personnel help perform the cost-benefit analyses on proposed projects. They may also monitor ongoing project costs to keep them within budget. Accounting personnel undoubtedly will find themselves involved with systems development at various points throughout their careers.

For the Finance Major

Finance personnel are frequently involved with the financial issues that accompany any large-scale systems development project (for example, budgeting). They also are involved in cost-benefit and risk analyses. To perform these tasks they need to stay abreast of the emerging techniques used to determine project costs and ROI. Finally, because they must manage vast amounts of information, finance departments are also common recipients of new systems.

For the Marketing Major

In most organizations, marketing, like finance, involves massive amounts of data and information. Like finance, then, marketing is also a hotbed of systems development. Marketing personnel will increasingly find themselves participating on systems development teams. Such involvement increasingly means helping to develop systems, especially Web-based systems that reach out directly from the organization to its customers.

For the Production/Operations Management Major

Participation on development teams is also a common role for production/operations people. Manufacturing is becoming increasingly computerized and integrated with other allied systems, from design to logistics to customer support. Production systems interface frequently with marketing, finance, and human resources. In addition, they may be part of a larger, enterprisewide system. Also, many end users in POM either develop their own systems or collaborate with IT personnel on specific applications.

For the Human Resources Management Major

The human resources department is closely involved with several aspects of the systems acquisitions process. Acquiring new systems may require hiring new employees, changing job descriptions, or terminating employees. Human resources performs all of these tasks. Furthermore, if the organization hires consultants for the development project or outsources it, the human resources department may handle the contracts with these suppliers.

For the MIS Major

Regardless of the approach that the organization adopts for acquiring new systems, the MIS department spearheads it. If the organization chooses either to buy or to lease the application, the MIS department leads in examining the offerings of the various vendors and in negotiating with the vendors. If the organization chooses to develop the application in-house, then the process falls to the MIS department. MIS analysts work closely with users to develop their information requirements. MIS programmers then write the computer code, test it, and implement the new system.

Summary

1. Describe the IT planning process.

IT planning begins with reviewing the strategic plan of the organization. The organizational strategic plan and the existing IT architecture provide the inputs in developing the *IT strategic plan*, which describes the IT architecture and major IS initiatives needed to achieve the goals of the organization. The IT strategic plan may also require a new IT architecture, or the existing IT architecture may be sufficient. In either case, the IT strategic plan leads to the *IS operational plan*, which is a clear set of projects that will be executed by the IS/IT department and by functional area managers in support of the IT strategic plan.

2. Describe the IT justification process and methods.

The justification process is basically a comparison of the expected costs versus the benefits of each application. Although measuring costs generally is not complex, measuring benefits is, due to the many intangible benefits involved. Several methodologies exist for evaluating costs and benefits, including net present value, return on investment, breakeven analysis, and the business case approach.

3. Describe the SDLC and its advantages and limitations.

The systems development life cycle (SDLC) is the traditional method used by most organizations today. The SDLC is a structured framework that consists of distinct sequential processes: systems investigation, systems analysis, systems design, programming, testing, implementation, operation, and maintenance. These processes, in turn, consist of well-defined tasks. Some of these tasks are present in most projects, while others are present in only certain types of projects. That is, smaller development projects may require only a subset of tasks, whereas large projects typically require all tasks. Using the SDLC guarantees quality and security, but it is slow and expensive.

4. Describe the major alternative methods and tools for building information systems.

A common alternative for the SDLC is quick prototyping, which helps to test systems. Useful prototyping tools for SDLC are joint application design (for finding information needs) and rapid application development (which uses CASE tools). For smaller and rapidly needed applications, designers can use agile development, component-based development, and object-oriented development tools, which are popular in Web-based applications.

5. List the major IT acquisition options and the criteria for option selection.

The major options are buy, lease, and build (develop in-house). Other options are joint ventures and use of e-marketplaces or exchanges (private or public). Building in-house can be done by using the SDLC, prototyping, or other methodologies. It can be done by outsourcers, hosting vendors, the IS department employees, or end users (individually or together).

6. Describe the role of hosting vendors.

Hosting vendors provide the IT platform that client companies can use to run their applications. Hosting vendors provide hardware resources in the form of utility computing, software resources in the form of software-as-a-service, and high-speed communications links to clients.

7. Describe the process of vendor and software selection.

The process of vendor and software selection is composed of six steps: identify potential vendors, determine evaluation criteria, evaluate vendors and packages, choose the vendor and package, negotiate a contract, and establish service level agreements.

Chapter Glossary

agile development A software development methodology that delivers functionality in rapid iterations, measured in weeks, requiring frequent communication, development, testing, and delivery.

application portfolio The set of recommended applications resulting from the planning and justification process in application development.

application service provider (ASP) An agent or vendor who assembles the software needed by enterprises and packages them with outsourced development, operations, maintenance, and other services.

component-based development A software development methodology that uses standard components to build applications.

computer-aided software engineering (CASE) Development approach that uses specialized tools to automate many of the tasks in the SDLC; upper CASE tools automate the early stages of the SDLC, and lower CASE tools automate the later stages.

direct conversion Implementation process in which the old system is cut off and the new system is turned on at a certain point in time.

feasibility study Investigation that gauges the probability of success of a proposed project and provides a rough assessment of the project's feasibility.

implementation The process of converting from an old computer system to a new one.

integrated CASE (ICASE) tools CASE tools that provide links between upper CASE and lower CASE tools.

IT steering committee A committee, comprised of a group of managers and staff representing various organizational units, set up to establish IT priorities and to ensure that the MIS function is meeting the needs of the enterprise.

IT strategic plan A set of long-range goals that describe the IT infrastructure and major IT initiatives needed to achieve the goals of the organization.

joint application design (JAD) A group-based tool for collecting user requirements and creating system designs.

logical system design Abstract specification of what a computer system will do.

outsourcing Use of outside contractors or external organizations to acquire IT services.

phased conversion Implementation process that introduces components of the new system in stages, until the entire new system is operational.

physical system design Actual physical specifications that state how a computer system will perform its functions.

pilot conversion Implementation process that introduces the new system in one part of the organization on a trial basis; when the new system is working properly, it is introduced in other parts of the organization.

programming The translation of a system's design specifications into computer code.

prototyping Approach that defines an initial list of user requirements, builds a prototype system, and then improves the system in several iterations based on users' feedback.

rapid application development (RAD) A development method that uses special tools and an iterative approach to rapidly produce a high-quality system.

request for proposal (RFP) Document that is sent to potential vendors inviting them to submit a proposal describing their software package and how it would meet the company's needs.

scope creep Adding functions to an information system after the project has begun.

service level agreements (SLAs) Formal agreements regarding the division of work between a company and its vendors.

systems analysis The examination of the business problem that the organization plans to solve with an information system.

systems analysts IS professionals who specialize in analyzing and designing information systems.

systems design Describes how the new system will provide a solution to the business problem.

systems development life cycle (SDLC) Traditional structured framework, used for large IT projects, that consists of sequential processes by which information systems are developed.

systems stakeholders All people who are affected by changes in information systems.

technical specialists Experts on a certain type of technology, such as databases or telecommunications.

waterfall approach SDLC approach in which tasks in one stage were completed before the work proceeded to the next stage.

Discussion Questions

1. Discuss the advantages of a lease option over a buy option.
2. Why is it important for all business managers to understand the issues of IT resource acquisition?
3. Why is it important for everyone in business organizations to have a basic understanding of the systems development process?
4. Should prototyping be used on every systems development project? Why or why not?
5. Discuss the various types of feasibility studies. Why are they all needed?
6. Discuss the issue of assessing intangible benefits and the proposed solutions.
7. Discuss the reasons why end-user-developed information systems can be of poor quality. What can be done to improve this situation?
8. Why is the attractiveness of ASPs increasing?

Problem-Solving Activities

1. Access *www.ecommerce-guide.com*. Find the product review area and read reviews of three software payment solutions. Assess the payment solutions as possible components.
2. Use an Internet search engine to obtain information on CASE and ICASE tools. Select several vendors and compare and contrast their offerings.
3. Access *www.ning.com*, *www.coghead.com*, *www.teqlo.com*, and *www.dabbledb.com*. Observe how each site provides components for you to use to build applications. Build a small application at each site.

Web Activities

1. Enter *www.ibm.com/software*. Find its WebSphere product and read recent customers' success stories. What makes this software so popular?
2. Enter the Web sites of the GartnerGroup (*www.gartnergroup.com*), the Yankee Group (*www.yankeegroup.com*), and CIO (*www.cio.com*). Search for recent material about ASPs and outsourcing, and prepare a report on your findings.
3. StoreFront (*www.storefront.net*) is a vendor of e-business software. At its site, the company provides demonstrations illustrating the types of storefronts that it can create for shoppers. The site also provides demonstrations of how the company's software is used to create a store.
   a. Run the StoreFront demonstration to see how this is done.
   b. What features does StoreFront provide?
   c. Does StoreFront support smaller or larger stores?
   d. What other products does StoreFront offer for creating online stores? What types of stores do these products support?

Team Assignments

1. Assessing the functionality of an application is part of the planning process (Step 1). Select three to five Web sites that cater to the same type of buyer (for instance, several Web sites that offer CDs or computer hardware), and divide the sites among the teams. Each team will assess the functionality of its assigned Web site by preparing an analysis of the different sorts of functions provided by the sites. In addition, the team should

compare the strong and weak points of each site from the buyer's perspective.

2. Divide into groups, with each group visiting a local company (include your university). At each firm, study the systems acquisition process. Find out the methodology or methodologies used by each organization and the type of application each methodology applies. Prepare a report and present it to the class.

3. As a group, design an information system for a startup business of your choice. Describe your chosen IT resource acquisition strategy, and justify your choices of hardware, software, telecommunications support, and other aspects of a proposed system.

Huge Problems at Britain's National Health System

THE BUSINESS PROBLEM Established in 1948, the National Health Service (NHS) in the United Kingdom is the largest healthcare organization in Europe. Controlled by the British government, it is also a vast bureaucracy, employing more than 1 million workers and providing a full range of healthcare services to the country's 60 million citizens.

The inspiration to digitize this huge bureaucracy first surfaced in 2001. At that time, much of the NHS was paper-based and was severely lagging in its use of technology, largely because of years of underinvestment. Hospitals throughout the U.K. were dealing with multiple vendors, many of them small to midsize U.K. software companies. Predictably, the NHS had become a hodgepodge of incompatible systems from different suppliers, with differing levels of functionality. The NHS had created silos of information that were not shared, or even sharable.

In an attempt to resolve these problems, in 2002 the British government initiated the National Program for Information Technology (NPIT), which includes England, Northern Ireland, and Wales (but not Scotland). The overall objective of the NPIT was to build a single, electronic healthcare record for every individual. In effect, this record would be a comprehensive, lifelong history of the patient's healthcare information, regardless of where, when, and by whom he or she was treated. In addition, the NPIT would provide healthcare professionals with access to a national data repository. Finally, it would support the NHS in collecting and analyzing information and monitoring health trends to make the best use of clinical and other resources.

A major obstacle for the NPIT was the sheer size of England's healthcare system. For example, in one year, the system served some 52 million people; it dealt with 325 million consultations in primary care, 13 million outpatient consultations, and 4 million emergency admissions; and it issued 617 million prescriptions.

THE IT SOLUTION The NPIT is a 10-year project designed to build new information systems to (1) connect more than 100,000 doctors, 380,000 nurses, and 50,000 other healthcare professionals; (2) allow for the electronic storage and retrieval of patient medical records; (3) permit patients to set up appointments via their computers; and (4) let doctors electronically transmit prescriptions to local pharmacies.

Specifically, the information systems that the NHS is attempting to deliver include the following:

- *The National Spine.* The National Spine is a database at the heart of the NPIT. The Spine encompasses individual electronic NHS lifelong care records for every patient in England, securely accessible by the patient and his or her health providers. The Spine will enable patients and providers to securely access integrated patient data, prescription ordering, proactive decision support, and best-practice reference data.
- *Choose and Book.* Choose and Book provides convenience for patients in electronically selecting the date, place, and time of their appointments.
- *N3.* The N3 national network is a massive, secure, broadband, virtual private network that provides the IT infrastructure and broadband connectivity for the NHS so that it can share patient information with various organizations. The N3 supports Choose and Book, electronic prescriptions, and electronic transfer of patient information.

The NHS first had McKinsey and Company conduct a study of the U.K. healthcare system. McKinsey concluded that the project was too large for any one vendor to act as prime contractor for all of it. Consequently, the NHS divided England into five regions—London, Eastern, Northeast, Northwest, and Southern—each with about 12 million people. Each of the five regions would be serviced by a prime IT vendor, known as a Local Service Provider (LSP).

The vendor-selection process was conducted with great secrecy. Unfortunately, the secrecy led to the exclusion of most frontline healthcare providers from the vendor selection process. The NHS offered 10-year service contracts to the LSPs for the five regions, each worth about $2 billion.

The LSPs are responsible for developing and integrating information systems at a local level. The LSPs are also responsible for implementing clinical and administrative applications, which support the delivery of patient care and enable trusts to exchange data with the National Spine. (A trust is a regional healthcare agency that administers England's national healthcare programs.) In addition, the LSPs provide the data centers to run all the applications.

Significantly, all of the NHS's contracts with the LSPs stipulated that vendors would not be paid until they delivered working systems. Because the vendors were the prime contractors, this stipulation also meant that the subcontractors would not be paid until they delivered working systems.

Accenture was named LSP for two regions, and Computer Sciences Corporation (CSC), British Telecom (BT), and a Fujitsu-led alliance were named LSPs for the other three regions. BT was also given the contract to build both the N3 network and the National Spine. Atos Origin was chosen to provide Choose and Book.

As previously explained, the LSPs were to act as prime contractors for their respective regions, and they were able to choose their own software vendors and subcontractors. BT and the Fujitsu group selected IDX (now part of GE Healthcare), an established healthcare services and software provider, to develop health records software. Accenture and CSC chose iSoft, a U.K.-based supplier of healthcare software, for that function.

Developing this software presented many challenges. Both iSoft and IDX had to write some of the software from scratch. The difficulty was that the programmers and systems developers did not comprehend some of the terminology used by the British health system, and more importantly, how the British health system actually operated.

Compounding these problems was Accenture and CSC's decision to select iSoft as their clinical and administrative software vendor. These companies were depending on iSoft's Lorenzo application suite, which at that time was still in development. However, iSoft seriously underestimated the time and effort necessary to develop the Lorenzo suite. As a result, under the collect-on-implementation contract that the LSPs had signed with the NHS, neither Accenture nor iSoft could generate revenue. In a Catch-22 situation, this lack of revenue left iSoft short of the cash it needed to finish developmental work on Lorenzo.

The ongoing delay of Lorenzo left Accenture and CSC in a quandary. Should they continue to wait for Lorenzo, or should they lock into older, existing applications?

Accenture opted to wait and use Lorenzo. In contrast, CSC chose to implement iSoft's existing line of products.

While waiting for Lorenzo, Accenture worked with general practitioners, as opposed to CSC, which focused almost entirely on hospitals. Accenture's problem was that the general practitioner implementation was extremely difficult because there are so many of them and the NHS had given them an option called GP Systems of Choice. This option stipulated that the doctors did not have to follow Accenture's lead in selecting a system, but instead could choose on their own. This choice, in turn, further complicated the transfer of more than 10 years of data from old systems to the Spine-compliant systems being provided by Accenture. Typically, it cost about $9,000 and took six months to transfer the data of each practitioner.

Meanwhile, there were concerns with GE Healthcare's IDX as well. Fujitsu and BT had agreed to develop a Common Solution Program, meaning that the two LSPs would develop common applications for two of England's regions. Due to time delays at IDX, Fujitsu and BT replaced the firm with Cerner, a U.S. healthcare IT company. This replacement caused additional time delays for the project.

THE RESULTS The NPIT was originally budgeted at $12 billion, but that figure has risen to $24 billion as a result of the many problems encountered in developing the NPIT. By mid-2007, the NHS had delivered some of the program's key elements. For example, 1 million patient referrals to specialist care were made through Choose and Book, and 97 percent of doctors' offices were connected to the N3 network.

However, many deliverables of the project have been delayed. In addition, the N3 network experienced more than 100 failures in 2006. One network outage disrupted mission-critical computer services such as patient administration systems for three days.

Another problem is that the project has little support among healthcare workers. This problem stemmed from excluding frontline healthcare professionals in the early phases of the project. Therefore, it fell largely to the vendors and the bureaucrats to create the system. Physicians complained that the system focuses too much on administrative needs and not enough on clinicians' concerns. A survey conducted in 2006 showed that only 38 percent of British general practitioners and nurses believe that the project was an important priority for the NHS, and only 13 percent believe that the project represents a good use of NHS resources.

The NHS policy to pay vendors only on delivery of working systems was shortsighted, because the policy provided no flexibility to deal with vendors that encountered unexpected problems. In late 2006, Accenture announced that it was walking away from its contract with the NHS. Accenture did not say why it was exiting the project, but the company had set aside some $500 million to cover losses from its work in England.

As of mid-2007, the NHS itself had run short of funding, resulting in huge layoffs, possible closings of hospitals, and reductions in services. These problems were so serious that they prompted the British government to initiate an effort to bring costs under control. Some experts estimate that it will take another $15 billion (over the $24 billion already spent) to get the NPIT initiative fully functional.

Sources: T. Shifrin, "U.K. Gov't 'Loses' $1.7 Billion in Data Transfer," *Computerworld,* April 27, 2007; H. Havenstein, "U.K. Agency Hopes Integration Tools Boost Quality of Health Data," *Computerworld,* January 30, 2006; S. Gibson, "Accenture Stumbles on U.K. Health Work," *eWeek,* March 29, 2006; P. McDougall, "One Sick IT Project," *InformationWeek,* June 5, 2006; L. McCartney, "U.K. Dept of Health: Prescription for Disaster," *Baseline Magazine,* November 13, 2006; V. Loh, "Stupid Technology Tricks of 2006," *eWeek,* December 10, 2006; "NHS Software Supplier Reshuffles CEO," *CIO,* June 15, 2006; *www.connectingforhealth.nhs.uk/,* accessed May 7, 2007.

QUESTIONS

1. You are the director of Britain's National Health Service. What would you do to get the project back on track?
2. Is the NPIT project simply too big for anyone to attempt? Why or why not?

Web Resources wiley.com/college/rainer

Student Web Site
- Web Quizzes
- Student Lecture Slides in PowerPoint
- Virtual Company ClubIT: Website and Assignments

WileyPLUS
- e-book
- Flash Cards
- How-To Animations for Microsoft Office

Acquiring Information Systems for Club IT

The assignments on the *WileyPLUS* Web site will ask you to make recommendations for overall improvements on how to upgrade the club's information management capabilities.

wiley.com/college/rainer

Technology Guide 1

Computer Hardware

Learning Objectives

1. Identify the major hardware components of a computer system.
2. Describe the design and functioning of the central processing unit.
3. Discuss the relationships between microprocessor component designs and performance.
4. Describe the main types of primary and secondary storage.
5. Distinguish between primary and secondary storage along the dimensions of speed, cost, and capacity.
6. Define enterprise storage, and describe the various types of enterprise storage.
7. Describe the hierarchy of computers according to power and their respective roles.
8. Differentiate the various types of input and output technologies and their uses.
9. Discuss the innovations in hardware utilization.
10. Discuss strategic issues that link hardware design to business strategy.

TG1.1 Introduction

Decisions about hardware focus on three interrelated factors: appropriateness for the task, speed, and cost. The incredible rate of innovation in the computer industry complicates hardware decisions, because computer technologies become obsolete more quickly than other organizational technologies.

This Technology Guide will help you better understand the computer hardware decisions in your organization as well as your personal computing decisions. Many of the design principles presented here apply to computers of all sizes, from an enterprise-wide system to a personal PC. In addition, the dynamics of innovation and cost that we discuss can affect corporate as well as personal hardware decisions.

You might be wondering: Why do I have to know anything about hardware? There are several reasons why it is advantageous to know hardware basics. First, regardless of your major (and future functional area in an organization), you will be using hardware throughout your career. Second, you will have input concerning the hardware you are using, such as whether it is performing adequately for your needs; if not, what problems you are having with it, and many other such issues. Third, you will also have input into decisions such as when your functional area or organization upgrades its hardware. MIS employees will act as advisers, but you will provide important input into such decisions. Finally, in some organizations, the budget for hardware is allocated to functional areas or departments, meaning that you might be making hardware decisions (at least locally) yourself.

As we noted in Chapter 1, *hardware* refers to the physical equipment used for the input, processing, output, and storage activities of a computer system. It consists of the following:

- *Central processing unit (CPU)*. Manipulates the data and controls the tasks performed by the other components.
- *Primary storage*. Temporarily stores data and program instructions during processing.
- *Secondary storage*. Is external to the CPU; stores data and programs for future use.
- *Input technologies*. Accept data and instructions and convert them to a form that the computer can understand.
- *Output technologies*. Present data and information in a form people can understand.
- *Communication technologies*. Provide for the flow of data from external computer networks (e.g., the Internet and intranets) to the CPU, and from the CPU to computer networks.

Before you go on . . .

1. Decisions about hardware focus on what three factors?
2. Define hardware and list the major hardware components.

TG1.2 The Central Processing Unit

The **central processing unit (CPU)** performs the actual computation or "number crunching" inside any computer. The CPU is a **microprocessor** (for example, an Itanium2 by Intel) made up of millions of microscopic transistors embedded in a circuit on a silicon wafer or *chip*. Hence, microprocessors are commonly referred to as chips.

As shown in Figure TG1.1, the microprocessor has different parts, which perform different functions. The **control unit** sequentially accesses program instructions, decodes them, and controls the flow of data to and from the ALU, the registers, the caches, primary

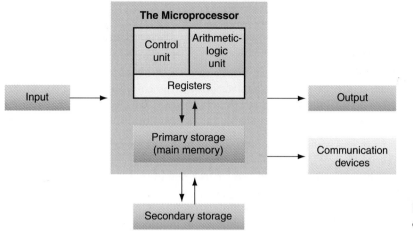

FIGURE TG1.1   Parts of a microprocessor.

storage, secondary storage, and various output devices. The **arithmetic-logic unit** (**ALU**) performs the mathematic calculations and makes logical comparisons. The **registers** are high-speed storage areas that store very small amounts of data and instructions for short periods of time.

How the CPU Works

In the CPU, inputs enter and are stored until needed. When needed, they are retrieved and processed, and the output is stored and then delivered somewhere. Figure TG1.2 illustrates this process, which works as follows.

- The inputs consist of data and brief instructions about what to do with the data. These instructions come from software in other parts of the computer. Data might be entered by the user through the keyboard, for example, or read from a data file in another part of the computer. The inputs are stored in registers until they are sent to the next step in the processing.

- Data and instructions travel in the chip via electrical pathways called buses. The size of the bus—analogous to the width of a highway—determines how much information can flow at any time.

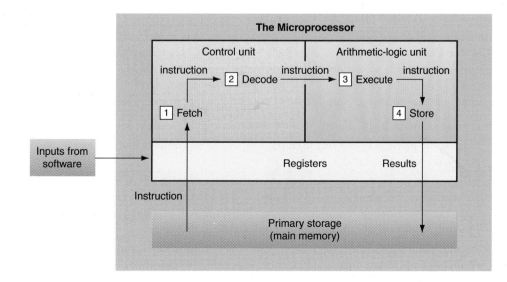

FIGURE TG1.2   How the CPU works.

- The control unit directs the flow of data and instructions within the chip.

- The arithmetic-logic unit (ALU) receives the data and instructions from the registers and makes the desired computation. These data and instructions have been translated into **binary form**, that is, only 0s and 1s. The CPU can process only binary data.

- The data in their original form and the instructions are sent to storage registers and then are sent back to a storage place outside the chip, such as the computer's hard drive (discussed below). Meanwhile, the transformed data go to another register and then on to other parts of the computer (to the monitor for display or to storage, for example).

Intel offers excellent demonstrations of how CPUs work: see *http://www97.intel.com/discover/ JourneyInside/TJI_Curriculum/default.aspx.*

This cycle of processing, known as a **machine instruction cycle**, occurs billions of times per second. Processing speed depends on clock speed, word length, bus width, and the number of transistors on the chip.

The **clock speed** is the preset speed of the clock that times all chip activities, measured in *megahertz* (MHz, millions of cycles per second) and *gigahertz* (GHz, billions of cycles per second). The **word length** is the number of binary units, or **bits** (0s and 1s) that the CPU can process in one machine cycle. Current chips handle 64-bit word lengths, meaning that a chip can process 64 bits of data in one machine cycle. The larger the word length, the faster the chip.

As previously discussed, the **bus width** is the size of the physical paths down which the data and instructions travel as electrical impulses. The wider the bus, the more data can be moved and the faster the processing.

We want to pack as many transistors into the chip as possible. If the chip is very compact and efficiently laid out, then data and instructions do not have far to travel while being stored or processed. The distance between transistors is known as **line width**. Line width is expressed in nanometers (billionths of a meter). Technological advances are creating CPUs with 45-nanometer line widths (0.045 micron), enabling the chip to have one billion transistors. The smaller the line width, the more transistors that can be packed onto a chip, and the faster the chip.

Although these four factors are quantifiable, differences in the factors between one chip and another make it difficult to compare the speeds of different processors. As a result, Intel and other chip manufacturers have developed a number of benchmarks to compare processor speeds.

Advances in Microprocessor Design

Innovations in chip designs are coming at a faster and faster rate, as described by **Moore's Law**. In 1965, Gordon Moore, a co-founder of Intel Corporation, predicted that microprocessor complexity would double approximately every two years. His prediction has been amazingly accurate.

The advances predicted from Moore's Law come mainly from the following changes:

- Producing increasingly miniaturized transistors.

- Making the physical layout of the chip's components as compact and efficient as possible; that is, decreasing line width.

- Using materials for the chip that improve the *conductivity* (flow) of electricity. Chips traditionally have been made of silicon, which is a semiconductor of electricity; that is, electrons can flow through it at a certain rate. Materials such as gallium arsenide and silicon germanium allow even faster electron travel, although they are more expensive.

- Placing multiple processors on a single chip. Chips with more than one process are called *multicore* chips. For example, the Cell chip, produced by a consortium of Sony, Toshiba, and

IBM, contains nine processors. The Cell chip enables graphics-rich computing, and is also used in TV sets and home theaters capable of downloading and showing large numbers of high-definition programs. Intel (*www.intel.com*) and AMD (*www.amd.com*) have chips with four processors, called quad-core chips. In addition, Intel is developing a chip with 80 processors that will be able to perform more than 1 trillion floating point operations per second, or 1 *teraflop*. A floating point operation is an arithmetic operation involving decimals.

In addition to increased speeds and performance, Moore's Law has had an impact on costs. For example, in 1997 a personal computer with a 233-MHz Intel Pentium II chip, 64 megabytes of RAM, a 4-gigabyte hard disk, and a 17-inch monitor cost about $4,000. As of mid-2007, a personal computer with a dual-core Intel chip (two processors on one chip), one gigabyte of RAM, a 250-gigabyte hard drive, the Windows Vista operating system, Office Productivity and Security software, and a 19-inch flat-screen monitor cost about $1,700 (from *www.dell.com*).

Although organizations certainly benefit from microprocessors that are faster, they also benefit from chips that are less powerful but are smaller and less expensive. These chips, known as **microcontrollers**, are embedded in countless products and technologies, from cellular telephones to toys to automobile sensors. Microprocessors and microcontrollers are similar except that microcontrollers usually cost less and work in less demanding applications.

Before you go on . . .

1. Briefly describe how a microprocessor functions.
2. What factors determine the speed of the microprocessor?
3. How are microprocessor designs advancing?

TG1.3 Computer Memory

The amount and type of memory that a computer possesses has a great deal to do with its general utility. A computer's memory can affect the types of programs it can run, the work it can do, its speed, the cost of the machine, and the cost of processing data. There are two basic categories of computer memory. The first, *primary storage*, is called "primary" because it stores small amounts of data and information that will be used immediately by the CPU. The second, *secondary storage*, stores much larger amounts of data and information (an entire software program, for example) for extended periods of time.

Memory Capacity

As we have seen, CPUs process only binary units—0s and 1s—which are translated through computer languages (covered in Technology Guide 2) into bits. A particular combination of bits represents a certain alphanumeric character or a simple mathematical operation. Eight bits are needed to represent any one of these characters. This 8-bit string is known as a **byte**. The storage capacity of a computer is measured in bytes. Bits typically are used as units of measure only for telecommunications capacity, as in how many million bits per second can be sent through a particular medium.

The hierarchy of terms used to describe memory capacity is as follows:

- **Kilobyte**. *Kilo* means 1 thousand, so a kilobyte (KB) is approximately 1,000 bytes. Actually, a kilobyte is 1,024 bytes.
- **Megabyte**. *Mega* means 1 million, so a megabyte (MB) is approximately 1 million bytes. Most personal computers have hundreds of megabytes of RAM memory (a type of primary storage, discussed later).

- **Gigabyte**. *Giga* means 1 billion, so a gigabyte (GB) is approximately 1 billion bytes. The storage capacity of a hard drive (a type of secondary storage, discussed shortly) in modern personal computers is hundreds of gigabytes.
- **Terabyte**. A terabyte is approximately 1 trillion bytes.
- **Petabyte**. A petabyte is approximately 1,000 terabytes.
- **Exabyte**. An exabyte is approximately 1,000 petabytes.
- **Zettabyte**. A zettabyte is approximately 1,000 exabytes.

To get a feel for these amounts, consider the following example. If your computer has 320 GB of storage capacity on its hard drive (a type of secondary storage), it can store approximately 320 billion bytes of data. If the average page of text has about 2,000 bytes, then your hard drive could store some 160 million pages of text.

Primary Storage

Primary storage, or *main memory*, as it is sometimes called, stores three types of information for very brief periods of time: (1) data to be processed by the CPU, (2) instructions for the CPU as to how to process the data, and (3) operating system programs that manage various aspects of the computer's operation. Primary storage takes place in chips mounted on the computer's main circuit board, called the *motherboard*, which are located as close as physically possible to the CPU chip. (See Figure TG1.3.) As with the CPU, all the data and instructions in primary storage have been translated into binary code.

The four main types of primary storage are (1) register, (2) random access memory (RAM), (3) cache memory, and (4) read-only memory (ROM). The logic of primary storage is that those components that will be used immediately are stored in very small amounts as close to the CPU as possible. Remember that, as with CPU chip design, the shorter the distance the electrical impulses (data) have to travel, the faster they can be transported and processed.

Registers. As indicated earlier, registers are part of the CPU. They have the least capacity, storing extremely limited amounts of instructions and data only immediately before and after processing.

Random Access Memory. **Random access memory (RAM)** is the part of primary storage that holds a software program and small amounts of data for processing. When you start most software programs on your computer (such as Microsoft Word), the entire program is brought from secondary storage into RAM. As you use the program, small parts of the program's instructions and data are sent into the registers and then to the CPU. Compared with the registers, RAM stores more information and is located farther away from the CPU. However, compared with secondary storage, RAM stores less information and is much closer to the CPU. Again, getting the data and instructions as close to the CPU as possible is vital to the computer's speed. Also vital is the fact that the RAM is a type of microprocessor chip. As we shall discuss later, microprocessor chips are much faster (and more costly) than secondary storage devices. It is easy and inexpensive to add RAM to a computer system. As of mid-2007, 1 gigabyte of RAM cost less than $280.

RAM is temporary and, in most cases, *volatile*. That is, RAM chips lose their contents if the current is lost or turned off, as in a power surge, brownout, or electrical noise generated by lightning or nearby machines. However, there are nonvolatile RAM technologies, such as magnetic RAM, discussed below. RAM chips are located directly on the motherboard or in other chips located on peripheral cards that plug into the main circuit board.

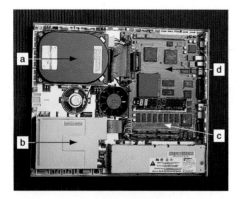

FIGURE TG1.3   Internal workings of a common personal computer: (a) hard disk drive; (b) floppy disk drive; (c) RAM; (d) CPU board with fan. *Source*: Jerome Yeats/Photo Researchers, Inc.

The two main types of RAM are *dynamic RAM* (*DRAM*) and *static RAM* (*SRAM*). DRAM memory chips offer the greatest capacities and the lowest cost per bit, but they are relatively slow. SRAM costs more than DRAM, but it is faster. For this reason, SRAM is the preferred choice for performance-sensitive applications, including the external L2 and L3 caches (discussed below) that speed up microprocessor performance.

An emerging technology is *magnetic RAM (MRAM)*. As its name suggests, MRAM uses magnetism, rather than electricity, to store data. One major advantage of MRAM over DRAM and SRAM is that it is nonvolatile. DRAM wastes a lot of electricity because it needs to be supplied with a constant current to store data. MRAM requires only a tiny amount of electricity. In essence, MRAM combines the high speed of SRAM, the storage capacity of DRAM, and the nonvolatility of flash memory (discussed later in this Technology Guide).

Cache Memory.   **Cache memory** is a type of high-speed memory that enables the computer to temporarily store blocks of data that are used more often and that a processor can access more rapidly than main memory (RAM). It augments RAM in the following way: Many modern computer applications (Microsoft Windows Vista, for example) are very complex and have huge numbers of instructions. It takes considerable RAM capacity (usually a minimum of 512 megabytes) to store the entire instruction set. Also, many applications might exceed your RAM. In either case, your processor must go to secondary storage to retrieve the necessary instructions. To alleviate this problem, software is often written in smaller blocks of instructions. As these blocks are needed, they can be brought from secondary storage into RAM. This process is still slow, however.

Cache memory is a place closer to the CPU than RAM where the computer can temporarily store those blocks of instructions that are used most often. Blocks used less often remain in RAM until they are transferred to cache; blocks used infrequently remain in secondary storage. Cache memory is faster than RAM because the instructions travel a shorter distance to the CPU.

Read-only Memory.   Most of us have lost data at one time or another due to a computer "crash" or a power failure. What is usually lost is whatever is in RAM, cache, or the registers at the time, because these types of memory are volatile. Therefore, we need greater security when we are storing certain types of critical data or instructions. Cautious computer users frequently save data to nonvolatile memory (secondary storage). In addition, most modern software applications have autosave functions. Programs stored in secondary storage, even though they are temporarily copied into RAM when they are being used, remain intact because only the copy is lost, not the original.

Read-only memory (ROM) is the place—actually, a type of chip—where certain critical instructions are safeguarded. ROM is nonvolatile, so it retains these instructions when the power to the computer is turned off. The read-only designation means that these instructions can only be read by the computer and cannot be changed by the user. An example of ROM is the instructions needed to start or "boot" the computer after it has been shut off.

Secondary Storage

Secondary storage is designed to store very large amounts of data for extended periods of time. Secondary storage can have memory capacity of several terabytes or more. Significantly, only small portions of that data are placed in primary storage at any one time. Secondary storage has the following characteristics:

- It is nonvolatile.
- It takes more time to retrieve data from secondary storage than it does from RAM.

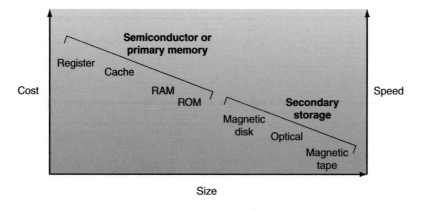

FIGURE TG 1.4
Primary memory
compared to secondary
storage.

- It is cheaper than primary storage (see Figure TG1.4).
- It can take place on a variety of media, each with its own technology, as we discuss next. The overall trends in secondary storage are toward more direct-access methods, higher capacity with lower costs, and increased portability.

Magnetic Media. **Magnetic tape** is kept on a large open reel or in a smaller cartridge or cassette. Although this is an old technology, it remains popular because it is the cheapest storage medium, and it can handle enormous amounts of data. The downside is that it is the slowest method for retrieving data, because all the data are placed on the tape sequentially. **Sequential access** means that the system might have to run through the majority of the tape before it comes to the desired piece of data.

Magnetic tape storage often is used for information that an organization must maintain but uses only rarely or does not need immediate access to. Industries with huge numbers of files (e.g., insurance companies) use magnetic tape systems. Modern versions of magnetic tape systems use cartridges and often a robotic system that selects and loads the appropriate cartridge automatically. There are also some tape systems, like digital audio tapes (DAT), for smaller applications such as storing copies of all the contents of a personal computer's secondary storage ("backing up" the storage).

Magnetic disks are a form of secondary storage on a magnetized disk that is divided into tracks and sectors that provide addresses for various pieces of data. They come in a variety of styles and are popular because they allow much more rapid access to the data than does magnetic tape. Magnetic disks, called **hard drives** or fixed disk drives, are the most commonly used mass storage devices because of their low cost, high speed, and large storage capacity. Hard disk drives read from, and write to, stacks of rotating (at up to 15,000 RPM) magnetic disk platters mounted in rigid enclosures and sealed against environmental and atmospheric contamination. These disks are permanently mounted in a unit that may be internal or external to the computer.

Hard drives store data on platters that are divided into concentric tracks. Each track is further divided into segments called *sectors*. To access a given sector, a read/write head pivots across the rotating disks to locate the right track, which is calculated from an index table. The head then waits as the disk rotates until the right sector is underneath it (see Figure TG1.5). Because the head floats just above the surface of the disk (less than 25 microns), any bit of dust or contamination can disrupt the device. When this happens, it is called a *disk crash*, and it usually results in catastrophic loss of data. For this reason, hard drives are hermetically sealed when they are manufactured.

Every piece of data has an address attached to it, corresponding to a particular track and sector. Any piece of desired data can be retrieved in a nonsequential manner, by direct access.

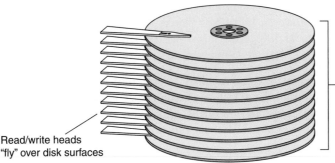

11 disks
20 recording surfaces
3,500 RPMs

Read/write heads
"fly" over disk surfaces

FIGURE TG1.5
Read/write heads.

This is why hard disk drives are sometimes called *direct access storage devices*. The read/write heads use the data's address to quickly find and read the data (see Figure TG1.5). Unlike magnetic tape, the system does not have to read through all the data to find what it wants.

Modern personal computers typically have internal hard drives with storage capacity ranging from hundreds of gigabytes to several terabytes. Data access is very fast, measured in milliseconds, though still much slower than RAM. Because they are somewhat susceptible to mechanical failure, and because users may need to take all their hard drive's contents to another location, many users back up their hard drive's contents with either a portable hard disk drive system or thumb drives (discussed later in this chapter).

To take advantage of the new, faster technologies, disk drive interfaces must also be faster. Most PCs and workstations use one of two high-performance disk interface standards: *Enhanced Integrated Drive Electronics* (*EIDE*) or *Small Computer Systems Interface* (*SCSI*). EIDE offers good performance, is inexpensive, and supports up to four disks, tapes, or CD-ROM drives. In contrast, SCSI drives are more expensive than EIDE drives, but they offer a faster interface and support more devices. SCSI interfaces are therefore used for graphics workstations, server-based storage, and large databases.

Optical Storage Devices. Unlike magnetic media, **optical storage devices** do not store data via magnetism. Rather, a laser reads the surface of a reflective plastic platter. Optical disk drives are slower than magnetic hard drives, but they are less susceptible to damage from contamination and are less fragile.

In addition, optical disks can store a great deal of information, both on a routine basis and when combined into storage systems. Optical disk storage systems are often implemented in the form of optical jukeboxes, which store many disks and operate much like the automated phonograph record changers for which they are named. Types of optical disks include compact disk read-only memory (CD-ROM) and digital video disk (DVD).

Compact Disk, Read-Only Memory. **Compact disk, read-only memory (CD-ROM)** storage devices feature high capacity, low cost, and high durability. However, because a CD-ROM is a read-only medium, it cannot be written on. Compact disk, rewritable (CD-RW) adds rewritability to the recordable compact disk market.

Digital Video Disk. The **digital video disk (DVD)** is a 5-inch disk with the capacity to store about 135 minutes of digital video. DVD provides sharp detail, true color, no flicker, and no snow. DVDs can also perform as computer storage disks, providing storage capabilities of 17 gigabytes. DVD players can read current CD-ROMs, but current CD-ROM players cannot read DVDs. The access speed of a DVD drive is faster than that of a typical CD-ROM drive.

Today, two standards are competing to replace the standard DVD: Blu-Ray and High-Density DVD (HD DVD). The two technologies do not work together, and it is unlikely that both will survive. Blu-Ray offers greater capacity (25 gigabytes per side) than HD DVD (15 gigabytes per side). However, HD DVD devices are much cheaper (about $500) than Blu-ray devices ($1,000 to $1,500). Experts say that the best choice for consumers is to wait until one standard wins, because you do not want to be stuck with an obsolete technology.

__Holographic Memory.__ **Holographic memory** is an optical technology that uses a three-dimensional medium to store data. InPhase Technologies (*www.inphase-technologies.com*) has produced a write-once, read-many (WORM) optical disk that stores 300 gigabytes. Each disk has 63 times the capacity of a DVD and can store more than 35 hours of broadcast-quality video.

Flash Memory Devices. **Flash memory** is nonvolatile computer memory that can be electrically erased and reprogrammed. This technology can be built into a system or installed on a personal computer card.

Flash memory devices (or *memory cards*) are electronic storage devices that contain no moving parts and use 30 times less battery power than hard drives. Flash devices are also smaller and more durable than hard drives. The trade-offs are that flash devices store less data than hard drives and are more expensive.

There are many different types of flash devices, and they are used in many different places. For example, flash devices are used with digital cameras, handheld and laptop computers, telephones, music players, and video game consoles. Apple (*www.apple.com*) replaced the micro-hard-drive-based iPod Mini with the flash-based iPod Nano for four reasons: (1) rapid improvements in the storage capacity of flash memory chips, (2) rapid decreases in cost, (3) much longer battery life, and (4) smaller size.

One popular flash memory device is the **thumb drive** (also called *memory stick, jump drive*, or *flash drive*). These devices fit into Universal Serial Bus (USB) ports on personal computers and other devices, and they can store many gigabytes. Thumb drives have replaced magnetic floppy disks for portable storage (see Figure TG1.6).

Enterprise Storage Systems

To deal with ever-expanding volumes of information, companies employ enterprise storage systems. An **enterprise storage system** is an independent, external system that includes two or more storage devices. Enterprise storage systems provide large amounts of storage, high-performance data transfer, a high degree of availability, protection against data loss, and sophisticated management tools.

The performance of enterprise storage system hardware has improved very rapidly. In 1956, the first disk storage unit was the size of two refrigerators, and it stored 5 megabytes of information. Current disk storage units are half that size, and they store 320 terabytes. The three major types of enterprise storage systems are redundant arrays of independent disks, storage area networks, and network-attached storage.

FIGURE TG1.6 Thumb drive. *Source: www.dansdata.com/images/pclock/rx800.jpg*

Redundant Arrays of Independent Disks. Hard drives in all computer systems are susceptible to failures caused by temperature variations, head crashes, motor failure, and changing voltage conditions. To improve reliability and to protect the data in their enterprise storage systems, many organizations use **redundant arrays of independent disks (RAID)** storage products. RAID links groups of standard hard drives to a specialized microcontroller. The microcontroller coordinates the drives so that they appear as a single logical drive, but they take advantage of the multiple physical drives by storing data redundantly, meaning data that are duplicated in multiple places. This arrangement protects against data loss due to the failure of any single drive.

Storage Area Network.   A **storage area network (SAN)** is an architecture for building special, dedicated networks that allow rapid and reliable access to storage devices by multiple servers. **Storage over IP**, sometimes called *IP over SCSI* or *iSCSI*, is a technology that uses the Internet Protocol to transport stored data among devices within a SAN. SANs employ **storage visualization software** to graphically plot an entire network and allow storage administrators to monitor all networked storage devices from a single console.

Network-Attached Storage.   A **network-attached storage (NAS)** device is a special-purpose server that provides file storage to users who access the device over a network. The NAS server is simple to install (i.e., plug-and-play) and works exactly like a general-purpose file server, so no user retraining or special software is needed.

Table TG1.1 compares the advantages and disadvantages of the various secondary storage media.

Secondary Storage

Type	Advantages	Disadvantages	Application
Magnetic Storage Devices			
Magnetic tape	Lowest cost per unit stored.	Sequential access means slow retrieval speeds.	Corporate data archiving.
Hard drive	Relatively high capacity and fast retrieval speed.	Fragile; high cost per unit stored.	Personal computers through mainframes.
RAID	High capacity; designed for fault tolerance and reduced risk of data loss; low cost per unit stored.	Expensive, semipermanent installation.	Corporate data storage that requires frequent, rapid access.
SAN	High capacity; designed for large amounts of enterprise data.	Expensive.	Corporate data storage that requires frequent, rapid access.
NAS	High capacity; designed for large amounts of enterprise data.	Expensive.	Corporate data storage that requires frequent, rapid access.
Memory cards	Portable; easy to use; less failure-prone than hard drives.	Expensive.	Personal and laptop computers.
Thumb drives	Extremely portable and easy to use.	Relatively expensive.	Consumer electronic devices; moving files from portable devices to desktop computers.
Optical Storage Devices			
CD-ROM	Moderate capacity; moderate cost per unit stored; high durability.	Slower retrieval speeds than hard drives; only certain types can be rewritten.	Personal computers through corporate data storage.
DVD	Moderate capacity; moderate cost per unit stored.	Slower retrieval speeds than hard drives.	Personal computers through corporate data storage.

Table TG1.1

Before you go on . . .

1. Describe the four main types of primary storage.
2. Describe different types of secondary storage.
3. How does primary storage differ from secondary storage in terms of speed, cost, and capacity?
4. Describe the three types of enterprise storage systems.

TG1.4 Computer Hierarchy

Computer hardware has evolved through five stages, or generations of technology: vacuum tubes, transistors, integrated circuits, ultra-large-scale integrated circuits, and massively parallel processing. Each generation has provided increased processing power and storage capacity while simultaneously exhibiting decreasing costs.

The traditional way of comparing classes of computers is by their processing power. Analysts typically divide computers—called the *platform* in the computer industry—into six categories: supercomputers, mainframes, midrange computers (minicomputers and servers), workstations, microcomputers, and computing devices. Recently, the lines among these categories have become blurred. This section presents each class of computers, beginning with the most powerful and ending with the least powerful.

Supercomputers

The term **supercomputer** does not refer to a specific technology. Rather, it indicates the fastest computing engines available at any given time. Supercomputer speeds can exceed 100 teraflops.

People generally use supercomputers for computationally demanding tasks on very large data sets. Rather than transaction processing and business applications—the forte of mainframes and other multiprocessing platforms—supercomputers typically run military and scientific applications. Although they cost millions of dollars, they are being used for commercial applications where huge amounts of data must be analyzed.

Mainframe Computers

Although mainframe computers are increasingly viewed as just another type of server, albeit at the high end of the performance and reliability scales, they remain a distinct class of systems differentiated by hardware and software features. **Mainframes** remain popular in large enterprises for extensive computing applications that are accessed by thousands of concurrent users. Examples of mainframe applications are airline reservation systems, corporate payroll programs, Web site transaction processing systems (e.g., Amazon and eBay), and student grade calculation and reporting.

Source: Courtesy of International Business Machines Corporation. Unauthorized use is not permitted.

Mainframes are less powerful and generally less expensive than supercomputers. A mainframe system can have up to hundreds of gigabytes of primary storage. Secondary storage (see the earlier discussion of enterprise storage systems) may use high-capacity magnetic and optical storage media with capacities in the terabyte range. Typically, several hundred or thousands of online computers can be linked to a single mainframe. Today's most advanced mainframes perform at teraflop speeds and can handle billions of transactions per day.

Some large organizations that began moving away from mainframes toward distributed systems now are moving back toward mainframes because of their centralized administration, high reliability, and increasing flexibility. This process is called *recentralization*. This shift has occurred for several reasons, including the following:

- Supporting the high transaction levels associated with e-commerce
- Reducing the total cost of ownership of distributed systems
- Simplifying administration
- Reducing support-personnel requirements
- Improving system performance

In addition, mainframe computing provides a secure, robust environment in which to run strategic, mission-critical applications.

Midrange Computers

Larger midrange computers, called **minicomputers**, are relatively small, inexpensive, and compact computers that perform the same functions as mainframe computers, but to a more limited extent. In fact, the lines between minicomputers and mainframes have blurred in both price and performance. Minicomputers are a type of **server**, supporting computer networks and enabling users to share files, software, peripheral devices, and other resources. Note that mainframes are a type of server as well, providing support for entire enterprise networks.

Minicomputers can provide flexibility to organizations that do not want to spend IT dollars on mainframes, which are less scalable. Scalable computers are inexpensive enough so that adding more computers of that type is not prohibitive. Because mainframes are so expensive, we say that they are not very scalable.

Organizations with heavy transaction-processing requirements often utilize multiple servers in *server farms*. As companies pack greater numbers of servers in their server farms, they increasingly use pizza-box-sized servers called *rack servers* that can be stacked in racks. These computers run cooler and thus can be packed more closely, requiring less space. To further increase density, companies use a server design called a blade. A *blade* is a card about the size of a paperback book on which the memory, processor, and hard drives are mounted.

Workstations

Computer vendors originally developed desktop engineering workstations, or workstations for short, to provide the high levels of performance demanded by engineers. That is, **workstations** run computationally intensive scientific, engineering, and financial applications. Workstations are typically based on RISC architecture and provide both very high-speed calculations and high-resolution graphic displays. These computers are widely used within the scientific and business communities. Workstation applications include electronic and mechanical design, medical imaging, scientific visualization, 3-D animation, and video editing. Today, the distinction between workstations and personal computers is negligible.

Microcomputers

Microcomputers—also called *micros, personal computers*, or *PCs*—are the smallest and least expensive category of general-purpose computers. It is important to point out that the term, PC, often connotes using the Microsoft Windows operating system. In fact, a variety of PCs are available, many of which do not use Windows, such as the Apple MacIntosh which uses the MacIntosh OS X operating system (discussed in Technology Guide 2).

Microcomputers can be subdivided into five classifications based on their size: desktops, thin clients, notebooks and laptops, and ultra-mobile PCs.

Desktop PCs.   The *desktop personal computer* has become the dominant method of accessing workgroup and enterprisewide applications. It is the typical, familiar microcomputer system that has become a standard tool for business and the home. It typically has a CPU and a separate but connected monitor and keyboard. In general, modern microcomputers have a several gigabytes of primary storage, a rewriteable CD-ROM and a DVD drive, and hundreds of gigabytes of secondary storage.

Thin-Client Systems. **Thin-client systems** are desktop computer systems that do not offer the full functionality of a PC. Compared to a PC, or **fat client**, thin clients are less complex, particularly because they lack locally installed software. That is, a thin client would not have Microsoft Office installed on it. Thus, they are easier and less expensive to operate and support than PCs. The benefits of thin clients include fast application deployment, centralized management, lower cost of ownership, and easier installation, management, maintenance, and support. The main disadvantage of thin clients is that if the network fails, then users can do very little on their computers. For example, if users have fat clients and the network fails, then they can still use Microsoft Office because it is installed on their computers.

Laptop and Notebook Computers. As computers have become much smaller and vastly more powerful, they also have become portable. **Laptop and notebook computers** are small, easily transportable, lightweight microcomputers that fit easily into a briefcase. In general, notebook computers are smaller than laptops. Notebooks and laptops are designed for maximum convenience and transportability. They provide users with access to processing power and data outside an office environment. At the same time, they cost more than desktops for similar functionality.

Ultra-mobile PCs. **Ultra-mobile personal computers (PCs)** are small, mobile computers that run various mobile operating systems. Ultra-mobile PCs have the full functionality of a desktop computer, but they are smaller and lighter than traditional laptop and notebook computers. These computers have multiple input methods, including touch screen, stylus, speech, and Bluetooth or traditional keyboard. Figure TG1.7 shows an ultra-mobile PC.

Computing Devices

Improved computer technology has led to the development of improved, ever-smaller computing/communication devices. Technology such as wearable computing/communication devices is now common. This section briefly looks at some of these new computing devices.

Wearable computers (wearable devices) are designed to be worn and used on the body. Industrial applications of wearable computers include systems for factory automation, warehouse management, and performance support, such as viewing technical manuals and diagrams while building or repairing something. The technology is already widely used in such diverse industries as freight delivery (e.g., the electronic tablet that your UPS courier carries), aerospace, securities trading, law enforcement, and the military.

Embedded computers are placed inside other products to add features and capabilities. For example, the average mid-sized automobile has more than 3,000 embedded computers, called *controllers*, that monitor every function from braking to engine performance to seat controls with memory.

Other small-sized computing devices are active badges and memory buttons. *Active badges* can be worn as ID cards by employees who wish to stay in touch at all times while moving around the corporate premises. *Memory buttons* are nickel-sized devices that store a small database relating to whatever they are attached to. These devices are similar to a bar code, but they contain far more information.

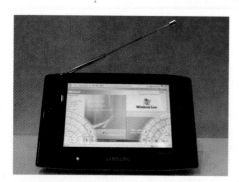

FIGURE TG1.7 Ultra-mobile PC.
Source: Andreas Rentz/Getty Images/ NewsCom.

FIGURE TG1.8 Bluetooth laser virtual keyboard. *Source*: WENN Photos/NewsCom.

TG1.5 Input and Output Technologies

Input technologies allow people and other technologies to put data into a computer. The two main types of input devices are human data entry devices and source-data automation devices. As their name implies, *human data entry* devices require a certain amount of human effort to input data. Examples are keyboard, mouse, pointing stick, trackball, joystick, touchscreen, stylus, and voice-recognition.

An interesting development in keyboard technology is the Bluetooth laser virtual keyboard (see Figure TG1.8). This device, only 3.5 inches high, uses a laser to project a full QWERTY keyboard on any flat surface. (QWERTY are the first six alphabetic keys, from left to right, on a standard keyboard.) The device connects to smart phones and computers using Bluetooth (discussed in Chapter 7).

In contrast, *source-data automation* devices input data with minimal human intervention. These technologies speed up data collection, reduce errors, and gather data at the source of a transaction or other event. Barcode readers are an example of source-data automation. Table TG1.2 describes the various input devices.

The output generated by a computer can be transmitted to the user via several output devices and media. These devices include monitors, printers, plotters, and voice. Table TG1.3 describes the various output devices.

Multimedia technology is the computer-based integration of text, sound, still images, animation, and digitized motion video. It merges the capabilities of computers with televisions, VCRs, CD players, DVD players, video and audio recording equipment, and music and gaming technologies. Multimedia usually represents a collection of various input and output technologies. High-quality multimedia processing requires powerful microprocessors and extensive memory capacity, including both primary and secondary storage.

TG1.6 Innovations in Hardware Utilization

To fully understand hardware, we should have an idea of how fast hardware is changing. In this section we discuss how companies are using their hardware resources in innovative ways, including server farms, virtualization, grid computing, utility computing, edge computing, autonomic computing, and nanotechnology.

Input Devices

Input Device	Description
Human Data Entry Devices	
Keyboards	Most common input device (for text and numerical data).
Mouse	Handheld device used to point cursor at point on screen, such as an icon; user clicks button on mouse instructing computer to take some action.
Optical mouse	Mouse is not connected to computer by a cable; mouse uses camera chip to take images of surface it passes over, comparing successive images to determine its position.
Trackball	User rotates a ball built into top of device to move cursor (rather than moving entire device such as a mouse).
Pointing stick	Small button-like device; cursor moves in the direction of the pressure you place on the stick.
Touchpad	User moves cursor by sliding finger across a sensitized pad and then can tap pad when cursor is in desired position to instruct computer to take action (also called *glide-and-tap pad*).
Graphics tablet	A device that can be used in place of, or in conjunction with, a mouse or trackball; has a flat surface for drawing and a pen or stylus that is programmed to work with the tablet.
Joystick	Joystick moves cursor to desired place on screen; commonly used in workstations that display dynamic graphics and in video games.
Touch screen	Users instruct computer to take some action by touching a particular part of the screen; commonly used in information kiosks such as ATM machines.
Stylus	Pen-style device that allows user either to touch parts of a predetermined menu of options or to handwrite information into the computer (as with some PDAs); works with touch-sensitive screens.
Digital pen	Mobile device that digitally captures everything you write; built-in screen confirms what you write has been saved; also captures sketches, figures, etc.; on-board flash memory can store up to 50 pages.
Web camera (Webcam)	A real-time video camera whose images can be accessed via the Web or instant messaging.
Voice recognition	Converts voice wave sounds into digital input for computer; critical technology for physically challenged people who cannot use other input devices.
Source-Data Automation Input Devices	
Automated teller machine	A device that includes source-data automation input in the form of a magnetic stripe reader; human input via a keyboard; and output via a monitor, printer, and cash dispenser.
Magnetic stripe reader	A device that reads data from a magnetic stripe, usually on the back of a plastic card (for example, credit or debit cards).
Point-of-sale terminals	Computerized cash registers that also may incorporate touchscreen technology and barcode scanners (see below) to input data such as item sold and price.
Barcode scanners	Devices scan black-and-white barcode lines printed on merchandise labels.
Optical mark reader	Scanner for detecting presence of dark marks on predetermined grid, such as multiple-choice test answer sheets.

Magnetic ink character reader	Read magnetic ink printed on checks, which identify the bank, checking account, and check number.
Optical character recognition	Software that converts text into digital form for input into computer.
Sensors	Collect data directly from the environment and input data directly into computer; examples include your car's airbag activation sensor and radio frequency identification tags.
Cameras	Digital cameras capture images and convert them into digital files.
Retinal scanning displays	Projects an image, pixel by pixel, directly onto a viewer's retina; used with mobile devices; see Microvision's (*mvis.com*) Nomad and Xybernaut's (*xybernaut.com*) Poma.
Radio frequency identification (RFID)	Uses active or passive tags (transmitters) to wirelessly transmit product information to electronic readers.

Output Devices

Output Device	Description
Monitors	
Cathode ray tubes	Video screens on which an electron beam illuminates pixels on display screen.
Liquid crystal display (LCDs)	Flat displays that have liquid crystals between two polarizers to form characters and images on a backlit screen.
Organic light-emitting diodes (OLEDs)	Displays that are brighter, thinner, lighter, cheaper, and faster and take less power to run than LCDs.
Retinal scanning displays	Project image directly onto a viewer's retina; used in medicine, air traffic control, and controlling industrial machines.
Printers	
Laser	Use laser beams to write information on photosensitive drums; produce high-resolution text and graphics.
Inkjet	Shoot fine streams of colored ink onto paper; usually less expensive to buy than laser printers, but can be more expensive to operate; can offer resolution quality equal to laser printers.
Plotters	Use computer-directed pens for creating high-quality images, blueprints, schematics, drawing of new products, and so on.
Voice Output	A speaker/headset, which can output sounds of any type; voice output is a software function that uses this equipment.

Server Farms

Many companies are finding that they do not have enough computer processing power to meet their needs. In particular, they have an increasing shortage of facilities needed to manage, transmit, and store the data flowing from Web-based applications. To address this problem, they are building massive data centers called **server farms**, which contain hundreds of thousands of networked computer servers (see Figure TG1.9).

FIGURE TG1.9 Server Farm. *Source*: Courtesy of International Business Machines Corporation. Unauthorized use is not permitted.

The huge number of servers in a server farm provides redundancy and fault tolerance in case one or more servers fail. Server farms require massive amounts of electrical power, air conditioning, backup generators, security, and money. They also need to be located fairly closely to fiber-optic communications links.

Locations that satisfy these requirements are difficult to find. For example, Yahoo and Microsoft are building huge server farms in Quincy, Washington, to take advantage of cheap, local hydroelectric power. Google has already built a massive server farm in Oregon for the same reason.

Virtualization

According to Gartner Inc. (*www.gartner.com*), a research firm, utilization rates on servers range from 5 to 10 percent. That is, most of the time, organizations are using only a small percentage of their total computing capacity. One reason for this low rate is that most organizations buy a new server every time they implement a new application. CIOs tolerate this inefficiency in order to make certain that they can supply enough computing resources to users when they are needed. Also, server prices have dropped more than 80 percent in the last decade, making it easier and cheaper to buy another server than to increase the utilization of the servers the company already has. However, virtualization has changed this situation.

Virtualization means that servers no longer have to be dedicated to a particular task. **Server virtualization** uses software-based partitions to create multiple virtual servers (called *virtual machines*) on a single physical server. Therefore, multiple applications can run on a single physical server, with each running within its own software environment.

As an example of virtualization, consider Welch Foods (*www.welchs.com*), the food-processing and marketing arm of the National Grape Cooperative Association. Welch makes and sells Welch's juices and jellies, and it distributes the proceeds to the growers. The company deployed virtualization for flexibility in daily operations, backup and recovery, and expense savings. The company realized greater efficiency from each virtualized server, which translated to savings of more than $300,000 per year. In addition, when Welch wants to implement a new application, it creates a new partition on an existing server, and it has the application up and running in less than an hour. In the past, Welch would have purchased a new server, and it would have taken 16 to 32 days to fully implement the new application.

Grid Computing

Grid computing applies the unused processing resources of many geographically dispersed computers in a network to form a virtual supercomputer. Target problems are usually scientific or technical in nature and require a great number of computer processing cycles or access to large amounts of data.

An example of grid computing is the World-wide In Silico Docking on Malaria (WISDOM) project. Malaria is the world's most common parasitic infection, affecting more than 500 million people annually and killing more than 1 million. Utilizing 5,000 computers in 25 countries for 4 months, the project analyzed 140 million drug compounds to test their effectiveness against malaria. Project leaders estimated that in 4 months the grid approach provided the processing power that would have taken 420 years of computing on a single personal computer.

Other notable grid-computing efforts are analyzing drug compounds to target the avian flu, anthrax, smallpox, Ebola, and other infectious diseases. The IBM World Community Grid (*www.worldcommunitygrid.org*) is now being used to study the human immune-deficiency virus (HIV).

Utility Computing

In **utility computing**, a service provider makes computing resources and infrastructure management available to a customer as needed. The provider then charges the customer for specific usage rather than a flat rate. Utility computing is also called *subscription computing* and *on-demand computing*. Utility computing enables companies to efficiently meet fluctuating demands for computing power by lowering the cost of owning hardware infrastructure.

Utility computing also provides fault tolerance, redundancy, and scalability. That is, if one server fails, another takes it place. Scalability means that if an application requires additional servers, they can easily be added as they are needed.

Applied Biosystems (*www.appliedbiosystems.com*) used the Sun Grid for computational genetics. Sun Microsystems (*www.sun.com*) developed the Sun Grid to provide computer power for $1 per CPU hour (that is, the amount of computing that one processor can deliver per hour). Applied Biosystems rented time on 1,000 computers, which were able to complete the job in one week. The same job would have taken three months on the company's own servers.

Edge Computing

Edge computing is the process in which parts of Web site content and processing are located close to the user to decrease response time and lower processing costs. The three components in edge computing are: (1) the computer that you use to access a Web site; (2) small, relatively inexpensive servers—called *edge servers*—that are located in your Internet service provider (ISP); and (3) the servers of the company whose Web site you are accessing. Companies such as Akamai (*www.akamai.com*) provide edge servers, where Web content is cached for rapid access. When you make a request to a company's Web site, edge servers process it first and provide your information if it is available. If additional processing or information is necessary, your request goes to the company's servers.

Autonomic Computing

Modern IT environments are becoming more complex as the number of networked computing devices (wireline and wireless) increases and the software on these devices becomes more sophisticated. As a result, IT environments are rapidly becoming impossible for humans to adequately manage and maintain. To help resolve this problem, experts have designed **autonomic systems** that manage themselves without direct human intervention.

Organizations using autonomic systems set business policies and objectives for the self-management process. The system configures itself optimally to meet the requirements, finds and repairs hardware and software problems, and protects itself against attacks and failures. For example, much work is being done in information security to develop proactive defenses to automatically detect malicious software and disable it, even if that software has not been seen before (see Chapter 3).

Nanotechnology

Finally, **nanotechnology** refers to the creation of materials, devices, and systems at a scale of 1 to 100 nanometers (billionths of a meter). In the near future, still-experimental computers will be constructed on a nanotechnology scale and could be used literally anywhere. They will require very little power, yet they will have huge storage capacities. In an interesting application, one company, Nano Tex, incorporates nanotechnology into its fabrics to make them wrinkle free and stain resistant. For a demonstration, see *www.nano-tex.com*.

Before you go on . . .

1. What are server farms? virtualization? grid computing? utility computing? edge computing? autonomic computing?

2. What is nanotechnology?

TG1.7 Strategic Hardware Issues

This technology guide has explained how hardware is designed and how it works. However, for most businesspeople, the more complex and important issues are what the hardware enables, how it is advancing and how rapidly. In many industries, exploiting computer hardware is a key to achieving competitive advantage. Successful hardware exploitation comes from thoughtful consideration of the following questions:

- How do organizations keep up with the rapid price and performance advancements in hardware? For example, how often should an organization upgrade its computers and storage systems? Will upgrades increase personal and organizational productivity? How can organizations measure such increases?

- How should organizations determine the need for the new hardware infrastructures, such as server farms, virtualization, grid computing, and utility computing?

- Portable computers and advanced communications technologies have enabled employees to work from home or from anywhere. Will these new work styles benefit employees and the organization? How do organizations manage such new workstyles?

Before you go on . . .

1. How do you think the various types of computer hardware affect personal productivity? organizational productivity?

2. What are some disadvantages of advances in microprocessor design?

What's in IT for Me?

For All Business Majors

Practically all professional jobs in business today require computer literacy and skills for personal productivity. Going further, all industries use computer technology for one form of competitive advantage or another.

Clearly, the design of computer hardware has profound impacts for businesspeople. It is also clear that personal and organizational success can depend on an understanding of hardware design and a commitment to knowing where it is going and what opportunities and challenges innovations will bring. Because these innovations can occur so rapidly, hardware decisions at both the individual and organizational level are difficult.

At the *individual level*, most people who have a home or office computer system and want to upgrade it, or people who are contemplating their first computer purchase, are faced with the decision of *when* to buy as much as *what* to buy and at what cost. At the *organizational level*, these same issues plague IS professionals.

However, they are more complex and more costly. Most organizations have many different computer systems in place at the same time. Innovations may come to different classes of computers at different times or rates. Therefore, managers must decide when old hardware *legacy systems* still have a productive role in the IS architecture and when they should be replaced.

IS management at the corporate level is one of the most challenging careers today, due in no small part to the constant innovation in computer hardware. That may not be your career objective, but an appreciation of that area is beneficial. After all, the people who keep you equipped with the right computing hardware, as you can now see, are very important allies in your success.

1. **Identify the major hardware components of a computer system.**

Today's computer systems have six major components: the central processing unit (CPU), primary storage, secondary storage, input technologies, output technologies, and communications technologies.

2. **Describe the design and functioning of the central processing unit.**

The CPU is made up of the arithmetic-logic unit (ALU), which performs the calculations; the registers, which store minute amounts of data and instructions immediately before and after processing; and the control unit, which controls the flow of information on the microprocessor chip. After processing, the data in their original form and the instructions are sent back to a storage place outside the chip.

3. **Discuss the relationships between microprocessor component designs and performance.**

Microprocessor designs aim to increase processing speed by minimizing the physical distance that the data (as electrical impulses) must travel and by increasing the bus width, clock speed, word length, and number of transistors on the chip.

4. **Describe the main types of primary and secondary storage.**

There are four types of primary storage: registers, random access memory (RAM), cache memory, and read-only memory (ROM). All are direct access memory; only ROM is nonvolatile. Secondary storage includes magnetic media (tapes, hard drives, and thumb, or flash, drives) and optical media (CD-ROM, DVD, and optical jukeboxes).

5. **Distinguish between primary and secondary storage along the dimensions of speed, cost, and capacity.**

Primary storage has much less capacity than secondary storage, and it is faster and more expensive per byte stored. It is located much closer to the CPU than is secondary storage. Sequential-access secondary storage media such as magnetic tape are much slower and less expensive than direct access media (for example, hard drives, optical media).

6. **Define enterprise storage, and describe the various types of enterprise storage.**

An enterprise storage system is an independent, external system with intelligence that includes two or more storage devices. There are three major types of enterprise storage subsystems: redundant arrays of independent disks (RAIDs), storage area networks (SANs), and network-attached storage (NAS). RAID links groups of standard hard drives to a specialized microcontroller. SAN is an architecture for building special, dedicated networks that allow access to storage devices by multiple servers. A NAS device is a special-purpose server that provides file storage to users who access the device over a network.

Summary

7. Describe the hierarchy of computers according to power and their respective roles.

Supercomputers are the most powerful computers, designed to handle the maximum computational demands of science and the military. Mainframes are not as powerful as supercomputers, but they are powerful enough for large organizations to use for centralized data processing and large databases. Minicomputers are smaller and less powerful versions of mainframes that are often devoted to handling specific subsystems. Workstations fall in between minicomputers and personal computers in speed, capacity, and graphics capability. Desktop personal computers (PCs) are the most common personal and business computers. Laptop or notebook computers are small, easily transportable PCs. Mobile devices are now as functional as low-end laptops, and they enable employees to compute anywhere, everywhere, and anytime. Wearable computers free their users' movements. Embedded computers are placed inside other products to add features and capabilities. Employees may wear active badges as ID cards. Memory buttons store a small database relating to whatever they are attached.

8. Differentiate the various types of input and output technologies and their uses.

Principal human data entry input technologies include the keyboard, mouse, optical mouse, trackball, touchpad, joystick, touchscreen, stylus, and voice-recognition systems. Principal source-data automation input devices are ATMs, POS terminals, barcode scanners, optical mark readers, magnetic ink character readers, optical character readers, sensors, cameras, radio frequency identification, and retinal scanning displays. Common output technologies include various types of monitors, impact and nonimpact printers, plotters, and voice output.

9. Discuss innovations in hardware utilization.

Server farms contain hundreds of thousands of networked computer servers, which provide redundancy, fault tolerance, and automatic rollover in case one or more servers fail. Server virtualization means that multiple applications can run on a single physical server. Another type of virtualization enables multiple physical servers to appear as one logical server to the user. Grid computing applies the unused processing resources of many geographically dispersed computers in a network to form a virtual supercomputer. In utility computing, a service provider makes computing resources and infrastructure management available to a customer as needed. Edge computing locates parts of Web site content and processing close to the user to increase response time and lower technology costs. Autonomic systems are designed to manage themselves without direct human intervention. Nanotechnology refers to the creation of materials, devices, and systems at a scale of 1 to 100 nanometers (billionths of a meter).

10. Discuss strategic issues that link hardware design to business strategy.

Strategic issues linking hardware design to business strategy include: How do organizations keep up with the rapid price/performance advancements in hardware? How often should an organization upgrade its computers and storage systems? How can organizations measure benefits gained from price/performance improvements in hardware?

Chapter Glossary

arithmetic-logic unit (ALU) Portion of the CPU that performs the mathematic calculations and makes logical comparisons.

autonomic systems (also called **autonomic computing**) Computer systems designed to manage themselves without human intervention.

binary form The form in which data and instructions can be read by the CPU—only 0s and 1s.

bits Short for binary digit (0s and 1s), the only data that a CPU can process.

bus width The size of the physical path down which the data and instructions travel as electrical impulses on a computer chip.

byte An 8-bit string of data, needed to represent any one alphanumeric character or simple mathematical operation.

cache memory A type of primary storage where the computer can temporarily store blocks of data used more often and which a processor can access more rapidly than main memory (RAM).

central processing unit (CPU) Hardware that performs the actual computation or "number crunching" inside any computer.

clock speed The preset speed of the computer clock that times all chip activities, measured in megahertz and gigahertz.

compact disk, read-only memory (CD-ROM) A form of secondary storage that can be only read and not written on.

control unit Portion of the CPU that controls the flow of information.

digital video disk (DVD) An optical storage device used to store digital video or computer data.

edge computing Process in which parts of a Web site's content and processing are located close to the user to decrease response time and lower costs.

enterprise storage system An independent, external system with intelligence that includes two or more storage devices.

fat-client systems Desktop computer systems that offer full functionality.

flash memory A form of nonvolatile computer memory that can be electrically erased and reprogrammed.

flash memory devices Electronic storage devices that are compact, portable, require little power, and contain no moving parts.

grid computing Applying the resources of many computers in a network to a single problem at the same time.

hard drives A form of secondary storage that stores data on platters divided into concentric tracks and sectors, which can be read by a read/write head that pivots across the rotating disks.

holographic memory An optical technology that uses a three-dimensional medium to store data.

laptop and notebook computers Small, easily transportable, lightweight microcomputers.

line width The distance between transistors; the smaller the line width, the faster the chip.

machine instruction cycle The cycle of computer processing, whose speed is measured in terms of the number of instructions a chip processes per second.

magnetic disks A form of secondary storage on a magnetized disk divided into tracks and sectors that provide addresses for various pieces of data; also called hard disks.

magnetic tape A secondary storage medium on a large open reel or in a smaller cartridge or cassette.

mainframes Relatively large computers used in large enterprises for extensive computing applications that are accessed by thousands of users.

microcomputers The smallest and least expensive category of general-purpose computers; also called micros, personal computers, or PCs.

microcontrollers Embedded computer chips that usually cost less and work in less-demanding applications than microprocessors.

microprocessor The CPU, made up of millions of transistors embedded in a circuit on a silicon wafer or chip.

minicomputers Relatively small, inexpensive, and compact midrange computers that perform the same functions as mainframe computers, but to a more limited extent.

Moore's law Prediction by Gordon Moore, an Intel co-founder, that microprocessor complexity would double approximately every two years.

multimedia technology Computer-based integration of text, sound, still images, animation, and digitized full-motion video.

nanotechnology The creation of materials, devices, and systems at a size of 1 to 100 nanometers (billionths of a meter).

network-attached storage (NAS) An enterprise storage system in which a special-purpose server provides file storage to users who access the device over a network.

notebook computer (see **laptop computer**)

optical storage devices A form of secondary storage in which a laser reads the surface of a reflective plastic platter.

primary storage (also called **main memory**) High-speed storage located directly on the motherboard that stores data to be processed by the CPU, instructions telling the CPU how to process the data, and operating systems programs.

random access memory (RAM) The part of primary storage that holds a software program and small amounts of data when they are brought from secondary storage.

read-only memory (ROM) Type of primary storage where certain critical instructions are safeguarded; the storage is nonvolatile and retains the instructions when the power to the computer is turned off.

redundant arrays of independent disks (RAID) An enterprise storage system that links groups of standard hard drives to a specialized microcontroller that coordinates the drives so they appear as a single logical drive.

registers High-speed storage areas in the CPU that store very small amounts of data and instructions for short periods of time.

secondary storage Technology that can store very large amounts of data for extended periods of time.

sequential access Data access in which the computer system must run through data in sequence in order to locate a particular piece.

server Smaller midrange computers that support networks, enabling users to share files, software, and other network devices.

server farm Massive data center containing thousands of servers.

server virtualization Using software to partition a server into separately operating virtual machines

storage area network (SAN) An enterprise storage system architecture for building special, dedicated networks that allow rapid and reliable access to storage devices by multiple servers.

storage over IP Technology that uses the Internet Protocol to transport stored data between devices within a SAN; sometimes called IP over SCSI or iSCSI.

storage visualization software Software used with SANs to graphically plot an entire network and allow storage administrators to monitor all devices from a single console.

supercomputer Computer with the greatest processing power available; used primarily in scientific and military work for computationally demanding tasks on very large data sets.

thin-client systems Desktop computer systems that do not offer the full functionality of a PC.

thumb drive Storage device that fits into the USB port of a personal computer and is used for portable storage.

Ultra-mobile personal computer Small, mobile computer that has the full functionality of a desktop computer, but is smaller and lighter than traditional laptops and notebooks.

utility computing A type of computing whereby a service provider makes computing resources available to a customer as needed.

word length The number of bits (0s and 1s) that can be processed by the CPU at any one time.

workstations Powerful desktop-size computers that run computationally intensive scientific, engineering, and financial applications.

Discussion Questions

1. What factors affect the speed of a microprocessor?
2. If you were the chief information officer (CIO) of a firm, what factors would you consider when selecting secondary storage media for your company's records (files)?
3. Given that Moore's Law has proven itself over the past two decades, speculate on what chip capabilities will be 10 years in the future. What might your desktop PC be able to do?
4. If you were the chief information officer (CIO) of a firm, how would you explain the workings, benefits, and limitations of thin clients as opposed to using fat clients?
5. Where might you find embedded computers at home, at school, and/or at work?
6. What is the value of server farms, virtualization, and grid computing to any large organization?

Web Activities

1. Access the Web sites of the major chip manufacturers, for example, Intel (*www.intel.com*), Motorola (*www.motorola.com*), and Advanced Micro Devices (*www.amd.com*), and obtain the latest information regarding new and planned chips. Compare performance and costs across these vendors.
2. Access The Journey Inside on Intel's Web site (*http://www.intel.com/education/journey/index.htm*). Prepare a presentation of each step in the machine instruction cycle.
3. Investigate the status of utility computing by visiting *www.utilitycomputing.com/forum*, *www.aspnews.com* (discussion forum), *www.google.com*, *www.ibm.com*, *www.oracle.com*, and *www.cio.com*. Prepare a report that will highlight the progress today and current inhibitors.

Technology Guide 2

Computer Software

Learning Objectives

1. Differentiate between the two major types of software.

2. Describe the general functions of the operating system.

3. Describe the major types of application software.

4. Describe the major software issues that organizations face today.

5. Discuss the advantages and disadvantages of open-source software.

6. Explain how software has evolved and consider trends for the future.

TG2.1 Significance of Software

Computer hardware is only as effective as the instructions we give it, and those instructions are contained in **software**. The importance of computer software cannot be overestimated. The first software applications of computers in business were developed in the early 1950s. Software was less costly in computer systems then. Today, software comprises a much larger percentage of the cost of computer systems because the price of hardware has dramatically decreased at the same time that the complexity and price of software have dramatically increased.

Software's increasing complexity also leads to increased potential for errors or *bugs*. Large applications today can contain millions of lines of computer code, written by hundreds of people over the course of several years. The potential for error is huge, and testing and *debugging* software is expensive and time-consuming.

Regardless of the overall trends in software (increased complexity, increased cost, and increasing numbers of defects), software has become an everyday feature of our business and personal lives. Keep in mind that, regardless of your major, you will be using many different types of software throughout your career. In addition, you will provide input about the current types of software that you use, such as: does the software help you do your job; is it easy to use; do you need more functionality and if so, what functionality would be helpful to you; and many others. In your functional area, MIS employees will act as your advisers, but you will have definitive input into the software needed to do your job. In some organizations, the budget for software is allocated to functional areas or departments, meaning that you might be making software decisions (at least locally) yourself. Finally, when your functional area or organization considers acquiring new applications (discussed in Chapter 10), you will again have input into these decisions.

Software consists of **computer programs**, which are sequences of instructions for the computer. The process of writing, or *coding*, programs is called *programming*. Individuals who perform this task are called *programmers*.

Unlike the hardwired computers of the 1950s, modern software uses the **stored program concept**, in which software programs are stored in the computer's hardware. These programs are accessed and their instructions are executed (followed) in the computer's CPU. Once the program has finished executing, a new program is loaded into the main memory, and the computer hardware addresses another task.

Computer programs include **documentation**, which is a written description of the program's functions. Documentation helps the user operate the computer system, and it helps other programmers understand what the program does and how it accomplishes its purpose. Documentation is vital to the business organization. Without it, if a key programmer or user leaves, the knowledge of how to use the program or how it is designed may be lost.

The computer is able to do nothing until it is instructed by software. Although computer hardware is, by design, general purpose, software enables the user to instruct a computer system to perform specific functions that provide business value. There are two major types of software: systems software and application software. The relationship among hardware, systems software, and application software is illustrated in Figure TG2.1.

Systems software is a set of instructions that serves primarily as an intermediary between computer hardware and application programs. Systems software provides important self-regulatory functions for computer systems, such as loading itself when the computer is first turned on and providing commonly used sets of instructions for all applications. *Systems programming* refers to both the creation and maintenance of systems software.

Application software is a set of computer instructions that provide more specific functionality to a user. That functionality may be broad, such as general word processing, or

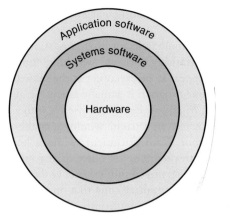

FIGURE TG2.1
Systems software
services as intermediary
between hardware and
functional applications.

narrow, such as an organization's payroll program. Essentially, an application program applies a computer to a certain need. *Application programming* refers to both the creation and modification and improvement of application software. Application software may be proprietary or off-the-shelf. As we shall see, organizations today use many different software applications.

Before you go on . . .

1. What does this statement mean: "Hardware is useless without software?"
2. What are differences between systems software and application software?

TG2.2 Systems Software

As we discussed earlier, systems software is the class of programs that control and support the computer system and its information processing activities. Systems software also facilitates the programming, testing, and debugging of computer programs. Systems software programs support application software by directing the basic functions of the computer. For example, when the computer is turned on, the initialization program (a systems program) prepares and readies all devices for processing. Systems software can be grouped into two major functional categories: system control programs and system support programs.

System Control Programs

System control programs control use of the hardware, software, and data resources of a computer system. The main system control program is the operating system. The **operating system (OS)** supervises the overall operation of the computer. One of its key functions is to monitor the computer's status and scheduling operations, including the input and output processes. In addition, the operating system allocates CPU time and main memory to programs running on the computer. It also provides an interface between the user and hardware. This interface hides the complexity of the hardware from the user. That is, you do not have to know how the hardware actually operates. You simply have to know what the hardware will do and what you need to do to obtain desired results.

Functions of the Operating System. The operating system manages the program or programs (also called *jobs* or *tasks*) running on the processor at a given time. Operating systems provide various types of program management, such as multitasking, multithreading, and multiprocessing.

The management of two or more tasks, or programs, running on the computer system at the same time is called **multitasking**. Because switching among these programs occurs so rapidly, all of the programs appear to be executing at the same time. However, because there is only one processor, only one program is actually executing at any one time. For example, you may create a graph with Microsoft Excel and insert it into a Word document. Both programs can be open on your screen in separate windows, enabling you to create your graph, copy it, and paste it into your Word document, without having to exit Excel and start Word. However, although both programs are open, at any given moment you are working in either Excel or Word. The programs cannot execute at the same time.

Multithreading is a form of multitasking that involves running multiple tasks, or threads, within a single application simultaneously. For example, a word processor application may edit one document while spell-checking another. **Multiprocessing** occurs when a computer system with two or more processors can run more than one program at a given time by assigning them to different processors.

In addition to managing programs executing on computer hardware, operating systems must also manage main memory and secondary storage. Operating systems enable a process called **virtual memory**, which simulates more main memory than actually exists in the computer system. It allows a program to behave as if it had access to the full storage capacity of a computer rather than just access to the amount of primary storage installed on the computer. Virtual memory divides an application program or module into fixed-length portions called *pages*. The system executes some pages of instructions while pulling others from secondary storage. In effect, virtual memory allows users to write programs as if primary storage were larger than it actually is.

The ease or difficulty of the interaction between the user and the computer is determined largely by the *interface design*. Older, text-based interfaces like DOS (*d*isk *o*perating *s*ystem) required the user to type in cryptic commands. In an effort to make computers more user friendly, programmers developed the graphical user interface. The **graphical user interface (GUI)** allows users to exercise direct control of visible objects (such as icons) and actions that replace complex commands. The GUI was developed by researchers at Xerox Palo Alto Research Center (PARC) and then popularized by the Apple MacIntosh computer. Microsoft soon introduced its GUI-based Windows operating system for IBM-style PCs.

The next generation of GUI technology will incorporate features such as virtual reality, head-mounted displays, speech input (user commands) and output, pen and gesture recognition, animation, multimedia, artificial intelligence, and cellular/wireless communication capabilities. Future GUIs also will provide social interfaces. A **social interface** is a user interface that guides the user through computer applications by using cartoon-like characters, graphics, animation, and voice commands. The cartoon-like characters can be cast as puppets, narrators, guides, inhabitants, or avatars (computer-generated humanlike figures).

Types of Operating Systems.   As we previously discussed, operating systems are necessary in order for computer hardware to function. **Operating environments** are sets of computer programs that add features that enable system developers to create applications without directly accessing the operating system; they function only *with* an operating system. That is, operating environments are not operating systems, but they work only with an operating system. For example, the early versions of Windows were operating environments that provided a graphical user interface and were functional only with MS-DOS.

Operating systems are classified into different types depending on the type of computer on which they run and the number of users they support. *Operating systems for mobile devices* are designed to support a single person using a mobile, handheld device or information appliance. Small computer operating systems (*notebooks, laptops, desktops,* and *workstations*) are designed to support a single user or a small workgroup of users. Large computer operating systems (*midrange computers* and *mainframes*) typically support between a few dozen and thousands of concurrent users. Large computer operating systems offer greater functionality than the other types, including reliability, backup, security, fault tolerance, and rapid processing speeds. One important exception to this generalization is the user interface, which is most sophisticated on desktop operating systems and least sophisticated on large computer operating systems.

We are most familiar with small computer operating systems because we use them daily. Examples are Windows XP and Vista, the Apple Macintosh operating system X (Mac OS X), and Linux. The Windows family of operating systems is the dominant small-computer operating system. Various versions run on laptops, notebooks, desktops, and servers.

Today's desktop operating systems use GUIs with icons to provide instant access to common tasks and plug-and-play capabilities. **Plug-and-play** is a feature that can automate the installation of new hardware by enabling the operating system to recognize new hardware and then automatically install the necessary software, called *device drivers.* These operating systems also provide transparent, three-dimensional windows to make it easier to see files and other windows on your monitor. Your screen itself can be a movie or an animated image. Plug-and-play provides you with an area of your screen where you can put mini-applications such as clocks, stock tickers, calendars, and RSS readers (discussed in Chapter 5). You can view all open windows in a fanned-out, playing card view, and you have a GUI for finding and organizing directories, folders and files.

Current desktop operating systems allow your computer to become a digital hub. For example, you can easily store and wirelessly transmit pictures from your computer to digital picture frames placed around your house as well as to other computers. In addition, you can easily listen to your digital music and wirelessly stream your tunes to speakers located around your home. You can also view videos (including movies) on your computer.

System Support Programs

The second major category of systems software, **system support programs**, supports the operations, management, and users of a computer system by providing a variety of support services. Examples of system support programs are system utility programs, performance monitors, and security monitors.

System utilities are programs that have been written to accomplish common tasks such as sorting records and creating directories and subdirectories. These programs also restore accidentally erased files, locate files within the directory structure, and manage memory usage. **System performance monitors** are programs that monitor the processing of jobs on a computer system. They monitor performance in areas such as processor time, memory space, input/output devices, and system and application programs. **System security monitors** are programs that monitor the use of a computer system to protect it and its resources from unauthorized use, fraud, and destruction.

Before you go on . . .

1. What are the two main types of systems software?
2. What are the major differences among mobile device, desktop, and mainframe operating systems?

Personal Application Software

Category of Personal Application Software	Major Functions	Examples
Spreadsheets	Use rows and columns to manipulate primarily numerical data; useful for analyzing financial information, and for what-if and goal-seeking analyses.	Microsoft Excel Corel Quattro Pro
Word Processing	Allows users to manipulate primarily text with many writing and editing features.	Microsoft Word Corel WordPerfect
Desktop Publishing	Extends word processing software to allow production of finished, camera-ready documents, which may contain photographs, diagrams, and other images combined with text in different fonts.	Microsoft Publisher QuarkXPress 7
Data Management	Allows users to store, retrieve, and manipulate related data.	Microsoft Access FileMaker Pro
Presentation	Allows users to create and edit graphically rich information to appear on electronic slides.	Microsoft PowerPoint Corel Presentations
Graphics	Allows users to create, store, and display or print charts, graphs, maps, and drawings.	Adobe PhotoShop Corel DRAW
Personal Information Management	Allows users to create and maintain calendars, appointments, to-do lists, and business contacts.	IBM Lotus Notes Microsoft Outlook
Personal Finance	Allows users to maintain checkbooks, track investments, monitor credit cards, bank and pay bills electronically.	Quicken Microsoft Money
Web Authoring	Allows users to design Web sites and publish them on the Web.	Microsoft FrontPage Macromedia Dreamweaver
Communications	Allows users to communicate with other people over any distance.	Novell Groupwise Netscape Messenger

TG2.3 Application Software

As we discussed earlier, application software consists of instructions that direct a computer system to perform specific information processing activities and that provide functionality for users. Because there are so many different uses for computers, there are a correspondingly large number of different application software programs.

Types of Application Software

Application software includes both proprietary and off-the-shelf software. **Proprietary application software** addresses a company's specific or unique business need. This type of software may be developed in-house by the organization's information systems personnel, or it may be commissioned from a software vendor. Specific software programs developed for a particular company by a vendor are called **contract software**.

Alternatively, **off-the-shelf application software** can be purchased, leased, or rented from a vendor that develops programs and sells them to many organizations. Off-the-shelf software may be a standard package, or it may be customizable. Special-purpose programs or "packages" can be tailored for a specific purpose, such as inventory control or payroll. The word **package** is a commonly used term for a computer program (or group of programs) that has been developed by a vendor and is available for purchase in a prepackaged form. We discuss the methodology involved in acquiring application software, whether proprietary or off-the-shelf, in Chapter 10.

Categories of Personal Application Software

General-purpose, off-the-shelf application programs designed to help individual users increase their productivity are referred to as **personal application software**. Some of the major types of personal application software are listed in Table TG2.1. *Software suites* combine some of these packages and integrate their functions.

Speech-recognition software is an input technology, rather than strictly an application, that can feed systems software and application software. **Speech-recognition software**, also called *voice recognition*, recognizes and interprets human speech, either one word at a time (discrete speech) or in a conversational stream (continuous speech). Advances in processing power, new software algorithms, and better microphones have enabled developers to design extremely accurate voice-recognition software. Experts predict that, in the near future, voice-recognition systems will likely be built into almost every device, appliance, and machine that people use. Applications for voice-recognition technology abound. Consider these examples:

- Call centers are using the technology. The average call-center call costs $5 if it is handled by an employee, but only 50 cents with a self-service, speech-enabled system. The online brokerage firm E-Trade Financial uses Tellme (*www.tellme.com*) to field about 50,000 calls per day, thereby saving at least $30 million annually.

- IBM's Embedded ViaVoice software (*http://www-306.ibm.com/software/voice/viavoice/*) powers GM's OnStar and other dashboard command systems, such as music players and navigational systems.

- Apple's MacIntosh OS X and Microsoft's Vista operating system come with built-in voice technology.

- Nuance's Dragon NaturallySpeaking (*www.nuance.com*) allows for accurate voice-to-text and e-mail dictation.

- Vocera Communications (*www.vocera.com*) has developed a communicator badge that combines voice recognition with wireless technologies. Among its first customers were medical workers, who use the badge to search through hospital directories by voice and find the right person to help with a patient problem or to find medical records.

- Vox-Tec's (*www.voxtec.com*) Phraselator, a handheld device about the size of a checkbook, listens to requests for a phrase and then delivers a translation in any of 41 specified languages. It is being used by U.S. troops in Iraq and Afghanistan to provide translations in Arabic, Pashto, and local dialects.

Before you go on . . .

1. Which classes of personal application software are essential for the productivity of a business or other organization with which you are familiar? Which are nonessential?

2. What do you see as advantages of speech recognition software? disadvantages?

TG2.4 Software Issues

The importance of software in computer systems has brought new issues to the forefront for organizational managers. These issues include software defects (bugs), software evaluation and selection, licensing, open systems, open-source software, and software-as-a-service.

Software Defects

All too often, computer program code is inefficient, poorly designed, and riddled with errors. The Software Engineering Institute (SEI) at Carnegie Mellon University in Pittsburgh defines good software as usable, reliable, defect free, cost effective, and maintainable. As we become increasingly dependent on computers and networks, the risks associated with software defects are accelerating.

The SEI maintains that, on average, professional programmers make between 100 and 150 errors in every 1,000 lines of code they write. Fortunately, the software industry recognizes this problem, but unfortunately, the problem is enormous, and the industry is taking only initial steps to resolve it. One critical step is better design and planning at the beginning of the development process (discussed in Chapter 10).

Software Evaluation and Selection

The software evaluation and selection decision is a difficult one because it is affected by many factors; Table TG2.2 summarizes these selection factors. The first part of the selection process involves understanding the organization's software needs and identifying the criteria that will be used in making the eventual decision. After the organization establishes its software

Table TG2.2

Software Selection Factors

Factor	Considerations
Size and location of user base	□ Does the proposed software support a few users in a single location?
	□ Can it accommodate large numbers of geographically dispersed users?
Availability of system	□ Does the software offer tools that monitor system usage?
	□ Does it maintain a list of authorized users and provide the level of security needed?
Costs—initial and subsequent	□ Is the software affordable, taking into account all costs, including installation, training, and maintenance?
System capabilities	□ Does the software meet both current and anticipated future needs?
Existing computing environment	□ Is the software compatible with existing hardware, software, and communications networks?
In-house technical skills	□ Should the organization develop software applications in-house?
	□ Should the organization purchase applications off the shelf or contract software out of house?

requirements, it should evaluate specific software. To accomplish this task, it should create an evaluation team composed of representatives from every group that will have a role in using the software. The team will study the proposed alternatives and find the software that promises the best match between the organization's needs and the software capabilities.

Software Licensing

Although many people do so routinely, copying software is illegal. The Software Publishers Association (SPA) has stated that software piracy costs software vendors around the world approximately $15 billion annually.

To protect their investment, software vendors must prevent their software from being copied and distributed by individuals and other software companies. A company can copyright its software, which means that the U.S. Copyright Office grants the company the exclusive legal right to reproduce, publish, and sell that software. (We discuss copyrights and patents in Chapter 3.) The SPA enforces software copyright laws in corporations by auditing the corporations to ensure that the software they are using is properly licensed.

As the number of desktop computers continues to increase and businesses continue to decentralize, it becomes more and more difficult for IS managers to supervise their software assets. As a result, new firms have arisen that specialize in tracking software licenses for a fee. Firms such as ASAP Software (*www.asap.com*), Software Spectrum (*www.insight.com*), and others will track and manage a company's software licenses to ensure that company's compliance with U.S. copyright laws.

Open Systems

The concept of **open systems** refers to a model of computing products that work together. Achieving this goal is possible through use of the same operating system with compatible software on all the different computers that would interact with one another in an organization. A complementary approach is to produce application software that will run across all computer platforms. If hardware, operating systems, and application software are designed as open systems, the user will be able to purchase the best software, called *best of breed*, for the job without worrying about whether it will run on particular hardware.

Open-source Software

In many cases in the software industry, the trend is moving away from proprietary software toward open-source software. Proprietary software is software that has been developed by a company and has restrictions on its use, copying, and modification. The company developing such software spends money and time on research and development of its software product, and then sells it in the marketplace. The proprietary nature of the software means that the company keeps the source code—the actual computer instructions—private (as Coca-Cola does with its formula).

On the other hand, **open-source software** is software whose source code is available at no cost to developers or users. Open-source software is not shareware or freeware. *Shareware* typically allows no access to the underlying source code. *Freeware* is copyrighted software that is made available to the user free of charge for an unlimited time. In contrast, open-source software is copyrighted and distributed with license terms ensuring that the source code will always be available.

Open-source software products have worldwide "communities" of developers who write and maintain the code. Inside each community, however, only a small group of developers, called *core developers*, is allowed to modify or submit changes to the code. Other developers submit code to the core developers.

Implementing open-source software in an organization has both advantages and disadvantages. According to OpenSource (*www.opensource.org*), open-source development produces high-quality, reliable, flexible (code can be changed to meet the needs of the user), low-cost software. In many cases, open-source software is more reliable than commercial software. Because the code is available to many developers, more bugs are discovered early and quickly and are fixed immediately. Support for open-source software is also available from firms that provide products derived from the software. An example is Red Hat for Linux (*www.redhat.com*). These firms provide education, training, and technical support for the software for a fee.

Open-source software also has disadvantages. To begin with, organizations that do not have in-house technical experts will have to buy maintenance-support contracts from a third party. In addition, questions have arisen concerning the ease of use of open-source software, the amount of time and expense needed to train users, and the compatibility with existing systems or with the systems of business partners.

There are many examples of open-source software, including the GNU (GNU's Not UNIX) suite of software (*www.gnu.org*) developed by the Free Software Foundation (*www.fsf.org*); the Linux operating system (see *www.linuxhq.com*); the Apache Web server (*www.apache.org*); the sendmail SMTP (Send Mail Transport Protocol) e-mail server (*www.sendmail.org*); the Perl programming language (*www.perl.org*); the Firefox 2 browser from Mozilla (*www.mozilla.com*); and Sun's StarOffice applications suite (*www.sun.com/software/star/staroffice/index.jsp*). There are about 140,000 open-source projects under way on SourceForge (*www.sourceforge.net*), the popular open-source hosting site.

Linux and Apache are excellent examples of how open-source software is moving to the mainstream. Linux is gaining market share in servers, now running on approximately one-fourth of all servers, where Microsoft runs on about two-thirds of all servers. Furthermore, almost two-thirds of the world's Web servers now run Apache, compared to one-third for Microsoft.

Software-as-a-Service

Software-as-a-Service (SaaS) is a method of delivering software in which a vendor hosts the applications. Customers access these applications over a network, typically the Internet. Customers do not own the software but pay for using it. The Google and Amazon cases presented in Chapter 1 provide examples of SaaS.

Before you go on . . .

1. What are some of the legal issues involved in acquiring and using software in most business organizations?
2. What are some of the criteria used for evaluating software when planning a purchase?
3. What is open-source software, and what are its advantages?

TG2.5 Programming Languages

Programming languages allow people to write instructions that tell computers what to do and are the means by which all systems and application software are developed. Because computers do exactly what they are told, programming languages require a high degree of precision and completeness. Also, digital computers only understand 0s and 1s, or binary digits. Therefore, all computer languages, except machine language, must be translated into binary digits for processing. This process is accomplished by a type of systems software called a **compiler**. Table TG2.3 provides a description of common categories of programming languages.

Programming Languages

Table TG2.3

Category	Characteristics
First-Generation Language (Machine)	Consists of 0's and 1's; extremely difficult to use by programmers.
Second-Generation Language (Assembly)	More user friendly than machine language; uses mnemonics for people to use, such as ADD for add, SUB for subtract, and MOV for move.
Third-Generation Language (Procedural)	Requires the programmer to specify, step by step, exactly how the computer must accomplish a task. Examples include C, Basic, FORTRAN, and COBOL.
Fourth-Generation Language (Nonprocedural)	Allows the user to specify the desired result without having to specify step-by-step procedures; simplify and accelerate programming process. Examples include SAS, SPSS, and APL.
Visual Programming Languages	Employed within a graphical environment and uses a mouse, icons, symbols on the screen, or pull-down menus to make programming easier. An example is Visual Basic.

It will be unusual for most of you to write computer programs at work using the programming languages listed in Table TG2.3 or object-oriented programming languages. (MIS majors may not do much programming either.) However, you should have a basic knowledge of these languages because your organization's computer programmers will use some of them to develop the applications you will use.

Object-oriented languages work differently than the languages in Table TG2.3. **Object-oriented languages** are based on the idea of taking a small amount of data and the instructions about what to do with that data, which are called **methods**, and combining them into what is called an **object**. When the object is selected or activated, the computer has the desired data and takes the desired action. This is what happens when you click on an icon on your GUI-equipped computer screen. For example, when you click on the Internet Explorer icon on your desktop (which is an object), the IE window will open. The IE icon object contains the program code for opening a window.

Object-oriented languages also have a **reusability feature**, which means that objects created for one purpose can be used in a different object-oriented program if desired. For example, a student object in a university system can be used for applications ranging from grades to fees to graduation checks. Java is a powerful and popular object-oriented language, and we look at it here in more detail.

Java is an object-oriented language, developed by Sun Microsystems, that enables programmers to develop applications that work across the Internet. Java can handle text, data, graphics, sound, and video, all within one program. Java is used to develop small applications, called **applets**, which can be included in an HTML page on the Internet. When an individual uses a Java-compatible browser to view a page that contains a Java applet, the applet's code is transferred to the user's system and is executed by the user's browser.

Applications written in Java can be stored on Internet servers, downloaded as needed, and then erased from the local computer when the processing is completed. This feature means that users no longer need to store copies of the application on the hard drive of their PCs.

Hypertext Markup Language and Extensible Markup Language

Hypertext markup language and extensible markup language are programming languages that are used to build rich multimedia Web pages, Web sites, and Web-based applications. For example, you may use these languages to build your own Web page.

Hypertext markup language (HTML) is used for creating and formatting documents on the World Wide Web. HTML gives users the option of controlling visual elements such as fonts, font size, and paragraph spacing without changing the original information.

Hypertext is an approach to document management in which documents are stored in a network of nodes connected by links, which are called **hyperlinks**. Users access data through an interactive browsing system. The combination of nodes, links, and supporting indexes for any particular topic constitutes a **hypertext document**. A hypertext document may contain text, images, and other types of information such as data files, audio, video, and executable computer programs.

Extensible markup language (XML) improves the functionality of Web documents by describing what the data in documents actually mean, as well as the business purpose of the documents themselves. As a result, XML improves the compatibility among the disparate systems of business partners by allowing XML documents to be moved to any format on any platform without the elements losing their meaning. As a result, the same information can be published to a Web browser, a PDA, or a smartphone, and each device would use the information appropriately.

XML and HTML are not the same. The purpose of HTML is to help build Web pages and display data on Web pages, whereas the purpose of XML is to describe data and information. It does not say *how* the data will be displayed (which HTML does). XML can be used to send complex messages that include different files (and HTML cannot).

Figure TG2.2 compares HTML and XML. Notice that HTML describes only where an item appears on a page, whereas XML describes what the item is. For example, HTML shows only that "Introduction to MIS" appears on line 1, whereas XML shows that "Introduction to MIS" is the Course Title.

Before you go on . . .

1. Differentiate between HTML and XML.
2. What are the strategic advantages of using object-oriented programming languages?

English Text	HTML	XML
MNGT 3070	<TITLE>Course Number</TITLE>	<Department and course="MNGT 3070">
Introduction to MIS	<BODY>	<COURSE TITLE>Introduction to MIS<COURSE>
<TITLE>		
3 semester hours	<UL>	<HOURS UNIT="Semester">3</NUMBER OF HOURS>
Professor Smith	<LI>Introduction to MIS	<INSTRUCTOR>Professor Smith<INSTRUCTOR>
	<LI>3 semester hours	
	<LI>Professor Smith	
	</UL></BODY>	

FIGURE TG2.2   Comparison of HTML and XML.

What's in **IT** for Me?

For the Accounting Major

Accounting application software performs the organization's accounting functions, which are repetitive and high volume. Each business transaction (e.g., a person hired, a paycheck produced, an item sold) produces data that must be captured. After accounting applications capture the data, they manipulate them as necessary. Accounting applications adhere to relatively standardized procedures, handle detailed data, and have a historical focus (i.e., what happened in the past).

For the Finance Major

Financial application software provides information about the firm's financial status to persons and groups inside and outside the firm. Financial applications include forecasting, funds management, and control applications. Forecasting applications predict and project the firm's future activity in the economic environment. Funds management applications use cash flow models to analyze expected cash flows. Control applications enable managers to monitor their financial performance, typically by providing information about the budgeting process and performance ratios.

For the Marketing Major

Marketing application software helps management solve problems that involve marketing the firm's products. Marketing software includes marketing research and marketing intelligence applications. Marketing applications provide information about the firm's products and competitors, its distribution system, its advertising and personal selling activities, and its pricing strategies. Overall, marketing applications help managers develop strategies that combine the four major elements of marketing: product, promotion, place, and price.

For the Production/Operations Management Major

Managers use production/operations management applications software for production planning and as part of the physical production system. POM applications include production, inventory, quality, and cost software. These applications help management operate manufacturing facilities and logistics. Materials requirements planning (MRP) software is also widely used in manufacturing. This software identifies which materials will be needed, how much will be needed, and the dates on which they will be needed. This information enables managers to be proactive.

For the Human Resources Management Major

Human resources management application software provides information concerning recruiting and hiring, education and training, maintaining the employee database, termination, and administering benefits. HRM applications include workforce planning, recruiting, workforce management, compensation, benefits, and environmental reporting subsystems (e.g., equal employment opportunity records and analysis, union enrollment, toxic substances, and grievances).

MIS

If your company decides to develop software itself, the MIS function is responsible for managing this activity. If the company decides to buy software, the MIS function deals with software vendors in analyzing their products. The MIS function is also responsible for upgrading software as vendors release new versions.

Summary

1. Differentiate between the two major types of software.

Software consists of computer programs (coded instructions) that control the functions of computer hardware. There are two main categories of software: systems software and application software. Systems software manages the hardware resources of the computer system; it functions between the hardware and the application software. Systems software includes the system control programs (operating systems) and system support programs. Application software enables users to perform specific tasks and information processing activities. Application software may be proprietary or off-the-shelf.

2. Describe the general functions of the operating system.

Operating systems manage the actual computer resources (i.e., the hardware). They schedule and process applications (jobs), manage and protect memory, manage the input and output functions and hardware, manage data and files, and provide clustering support, security, fault tolerance, graphical user interfaces, and windowing.

3. Describe the major types of application software.

The major types of application software are spreadsheet, data management, word processing, desktop publishing, graphics, multimedia, communications, speech recognition, and groupware. Software suites combine several types of application software (e.g., word processing, spreadsheet, and data management) into an integrated package.

4. Describe the major software issues that organizations face today.

Computer program code often contains errors. The industry recognizes the problem of software defects, but it is so enormous that only initial steps are being taken. The software evaluation and selection decision is a difficult one because it is affected by many factors. Software licensing is yet another issue for organizations and individuals. Copying software is illegal. Software vendors copyright their software to protect it from being copied. As a result, companies must license vendor-developed software to use it.

5. Discuss the advantages and disadvantages of open-source software.

Advantages of open-source software include high quality, reliability, flexibility (code can be changed to meet the needs of the user), and low cost. Open-source software can be more reliable than commercial software. Because the code is available to many developers, more bugs are discovered early and quickly and are fixed immediately. Disadvantages include cost of maintenance support contracts, ease of use, amount of time and expense needed to train users, and compatibility with existing systems or with systems of business partners.

6. Explain how software has evolved and consider trends for the future.

Software and programming languages continue to become more user oriented. Programming languages have evolved from the first generation of machine languages, which is directly understandable to the CPU, to higher levels that use more natural language and do not require users to specify the detailed procedures for achieving desired results. Software itself is becoming much more complex, expensive, and time-consuming to develop.

Chapter Glossary

applets Small Java applications that can be included in an HTML page on the Internet.

application software The class of computer instructions that directs a computer system to perform specific processing activities and provide functionality for users.

compiler A type of systems software that converts other computer languages into machine language.

computer programs The sequences of instructions for the computer, which comprise software.

contract software Specific software programs developed for a particular company by a vendor.

documentation Written description of the functions of a software program.

extensible markup language (XML) A programming language designed to improve the functionality of Web documents by providing more flexible and adaptable data identification.

graphical user interface (GUI) System software that allows users to have direct control of visible objects (such as icons) and actions, which replace command syntax.

hyperlinks The links that connect document nodes in hypertext.

hypertext An approach to document management in which documents are stored in a network of nodes connected by links and are accessed through interactive browsing.

hypertext document The combination of nodes, links, and supporting indexes for any particular topic in hypertext.

hypertext markup language (HTML) The standard programming language used on the Web to create and recognize hypertext documents.

Java Object-oriented programming language, developed by Sun Microsystems, that gives programmers the ability to develop applications that work across the Internet.

methods In object-oriented programming, the instructions about what to do with encapsulated data objects.

multiprocessing Simultaneously processing more than one program by assigning them to different processors (multiple CPUs).

multitasking The management of two or more tasks, or programs, running concurrently on the computer system (one CPU).

multithreading A form of multitasking that runs multiple tasks within a single application simultaneously.

object In object-oriented programming, the combination of a small amount of data with instructions about what to with the data.

object-oriented languages Programming languages that encapsulate a small amount of data with instructions about what to do with the data.

off-the-shelf application software Software purchased, leased, or rented from a vendor that develops programs and sells them to many organizations; can be standard or customizable.

open-source software Software made available in source code form at no cost to developers.

open systems A model of computing products that work together by use of the same operating system with compatible software on all the different computers that would interact with one another in an organization.

operating environments A set of computer programs adds features enabling developers to create applications without directly accessing the operating system; function only with an operating system.

operating system (OS) The main system control program, which supervises the overall operations of the computer, allocates CPU time and main memory to programs, and provides an interface between user and hardware.

package Common term for a computer program developed by a vendor and available for purchase in prepackaged form.

personal application software General-purpose, off-the-shelf application programs that support general types of processing, rather than being linked to any specific business function.

plug-and-play Feature that enables the operating system to recognize new hardware and install the necessary software (called device drivers) automatically.

proprietary application software Software that addresses a specific or unique business need for a company; may be developed in-house or may be commissioned from a software vendor.

reusability feature Feature of object-oriented languages that allows objects created for one purpose to be used in a different object-oriented program if desired.

social interface A user interface that guides the user through computer applications by using cartoon-like characters, graphics, animation, and voice commands.

software A set of computer programs that enable the hardware to process data.

Software-as-a-Service (SaaS) A method of delivering software in which a vendor hosts the applications, and customers access them over a network and pay only for using them.

speech-recognition software Software that recognizes and interprets human speech, either one word at a time (discrete speech) or in a stream (continuous speech).

stored program concept Modern hardware architecture in which stored software programs are accessed and their instructions are executed (followed) in the computer's CPU, one after another.

system control programs Software programs that control use of the hardware, software, and data resources of a computer system.

system performance monitors Programs that monitor the processing of jobs on a computer system and monitor system performance in areas such as processor time, memory space, and application programs.

system security monitors Programs that monitor a computer system to protect it and its resources from unauthorized use, fraud, or destruction.

system support programs Software that supports the operations, management, and users of a computer system by providing a variety of support services (e.g., system utility programs, performance monitors, and security monitors).

system utilities Programs that accomplish common tasks such as sorting records, creating directories and subdirectories, locating files, and managing memory usage.

systems software The class of computer instructions that serve primarily as an intermediary between computer hardware and application programs; provides important self-regulatory functions for computer systems.

virtual memory A feature that simulates more main memory than actually exists in the computer system by extending primary storage into secondary storage.

Discussion Questions

1. You are the CIO of your company and you have to develop an application of strategic importance to your firm. Do you buy an off-the-shelf application, develop an application in-house, or use open-source software? Support your answer by explaining the pros and cons of each choice.

2. You have to take a programming course, or maybe more than one, in your MIS program. Which programming language(s) would you choose to study? Why? Should you even have to learn a programming language? Why or why not?

Web Activities

1. A great deal of software is available free over the Internet. Go to *www.pcmag.com/article2/0,1895,2090787,00 .asp* and observe all the software available for free. Choose one software program and download it to your computer. Prepare a brief discussion about the software for your class.

2. Enter the IBM Web site (*www.ibm.com*) and search on "software." Click on the drop box for Products, and notice how many software products IBM produces. Is IBM only a hardware company?

Technology Guide 3

Protecting Your Information Assets

Learning Objectives

1. Identify the various behavioral actions you can take to protect your information assets.

2. Identify the various computer-based actions you can take to protect your information assets.

365

TG3.1 Introduction

We travel in our work, we work from home, and we access the Internet from home for personal reasons (for example, shopping, ordering products, planning trips, gathering information, staying in touch with friends and family via e-mail). Therefore, in this Technology Guide we discuss how to protect your information assets when computing at home or while you are traveling.

It is important to note that, when you are at work or when you access your university's network from home or on the road, you hopefully have the advantage of "industrial strength" information security that your university's information systems department has implemented. In all other cases, however, you are on your own, and it is up to you to protect yourself. Protecting yourself is even more critical as organized crime increasingly is turning its attention to home users. As businesses improve their information security, consumers become the next logical target. According to Symantec (*www.symantec.com*), if you connected an unprotected personal computer to the Internet in 2003, it would be attacked within 15 minutes. Today, that personal computer will be attacked within seconds.

You can take two types of actions to protect your information assets: behavioral actions and computer-based actions. Behavioral actions are those actions that do not specifically involve a computer; computer-based actions relate to safe computing. If you take both types of action, you will protect your information and greatly reduce your exposure to fraud and identity theft.

Before you go on . . .

1. Why is it so important for you to protect yourself?
2. What are the two types of action you can take to protect yourself?

TG3.2 Behavioral Actions to Protect Your Information Assets

General Behavioral Actions

You should not provide personal information to strangers in any format (physical, verbal, or electronic). From our discussion of social engineering in Chapter 3, remember that you will face social engineering attacks at home as well as at work. You must be on your guard at all times. For example, before you provide personal information over the telephone, verify that you are talking to authorized personnel. To accomplish this verification, you should hang up and call the person or company back.

A critically important behavioral action that you can take is to protect your Social Security number. Unfortunately, far too many organizations use your Social Security number to uniquely identify you. When you are asked to provide your Social Security number, ask why you cannot provide some other combination of nine numbers and letters as unique identification. If the person asking for your Social Security number, for example your physician's clerk, is not responsive, ask to speak with a supervisor. There is a movement underway to avoid using Social Security numbers everywhere for identification. If this movement is successful, then you might have to remember many more identifiers. However, your information security would improve. Remember, you have to take the initiative here.

Another critical consideration involves your credit cards. The actions you can take with your credit cards are important because fraudulent credit card use is so widespread. Use credit cards with your picture on them. Although cashiers probably cannot read your

signature on the back of your card, they can certainly compare your picture to your face. For example, the Bank of America will place your picture on several of its credit cards for free (visit *www.bankofamerica.com/creditcards* and click on Security Features at the bottom of the left-hand column).

You may also want to use virtual credit cards that offer you the option of shopping online with a disposable credit card number. For no extra charge, you sign up at your credit card's Web site and typically download software onto your computer. When you are ready to shop, you receive a randomly generated substitute 16-digit number that you can use at the online store. The number can be used once or, in some cases, repeated at the same store. The card number can also be used to buy goods and services over the phone and through the mail, but it cannot be used for in-store purchases that require a traditional plastic card. Two card issuers that offer virtual cards are Citibank and Discover.

Also, pay very close attention to your credit card billing cycles. You should know, to within a day or two, when your credit card bills are due. If a credit card bill does not arrive when expected, call your credit card company immediately. If your credit card is stolen and is being used fraudulently, the first thing the thief does is change the address on the account so that you do not receive the bill.

Another important action is to limit your use of debit cards. Debit cards are linked to your bank account, meaning that a person who steals your debit card and personal identification number (PIN) can clean out your bank account. In contrast, your liability with credit cards is usually zero (or a small amount). Your credit card company bears the liability for fraudulent charges, provided that you notify the company within 60 days of the theft.

Do not use a personal mailbox at your home or apartment for anything other than catalogs and magazines. Use a private mailbox or a Post Office box. It is far too easy for thieves to steal mail from home mailboxes when there is no one at home for much of the day. Think about the wealth of information that could be stolen from your mailbox: credit card statements, bank statements, investment statements, and so on.

When you discard mail or old records, use a cross-cut, or confetti, shredder to cut them up. Recall our discussion of dumpster diving in Chapter 3. A single-cut shredder is not sufficient because, with enough time, a thief can reassemble the strips.

Another security option is to sign up with a company that provides proactive protection of your personal information. Examples of such companies are LifeLock (*www.lifelock.com*), TrustedID (*www.trustedid.com*), and CardCops (*www.cardcops.com*).

LifeLock and TrustedID allow customers to lock their credit files so that new lines of credit cannot be opened unless customers first unlock their existing files. Locking credit files means that merchants and banks must have verbal or written permission from customers before opening new credit in their names. Ordinarily, the locking process involves sending registered mail to each of the three major credit agencies every 90 days. These three agencies are Equifax (*www.equifax.com*), Experian (*www.experian.com*), and TransUnion (*www.transunion.com*). LifeLock and TrustedID do that for you, and thus proactively monitor your various credit files.

CardCops provides an early warning service that notifies its customers that the company has found your personal information circulating on the Internet. It also collects compromised data on the Internet and makes it available to its customers and to merchants.

If you follow the behavioral and computer-based action recommendations in this Technology Guide, you will greatly reduce, but not eliminate, the chances that your identity will be stolen. If your identity is stolen despite these precautions, you should follow these steps to recover:

- First, get a lawyer.
- Get organized. Keep a file with all your paperwork, including the names, addresses, and phone numbers of everyone you contact about this crime.

- File a detailed police report. Send copies of this report to creditors and other agencies that may require proof of the crime.
- Get the name and phone number of your police investigator, and give it to your creditors.
- In all communications about this crime, use certified, return-receipt mail. Report that you are the victim of ID theft to the fraud divisions of all three credit reporting agencies: Equifax, Experian, and TransUnion. Due to the increased incidence of identity theft, federal law now gives you the right to have one free credit report per year. If you request your free annual credit report from each of the three agencies, you will receive one free report every four months.
- Be sure to get your unique case number from each credit agency, and ask each agency to send you your credit report.
- Tell each agency to issue a fraud alert. The fraud alert requires mortgage brokers, car dealers, credit card companies, and other lenders to scrutinize anyone who opens an account in your name for 90 days.
- Get the document that you need to file a long-term fraud alert, which lasts for seven years and can be canceled at any time.
- Ask the credit agencies for names and phone numbers of lenders with whom fraudulent accounts have been opened.
- Point out all entries generated due to fraud to each agency. Ask each agency to remove the specified fraudulent entries.
- Tell each agency to notify anyone who received your report in the last six months that you are disputing the information.
- Californians can order a "credit freeze" with all three major credit agencies. This freeze requires lenders, retailers, utilities, and other businesses to get special access to your credit report through a PIN-based system. It also helps prevent anyone from getting any new loans or credit in your name. Similar legislation has been introduced in other states.
- Call your credit card companies directly.
- Change all your credit cards immediately. Get replacements with new account numbers, and close your old accounts.
- Be alert for change-of-address forms in your mail. The post office must send notifications to your old and new addresses. If someone tries to change your mailing address, it is a major indication that you have been victimized.
- Fill out fraud affidavits for creditors. The Federal Trade Commission (FTC) provides a form that many creditors accept: *www.ftc.gov/bcp/conline/pubs/credit/affidavit.pdf*
- If debt collectors demand payment of fraudulent accounts, write down the name of the company as well as the collector's name, address, and phone number. Tell the collector that you are the victim of identity theft. Send the collection agency a certified letter with a completed FTC form. If this does not work, refer the agency to your lawyer.

In addition to these behavioral actions, the computer-based actions we discuss in the next section will further help you protect yourself.

TG3.3 Computer-Based Actions to Protect Your Information Assets

As shown in this section, you can take many computer-based actions to help increase the security of your information. Note that our discussion centers around Microsoft Windows XP. In mid-2007, Microsoft released Windows Vista, which is reported to have much improved

security features. We will keep up with Vista's security features on this book's Web site (*www.wiley.com/college/rainer*). We stick to Microsoft Windows XP and Vista because XP currently (mid-2007) dominates the desktop market and Vista probably will also. We do not discuss other operating systems due to space limitations.

Determining Where People Have Visited on the Internet Using Your Computer

At home, you may have a single computer or several computers connected to a network. Although you may practice "safe computing," not everyone using your computer may do the same. For example, you might have roommates who use your computer. Their friends could be using your computer as well.

You can check to see where anyone who may have used your computer has visited on the Internet. To accomplish this, check the Browser history by following these steps in Internet Explorer:

- Click on My Computer.
- Click on Control Panel.
- Click on Network and Internet Connections.
- Click on Internet Options.
- Click on Temporary Internet Files.
- Click on Settings.
- Click on View Files.
- If the Browser History is empty, it means that someone has either (1) not been surfing the Internet at all or (2) has erased the browser history.
- If you now check the Recycle Bin and it is also empty, this means that someone has also emptied the Recycle Bin. At this time, you should consider installing monitoring software on your computer (discussed later).

The Dangers of Social Networking Sites

You should never post personal information about yourself or your family in chat rooms or on social networking sites. In fact, you should access these Web sites and review any entries that you have made. The reason for these precautions is that potential employers are now searching these Web sites for information about you. Well-known social networking sites include MySpace, Friendster, Xanga, YouTube, FaceBook, and Flickr.

One company, Reputation Defender (*www.reputationdefender.com*), states that its goal is to search out all information about you on the Internet and present it to you in the form of a report. Then, at your command, the company states that it will "destroy all inaccurate, inappropriate, hurtful, and slanderous information about you."

Determining If Your Computer Is Infected

Your first action is to determine if your computer system is infected with malicious software. Here are the signs to look for:

- Your computer shuts down unexpectedly by itself.
- Your computer refuses to start normally.
- Running the DOS CHKDSK (**CH**EC**K D**I**SK**) command shows that less than 655,360 (640 kilobytes) bytes are available. To run the CHKDSK command, follow these steps:
  - Click on Start.
  - Click on All Programs.

- Click on Accessories.
- Click on Command Prompt.
- Type in CHKDSK and hit Enter.

- Your computer exhibits erratic behavior, exhibiting some or all of these characteristics:

  - Your system unexpectedly runs out of memory on your computer's hard drive.
  - Your system continually runs out of main memory (RAM).
  - Programs take longer to load than normal.
  - Programs act erratically.
  - Your monitor displays strange graphics or messages.
  - Your system displays an unusually high number of error messages.
  - Your e-mail program sends messages to all the contacts in your address book, without your knowledge or permission.

If you note any or all of these signs, then your computer might be infected with malware. You can then take the computer-based actions discussed later in this chapter to rid your computer of this software. However, if you take the actions discussed in the next section, it will reduce your chances of getting such an infection in the first place.

Computer Actions to Prevent Malware Infections

Many of the actions we discuss in this section are common sense, but surprisingly large numbers of people do not pay attention to them. Taking these steps will help you prevent a malware infection of your computer system.

We begin by considering actions that you must *never* take with your computer. Never open unrequested attachments to e-mail files, even those from people you know and trust. Their computers may have been compromised without their knowledge, in which case the e-mail could be a phishing attack.

Never open attachments or Web links in e-mails from people you do not know. These attachments can infect your system with a worm or virus. Similarly, these Web links can be a phishing attack that can infect your system with a Trojan horse, turning your computer into a zombie, or bot (short for robot). As we saw in Chapter 3, when this occurs your computer is no longer under your control.

Never accept files transferred to you during Internet chat or instant messaging sessions. These files are usually not from people you know and they can infect your system with malware.

Never download any files or software over the Internet from Web sites that you do not know. Never download files or software that you have not requested.

Test Your System. It is a good idea to test your system. Several Web sites provide free security tests. These tests send different types of messages to your computer to evaluate how well your system is protected from a variety of attacks. Free testing Web sites include: Hacker-Whacker (*www.hackerwhacker.com*), Shields Up! (*www.grc.com*), Symantec Security Check (*http://security.norton.com*), McAfee MySecurity Status (*http://us.mcafee.com/MySecurityStatus/*), and AuditMyPC (*www.auditmypc.com*).

Microsoft provides a scanning tool called the Microsoft Baseline Analyzer. This useful tool scans Windows-based computers for common security problems and generates individual security reports for each computer that it scans. The Baseline Analyzer is a free download available at this Web site: *www.microsoft.com/technet/security/tools/mbsa2/default.mspx*.

You can also run free malware scans on your computer. Several companies will scan your computer to identify viruses, worms, and other malware, and also offer suggestions about how to clean your system if it is infected. These companies include:

- Trend Micro (*http://housecall.trendmicro.com*)
- McAfee (*http://us.mcafee.com/root/mfs/default.asp*)
- Panda Software (*www.pandasoftware.com/activescan/com/activescan_principal.htm*)

Install a Security Suite on Your Computer.   Security suites are software packages that contain a variety of security products, such as anti-malware software, spam protection, e-mail fraud protection, spyware detection, intrusion detection, monitoring software, and others. As you can see, these suites provide a great deal of functionality in one package. There is a question whether the individual functions in a security suite can match the combined functions of a group of individual products. Therefore, we discuss individual products in the next sections.

Well-known security suites include the following, but there are many others:

- ZoneAlarm Security Suite (*www.zonelabs.com*)
- McAfee Internet Security Suite (*www.mcafee.com*)
- Norton Internet Security (*www.symantec.com*)
- PC-cillin Internet Security (*www.trendmicro.com*)

Install an Anti-malware Product on Your Computer.   You should install an anti-malware product on your computer and use it, ideally at least once per week. Remember that every time you scan your computer for malware with your anti-malware product, you must update your malware definitions before you scan. Typically, anti-malware product vendors automatically update your malware definitions over the Web.

There are free anti-malware products and commercial anti-malware products. In general, the free products are adequate, but the commercial products offer more functionality. Thefreecountry.com is an excellent resource offering a great deal of information on free anti-malware products, as well as many other security products. For free anti-malware products, see *www.thefreecountry.com/security/anti-malware.shtml*.

Well-known commercial anti-malware products include the following, but there are many others: Norton Anti-malware (*www.symantec.com*), PC-cillin (*www.trendmicro.com*), and VirusScan (*www.mcafee.com*).

Install a Firewall on Your Computer.   A personal firewall is software installed on your home computer that controls communications to and from your computer by permitting or denying communications based on your security settings. A personal firewall will not usually protect any more than the computer on which the software is installed. Nevertheless, firewalls perform essential functions.

Essentially, firewalls should make your computer invisible. This means that your firewall should not respond to Internet requests to ports—that is, communications links to your computer—that are not used for common Internet use. In effect, your computer operates in stealth mode on the Internet.

Firewalls also should alert you to suspicious behavior. They should tell you when a program or connection is attempting to do something unwanted, such as download software or run a program such as ActiveX.

ActiveX (by Microsoft), which can execute programs downloaded from Internet Explorer, can be exploited by attackers trying to compromise your computer. To manage ActiveX in Internet Explorer, follow these steps:

- Click on Start.
- Click on All Programs.

- Click on Accessories.
- Click on System Tools.
- Click on Security Center.
- Click on Internet Options.
- Click on the Security tab.
- Click on the button that says "Custom level. . . ."
- Scroll down and choose the following:
  - The button for Prompt "Download signed ActiveX controls."
  - The button for Disable "Download unsigned ActiveX controls."

Finally, firewalls should block outbound connections that you do not initiate. Your firewall should not let your computer access the Internet on its own. If your computer tries to access the Internet by itself, this is a sure sign that it is infected with malware.

As with anti-malware programs, there are both free firewall products and commercial firewall products. Again, the free products are adequate, but the commercial products offer more functionality. For a list of free firewall software visit: *http://netsecurity.about.com/od/ personalfirewalls/a/aafreefirewall.htm*.

Because Microsoft Windows XP is in such wide use, we briefly discuss its personal firewall here. Microsoft Windows XP Service Pack 2 includes the Windows Security Center and free firewall software. However, this product only protects against unwanted inbound connections. It does not stop existing malware on your computer from making outbound connections.

Many companies offer commercial firewall software. Some of the best-known commercial firewall products are:

- ZoneAlarm Security Suite (*www.zonelabs.com*)
- Norton Internet Security (*www.symantec.com*)
- PC-cillin Internet Security (*www.trendmicro.com*)
- McAfee Internet Security (*www.mcafee.com*)
- Black ICE PC Protection (*www.blackICE.iss.net*)
- F-Secure Internet Security (*www.f-secure.com*)
- Panda Platinum Internet Security (*www.pandasoftware.com*)

It is a good idea to test your firewall. However, it is best to use only those Web sites that are run by actual firewall or security software companies. A good firewall test site is the McAfee Hackerwatch site at *www.hackerwatch.org/probe/*. This site allows you to do a basic probe test on your computer to see if your firewall is blocking ports that may be vulnerable.

Install an Antispyware Product on Your Computer. As with anti-malware products and firewalls, free antispyware products are adequate, but commercial antispyware products offer more functionality. Free antispyware products include Ad-Aware SE Personal (*www.lavasoft.com*) and Spybot Search&Destroy (*www.safer-networking.org*).

Well-known commercial antispyware products include the following, but there are many others: CounterSpy (*www.sunbeltsoftware.com*), Spy Sweeper (*www.webroot.com*), Ad-Aware (*www.lavasoft.com*), SpyCatcher (*www.tenebril.com*), and Spyware Eliminator (*www .aluriasoftware.com*).

Several companies offer free spyware scans. Take a look at Spy Audit (*www.webroot.com*), Zonelabs (*www.zonelabs.com*), and Norton (*www.symantec.com*).

Install Monitoring Software on Your Computer. Monitoring software logs keystrokes, e-mails, applications, windows, Web sites, Internet connections, passwords, chat conversations, Web cams, and even screenshots. Companies that offer monitoring software include SpyAgent (*www.spytech-web.com*), SpyBuddy (*www.exploreanywhere.com*), WinSpy (*www.win-spy.com*), and SpectorSoft (*www.spectorsoft.com*).

Install Content Filtering Software on Your Computer.   Content filtering software performs many functions. It can block access to undesirable Web sites, and record and view all Web sites visited. It can also record both sides of chat conversations from AOL Instant Messenger (AIM and AIM Triton), Yahoo Messenger, and MSN Messenger.

This software provides many filter categories, enabling you to selectively filter content. Companies that offer content filtering software include Cybersitter (*www.cybersitter.com*), NetNanny (*www.netnanny.com*), and CyberSpy (*www.cyberspyware.com*). In addition, a free content filtering software product may be found at *www.we-blocker.com*.

Internet Explorer's Content Advisor utility allows you to block access to Web sites that meet specified criteria and to set your own tolerance levels for various types of Internet content. To activate and configure Content Advisor, follow these steps:

- Click on My Computer.
- Click on Control Panel.
- Click on Network and Internet Connections.
- Click on Internet Options.
- When the Internet Options dialog box appears, select the Content Tab.
- Click on the Enable button.
- You will see four categories: language, nudity, sex, violence. For each category, you can move the slide bar for increased restriction.
- After you have set the slide bar for each category, click OK.

You can also block selected Web sites. To do so, follow these steps:

- Click on My Computer.
- Click on Control Panel.
- Click on Network and Internet Connections.
- Click on Internet Options.
- When the Internet Options dialog box appears, select the Content Tab.
- Click on the Enable button.
- Click the Approved Sites tab.
- Enter the Web sites you wish to block, and click Never.
- Click OK.

Install Antispam Software on Your Computer.   Antispam software helps you to control spam. Well-known commercial antispam products include the following, but there are many others:

- Cloudmark (*www.cloudmark.com*)
- MailFrontier Desktop (*www.mailfrontier.com*)
- SpamKiller (*www.mcafee.com*)
- Norton Antispam (*www.symantec.com*)
- SpamGourmet (*www.spamgourmet.com*)
- SpamAssassin (*http://spamassassin.apache.org/*)

You might also want to set up multiple free e-mail accounts, such as accounts on hotmail and gmail. Then, as you surf the Internet and are asked for your e-mail address, you use one of these accounts and not your home or business e-mail account. When your free e-mail accounts are full of spam, you can close them and open new accounts.

Install Proactive Intrusion Detection and Prevention Software on Your Computer. As we have discussed, anti-malware software is reactive in nature, leaving you vulnerable to zero-day attacks (discussed in Chapter 3). For this reason, it is important to add proactive intrusion detection and prevention software to your defenses. One such product is Prevx (*www.prevx.com*). You can download and install Prevx for free, and it will scan your computer for malicious software. If it finds any, it will activate a free 30-day clean-up account and remove the malware from your computer. Once this period runs out, Prevx will continue to scan incoming programs and protect your computer from them. However, if you subsequently get infected and want to continue using Prevx, you must pay for one year of protection.

Manage Patches. You should download and install all patches immediately (for example, patches for Windows). Software patches are typically released to repair security problems. As soon as patches are announced and released, hackers use zero-day attacks to exploit them before unwary users react. Therefore, if you do not download and install patches quickly, your computer will be extremely vulnerable to attack.

Microsoft provides an automatic method that checks for, and downloads, any new patches. To enable Automatic Update in Windows XP, follow these steps:

- Right click on Start.
- Click on Explore.
- Scroll down and click on Control Panel.
- Click on System.
- Click on the Automatic Updates tab at the top of the box.
- You can now configure when you want to download and install updates.

To open the Microsoft Update window in Windows XP, follow these steps:

- Click on Start.
- Click on All Programs.
- Click on Windows Update.

If you click the Express button, your system will be scanned, and you will be notified if any new updates are available. You can then review suggested updates and install them.

Use a Browser Other Than Internet Explorer. You might want to use a browser other than Internet Explorer, such as Firefox (*www.mozilla.org*), Opera (*www.opera.com*), or Safari from Apple (*http://www.apple.com/macosx/features/safari/*). These browsers are not impregnable, but they are less prominent, and hackers, at least so far, have paid less attention to them. Even if you decide to use a browser other than Internet Explorer, however, you should still implement all of the security measures discussed.

You should also keep your browser updated. For browser updates of Internet Explorer 6, see this site: *www.microsoft.com/windows/ie/downloads/critical/*. Internet Explorer 7 has recently been released, and does not yet have its own updates link.

Use an Operating System Other Than Windows. The two main alternatives to Windows XP and Vista are Apple's Mac OS X and Linux. These two operating systems are not invulnerable but they are both based on UNIX, which makes them inherently more secure than any version of Windows. (UNIX is an operating system developed by AT&T in the 1960s and 1970s that usually runs on servers rather than desktops.) In addition, Linux and Mac OS X have much smaller market shares than Windows, and thus they are less attractive targets for malware.

- Click on Start.
- Click on All Programs.
- Click on Accessories.
- Click on Notepad.
- In Notepad, click on File and then on Open.
- Type in c:\netstat.txt in the box provided.
- You will see a number of active connections in a Listening state. Each active connection will have a local address. The local address will be in a form like this:

    0.0.0.0.xxxxx (where the x's refer to a sequence of numbers)

- If a Trojan horse is present, your system will be listening for one of the addresses listed here. Netstat addresses for a few common Trojans:
  - Back Orifice   0.0.0.0.31337 or 0.0.0.0.31338
  - Deep Throat   0.0.0.0.2140 or 0.0.0.0.3150
  - NetBus   0.0.0.0.12345 or 0.0.0.0.12346
  - Remote Grab   0.0.0.0.7000
- For a complete list of Trojan horse addresses, see *http://www.doshelp.com/Ports/Trojan_Ports.htm*

How to Turn Off Peer-to-Peer (P2P) File Sharing.   Peer-to-peer (P2P) networks do not use central file servers. Instead, the computers on P2P networks act as both clients and servers. These networks, such as Kazaa, Limewire, Ares, and Gnutella, are very poorly protected from viruses, and various types of malware spread through them especially easily.

When you join a P2P file-sharing network, you are no longer an anonymous computer on the Internet. Attackers often focus on P2P networks because computers on these networks can be easy targets. Therefore, you may find it advisable to turn off P2P file sharing on your computer. To do so, follow these steps in Windows XP:

- First, you must have Administrator privileges (which you will have at home).
- Click on My Computer.
- Click on Control Panel.
- Click on Network and Internet Connections.
- Click on Network Connections.
- Click on Local Area Connection icon.
- Click on Properties in the Local Area Connection Status box.
- Click on File and Printer Sharing for Microsoft Networks.
- Click Uninstall.

How to Look for New and Unusual Files.   When an attacker compromises your computer, he or she leaves one or more new files somewhere on your hard drive. In Windows XP, you can use the Search Companion utility to look for newly created files. Follow these steps in Windows XP:

- Right click on Start.
- Click on Search.
- When Search window opens, select All Files and Folders.
- When the Search Companion window appears, enter *.* in the All or Part of the File Name blank.

- Click the When Was It Modified button, and select Within the Last Week.
- Click the Search button.
- Windows will return a list of files modified any time within the last week. Study this list for any files that look suspicious.

How to Detect Fake Web Sites. A fake Web site is typically created to look like a well-known, legitimate site with a slightly different or confusing URL. The attacker tries to trick people into going to the spoofed site by sending out e-mail messages, hoping that some users will not notice the incorrect URL and give away important information. We discussed this attack, known as phishing, in Chapter 3. Examples of products that help detect fake Web sites are the SpoofStick, the Verification Engine, and McAfee's SiteAdvisor. These products are not definitive solutions, but they are helpful.

The SpoofStick (*www.spoofstick.com*) helps users detect fake Web sites by prominently displaying a new tool bar in your browser that shows you which site you are actually surfing. For example, if you go to Amazon's Web site, the SpoofStick tool bar says "You're on amazon.com." However, if you go to a fake Web site that pretends to be Amazon, the Spoof-Stick tool bar shows the actual IP address of the Web site you are surfing, saying, for example, "You're on 137.65.23.117."

Similarly, the Verification Engine (*www.vengine.com*) allows you to verify that the site you are visiting or are directed to via e-mail can be trusted. If you mouse to the logo brand or image you want to verify, the Verification Engine will authenticate the trust credentials of the site you are surfing. In addition, during a secure communications session with Internet Explorer, you can mouse over the padlock to verify: (1) that the padlock is genuine and not a fraudulent graphic and (2) that the site uses a secure sockets layer (SSL) certificate (discussed in Chapter 3) containing the correct information about the company to which you are connected.

McAfee's SiteAdvisor (*www.siteadvisor.com*) sticks a green, yellow, or red safety logo next to search results on Google, Yahoo, and MSN. The product puts a color-coded button in the Internet Explorer toolbar. Mousing over the button displays details about why the Web site is good or bad. SiteAdvisor also scores Web sites on excessive use of pop-up advertisements, how much spam the Web site will generate if you reveal your e-mail address, and if the Web site spreads spyware and adware.

Protecting Your Privacy

In today's hostile Internet environment, you must use strong passwords (discussed in Chapter 3). You may also wish to protect your privacy by surfing the Web and e-mailing anonymously.

Use Strong Passwords. You can use the Secure Password Generator at PCTools (*www.pctools.com/guides/password*) to create strong passwords. The Generator lets you select the number and type of characters in your password.

Remembering multiple passwords is difficult. You can use free software such as Password Safe (*http://passwordsafe.sourceforge.net/*) or Roboform (*www.roboform.com*) to help you remember your passwords and maintain them securely.

How to Surf the Web Anonymously. Many users worry that knowledge of their IP addresses is enough for outsiders to connect their online activities to their "real-world" identities. Depending on his or her technical, physical, and legal access, a determined party (such as a government prosecutor) may be able to do so, especially if he or she is assisted by the records of the ISP that has assigned the IP address. As a result, many people surf the Web and e-mail anonymously.

Surfing the Web anonymously means that you do not make your IP (Internet Protocol) address or any other personally identifiable information available to the Web sites you are visiting. There are two ways to go about surfing the Web anonymously: you can use an anonymizer Web site as a proxy server, or you can use an anonymizer as a permanent proxy server in your Web browser.

A proxy server is a computer to which you connect, that in turn connects to the Web site you wish to visit. You remain anonymous because only the information on the proxy server is visible to outsiders.

For example, consider Anonymouse (*http://anonymouse.org*). When you access this site, you can click on a link called "Your calling card without Anonymouse." You will see the information that is available to any Web site you visit when you surf normally.

If you want to surf anonymously, enter the URL of the site you want to visit on the Anonymouse Web site where it says "Enter URL." For example, suppose you wish to visit *www.amazon.com*. You enter Amazon's URL where indicated on the Anonymouse Web site. When the Amazon Web site opens on your computer, the URL will look like this: *http://anonymouse.org/cgi-bin/anon-www.cgi/http://www.amazon.com/gp/homepage.html/102-8701104-7307331*. You are now anonymous at Amazon because Anonymouse is a proxy server for you and Amazon sees only the information from Anonymouse. Keep in mind that although anonymous surfing is more secure than regular surfing, it is also typically slower.

Other anonymizers include Anonymize (*www.anonymize.net*), Anonymizer (*www.anonymizer.com*), IDZap (*www.idzap.com*), Ultimate Anonymity (*www.ultimate-anonymity.com*), The Cloak (*www.the-cloak.com*), and GhostSurf Platinum (*www.tenebril.com/consumer*).

Another way to surf the Web anonymously is to use an anonymizer as a permanent proxy server on your computer. To do so, here are the steps to take:

- Click on My Computer.
- Click on Control Panel.
- Click on Networking and Internet Connections.
- Click on Internet Options.
- Select the Connections tab.
- Click on LAN Settings.
- When the Local Area Network (LAN) Settings dialog box opens, check the "Use A Proxy Server for Your LAN" option.
- Enter the anonymizer's Web address in the Address field (it is your choice of which anonymizer you wish to use).
- Enter 8080 in the Port box.
- Click OK.

How to E-Mail Anonymously.   The reasons for anonymous e-mail are the same as those for surfing the Web anonymously. Basically, you want to protect your privacy. Anonymous e-mail means that your e-mail messages cannot be tracked back to you personally, to your location, or to your computer. That is, your e-mail messages are sent through another server belonging to a company—known as a re-mailer—that provides anonymous e-mail services. The recipient of your e-mail sees only the re-mailer's header on your e-mail. In addition, your e-mail messages are encrypted so that if they are intercepted, they cannot be read. If you do use a re-mailer, it is possible that your intended recipient will not open your e-mail because he or she will not know it is from you.

Leading commercial re-mailers include CryptoHeaven (*www.cryptoheaven.com*), Ultimate Anonymity (*www.ultimate-anonymity.com*), and Hushmail (*www.hushmail.com*). The commercial version of Pretty Good Privacy (PGP) is available at *www.pgp.com*.

There are free products for anonymous e-mailing and encryption widely available. For example, the free, open-source version of Pretty Good Privacy, called Open PGP, is available at *www.pgpi.org*. For a list of these free products and a discussion of each one, visit: *http://netsecurity.about.com/cs/hackertools/a/aafreecrypt.htm.*

The Outlook e-mail that comes with Microsoft Office also allows you to encrypt outgoing e-mail messages. This product is based on public key technology (discussed in Chapter 3), so you must download and purchase a digital certificate. The first time you send an encrypted message, Microsoft takes you through the steps necessary to obtain your digital certificate.

The steps necessary to use e-mail encryption in Outlook are as follows:

- Open Outlook and compose your message.
- Click the Options button.
- When the Message Options window opens, click the Security Settings button.
- The Security Properties window now opens.
- Check the Encrypt message contents and attachments checkbox.
- For the time being, you should not check the Add digital signature to this message checkbox, because you first need to install a digital certificate.
- Click OK in the Security Properties dialog box.
- You should now be returned to your message.
- Choose an address to send the message to.
- Click the Send button.
- You see the Welcome to Secure E-mail window.
- Click the Get Digital ID. . . . button.
- You now are taken to a Microsoft Web site with links to two digital certificate providers: GeoTrust and VeriSign.
- You have to register for the digital certificate at each provider; you need access to your e-mail (and your telephone for GeoTrust).
- After the registration process, you click an installation button to install the digital certificate.
- When you start the installation, Microsoft may display a Potential Scripting Violation warning; click Yes to continue.
- Once you get the digital certificate installed, you can click the Send button in Microsoft Outlook.
- You may encounter problems if the people you are sending encrypted messages to do not have digital certificates; also, some e-mail systems may not accept encrypted messages because anti-virus scanners cannot scan encrypted e-mail.

Thawte (*www.thawte.com*) offers a free personal digital e-mail certificate. See *http://www.thawte.com/secure-email/personal-email-certificates/index.html.*

It is a good idea to periodically check the trusted certificate authorities that are configured in your browser and verify that those companies can be trusted. In Internet Explorer, follow these steps:

- Click on Start.
- Right click on Explore.
- Click on Control Panel.
- Click on Security Center.
- Click on Internet Options.
- Click on Content tab.
- Click on Certificates button.

- Click on Intermediate Certification Authorities tab and check that the companies listed can be trusted.
- Click on Trusted Publishers tab and check that the companies listed can be trusted.

The StealthSurfer II ID Protect.   The StealthSurfer II ID Protect (*www.stealthsurfer.biz*) is a thumb drive that allows you to surf the Web with anonymity from any computer, even if you use a wireless (Wi-Fi) connection. Using the device's integrated Web browser, you surf in an encrypted mode that masks your IP address and secures your data from interception by outsiders. The device is ideal for frequent coffee shop surfers, airport travelers, Internet café goers, or anyone who uses his or her laptop wirelessly in a public "hotspot."

When you use StealthSurfer, all your sensitive Internet files such as cookies, Internet history, and cache are stored on the device instead of your computer. Should your StealthSurfer fall into unwanted hands, password protection maintains your data's privacy and security. StealthSurfer helps stop identity theft by concealing your Web surfing habits, files, and visited Web sites from anyone who has physical access to your computer.

Small enough to carry on a keychain, the thumb drive plugs into the USB port of your computer. The device contains a comprehensive privacy solution, which includes the following packages already integrated on the device:

- The Firefox Internet browser (*www.mozilla.com/firefox/*).
- Anonymizer: This product provides for anonymous Web surfing (discussed above).
- RoboForm: This Internet privacy product simplifies the process of filling out online forms by storing your user identity, including name, address, phone number, and other important information. It securely stores confidential data such as passwords, bank accounts, and credit card numbers using strong encryption.
- Thunderbird: This product allows for portable, secure e-mail access.
- Hushmail: Discussed above.

How to Adjust Your Privacy Settings on Your Computer.   Windows XP allows you to select the level of privacy that you want when using your computer. Follow these steps to adjust your privacy settings:

- Click on My Computer.
- Click on Control Panel.
- Click on Security Center.
- Click on Internet Options.
- Click on Privacy tab at the top.
- Adjust the slide bar.
- Manipulate the slide bar to determine the level of privacy you desire.
- You will see an explanation of what each level means as you use the slide bar.

- The levels of privacy and their meanings are:
  - Lowest (Accept All Cookies)
    - All cookies will be saved on this computer.
    - Existing cookies on this computer can be read by the Web sites that created them.
  - Low
    - Restricts third-party cookies that do not have a compact privacy policy.
    - Restricts third-party cookies that use personally identifiable information without your implicit consent.

- Medium
  - Blocks third-party cookies that do not have a compact privacy policy.
  - Blocks third-party cookies that use personally identifiable information without your implicit consent.
  - Restricts first-party cookies that use personally identifiable information without your implicit consent.
- Medium High
  - Blocks third-party cookies that do not have a compact privacy policy.
  - Blocks third-party cookies that use personally identifiable information without your explicit consent.
  - Blocks first-party cookies that use personally identifiable information without your explicit consent.
- High
  - Blocks cookies that do not have a compact privacy policy.
  - Blocks cookies that use personally identifiable information without your explicit consent.
- Very High (Block All Cookies)
  - Cookies from all Web sites will be blocked.
  - Existing cookies on your computer cannot be read by Web sites.

Note: A first-party cookie either originates on, or is sent to, the Web site you are currently viewing. These cookies are commonly used to store information, such as your preferences when visiting that site. In contrast, a third-party cookie either originates on, or is sent to, a different Web site from the one you are currently viewing. Third-party Web sites usually provide some content on the Web site you are viewing. For example, many sites use advertising from third-party Web sites, and those third-party Web sites may use cookies. A common use for this type of cookie is to track your Web page use for advertising or other marketing purposes.

Erasing Your Google Search History.   If you have signed up for Google's Personalized Search, you can follow these steps to erase your search history. First you sign in to your Google account at *www.google.com/psearch*. You can examine the Search History page and choose days on the calendar to see every search you have made since you created your Google account. Click on the Remove Items button. Remember, however, that even after you remove items from your computer, logs and backups will still exist on Google's servers. To prevent Google from collecting this information in the future, select items such as Web, Images, and News about which you do not want data collected, and then press the Pause button.

Personal Disaster Preparation

As with a business, you can experience a disaster at home (for example, fires and floods). There are steps you should take to protect your information assets, whether they are stored on your computer (digital form) or in another form (hardcopy). First and foremost, you should have a safety deposit box at your bank for your important papers. You should also have a fireproof safe at home where you can store other important papers. You should keep the Windows XP installation CD and the installation CDs for all your programs in this safe. In addition, you should make a regular backup of your key files, and keep these backups in the safe as well. You might also want to encrypt your backup files if they contain sensitive information.

Restoring Backup Files

You can use the Windows Backup utility to restore the backup copies to your hard disk. In Windows XP, you launch Backup by:

- Click Start.
- Click All Programs.
- Click Accessories.
- Click System Tools.
- Click Backup.

Windows XP has a utility called Windows System Restore. This utility automatically restores key system files to the state they were in before you had problems. System Restore creates a "mirror" of key system files and settings—called a restore point—every ten hours, whenever you install a new piece of software, or whenever you manually indicate. When something goes wrong on your system, such as being infected with a virus or worm, you can revert to a restore point from before the problem occurred, thereby putting your system back in working order.

To use System Restore:

- Click Start.
- Click More Programs.
- Click Accessories.
- Click System Tools.
- Click System Restore.
- When the System Restore window opens, choose the Restore My Computer To An Earlier Time Option.
- Click Next.
- When the Select A Restore Point screen appears, you will see a calendar showing the current month. Any date highlighted in bold contains a restore point. Select a restore point, and click the Next button.
- When the confirmation screen appears, click Next.

Wireless Security

Many home users have implemented a wireless local area network. The security considerations for these networks are greater than those for a wired home network. The reason is simple: if you are wirelessly computing and communicating, then you are broadcasting and therefore, by definition, are nonsecure. The most common reason for intruders to connect to a nonsecure wireless network is to gain access to the Internet. Intruders might also connect in order to use your network as a base for spamming or other unethical or illegal activities, or in order to gain access to your sensitive personal information.

Unfortunately, recent studies have shown that three-fourths of all home wireless users have not activated any security features to protect their information. Unless you take the steps we discuss here, your information assets are extremely vulnerable.

Hide Your Service Set Identifier (SSID).   Your wireless router, which connects your home network with your ISP, comes with a default SSID that is the same for thousands or millions of routers made by the manufacturer. Therefore, an attacker can search for wireless networks by looking for a relatively small number of default SSIDs. For this reason, you should change your default SSID to a unique SSID and tell your wireless home network to stop broadcasting its SSID. A step-by-step guide is available here: *http://netsecurity.about .com/od/stepbystep/ss/change_ssid .htm.*

Use Encryption.   To avoid broadcasting in the clear, you must use encryption with your wireless home network. Wireless equivalent protocol (WEP) is an old protocol that is now very easy to crack and should not be used. Instead, you should use Wi-Fi Protected Access

(WPA2), which is the second generation of WPA. WPA2 is much stronger than WEP and will strengthen your encryption from attackers trying to crack it. Note: Your wireless router must support WPA2. Otherwise, use WPA rather than WEP. In addition, you should use a strong passphrase of at least 20 random characters on your router.

Filter Out Media Access Control (MAC) Addresses. Every piece of networking hardware has a unique identification number called a media access control (MAC) address that looks like this: 00-00-00-00-00-00. (Note that this MAC address is an example.) You should get the MAC address of all computers on your home wireless network. Then, instruct your router to connect only with these computers and deny access to all other computers attempting to connect with your network.

- To find the MAC address of your computer, follow these steps:
  - Click on Start.
  - Click on All Programs.
  - Click on Accessories.
  - Click on Command Prompt.
  - At the cursor, type ipconfig/all.
  - Hit Enter.
  - The MAC address will be the Physical Address.

Limit Internet Protocol (IP) Addresses. You should instruct your router to allow only a certain number of IP addresses to connect to your network. Ideally, the number of IP addresses will be the same as the number of computers on your network.

Sniff Out Intruders. A variety of wireless intrusion detection systems will monitor your wireless network for intruders, tell you they are on your network, show their IP addresses and their activity, and even tell them you know that they are there. Commercial products include the Internet Security Systems (*www.iss.net*) wireless scanner and AirDefense Personal (*www.airdefense.net*). AirSnare is a free wireless intrusion detection system (see *http://home.comcast.net/~jay.deboer/airsnare*).

Using a Public Hotspot. When you travel, keep in mind that most public wireless providers and hotspots use no security at all. As a result, everything you send and receive is in the clear with no encryption. Many intruders go to public hotspots and listen in on wireless computing and communications taking place there. If you must computer wirelessly at a public hotspot, here are several things you should do before you connect.

- Use virtual private networking (VPN) technology to connect to your organization's network (discussed in Chapter 3).
- Use Remote Desktop to connect to a computer that is running at your home.
- Configure Windows firewall to be "on with no exceptions."
- Only use Web sites that use Secure Sockets Layer (SSL) for any financial or personal transactions.

Other Good Information. Microsoft provides excellent resources for wireless networking and wireless security. For an explanation of the Wireless Network Setup Wizard in Windows XP Service Pack 2, see: *www.microsoft.com/technet/community/columns/cableguy/cg0604.mspx*. This overview provides the background for applying the security measures we discussed previously. For an overview of WPA Wireless Security for Home Networks, see: *http://www.microsoft.com/windowsxp/using/networking/expert/bowman_03july28.mspx*.

Now that you have finished all the steps necessary to protect your wireless home network, it is a good idea to test your wireless network for vulnerabilities. eEye has created a free Wi-Fi vulnerability scanner that you can download here: *www.eeye.com/html/resources/downloads/wifi/RetinaWiFi.html*. This tool is a comprehensive scanner that scans your vicinity looking for wireless devices to test. Once run, it will generate a detailed report outlining all the security problems it finds.

Wireless Security Software.   For extra security, you can buy wireless security programs. Trend Micro (*www.trendmicro.com*) has added Wi-Fi Intrusion Detection to PC-cillin, which also includes a personal firewall, antivirus software, and antispyware software. The software warns you when an unknown user tries to access your wireless network. Zonelabs (*www.zonelabs.com*) has a product called ZoneAlarm Wireless Security; this software automatically detects wireless networks and helps secure them.

McAfee (*www.mcafee.com*) provides a free scan to check the security of the wireless network connection that you are using. The scan works only with Internet Explorer. For the scan, go to *www.mcafee.com*, click the section for home users, and look under Free Services for McAfee Wi-Fi scan.

1. Identify the various behavioral actions you can take to protect your information assets.
- Do not provide personal information to strangers in any format (physical, verbal, or electronic).
- Protect your Social Security number.
- Use credit cards with your picture on them.
- Pay very close attention to your credit card billing cycles.
- Limit your use of debit cards.
- Do not use a personal mailbox at your home for anything other than catalogs and magazines.
- Use a cross-cut, or confetti, shredder.
- Sign up with a company that provides proactive protection of your personal information.
- Check to see where anyone who may have used your computer has visited on the Internet.
- Never post personal information about yourself or your family in chat rooms or on social networking sites.

2. Identify the various computer-based actions you can take to protect your information assets.
- Never open unrequested attachments to e-mail files, even those from people you know and trust.
- Never open attachments or Web links in e-mails from people you do not know.
- Never accept files transferred to you during Internet chat or instant messaging sessions.
- Never download any files or software over the Internet from Web sites that you do not know.
- Never download files or software that you have not requested.
- Test your system.
- Run free malware scans on your computer.
- Have an anti-malware product on your computer and use it (ideally at least once per week).
- Have a firewall on your computer.
- Have an antispyware product on your computer.
- Have a rootkit detection product on your computer.

- Have monitoring software on your computer.
- Have content filtering software on your computer.
- Have antispam software on your computer.
- Have proactive intrusion detection and prevention software on your computer.
- Manage patches.
- Use a browser other than Internet Explorer.
- Travel with a "sterile" laptop or no laptop.
- Use a laptop security system.
- Use two-factor authentication.
- Use encryption.
- Use laptop tracing tools or device reset/remote kill tools.
- Turn off peer-to-peer (P2P) file sharing.
- Look for new and unusual files.
- Detect fake Web sites.
- Use strong passwords.
- Surf the Web anonymously.
- E-mail anonymously.
- Adjust the privacy settings on your computer.
- Erase your Google search history.
- Personal disaster preparation: backup, backup, backup!
- Wireless Security

  - Hide your Service Set Identifier (SSID).
  - Use encryption.
  - Filter out media access control (MAC) addresses.
  - Limit Internet Protocol (IP) addresses.
  - Sniff out intruders.
  - Change the default administrator password on your wireless router to something not easily guessed.
  - Use virtual private networking (VPN) technology to connect to your organization's network.
  - Use Remote Desktop to connect to a computer that is running at your home.
  - Configure Windows firewall to be "on with no exceptions."
  - Only use Web sites that use Secure Sockets Layer (SSL) for any financial or personal transactions (discussed in Chapter 3).
  - Use wireless security programs.

Discussion Questions

1. Why is it so important for you to protect your information assets? Can you assume that your organization's MIS department will do it for you?

2. Discuss the differences between behavioral and computer-based actions that you should take.

Web Activities

1. Using one product suggested in this Technology Guide or a product you find, do the following:
- Test or scan your computer for malware.
- Test your firewall.
- Scan your computer for spyware.

2. Follow the steps in this Guide to see if you have a Trojan Horse on your computer.

Basics of Telecommunications and Networks

Learning Objectives

1. Understand the basic telecommunications system.
2. Describe the major types of transmission technologies.
3. Describe the two major types of networks.
4. Describe the Ethernet and TCP/IP protocols.
5. Differentiate between client/server computing and peer-to-peer computing.

TG4.1 The Telecommunications System

A **telecommunications system** consists of hardware and software that transmit information from one location to another. These systems can transmit text, data, graphics, voice, documents, or full-motion video information with two basic types of signals, analog and digital. **Analog signals** are continuous waves that transmit information by altering the characteristics of the waves. Analog signals have two parameters: amplitude and frequency. For example, voice and all sounds are analog, traveling to human ears in the form of waves. The higher the waves (or amplitude), the louder the sound; the more closely packed the waves, the higher the frequency or pitch. In contrast, **digital signals** are discrete pulses that are either on or off, representing a series of *bits* (0s and 1s). This quality allows them to convey information in a binary form that can be clearly interpreted by computers. See Figure TG4.1 for a graphic representation of analog and digital signals.

The major components of a telecommunications system include the following: devices, communications processors, and communications channels and media. Devices include all types of hardware, from smart phones to supercomputers. Figure TG4.2 shows a typical telecommunications system. Note that these systems communicate in both directions, so devices serve as both transmitters and receivers.

Communications Processors

Communications processors are hardware devices that support data transmission and reception across a telecommunications system. These devices include modems, multiplexers, and front-end processors.

Modems. The function of **modems** is to convert digital signals to analog signals (a process called *modulation*) and analog signals to digital signals (a process called *demodulation*). Modems are used in pairs. The modem at the sending end converts a computer's digital information into analog signals for transmission over analog lines. At the receiving end, another modem converts the analog signal back into digital signals for the receiving computer. There are three types of modems: dial-up modems, DSL modems, and cable modems.

Analog Signal
(Wave Signals)

Digital Signal
(Stream of Bits)

FIGURE TG4.1
Analog and digital signals.

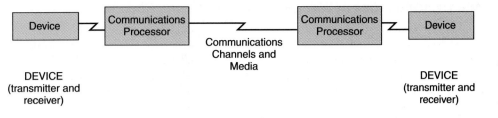

FIGURE TG4.2
Typical telecommunications system.

The U.S. public telephone system was originally designed as an analog network to carry voice signals or sounds in an analog wave format. In order for this type of circuit to carry digital information, that information must be converted into an analog wave pattern by a dial-up modem. Dial-up modems have transmission speeds of up to 56 Kbps.

Cable modems are modems that operate over coaxial cable (for example, cable TV). They offer high-speed access to the Internet or corporate intranets. Cable modems use a shared line. Therefore, when large numbers of users access the same modem, they can slow down the access speed.

DSL (digital subscriber line, discussed later in this Technology Guide) *modems* operate on the same lines as voice telephones and dial-up modems, but DSL signals do not interfere with voice service. Also, DSL modems always maintain a connection, so an Internet connection is immediately available.

Multiplexer.   A **multiplexer** is an electronic device that allows a single communications channel to carry data transmissions simultaneously from many sources. Multiplexing can be accomplished by dividing a high-speed channel into multiple channels of slower speeds or by assigning each transmission source a very small amount of time for using the high-speed channel. Multiplexers lower communication costs by allowing devices to share communications channels. Multiplexing thus makes more efficient use of these channels by merging the transmissions of several computers (for example, personal computers) at one end of the channel, while a similar unit separates the individual transmissions at the receiving end (for example, a mainframe).

Front-End Processor.   With most mainframe and minicomputers, the central processing unit (CPU) must communicate with multiple computers at the same time. Routine communication tasks can absorb a large proportion of the CPU's processing time, leading to degraded performance on more important jobs. In order not to waste valuable CPU time, many computer systems have a small secondary computer dedicated solely to communication. Known as a **front-end processor**, this specialized computer manages all routing communications with peripheral devices.

Communications Media and Channels

For data to be communicated from one location to another, some form of pathway or medium must be used. These pathways are called **communications channels**. The communications channels are listed below. Note that they are divided into two types of media: cable (twisted-pair wire, coaxial cable, and fiber-optic cable) and broadcast (microwave, satellite, radio, and infrared).

Cable or **wireline media** use physical wires or cables used to transmit data and information. Twisted-pair wire and coaxial cable are made of copper, and fiber-optic cable is made of glass. The alternative is communication over **broadcast** or **wireless media**. The key to mobile communications in today's rapidly moving society is data transmissions over

Table TG4.1

Advantages and Disadvantages of Wireline Communications Channels

Channel	Advantages	Disadvantages
Twisted-pair wire	Inexpensive Widely available Easy to work with Unobtrusive	Slow (low bandwidth) Subject to interference Easily tapped (low security)
Coaxial cable	Higher bandwidth than twisted-pair Less susceptible to electromagnetic interference	Relatively expensive and inflexible Easily tapped (low-to-medium security) Somewhat difficult to work with
Fiber-optic cable	Very high bandwidth Relatively inexpensive Difficult to tap (good security)	Difficult to work with (difficult to splice)

electromagnetic media—the "airwaves." In this section we discuss the three wireline channels. Table TG4.1 summarizes the advantages and disadvantages of each of these channels. We discuss wireless media in Chapter 7.

Twisted-Pair Wire. **Twisted-pair wire** is the most prevalent form of communications wiring; it is used for almost all business telephone wiring. Twisted-pair wire consists of strands of copper wire twisted in pairs (see Figure TG4.3). It is relatively inexpensive to purchase, widely available, and easy to work with. It can be made relatively unobtrusive by running it inside walls, floors, and above ceilings. However, twisted-pair wire has some significant disadvantages. It is relatively slow for transmitting data, it is subject to interference from other electrical sources, and it can be easily tapped by unintended receivers for gaining unauthorized access to data.

Coaxial Cable. **Coaxial cable** (Figure TG4.4) consists of insulated copper wire. It is much less susceptible to electrical interference than is twisted-pair wire, and it can carry much more data. For these reasons, it is commonly used to carry high-speed data traffic as well as television signals (thus the term *cable TV*). However, coaxial cable is more expensive and more difficult to work with than twisted-pair wire. It is also somewhat inflexible.

Fiber Optics. **Fiber-optic cables** (Figure TG4.5) consist of thousands of very thin filaments of glass fibers that transmit information via light pulses generated by lasers. The fiber-optic cable is surrounded by cladding, a coating that prevents the light from leaking out of the fiber.

FIGURE TG4.3
Twisted-pair wire.

FIGURE TG4.4   Coaxial cable.

FIGURE TG4.5   Fiber-optic cable.

Fiber-optic cables are significantly smaller and lighter than traditional cable media. They also can transmit far more data, and they provide greater security from interference and tapping. As of mid-2007, optical fiber has reached data transmission rates over 25 trillion bits (terabits) per second. Fiber-optic cable is typically used as the backbone for a network, while twisted-pair wire and coaxial cable connect the backbone to individual devices on the network.

One problem associated with fiber optics is *attenuation*, the reduction in the strength of a signal. Attenuation occurs for both analog and digital signals. To resolve attenuation problems, manufacturers must install equipment to receive the weakened or distorted signals, amplify them to their original strength, and then send them out to the intended receiver.

Transmission Speed

Bandwidth refers to the range of frequencies available in any communications channel. Bandwidth is a very important concept in communications because the transmission capacity of any channel (stated in bits per second, or bps) is largely dependent on its bandwidth. In general, the greater the bandwidth, the greater the channel capacity.

Narrowband channels typically provide low-speed transmission speeds up to 64 Kbps but can now reach speeds of up to 2 Mbps. **Broadband** channels provide high-speed transmission rates ranging from 256 Kbps up to several terabits per second.

The speeds of particular communications channels are as follows:

- Twisted-pair wire: up to 100 Mbps (million bits per second)
- Microwave: up to 200 Mbps
- Satellite: up to 200 Mbps
- Coaxial cable: up to 200 Mbps
- Fiber-optic cable: over 25 Tbps (trillion bits per second)

Transmission Technologies

A number of telecommunications technologies enable users to transmit high-volume data quickly and accurately over any type of network.

Integrated Services Digital Network. **Integrated services digital network (ISDN)** is an older international telephone standard for network access that uses existing telephone lines and allows users to transfer voice, video, image, and data simultaneously.

Digital Subscriber Line.   **Digital subscriber lines (DSLs)** provide high-speed, digital data transmission from homes and businesses over existing telephone lines. Because the existing lines are analog and the transmission is digital, you need DSL modems.

Asynchronous Transfer Mode.   **Asynchronous transfer mode (ATM)** networks permit almost unlimited bandwidth on demand. ATM offers several advantages: it makes possible large increases in bandwidth; and it provides support for data, video, and voice transmissions on a single communications line. ATM currently requires fiber-optic cable, but it can transmit up to 2.5 gigabits per second. On the downside, ATM is more expensive than ISDN and DSL.

Synchronous Optical Network.   **Synchronous optical network (SONET)** is an interface standard for transporting digital signals over fiber-optic lines that allow users to integrate transmissions from multiple vendors. SONET defines optical line rates, known as optical carrier (OC) signals. The base rate is 51.84 Mbps (OC-1), and higher rates are direct multiples of the base rate. For example, OC-3 runs at 155.52 Mbps, or three times the rate of OC-1.

T-Carrier System.   The **T-carrier system** is a digital transmission system that defines circuits that operate at different rates, all of which are multiples of the basic 64 Kbps used to transport a single voice call. These circuits include T1 (1.544 Mbps, equivalent to 24 channels); T2 (6.312 Mbps, equivalent to 96 channels); T3 (44.736 Mbps, equivalent to 672 channels); and T4 (274.176 Mbps, equivalent to 4,032 channels).

Before you go on . . .

1. Describe the basic telecommunications system.
2. Compare and contrast the three wireline communications channels.
3. Describe the various technologies that enable users to send high-volume data over any network.

TG4.2 Types of Networks

A **computer network** is a system that connects computers via communications media so that data can be transmitted among them. Computer networks are essential to modern organizations for many reasons. First, networked computer systems enable organizations to be more flexible so that they can adapt to rapidly changing business conditions. Second, networks enable companies to share hardware, computer applications, and data across the organization and among organizations. Third, networks make it possible for geographically dispersed employees and workgroups to share documents, ideas, and creative insights. This sharing encourages teamwork, innovation, and more efficient and effective interactions. Finally, networks are a critical link between businesses and their customers.

There are various types of computer networks, ranging from small to worldwide. Types of networks include (from smallest to largest) personal area networks (PANs), local area networks (LANs), metropolitan area networks (MANs), wide-area networks (WANs), and the Internet. PANs are short-range (typically a few meters) networks used for communication among devices close to one person. PANs can be wired or wireless. We discuss wireless PANs in Chapter 7. MANs, relatively large computer networks that cover a metropolitan area, fall between LANs and WANs in size. In this section, we discuss local area and wide-area networks. We look at the basics of the Internet and the World Wide Web in Technology Guide 5.

Local Area Networks

A **local area network (LAN)** connects two or more devices in a limited geographical region, usually within the same building, so that every device on the network can communicate with every other device. Figure TG4.6 shows a LAN with four computers and a printer that connect via a **switch**, which is a special-purpose computer that allows the devices in a LAN to communicate directly with each other. Every device in a LAN has a **network interface card** (NIC) that allows the device to physically connect to the LAN's communications medium. This medium is typically unshielded twisted-pair wire (UTP).

Although not required, many LANs have a **file server** or **network server**. File servers are often powerful microcomputers with large, fast-access hard drives. The server typically contains various software and data for the network, and houses the LAN's network operating system, which manages the server and routes and manages communications on the network.

The network gateway connects the LAN to external networks—either public or corporate—so that it can exchange information with them. A **gateway** is a communications processor that connects dissimilar networks by translating from one set of protocols (rules that govern the functioning of a network) to another. A communications processor that connects two networks of the same type is called a **bridge**. A **router** is a communications processor that routes messages through several connected LANs or across a wide-area network such as the Internet.

As we mentioned earlier, because a LAN is restricted to a small area, the nodes can be connected either through cables or via wireless technologies. *Wireless local area networks* (*WLANs*) provide LAN connectivity over short distances, typically less than 150 meters. We discuss WLANs and other wireless technologies in Chapter 7.

Wide-Area Networks

When businesses have to transmit and receive data beyond the confines of the LAN, they use wide-area networks. **Wide-area networks (WANs)** are networks that cover large geographic areas and typically connect multiple LANs. WANs generally are provided by

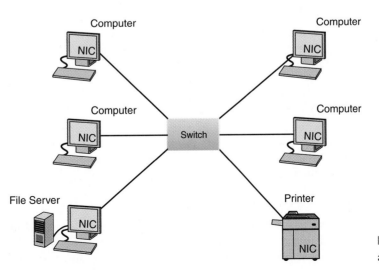

FIGURE TG4.6   Local area network.

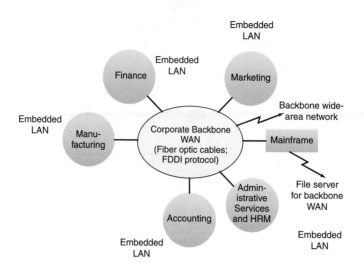

FIGURE TG4.7
Enterprise network.

common carriers such as telephone companies and the international networks of global communications services providers. WANs have large capacity, and they typically combine multiple channels (for example, fiber-optic cables, microwave, and satellite). The Internet, which we discuss in the next section, is an example of a WAN.

One important type of WAN is the **value-added network (VAN)**. VANs are private, data-only networks managed by outside third parties that provide telecommunication and computing services to multiple organizations. Many companies use VANs to avoid the expenses of creating and managing their own networks.

Enterprise Networking

Organizations today have multiple LANs and may have multiple WANs, which are interconnected to form an **enterprise network**. Figure TG4.7 shows a model of enterprise computing. Note that the enterprise network in the figure has a backbone network composed of fiber-optic cable. Corporate **backbone networks** are high-speed central networks to which multiple smaller networks (such as LANs and smaller WANs) connect. The LANs are called *embedded LANs* because they connect to the backbone WAN.

Before you go on . . .

1. What are the main business reasons for using networks?

2. What is the difference between LANs and WANs?

3. Describe an enterprise network.

TG4.3 Network Fundamentals

This section addresses network protocols and types of network processing. These topics describe how networks actually transmit and process data and information over the basic telecommunications system.

Network Protocols

Computing devices that are connected to the network access and share the network to transmit and receive data. These components are often referred to as "nodes" of the network. They work together by adhering to a common set of rules that enable them to communicate with one another. This set of rules and procedures that govern transmission across a network is a **protocol**.

Ethernet.   A common LAN protocol is **Ethernet**. Most large corporations use gigabit Ethernet in which the network provides data transmission speeds of 1 billion bits per second. However, 10-gigabit Ethernet is becoming the standard (10 billion bits per second).

Transmission Control Protocol/Internet Protocol.   The **Transmission Control Protocol/Internet Protocol (TCP/IP)** is the protocol of the Internet. TCP/IP uses a suite of protocols, the main ones being the Transmission Control Protocol (TCP) and the Internet Protocol (IP). The TCP performs three basic functions: (1) It manages the movement of packets (discussed below) between computers by establishing a connection between the computers, (2) it sequences the transfer of packets, and (3) it acknowledges the packets that have been transmitted. The **Internet Protocol (IP)** is responsible for disassembling, delivering, and reassembling the data during transmission.

Before data are transmitted over the Internet, they are broken down into small, fixed bundles of data called packets. The transmission technology that breaks up blocks of text into packets is called **packet switching**. Each packet carries the information that will help it reach its destination—the sender's Internet Protocol (IP) address (discussed in Technology Guide 5), the intended receiver's IP address, the number of packets in this message, and the number of this particular packet within the message. Each packet travels independently across the network and can be routed through different paths in the network. When the packets reach their destination, they are reassembled into the original message. The packets use TCP/IP to carry their data.

TCP/IP functions in four layers (see Figure TG4.8). The *application layer* enables client application programs to access the other layers and defines the protocols that applications use to exchange data. One of these application protocols is the **hypertext transfer protocol (HTTP)**, which defines how messages are formulated and transmitted. The *transport layer* provides the application layer with communication and packet services; this layer includes TCP and other protocols. The *Internet layer* is responsible for addressing, routing, and packaging data packets. The Internet Protocol is one of the protocols in this layer. The *network interface layer* places packets on and receives them from the network medium, which could be any networking technology.

Two computers using TCP/IP can communicate even if they use different hardware and software. Data sent from one computer to another proceed downward through all four layers, beginning with the sending computer's application layer and going through its network interface layer. After the data reach the receiving computer, they travel up the layers.

TCP/IP enables users to send data across sometimes-unreliable networks with the assurance that the data will arrive in uncorrupted form. TCP/IP is very popular with business organizations owing to its reliability and the ease with which it can support intranets and related functions. Figure TG4.9 illustrates a message being sent from New York City to Los Angeles over a packet-switching network.

Types of Network Processing

Organizations typically use multiple computer systems across the firm. **Distributed processing** divides processing work among two or more computers. This process enables computers in different locations to communicate with one another via telecommunications links. A common type of distributed

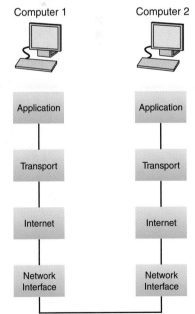

FIGURE TG4.8   The four layers of the TCP/IP reference model.

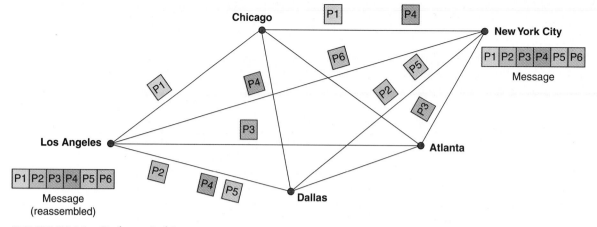

FIGURE TG4.9 Packet switching.

processing is client/server processing. A special type of client/server processing is peer-to-peer processing.

Client/Server Computing. **Client/server computing** links two or more computers in an arrangement in which some machines (called **servers**) provide computing services for user PCs (called **clients**). Usually, an organization does the bulk of its processing or application/data storage on suitably powerful servers that can be accessed by less powerful client machines. The client requests applications, data, or processing from the server, which acts on these requests by "serving" the desired commodity.

Client/server computing leads to the ideas of "fat" clients and "thin" clients. *Fat clients* have large storage and processing power and can still run local programs (for example, Microsoft Office) if the network is down. *Thin clients* may have no local storage and limited processing power. Thus, they must depend on the network to run applications.

Peer-to-Peer Processing. **Peer-to-peer (P2P) processing** is a type of client/server distributed processing in which each computer acts as *both* a client and a server. Each computer can access (as assigned for security or integrity purposes) all files on all other computers.

There are three basic types of peer-to-peer processing. The first accesses unused CPU power among networked computers. A well-known application of this type is SETI@home (*http://setiathome.ssl.berkeley.edu*) (Figure TG4.10). These applications are from open-source projects and can be downloaded at no cost.

The second form of peer-to-peer is real-time, person-to-person collaboration, such as America Online's Instant Messenger. Companies such as Groove Networks (*www.groove.net*) have introduced P2P collaborative applications that use buddy lists to establish a connection and allow real-time collaboration within the application.

The third peer-to-peer category is advanced search and file sharing. This category is characterized by natural language searches of millions of peer systems and lets users discover other users, not just data and Web pages. One example of this is BitTorrent.

BitTorrent (*www.bittorrent.com*) is an open-source, free, peer-to-peer file-sharing application that is able to simplify the problem of sharing large files by dividing them into tiny pieces, or "torrents." BitTorrent addresses two of the biggest problems of file sharing: (1) Downloading bogs down when many people access a file at once, and (2) some people leech, downloading content but refusing to share. BitTorrent eliminates the bottleneck by having everyone share little pieces of a file at the same time—a process called

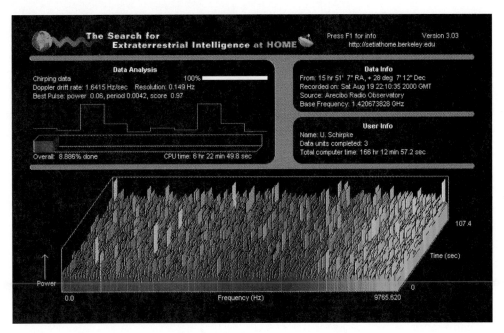

FIGURE TG4.10
SETI@home.

swarming. The program prevents leeching because users must upload a file while they download it. This means that the more popular the content, the more efficiently it zips over a network.

Before you go on . . .

1. Compare and contrast the ATM, SONET, and T-carrier systems.
2. What is a network protocol?
3. Describe the Ethernet and TCP/IP protocols.
4. Differentiate between client/server computing and peer-to-peer processing.

---

1. **Understand the basic telecommunications system.**
   Telecommunications systems are composed of computers, which act as transmitters and receivers of information; communications processors (e.g., modems, multiplexers, and front-end processors); communications channels and media; and networking software.

2. **Describe the major types of transmission technologies.**
   Integrated services digital network (*ISDN*) technology allows users to transfer voice, video, image, and data simultaneously at high speed, using existing telephone lines. *Digital subscriber lines* provide high-speed, digital data transmission, also over existing telephone lines. *Cable modems* operate over coaxial cable (for example, cable TV). *Asynchronous transfer mode* (*ATM*) networks allow for almost unlimited bandwidth on demand. *Synchronous optical network* (*SONET*) is an interface standard for transporting digital signals over fiber-optic lines, allowing integration of transmissions from multiple vendors. The *T-carrier system* is a digital transmission system, whose circuits operate at different rates, all of which are multiples of 64 Kbps.

Summary

3. **Describe the two major types of networks.**

The two major types of networks are local area networks (LANs) and wide-area networks (WANs). LANs encompass a limited geographic area and are usually composed of one communications medium. In contrast, WANs encompass a broad geographical area and are usually composed of multiple communications media.

4. **Describe the Ethernet and TCP/IP protocols.**

A common LAN protocol is *Ethernet.* Large corporations typically use gigabit Ethernet, which provides data transmission speeds of 1 billion bits per second. The *Transmission Control Protocol/Internet Protocol* (*TCP/IP*) is a file-transfer, packet-switching protocol that can send large files of information with the assurance that the data will arrive in uncorrupted form. TCP/IP is the communications protocol of the Internet.

5. **Differentiate between client/server computing and peer-to-peer computing.**

Client/server architecture divides processing between clients and servers. Both are on the network, but each processor is assigned those functions it is best suited to perform. Peer-to-peer processing is a type of client/server distributed processing that allows two or more computers to pool their resources, so that each computer acts as both a client and a server.

Discussion Questions

1. What are the implications of having fiber-optic cable to everyone's home?
2. What are the implications of BitTorrent for the music industry? for the motion picture industry?
3. Discuss the pros and cons of P2P networks.

Web Exercise

1. Access several P2P applications, such as SETI@home. Describe the purpose of each and which ones you would like to join.

Chapter Glossary

analog signals Continuous waves that transmit information by altering the amplitude and frequency of the waves.

asynchronous transfer mode (ATM) Data transmission technology that uses packet switching and allows for almost unlimited bandwidth on demand.

backbone network The main fiber-optic network that links the nodes of a network.

bandwidth The range of frequencies available in a communications channel, stated in bits per second.

bridge A communications processor that connects two networks of the same type.

broadband A transmission speed ranging from 256 Kbps up to several terabits per second.

broadcast media (also called wireless media) Communications channels that use electromagnetic media (the "airwaves") to transmit data.

cable media (also called wireline media) Communications channels that use physical wires or cables to transmit data and information.

cable modems A modem that operates over coaxial cable and offers high-speed access to the Internet or corporate intranets.

clients Computers, such as users' personal computers, that use any of the services provided by servers.

client/server computing Form of distributed processing in which some machines (servers) perform computing functions for end-user PCs (clients).

coaxial cable Insulated copper wire; used to carry high-speed data traffic and television signals.

communications channels Pathway for communicating data from one location to another.

communications processors Hardware devices that support data transmission and reception across a telecommunications system.

computer network A system connecting communications media, hardware, and software needed by two or more computer systems and/or devices.

digital signals Discrete pulses, either on or off, that convey information in a binary form.

digital subscriber lines (DSLs) A high-speed, digital data-transmission technology using existing analog telephone lines.

distributed processing Network architecture that divides processing work between two or more computers, linked together in a network.

enterprise network A network composed of interconnected multiple LANs and WANs.

Ethernet A common local area network protocol.

fiber-optic cables Thousands of very thin filaments of glass fibers, surrounded by cladding, that transmit information via light pulses generated by lasers.

file server (also called **network server**) A computer that contains various software and data files for a local area network, and contains the network operating system.

front-end processor A small secondary computer, dedicated solely to communication, that manages all routing communications with peripheral devices.

gateway A communications processor that connects dissimilar networks by translating from one set of protocols to another.

hypertext transport protocol (HTTP) The communications standard used to transfer pages across the WWW portion of the Internet; defines how messages are formulated and transmitted.

integrated services digital network (ISDN) A high-speed technology that allows users to transfer voice, video, image, and data simultaneously, over existing telephone lines.

Internet Protocol (IP) A set of rules responsible for disassembling, delivering, and reassembling packets over the Internet.

local area network (LAN) A network that connects communications devices in a limited geographical region (e.g., a building), so that every user device on the network can communicate with every other device.

modem Device that converts signals from analog to digital and vice versa.

multiplexer Electronic device that allows a single communications channel to carry data transmissions simultaneously from many sources.

narrowband A transmission speed up to 64 Kbps that can now reach speeds of up to 2 Mbps.

network interface card A type of computer hardware that allows devices in a local area network to physically connect to the LAN's communications medium.

network server (see **file server**)

packet switching The transmission technology that breaks up blocks of text into packets.

peer-to-peer (P2P) processing A type of client/server distributed processing that allows two or more computers to pool their resources, making each computer both a client and a server.

protocol The set of rules and procedures governing transmission across a network.

router A communications processor that routes messages through several connected LANs or to a wide-area network.

server A computer that provides access to various network services, such as printing, data, and communications.

switch A special-purpose computer that allows devices in a LAN to communicate directly with each other.

synchronous optical network (SONET) An interface standard for transporting digital signals over fiber-optic lines; allows the integration of transmissions from multiple vendors.

T-carrier system A digital transmission system that defines circuits that operate at different rates, all of which are multiples of the basic 64 Kbps used to transport a single voice call.

telecommunications system The hardware and software that transmit information from one location to another.

Transmission Control Protocol/Internet Protocol (TCP/IP) A file transfer protocol that can send large files of information across sometimes unreliable networks with the assurance that the data will arrive uncorrupted.

twisted-pair wire Strands of copper wire twisted together in pairs.

value-added network (VAN) A private, data-only network that is managed by an outside third party and used by multiple organizations to obtain economies in the cost of network service and network management.

wide-area network (WAN) A network, generally provided by common carriers, that covers a wide geographic area.

wireless media (see **broadcast media**)

wireline media (see **cable media**)

Technology Guide 5

Basics of the Internet and the World Wide Web

Outline

Learning Objectives

1. Differentiate among the Internet, the World Wide Web, intranets, and extranets.
2. Describe how the Internet operates.
3. Discuss the various ways to connect to the Internet.
4. Describe the parts of an Internet address.

TG5.1 The Internet

The Internet ("the Net") is a global wide-area network (WAN) that connects approximately 1 million organizational computer networks in more than 200 countries on all continents, including Antarctica. Participating computer systems, called nodes, include PCs, local area networks, databases, and mainframes.

The computers and organizational nodes on the Internet can be of different types and makes. They are connected to one another by data communications lines of different speeds. The main network connections and telecommunications lines that link the nodes are referred to as the backbone. For the Internet, the backbone is a fiber-optic network that is operated mainly by large telecommunications companies.

As a network of networks, the Internet enables people to access data in other organizations and to communicate, collaborate, and exchange information seamlessly around the world, quickly and inexpensively. Thus, the Internet has become a necessity in the conduct of modern business.

The Internet grew out of an experimental project of the Advanced Research Project Agency (ARPA) of the U.S. Department of Defense. The project began in 1969 as the *ARPAnet*. Its purpose was to test the feasibility of a WAN over which researchers, educators, military personnel, and government agencies could share data, exchange messages, and transfer files. Today, Internet technologies are being used both within and among organizations. An **intranet** is a network designed to serve the internal informational needs of a single organization. Intranets support discovery (easy and inexpensive browsing and search), communication, and collaboration. For the numerous uses of intranets, see *www.intranetjournal.com*.

In contrast, an **extranet** connects parts of the intranets of different organizations and allows secure communications among business partners over the Internet using virtual private networks. Extranets offer limited accessibility to the intranets of participating companies, as well as necessary interorganizational communications. They are widely used in the areas of business-to-business (B2B) electronic commerce (see Chapter 6) and supply chain management (SCM; see Chapter 8).

Darknets are private networks that run on the Internet but are open only to users who belong to the network. Typically, relatively few people or organizations have access to a darknet, owing to security concerns. These users swap passwords or digital keys so that they can communicate securely with one another. The data flowing between computers often are encrypted, making darknets more secure than typical corporate intranets, because companies usually do not encrypt data located inside corporate firewalls. There are three major uses for darknets: to provide freedom of speech in countries where censorship exists; to ensure corporate security where companies create highly secure networks to protect sensitive data; and unfortunately to infringe on copyrights where people use file-sharing software to illegally share music, movies, and software.

No central agency manages the Internet. Instead, the cost of its operation is shared among hundreds of thousands of nodes. Thus, the cost for any one organization is small. Organizations must pay a small fee if they wish to register their names, and they need to have their own hardware and software for the operation of their internal networks. The organizations are obliged to move any data or information that enter their organizational network, regardless of their source, to their destination, at no charge to the senders. The senders, of course, pay the telephone bills for using either the backbone or regular telephone lines.

Accessing the Internet

There are several ways to access the Internet. From your place of work or your university, you can access the Internet via your organization's LAN. A campus or company backbone connects all the various LANs and servers in the organization to the Internet. You can also log onto the Internet from your home or on the road, with either wireline or wireless connections.

Connecting via an Online Service.   You can also access the Internet by opening an account with an Internet service provider. An **Internet service provider (ISP)** is a company that offers Internet connections for a fee. Large ISPs include America Online (*www.aol.com*), Juno (*www.juno.com*), Earthlink (*www.earthlink.com*), and NetZero (*www.netzero.net*). In addition, many telephone providers and cable companies sell Internet access, as do computer companies such as Microsoft. To use this service, you need a modem and standard communications software. To find a local ISP, access *www.thelist.com*. There, you can search by your telephone area code for an ISP that services your area.

ISPs connect to one another through **network access points (NAPs)**. NAPs are an exchange point for Internet traffic, and they determine how traffic is routed. NAPs are key components of the Internet backbone. Figure TG5.1 shows a schematic of the Internet. Note that the white links at the top of the figure represent the Internet backbone. In this figure, the brown dots where the white links meet are the NAPs.

Connecting via Other Means.   Several attempts have been launched to make access to the Internet cheaper, faster, and easier. For example, terminals known as **Internet kiosks** have been located in public places such as libraries and airports (and even in convenience stores in some countries) for use by people who do not have their own computers. Accessing the Internet from cell phones and pagers is also becoming more common, as is fiber-to-the-home (FTTH). FTTH involves placing fiber-optic cable directly to individual homes. In practice, this is usually done only in new residential developments, but it is rapidly spreading. Table TG5.1 summarizes the various means that you can use to connect to the Internet.

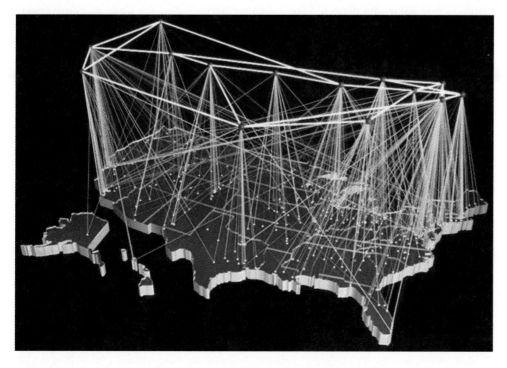

FIGURE TG5.1
Internet (backbone in white) *Source:* neosoft.com

Internet Connection Methods

Service	Description	Typical Bandwidth
Dial-up	Still used in the United States where broadband is not available.	56.6 Kbps
ISDN	More expensive than broadband connections.	128 Kbps
DSL	Broadband access via telephone companies.	Upload: 1.5 Mbps Download: 3 Mbps
Cable Modem	Access over your cable TV coaxial cable. Can have degraded performance if many of your neighbors are accessing the Internet at once.	Upload: 768 Kbps Download: up to 100 Mbps
Satellite	Access where cable and DSL are not available.	Upload: 50 Kbps Download: 5 Mbps
Wireless	Very convenient, and WiMax will increase the use of broadband wireless.	Up to 75 Mbps (theoretically)
Fiber to the Home (FTTH)	Expensive and usually only placed in new housing developments.	Up to 100 Mbps

Addresses on the Internet.   Each computer on the Internet has an assigned address, called the **Internet Protocol (IP) address**, that distinguishes it from all other computers. The IP address consists of numbers, in four parts, separated by dots. For example, the IP address of one computer might be 135.62.128.91. You can access a Web site by typing this number in the address bar of your browser.

Most computers also have names, which are easier for people to remember than IP addresses. These names are derived from a naming system called the **domain name system (DNS)**. Companies called *registrars* are accredited to register domain names by the Internet Corporation for Assigned Names (ICANN) (*www.icann.org*).

Domain names consist of multiple parts, separated by dots, which are read from right to left. For example, consider the domain name *software.ibm.com*. The rightmost part of an Internet name is its **top-level domain (TLD)**. The letters "com" in software.ibm.com indicate that this is a commercial site. Popular TLDs are:

com   commercial sites
edu   educational sites
mil   military government sites
gov   civilian government sites
org   organizations

To finish our domain name example, "ibm" is the name of the company (IBM), and "software" is the name of the particular machine (computer) within the company to which the message is being sent.

In other countries, the country name or designator is the TLD. The use of TLDs within a country is up to that country. Those countries that use TLDs may or may not follow the U.S. TLD system. For example, the United Kingdom uses ".co" where the U.S. uses ".com" and ".ac" (for academic) where the U.S. uses ".edu." Many non-U.S. Web sites do use U.S. TLDs, especially ".com."

IP Addressing Schemes.   Currently, there are two IP addressing schemes. The first scheme, IPv4, is the most predominant. IP addresses using IPv4 consist of 32 bits, meaning that there are 2^{32} possibilities for IP addresses (or 4,294,967,295 distinct addresses). At the time that IPv4 was developed, there were not as many computers that needed addresses as there are today. Therefore, a new IP addressing scheme has been developed, called IPv6.

IP addresses using IPv6 consist of 128 bits, meaning that there are 2^{128} possibilities for distinct IP addresses, which is an unimaginably large number. IPv6, which is replacing IPv4, will accommodate the rapidly increasing number of devices that need IP addresses, such as smart phones.

The Future of the Internet

Despite the massive scope and potential of the Internet, in some cases it is too slow for data-intensive applications. Examples of such applications are full-motion video files (movies) or large medical files (X-rays). In addition, the Internet is unreliable and is not secure. As a result, Internet2 has been developed by more than 200 U.S. universities working with industry and government. **Internet2** develops and deploys advanced network applications such as remote medical diagnosis, digital libraries, distance education, online simulation, and virtual laboratories. Internet2 is designed to be fast, always on, everywhere, natural, intelligent, easy, and trusted. It is not a separate physical network from the Internet. For more detail, see *www.internet2.edu*.

Before you go on . . .

1. Describe the evolution of the Internet and describe Internet2.
2. Describe the various ways that you can connect to the Internet.
3. Describe the parts of an Internet address.

TG5.2 The World Wide Web

Many people equate the Internet with the World Wide Web. However, they are not the same thing. The Internet functions as a transport mechanism, whereas the World Wide Web is an application that uses those transport functions. Other applications, such as e-mail, also run on the Internet.

The **World Wide Web (the Web, WWW,** or **W3)** is a system of universally accepted standards for storing, retrieving, formatting, and displaying information via a client/server architecture. The Web handles all types of digital information, including text, hypermedia, graphics, and sound. It uses graphical user interfaces, so it is very easy to navigate.

Organizations that wish to offer information through the Web must establish a **home page**, which is a text and graphical screen display that usually welcomes the user and explains the organization that has established the page. In most cases, the home page will lead users to other pages. All the pages of a particular company or individual are collectively known as a **Web site**. Most Web pages provide a way to contact the organization or the individual. The person in charge of an organization's Web site is its **Webmaster** (*note:* Webmaster is not gender-specific).

To access a Web site, the user must specify a **uniform resource locator (URL)**, which points to the address of a specific resource on the Web. For instance, the URL for Microsoft is http://www.microsoft.com. HTTP stands for hypertext transport protocol, which we discussed in Technology Guide 4. The remaining letters in this URL—www.microsoft.com— indicate the domain name that identifies the Web server storing the Web site.

Users access the Web primarily through software applications called **browsers**. Browsers provide a graphical front end that enable users to point-and-click their way across the Web, a process called **surfing**. Web browsers became a means of universal access because they deliver the same interface on any operating system under which they run. Leading browsers include Internet Explorer from Microsoft, Firefox from Mozilla (*www.mozilla.org*), and Safari from Apple.

Before you go on . . .

1. What are the roles of browsers?
2. Describe the difference between the Internet and the World Wide Web.
3. What is a URL?

Summary

1. **Differentiate among the Internet, the World Wide Web, intranets, and extranets.**

   The Internet is a global network of computer networks, using a common communications protocol, TCP/IP. The *World Wide Web* is a system that stores, retrieves, formats, and displays information accessible through a browser. An *intranet* is a network designed to serve the internal informational needs of a company, using Internet concepts and tools. An *extranet* connects portions of the intranets of different organization and allows secure communications among business partners over the Internet.

2. **Describe how the Internet operates.**

   The set of rules used to send and receive packets from one machine to another over the Internet is known as the Internet Protocol (IP). Other protocols are used in connection with IP. The best known of these is the *Transmission Control Protocol* (*TCP*). The IP and TCP protocols are so commonly used together that they are referred to as the *TCP/IP protocol*, which we discussed in Technology Guide 4.

3. **Discuss the various ways to connect to the Internet.**

   Table TG 5.1 summarizes various ways to connect to the Internet.

4. **Describe the parts of an Internet address.**

   Each computer on the Internet has an assigned address, called the Internet Protocol (IP) address, that distinguishes it from all other computers. The IP address consists of numbers, in four parts, separated by dots. For example, the IP address of one computer might be 135.62.128.91. You can access a Web site by typing this number in the address bar of your browser.

   Most computers also have names, which are easier for people to remember than IP addresses. These names are derived from a naming system called the domain name system (DNS). Domain names consist of multiple parts, separated by dots, which are read from right to left. For example, consider the domain name *software.ibm.com*. The rightmost part of an Internet name is its top-level specification, or the zone. It designates the type of organization that owns the site. The letters "com" in software.ibm.com indicate that this is a commercial site. To finish our domain name example, "ibm" is the name of the company (IBM), and "software" is the name of the particular machine (computer) within the company to which the message is being sent. In some domain names, you will find two letters to the right of the top-level specification. These two letters represent the country of the Web site. For example, "us" stands for the United States, "de" for Germany, "it" for Italy, and "ru" for Russia.

Discussion Questions

1. Should the Internet be regulated? If so, by whom?
2. Discuss the pros and cons of delivering this book over the Internet.
3. Explain how the Internet works. Assume you are talking with someone who has no knowledge of information technology (in other words, keep it very simple).
4. Do some Web pages take longer to download than others? If so, why? Explain your answer.

Web Exercises

1. Access *www.ipv6.org* and learn about more advantages of IPv6.
2. Access *www.icann.org* and learn more about this important organization.
3. You want to set up your own Web site using your name for the domain name (for example, KellyRainer).
   a. Explain the process for registering a domain.
   b. Which top-level domain will you use and why?
   c. Access *www.icann.org* and obtain the name of an agency or company that can register a domain for the TLD that you selected. What is the name of that agency or company?
   d. Access the Web site for that agency or company to learn the process that you must use. How much will it initially cost to register your domain name? How much will it cost to maintain that name in the future?

Chapter Glossary

browsers Software applications through which users primarily access the Web.

darknet A private network that runs on the Internet but is open only to users who belong to it.

domain name The name assigned to an Internet site, consisting of multiple parts, separated by dots, which are translated from right to left.

domain name system (DNS) The system administered by the Internet Corporation for Assigned Names (ICANN) that assigns names to each site on the Internet.

extranet A network that connects parts of the intranets of different organizations.

home page A text and graphical screen display that welcomes users and describes the organization that has established the page.

The Internet ("the Net") The massive network that connects computer networks of businesses, organizations, government agencies, and schools around the world, quickly, seamlessly, and inexpensively.

Internet2 A new, faster telecommunications network that deploys advanced network applications such as remote medical diagnosis, digital libraries, distance education, online simulation, and virtual laboratories.

Internet kiosks Terminals for public Internet access.

Internet service provider (ISP) Company that provides Internet connections for a fee.

intranet A private network that uses Internet software and TCP/IP protocols.

Internet Protocol (IP) address An assigned address that uniquely identifies a computer on the Internet.

network access points (NAPs) Computers that act as exchange points for Internet traffic and determine how traffic is routed.

surfing The process of navigating around the Web by pointing and clicking a Web browser.

top-level domain (TLD) The rightmost part of an Internet name, indicating the type of organization that owns the site.

uniform resource locator (URL) The set of letters that identifies the address of a specific resource on the Web.

Web site Collectively, all of the Web pages of a particular company or an individual.

Webmaster The person in charge of an organization's Web site.

World Wide Web (the Web, WWW, or W3) A system of universally accepted standards for storing, retrieving, formatting, and displaying information via a client/server architecture; uses the transport functions of the Internet.

Glossary

access controls Controls that restrict unauthorized individuals from using information resources and are concerned with user identification.

accountability A term that means a determination of who is responsible for actions that were taken.

ad-hoc (on-demand) reports Nonroutine reports.

adware Alien software designed to help pop-up advertisements appear on your screen.

affinity portal A Web site that offers a single point of entry to an entire community of affiliated interests.

aggregators Web sites that provide collections of content from the Web.

agile development A software development methodology that delivers functionality in rapid iterations, measured in weeks, requiring frequent communication, development, testing, and delivery.

AJAX A Web development technique that allows portions of Web pages to reload with fresh data instead of requiring the entire Web page to reload.

alien software Clandestine software that is installed on your computer through duplicitous methods.

analog signals Continuous waves that transmit information by altering the amplitude and frequency of the waves.

anti-anti-malware systems (antivirus software) Software packages that attempt to identify and eliminate viruses, worms, and other malicious software.

applets Small Java applications that can be included in an HTML page on the Internet.

application controls Controls that protect specific applications.

application portfolio The set of recommended applications resulting from the planning and justification process in application development.

application program (also called **program**) A computer program designed to support a specific task or business process.

application service provider (ASP) An agent or vendor who assembles the software needed by enterprises and packages them with outsourced development, operations, maintenance, and other services.

application software The class of computer instructions that directs a computer system to perform specific processing activities and provide functionality for users.

arithmetic-logic unit (ALU) Portion of the CPU that performs the mathematic calculations and makes logical comparisons.

artificial intelligence (AI) A subfield of computer science concerned with studying the thought processes of humans and representing the effects of those processes via machines.

asynchronous transfer mode (ATM) Data transmission technology that uses packet switching and allows for almost unlimited bandwidth on demand.

attribute Each characteristic or quality describing a particular entity.

auction A competitive process in which either a seller solicits consecutive bids from buyers or a buyer solicits bids from sellers, and prices are determined dynamically by competitive bidding.

audit An examination of information systems, their inputs, outputs, and processing.

authentication A process that determines the identity of the person requiring access.

authorization A process that determines which actions, rights, or privileges the person has, based on verified identity.

autonomic systems (also called **autonomic computing**) Computer systems designed to manage themselves without human intervention.

back door Typically a password, known only to the attacker, that allows the attacker to access the system without having to go through any security procedures.

backbone network The main fiber-optic network that links the nodes of a network.

bandwidth The range of frequencies available in a communications channel, stated in bits per second.

banners Electronic billboards, which typically contain a short text or graphical message to promote a product or a vendor.

batch processing TPS that processes data in batches at fixed periodic intervals.

best practices The most successful solutions or problem-solving methods for achieving a business outcome.

binary form The form in which data and instructions can be read by the CPU—only 0s and 1s.

biometrics The science and technology of authentication (i.e., establishing the identity of an individual) by measuring the subject's physiologic or behavioral characteristics.

bit A binary digit; that is, a 0 or a 1.

bits Short for binary digit (0s and 1s), the only data that a CPU can process.

blacklisting A process in which a company identifies certain types of software that are not allowed to run in the company environment.

blog (short for **Weblog**) A personal Web site, open to the public, in which the site creator expresses his or her feelings or opinions.

blogosphere The term for the millions of blogs on the Web.

Bluetooth Chip technology that enables short-range connection (data and voice) between wireless devices.

bricks-and-mortar organizations Organizations in which the product, the process, and the delivery agent are all physical.

bridge A communications processor that connects two networks of the same type.

broadband A transmission speed ranging from 256 Kbps up to several terabits per second.

broadcast media (also called wireless media) Communications channels that use electromagnetic media (the "airwaves") to transmit data.

browsers Software applications through which users primarily access the Web.

brute force attack Attacks that use massive computing resources to try every possible combination of password options to uncover a password.

bullwhip effect Erratic shifts in orders up and down the supply chain.

bundling A type of cross-selling in which a combination of products is sold together at a lower price than the combined costs of the individual products.

bus width The size of the physical path down which the data and instructions travel as electrical impulses on a computer chip.

business intelligence Applications and technologies for consolidating, analyzing, and providing access to vast amounts of data to help users make better business and strategic decisions.

business intelligence (BI) systems Information systems that provide computer-based support for complex, non-routine decisions, primarily for middle managers and knowledge workers.

business model The method by which a company generates revenue to sustain itself.

business process A set of related steps or procedures designed to produce a specific outcome.

business-to-business (B2B) Electronic commerce in which both the sellers and the buyers are business organizations.

business-to-consumer (B2C) Electronic commerce in which the sellers are organizations and the buyers are individuals; also known as e-tailing.

business-to-employee (B2E) An organization using electronic commerce internally to provide information and services to its employees.

buy-side marketplace B2B model in which organizations buy needed products or services from other organizations electronically, often through a reverse auction.

byte An 8-bit string of data, needed to represent any one alphanumeric character or simple mathematical operation.

cable media (also called **wireline media**) Communications channels that use physical wires or cables to transmit data and information.

cable modems A modem that operates over coaxial cable and offers high-speed access to the Internet or corporate intranets.

cache memory A type of primary storage where the computer can temporarily store blocks of data used more often and which a processor can access more rapidly than main memory (RAM).

cellular telephones (also called **cell phones**); telephones that use radio waves to provide two-way communications.

central processing unit (CPU) Hardware that performs the actual computation or "number crunching" inside any computer.

certificate authority A third party that acts as a trusted intermediary between computers (and companies) by issuing digital certificates and verifying the worth and integrity of the certificates.

channel conflict The alienation of existing distributors when a company decides to sell to customers directly online.

chat room A virtual meeting place where groups of regulars come to "gab" electronically.

chief information officer (CIO) The executive in charge of the information systems department in an organization.

clicks-and-mortar organizations Organizations that do business in both physical and digital dimensions.

clickstream data Data collected about user behavior and browsing patterns by monitoring users' activities when they visit a Web site.

client/server computing Form of distributed processing in which some machines (servers) perform computing functions for end-user PCs (clients).

clients Computers, such as users' personal computers, that use any of the services provided by servers.

clock speed The preset speed of the computer clock that times all chip activities, measured in megahertz and gigahertz.

coaxial cable Insulated copper wire; used to carry high-speed data traffic and television signals.

code of ethics A collection of principles that are intended to guide decision making by members of the organization.

cold site A backup location that provides only rudimentary services and facilities.

collaboration Mutual efforts by two or more individuals who perform activities in order to accomplish certain tasks.

commercial (public) portal A Web site that offers fairly routine content for diverse audiences; offers customization only at the user interface.

communications channels Pathway for communicating data from one location to another.

communications controls (see also **network controls**) Controls that deal with the movement of data across networks.

communications processors Hardware devices that support data transmission and reception across a telecommunications system.

compact disk, read-only memory (CD-ROM) A form of secondary storage that can be only read and not written on.

comparative reports Reports that compare performances of different business units or time periods.

competitive advantage An advantage over competitors in some measure such as cost, quality, or speed; leads to control of a market and to larger-than-average profits.

competitive forces model A business framework devised by Michael Porter, which analyzes competitiveness by recognizing five major forces that could endanger a company's position.

compiler A type of systems software that converts other computer languages into machine language.

component-based development A software development methodology that uses standard components to build applications.

computer network A system connecting communications media, hardware, and software needed by two or more computer systems and/or devices.

computer programs The sequences of instructions for the computer, which comprise software.

computer-aided software engineering (CASE) Development approach that uses specialized tools to automate many of the tasks in the SDLC; upper CASE tools automate the early stages of the SDLC, and lower CASE tools automate the later stages.

computer-based information system (CBIS) An information system that uses computer technology to perform some or all of its intended tasks.

consumer-to-consumer (C2C) Electronic commerce in which both the buyer and the seller are individuals (not businesses).

contract software Specific software programs developed for a particular company by a vendor.

control unit Portion of the CPU that controls the flow of information.

controls Defense mechanisms, also called countermeasures, employed by organizations to protect their information assets.

controls evaluation A process in which the organization identifies security deficiencies and calculates the costs of implementing adequate control measures.

cookies Small amounts of information that Web sites store on your computer, temporarily or more or less permanently.

copyright A grant that provides the creator of intellectual property with ownership of it for the life of the creator plus 70 years.

corporate portal A Web site that provides a single point of access to critical business information located inside and outside of an organization.

cross-selling The marketing of complementary products to customers.

customer relationship management (CRM) An enterprisewide effort to acquire and retain customers, often supported by IT.

customer touch point Any method of interaction with a customer.

cyberbanking Various banking activities conducted electronically from home, a business, or on the road instead of at a physical bank location.

cybercafés Public places in which Internet terminals are available, usually for a small fee.

cybercrime Illegal activities executed on the Internet.

cybersquatting Registering domain names in the hope of selling them later at a higher price.

cyberterrorism A premeditated, politically motivated attack against information, computer systems, computer programs, and data that results in violence against noncombatant targets by subnational groups or clandestine agents.

cyberwarfare War in which a country's information systems could be paralyzed from a massive attack by destructive software.

darknet A private network that runs on the Internet but is open only to users who belong to it.

dashboards (also called **digital dashboards)** Information systems that support all managers of the organization by providing rapid access to timely information and direct access to structured information in the form of reports.

data dictionary Collection of definitions of data elements, data characteristics that use the data elements, and the individuals, business functions, applications, and reports that use this data element.

data governance An approach to managing information across an entire organization.

data items An elementary description of things, events, activities, and transactions that are recorded, classified, and stored but are not organized to convey any specific meaning.

data mart A small data warehouse designed for a strategic business unit (SBU) or a department.

data mining The process of searching for valuable business information in a large database, data warehouse, or data mart.

data model Definition of the way data in a DBMS are conceptually structured.

data warehouse A repository of subject-oriented historical data that are organized to be accessible in a form readily acceptable for analytical processing.

database A group of logically related files that stores data and the associations among them.

database management system (DBMS) The software program (or group of programs) that provides access to a database.

decision room A face-to-face setting for a group DSS, in which terminals are available to the participants.

decision support system (DSS) Business intelligence systems that evolved from decision support systems; they combine models and data in an attempt to solve semi-structured and some unstructured problems with extensive user involvement.

demilitarized zone (DMZ) A separate organizational local area network that is located between an organization's internal network and an external network, usually the Internet.

denial-of-service attack A cyberattack in which an attacker sends a flood of data packets to the target computer, with the aim of overloading its resources.

dictionary attack Attacks that try combinations of letters and numbers that are most likely to succeed, such as all words from a dictionary.

digital certificate An electronic document attached to a file certifying that this file is from the organization it claims to be from and has not been modified from its original format or content.

digital dashboard A business intelligence system that provides rapid access to timely information and direct access to management reports.

digital divide The gap between those who have access to information and communications technology and those who do not.

digital dossier An electronic description of a user and his or her habits.

digital radio (see **satellite radio**).

digital signals Discrete pulses, either on or off, that convey information in a binary form.

digital subscriber lines (DSLs) A high-speed, digital data-transmission technology using existing analog telephone lines.

digital video disk (DVD) An optical storage device used to store digital video or computer data.

digital wallet (e-wallet) A software component in which a user stores secured personal and credit card information for one-click reuse.

direct conversion Implementation process in which the old system is cut off and the new system is turned on at a certain point in time.

disintermediation Elimination of intermediaries in electronic commerce.

distance learning (DL) Learning situations in which teachers and students do not meet face to face.

distributed denial-of-service attack A denial-of-service attack that sends a flood of data packets from many compromised computers simultaneously.

distributed processing Network architecture that divides processing work between two or more computers, linked together in a network.

documentation Written description of the functions of a software program.

domain name The name assigned to an Internet site, consisting of multiple parts, separated by dots, which are translated from right to left.

domain name system (DNS) The system administered by the Internet Corporation for Assigned Names (ICANN) that assigns names to each site on the Internet.

drill-down reports Reports that show a greater level of detail than is included in routine reports.

e-business A broader definition of electronic commerce, including buying and selling of goods and services, as well as servicing customers, collaborating with business partners, conducting e-learning, and conducting electronic transactions within an organization.

e-government The use of electronic commerce to deliver information and public services to citizens, business partners, and suppliers of government entities, and those working in the public sector.

e-learning Learning supported by the Web; can be done inside traditional classrooms or in virtual classrooms.

e-procurement Purchasing by using electronic support.

e-wallet (see **digital wallet**).

edge computing Process in which parts of a Web site's content and processing are located close to the user to decrease response time and lower costs.

electronic commerce (e-commerce) The process of buying, selling, transferring, or exchanging products, services, or information via computer networks, including the Internet.

electronic commerce systems A type of interorganizational information system that enables organizations to conduct transactions with other businesses and with customers.

electronic data interchange (EDI) A communication standard that enables the electronic transfer of routine documents between business partners.

electronic mall A collection of individual shops under one Internet address.

electronic marketplace A virtual market space on the Web where many buyers and many sellers conduct electronic business activities.

electronic payment systems Computer-based systems that allow customers to pay for goods and services electronically, rather than writing a check or using cash.

electronic retailing (e-tailing) The direct sale of products and services through storefronts or electronic malls, usually designed around an electronic catalog format and/or auctions.

electronic storefront The Web site of a single company, with its own Internet address, at which orders can be placed.

electronic surveillance Monitoring or tracking people's activities with the aid of computers.

employee monitoring systems Systems that monitor employees' computers, e-mail activities, and Internet surfing activities.

encryption The process of converting an original message into a form that cannot be read by anyone except the intended receiver.

enterprise network A network composed of interconnected multiple LANs and WANs.

enterprise resource planning (ERP) systems Systems that tightly integrate the functional area information systems via a common database.

enterprise storage system An independent, external system with intelligence that includes two or more storage devices.

entity A person, place, thing, or event about which information is maintained in a record.

entity classes A grouping of entities of a given type.

entity-relationship (ER) diagram Document that shows data entities and attributes and relationships among them.

entity-relationship (ER) modeling The process of designing a database by organizing data entities to be used and identifying the relationships among them.

entry barrier Product or service feature that customers expect from organizations in a certain industry; an organization trying to enter this market must provide this product or service at a minimum to be able to compete.

ergonomics The science of adapting machines and work environments to people, focusing on creating an environment that is safe, well lit, and comfortable.

Ethernet A common local area network protocol.

ethics A term that refers to the principles of right and wrong that individuals use to make choices to guide their behaviors.

exception reports Reports that include only information that exceeds certain threshold standards.

exchange (see **public exchange**).

expert systems (ES) Information systems that attempt to duplicate the work of human experts by applying reasoning capabilities, knowledge, and expertise within a specific domain.

explicit knowledge The more objective, rational, and technical types of knowledge.

exposure The harm, loss, or damage that can result if a threat compromises an information resource.

extensible markup language (XML) A programming language designed to improve the functionality of Web documents by providing more flexible and adaptable data identification.

extranet A network that connects parts of the intranets of different organizations.

fat-client systems Desktop computer systems that offer full functionality.

feasibility study Investigation that gauges the probability of success of a proposed project and provides a rough assessment of the project's feasibility.

fiber-optic cables Thousands of very thin filaments of glass fibers, surrounded by cladding, that transmit information via light pulses generated by lasers.

field A grouping of logically related characters into a word, a small group of words, or a complete number.

file A grouping of logically related records.

file server (also called **network server**) A computer that contains various software and data files for a local area network, and contains the network operating system.

firewall A system (either hardware, software, or a combination of both) that prevents a specific type of information from moving between untrusted networks, such as the Internet, and private networks, such as your company's network.

flash memory A form of nonvolatile computer memory that can be electrically erased and reprogrammed.

flash memory devices Electronic storage devices that are compact, portable, require little power, and contain no moving parts.

forward auction An auction that sellers use as a selling channel to many potential buyers; the highest bidder wins the items.

front-end processor A small secondary computer, dedicated solely to communication, that manages all routing communications with peripheral devices.

functional area information systems (FAISs) Information systems designed to summarize data and prepare reports for the functional areas, such as accounting and marketing.

functional exchanges Electronic marketplaces where needed services such as temporary help or extra office space are traded on an "as-needed" basis.

gateway A communications processor that connects dissimilar networks by translating from one set of protocols to another.

geographic information system A computer-based system for capturing, integrating, manipulating, and displaying data using digitized maps.

global information systems Interorganizational systems that connect companies located in two or more countries.

global positioning system (GPS) A wireless system that uses satellites to enable users to determine their position anywhere on earth.

globalization The integration and interdependence of economic, social, cultural, and ecological facets of life, enabled by rapid advances in information technology

goal-seeking analysis Study that attempts to find the value of the inputs necessary to achieve a desired level of output.

graphical user interface (GUI) System software that allows users to have direct control of visible objects (such as icons) and actions, which replace command syntax.

grid computing Applying the resources of many computers in a network to a single problem at the same time.

group decision support system (GDSS) An interactive computer-based system that supports the process of finding solutions by a group of decision makers.

group purchasing The aggregation of purchasing orders from many buyers so that a volume discount can be obtained.

groupware Software products that support groups of people who collaborate on a common task or goal and that provide a way for groups to share resources.

hard drives A form of secondary storage that stores data on platters divided into concentric tracks and sectors, which can be read by a read/write head that pivots across the rotating disks.

hardware A set of devices (for example, processor, monitor, keyboard, printer) that together accept data and information, process them, and display them.

holographic memory An optical technology that uses a three-dimensional medium to store data.

home page A text and graphical screen display that welcomes users and describes the organization that has established the page.

horizontal exchanges Electronic marketplaces that connect buyers and sellers across many industries, used mainly for MRO materials.

hot sites A fully configured computer facility, with all information resources and services, communications links, and physical plant operations, that duplicate your company's computing resources and provide near real-time recovery of IT operations.

hotspot A small geographical perimeter within which a wireless access point provides service to a number of users.

hyperlinks The links that connect document nodes in hypertext.

hypertext An approach to document management in which documents are stored in a network of nodes connected by links and are accessed through interactive browsing.

hypertext document The combination of nodes, links, and supporting indexes for any particular topic in hypertext.

hypertext markup language (HTML) The standard programming language used on the Web to create and recognize hypertext documents.

hypertext transport protocol (HTTP) The communications standard used to transfer pages across the WWW portion of the Internet; defines how messages are formulated and transmitted.

identifier An attribute that identifies an entity instance.

identity theft Crime in which someone steals the personal information of others to create a false identity and then uses it for some fraud.

implementation The process of converting from an old computer system to a new one.

industrywide portal A Web-based gateway to information and knowledge for an entire industry.

information Data that have been organized so that they have meaning and value to the recipient.

information system (IS) A process that collects, processes, stores, analyzes, and disseminates information for a specific purpose; most ISs are computerized.

information systems controls The procedures, devices, or software aimed at preventing a compromise to a system.

information technology Technology that relates to any computer-based tool that people use to work with information and support the information and information processing needs of an organization.

information technology (IT) architecture A high-level map or plan of the information assets in an organization.

information technology (IT) infrastructure The physical facilities, IT components, IT services, and IT personnel that support the entire organization.

infrared A type of wireless transmission that uses red light not commonly visible to human eyes.

instance A particular entity within an entity class.

integrated CASE (ICASE) tools CASE tools that provide links between upper CASE and lower CASE tools.

integrated services digital network (ISDN) A high-speed technology that allows users to transfer voice, video, image, and data simultaneously, over existing telephone lines.

intellectual capital (intellectual assets) Other terms for knowledge.

intellectual property The intangible property created by individuals or corporations, which is protected under trade secret, patent, and copyright laws.

intelligent systems A term that describes the various commercial applications of artificial intelligence.

Internet kiosks Terminals for public Internet access.

Internet Protocol (IP) A set of rules responsible for disassembling, delivering, and reassembling packets over the Internet.

Internet Protocol (IP) address An assigned address that uniquely identifies a computer on the Internet.

Internet service provider (ISP) Company that provides Internet connections for a fee.

Internet telephony (voice-over Internet protocol or VoIP) Use of the Internet as the transmission medium for telephone calls.

Internet2 A new, faster telecommunications network that deploys advanced network applications such as remote medical diagnosis, digital libraries, distance education, online simulation, and virtual laboratories.

interorganizational information system (IOS) An information system that supports information flow among two or more organizations.

intranet A private network that uses Internet software and TCP/IP protocols.

intrusion detection system A system designed to detect all types of malicious network traffic and computer usage that cannot be detected by a firewall.

IT steering committee A committee, comprised of a group of managers and staff representing various organizational units, set up to establish IT priorities and to ensure that the MIS function is meeting the needs of the enterprise.

IT strategic plan A set of long-range goals that describe the IT infrastructure and major IT initiatives needed to achieve the goals of the organization.

java Object-oriented programming language, developed by Sun Microsystems, that gives programmers the ability to develop applications that work across the Internet.

joint application design (JAD) A group-based tool for collecting user requirements and creating system designs.

key-indicator reports Reports that summarize the performance of critical activities.

keystroke loggers (keyloggers) Hardware or software that can detect all keystrokes made on a compromised computer.

knowledge Data and/or information that have been organized and processed to convey understanding, experience, accumulated learning, and expertise as they apply to a current problem or activity.

knowledge management (KM) A process that helps organizations identify, select, organize, disseminate, transfer, and apply information and expertise that are part of the organization's memory and that typically reside within the organization in an unstructured manner.

knowledge management systems (KMSs) Information technologies used to systematize, enhance, and expedite intra- and interfirm knowledge management.

knowledge workers Professional employees who are experts in a particular subject area and create information and knowledge.

laptop and notebook computers Small, easily transportable, lightweight microcomputers.

least privilege A principle that users be granted the privilege for some activity only if there is a justifiable need to grant this authorization.

liability A legal concept meaning that individuals have the right to recover the damages done to them by other individuals, organizations, or systems.

line width The distance between transistors; the smaller the line width, the faster the chip.

local area network (LAN) A network that connects communications devices in a limited geographical region (e.g., a building), so that every user device on the network can communicate with every other device.

location-based commerce (L-commerce) Mobile commerce transactions targeted to individuals in specific locations, at specific times.

logic bombs Segments of computer code embedded within an organization's existing computer programs.

logical system design Abstract specification of what a computer system will do.

machine instruction cycle The cycle of computer processing, whose speed is measured in terms of the number of instructions a chip processes per second.

magnetic disks A form of secondary storage on a magnetized disk divided into tracks and sectors that provide addresses for various pieces of data; also called hard disks.

magnetic tape A secondary storage medium on a large open reel or in a smaller cartridge or cassette.

mainframes Relatively large computers used in large enterprises for extensive computing applications that are accessed by thousands of users.

make-to-order The strategy of producing customized products and services.

malware Malicious software such as viruses and worms.

management A process by which organizational goals are achieved through the use of resources.

management information systems Systems that deal with the planning for, development, management, and use of information technology tools to help people perform all tasks related to information processing and management.

mashup A Web site that takes content from a number of other Web sites and mixes them together to create a new kind of content.

mass customization A production process in which items are produced in large quantities but are customized to fit the desires of each customer.

master data A set of core data, such as customer, product, employee, vendor, geographic location, and so on that span the enterprise information systems.

master data management A process that provides companies with the ability to store, maintain, exchange, and synchronize a consistent, accurate, and timely "single version of the truth" for the company's core master data.

Mesh network A network composed of motes in the physical environment that "wake up" at intervals to transmit data to their nearest neighbor mote.

metasearch engine A computer program that searches several engines at once and integrates the findings of the various search engines to answer queries posted by users.

methods In object-oriented programming, the instructions about what to do with encapsulated data objects.

microbrowser Internet browsers with a small file size that can work within the low-memory constraints of wireless devices and the low bandwidths of wireless networks.

microcomputers The smallest and least expensive category of general-purpose computers; also called micros, personal computers, or PCs.

microcontrollers Embedded computer chips that usually cost less and work in less-demanding applications than microprocessors.

microprocessor The CPU, made up of millions of transistors embedded in a circuit on a silicon wafer or chip.

microwave transmission A wireless system that uses microwaves for high-volume, long-distance, point-to-point communication.

minicomputers Relatively small, inexpensive, and compact midrange computers that perform the same functions as mainframe computers, but to a more limited extent.

mobile commerce (m-commerce) Electronic commerce transactions that are conducted in a wireless environment, especially via the Internet.

mobile computing A real-time, wireless connection between a mobile device and other computing environments, such as the Internet or an intranet.

mobile portal A portal that aggregates and provides content and services for mobile users.

mobile wallet A technology that allows users to make purchases with a single click from their mobile devices.

model (in decision making) A simplified representation, or abstraction, of reality.

modem Device that converts signals from analog to digital and vice versa.

Moore's law Prediction by Gordon Moore, an Intel co-founder, that microprocessor complexity would double approximately every two years.

multichanneling A process through which a company integrates its online and offline channels.

multidimensional structure The manner in which data are structured in a data warehouse so that they can be analyzed by different views or perspectives, which are called dimensions.

multimedia technology Computer-based integration of text, sound, still images, animation, and digitized full-motion video.

multiplexer Electronic device that allows a single communications channel to carry data transmissions simultaneously from many sources.

multiprocessing Simultaneously processing more than one program by assigning them to different processors (multiple CPUs).

multitasking The management of two or more tasks, or programs, running concurrently on the computer system (one CPU).

multithreading A form of multitasking that runs multiple tasks within a single application simultaneously.

nanotechnology The creation of materials, devices, and systems at a size of 1 to 100 nanometers (billionths of a meter).

narrowband A transmission speed up to 64 Kbps that can now reach speeds of up to 2 Mbps.

natural language generation (also **voice synthesis**) Technology that enables computers to produce ordinary language, by "voice" or on the screen, so that people can understand computers more easily.

natural language processing (NLP) Communicating with a computer in the user's native language.

natural language understanding (also **speech or voice recognition**) The ability of a computer to comprehend instructions given in ordinary language, via the keyboard or by voice.

near-field communications (NFC) The smallest of the short-range wireless networks that is designed to be embedded in mobile devices such as cell phones and credit cards.

network A connecting system (wireline or wireless) that permits different computers to share their information.

network access points (NAPs) Computers that act as exchange points for Internet traffic and determine how traffic is routed.

network controls (see **communications controls**).

network interface card A type of computer hardware that allows devices in a local area network to physically connect to the LAN's communications medium.

network server (see **file server**).

network-attached storage (NAS) An enterprise storage system in which a special-purpose server provides file storage to users who access the device over a network.

neural network A system of programs and data structures that approximates the operation of the human brain.

normalization A method for analyzing and reducing a relational database to its most streamlined form for minimum redundancy, maximum data integrity, and best processing performance.

notebook computer (see **laptop computer**).

object In object-oriented programming, the combination of a small amount of data with instructions about what to do with the data.

object-oriented languages Programming languages that encapsulate a small amount of data with instructions about what to do with the data.

off-the-shelf application software Software purchased, leased, or rented from a vendor that develops programs and sells them to many organizations; can be standard or customizable.

office automation systems (OASs) Information systems that typically support the clerical staff, lower and middle managers, and knowledge workers.

online analytical processing (OLAP) The analysis of accumulated data by end users.

online transaction processing (OLTP) TPS that processes data after transactions occur, frequently in real time.

open systems A model of computing products that work together by use of the same operating system with compatible software on all the different computers that would interact with one another in an organization.

open-source software Software made available in source code form at no cost to developers.

operating environments A set of computer programs that adds features enabling developers to create applications without directly accessing the operating system; functions only with an operating system.

operating system (OS) The main system control program, which supervises the overall operations of the computer, allocates CPU time and main memory to programs, and provides an interface between user and hardware.

opt-in model A model of informed consent, where a business is prohibited from collecting any personal information unless the customer specifically authorizes it.

opt-out model A model of informed consent that permits the company to collect personal information until the customer specifically requests that the data not be collected.

optical storage devices A form of secondary storage in which a laser reads the surface of a reflective plastic platter.

organizational decision support system (ODSS) A DSS-BI system that focuses on an organizational task or activity involving a sequence of operations and decision makers.

organizational social responsibility Efforts by organizations to solve various social problems.

outsourcing Use of outside contractors or external organizations to acquire IT services.

package Common term for a computer program developed by a vendor and available for purchase in prepackaged form.

packet switching The transmission technology that breaks up blocks of text into packets.

passphrase A series of characters that is longer than a password but that can be memorized easily.

password A private combination of characters that only the user should know.

password attack (see **brute force attack** and **dictionary attack**).

patent A document that grants the holder exclusive rights on an invention or process for 20 years.

peer-to-peer (P2P) processing A type of client/server distributed processing that allows two or more computers to pool their resources, making each computer both a client and a server.

penetration test A method of evaluating the security of an information system by simulating an attack by a malicious perpetrator.

people Those individuals who use the hardware and software, interface with it, or use its output.

permission marketing Method of marketing that asks consumers to give their permission to voluntarily accept online advertising and e-mail.

person-to-person payments A form of electronic cash that enables the transfer of funds between two individuals, or between an individual and a business, without the use of a credit card.

personal application software General-purpose, off-the-shelf application programs that support general types of processing, rather than being linked to any specific business function.

personal area network A computer network used for communication among computer devices close to one person.

pervasive computing (also called **ubiquitous computing**) A computer environment in which virtually every object has processing power with wireless or wired connections to a global network.

phased conversion Implementation process that introduces components of the new system in stages, until the entire new system is operational.

phishing attack An attack that uses deception to fraudulently acquire sensitive personal information by masquerading as an official-looking e-mail.

physical controls Controls that restrict unauthorized individuals from gaining access to a company's computer facilities.

physical system design Actual physical specifications that state how a computer system will perform its functions.

pilot conversion Implementation process that introduces the new system in one part of the organization on a trial basis; when the new system is working properly, it is introduced in other parts of the organization.

piracy Copying a software program without making payment to the owner.

platform The hardware, software and communications compounds that organisations use to process and manage information.

plug-and-play Feature that enables the operating system to recognize new hardware and install the necessary software (called device drivers) automatically.

podcast A digital audio file that is distributed over the Web using Really Simple Syndication for playback on portable media players or personal computers.

pop-under ad An advertisement that is automatically launched by some trigger and appears underneath the active window.

pop-up ad An advertisement that is automatically launched by some trigger and appears in front of the active window.

portal A Web-based personalized gateway to information and knowledge that provides information from disparate information systems and the Internet, using advanced search and indexing techniques.

primary activities Those business activities related to the production and distribution of the firm's products and services, thus creating value.

primary key The identifier field or attribute that uniquely identifies a record.

primary storage (also called **main memory**) High-speed storage located directly on the motherboard that stores data to be processed by the CPU, instructions telling the CPU how to process the data, and operating systems programs.

privacy The right to be left alone and to be free of unreasonable personal intrusion.

privacy codes (see **privacy policies**).

privacy policies An organization's guidelines with respect to protecting the privacy of customers, clients, and employees.

privilege A collection of related computer system operations that can be performed by users of the system profiling.

procedures The set of instructions about how to combine components of information systems in order to process information and generate the desired output.

productivity The ratio between the inputs to a process and the outputs from that process.

profiling The process of compiling a digital dossier on a person.

programming The translation of a system's design specifications into computer code.

propagation delay The one-quarter-second transmission delay in communication to and from GEO satellites.

proprietary application software Software that addresses a specific or unique business need for a company; may be developed in-house or may be commissioned from a software vendor.

protocol The set of rules and procedures governing transmission across a network.

prototyping Approach that defines an initial list of user requirements, builds a prototype system, and then improves the system in several iterations based on users' feedback.

public exchange (or exchange) Electronic marketplace in which there are many sellers and many buyers, and entry is open to all; it is frequently owned and operated by a third party.

public-key encryption (also called **asymmetric encryption**) A type of encryption that uses two different keys, a public key and a private key.

query by example (QBE) Database language that enables the user to fill out a grid (form) to construct a sample or description of the data wanted.

radio frequency identification (RFID) technology A wireless technology that allows manufacturers to attach tags with antennas and computer chips on goods and then track their movement through radio signals.

radio transmission System that uses radio-wave frequencies to send data directly between transmitters and receivers.

random access memory (RAM) The part of primary storage that holds a software program and small amounts of data when they are brought from secondary storage.

rapid application development (RAD) A development method that uses special tools and an iterative approach to rapidly produce a high-quality system.

read-only memory (ROM) Type of primary storage where certain critical instructions are safeguarded; the storage is nonvolatile and retains the instructions when the power to the computer is turned off.

Really Simple Syndication (RSS) Allows anyone to syndicate (publish) his or her blog, or any other content, to anyone who has an interest in subscribing.

record A grouping of logically related fields.

redundant arrays of independent disks (RAID) An enterprise storage system that links groups of standard hard drives to a specialized microcontroller that coordinates the drives so they appear as a single logical drive.

registers High-speed storage areas in the CPU that store very small amounts of data and instructions for short periods of time.

regular ID card An identification card that typically has the person's picture and, often, his or her signature.

relational database model Data model based on the simple concept of tables in order to capitalize on characteristics of rows and columns of data.

request for proposal (RFP) Document that is sent to potential vendors inviting them to submit a proposal describing their software package and how it would meet the company's needs.

responsibility A term that means you accept the consequences of your decisions and actions.

reusability feature Feature of object-oriented languages that allows objects created for one purpose to be used in a different object-oriented program if desired.

reverse auction An auction in which one buyer, usually an organization, seeks to buy a product or a service, and suppliers submit bids; the lowest bidder wins.

reverse social engineering A type of attack in which employees approach the attacker.

risk The likelihood that a threat will occur.

risk acceptance A strategy in which the organization accepts the potential risk, continues to operate with no controls, and absorbs any damages that occur.

risk analysis The process by which an organization assesses the value of each asset being protected, estimates the probability that each asset might be compromised, and compares the probable costs of each being compromised with the costs of protecting it.

risk limitation A strategy in which the organization limits its risk by implementing controls that minimize the impact of a threat.

risk management A process that identifies, controls, and minimizes the impact of threats, in an effort to reduce risk to manageable levels.

risk mitigation A process whereby the organization takes concrete actions against risks, such as implementing controls and developing a disaster recovery plan.

risk transference A process in which the organization transfers the risk by using other means to compensate for a loss, such as by purchasing insurance.

router A communications processor that routes messages through several connected LANs or to a wide-area network.

routine reports Reports produced at scheduled intervals.

satellite radio (also called **digital radio**) A wireless system that offers uninterrupted, near CD-quality music that is beamed to your radio from satellites.

satellite transmission A wireless transmission system that uses satellites for broadcast communications.

scope creep Adding functions to an information system after the project has begun.

screen scraper Software that records a continuous "movie" of a screen's contents rather than simply recording keystrokes.

search engine A computer program that searches for specific information by keywords and reports the results.

secondary keys An identifier field or attribute that has some identifying information, but typically does not identify the file with complete accuracy.

secondary storage Technology that can store very large amounts of data for extended periods of time.

secure socket layer (SSL) (see also **transport layer security**) An encryption standard used for secure transactions such as credit card purchases and online banking.

sell-side marketplace B2B model in which organizations sell to other organizations from their own private e-marketplace and/or from a third-party site.

sensitivity analysis The study of the impact that changes in one (or more) parts of a model have on other parts.

sequential access Data access in which the computer system must run through data in sequence in order to locate a particular piece.

server A computer that provides access to various network services, such as printing, data, and communications.

server farm Massive data center containing thousands of servers.

server virtualization Using software to partition a server into separately operating virtual machines.

service level agreements (SLAs) Formal agreements regarding the division of work between a company and its vendors.

service-oriented architecture (SOA) An IT architecture that makes it possible to construct business applications using Web services, which can be reused across an organization in other applications.

short message service (SMS) A service provided by digital cell phones that can send and receive short text messages (up to 160 characters in length).

signature recognition The user signs his or her name, and the system matches this signature with one previously recorded under controlled, monitored conditions.

smart card A card that contains a microprocessor (chip) that enables the card to store a considerable amount of information (including stored funds) and to conduct processing.

smart ID cards Cards with a chip embedded in them with pertinent information about the user.

social engineering Getting around security systems by tricking computer users inside a company into revealing sensitive information or gaining unauthorized access privileges.

social interface A user interface that guides the user through computer applications by using cartoon-like characters, graphics, animation, and voice commands.

social networking Web sites that allow users to upload their content to the Web, in the form of text (for example, blogs), voice (for example, podcasts), images, and videos (for example, videocasts).

software A set of computer programs that enable the hardware to process data.

Software-as-a-Service (SaaS) A method of delivering software in which a vendor hosts the applications, and customers access them over a network and pay only for using them.

spam Unsolicited e-mail.

spamming Indiscriminate distribution of e-mail without the receiver's permission.

spamware Alien software that uses your computer as a launch platform for spammers.

speech-recognition software Software that recognizes and interprets human speech, either one word at a time (discrete speech) or in a stream (continuous speech).

spyware Alien software that can record your keystrokes and/or capture your passwords.

storage area network (SAN) An enterprise storage system architecture for building special, dedicated networks that allow rapid and reliable access to storage devices by multiple servers.

storage over IP Technology that uses the Internet Protocol to transport stored data between devices within a SAN; sometimes called IP over SCSI or iSCSI.

storage visualization software Software used with SANs to graphically plot an entire network and allow storage administrators to monitor all devices from a single console.

stored program concept Modern hardware architecture in which stored software programs are accessed and their instructions are executed (followed) in the computer's CPU, one after another.

stored-value money card A form of electronic cash on which a fixed amount of prepaid money is stored; the amount is reduced each time the card is used.

strategic information systems (SISs) Systems that help an organization gain a competitive advantage by supporting its strategic goals and/or increasing performance and productivity.

strong passwords A password that is difficult to guess, longer rather than shorter, contains upper and lower case letters, numbers, and special characters, and is not a recognizable word or string of numbers.

structured query language (SQL) Popular relational database language that enables users to perform complicated searches with relatively simple instructions.

supercomputer Computer with the greatest processing power available; used primarily in scientific and military work for computationally demanding tasks on very large data sets.

supply chain The flow of materials, information, money, and services from raw material suppliers through factories and warehouses to the end customers; includes the organizations and processes involved.

supply chain management (SCM) The planning, organizing, and optimization of one or more of the supply chain's activities.

support activities Business activities that do not add value directly to a firm's product or service under consideration but support the primary activities that do add value.

surfing The process of navigating around the Web by pointing and clicking a Web browser.

switch A special-purpose computer that allows devices in a LAN to communicate directly with each other.

synchronous optical network (SONET) An interface standard for transporting digital signals over fiber-optic lines; allows the integration of transmissions from multiple vendors.

system control programs Software programs that control use of the hardware, software, and data resources of a computer system.

system performance monitors Programs that monitor the processing of jobs on a computer system and monitor system performance in areas such as processor time, memory space, and application programs.

system security monitors Programs that monitor a computer system to protect it and its resources from unauthorized use, fraud, or destruction.

system support programs Software that supports the operations, management, and users of a computer system by providing a variety of support services (e.g., system utility programs, performance monitors, and security monitors).

system utilities Programs that accomplish common tasks such as sorting records, creating directories and subdirectories, locating files, and managing memory usage.

systems analysis The examination of the business problem that the organization plans to solve with an information system.

systems analysts IS professionals who specialize in analyzing and designing information systems.

systems design Describes how the new system will provide a solution to the business problem.

systems development life cycle (SDLC) Traditional structured framework, used for large IT projects, that consists of sequential processes by which information systems are developed.

systems software The class of computer instructions that serve primarily as an intermediary between computer hardware and application programs; provides important self-regulatory functions for computer systems.

systems stakeholders All people who are affected by changes in information systems.

T-carrier system A digital transmission system that defines circuits that operate at different rates, all of which are multiples of the basic 64 Kbps used to transport a single voice call.

table A grouping of logically related records.

tacit knowledge The cumulative store of subjective or experiential learning; highly personal and hard to formalize knowledge.

tag A keyword or term, chosen by users, that describes a piece of information (for example, a blog, a picture, an article, or a video clip).

technical specialists Experts on a certain type of technology, such as databases or telecommunications.

telecommuting A work arrangement whereby employees work at home, at the customer's premises, in special workplaces, or while traveling, usually using a computer linked to their place of employment.

telecommunications system The hardware and software that transmit information from one location to another.

teleconferencing The use of electronic communication that allows two or more people at different locations to have a simultaneous conference.

telemetry The wireless transmission and receipt of data gathered from remote sensors.

The Internet ("the Net") The massive network that connects computer networks of businesses, organizations, government agencies, and schools around the world, quickly, seamlessly, and inexpensively.

thin-client systems Desktop computer systems that do not offer the full functionality of a PC.

threat Any danger to which an information resource may be exposed.

thumb drive Storage device that fits into the USB port of a personal computer and is used for portable storage.

tokens Devices with embedded chips and a digital display that presents a login number that the employees use to access the organization's network.

top-level domain (TLD) The rightmost part of an Internet name, indicating the type of organization that owns the site.

topology The physical layout and connectivity of a network.

trade secret Intellectual work, such as a business plan, that is a company secret and is not based on public information.

trans-border data flow The flow of corporate data across nations' borders.

transaction Any business event that generates data worth capturing and storing in a database.

transaction processing system (TPS) An information system that supports the monitoring, collection, storage, processing, and dissemination of data from the organization's basic business transactions.

Transmission Control Protocol/Internet Protocol (TCP/IP) A file transfer protocol that can send large files of information across sometimes unreliable networks with the assurance that the data will arrive uncorrupted.

transport layer security (TLS) (see **secure socket layer**).

trap doors (see **back door**).

Trojan horses A software program containing a hidden function that presents a security risk.

tunneling A process that encrypts each data packet to be sent and places each encrypted packet inside another packet.

Turing test A test for artificial intelligence in which a human interviewer, conversing with both an unseen human being and an unseen computer, cannot determine which is which; named for English mathematician Alan Turing.

twisted-pair wire Strands of copper wire twisted together in pairs.

ubiquitous computing (see **pervasive computing**).

Ultra-mobile personal computer Small, mobile computer that has the full functionality of a desktop computer, but is smaller and lighter than traditional laptops and notebooks.

ultra-wideband (UWB) A high-bandwidth wireless technology with transmission speeds in excess of 100 Mbps that can be used for applications such as streaming multimedia from, say, a personal computer to a television.

uniform resource locator (URL) The set of letters that identifies the address of a specific resource on the Web.

up-selling The marketing of higher-value products and services to new or existing customers.

utility computing A type of computing whereby a service provider makes computing resources available to a customer as needed.

value chain model Model that shows the primary activities that sequentially add value to the profit margin; also shows the support activities.

value system System that includes the producers, suppliers, distributors, and buyers, all with their value chains.

value-added network (VAN) A private, data-only network that is managed by an outside third party and used by multiple organizations to obtain economies in the cost of network service and network management.

vendor-managed inventory (VMI) Strategy in which the supplier monitors a vendor's inventory levels and replenishes products when needed.

vertical exchanges Electronic marketplaces that connect buyers and sellers in a given industry.

vertical integration Strategy of integrating the upstream part of the supply chain with the internal part, typically by purchasing upstream suppliers, in order to ensure the timely availability of supplies.

videocast A digital video file that is distributed over the Web using Really Simple Syndication for playback on portable media players or personal computers.

videoconference A virtual meeting in which participants in one location can see and hear participants at other locations and can share data and graphics by electronic means.

viral marketing Online word-of-mouth marketing.

virtual bank A banking institution dedicated solely to Internet transactions.

virtual collaboration The use of digital technologies that enable organizations or individuals to collaboratively plan, design, develop, manage, and research products, services, and innovative information systems and electronic commerce applications.

virtual group (team) A work group whose members are in different locations and who meet electronically.

virtual memory A feature that simulates more main memory than actually exists in the computer system by extending primary storage into secondary storage.

virtual organizations Organizations in which the product, the process, and the delivery agent are all digital; also called pure-play organizations.

virtual private network (VPN) A private network that uses a public network (usually the Internet) to securely connect users by using encryption.

virtual reality Interactive, computer-generated, three-dimensional graphics delivered to the user through a head-mounted display.

virtual universities Online universities from which students take classes from home or an off-site location, via the Internet.

virus Malicious software that can attach itself to (or "infect") other computer programs without the owner of the program being aware of the infection.

voice over Internet Protocol (VoIP; also Internet telephony) A communications system in which analog voice signals are digitized, sectioned into packets, and then sent over the Internet.

voice portal A Web site with an audio interface.

voice recognition System whereby the user speaks a phrase that has been previously recorded under controlled, monitored conditions, and the voice recognition system matches the two voice signals.

vulnerability The possibility that an information resource will suffer harm by a threat.

vulnerability management system A system that handles security vulnerabilities on unmanaged, remote devices and, in doing so, extends the security perimeter that exists for the organization's managed devices.

warm site A site that provides many of the same services and options of the hot site, but does not include the company's applications.

waterfall approach SDLC approach in which tasks in one stage were completed before the work proceeded to the next stage.

Web 2.0 A loose collection of information technologies and applications, and the Web sites that use them; the Web sites enrich the user experience by encouraging user participation, social interaction, and collaboration.

Web services Self-contained business/consumer modular applications delivered over the Internet.

Web site Collectively, all of the Web pages of a particular company or an individual.

weblog A personal Web site, open to the public, in which the site owner expresses his or her feelings or opinions.

Webmaster The person in charge of an organization's Web site.

what-if analysis The study of the impact of a change in the assumptions (input data) on the proposed solution.

whiteboards An area on a computer display screen on which multiple users can write or draw; multiple users can use a single document "pasted" onto the screen.

whitelisting A process in which a company identifies acceptable software and permits it to run, and either prevents anything else from running or lets new software run in a quarantined environment until the company can verify its validity.

wide-area network (WAN) A network, generally provided by common carriers, that covers a wide geographic area.

wiki A Web site on which anyone can post material and make changes quickly, without using difficult commands.

wireless Telecommunications in which electromagnetic waves carry the signal between communicating devices.

wireless access point An antenna connecting a mobile device to a wired local area network.

wireless application protocol (WAP) The standard that enables wireless devices with tiny display screens, low-bandwidth connections, and minimal memory to access Web-based information and services.

wireless fidelity (Wi-Fi) A set of standards for wireless local area networks based on the IEEE 802.11 standard.

wireless local area network (WLAN) A computer network in a limited geographical area that uses wireless transmission for communication.

wireless media (see **broadcast media**).

wireless network interface card (WNIC) A device that has a built-in radio and antenna and is essential to enable a computer to have wireless communication capabilities.

wireless sensor networks (WSN) Networks of interconnected, battery-powered, wireless sensors placed in the physical environment.

wireline media (see **cable media**).

word length The number of bits (0s and 1s) that can be processed by the CPU at any one time.

work group Two or more individuals who act together to perform some task, on either a permanent or temporary basis.

workflow The movement of information as it flows through the sequence of steps that make up an organization's work procedures.

workstations Powerful desktop-size computers that run computationally intensive scientific, engineering, and financial applications.

World Wide Web (the Web, WWW, or W3) A system of universally accepted standards for storing, retrieving, formatting, and displaying information via a client/server architecture; uses the transport functions of the Internet.

worm Destructive programs that replicate themselves without requiring another program to provide a safe environment for replication.

zero-day attack An attack that takes advantage of a newly discovered, previously unknown vulnerability in a particular software product; perpetrators attack the vulnerability before the software vendor can prepare a patch for it, or sometimes before the vendor is even aware of the vulnerability.

Index